SOLOMON ISLANDS CHRISTIANITY

SOLOMON ISLANDS CHRISTIANITY

A Study in Growth and Obstruction

ALAN R. TIPPETT

The William Carey Library presents this reprinting of the first edition as it appeared in 1967. The reader is asked to bear in mind that certain facts and details have changed with time.

William Carey Library

Copyright © 1967 by ALAN R. TIPPETT

All rights reserved.

Second Printing

First published   1967   by   Lutterworth Press, LONDON

ON BEHALF OF THE COMMISSION ON WORLD MISSION AND EVANGELISM OF THE WORLD COUNCIL OF CHURCHES

Library of Congress Catalog Card Number: 75-15143
International Standard Book Number 0-87808-724-9

Published by the William Carey Library
533 Hermosa Street
South Pasadena, Calif. 91030
Telephone 213-799-4559

PRINTED IN THE UNITED STATES OF AMERICA

Solomon Islands

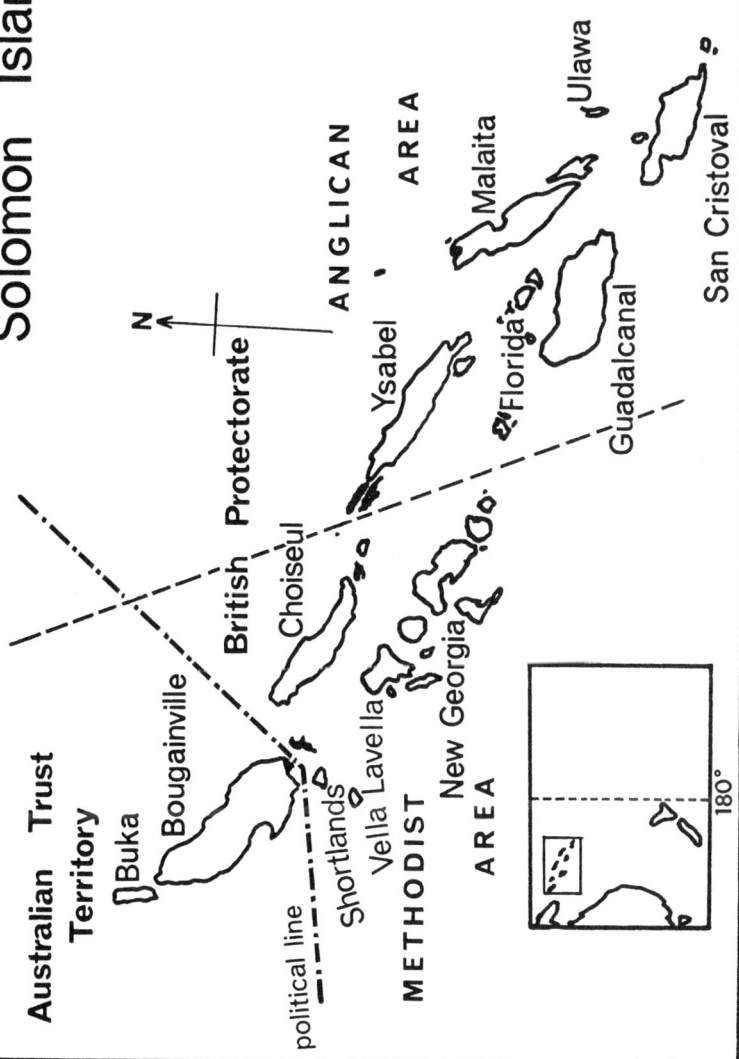

Australian Trust Territory

Buka

Bougainville

British Protectorate

political line

Shortlands

Vella Lavella

New Georgia

METHODIST AREA

Choiseul

Ysabel

Florida

Guadalcanal

ANGLICAN AREA

Malaita

Ulawa

San Cristoval

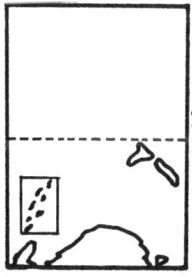

N

180°

CONTENTS

PAGE

Editorial Foreword   ix

INTRODUCTION   xiii

CHAPTER

PART ONE
THE SOLOMON ISLANDS AS THEY WERE   I
1. Pre-Christian Religion   3
2. Early Culture Contact   20

PART TWO
PATTERNS OF CHURCH GROWTH   27
3. Levels for Studying Church Growth   29
4. The Growth of the Church in the Eastern Solomons   33
5. The Growth of the Church in the Western Solomons   54

PART THREE
PROBLEMS OF MISSIONARY ATTITUDE AND THEORY   77
Introductory Note   79
6. Problems of Theory and Practice   82
7. Problems of Encounter   100
8. Problems of Institutions and Education   119

PART FOUR
THE RELEVANCE OF ANTHROPOLOGICAL DIMENSIONS   137
9. The Transmission and Control of Authority and Leadership   139
10. The Head-hunting and Slavery Complex and Socio-religious
    Change   147
11. How Village Structure Reflects Christian Patterns   161
12. Exchange Economy and Christian Innovation   171
13. Feud and Reconciliation   190
14. Comparative Analysis of Nativistic Movements   201

PART FIVE
THE WESTERN SOLOMONS SCHISM   217
15. The Prophet and the Situation   219
16. The Group Experiences of Etoism   232
17. Theological Analysis of Etoism   248
    Concluding Summary to Part Five   265

v

CHAPTER   PAGE

PART SIX

THEOLOGICAL DEPTHS OF THE CURRENT SITUATION   267
18. The Process from Animist to Christian Forms   269
19. Hymns as a Theological Index   286
20. The Bible in the Village Situation   297
21. Measuring Congregational Piety by Curves   308
22. Half-Christian Half-Pagan Villages   319
23. Urban and Industrial Situations   330

CONCLUSION   346

Notes   353

Bibliography   378

Index of Persons   394

General Index   399

ACKNOWLEDGEMENTS

THE WRITER wishes to thank the Lord Bishop of Melanesia and the Chairman of the Methodist Mission for their personal help in opening the facilities of their respective missions to him and for the loan of books which have added much to this study.

The undermentioned libraries and archival institutions were used for checking and cross-checking references and data; thanks are due to their respective authorities and employees—the library of the University of Oregon, Eugene, U.S.A., the Mitchell Library, Sydney, the State Library of Victoria, the La Trobe Library of Melbourne and the libraries of the Australian National University, Canberra; the collections of the Melanesian Mission in Auckland, of the Methodist Foreign Missions in the same city, and of the Secretariat in Honiara, British Solomons; the archives of the Methodist Overseas Missions in Sydney, and of the Methodist Church in Fiji at Suva; the Methodist Mission records and files at Munda in the Solomons; and the Western Pacific High Commission Archives, together with the Alport Barker and Harold Gatty Collections in Suva, Fiji, where some valuable preparatory work was done *en route* to the Solomons.

The writer also thanks the kind folk who attended to the organization of his itinerary in the Solomons, to Archdeacon Reynolds and the Melanesian Mission business manager, Mr. G. Morgan, and in particular to the Rev. and Mrs. A. C. Watson for making their home his headquarters in Honiara and placing every convenience at his disposal. Dr. C. E. Fox and Rev. B. Ayres of Taroaniara, and Mr. David Hilliard of the Australian National University, Canberra, also gave much help.

The village depth studies were possible only because of scores of indigenous informants. One ought to list twenty or thirty of them but two certainly cannot be omitted—Father George Kiriau, the Anglican priest, and Joeli Zio, the Methodist catechist. These two devoted servants of the Lord gave their time and help without stint, and without their aid the project just could not have been attempted.

Many returned missionaries were helpful in clarifying issues with respect to localities the investigator was unable to visit. Especially should be mentioned the Rev. A. H. Voyce and J. R. Metcalfe and their wives and the Rev. G. A. R. Cornwell, all of whom generously made available much valuable data used in this volume.

When one looks back over the experience in the islands and makes a list of the missionaries who helped with interviews and hospitality, one is confronted by a formidable list of names. It is easier to say thank-you to all the folk at Honiara, Taroaniara, Fauambu, Munda and Banga. One appreciates having been taken over hospitals, schools and other institutions, and having been able to meet theological students both in the east and west. Many good lay folk invited him into their homes and put their cars at his disposal. He cannot adequately express his thanks to them all. Finally, without the clerical assistance of his wife the task could not have been done.

EDITORIAL FOREWORD

LIKE ALL other books in this series, this study deals with the inter-relatedness of the local church and the community which surrounds it, and examines the influence of each upon the other. As with other studies, it also has its own particular variation upon the main theme; in this case, it is the factors which favour and those which obstruct the natural growth of the church, in terms both of numerical expansion and of spiritual maturity.

Over three years ago the W.C.C. Department of Missionary Studies convened a special consultation at Iberville, near Quebec, to study the question of church growth. In the statement which resulted from the conference, the following assertions were made:

> In surveying the world missionary situation, generalities are of little help. Each population presents its own distinctive problems regarding church growth, and solutions from one area must not be naïvely projected, without examination, into another. Analytical techniques can help immensely towards recognition and understanding of the facts, and at this point careful statistics are of great use. If we are willing to replace defensive prejudices by comparative study of situations in which the churches have or have not grown, we shall find much to learn . . .
>
> Experience has demonstrated that many missionary methods used in the past are wrong, yet these continue to be repeated and defended, because they are not honestly examined in the light of their results. . . .
>
> Much of what is being undertaken by missions, with foreign resources, would be immeasurably more effective as a witness to the Gospel if spontaneously undertaken, according to their own means, by members of the local church . . .
>
> We have considered many illustrations of factors which favour or retard church growth, of the complexities which require examination before situations can be adequately understood, and of the prevalence of mistaken ideas on this subject which call for radical correction. These have left us more than ever convinced of the need for scientific research into many different matters, some related to sociology, anthropology and similar disciplines, others to church administration and structures, all to the strategy of the Church's mission.

Dr. Alan Tippett took part in that consultation—but that is the least of his qualifications for undertaking the study he here presents in such a readable, painstaking, and thought-provoking way. He spent twenty years as a missionary in Fiji, for the last four of which he was principal of the Methodist Theological Seminary; he gained his doctorate in anthropology from the University of Oregon; and he is now professor of missionary anthropology at the graduate School of World Mission of Fuller Theological Seminary, Pasadena, California. It would be an entire misunderstanding of the significance of this book, and of the purpose of this series, to think that its relevance

ix

is confined to the Pacific. Not only is it pertinent to the churches'
life in any region of the world where peoples are moving from tribal
communities into modern society, but it will be found to have a bearing
upon problems of church growth in many kinds of more sophisticated
areas.

We wish to express our gratitude to the mission boards which contributed, through the National Missionary Council of Australia, a
large share of Dr. Tippett's salary during the year he was engaged
in this research. We also thank the co-operating churches and missionaries in the Solomon Islands, without whose help this project could not
have been undertaken.

VICTOR E. W. HAYWARD

Geneva,   *Executive Secretary, W.C.C. Dept. on*
December 1966.   *Studies in Mission and Evangelism*

MAPS AND DIAGRAMS

Map of the Solomon Islands   *Frontispiece*
Map of Malaita: Distribution of Mission Stations   47
Policy of Decentralization: Bougainville and Buka   74
The Lineage of Gove through Pequ Vovoso   140
How an increase of head-hunting and slavery maintains its own
    equilibrium   149
Plan of Rarumana Village   161
Plan of Fouia Village   164
Plan of Sulufou Village   167
Senga-Vurulata Feud   191
Map of Choiseul: Districts and villages involved in the feud   195
Instability and Irregularity in Church Growth due to Nativistic
    Movements (Western Solomons)   210
Effect of Nativistic Movements on the Growth of Congregations
    (Western Solomons)   213
Map: Distribution of Etoism   230
From Church Agent to Nativistic Prophet   242
Dynamics of the Emergence of Etoism   246
The Spiritual Importance of Functional Substitutes   271
Range of Hymn Usage (Graph)   295
Acceptance and Rejection of Christianity   324
The Concept of the Family among the Salt-water People of
    Malaita   327

INTRODUCTION

Iᴍᴍᴇᴅɪᴀᴛᴇʟʏ ᴀꜰᴛᴇʀ the war the head of a Christian mission returned to what had been his station headquarters. The area was still under army occupation and physically all was desolation. Yet his report was one of thanksgiving. His people "had suffered hunger, nakedness, peril and persecution", but he was convinced of "the indestructibility of the Christian faith". He listed the congregations which had rebuilt the churches destroyed by enemy action and named many "strong Christian leaders", who had endured much and would certainly rebuild the Church of the future.[1] Nevertheless, within a few years, some 3,000 persons from those very Christian communities he listed, under some of the leaders he had specifically mentioned, had rejected his Church and followed an indigenous prophet with a Christopagan theology.

Solomon Islands Christianity presents us with a study in *growth* and *obstruction*. In both the first and second generations we face success and failure. When a historian and anthropologist is called in to investigate such a situation, the report which emerges is bound to be problem-orientated. This does not mean, however, that he is unaware of the splendid pioneering work done by the various missions involved. It would be much easier for him to write a pleasant record of achievement. Such a record would be true—but it would not be the whole truth. The Department of Missionary Studies of the World Council of Churches determined on a research project for this region during 1964-65. This volume is the result.

METHODOLOGY

This study is historical but it is not a history. The record of each Mission concerned has been written by its own competent historian. However, to understand the current problems faced by the churches some historical perspectives are essential. Solomon Island Christianity has grown and developed with clearly marked trends over the years. The study is historical also in that the techniques of historical method have been applied to the documents and other sources of information used. Most of this has been done from primary sources, secondary sources being evaluated in the light of their own specific purposes at the period in which they were written, rather than the period about which they were written.

This study is anthropological, but it is not an anthropology. It makes no attempt at presenting a total cultural analysis of a race of people or a village community, either diachronically or synchronically. Nevertheless in methods of research, by participant observation in selected villages, in methods of handling informants and cross-checking their testimonies, this may be called anthropological research.

Essentially this is a religious study. It examines two of the young churches of the Solomon Islands, using historical and anthropological data to interpret the character of the local situations in which the churches have emerged or are at present emerging. It attempts to show something of the patterns by which people have come and are coming out of paganism into Christianity. It analyses the effects of social conditions and mission policies, in either stimulating or obstructing growth. It probes the problematics of both first- and second-generation Christianity. If the methodology is historical and anthropological, the purpose of the book is entirely religious. At heart many of the problems are ultimately theological.

One had to settle on some specific limits for the project. Regionally we are concerned with what is popularly known as the *Solomon Islands*, the group of islands stretching from Buin and Bougainville to San Cristoval and Ulawa.[2] Within these geographical limits I have confined myself to the Melanesian people. I am well aware of the presence of Polynesians, Micronesians and others in the region, and I recognize that in reality they are part of the situation—but so complicated a part that they warrant a special study of their own.[3]

At one or two specific points studies have been conducted in depth, by my living with a village congregation for a period of time and sharing their religious and daily life. One research worker, even in a lifetime, could never learn everything of the Solomon Island situation, and I hasten to admit awareness of the shortcomings of my research and knowledge. Many missionaries understand their localities better. My only advantage has been to see things over a fairly wide panorama, and to be able to look at them objectively, regardless of mission policy and administrative restrictions. My whole task was to discover what it means to be a Melanesian Christian in Melanesia today.

My task also involved me in a great deal of archival and library research in the scattered repositories of Oceanic documentary material, and in interviews with many retired missionaries in Fiji, Australia and New Zealand. I hope the total picture benefits from this expenditure of money, time and effort.

The patterns reconstructed in this book are vignettes of the island life. Here the Church grew. There it stopped growing. Here one finds dramatic action. There one meets indifference. Here we meet a first-generation social group, in a face to face encounter with the powers of darkness. There the problematics of individuals drifting from marginality to nominality confront us. All these are real life situations. As the subject is inexhaustible I make no claim for completeness in the study. Missionaries in the area may feel there are important omissions. I can only claim their forbearance, for the number of localities I could visit in the time was certainly limited.

Before undertaking this study I had myself served the Church for twenty years in another part of Melanesia. This gave me some background for the analysis of Melanesian patterns in the Solomons, which were both similar and dissimilar to those which I had known.

As the two Missions which contributed to this project had observed half a century of comity agreement, their areas of operation were sufficiently discrete to permit an independent observer to make objective comparisons of their respective developments. The tragedy was that a third Mission, which could have received much from and contributed much to the project, declined to co-operate. This decision was made some months before my arrival in the islands and was based on what I believe to be a mistaken attitude towards the World Council of Churches.[4]

It is true that any Mission takes a risk in throwing open its portals to a complete stranger, whose training in history and anthropology is bound to make him a critical observer. This makes me all the more appreciative of the sincerity of the co-operating Missions. I hope any critical findings will not be regarded as uncharitable. I feel obligated to provide a straightforward and honest appraisal of the situations they confront in their respective areas, and I take it that they contributed to the project for this express purpose. I am deeply indebted to them for opening their stations, records and village churches to my wife and myself, for the welcome and hospitality we received wherever we went, and for the generous manner in which they placed their shipping facilities at our disposal. I can only say that we felt our own spiritual experience was enriched by serving the World Church for a time across these denominational and cultural barriers.

I realize that my suggestions are the objective observations of an outsider, and that to the insider there may well be administrative and procedural objections for which I have not allowed; yet I believe that all the matters raised in this report do call for serious consideration from those who frame the policy of the Church in our time, and for those who apply it at the 'grass-roots' level.

·   ·   ·   ·   ·

If I am to generalize and put the Solomon Island situation into a single proposition, perhaps it should be put like this—*Two decades ago the need for new thinking lay with the missionaries, but today it is most urgently needed at the level of the village congregation.*

What is the village congregation's conception of its own role in the local scene? What is its obligation to its pagan neighbour? Has it a responsibility to cultivate social graces and to deal with social backwardness? Can it see itself as *the Church* in the village scene, or is it dependent on outside resources and decisions? What is the place of the conversion experience in the village congregation in second-generation Christianity? What is the Solomon Island Christian's own answer to these questions? My feeling is that he has no answer. But these are basic questions of church growth—conversion, quality and organic growth. The Solomon Island situation demands an answer.

The social structure of the Solomon Islands is changing rapidly today, though the country is still far too backward and undeveloped. With the world in its present mood, the social development of the Solomons must be speeded up further. The Government leaves too much to the Missions. Government officials and Europeans still speak too much of *Missions*, and act through *Missions*, though they now use the word *Churches* in their White Papers. The village Christian also is far more aware of the *Mission* than of the *Church*. The question of whether or not the Solomon Island Churches can take over from the Missions is a major problem. Can the Churches take over the loads the Missions have hitherto carried—educational and medical work, for instance? Should they attempt to do so? What is the role of such a mission institution, financed from outside, in an indigenous church? Church growth—in an organizational sense—may expect some 'growing pains' in the next two decades.

The Government will have to endure more free speech and criticism. The country badly needs an organ for the expression of public opinion, a newspaper or radio, free from official control. When this comes, social change will speed up in many ways. There is considerable unrest among private citizens about the lack of free speech. Where does the island Church fit into this?

A new social balance is emerging, with new classes (like the Fijians in the townships, for example) bringing about change. The distinction between town and country is becoming more significant. How different then is the relevance of the Church in an emerging atmosphere of commercial and competitive materialism, from its relevance in a half-pagan half-Christian village where the main issue is still whether Christ or the ancestral ghost is Saviour?

In this world of dynamic change every local situation is unique and requires a creative, vital Church in its midst. We cannot say that the crisis is shifting from country to town. The crisis is everywhere. Every local church must stand on its own feet. This is why the station-centred missions have to give way to the Church. It is not enough for missionaries to be willing and even anxious to decrease, though this must be so. Nor is it enough to appoint a few good Melanesians to higher office, though this also is desirable. Nor do I think a trained *élite* can handle the situation. There must be a response towards increased responsibility from the local congregations themselves.

It is possible for the local church to be thoroughly indigenous as a pious worshipping body, meeting the personal needs of those within its loyal ranks, yet be thoroughly cut off and irrelevant to the other half of the village outside. Many static churches in the Solomons could be growing churches—by the conversion of pagans in one area and the revival of nominal Christians in another. This is a primary problem. *Enclosed* congregations, without outreach, are numerous. The enclosure of a congregation may be the result of self-satisfaction, of formalism or thoughtlessness, or it may be the result of excessive dependence on a mission or on the mission teacher.

Nor is it adequate to train better indigenous leaders—although this certainly must be done—if these leaders are merely replicas of the foreign missionary. They must be leaders who can effect renewal at the level of the village congregation. The test for any leader must lie at the effect his leadership produces at the 'grass-roots' level—whether this be direct or transmitted through others. I am all for raising the levels of education, improving the quality of preaching and making the business meetings more efficient. But if any leader is unable to bring his congregation to a conversion experience, and to translate that experience into action in the village outside, he has failed and his congregation will be enclosed and static. It is possible for missionaries and mission stations to concentrate effectively on raising standards, yet overlook the basic encounter of the village congregation with its environment. The stress should not be on raised educational standards *per se*, but on standards that can be translated into relevant encounter on the part of the local group. I think this is a question to which the Church in the Solomons ought to give some serious thought.

I note that in his last Synod Charge the Anglican Bishop, after having commented on the various ways in which Melanesian responsibility was being increased, expressed his feeling that there was "indeed a need for further development of spiritual life in our villages".[5] The success or failure of the Church in the Solomons with this generation will be determined there—at the local congregational level. Mission policy and leadership can stimulate this growth or obstruct it, can help or hinder the emergence of the Church—but in the final analysis the local Church has to emerge itself, and demonstrate its own relevance within every village situation.

Part One

THE SOLOMON ISLANDS AS THEY WERE

1 Pre-Christian Religion
     The Creator
     Ghosts and Spirits
     Skulls
     Ceremonial Inhumanity
     Magico-religious Ritual
     Concepts of Sin and Salvation

2 Early Culture Contact
     The Labour Trade
     Depopulation
     Reprisals and Punitive Expeditions
     The Missionary Advocate
     Colonialism
     The Psychological Factor

CHAPTER 1

Pre-Christian Religion

THE CREATOR

SOLOMON ISLAND origin myths conceptualize a high god responsible for the work of creation. The myths vary in each island but Bañara of Vella Lavella, Bañara la'ata of Choiseul, Koevasi of Guadalcanal and the Great Spirit of Roviana were remarkably similar. They supposedly produced their respective islands out of chaos, gave them form and order, created the original human beings and classified them into their present social groups.

They have another point in common: having completed the work of creation and having grown old, they had 'retired', as it were, from the active life of being *working* gods. As a result they were seldom worshipped. Each could be described, as Nicholson spoke of Bañara of Vella Lavella, as the *Great Outsider*. Except for references in the myths and folksongs, they might well have been forgotten.

The myths survive, partly because they provide the rhythmic accompaniment for social festivities, but also because they reinforce local tradition and customs. They serve the purpose of law. If a foreigner questions a custom, the islander may well answer him thus:

This is the way we do it, because we were taught to do it this way. Our ancestors were instructed in this by the great creator at the beginning.

This is common over all Melanesia. It is a satisfactory explanation of why some folk live in the mountains and some by the sea, why some foods are taboo to some groups and not to others, why tattooing is for males in one place and for females in another. The prehistoric *kesa* money was made by Bañara la'ata and its uses determined by him. Fishing and planting procedures and marriage patterns were determined in antiquity by these high gods who have now officially finished their work and retired.

The creator was not always a male. Koevasi was a female. Her husband, Sivatohu, was the great warrior of the sky. In this case the myth shows them, not only as progenitors of male and female, but also as the originators of the male and female roles of war and work.

Writing of Roviana beliefs in 1908, Goldie described the great and good Spirit[1] as omnipotent and omniscient, and as responsible for the creation of all things which exist. But this great Spirit was not to be approached by mortals; hence human beings pay more attention to those lesser spirits which control the daily fortunes of man. Prayers, sacrifices and sacred places are for them and not the great unapproachable Spirit.

3

In Bougainville, among the people of Siwai, the concept of the
Supreme Being is not a unity, nor even a male-female dichotomy as in
Guadalcanal. The role has been subdivided, so that three names are
much eulogized in the myths (though there are others also)—Tantanu
(Maker), Hongging (Headman of Paradise) and Panangga (Orphan).
The first of these, after having created all the food plants, finally went
up to dwell in the sky.[2] Both the Methodists and Roman Catholics have
found their God-concept in this term, qualifying it Tantanu Mekusim
(True Maker)—and in this way, says Oliver, they reinforced the
traditional beliefs about Maker himself. Headman of Paradise created
the afterworld (Ru'no'no) and established himself there. Orphan
became the creator of techniques, something like the biblical characters
of Jubal and Tubal Cain (Gen. 4: 21–22). He gave them the arts of war,
hunting, fishing and sexual patterns, and is a popular figure. However,
the Siwai conform to type as far as worship is concerned. These deities
belong to mythology, not to the vital protections and successes of
daily life.[3]

GHOSTS AND SPIRITS

The creator having retired, then, who is responsible for the affairs
of daily life? To whom can man appeal concerning those needs that
require some power beyond his own natural resources? This requirement is met everywhere by a belief in spirits—either the ghosts of the
dead, or free spirits which never had human form. In some parts of
Melanesia we meet a clear cult of the deified original human ancestor
of the lineage, but this does not appear to have developed in the
Solomons. Rather there is a widespread readiness to call on the ghosts
of the dead, who have died in living memory or within the last three
or four generations, and who are particularly remembered for their
prowess in some important aspect of life. They were famous as either
warriors, gardeners, fishermen or magicians. Such ghosts would be
called on to supply mana[4] to the living with respect to these proficiencies.
Ghosts of ordinary people were confined to humble responsibilities for
the health and welfare of those in their immediate domestic households.
Sacrifices were offered at a burial to ensure they rested in peace and
did not become troublesome spirits afterwards. Similar performances,
with rites and simple sacrifices, are made to assure that people who
might have died disgruntled because of misfortune, death before
maturity, or through sorcery, are satisfied and at peace.

The ancestral skull was preserved by each household as a repository
of mana, the ghost of the ancestor being supposed to have the interests
of his progeny at heart. Other skulls of relatives and enemies served
also to increase the supply of mana, and this could be drawn on for
profit or proficiency or for protection. In some localities special constructions or receptacles were built to house the skulls, or perhaps they
would be preserved in or under a sacred tree; but whatever the form,
all villages had some sacred place or structure for this purpose. Even
with the lesser spirits, concerned purely with domestic concord and
health, there was always some material but sacred vehicle—a bamboo,

a net or maybe a basket—where sacred objects were preserved and reverenced for purposes of sacrifices and magic. One of my Malaita informants told me that a ghost could inhabit a basket or bamboo section in which, say, a tooth or jaw-bone was housed. He described a sacrifice (*lui agalo*) performed by an enemy to deprive the householder of the protective *mana* of this ghost. This made the householder vulnerable through loss of protective *mana*.

The question of the *mana* of a Roviana warrior was investigated by Williamson, while those people were yet pagan. He found that the *mana* obtained from the ghost of a great warrior was accumulated in a repository of some kind, an amulet or stone hung round the neck, a tuft of leaves in the belt, a tooth hung on the finger of the warrior's spear hand, or in a form of ritual words. Upon his death this *mana* would adhere to his own ghost, so that here again we have the concept of the cumulative store of *mana*.[5] Necklaces of human teeth from dead relatives were worn, but these were sacred, and not for trade exchange like other necklaces.[6] In all such cases the *mana* of the repository could be activated by the person, but the *mana* belonged to the ghost, who was named or called by a ritual word. The *mana* is always resident in the material repository. If we are to understand subsequent conversion behaviour, this point must be clear to us.

There is at the Methodist museum of Munda a most interesting magical repository known as *loqomo*. It comprises a small plaited bag with the tooth of a dead man. It was attached to the handle of a warrior's shield, and then placed round his neck during fighting, so that the wearer could communicate better with the ghost. With this aid he could run faster without falling, he could detect the hiding-place of his enemy, and obtain other benefits and protections. The object was regarded as an entity but was theologically conceptualized as having both form and spirit.

We see, then, that Solomon Island religion was more the worship of ghosts and spirits than of the almost-forgotten creator. When Christianity arrived the religious encounter was not between a pagan deity and the Christian God, Creator and Ruler of the Universe and Father of Mankind. The encounter had to take place on the level of daily life against those powers which dealt with the relevant problems of gardening, fishing, war, security, food supply and the personal life crises. For all of these, *mana* was needed. In the eyes of any potential Melanesian convert to Christianity, therefore, the issue was one of *power in daily life*. The convert could not stand with the missionary and conceptualize in terms of psychology and western thought-forms. Rather the missionary had to stand with the convert and help him to understand what Christ meant in terms of power encounter:

> Behold I give you power (exousia) ... over all the power (dunamis) ... (Luke 10: 19)

The implications of this will be dealt with in the section of this report on the 'Problems of Encounter'. Elsewhere I have also written of this as coming "to grips at the level of experience" rather than at "the level of intellect".[7]

The Melanesian was confronted with both positive and negative religious needs. There were those needs which provided for the continuation of life, the effectiveness of food production, fishing trade and exchange, and for communal cohesion.[8] These made him turn to religion for positive and practical satisfactions. On the other hand there were dangers, losses, failures, jealousies, hostile magic and other disruptive factors, which had to be prevented or countered. These resulted from anger, jealousy or offence, either of the spirits themselves or of some vindictive persons who stimulated them. This *mana* of hostility had to be appeased or turned aside or driven away or overcome by a more powerful *mana*. It was a world of continual encounter, and a gospel of encounter between Christ and Satan was quite meaningful to these people.

Each locality had its own way of structuring concepts with respect to the functioning of the spirits, and some terms have dual meanings—representing either the spirits of the dead (which I shall call *ghosts* in this report) or spirits which never had any human form (which I shall speak of as *spirits*). The differentiation was made, however, either by the use of alternative terms or restrictive adjectives. The distinction between ghost and spirit is indigenous.[9]

The ghosts were usually resident in the region of the dead, a specific locality, but were available for assisting human beings when suitable prayers and sacrifices were offered to them. In some places a ghost of special prowess, when regularly called by a devotee, was said to be *owned* by him (e.g. *li'oa*—Sa'a and Ulawa). Marett gives us the term *tindalo mana*, ghost of power, for the ghost of a person eminent in his lifetime.

Spirits which never had a human form were associated with specific localities, and frequently with some living creature like a snake or shark, or with natural phenomena like cloud, a stone pillar or some rock of peculiar shape. This physical manifestation of this spirit is variously described as its *shrine*, or *vehicle* or *incarnation*. Although the functions and the shrines vary in each locality, the concept is widespread throughout the Solomons. Some of the terms used reveal affinity, others do not: one meets *Hi'ona* (Ulawa), *Vigona* (Florida) and *Figona* (San Cristoval) but in the north-west *Halelehan*. In Roviana we meet *Tigona-na* for a fetish, idol or image. It was the shrine inhabited by the spirit, not the spirit itself, which is *Tomate*. Supplication is made to the spirit through the shrine.

In addition to these ghosts and spirits, most localities had their goblins and mischievous imps—more trouble-makers than feared, but their names suggest no linguistic connections.[10]

In one locality it is said that there are three kinds of important spirits—ghosts of important warriors, spirits that appear in sharks, and spirits that appear in snakes. These are responsible for fortunes in war, fishing and gardening respectively, the first and second being related to the affairs of men and the third to those of women. This is met in Guadalcanal and the ghosts of lesser people are known as 'little spirits', whose duties are confined to maintaining domestic health and happiness.

A Roman Catholic source,[11] generalizing for the Solomons, but I imagine at this point based on Guadalcanal evidence, classified spirit beings in two categories, living spirits and dead (ghosts), and confirms the widespread tendency to worship the ghosts of celebrated persons. This writer stresses the universality of some belief in an after-life.[12]

The basic generalizations that are of significance for this report in that they have bearing on present-day attitudes, and in particular on the neo-pagan resurgence of today, are three:

1. *The Solomon Islanders conceptualized the creator as a great* Outsider, *who, having completed his creative work and having laid down custom and traditional procedure, had now retired from being an active god.*
2. *The relevant religion for life concerned the activities of ghosts and spirits. These had supplies of* mana *and could be propitiated, so that the* mana *could be manipulated to meet both the positive and negative needs of man in daily life.*
3. *Ghosts were the spirits of the dead who had demonstrated prowess during their lifetime. Spirits had never been human, and presented themselves in shrines—living creatures or natural phenomena.*

SKULLS

One achieved great virtue by placing the skulls of one's enemies in one's skull-house. One Solomon Islander put it like this:

> To the Solomon Islanders the heads of their enemies had more soul-value than anything else, and it was believed that the more human heads one secured, the better the time he would have when he passed into the spirit world.[13]

This was written by a man from a head-hunting area. Expeditions were made to collect skulls. Heads were the approved offering for numerous occasions—the building of a canoe-house, the launching of a war-canoe, the opening of a ceremonial house, for example. The fortunes of these structures depended in the build-up of *mana* in the presentation of heads. These were communal projects for the accumulation of 'merit' in this world to ensure happiness in the next. This depended not merely on the heads, but on the manner of their preparation, decoration and presentation. The ritual had to be perfect, lest the spirits be offended. On a smaller scale, individuals built up their personal supplies of *mana* in the same way. Again faulty ritual might well cause the *mana* to rebound against the person seeking its help. This could cause his soul to leave his body. Without doubt these people lived in a state of fear and suspicion, but the fear of the neighbouring clan was greater than that of a malignant neighbour, because it was continuous and unrelenting.

About eight miles from the Babatana mission station on Choiseul was a place known as the Island of Skulls. My informant saw some thirty skulls there. It was a burial place where bodies were cremated, mostly bodies of their own folk, and where the skulls were preserved to provide a reservoir of soul-force to be available for worshippers within the lineage, who approached with the correct offering and presented it correctly with the prescribed incantations. At another place nearer still to the station, skulls were hung in the branches of a banyan tree together with ceremonial armlets.

There were thus two complexes of skull-preparation and preservation, one for the skulls of enemies and the other for those of one's relations. Both represented repositories of *mana*. At the skull-house where the ancestral skull was set up, the ghost was honoured and propitiated with this sacred skull as central medium. Sometimes this skull had a small hole through which the ghost himself could come and go. In some localities, mainly in the far east of the Group, ancestral skulls were preserved in carved boxes which represented the shape of a shark or bonito.[14] Skulls of enemies were the most suitable type of offering to be presented before this honoured skull of the ancestor, and greatly increased the *mana* reserves of the latter. Thus skulls could be both objects before which offerings were presented or they could be themselves presented as offerings.

In any case the skull was so significant a point of reference in the system that with the acceptance of Christianity some ocular demonstration of disposal was necessary. In some areas this was a mass burial in a common grave without a cross, and especially in Anglican areas these may be distinguished from Christian graves in this way. The people always hasten to explain why there is no cross on the common grave.

Where the shrine or vehicle was an image or wooden figure, ceremonial disposal was likewise required. These 'idols' were widely distributed throughout the western islands. Many were associated with the war patterns. Usually a conch shell was kept at the site and blown to signify that an enemy had been taken or killed. In Choiseul large deposits of human bones were found at these 'idol' sites. This signified the possibility of large gatherings of ghosts at the place. Other trophies of war were also collected there. When the people became Christian they usually disposed of the 'idol'. Sometimes they handed it over to the missionary, and, if small enough, it might be taken from place to place to serve as a preaching text. Some indigenous evangelists did most effective preaching in this manner, because they were obviously unafraid of the *mana* of the image. The wooden figure of Higaloze, which overlooked Kusage right up to the days of the last war, had never been ceremonially disposed of. Eventually it fell into decay by neglect. Weatherworn offerings of custom-money were still there in 1940.[15] The people involved had avoided the power encounter of conversion. It is interesting to find that the whole of this area is now involved in a neo-pagan perversion of Christianity.

CEREMONIAL INHUMANITY

All the rites and ceremonies which humanitarianism (either mission or administrative) resisted were basically religious. In cannibalism the enemy was eaten, not so much because of the love of flesh,[16] but rather that the eater might obtain the strength and *mana* of the victim to add to his own supply—conceptualized as both a personal and a tribal acquisition of *mana* in terms of fighting capacity. The more spiritual dimensions of power or *mana* were acquired for the ancestral ghost by the eating of the enemy, the satisfaction of revenge that it provided and the presentation of bodies provided for the solemn and triumphant sacrifice. Often a small token portion of the body was burned as a sacrifice, the remainder being used for the feast.

To fight until the warriors had secured a group of victims for the oven, meant reducing the *mana* of the enemy lineage as well as building up their own. In some localities this was done as an act of defiance and contempt for the white man long after the establishment of the Protectorate. Such defiance in itself increased the supply of *mana*. During those days when the Malaita bushmen had a price on the head of missionary Hopkins, there was a *mana* scale of values for bodies and/or skulls:

pig——▸woman——▸man——▸warrior——▸chief——▸white man[17]

Widows were strangled because it was fitting for them to accompany their husbands into the spirit world. Infanticide was thought to be better than leaving a weakling child to live and perhaps become a disgruntled spirit at death. Her ghost (it was more often a girl) would be happier thus than to become ultimately the ghost of a woman who had been shamed because of her inability to perform her gardening duties during her lifetime. If a mother mourned a child too greatly the ghost of the child would refuse to leave the locality. The mother would therefore be strangled to accompany the ghost of the child to the abode of the dead. After all it is the ghost that is real and lives on. Reclus found that in one locality

> the skull is placed at one end of the grave, the youngest wife and an infant are thrown in with the most valuable property of the chief, and with the offerings of his friends. Then all is broken and trodden down and covered with stones. At the same time the assembly breaks into wailing.[18]

A supply of slaves was kept for sacrifice, cannibal feasting and for accompanying the dead into the after-life. A great many of these detribalized and insecure persons found their way to mission stations and became Christian, especially in the western islands. They represent one specific configuration of the conversion pattern.

Each person was thought to have two souls. One was a source of trouble throughout this life. When it left the body the person became sick. It finally departed at death to inhabit some other body or object. The other soul was the person's own individuality, and was freed by the death of the body to continue its existence as a ghost with power. However, normally the ghost went to the place of the dead, whence it had to be recalled by a magical rite before it could render any desired service.

One Roman Catholic source claims an indigenous dichotomy of

paradise and hell, setting the former at Malapa and the latter at a place near Visale, at the opposite ends of Guadalcanal.[19] The chiefs, especially those of one's own people, would most certainly go to paradise, but one's enemies mostly went to hell. However, near to hell was a place where ghosts could do 'penance', so this Roman Catholic writer finds a confused idea something like that of purgatory. Clearly there was here at least a capacity for receiving Roman Catholic doctrine; although unless deliberate teaching to the contrary were to be provided, it is almost certain these people would conceptualize heaven and hell as located somewhere in geographical terms. The very capacity for theological conceptualization had with it dangers of misunderstanding and misrepresentation, unless the follow-up nurture were faithfully done. This applied to both Protestant and Catholic alike. The same writer narrates a case of the arrival of a flotilla of canoes loaded with pagans while the original mission party was engaged in celebrating mass. The pagan chief interpreted it to be a ceremony offered to the ghost of Mendaña, and sent the missionaries an offering for the ghost— half the body of a child. He was mystified and annoyed when the body was respectfully buried.[20]

The concept of judgement after death was found with the Roviana people, being vested in the verdict of an old woman (the society being matrilineal), who stands at the parting of the way which divides for each person after death. One road leads to a place of happiness and the other to the locality of evil departed spirits. Strangely enough the name Sondo, by which Goldie speaks of this locality of departed spirits, is the Roviana name for the Shortlands and Bougainville. These were localities on earth. When the Methodist missionaries wanted a word for heaven they chose to use the term for the sky, or the vacant space above (mañauru), and avoided the indigenous concept of the two localities on earth, one for good and one for evil spirits or ghosts. This selection fixed the idea of the Christian heaven as something transcendent. It also separated Christian concepts of the after-life from all the customs of ceremonial inhumanity.

MAGICO-RELIGIOUS RITUAL

Before we can appreciate fully the operation and function of magical or religious ceremonial we must clarify the use of the words *magic* and *sorcery*. I shall avoid the terms *witch* and *witchcraft*, although they are both common in the early missionary records. Witchcraft, as defined by Parrinder in the best work I know on the subject,[21] I have never found in the South Pacific in twenty years of enquiring into these things. Those who have spoken of Oceanic witches and witchcraft have grouped together all kinds of phenomena associated with animism, without any attempt at differentiating their respective functions and processes, or the popular attitudes towards them. Medicine men and sorcerers are equated, without reference to the motives, hopes or fears of those who lived in daily confrontation with them.

We must recognize that the animist expressed an intense *desire* for one type of magic and an intense *fear* of the other. The popular attitude towards the respective practitioners was *appreciation* in one case, *hostility* in the other. Whether the processes were operating on a communal, family or individual level, it appears we have two types— helpful and hostile. The word witchcraft does not cover this but involves a quite different psychological set. The area of magic covers the activating of spirit forces for protective, preventive, corrective, purification or productive purposes. The practitioner may be a medicine-man, a magic-man, a wise-woman, a priest or the elder of the family. The area of sorcery covers hostile magic to cause sickness, to kill, to destroy security or do some other kind of injury. The practitioner is a sorcerer or sorceress. The former is approved, the latter feared. The former is concerned with good health, production of food supply, military strength, craft efficiency, success in fishing and hunting and of social cohesion. The latter operates against all these things and is motivated by jealousy, anger, ambition or hope of gain. The friendly magic is used by the people on all levels daily. The latter is disapproved and resisted by specific social and magical mechanisms. The magic-man is called in to counter the work of the sorcerer, so that the former is ultimately communally disposed, but the latter is individualistic. The only instances of hostile magic made use of by the former are socially and protectively conceptualized—as, for instance, an operation against a common enemy or to counter sorcery or to eliminate some individual who is popularly regarded as a danger to communal co-hesion. It was at this point that it was sometimes applied against Christian converts, when they were regarded as destroyers of social cohesion. One may speak of magic, or white magic or magico-religion on the one hand, and of black magic or sorcery on the other; but the distinction is of fundamental importance in understanding the Christian encounter with Melanesian animism.

In all cases of both magic and sorcery, or any other process involving the acquisition or activating of *mana*, the process must be correctly executed, otherwise the *mana* may rebound on the practitioner. *Mana* must be activated by the correct person, under the correct circumstances, in the correct place, by means of the correct formula. That mistakes be not made, special persons are appointed. However any unsocial person may set himself up as a sorcerer. The risk is great nevertheless. He becomes enslaved, as it were, by his own mechanisms, and the penalties of error are fatal. Most sorcerers come to a tragic end. Both magic and sorcery are marketable property: in trade exchange the value of medicines, charms and formulae is high.

Pagan ritual comprised prayers, incantations and recited charms; the presentation of offerings and sacrifices, symbolic acts, the use of sacred objects and the imposition of taboos. Although these varied considerably in form in various parts of the Solomons, they were never-theless universal features of Solomon Island animism.

Knowledge of the use of magical plants and the recipes and rituals for preparing them for use was a form of wealth. These jealously guarded secrets were occasionally traded in the inter-district exchanges. One of the features of the post-war pattern is the extension of this kind of trade through the meeting of persons from various islands in labour concentrations on plantations and in the towns. That which threatened to die out with the suppression of the slavery and head-hunting trade configurations is now reviving within the current structures of commerce and labour. The use of plants is important to both magic-man and sorcerer, and sometimes they use the same plants to their different ends. Even so, there is a group of a dozen or so plants universally used for magical purposes. The most important of these is probably the dracaena.

A study of magic includes details of such ceremonials as those associated with the clearing and planting of land, harvesting of crops, fishing, with all kinds of craftwork from large communal projects like canoe and house building to individual workmanship in hand-carving. It was not, by any means, confined to war. Magic was involved in the very stuff of life and should Christianity take the place of animism, these social services of animism should not be left as voids in the daily life.

Let us take, for example. the use of the incantation and ritual charm. These were used for a number of purposes both in magico-religion and in sorcery. They may be summarized thus:

(a) In magic —to control the weather, to restore a sick person to health, to bring success in fishing or gardening, to give travellers protection against spirits on land and sea, in divination and in ordeals, to accompany sacrifices or ceremonial purification rites, for calling on the help of ghosts and for winning the affection of women.

(b) In sorcery—to be said over fragments of food, afterbirth, finger-nail clippings, etc., in causing sickness or death; for preparing magical paraphernalia and concoctions; and in terminating effective sorcery after the death of the victim.

Quite often these incantations were preceded or followed by an invocation to the ghost or spirit supplying the necessary *mana*. Supposedly these invocations gave potency to the incantation. Those two lists should serve to show that, although the mode of approach through ritual forms and prayers may be variously used, and to very different ends, we have two quite clear categories, which I have called magico-religion or magic, and sorcery. These categories are indigenous concepts.[22]

The question with which we are concerned in this book is: what kind of a church emerges out of this situation when these people turn to Christ? An attempt is made to answer this question in the part on theological depths of the current situation, where Christian prayer patterns and liturgy are discussed as functional substitutes.

The old religious patterns made much use of divinatory processes for disclosing things which called for investigation: Who was the thief? Who or what was responsible for this man's sickness? Is it advisable to take the proposed journey, or to go to war? Is this fishing expedition likely to be a success? Behind all this lies the belief that spirit forces are continually active, so that it is difficult and unwise for man to operate in opposition to their will and power. With this passage from spirit worship to Christianity, acceptance of the belief in the divine sovereign will was not difficult, but—short of a Hebrew *Urim* and *Thummim* and a Christian *promise box*—how does a converted animist discover the will of the Christian God?

Sacrifices comprised offerings of nuts, yams, betel nut, various forms of custom-money, pigs and human beings. These offerings were made at specific localities—in a village, or at a sacred grove, in a canoe-house, beside the sea or under a sacred tree. The sacrificial location was frequently known as the *sacred fire*. These fires were held according to a kind of religious protocol. A pig, for instance, could not be sacrificed at a fire of lower status than the priest offering the sacrifice. In cases where skulls and other bones were preserved for veneration inside the house, they were usually placed in a basket in such a position that the sacrifice could be burnt below, allowing the smoke to ascend to the sacred basket. Or if a number of skulls were arranged on a platform, the sacrifice would be burnt beneath, for the same reason.

Human sacrifices were the most important of all. For this purpose slaves were kept. But the sacrifice of a pig was also important. This was a propitiation, the pig taking the place of a guilty person. Human sacrifices were applied to occasions of communal consequence like the launching of a war-canoe, the building of a communal house, or a change in the head of a lineage through the death of a chief. Such occasions were both social and political events. Above all there should be no possibility of the ghost being dissatisfied with the generosity of the sacrifice. In most of these cases the sacrifices were completely destroyed; there were others, however, when only a token portion of the man or pig was actually consumed for the ghost—the remainder being used for feasting. This was possible when the slave or pig had been previously dedicated to the ghost, so that the creature belonged to him in entirety and had been fattened for such an occasion as this.

In other cases the ghost received only the spirit part of the sacrifice. Some would call these offerings, rather than sacrifices. They included the offering of the first-fruit, the ceremonial commencement of the fishing season, the beginning of the 'almond' harvest and offerings of appeasement. These were all obligatory but not substitutionary. Another series of offerings was associated with ceremonial defilement and purification, especially following such incidents as sickness, childbirth and funerary occasions. These are what Van Gennep calls *rites of incorporation*, when folk are received back into normal society again after periods of separation.

All this is far removed from individualistic sorcery. These magical or religious rites spring from the social situations of daily life. The pagan magico-religion was at least a sincere attempt at being relevant within its environment. If Christianity was to replace it, it was in this type of situation that the new faith had to be relevant. Later we will examine the conceptual stepping-stones from this world into that of Christian theology.

Another element of the pattern was that of *spirit-possession*. When a person was possessed, it was said in some localities that a spirit had *embarked* the victim. Such a spirit had to be exorcised. Thus there were two theories of sickness. In one, a man's soul was stolen or partly stolen by some spirit.[23] In the other case he was possessed. In the former the soul had to be retrieved by the magician, in the latter exorcised. The former was usually declared to be the work of some sorcerer, especially if the victim died. In this event it was appropriate for the next of kin to exact a requittal. I say 'usually', because sickness could be caused by the 'friendly' ghost, who was grieved because the living had neglected the sacrifices to him. If divination indicated this reason, the matter was corrected by appeasement.

Exorcism had an elaborate ritual. Medicinal concoctions were prepared from lime and dracaena leaves and, accompanied by the correct incantations, a symbolic performance of catching the ghost was enacted. Exorcism has its place in Scripture, and frequently when communities became Christian the missionary was called to exorcise the spirit from the locality where the new church was to be built. Several descriptions of this have been preserved. Thus exorcism could be either personal or locational in application.

I have come across only one case of what might be called *Shamanism*. It seems to savour of South-east Asia rather than of Melanesia. A man named Siama worked with three spirits at Barasaka. He conversed with Tadone, Niodi and Gonu by means of dreams, and prepared leaves and spices under their instruction. He hung a bag of leaf-strips in his house, but did not sacrifice to it or to any ghosts or spirits. His paraphernalia included leaves in fragrant oil in a bag and scented beans in a tin matchbox. In times of sickness folk would seek his aid. Lying beside the sick person, his spirit would commune with those who troubled the sick man. He would argue with them that they ought to depart. If he did not succeed he would take other steps to secure their good will. His sole motivation was to restore the sick person to health.[24]

Clearly again this is far removed from sorcery, to which we must now turn. Sorcery, we have seen, is hostile, individual and anti-social. It was used to satisfy anger, jealousy, or to gain ends for personal profit. There were approved methods for dispensing primitive justice to sorcerers, and approved ordeals (like suspension for a day and night by the wrists or thumbs) by which they had to prove their innocence. One missionary reported numerous cases of this within a confined area. It helps us to see that sorcery, though accepted as a fact, was not socially approved, and those thought to be guilty of it were mercilessly treated. Woodford reported a case in which a woman was suspended for half a day by one wrist and for another half day by the other. She protested her innocence, but eventually confessed in order to escape the ordeal, producing some tobacco which was supposed to be her medium of applying the sorcery. The sick chief recovered, the diviner was proved correct, so the woman was strung up again, and subsequently being of no value as a worker she was sold to neighbouring islanders who took her away for eating.[25]

The forms of sorcery found in the Solomon Islands are as follows:

1. by a magical curse that causes disease (*toe*)
2. by hanging a knotted string over the intended victim's doorway (*tatari*)
3. by hiding a taboo ring in the victim's house (*tinomike*)
4. by hypnotism or possession, for destroying people by means of the 'evil eye' (*tomate njiama, pela*)
5. by causing paralysis of the arms and face with the aid of a plant concoction placed in the victim's house (*tuva*)
6. by preparing a bundle (*penupenu*) or a bamboo container for fragments of food or clothing, hair or finger-nail parings of the victim (*'arua, 'aru'aru, baha, si'onga*)
7. by symbolic burning or destruction of an object representing the victim himself (*bei*)
8. by stealing a man's soul from his body or part of his body (*aruya*)
9. by killing with the aid of a piece of chewed betel nut
10. by suddenly confronting the victim with a bag of magical charms (*vele, pela, fela*)

These are all ways of killing people by sorcery. Other methods may be used to produce other effects. A correct preparation of lime, ginger and dracaena (*toli loosinge*) causes a body to develop unpleasant sores, or establishes discord in a village or may be used to cause a woman to strangle herself.

Another group of processes may be used to captivate a woman for sexual purposes. The most common medium is tobacco, and the form which seemed to me to be the most currently active is known as *vinaroro*. *Doma*, originally a protective war charm, was revived under enemy occupation; it has since acquired some characteristics of sorcery, in that an individual can use it against his intended victim, that he 'may know nothing'.

These forms are mostly of limited distribution, but every locality has one form or another. In ancient times the counter used to be by appeal to the ancestral ghost by prayer, sacrifice, and charms. It was a *mana* encounter that resulted, not that of the sorcerer and his victim, but of the two spirits involved. This was specifically recorded long ago at Simbo by Hocart, who described it as an encounter between the *tomate mba* and *tomate kuri*—between the spirits (*tomate*) not the men.[26]

Individuals guilty of sorcery were killed by the kin of the victim, commonly determined by divination. Usually divination indicated some person of a rival territorial group. When the exposed sorcerer was within the local group, the accused was more often than not some unsocial scoundrel, whom society was happy to put away. Needless to say, such a social mechanism was often applied against would-be converts to Christianity in the early days.

Hogbin has described a more recent Malaita ceremony substituted for the traditional retaliation magic, now that the law prevents the old pattern. It involves the simple sacrifice of a pig, burning the kidneys. The priest of the group prays to the ancestral ghost, urging him to kill the sorcerer, who may or may not be named. The whole matter would be left to the ghost and was considered effectual—a new form of counter-magic which circumvents the law. The same writer insists that legislation cannot solve this problem. Only time and enlightenment can do this, because the efficacy of sorcery is bound up with the credulity of the victim.[27] Hocart pointed out that it is the emotional associations of the 'evil eye' that survive, not the theory. People are not interested in the theory, but they know the mechanism works and fear it. However, Hocart found that it came on like a fit and was not a continuous state. He regarded it as *possession*, although it was the effect of jealousy. A jealous man is subject to temptation and possession. Only by prayer can he induce the devil to depart. He acquired this perspective in Simbo, where he met the *evil eye* face to face.[28] Hogbin may look forward to a day when the Solomon Islander comes to disbelieve in evil spiritual forces, but this is not to say that the scientific materialist is right, or that we have ourselves yet fully explored such spiritual dimensions. However, be this as it may, the island world is currently one of spiritual encounter, and it is in such a world that religion, pagan or Christian, has to prove its relevance.

The matter of our concern is—what is the position of an islander converted to Christianity in this kind of situation? Does he face these hostile powers in the power of Christ? To what extent does he draw on Christian ritual, liturgy, prayer and symbolism to gain the victory? What does it mean to be a Solomon Island Christian?

CONCEPTS OF SIN AND SALVATION

For many years critics have maligned Christian missionaries for imposing western concepts of sin and salvation on their converts from animism. While it may be true that many of the emerging forms and denominational stresses have been western, the criticism has been largely misdirected in its assumption that sin and salvation, *per se*, are purely western concepts. They are, in point of fact, universals. The list of offences regarded as *sin* may differ greatly from culture to culture. Even within a confined region like the Solomons, chastity, for example, is demanded in Malaita but 'winked at' in the Shortlands. Forms of salvation vary similarly. But some sin concepts are always to be found, and with them the approved patterns for setting wrongs right.

Significantly, both these matters are usually treated as religious issues with social consequences, by the animist as well as by the Christian. Man is seen as an offender. He resorts to prayers, rituals, sacrifices, confessions and atonements, to set things right by appealing to some power beyond himself. He seeks to avoid offence by conformity to prescribed behaviour patterns and acts of worship. Religion is thus both protective and restorative. Had this not been so, the animist could not have received the Christian gospel at all. The way for Christian teaching had been prepared, and those who think of animism as entirely dark and bad should ask themselves how this 'animal' was able to understand the gospel at all.

Although, by his searching the animist had not found God, he had established a number of stepping-stones in the right direction. He thus had a capacity for Christianity. However, it does not follow that the form of Christianity had to be the same as that of the western world. The outworkings of the Good News might produce quite a different resultant pattern in the island world. Indeed, to be relevant, it had to do so.

We now turn briefly to the animist concepts of sin and the sin correctives of redemption and reconciliation. The Melanesian conceptualizes sin in any one of three dimensions, which for the purposes of description we shall call *anti-social, theological* and *extra-communal*. These are not necessarily exclusive categories, but are certainly three indigenous ways of regarding sin. It follows that patterns of reconciliation and redemption are applied according to the type of offence committed. It is all quite rational.

Anti-social sins are offences against the kin-group, or against an individual within the group; any failure to respect rights, authority, ownership, marriage and responsibility; any failure to fulfil one's responsibility in and to the group; or any act which jeopardizes the security, cohesion or entity of the group. The group recognizes the existence of other groups, but accepts no responsibility towards them, unless ceremonially bound by agreement in such matters as, say, coalition in war or trade exchanges. An offensive act towards a member of another group is not regarded as a sin, except in so far as it may bring reprisals for which the group is held responsible. In this sense it is a sin, not against the victim, but against the security of the offender's own kin-group. Sorcery comes under the head of anti-social sins, especially if applied against another member within the group. Every group had its approved discipline for application against the sorcerer.

Theological sins are offences against the tribal god or ancestral ghost. These include failure to obey the directions of the ghost, neglect of rituals performed on his behalf, carelessness about ritual forms (the role of the priest exists to avoid this), rejection of communal authority (which is by divine appointment), any neglect of custom laid down in tribal myths as of divine origin, any failure to observe taboos set in the name of the god or ghost. As these sins are not always as manifest as anti-social sins, many unexplained calamities are attributed to theological sins. Neglect of adequate sacrifice to a ghost is a common diagnosis of the diviner. As society depends on the assistance of the ghosts for success in gardening, fishing, hunting and war, neglect of sacrifices or erroneous ceremonials are regarded as serious offences.

Extra-communal sins are offences of groups, households or individuals against spirit forces outside the normal life of the society, especially spirits of the bush and sea; or any action that causes anger to some spirit, leading him to steal the soul of the offender or of a member of his family. Sickness, death and epidemics are often explained in this way. Such offences may be committed wittingly or unwittingly. A great network of taboos exists to warn the unwary of those localities frequented by such spirits. There may be some little ceremonial of respect (such as placing a spray of leaves on a stone) for the passer-by to perform.

Let us suppose a young man is suddenly taken ill and appears sick unto death. A diviner is called. He determines that the youth's father has offended a bush spirit by desecrating a sacred pool; or maybe the family ghost has been neglected in sacrifice; or perhaps the jealousy of a sorcerer is involved. Obviously the corrective applied will depend on the diagnosis of the diviner. In the first possibility the youth is either possessed by the bush spirit, or the spirit has stolen his soul. An exorcist or shaman will be employed. In the second case the correction lies within the family itself. The householder sacrifices a pig to the ghost, with a plea for forgiveness. In the third possibility the communal magic-man will be employed to apply counter-magic to overpower the *mana* of the sorcery. The fact that the diviner was able to ascribe the 'penalty' to any one of several offences, each with a different approved pattern for correction, should help us to see the importance of understanding these concepts of *right* and *wrong*, and the popular concern for *setting things right*.

By pondering this we learn why the conversion of individuals *out of* their groups can lead to persecution. If a conversion threatens the cohesion or totality of a group, and if the convert fails to perform his communal obligations (as he will when pagan acts are involved), he is guilty of anti-social sins which are quite manifest. His deliberate refusal to participate in the ghost cult, or to sacrifice, will make his sins also theological. He will be called irreligious at first. Then his group will realize they are involved in a power encounter. In such situations it is of great advantage if the group can be led to conversion as a total group. In the case of a group movement there is a direct substitution of 'loyalty to Christ' for 'loyalty to the ghost'; the solidarity of the group remains intact; and the conception of anti-social sin is Christianized but retains its essential structure. The concept of anti-social sin is one worth winning for Christ. It has a great deal of support in the New Testament, where the Church is conceptualized as a fellowship, a congregation, a community of believers and as a body. Under Christian influence, in time it may be extended also to those outside the group; but at the point of the sinfulness of anti-social acts, the animist has much to teach the western individualist.

Concepts of redemption and reconciliation are well developed with ceremonial units for confession, petition, restitution and reinstatement. In the Eastern Solomons redemption is covered by the word *tapaoli*, which, according to Ivens, comes from *tapa* (throw) and *oli* (in exchange). A *tapatapa* is an enclosure where an act of substitution is performed—an areca nut is thrown in, with a request for forgiveness or redemption. A more significant act of redemption is *tapaolite*, in which the exchange may be of porpoise teeth for ceremonial offences, or even a pig, by burnt sacrifice, as a substitution for a person.[29]

Where persons within the kin-group had become estranged, it was the duty of the chief or priest to restore them to concord. After agreement on the matter of restoration had been reached by discussion, it had to be ceremonially consummated at the sacred enclosure before the shrine (skull or stone) of the ancestral ghost. The offending parties presented their offerings in the same enclosure. Such a conception of reconciliation surely opened the way for the gospel, because it contained the basic ideas of reconciliation of man with brother man through a religious act, and suggested that the estrangement between human beings was also an estrangement between them and the spiritual Being who protected them.

In cases of affliction brought upon people, wittingly or unwittingly, by extra-communal offences, one could record an elaborate list of protective rituals, but they vary so much in each area that a generalization must suffice. There are charms, invocations, incantations and simple symbolic acts for protecting the unwary traveller by land or sea, the cultivator in his garden and the fisherman at his craft. These preserve him from harm and are usually performed in the name of his domestic ghost. There are similar devices and especially symbolic acts with sacred objects, for protecting houses, gardens, canoes and other property from any hostile *mana*. There is also a third category for protecting crops, output and returns; or may we say, to prevent the enemy sowing tares in one's crop. These are the three vulnerable points at which protection against extra-communal spirit forces is required—persons, property and harvests.

In addition to these are the ceremonial and seasonal occasions for the communal performance of rites of exorcism, purification and renewal. Some of these rites resemble the Hebrew ceremonial of the scapegoat taking the sins of the people away into the wilderness. In Ulawa, for instance, a dog was driven over a cliff and out to sea, to take away the sicknesses of the year, which were supposedly the penalties of the offences of the people. This was a symbolic purification and renewal rite.

All this, however non-western, is salvation psychology, in terms of sins, penalties and restoration. The orientation of popular desire was towards salvation and the direction of their exploration of salvation mechanisms was essentially religious. All this indicated a capacity for the gospel of Christ—and in the fullness of time God sent forth His Son.

CHAPTER 2

Early Culture Contact

THE LABOUR TRADE

THE INFLUENCE of the white man in the Solomon Islands before the encounter with Christianity was tragic. When early missionary work was beginning to take effect, culture contact continued to remain an obstructive factor to the growth of the Church. The attitude of the islanders towards the white missionaries was conditioned by the behaviour of the white men they knew. While the Church was growing apace in other parts of the Pacific, the Solomons remained basically hostile because of the long duration of the kidnapping trade. Even as late as the eighties, when this trade was supposedly under control, the relationships were bad. The American consular representative in the South Pacific at the time complained that American vessels were reporting trade closed to them, and of many outrages against Americans in islands where they had previously enjoyed good trade relations.[1] About the same time the British H.M.S. *Lark* visited Choiseul and found the inhabitants "cautious and suspicious". Guppy wrote of it:

> What happened to change this attitude, we could not learn. Evidently the good impression we had left behind us the year before had borne no fruit. Probably some inconsiderate action on the part of the crew of a trading vessel had undone our work.[2]

This was not new. It had been going on for half a century. The islands of Melanesia have a grim record of missionaries murdered because of the labour trade. Missionaries, being white, were equated with white traders, whalers, sandalwooders and slavers. As the kidnappers, seeking labour for Queensland, Fiji, Samoa, Central and South America, increased in numbers the record grew more brutal, and involved the displacement of a 1,500,000 persons and a serious disorganization of island life. The legitimate trader and the missionary suffered because of this, partly because they were white and partly because they were both engaged in trade.

The Solomon Islanders had their own slaving patterns and it is quite probable they saw the white man's slave trade for exactly what it was, and met it with the same forms of aggressive retaliation with which the Roviana or Simbo slaving raids would be met. Even after the turn of the century, when the Methodists were about to commence work in Roviana, the trader Wheatly listed sixty-two whites who had been murdered in that locality within a few years.[3] Thus there was a major obstruction to the gospel in this strong self-defensive psychological *set* against the reception of missionaries at all. Away back in 1845, when the first missionary experiment was made, the record began with the murder of the leader of the party.[4] It must also be admitted that the recruiters of the earlier period made deliberate capital on the better reputation of the missionary vessels, by white-washing their slave-ships, flying some missionary flag and posing themselves as missionaries until they had enticed enough victims on board. The verification of this grim record was collected at the time by Lorimer Fison, who, more than any single person, fought this nefarious trade.[5]

DEPOPULATION

Quite apart from these bad relations, there was the problem of the depopulation of the islands themselves. The figures are appalling. The Melanesian island of Erromanga, for example, which had an unhappy series of missionary murders, suffered a drop in population from 3,000 to 400.[6] That of Santa Maria fell from 5,000 to 2,000.[7] When Patteson began work on Mota he found 2,000 people there. In two decades it had dropped to half, and after a further two decades the figure stood at 350.[8] The excuse the Marovo chief gave for refusing Methodist entrance into his area was that Christianization meant depopulation, and he cited Ysabel as proof of his claim.[9]

Lambert insisted that the main cause of this depopulation was the introduction of diseases to which the people had no immunity.[10] Undoubtedly this was one reason, but it was certainly not the only one. We shall return to this when we examine the head-hunting complex, but let us observe here that the islanders were aware of the process of depopulation and attributed it to the rejection of the old religion for Christianity. This attitude was, in itself, obstructive to the spread of the gospel.

REPRISALS AND PUNITIVE EXPEDITIONS

The answer of the 'civilized' whites to the wrongs of the labour trade should have been a vigorous suppression of that trade in their own sea-ports. A policy of reprisals aggravated the island situation. A slave raid was followed by the murder of some innocent and unsuspecting white crew. This in turn led to a punitive expedition. The policy was used by the naval commanders and, after the establishment of the Protectorate, was continued by the Administration. The islanders saw it in terms of their own reprisal patterns, but the motives were quite different. The islanders did not appreciate the patterns of white authority, law and order, or what it meant to use punitive expeditions to 'teach them a lesson'. For a long time all white men were the same—kidnapper, legitimate trader, missionary and administrator—and any head could be taken for the loss of one of their own.

Guppy, when describing the murder of a British officer and crew by Florida people, admitted that this kind of thing was a monthly occurrence. A friendly trader, popular in one part of the Solomons for his trade relationships, was murdered in Bougainville as a reprisal for the activities of another white trader. This murder became the excuse for the former district making a war of reprisal on the Bougainville people. The murder of the captain meant some economic loss to them. Some of the crew of a ship, *Zephyr*, were massacred on Choiseul as a reprisal against kidnappers, and this in turn brought a punitive reprisal from H.M.S. *Emerald*. All these references come from one single source—cases met by Guppy on a single visit to the Solomons.[11]

This reciprocal belligerence obstructed missionary activity at several points. It prevented effective entrance into new areas and it endangered the lives of those establishing Christian posts. After the establishment of good contacts and the planting of a Christian teacher in a new locality, the visit of a kidnapper before the return of the missionary could lead to very unhappy results. Many an indigenous teacher lost his life in this way. After the turn of the century, when the Group fell under the rule of resident commissioners, and the missionaries became residents rather than making missionary visits, they still took a long time to establish themselves. The civil authority did not count for much, especially with the hill people, and the official punitive expeditions achieved very little.

Some of the missionaries established themselves eventually as supporters of the rights of the islanders and became important peacemakers. This in turn had bearing on the manner in which the Christian gospel was conceptualized in terms of a 'way of peace', with salvation as freedom from continual feuds, and the Christian encounter as one between the *mana* of the war ghosts and that of the Prince of Peace. The punitive expeditions of the Administration were seen in terms of "an eye for an eye and a tooth for a tooth", but frequently the people against whom the expedition was organized saw the Administration as coming in on the side of their enemies. The Administration seems never to have allowed for the fact that the camps involved in a feud kept accurate tally of offences and based everything on a specific concept of justice. Frequently missionaries came into the drama in the role of mediators and it is thus that they have recorded the patterns of feud and reconciliation. This role had a theological effect. While it is true that the continual feuds obstructed the growth of the Church, the Christian teachers and missionaries in these areas became involved in the work of reconciliation. When the long feuds brought about a state of exhaustion, sooner or later the mediators had their opportunity. After effective mediation there was always a burst of church growth, and naturally enough the peace ceremonials were identified with acceptance of the new faith in many cases. One of these cases has been analysed in detail in the anthropological section of this book.

References to Government punitive expeditions recur with monotonous regularity in the records. The official mission history of the western area mentions a number of them by locality—one at Hombu Peka, another with the hanging of an innocent man in the Marovo Lagoon, another at Roviana, one at Sasamunga, one more at Vella Lavella and still another at Buin.[12] This shows a wide distribution over the whole of the Western Solomons. The missionaries understood why they were regarded as *punitive*, but more often than not refused police protection and stood themselves beside the islanders, refusing to admit any justice in an expedition that merely balanced a score and made the innocent suffer for the guilty. This is not to say the islanders understood the missionary position either, but they often did see the missionary as a 'court of appeal' against what they felt to be Administrative injustice.

Sometimes a Resident Commissioner allowed a trader to drop hundreds of labourers, together with 'native police' without proper control, into some situation of tension. These would engage in a little head-hunting on the side. This was so in Vella Lavella, where the matter happens to be recorded in the archives because the gardens and property of both mission and local people suffered. On such occasions mission stations tended to become 'cities of refuge'. This happened also at Sasamunga after the burning of a number of villages by a punitive expedition. In the Marovo Lagoon incident the people against whom the expedition was launched insisted they were not guilty and missionary Goldie took up the case on their behalf. He secured the release of one prisoner but another, quite innocent, had unfortunately been hanged.[13]

Of all these cases none caused a greater disturbance than that of Sito, whose name was famous as a tribesman who ought to be brought to justice. The Government failed, but a missionary persuaded the Resident Commissioner that it was wrong to imprison a great number of people who were innocent, in lieu of the real offenders who were still at large. It was in this kind of role that the missionary was sometimes accepted by the people, especially in the western islands, long before there was any thought of their accepting the gospel. There are several lines of documentary material about Sito,[14] and some rather significant mission official correspondence about the policy of Government officials.[15] Goldie's comment in the Sito case is interesting because it shows the two wrongs Goldie was fighting: (1) no attempt at understanding the case and the issues it involved, and (2) the wrongness of the punitive pattern of letting the innocent suffer for the guilty.

> Sito had good ground for his action as his own wife and child had been murdered by a white official, and that in spite of the fact that though he had scores of easy opportunities, he never harmed a white man before. . . . All the traders and the boys belonging to the government did was to murder innocent men and women, burn their houses, and destroy their gardens. . . .[16]

Although it is doubtful if the islanders understood missionary ethics any better than the Government policy, they certainly appreciated protection from punitive plundering.

Most that I have written on this subject has concerned the western islands. Punitive expeditions were not confined to that locality, so it seems appropriate to show that the Melanesian Mission faced the same problems in the east.

> I contend that if we undertake to rule any people at all, we must act towards them, especially when they are as helpless as these people are, in a tender and fatherly way. We have no right to assume the position

of governors otherwise. We need more than the negative and repressive rule which now prevails here. The Resident Commissioners are more of the nature of glorified policemen than rulers. Their actions seem mainly confined to punitive measures and expeditions. Natives die by the thousand as the result of white men's acts and nothing is done. One white man dies by the hands of some lawless natives and instantly the authorities are awake, the native police are marched out, men-o'-war steam up, and the misguided natives are hunted to death, their gardens trampled down, their pigs shot, their villages desolated. Of positive help towards a better life these people receive nothing.[17]

THE MISSIONARY ADVOCATE

Once the missionary established himself as the islanders' advocate, he was bound to find himself involved in an advocacy on behalf of individual islanders. The following case will serve as an example:

> In 1920 Goldie found a government station being constructed at Buin with forced labour. One labourer, Chilion Kiau, recognized the mission ship and organized a deputation to wait on Goldie. He asked if they had to work against their will. The young police officer admitted this was the position, said he disapproved but was under orders. Goldie protested officially but got no reply. A senior officer arrived at Buin. Kiau, now accepted as leader by the labour, spoke on their behalf according to the normal island pattern. He was struck with a rifle, put under arrest, his books and papers burned. Goldie went to the Prime Minister in Melbourne. His secretary tried to brush aside these 'native tales', but Goldie had his facts and insisted on an investigation or he would give the facts to the press. He won his point, and had Kiau taken back and honourably reinstated by the officials.[18]

On another occasion this same missionary was asked by the islanders to represent them in a land alienation case in the Government Court. Who better? Goldie had a grasp of both the language of the people and British legal procedure. Large tracts of land were involved in a tense battle with Australian company lawyers and much was saved. Goldie was not by any means opposed to land sales but he had a reputation for watching the indigenous interests. In time the Government came to recognize his value and appointed him to the Advisory Council.[19]

I have stressed these aspects of justice for the Melanesian because they go back into the days of early culture contact and also have some aspects which survive to this present day. The current matrix of the problem is quite different but the moral dimension survives.

COLONIALISM

The cases I have been citing have been made public in the official mission histories. They have been cited to show how the missionary was forced to play a particular type of role. He fought for island rights, regardless of whether the islanders involved were pagans or Christians. However, this is not to say that the missionary was free from the general colonial outlook of his day—nor indeed, that he is yet free from it. He saw the master–servant relationship of brown and white as the planters saw it, and the church he established shows the influence of this orientation. While he was prepared to defend the islander desperately against inhumanity, plunder and other personal losses and protect his personal freedom, yet he still to this day tends to retain the master–servant frame of reference in his personal dealings with the Melanesian. A few missionaries have stepped down from this position and a few Melanesians have been elevated from their lowly status; but in general the basic attitudes are still the same. This attitude has hindered the emergence of the indigenous Church, especially in the west. The missionaries were fatherly masters who really loved and protected the "lesser breed" (a phrase from a hymn in the hymn-books of both churches involved in this survey) and were in turn loved for this protection. But for long years they remained reluctant to bring islanders forward into office, and they in turn accepted their dependent position. My feeling was that the stations, and their plantations, are still *very* colonial.

THE PSYCHOLOGICAL FACTOR

Culture contact has taken much out of these islands and put very little in. The plantation system has not built a sound economy. It depends on a single crop, and that mostly under foreign control. Early observers of the Solomon Island way of life said that a communistic system prevailed in each community. There was no individual ownership of land, canoes, houses or produce. The system was modified by the islanders themselves under the impact of culture clash, with the advent of the white trader. These traders, says Goldie, were adept in persuading the people to buy goods they did not require and running up debts for which they held individuals responsible. As more and more individuals in one tribe became so involved they were denied further purchases until payment had been made. This they accomplished by making private claims on what was really public property—coconut and sago palm produce, canoes and land. To assume ownership of these things against the communal group, the claimant resorted to the mechanism of the *tambu* or *taboo*. When a man set his tambu on a piece of land, or crops from certain trees, some spirit being involved thereby the fearful community did nothing about it. The man was thus able to establish his private ownership and pay his debts.[20] This question of land ownership is still a serious problem and the right and wrong of registering land is a subject for heated debate in many villages. Even in some very progressive villages there is still resistance to individual ownership.

The process of depopulation has only recently been arrested after a century of serious social dislocation. A volume of critical essays[21] has been devoted to this theme and reveals the features of culture contact that have been responsible—the introduction of arms and ammunition, the spread of foreign disease, the sale of intoxicating liquor, the unnatural conditions of plantation life, the elimination of social customs by the administration without any occupational substitutes, and the labour trade, to mention only some of them. The anthropologist

Rivers, who edited the volume, pressed also as most important *a psychological factor: a loss of interest in life.* He emphasized the loss of old customs, which though inhumane in many ways, were functional in the traditional patterns and had been discarded without the provision of functional substitutes.[22] He considered that Christianity was capable of supplying functional substitutes on the religious level and of giving people an interest in life, but was highly critical of the shortcomings of the economic substitutes for the suppressed customs. He considered the economic and religious factors to be closely related, and maintained that the missionary, as well as the administrator, must therefore have a positive attitude towards the economic dimensions of life. This involves the general interest in life, which in the final analysis determines survival. In the anthropological section of this book I have devoted some space to the economics of both the head-hunting and exchange patterns. These show the extent of the ramifications of interests and relationships in societies of this kind. The Church spread along many of these networks, but the changes in the respective configurations of head-hunting, slavery, and trade-exchange brought about by religious and moral change have taken something vital out of life itself. In the second generation this loss of interest in life has rebounded on the Church itself. For good or evil the emerging Church is involved in more than religion. The Christian is "bound in the bundle of life". The old animist saw religion as the integrator of the total life of society. Today it threatens to become a mere compartment.

Part Two*

PATTERNS OF CHURCH GROWTH

3 Levels for Studying Church Growth

4 The Growth of the Church in the Eastern Solomons
   Policy Laid Down by Selwyn
   Patteson's Contributions
   After Fifty Years
   Reasons for Slow Growth
   People-movements
   Social Factors
   The Second Fifty Years
   Why the Anglican Harvest failed in Malaita
   The Melanesian Brotherhood and the Companions

5 The Growth of the Church in the Western Solomons
   Origins
   The Roviana Phase (Pre-Great War)
   Types of Conversion
   The End of Australian Control
   Roman Catholic Methods
   Industrial Missions
   The 1928 Report and the Decade before the War

---

* This part is historical. It traces the growth of the Church in the Solomons from the beginning to the Pacific War.

CHAPTER 3

Levels for Studying Church Growth

THE STATEMENT drawn up by the Consultation on Church Growth, convened by the World Council of Churches Department of Missionary Studies at Iberville, Quebec, Canada, in 1963, began with the Church's mandate in the following terms:

the discipling of tribes and nations
the proclamation of the gospel to every human situation
the work of absorption into the fellowship
the growth within that fellowship
the outreach of that fellowship in concern for the world.

It was on a basis of this biblical position that policies, strategy, priorities and research techniques were examined.

In the Solomon Islands setting, as long as there are still ethnic units, families, villages and clans to be won from animism, there must be no relaxing of the effort to win them. True, the Solomon Islanders have responded to the missionary call to the New Guinea Highlands; but while there yet remain animist communities in Guadalcanal and Malaita there is still a missionary situation at their door. This situation has crystallized into an indifferent co-existence in some localities. These remaining pagan units are potential converts for any new ideology—philosophical, political or neo-pagan. The Great Commission is still relevant here.

There are all manner of situations in the nominally Christian villages, in the social and racial segments of the growing towns, in localities still feeling the aftermath of the war and the general effect of the acculturation process, where there is still direct discipling to be done. There are hundreds of folk of the second generation, who, though not animists, do not share the spiritual enthusiasm that brought their fathers out of animism. They are "of the world". We are confronted with the need of "discipling from the world" as well as from animism.

In these situations there exists a fellowship—the Church. It has been commissioned to proclaim Christ and to absorb those who respond (1 John 1: 3). As they are gathered in from "the highways and hedges" the fellowship should be expanding numerically.

Within the fellowship individuals should also be growing in grace. Two types of church growth are involved here—*quantitative* and *qualitative*. We are not concerned with a problem of *quantity or quality*. We are concerned with both. They are correlates.

The fellowship community, growing in numbers and in grace, must apply its experience to the human situations at its door. The Church is not an *enclosed* group, sealed off from the world around it—but something relevant, active, dynamic. The purpose of that action is not passive obedience to a command, but a gospel proclamation in order that those outside "may have fellowship with us". To this end the Church needs the guidance and strengthening of the Holy Spirit.

It is in this frame of reference of the Church's mandate that we examine *Solomon Islands Christianity*.

. . . . .

The growth of the Church, like the growth of a crop unto harvest is the work of God Himself, although He uses human agents in the process of cultivation. The Melanesian understands this two-fold responsibility. Even as an animist he differentiated between his own technical and agricultural knowledge, on the one hand, and the effect of sun and rain and many unknown factors which were outside his personal competence, on the other. His magico-religion recognized this dependence and sought aid from the power beyond. The Jews used a word *shutaf*, which suggested man's role as a *co-worker* with God in the processes of life. Although God Himself brings the crop to harvest, He relies on human agents to select good seed, to cultivate correctly, to weed carefully and to reap at the appropriate time. At many points wrong farming methods can adversely affect the quantitative and qualitative returns of the harvest. In using the imagery of harvest with reference to the growth of the Church, the Scriptures recognize this truth. Faulty missionary techniques can "quench the Spirit", to use one of Paul's phrases.

One of the purposes of this study is to examine missionary methods and discover which have been blessed by the Spirit with abundant harvests, and conversely which have retarded growth. This is not to say that everything depends on the technique alone. No farmer would ever claim *he* made the seed to grow, but nevertheless he would read carefully in the agricultural journal such articles as "Planting Methods that Stimulate or Hinder Growth", "The Importance of Weeding Techniques for Growth" and "The Right Time to Harvest for a Maximum Yield".

As I use the term *church growth* theoretically in three ways in this study, some definition is called for as we approach the historical unit of this book.

1. *Conversion Growth.* By conversion growth I mean that change of heart and mental set, which shows that a person has rejected his old way of life and found a place in the fellowship of Christians. This is possible in two ways:

 (*a*) in conversion from animism, registering the decision by burying the ancestral skull, destroying any fetish or sacred paraphernalia, turning to Christ and the fellowship of Christians;

 (*b*) in conversion from the world, a change of heart in which a materialist or agnostic or a mere nominal Christian experiences a confrontation with Christ and takes his place in the fellowship of Christians.

This is not a definition of conversion but of conversion *growth*. The convert must find his place in the fellowship or there is no church growth. This ought to be registered statistically in the records, if they are honestly kept. This has no bearing on the convert's knowledge of Christianity, but relates to the definite break with the past and incorporation into the Church community.

2. *Organic Growth.* There is a way in which a church grows when it emerges as the Church in a community, an indigenous body. It ceases to be part of a Mission. A biological analogy could be used of a cell separating from its parent cell and becoming an independent organism. This organic growth cannot always be registered statistically, but it has a physical way of proving its reality. The changing organizational patterns of the church often reflect growth going on. The appointment of deacons in the early Church showed that the Church was growing. The emergence of the Melanesian clergy, the appointment of Assistant Bishops, the new role of the Brotherhood, the statistics of the Boys' Brigade and other organizational developments are physical evidence of organic growth in certain directions. This is not numerical growth, but such organic growth may indirectly help statistical growth by providing new energy or eliminating old obstructions.

3. *Quality Growth.* The fellowship of Christians should be continually growing internally. Sometimes we speak of "growing in grace", sometimes of "the perfection of the saints" and sometimes of "sanctification". As to whether or not this kind of growth can be statistically recorded will depend on the theological content of the statistical frame of reference employed. The old traditional Methodist pattern, for example, does permit a record of quality growth. The child is baptized as "a lamb of the flock". When he registers his own personal decision to follow Christ he becomes a junior member. When this experience deepens to a more theological commitment he asks to become a member on trial, undergoes a course of instruction, serves a term on probation and is received into full membership at a special reception service or by confirmation. If he never comes to this point of spiritual maturity he remains an adherent. He may be a regular attender at worship and still remain an adherent. He is a Christian in that he is not an animist and he goes to church. Statistical records kept under this pattern do reflect quality growth, since the rolls were very carefully kept. This pattern operated in the Pacific in the early days and still does in some areas, although the Methodist Church in the Solomons has abandoned the system, which also provided for exhorters, prayer leaders, class leaders, preachers, and ministers—each registering a specific state of experience. The Anglicans bring their baptized infants on through stages of instruction to confirmation, and their adult converts likewise. The training steps have real spiritual significance. Both churches have levels for lay leadership participation, catechists and clergy. If all these are accurately recorded year by year, the statistics should reflect the organic and quality growth; but it must be admitted that many missionaries neglect this pastoral duty, and are satisfied with mere estimates which are quite unreliable.[1]

When the pastor keeps a record of pastoral counselling and confessions, he has recorded some physical evidence of quality growth or decline. The Roman Catholics do this. One Malaita Anglican priest told me that during Lent and Advent he had great numbers coming to get right again with God. He told me of the nature of their problems. I was impressed by the manner in which the Anglican emphasis on the key points of the Christian year brought a deeper desire for growth in grace on the part of his congregation.

By living in certain village communities and becoming a regular participant in their daily worship patterns, I explored ways and means for measuring quality, piety, theological emphasis and use of hymns and scripture. I feel that something was achieved in these depth studies and that by careful analysis much can be learned about organic and quality growth.

. . . . .

One could speak of *migration* or *transfer* growth also, but I shall only use this in one connection. Were I dealing with the migrating Micronesian communities in the Solomons, it would be important. We meet it in connection with the drift to the towns and plantations, and in reality it is not growth at all. The apparent growth of the church in Honiara registers as a corresponding loss in Malaita or Choiseul or wherever the folk have migrated from. Furthermore, if accurate statistics were always kept and transfers carefully attended to, we would discover that rather than any growth at all, we are confronted with a considerable loss through migration.

I will therefore mainly use these three categories of growth—conversion, organic and quality. Each is quite distinct, although they may be found together. Conversion growth, especially when it takes place in large people-movements, requires the follow-up of quality growth. The early experience of cutting oneself off from the pagan past is a definite encounter, but it must be consummated in quality growth, otherwise deep emotionally unsatisfied disturbances will emerge after a period of time. For church growth to be really effective, each of these dimensions of growth should be taking place together and interacting under the guidance and blessing of the Holy Spirit. I treat them separately for purposes of theoretical analysis, because one often finds one dimension developed and another neglected, and thereby the real growth of the church concerned is only partial and not full-orbed. Like the seven churches of Asia, many congregations are open for commendation at one point and criticism at another. This analysis of *Solomon Islands Christianity* thus becomes a study in growth and obstruction.

CHAPTER 4

The Growth of the Church in the Eastern Solomons

WRITTEN HISTORIES of the Anglican Church have a fairly fixed pattern based on the biographies of bishops. Events are 'things' which happened or were achieved in this or that episcopacy. In seeking documentary material one is confronted mainly with reports of the itineraries of the bishops or their responsible assistants. These record the number of baptisms, communions and confirmations of the itinerations, but often fail to give a clear picture of strength or growth. The episcopal structuring of church history has some advantages in helping to pin-point policies, changes and guiding principles, but the dynamics of growth are difficult to extract.

A survey of missions in the South Pacific immediately after the war showed the overall strength of the young church of the Melanesian Mission at 43,205—about three-quarters of these members being in the Solomons. This was the result of about a century of missionary activity. The pioneer of this work was Bishop G. A. Selwyn, who, after organizing the episcopate in New Zealand, turned to the islands in 1849. One could quite happily satisfy oneself by writing an appreciative account of this island church, distributed over a scattered archipelago, which had grown to about forty thousand in the face of great obstructions—international rivalry, the labour trade, and the processes of depopulation. This, however, would defeat our purpose.

In spite of the growth and present strength of this church in the Solomons, one has a feeling that it should be larger and stronger than it is. After a century there are still many unevangelized pockets in Guadalcanal and Malaita. The official Roman Catholic figures for 1964 estimated the pagans at about 12,000 in the South Solomons— nearly 10 per cent for the area concerned.[1] I visited a number of these pagan communities and found the people had adapted their paganism to the drastically modified way of life that has been forced on them by ruling conditions in the Protectorate. The local church seemed to have resigned itself to co-existence with a continuing paganism. This matter will shortly be investigated in more detail; meantime I assemble here a summary of what seem to me to be the principal policies of the Mission that have been used of God in the growth of this church, and set beside them any factors that have been obstructive.

POLICY LAID DOWN BY SELWYN

1. *Colonial Base:* Selwyn believed that the "surest way to spread the gospel to the uttermost parts of the earth, is by building up the

Colonial churches as missionary centres".[2] During the seven years he was establishing his episcopate in New Zealand, the islands to the north were continually in his mind. When the time came to establish the island mission, a New Zealand base and institutional centre was an integral part of the programme. Even though this was subsequently removed to Norfolk Island under a bishop for the islands alone, the New Zealand phase was an essential stepping-stone for Selwyn's approach to missions.

2. *Comity:* The Melanesian Mission came rather late into the Pacific field. The London Missionary Society (especially John Williams) and the Wesleyan Missionary Society (Walter Lawry in particular) had pan-Pacific vision and were well "on the march" before the arrival of Selwyn. A tour of the evangelized islands convinced Selwyn that the missionary world required some comity agreements. He determined to confine his own efforts in the islands to unoccupied areas and avoid missionary competition, such as he had experienced in New Zealand. Except for a very brief Roman Catholic experiment which failed, for fifty years the Anglicans had the Solomon Islands to themselves.

The reasons for comity were sound and practical:

(i) Comity permitted a strategic concentration of missionary effort on selected linguistic and culture areas.

(ii) This simplified the follow-up care of converts, organization of the church system, instruction, publication of scripture and aids for worship.

(iii) It prevented denominational competition and doctrinal disputes among the converts.

(iv) It obtained the maximum return for financial investment by concentrating travelling, shipping costs, etc., within a limited area of distribution.[3]

Faced with the great expanse of the Pacific before him, this was a wise policy. How long comity agreements should stand in the face of political and social change and present-day urbanization, is quite another matter. As a pioneering policy it was good.

3. *Commerce:* Most missions had some trade contacts in the early stages, either to pay for labour in establishing their stations, or as exchange for fresh food supplies. Most of them used the local trade economy for paying the first indigenous agents of the church,[4] but Selwyn, following the London Missionary Society, established regular markets in yams and pigs on a basis of weight and specific values.[5] He set out to establish a pattern of honest buying and selling without trickery.[6] Belshaw stresses how powerful a weapon commerce was in the battle for ideas, and cites trading references from Anglican sources which cannot be denied, though the matters cited date to Patteson's period of control. The policy was continued, and the editorial references in the journal cited show a general approval of the policy at home.[7]

4. *The Melanesian Mission Method:* The bishop specified the *object* of this trading (underscoring that word himself) in the following terms:

I give most of my goods to those who give me in turn what I want. [He is speaking at Marau, Guadalcanal.] Now what I want is to take some of your young people. . . . I want intelligent young lads, who can learn new habits and listen to a new teaching.[8]

The bishop was 'hiring' young men in return for trade goods—young men to go for a few months to his institution, where he hoped to bring them into a Christian experience and return them as evangelists to their own localities. This is the basic fact of the Melanesian Mission pioneering method. Young men were extracted from their societies, taken to a Christian settlement for a southern summer and then returned home, to be picked up again the following summer, and so on. In time many of these young men became the evangelical spearhead of the Mission, and from their efforts the Church in Melanesia grew. The system developed greatly under Patteson, Selwyn's successor. To work properly, family units had to be trained rather than individuals, and before long the bishop found himself asking for young women also, that the men might have Christian wives. In this market the bishop was 'wife-buying'! The pattern was legitimate in Melanesian ways, but it did lay the Mission open to much misunderstanding.[9]

The Melanesian Mission method of taking islanders to the Christian settlement in New Zealand (and later to Norfolk Island) aimed at "instilling into them all the Christianity, order and restraint possible", so that they would spread the truth among their own people upon their return. They were to observe Christianity in action and to acquire a desire for better health, better homes and also for education—"the redemption of the whole man".[10] This approach to missions has been called "evangelizing by civilizing" and is reflected in the prayer Selwyn wrote for the college he established for these islanders:

that true religion, sound learning and useful industry may here for ever flourish and abound.[11]

The method never did establish a high level of civilization in the villages. The Solomons are still socially among the backward areas of Pacific long-term mission activity. However, it did effect an entrance for the gospel into many places, it permitted the planting of churches, and the emergence of an indigenous ministry—and these are note-worthy accomplishments.

5. *The Melanesian Mission Ethos*:[12] Another conviction of the pioneer bishop was that the Church in Melanesia should be thoroughly Melan-esian. As many as possible of the ways and customs of the Melanesian should be retained within the Faith and approach of the Church of England. This was an important policy. As it worked out, it required that missionaries learn local languages, that Melanesian art forms be incorporated in church architecture, and above all it required a large team of island pastors and catechists. To live and worship today in an Anglican community in the Solomons is to become aware of the effect of a century of this policy—the Melanesian Mission ethos, a spirit among the missionaries reaching out towards a Melanesian Christianity expressing itself as a Melanesian Church. Nor are we surprised that

such an emphasis should produce a fine team of linguistic and anthropological writers among its missionaries, hard for any other single mission
to beat. The translation work of these men supplied the indigenous
pastors with the equipment they needed for making the Church indigenous, although this came after Selwyn's time. These Melanesian
agents were the most important element in the human side of the
Christian evangelistic thrust into the heart of animism,[13] even if the
method was a slow one.

6. *A Melanesian Diocese:* Selwyn's vision incorporated islands as
far north as New Guinea into his Mission. Realizing that this was
beyond his capacity operating from New Zealand, he worked for the
establishment of a bishop for Melanesia itself, though some years
passed before the appointment was actually made on February 24,
1861.[14]

PATTESON'S CONTRIBUTION

Much of Selwyn's policy survived as the permanent approach of the
Melanesian Mission. Patteson swung away from Selwyn's choice of
English as the *lingua franca* at the institution. He selected Mota, and
translation work developed from this moment. Mota became the
lingua franca because of the dominance of senior students from that
locality during the headmastership of Lonsdale Pritt (1861–67), who
relinquished that task when the institution was removed to Norfolk
Island, by which time the gospels of Luke and John and the book of
the Acts of the Apostles had been translated into Mota. Patteson
added to this before he died, although the whole Bible in Mota did
not appear until 1885. This was largely Codrington's work.

Patteson's translation emphasis was also directed towards the
Church's liturgy, and a particularly careful search for the correct
Melanesian terms for Christian theological concepts. He was patient
in developing theological dimensions and aimed at bringing a student
to a clear experience that was communicable to his friends and family
at home. He had a profound belief in the capacity of the Melanesian
for salvation, in which respect he thought of man collectively.[15] His
translation work included a scripture history, using the Old Testament
characters as types for Christian behaviour and piety; a set of questions
for Melanesian teachers to use with the folk they were instructing;
a primer which contained the Lord's Prayer, the Creed, the Ten
Commandments, some hymns and a few parables; and a catechism.[16]
Following on Selwyn's emphasis on the Christian life in action, Patteson
demonstrated the use of vernacular aids to worship as central in the
Christian life. Thus it has been Patteson, rather than Selwyn, who has
left the permanent imprint on Melanesian worship patterns today,
quite apart from the additional impression made by his martyr-
dom.

Patteson did not expect all the young men to return as missionaries;
but hoped that those who did not would at least prepare the way for
a friendly reception for the missionaries on their periodic itineraries. He
was prepared to proceed cautiously, believing that the slower way laid

the surer foundation. The policy of "remote control" from Norfolk Island was aimed at keeping the emerging church Melanesian in character, and maintaining the high standard of the *model*, on which the village devotional patterns were to be laid. This was certainly the slow way of doing it, and as more and more missions came into the field the policy of "remote control" had to go. It was, at best, an expensive method, and the presupposition that this kind of civilizing can be classified as evangelism is itself open to question.

An abstract of expenditure published for 1868 shows the dispensing of some £3,000 for the year. One third of this was expended on the running costs of the mission ship and another third covered the station capital costs—timber, fencing, labour, horses, cows, sheep and so on. Stipends required £480. Medical supplies, educational materials and printing costs were limited to £33 16s. 10d. Trade goods like hatchets and beads cost £56 8s. 10d. There was no direct item for evangelism, so it would seem that these were all conceptualized as the normal expenses of an evangelistic mission, evangelism itself being the total objective and not itemized. That a third of the funds should be used to itinerate from a distant station, and another third used to maintain that large and distant station, shows how expensive the system was.[17]

AFTER FIFTY YEARS

For fifty years the Anglicans had this field to themselves. During that time some 12,000 persons became Christian. For the period of time and the size of the population this was a comparatively small response by Oceanic standards. Furthermore, by far the majority of these converts had come into the Church in a short period of time by spontaneous people-movements, a type of conversion pattern which the Church Missionary Society had witnessed earlier in New Zealand before the arrival of Selwyn in that country, but which the Melanesian Mission had not actually sought. Had it not been for those people-movements in Ysabel and Florida, the growth for the half-century would have been very small indeed.

By the end of the century it was quite apparent the old system had to be changed, because the Melanesian Mission could neither handle the whole Solomon Group nor supply the staff to win it. In 1895 the policy was eased by the establishment of a station at Gela within the Solomon Island situation itself. By 1898 the French Marists arrived and the Melanesian catechists were hard pressed to deal with their arguments and competition. By 1904 Anglican policy changed and the missionaries moved into the front lines instead of operating from so far away. By negotiation with the Australian Methodists, a comity line was 'drawn' between Guadalcanal and New Georgia, and the Methodists took over the responsibility of winning the Western Solomons. The Anglicans removed from a small cause on Vella Lavella and strengthened their staff in the east. Nothing had been done on New Georgia, Choiseul or Bougainville. Thereafter the Methodists regarded these western islands as their comity area. The large populations on Guadalcanal, Malaita and San Cristoval, all in the Anglican area, were still unevangelized.

This was certainly more realistic for the available Anglican staff, but Bishop Wilson was unhappy at having to agree to this reduction of area.

The Anglican historian has explained the slow growth in the following manner:

> The failure of the Melanesian Mission to occupy the ground after fifty years was due to two reasons. First it had never had the men or money to do it, and secondly Selwyn's plan to take boys and educate them as missionaries to their own people was sure and sound, given time to complete it, but slower than that of the other missions who could send in numbers of European missionaries.[18]

This statement needs some evaluation. The Mission had every opportunity for half a century. How much time is needed to complete it? That other missions had more men and means, is open to doubt. The resources allocated for opening a new station in the western islands were smaller than the expenditure on the itineration from Norfolk Island for a single year. Missionaries who lived within the island situations were in continuous identification, not occasional visitors from a remote station. I do not think it was a statistical matter of men and money available but a need for deployment of men and means. Furthermore, when it comes to dealing with people–movement conversions, some of the greatest bursts of spontaneous growth in the Pacific have been effectively handled with very limited resources both in men and money.

One certainly cannot say the Anglican conversion experience was inferior or less evangelical. One is most impressed with the fervour of their indigenous evangelists, the manner in which they won social segments and communities, and the way in which some of these converted communities set out to win others.[19] There is a real atmosphere of a Melanesian Antioch here.

However, as one goes through the historical sources, one sometimes wonders if the slow process was not perhaps a little too deliberate. They demanded a long period before baptism, and a long period after that before confirmation. Although the posts for leadership were certainly open to Melanesians, the course of training was long, and the capacity to expand was restricted by the failure of the Church to raise a pastorate adequate for the evangelized areas. Even in later times the same evangelistic drive has been slowed down by the shortage of pastors, as we shall see when we discuss the Melanesian Brotherhood. When Bishop Wilson assumed office in 1894, there were only two Melanesian priests and seven deacons.

Although the ideal was stated from the start, it was not until Wilson's time that there appears to have been a real willingness to act upon it. He brought the number up to fourteen by the end of his term of office in 1911. An overall study of church growth patterns in the Pacific leads one to believe that there is some direct relation between the degree of authority given to indigenous church leaders and the growth of the church. It is possible for a Mission to have fine ideals with respect to indigeneity and yet to withhold action upon them.[20] To me as an objective observer, the great contribution of Bishop Wilson was his readiness to act on the ideals of Selwyn and Patteson and bring more and more Melanesians into responsible office. The step should have been taken at the time of the people-movements in Ysabel and Florida. Fifteen or twenty valuable years were lost. Now having rejected the historian's reasons for slow growth it is incumbent on me to suggest some constructive alternatives.

REASONS FOR SLOW GROWTH

Again as a purely objective observer, I suggest four reasons for this half century of slow growth:

1. Remote control techniques always suffer from a lack of direct *identification*. I had the pleasure of being taken to the location of Hopkins' station in Malaita and of talking to the local people about this missionary and his work. I am satisfied that he accomplished much by simply being resident there, and sharing the grim dangers of the small Christian party, by witnessing to his faith with a price on his head. I know that Selwyn and Patteson kept the missionaries behind the lines from the very good motive of ensuring that the emerging Church would not be western in character; but this was at the expense of direct identification, and I think it slowed down the growth potential.

2. The remote control system had the disadvantage of robbing the Mission witness of its *continuity*. The availability of a missionary as an advocate, peace-making mediator, adviser and dispenser of simple medicines, and the practical daily outworkings of the great faith he continuously proclaimed, all counted for much more than a seasonal visit—which to the Melanesian must have seemed to be for the economic ends of buying yams and pigs, and hiring youths and buying wives. In the one case the gospel was proclaimed in faith and works, in the other a business relationship was maintained. The former had continuity; the latter, like their own trade exchanges, was seasonal. When I say one "counted for more", I mean in terms of mission in obedience to the Great Commission. Quite apart from possible misunderstandings about the seasonal trade visit approach, its witness was at best intermittent. Certainly to Selwyn and Patteson, these were a means to an end—an end some years ahead, when the new teaching could be introduced by their own young couples. But what did these visits mean to the elders who let their young men go, and who bargained at the time for the trade goods? It was a business transaction, in which they made the best possible bargain, and that was an end of the matter in many cases. It must have slowed down the growth potential.

3. The remote control pattern was also *culturally defective* and operated against the very end it sought to attain. It extracted youths from the cultural matrix of their own society and subjected them to a form of life that must have been strange, however fine as a model

Christian community. If a youth found that the Christian way was acceptable and became a convert, then he had to return to his pagan society and live as an isolated figure in a hostile social complex, trying to demonstrate a life he had learned in an ideal Christian community. Not only was he deprived of the protection of the Christian authority but his very return confronted him with a primary decision—would he resume his pagan role within the pagan society from which he had come, and try to bring the group, through its legitimate councils, to Christianity; or would he accept a self-imposed ostracism and actively stand as a Christian opposed to his own social system? It was much easier to go to a completely pagan island than to return a Christian to his own pagan kin. This was certainly the hard way.[21] It tended to stir up resistance against the group acceptance of Christianity. Even when a man was personally attracted to Christianity after his first visit to New Zealand, his friends at home frequently tried to prevent his return a second time. Bishop Patteson admitted seventeen years after the start of the Mission that though some of the most advanced scholars did appear to value the mission "way of living", they "were comparatively few in number".[22] On the whole the cultural objections, especially the threat to group cohesion which individual conversion meant, slowed down the potential for church growth.

4. The remote control approach implied an expectancy of slow growth, because it accepted an *ultimate* rather than an *immediate* goal. It was "sure and sound", says the historian, "given time to complete it". After seventeen years Patteson still regarded it as "a day of small things". This expectancy of slow growth continued through the fifty years, except for that spontaneous outburst of people-movement which we will shortly examine.

Bishop G. A. Selwyn, like Marsden in Australia, was, by sympathy and method, a colonizer and a civilizer, as distinct from types like Henry Williams, later Bishop, who were described at the time as evangelizers. Selwyn believed that the great goal of evangelism *could not be reached* without simultaneous and even preliminary teaching of secular knowledge and methods of civilization.[23] The isolated institution therefore became necessary to separate young men deliberately from pagan society and teach them civilization in an ideal situation. One might say, an artificial and unreal situation. In some ways this equated Christianity with western civilization and thus operated against the very ideal of the Mission. To some extent the ideals within the structure were thus in conflict. Striving for a Melanesian character and striving for a 'civilized' way of life were antithetical.

Although Bishop Patteson introduced some fine spiritual qualities into the life and worship of his "sons and daughters", which still show their mark on Melanesian patterns today, he too emphasized the importance of material aspects—agricultural, industrial and commercial—that were western and remote from village conditions. Selwyn had stressed these things as "not merely useful but necessary". Surely this is to beg the question. Of course they are useful and necessary, but the question is really: are these the roots of the tree or the fruit of it? Where the civilizing process has been the immediate aim and the gospel the ultimate, the growth of the Church has always been delayed, and even then it has frequently come as a result of non-civilizing factors. An objective examination of the present case shows an outreach into Melanesian depths in worship patterns, but an applied Christianity which was quite western in character.

In study of the advocacy and acceptance of innovations, it must be recognized that the *real* innovator (the accepter) and the *would-be* innovator (advocate) do not necessarily see the innovation in identical terms. In this case Christianity is the innovation. In the Eastern Solomons the worship patterns advocated were accepted long ago and have become thoroughly indigenous; but many of the civilizing features have still not been accepted, as our village study will shortly reveal. Melanesian Christianity is by no means uniform, but there are many localities where the worship pattern is strong and effective, whereas the pattern of applied Christianity is defective. Western civilizing was not acceptable and no real Melanesian counterpart has yet been worked out. We shall return to this later, but meantime I believe this had some bearing on the slow growth of the Church during the first fifty years. I am suggesting that the advocacy of a complex innovation, combining structures that were religiously Melanesian and culturally western, met with an uneven response and slowed down the general acceptance of Christianity. Judging from responses in other parts of the Pacific, an immediate gospel for the people, which gave them victory over their animistic fears, rather than an ultimate one with civilizing complications, would have brought faster results. Provided the follow-up had been effective after the immediate acceptance of the gospel, a social and a civilizing application of a more Melanesian character would have been worked out locally.

In their desire for a truly Melanesian Church the Anglicans had a truly valuable insight, but a genuine Melanesian outworking of that Christianity in daily life and labour is still largely unexplored. As one stands looking back at all this from today, one is impressed by the fact that the real germinal ideas the century has produced, with respect to missionary outreach and stewardship, have come as *fruit* of the gospel *from the Melanesians themselves*. This is as it should be. When the gospel is put first, these things are added.

The slowness of growth during the first half century was recognized by the official historian. Perhaps it is easier for an outsider to examine a situation objectively than for one who has himself fought a good fight in the front lines. I believe the Anglican missionaries were dedicated, courageous and competent. They have left a splendid record and one does not feel disposed to find fault with them. Their policies, however, are open for examination, and it is at this point that I have dared to suggest reasons for the slow growth. I offer them only as suggestions, but I believe there is enough evidence for each of the four points to warrant its being taken seriously.

There were other factors slowing down growth, which applied to all missions regardless of policy—a tragic record of epidemics, which were interpreted religiously by the Melanesians; the trade in arms and ammunition; the labour trade; the illegitimate business of many traders and some planters, who actively opposed the establishment of missions;[24] and the rapid depopulation of many islands.[25] All this has to be allowed for. But such allowance having been made, the growth was nevertheless tragically slow.

PEOPLE-MOVEMENTS

During the seventies some indigenous agents had small groups ready for baptism when the mission ship arrived. Early growth took place in Mota, in the Banks Group south-east of the Solomons. Forty to fifty persons a year were added to the church there during this decade. By 1879 the island was half Christian—435 of a total population of 869. It took about twenty years to win Mota by a slow but steady flow. Ara, a small place with a population of a hundred, took six years to win. Immediately the young congregation sent out its own missionaries to three other communities.[26]

In the eighties the tempo of growth increased. The bishop might find 100 or 200 awaiting his arrival. This growth was taking place in the Solomons in Florida and Ysabel. In 1875 they each had one unstable school. The missionary visiting Ysabel found that a "horde of bush people in terror of head-hunters" had come to the location of the strongest chief to seek his protection. The missionary, who did not know the bush language, hoped it might lead to a general Christianization. In this state of general excitement it seemed to him that there was opening for the gospel, even though these bush people had not hitherto been exposed to any civilizing effects of missionary contact, as with the coast people.

On the nearby island of Florida missionary Penny was confronted by the beginnings of a people-movement, with a breaking up of the ghost worship. At Belaga, Hogo, Halavu, Olevuga, Ravu and Vura dramatic changes had suddenly taken place. Penny felt constrained to stay in the locality for twenty-two weeks, during which he not only saw the heathen forces overthrown, but brought some 200 persons to that state of Christian knowledge he considered adequate for baptism.

By 1885 some fairly strong churches had been established and the people-movement still continued. There were 189 adult baptisms in 1888 and in the following year over 1,000 Christians met the bishop, including groups who had been born and sworn enemies. They met in peace to witness the baptism of another 200 Christians. In 1892 a further 280 adult baptisms were reported, in 1893, 346 plus 180 children; in 1894, 118 confirmations and 200 more baptisms in 1895. This movement lasted for about twenty years and accounted for about 80 per cent of the total population of this particular locality.[27] The movement had a clear pattern based on the social structure, and passed from village to village.

Prior to this movement, evidence suggests that small groups, families or village sub-groups, had been turning to Christ. There are no references to Christian villages before about 1870, when we hear of Sapibuana and Lango. Except at Mota in the Banks Group, where some sub-groups had been won, there was no real abandonment of heathenism in the first twenty years. By the end of the third decade the Florida movement was under way. There were other movements in the eighties, though the localities were not always specified in the records. The bishop baptized 561 adults in 1886, 568, and later another 210, in 1889, showing that other places beside Florida were involved.[28] These appear to have been in Ysabel. The atmosphere of all this was more like that of the Church Missionary Society among the Maoris in New Zealand in the days of Henry Williams, and was not the type of response sought by Selwyn. We are bound to admit, on a solid body of evidence, that most of the 12,000 Christians in this Mission at the turn of the century had come from these people-movement responses, following patterns of culture and social structure, and not from responses to the civilizing process.

What experiments had been made in the latter direction had been largely confined to Mota, where Patteson had bought ten acres of land in 1867 for the establishment of a Christian village settlement. The Melanesian leader involved in this project gave long and faithful service and became a prominent and influential figure in Mota, but this project itself seems to have stimulated no real expansion of the Church. What missionary fire came from the Banks Group as a whole, came from the individual and group experiences of the converts, not from any ideas of Christian settlement. Indeed, in the second fifty years even that fire burned low and the second generation settled down to a state of missionary inaction.[29] This may be accounted for, however, partly by the depressing effect of the population drop from 2,000 to 350.

SOCIAL FACTORS

Social factors have played an important part in the winning of Solomon Islanders for Christ. This is demonstrated in such cases as that of Soga, of Bugotu, a chief in every way and a born leader, representative of a social unit. He had the capacity to teach himself to read and write and subsequently assisted in the translation of the Fourth Gospel. Soga was strongly influenced by Dr. Welchman and the two of them together brought many Ysabel people into Christianity between 1889 and 1898. By the end of that period churches and schools had been built, Christian teachers were established, and almost the entire population had been baptized or were receiving instruction for it. The place is solidly Anglican today. Any community of this size won for Christ in ten years is worthy of study. The chief element of the dynamics of church growth here would appear to be the co-operation of missionary and chief and their recognition of the ties and lines of the social structure. A European missionary who can fit himself into the culture pattern, together with a powerful chief, make a formidable team for winning men to Christ—not through intimidation, but because for tribal people this is a significant combination.

The changes brought about in Soga's life by conversion counted for much, especially with his enemies. The great efforts of his last days were directed at winning the bush people he had fought all his earlier life. Some of Welchman's adventures at bringing together such men have been narrated by the wife of Bishop Wilson in a useful volume, which should satisfy any reader that Welchman was aware of the importance of social structure and customary behaviour patterns, and that he would make use of any opportunity for reconciling enemies by using their own cultural mechanisms.[30]

During 1892 and 1893, when Welchman was using Soga for purposes of scripture translation, they also worked out together a Christian application of customary law—that is, a rule of behaviour for a Christian in the Melanesian way of life. There was no western civilizing about this. One wonders if this had anything to do with the higher standard of stewardship and applied Christianity in Ysabel today. Ysabel has certainly advanced further in this direction than the other eastern islands.

Although the people responded in social groups and in great numbers, Welchman was not blinded by mere numbers. He saw that group movements could still be multi-individual, and was concerned to know where each convert stood personally with respect to his experience. He did not hesitate to remove a segment of a group for further instruction before baptism. On one occasion he presented 101 for baptism, having satisfied himself personally that each one was ready, and having eliminated eighteen for further instruction. Three years earlier these candidates for baptism had been scattered in the bush, ready to kill on any pretext.

During these years the doors were opening for Christianity over a large part of the Eastern Solomons. Scores of family and village groups came into the Church. They were mostly activated and won by the indigenous servants of the Church. In the section on "Power Encounter" I shall deal at length with the experiences of Clement Marau, one of these effective evangelists. He may perhaps be taken as a type. Here again the importance of the social structure will be apparent. Although most of these young men had come into their Christian experience as individuals in Norfolk Island, yet they had to work out their own methods within the social structure. When they had made their adjustments they became effective evangelists, working through any individual convert into his family, from family to family, and thus into the larger social units. We have an actual description of the process from Marau's own pen.

It is therefore of importance that we observe that the majority of the 12,000 Christians in these islands after fifty years of mission activity had been won by people-movements of various size, religious movements pure and simple—i.e., by the confrontation of their animist deities and ghosts, and victory over the fear of them—with very little actual bearing on the civilizing process, which still has to be worked out in Melanesia itself.

THE SECOND FIFTY YEARS

In the second fifty years the Melanesian Mission was confronted by a quite different situation. The western islands were left to the Methodist Mission, which in turn agreed to keep out of the eastern part of the Group. Other missions encroached on the now reduced Anglican area. They were not prepared to discuss comity agreements, and were aware of the ripening fields. The Anglicans themselves, by this time, had moved into resident stations within the Solomons and had thereby eliminated one of the major obstructions to their growth. Bishop Wilson also demonstrated a readiness to act on the ideal of appointing more Melanesians to the full pastoral office,[31] an attitude which dramatically changed the picture. Despite the loss of potential converts by the encroachments of the non-comity missions, the Anglican community in the Eastern Solomons alone has now four times the numerical strength it had after the first fifty years.[32]

The most important innovation in this second half-century was probably the establishment of the Melanesian Brotherhood, which made the evangelistic thrust a thoroughly indigenous mechanism, and something quite unique in Pacific Missions.

The more rapid growth of the Church in the second fifty years may be accounted for by these three innovations: (1) the achievement of better identification and continuity of effort by the abandonment of remote control and bringing the entire staff into the field situation, (2) the readiness to act on the ideal of an indigenous ministry at all levels, and (3) the establishment of the Melanesian Brotherhood. It may well be that denominational competition had a stimulating effect, but I am not prepared to be dogmatic at this point. While it is true that the Malaita field ripened for harvest with the return of the labourers from Queensland,[33] I am not prepared to say this field was not ripe in the first period. Had the Mission commenced by direct identification of resident missionaries, it may have found this to have been so. However, we cannot be sure at this point.

One feature which has been carried over into the new century is the industrial emphasis. The fact that so much of the civilizing burden of the Protectorate is left by the Government to the Missions is a real problem. This includes far more than medicine and education. The mission shipping is practically alone in servicing many of the outer islands. What training is given to Melanesians in boat-building, engineering, printing and other civilizing pursuits is largely concentrated on mission stations like Taraoniara and Munda. In the western islands the plantation business is a major mission concern. No one can deny that these institutions are practical and important. To what extent they really belong to the missionary programme is problematic. They represent isolated station activities. The Melanesians living in these settlements are living in artificial situations very different from village conditions. They cannot therefore be classified as pilot projects, though they maintain a high level of religious life. In that they print the mission literature and keep the mission ships itinerating they may be considered essential, but one sometimes wonders whether this mission engagement in engineering and industry may not have hindered commercial development of these much-needed pursuits in the Protectorate. Taking over such industrial projects is a terrifying prospect for an emerging indigenous Church. When a Mission is in the process of becoming an indigenous Church, what happens to the economic structure of the civilizing adjuncts with which it has become entangled? This is a question which requires an answer.

WHY THE ANGLICANS FAILED TO REAP
THE FULL HARVEST IN MALAITA

From the writings of the Anglicans who lived as missionaries in Malaita, though none of them traces the course of church-planting, one has the impression of a gradual spread of Christianity throughout this large and populous island, firstly around the coastal ports and then from the trade exchange localities into the interior. One feels, however, that some of the earlier Christian settlements were new villages composed of segments of converts breaking away from pagan villages, often under the influence of labourers who had become Christian in Queensland.

The Anglicans had long been in this field, and their indigenous teachers had endured much danger and persecution. The mission had spent a great deal of money and had done the hard and back-breaking pioneering. Then they saw the field ripen unto harvest. Almost immediately other missions moved in and gathered much of the harvest into their own barns. The gospel they preached was at heart very much the same. It was largely a matter of having labourers available when the field was ripe, and perhaps being ready to deploy staff for the purpose of ingathering.

In the years of harvesting the Anglicans never could provide a *pastorate* to keep pace with the *evangelical spearhead*. They demanded high standards and experience from a Melanesian before ordaining him to the priesthood and were unable to supply an adequate number of European priests. They might well have met the situation by using new converts as exhorters or by providing a kind of class meeting where converts could testify, so that worship patterns could have been organized even without a catechist or priest, but this was not their way. Their system maintained the sacraments as central, and these required a priest, and the growth of the Church was determined, not by the capacity for the evangelistic thrust, but by the number of priests available to consolidate the work. Both Bishop Wilson and Bishop Steward, and some Anglican historical writers also, have bemoaned this effect of their policy of slow development. In the twenties and thirties the thrust of the Brotherhood into pagan areas was held up for this very reason and Brothers had to stay behind to do their own consolidation, contrary to their own rules.[34] Their evangelism is still today slowed down by this same factor, as the Bishop indicated in his Synod Charge in 1962.[35]

By the turn of the century the great people-movements in Florida and Ysabel had run their courses. Had these movements been fully

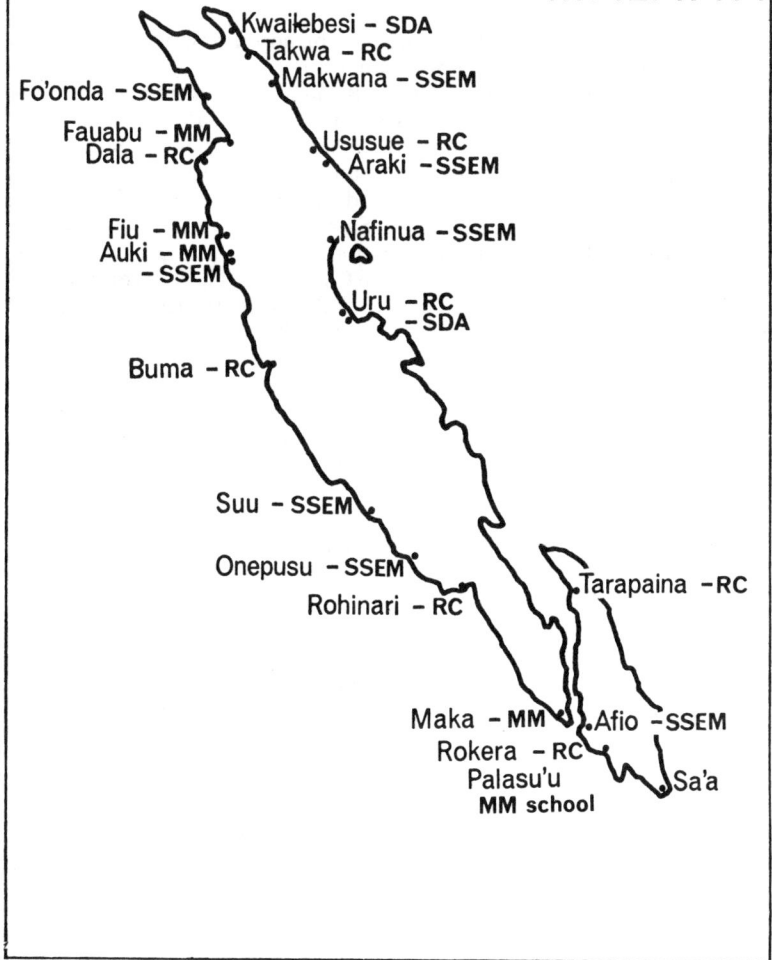

MALAITA

Kwaiłebesi – SDA
Takwa – RC
Makwana – SSEM
Fo'onda – SSEM
Fauabu – MM
Dala – RC
Ususue – RC
Araki – SSEM
Fiu – MM
Auki – MM
– SSEM
Nafinua – SSEM
Uru – RC
– SDA
Buma – RC
Suu – SSEM
Onepusu – SSEM
Rohinari – RC
Tarapaina – RC
Maka – MM
Afio – SSEM
Rokera – RC
Palasu'u
MM school
Sa'a

DISTRIBUTION OF MISSION STATIONS

MM   Melanesian Mission (Anglican)
SSEM   South Seas Evangelical Mission
RC   Roman Catholic
SDA   Seventh Day Adventists

(Jehovah's Witnesses and Baha'i also operate in the area)

The long portion of coast-line without mission stations is well-established
Anglican work, now under indigenous priests.

c

used to produce evangelists and pastors, there should have been a team of men ready for similar movements in Malaita when the field ripened to harvest. As a result of their policy Malaita has been won in different patterns.

It is now 108 years since an Anglican bishop first landed on Malaita and over a century since the first Malaita lads were taken away to the central institution for instruction. It is ninety-one years since the first Anglican teacher, Joseph Wate, was put on Malaita and set up a Christian school. Before the end of the century he had been ordained, the Sa'a people had become Christian and had six schools, several other communities had become Christian and the first resident white missionary had been appointed. The lower Sa'a area, all Christian before the turn of the century, the rendezvous for all Malaita, and a good place for the diffusion of ideas, had over 300 Christians. These formed a lively church which had emerged from a period of intense persecution, from a pagan league which had worked against them from 1886.

At the other end of Malaita the church-planting had commenced in 1902, where Malaita-men who had been converted in Fiji and Queensland were active. One of these, Jack Taloifuila, who was later ordained, introduced the Anglican Church into the Tai Lagoon area. His grave is today beside the church at Fouia, the village he himself founded as a Christian settlement. A second European missionary was placed in northern Malaita, in the Kwarade district, also about this time.

The Anglican men who worked in Malaita did splendid service under trying conditions. They lived close to the people and their written records reveal a depth of understanding of the *mores* of the people. They showed courage and faith and gave long service. Having read their literary work with care, I can testify to their thoroughness. I mention this to show that if the Anglicans did not reap the full harvest in Malaita, it was not the fault of the courage, competence or devotion of the missionaries. Nor was it the Anglican pattern of worship, which had much to commend itself to the people.

The return of the labourers from Fiji and Queensland provided both a new stimulus and a new set of problems. The men who had returned had seen Christianity and Christian schools and the benefits of law and order. They talked about these things with new attitudes. Whether their motives were right or wrong is not the point, but rather that doors began to open in all parts of Malaita on a basis of culture contact rather than social structure, as it had been in Ysabel and Florida. A populous island with some 50,000 people, though culturally segmented, was waiting to be won. A dramatic deployment of staff was called for. But the demand for "the continuing care for the flock" in Ysabel and Florida had a prior claim to "labourers for the vineyard" in Malaita. The care and preservation of areas already won did receive the priority and this reduced the capacity for growth from paganism. The opportunities being far more than the Anglicans could handle, the way was opened for other missions, with the result that Malaita is only half Anglican today, and a chain of denominational missions stretches along the coastline.

The Roman Catholics, for example, established themselves in the following localities:

Buma (1909), Rohinari and Tarapaina (1911), Rokera (1925), Takwa (1935), Dala (1950) and Ususue and Uru (1962).

This policy of progressive church-planting has brought their total number to 11,719 in Malaita, and a comparison of the 1963 and 1964 statistics reveals that their process of growth continues. As there were no Roman Catholic stations in Malaita before 1909, we must realize that the Anglicans here lost nearly 12,000 who were potential converts. A somewhat similar number have been won by the South Seas Evangelical Mission, and others by the Seventh Day Adventists. To return to our Roman Catholic figures, Malaita is part of the Vicariate of the South Solomons, which includes also San Cristoval and Guadalcanal of the Melanesian Mission area. In this total area the Roman Catholics now have 24,687 followers and have established themselves in four new localities since 1960. In each of these the Church is growing from paganism, their increases numbered 68, 48, 33 and 33 respectively last year, and they represent in all 3,069 conversions to Catholicism in four years.[36] The total number of pagans still remaining in this region we are discussing is about 12,000, so our analysis is currently relevant.

There is a principle of priority here that we might do well to consider for a moment. If the ripening of the harvest is the Lord's work and we are stewards in His service, is not the sending of labourers for the ingathering a just priority, even if it means a temporary reduction of those caring for the flock or making use of harvesters who are not fully trained? Is the ripening harvest itself a challenge to a Church to advance, to organize all its available personnel (indigenous and lay) for the ingathering? To limit the pastorate because of 'standards' at a time like this can mean a loss of the harvest. Better increase the number of pastors from the mature folk of the established congregation than lose the ripening harvests.

Reluctantly the Anglicans handed over their work in the west to the Methodists and deployed their staff to Guadalcanal Savo and Florida.[37] Why on earth to Florida, which had had about two decades for consolidation, when the harvest fields of Malaita were crying out for harvesters? As I see the Anglican problem, it was in their policy *at the working level*. They had the machinery to throw their Melanesian converts into action, but they delayed acting. They prolonged the period before baptism. They delayed confirmation. They held up ordination. They created strong worshipping fellowships where they operated but their slow process of perfectionism kept them nursing those congregations instead of thrusting their converts out into action. Today the Anglican village congregations with which I came in contact approve evangelism, and pray diligently for the Church's accredited evangelists, but the congregations themselves are not evangelistic. It is possible to devote so much attention to the nurture of the flock, that it becomes dependent on that nurture. It becomes a *fed* community within an enclosure, thoroughly dependent on the shepherd.

The movements of Ysabel and Florida should have been able to produce both evangelists and pastors adequate for the Malaita harvests. A competent Anglican observer recently wrote:

> Many converted by the Brothers could not be ministered to by the Church because of lack of staff. The people wanted the Anglican Church, but were taken up by the S.S.E.M., S.D.A., Jehovah's Witnesses, Baha'i or Roman Catholics.[38]

This I believe is true. Fox says "This happened in at least thirty cases".[39]

THE MELANESIAN BROTHERHOOD AND THE COMPANIONS

On October 28 we were living with the people of an Anglican village in Malaita. In the Christian Year the saints Simon and Jude are remembered on that day, but it has special significance for the Melanesians of Anglican areas, for this was the day that Ini Kopuria, founder of the *Melanesian Brotherhood,* took his vow. The Melanesian Brotherhood is the evangelistic arm of the Anglican Church in these islands, and was itself the outcome of a Melanesian vision.[40] The *Companions of the Brothers* are bodies of Christians in the villages, who meet daily to uphold the Brothers in prayer and to pray for the heathen among whom they work.[41]

The Melanesian Brotherhood has been an instrument greatly used by the Spirit of God during this century in bringing heathen people to Christ in the Eastern Solomons, and as far as New Britain and the Highlands of New Guinea. It stimulated both the missionary outreach of the Melanesian Church and the congregational concern for that outreach.

Ini Kopuria had been to Norfolk Island but returned to the Solomons to serve in the armed constabulary. After two years as a lance-corporal he met with an accident, was hospitalized and left slightly but permanently lamed. During his convalescence he thought much of the past and felt he had little to show for the favours he had received. Often in his schooldays, he had been chosen because of his promise and others left. Now a voice came to him:

> All this I gave to you:
> What have you given to me?

He accepted the challenge along the following lines. At Norfolk Island he had been inspired by Codrington's lectures in Church history. He had also been impressed by one of Bishop Steward's letters on Service, distributed by the *Southern Cross* a few years earlier. He now called on the Bishop, who guided his ideas into the form which eventually materialized as the Melanesian Brotherhood, and took him back to Norfolk Island, where five others of similar mind were found. They resolved to go obediently wherever the Bishop sent them.

The Brotherhood grew and developed into a series of small households, each under an Elder Brother chosen from among themselves, and each household assigned to a particular district. Within these districts the brothers itinerated in pairs among the heathen, seeking to open up the way for church-planting. The mission of the brothers was essentially a mission to the heathen and this is stated in the first rule:

> The work of the Brotherhood is to proclaim the teaching of Jesus Christ among the heathen, not to work among Christians.

Bishop Steward said that the second purpose was to ascertain by trial whether there was a vocation to the religious life among these Melanesians. Many held that the celibate life was impossible for them. Vows were made for one year and renewed annually on October 28. It was left open for a brother to retire if he desired to do so.

The brothers maintained a disciplinary check on each other, by discussion within the Chapter itself. A complaint about a brother was no matter for outside discussion. Final authority lay with the Father of the Order, the Bishop.

A centre was established at Tambiriu on land given by Ini, when he gave himself and his possessions to God with his vow of obedience and a resolution to take no payment from the Mission. Many young men, who had finished with school but had not yet settled down to the communal life, gave two or three valuable years of service in this way to the work of the Church. A great many of these eventually became catechists or priests. Some served as brothers for life.

With the economic changes and new opportunities that have come to the islands, it is not so easy a decision for a young man to make today—to turn away from remunerative openings to a vow of poverty. For quite a number of years the movement enlisted many young men who were not ready to settle down and marry, and thus directed their capacities and helped them retain their religious perspectives over those critical years of life. The situation is different now. The number of pagan localities in the Solomons has been reduced, wages for labour have increased, and many are now attracted to economic security rather than to the poverty of the Brotherhood. These economic roles have a different atmosphere, do not stimulate the same high motivation, or stabilize the religious experiences of the young men. The situation may be due for review.

Nevertheless, the Brotherhood has been a most important force in the Eastern Solomons, not only through its primary motive of converting the heathen, but especially because it was a Melanesian concept for Melanesian action—an indigenous growth in every sense of the word. The Melanesian people took the movement into their hearts and responded by establishing the Company of Companions, to pray for the brothers and their work. This was something really germinal in the character-building of the Melanesian Church.

At present there are about eighty members in seven households, though most of their current growth is outside the Solomons. Between 1955 and 1957 they were responsible for bringing forty-five pagan villages to Christ in New Britain and New Guinea, involving 9,500 persons.[42] I met a number of these young men in Malaita. They had come down to Sio Harbour from the mountains. Others were working among the bush people inland from Takataka. I had good reports of their effective evangelism at Bu and Ainikaula, and was impressed with those I had as travelling companions from time to time. My one reservation was not on their account, but on account of the village Christians, whom I often felt were inclined to regard the Brotherhood as the evangelistic 'wing' of the Church, to which all evangelism could be left.

Even so, there can be no doubt about the brothers opening up heathen areas to the light of the gospel. They were often roughly treated, but won their way in a remarkable manner, often by undertaking tasks which so astonished the heathen that they began to enquire about their gospel. They themselves call this "opening a heathen village".[43]

Yet the total effectiveness of the work of church-planting must depend on freeing these men for the exploration of more and more pagan areas. That requires pastors. If the number of men coming forward as catechists is small, the brothers have to carry on with the pastoral role and are deprived of the mobility which the evangelistic thrust requires. Potential growth is slowed down. Several bishops have recognized this and have regretted that the first rule of the Brotherhood has broken down. The whole question of the supply and maintenance of catechists calls for review. One Anglican observer in discussing this problem seems to assume that the role of the brothers in the Solomons has now to be applied "to follow-up work rather than to spearhead evangelism".[44] Apparently it is proposed to make the evangelistic order a teaching order. This is not necessarily the only solution. If there are still 12,000 pagans within the Eastern Solomons, there should be no relinquishing of spearhead evangelism (quite apart from this work in the more northern islands) unless the local congregations themselves are prepared to undertake the winning of their pagan neighbours.

If I may anticipate something that is still ahead of us in this book, in the post-war depth studies we are to be confronted by such things as the resurgence of pagan ideas in plantation settlements and towns, the growth of non-Christian pressure groups, the drift from marginality to nominality in village congregations, the absenteeism from village ways and worship through the labour system, the emergence of neo-pagan cults and the growth of new class stratification in the towns. Is there something in these situations that perhaps calls for a new type of evangelism? This is not follow-up. These are not new converts awaiting better instruction. These are new special segments in both town and country. There is a new paganism into which the young church has to make its evangelistic thrust.

Now either the Church will have to agree that this is the work of the total Church and every Christian has responsibility for it (in which case there is no further need at all for an evangelical Order perhaps), or the Brotherhood will have to explore these new situations within the new Solomons that call for new methods in gospel thrust. This is still pioneering work. The scene has certainly changed, but the need for evangelism is as great as ever. To suppose that an evangelistic Order has almost completed its work within the Solomons, is surely to forget that each generation has to be won for Christ. Whether this should be assigned to an Order or to specific lay programmes from the local congregations is for the Church to determine, but confrontation with the paganism in her midst cannot be avoided. The Church still needs an evangelistic effort (to bring commitment for Christ) and follow-up (to establish the convert in knowledge of the faith)—evangelists and pastors. A Church of the size of the one we are considering ought to be able to provide enough persons for both roles. If it cannot do so, then the matter calls for investigation by the leaders of the Church.

CHAPTER 5

The Growth of the Church in the Western Solomons

ORIGINS

METHODIST INTEREST in the Solomons came by way of Fiji, where Solomon Islanders provided labour for the canefields. Many had been kidnapped, others properly indentured. After the cession of Fiji the trade had been brought more under control, but it never had a clean name. Many descendants of these labourers still live in Fiji, much acculturated, but still closely knit sub-groups. They are cared for by the Melanesian Mission except in a few isolated localities where they have elected to affiliate with the Methodists.[1]

These people were pagan when they went to Fiji. Many were converted there by the Methodist Fijians, some going so far in their Christian experience as to become Methodist preachers. I allow John F. Goldie, who established Methodism in the Solomons, to give his own account of these beginnings.

> The call that moved the Methodist Church into action came from the Solomon Islanders themselves. This appeal came from the natives of Guadalcanal and Malaita, who had gone to plantations in Fiji. They found their way into Methodist schools and churches . . . What the gospel of Jesus Christ had done for Fiji, it could do for the Solomon Group. These men, though anxious to return, refused to do so unless missionaries accompanied them, and year after year they appealed to the Conference to send missionaries. The General Conference decided to begin work among these savages and Dr. Brown [the Mission Secretary] . . . recommended that we make our headquarters at Roviana, on the south-west of the main island of New Georgia. The Roviana people were the most powerful tribe of that locality . . . If they could be influenced, the missionary would experience little difficulty in teaching the others.[2]

In 1885 the Solomon Islanders petitioned the Wesleyan Synod in Fiji,[3] but the Wesleyans pointed out the significance of their comity agreement with the Melanesian Mission. The objection did not satisfy the petitioners, who found a champion in a layman named Beauclerc[4] and a mediator in Rev. Henry Worrall. They met sixty Guadalcanal men led by one of their accepted chiefs on April 19, 1896. There had been political changes in the Solomons and under great hope promised by the Protectorate, they were disposed to repatriate and wanted pastoral supervision. Some of their number had gone ahead and already needed it. They also argued that the Wesleyans were expanding in New Guinea, deploying personnel from Fiji. Worrall undertook to write to Dr. Brown in Australia.[5] These sessions were conducted in the Fijian language which was known to all parties. The Board stood by this agreement, urged the Solomon Islanders to join the Anglican Church, and Brown wrote to Bishop Wilson to facilitate their transfer. A reply was received but nothing came from it.[6] In 1897 Brown was in Fiji and again a deputation of Solomon Islanders waited on him. They presented a letter the text of which is preserved.[7] Nothing came of it. In September 1898 they pressed for a European missionary and a Fijian pastor for Guadalcanal. The following year Brown was visiting New Britain and returned to Sydney via the Solomon Islands. He visited plantations and the localities where missionary work was operating and realized that huge areas were quite out of reach of the gospel. He observed the Melanesian Mission had its hands full in the eastern part of the Group. Even though the Wesleyan Church had now been absorbed in the new Australian Methodist Church, he was not prepared to ignore the old comity agreement and therefore called on Bishop Wilson at Norfolk Island and settled upon New Georgia as a Methodist Mission area.[8] The bishop thought New Georgia would have been the last place he would have chosen. The few Anglicans in the western islands, as we have seen, were withdrawn to strengthen stations in the east and Methodist work began with a line of comity between New Georgia and Guadalcanal.[9] Even though the Methodists did enter the Solomons they did not satisfy the requests from Malaita and Guadalcanal, though they used a Fiji Guadalcanal convert as a teacher in the west.[10]

Goldie and Rooney arrived at Roviana, May 23, 1902. Their party comprised also a European carpenter, four Fijians, two Samoans, a Santo man and a Solomon Islander, both converted in Fiji.[11]

THE ROVIANA PHASE (PRE-GREAT WAR)

Wilson was surprised at the Methodist choice of Roviana, where the cultural conditions were not favourable for church-planting, as they were in Guadalcanal and Malaita. Although there were some Roviana men in Fiji, and these were interested,[12] the chiefly structure of most of New Georgia was opposed to Christianity, and the way of life was based on the operations of the head-hunting system. In the anthropological section of this book I show how this ramified through social life. Three reasons were officially given for the choice: (1) It was the darkest area and had the greatest need for the gospel. (2) It was untouched by other Protestant work. (3) The nearest Protestant Mission had agreed to the opening, as they were unable to develop serious occupancy of the area.[13] We may add that a number of planters in the area gave encouragement and opened their plantations to the missionaries. This is not stated officially as a reason, but it was a practical stepping-stone which secured the mission entrance into a forbidden area. It also tied Christianity with western commercial interests.[14]

Brown's reports show the door was not culturally open. Bera, who controlled the great Marovo Lagoon and the south-eastern end of New Georgia, was opposed to any mission because it would lead to epidemics and depopulation.[15] Brown himself decided that to ask

Ingava's permission for entry was to court refusal, for he had been told clearly Christianity was not wanted.[16] He was at a loss to know why, seeing the people had never met any missionaries, and he suspected prejudices stimulated by visiting vessels of bad character.[17] Yet the resident planters had good reason for wanting the mission, because, as Wheatley pointed out, sixty-two whites had been murdered in the past few years.[18] All this gave the new mission a foreign character.

In the process of establishment the Fijians and Samoans, who had volunteered for evangelical spearhead, were kept unduly long on the station, being fed on beef, biscuits and rice, instead of establishing themselves with the people and preparing a more stable food supply pattern.[19] This may have been partly because the doors in the villages were not open. In any case the mission commenced with a type of plantation pattern, with foreign bosses and local labour—thoroughly colonial.

The Christian group held evening worship each day after work and the pagan labourers were welcome to attend. They also received medical attention and other benefits of living on a Christian compound. This provided the European missionaries with an opportunity of collecting Roviana vocabulary and learning the structure of the language. This was so effective that Goldie felt able to attempt preaching in Rovianan to his labour gang after four months. Before long he had regular congregations of fifty or sixty, curious and interested, but as yet no converts. After two years he had fluctuating congregations of up to 500, but still no converts. He established mission outposts farther afield at Vella Lavella and Choiseul, and pressed his Board for more missionaries so that these islands could have permanently established stations. Rooney moved to Choiseul and three years later Nicholson went to Vella Lavella.[20]

A Sunday School had been opened. Confessions of Christ after five years were discouragingly few, though some 5,000 Solomon Islanders were attending worship services somewhere. There had been sickness and death among the mission party. Some localities had expressed willingness to accept Fijian and Samoan evangelists, and these were establishing themselves with the people. They were operating more within the cultural structure than those at the central stations, and were soon to obtain a different kind of response to the gospel they preached. From the start Goldie was a strong advocate of what he called *Industrial Missions* (not to be confused with the modern concept that goes by this name). Unfortunately the pattern was tied to colonialism. The Fijian agents, on the other hand, had come from areas of dramatic people-movement within the frame of reference of social structure. Both in theory and practice the methods were different and obtained different responses. Alas, all the official reports were (and still are) written from the stations, synod discussions emanated from the stations, it was a station or industrial mission perspective that coloured all the documents for the historian to work on, and this has become a permanent characteristic of the mission. Thus one reads page after page on station activities, while a spiritual movement in some remote but widespread area receives only a passing reference. Yet the growth that is statistically recorded took place away from the stations, and often by multi-individual people-movement, not by western individualism among folk culturally extracted from their social structure, as was so on the stations.

TYPES OF CONVERSION

Even the individual conversions on the stations, however, had their own sociological structure. I shall speak of these henceforth as *sodality conversions*, because they were not based on the structure of society itself, or kin groups or craft segments. They were loosely held groups on a basis of age and sex—youths or young women who were thrown together on a station, usually (but not always) detribalized persons, slaves and orphans in particular. For the purpose of decision-making they naturally conceptualized themselves as a group, but because of the loosely held character of that group and the fact that it contained both slaves and the sons of chiefs, I call it a sodality. A person who decided for Christ within this pattern found his life within the fellowship of the Church, but he isolated himself from any normal social unit to which he belonged. This was fraught with social and physical dangers and therefore tended to make the converts cling together. This new cohesion of the Christian fellowship became strong but tended to make the convert look to the mission station for his strength and support. It made the mission so indispensable that the emergence of a really indigenous Church was delayed thereby.

In the sixth year of the mission Goldie was awakened at midnight on Easter Sunday by about fifty boys who were living on the station. They were arguing the truth of the resurrection preaching of the day. Goldie placed this group in a special class and gave them twelve months' instruction with the hope of bringing them to baptism. This sodality acquired such cohesion as a Christian fellowship that forty-eight of them made the required standard and were received in a public baptismal service. The boys were roughly of the same age, but not by any means of similar social status. Each had to state his own personal experience in class, sons of chiefs and slaves together. The elders to whom these boys were socially responsible were not consulted, and felt slighted. Thoroughly angry, they waited outside the church, armed with spears and clubs.[21] The young men in the strength of their new experience were quite strong in the face of this danger and weathered the storm. There is no doubt about the genuineness of their conversions. However, the missionaries had extracted them from their social life, baptized them on a basis of western decision, completely by-passed the cultural mechanisms of family discussion and the traditional authority of the elders, and thereby had greatly endangered the lives both of the converts and of themselves. Indeed they might well have been driven out of these islands altogether, for to this point the mission had still never been admitted to New Georgia by traditional permission. It had forced its entrance through the traders rather than the chiefs—a complete departure from normal Methodist procedure in other islands.

Although the chiefs had not made war against their presence, and had permitted medical facilities, sewing classes and festivities (entertainment), yet they took violent exception to this act of baptism. The missionaries thought it was part of the general hostility to Christianity, but the hostility was due more to the fact that traditional authority and procedure had been flouted. Group action of this kind by youths, without the usual communal discussions that preceded all public decision-making, was viewed by the elders, not so much as a religious act as rebellion against the social patterns and the solidarity of society. Those who were most angered were those whose authority had been flouted.

The same reaction came shortly afterwards with the conversion of a sodality of girls. Let it be well noted that this time the hostility came, not from the chiefs, but from the 'witches' (sic) who were "the terror of the place".[22] They were rather the old women responsible for the protective and communal rites and ceremonies that had bearing on the life of the women of the tribe. They were not witches or sorceresses. They were feared, it is true, but they were socially approved and without their services it was thought that society could not escape disease nor could child-birth and other crises of the life of the woman function properly. They considered the behaviour of the girls their special concern, and their anger again was not so much that the girls wanted to become Christian, but because their authority had been counted as nothing. That the girls could take such a step showed they had lost their fear of the tribal belief regarding women's rites. This was of shattering significance to the practitioners of those rites. Grieved because they had been ignored, they predicted leprosy, insanity and other calamities because of such rejection of social procedure.

In both these cases pagan society as a whole would disapprove of any failure to respect traditional procedure, but would expect those who had 'lost face' by the incident to make the public objection—the tribal elders in the former case and the old women in the latter.

The responses among the young people, however, show that doors were beginning to open. At this stage, in some places, other missionaries had persuaded the elders to allow their sons become Christian, but this approach does not appear to have been made in Roviana. The elders, priests and old women were obstructive for a long time. The young converts were taught many Christian hymns. A new composition translating "Onward Christian Soldiers" swept round the Lagoon like a song 'hit'. The elders and old women felt that some of the Christian *mana* was coming from these hymns, which were regarded as magical; and therefore they banned their use.

When Ingava died a woman was sacrificed after the normal pattern, that her spirit might accompany his into the after-life. That all the inhabitants of the Roviana Lagoon might be associated with this sacrifice, her head was carried ceremonially through the villages.[23] The structure of life throughout the Lagoon was still solidly pagan. The Christian movement was station-centred, extra-cultural and confined to age and sex sodalities. Ingava died in 1906, and five or six more years were to pass before there was any growth of Christianity within the culture pattern of the Lagoon. Meantime the missionaries were suspect and have themselves recorded that they felt "the bushes had eyes and spears".

A station had been opened on Choiseul in 1904. In 1910 the first converts were baptized. The conversion pattern was identical, again a sodality of young people.[24] Within the following two years, life was unsettled in the villages near the mission station. The life of the missionary was threatened, and though he did not ask for protection, the Resident Commissioner at Gizo saw fit to send a small detachment of Tanna police to the locality.[25] It was 1913 before any people-movement on cultural lines was witnessed in this area.[26]

On Vella Lavella, where the work commenced in 1904 and a proper mission station was established under a missionary in 1907, the first baptisms came in 1910. Again they came as a sodality of seven young men. A year later eleven young women presented themselves for baptism according to the station pattern.[27]

We may say then, that the beginnings of mission work in the Western Solomons followed a fixed pattern—station-centred sodality groups, western in character, regardless of social status and by-passing the social decision-making patterns. This accounts for the cultural hostility of the period of early conversions.

However, some of the finest leaders of the emerging Church did come from these sodalities. The Choiseul group was led by Gandapeta, whose father was head of a clan and wealthy in land, nut-trees and shell-money. Gandapeta was an important conquest for Christ, even though still a youth and having assumed no office. As a Christian he never would, for his father's role had been to attend to post-war rituals, ancestral sacrifices and the torture of sorceresses. Strangely enough he was to play a significant role later on as a peacemaker in the termination of feuds and effecting of reconciliations.[28] From the Vella Lavella group came Daniel Bula, who became a strong leader and an independent thinker, quite western in many ways.[29]

The sodality type of conversion could take place only on a mission station, a plantation or some locality with an assemblage of people who were living under controls which were extra-tribal. There was no hope of converting villages in this manner. However, in the second decade, when the more influential of these converts went out into the villages, they frequently operated through kin and village mechanisms. There is a record of one man who went to his own Vella Lavella village and effected a complete transformation in a short space of time and built a fine church. Here there was no sodality of detribalized youths, but a total kin sub-group of sixty-five persons in a village community of 300. At the opening of the church he presented his father and mother, his uncles, brothers and sisters for baptism.[30] The Church had passed into the second phase of its growth: the years of people-movement had begun.

Along the lines of kin relationship, of indigenous trade routes and exchange markets, of marriage contacts and other social connections, news of the gospel spread, and before long chiefs began to ask the Mission for teachers. These lines of contact reached as far north as Bougainville. By the time of the Great War of 1914–18, pastor-teacher beach-heads had been established on all the major islands of the Western Solomons.

The people-movements are badly documented in the mission records, just isolated references among hundreds of pages of routine administrative and station reports. Even the revival movement on the head station, that we know continued for two years, was lightly reported. This particular movement was of the kind we might expect in a western high school community, reflecting a keenness about Christianity but without any great emotional overtones.[31] Meantime people-movements within the social structure were bursting spontaneously in remote pockets in many parts of the Group. Daniel Bula had won over the chief at Mundi Mundi and a movement was beginning there. At Kepi a group of thirty-five adults came forward for baptism, bringing a great number of children also—a total movement within an extended family like the Vella Lavella reference cited above.[32]

When Goldie made the point of the lack of excitement on the station, it is probable that he had in mind the more dramatic events of whole villages turning to Christ, where (as he described at Kepi) the people "destroyed the idols of their fathers" and the important heathen altar that was situated there.[33] Possibly this dichotomy of conversion pattern in the Western Solomons may have something to do with the failure of some of the station-trained agents to deal adequately with the village situations. It would not apply in all cases, but I am sure it did in many. A great many of them were already detribalized, and had nothing cultural to break with when they made their own decisions on the station; whereas in the villages a direct encounter with pagan culture could not be avoided. This was so for both men and women. We know, for example, that in Choiseul married women were forbidden by traditional taboo from entering any religious assembly and for nine years they were unable to enter the church despite the invitation open to all pagan listeners. The taboo was functional and based on the belief that in any religious ceremony the spirit(s) present might possess the woman there and be carried back to the village, thus causing sickness, and in particular upset the regularities of childbirth. In 1913 this taboo was ceremonially lifted.[34] Immediately the pagan women accepted the long-standing invitation to attend worship services, with the result that the following twelve months saw 130 of them come forward to be prepared for baptism at Sasamunga alone. This shows the importance of tribal sanctions. The barrier had to be removed in the ceremonial manner and then the way opened.

On the mission station a person's confession of faith was accepted at its face value as long as he could testify clearly of what he believed. In the village the confession of a change of faith had to be demonstrated by idol-destruction, skull-burial or some dramatic public act. Station-trained men were not always the best kind of agent for bringing about these dramatic encounters, because they had avoided this themselves by their station-conversions.

A great many of these station converts were refugees, slaves and persons rescued from despised death: people with no social contacts and without prestige, who might have been used at any time or sold for sacrificing. Let me cite a few cases from among the leaders of the Church in the years that followed. Lembu, who took over Daniel Bula's orphanage, was to have been sacrificed at birth but was saved and eventually found his way to the Christian orphanage. Mark Pivo, though the son of a Vella Lavella chief, was by a Ysabel slave woman and therefore of no social status. The slave mother came under the influence of the mission and brought her son to the station. Amos Tozaka had been enslaved as a child and converted in slavery. David Pausu of Siwai had been left by his mother as an unwanted child to drown, was recovered by his father's other wife, but upon the death of his parents was sold to visitors from Mono in exchange for a pig and some goods, which shows the variety of Mono–Siwai trade exchanges. He found his way to a plantation, thence to a labour ship, thence to a Tongan catechist, who brought him to the mission at Roviana. Gina, who went to New Zealand later for training, came from Ysabel slave stock two generations back. Isaac Kisini's wife, Salote, was enslaved as a child when her father was killed by the Kaloe people, and Isaac himself was saved from the same fate by Goldie. Moses Lakempa was buried alive as a child, dug up immediately by a Christian teacher and saved. One of the men sent to the New Guinea Highlands was left to die as an infant and another had been thrown into a river unwanted, rescued and educated by the Mission. Ever so many of the leading teachers and catechists came from this kind of social setting, refugees, socially dislocated, infants rescued from infanticide, and slaves without hope or status. For such, the mission stations offered hope, provided the person had some individual ability and a readiness to think for himself. They experienced genuine conversions, but they were psychologically different from the equally genuine conversions within the structure of families and social sub-groups.[35]

At this level the Fijian and Tongan agents and the converted Solomon men of status were the more effective evangelists. One of the earliest of the latter type, for example, was Zuvulu, an elder and a famous warrior, who, once converted to Christ, devoted his energies to convincing other warriors of the truth. Gandapeta was another.

At the time of the Great War the strength of the young church that was being built in these ways was as follows:

59 worshipping congregations, 31 of them with buildings
14 catechists (Fijians, Tongans and Samoans)
19 Solomon Island local preachers
10 Solomon Island class leaders
Indigenous members—full status   511
                 on trial   524
                          —— 1,035
Total converts from paganism (adherents)   6,625

This phase, then, leaves us with a clear pattern—strong central stations, dominantly youth-orientated, plucked out of their culture, but very much alive; and in the outstations under Fijians, Tongans and Samoans, the more regular type of Melanesian development. Within range of the central stations there was a tendency for the islanders to accept the Mission as socially useful, and its clinical work was breaking down some of the obstructive taboos. When the taboos broke down, areas were open for people-movements of the common Oceanic pattern. On the stations a demand for standards required twelve months for instruction before baptism.

THE END OF AUSTRALIAN CONTROL

The second phase continued until the district was handed over by the Australian Methodists to their New Zealand Church for administration, shortly after the war. This phase of the war and its immediate aftermath was a period of political readjustment, which would have to be considered at length were this a normal history. From our standpoint the feature of this period was the Church's involvement in inter-tribal issues. The role of the Church was conceptualized as restoring peace between the tribes, which had hitherto been continually at war with each other. The Mission attitude had two important aspects. It resisted the administrative approach at settling feuds by means of punitive expeditions, so that quite often the missionary found himself championing the rights of the islanders, and often against the Administration. Secondly, in the areas of strife and feud, Christianity was conceptualized as the way of peace, or the reconciling way of life, and thus Christ, as Saviour, was indeed the Prince of Peace. He was thus as much a communal as a personal Saviour. The anthropological analysis of the great Choiseul feud, later on in this book, will demonstrate this. It will also show the respective roles of missionary and indigenous evangelist in this drama of reconciliation.

In 1919 discussions were held which assigned this mission to the care of the Methodist Church of New Zealand. The staff was increased and twenty-two more island agents were brought from Fiji and Tonga. The further importation of such a large number of Fijians and Tongans was surely a strategic blunder, not because of any shortcomings on their part, but because it obstructed the organic growth of the Solomon Island Church itself. It aided the conversion growth but stopped the organic growth. From as early as 1913 Goldie had reported a strong class of 100 young Solomon Islanders meeting weekly at Roviana[36] and similar, though smaller groups were meeting at the other stations. By 1922 solid indigenous leadership should have come from those groups—I mean leadership on the levels of responsibility that was being given to Fijians and Tongans. We know that opportunity for class-meeting testimony had been given from an early date, and records show that some of those testimonies revealed considerable maturity of thought. Daniel Bula ran a fine institution and many were won for Christ there. One of his own converts took over after him.

When we consider the institutional strength of this mission and the intellectual character of the conversions, it is hard to see why twenty-two Fijians and Tongans had to be introduced, at what was clearly the point of time when those who made these decisions stood at the cross-roads that led one to an indigenous Church and the other to a paternalistic Mission. From this point the Christian cause became more and more dependent and drew further and further away from indigeneity. It continued thus until the Pacific War descended upon it. This was the moment for high faith and advance; the opportunity for the establishment of an indigenous ministry; for a missionary demonstration of their confidence in the experiences of their own converts. Real organic growth might have begun here. If ever the words of Brutus were true, it was at this hour in the Solomons:

> There is a tide in the affairs of men,
> Which taken at the flood leads on to fortune;
> Omitted, all the voyage of their life
> Is bound in shallows, and in miseries.
> On such a full sea are we now afloat;
> And we must take the current when it serves,
> Or lose our ventures.[37]

They did not take the current, and although there was great conversion growth there emerged a thoroughly paternalistic mission instead of an indigenous Church.

During the second period the Church had been growing statistically—forty-eight new congregations were planted during the decade and twenty-five new church buildings had been erected. The number of persons who had severed their connections with paganism and become Christian rose from 6,625 to 9,788, and the rise in membership figures shows that there had been some quality growth within—1,035 to 3,888. The number of local preachers had increased from nineteen to sixty-three. Standards at the central institution had risen sharply under the instruction of Leembruggen. In the face of the glowing reports of conversion and quality growth, it is all the more difficult to understand why the importations from Fiji and Tonga were needed in 1922 for those middle posts in the Church which really determine whether or not a young Church grows organically. The question may still be asked of this Church in the Solomons as it may also of the Administration in civil affairs.

During the following decade when doors were wide open in Bougainville and more and more Christian agents were needed for the evangelistic thrust there, the Solomon Islands District cried out year after year for teachers from New Britain—rather than elevate their own converts to responsibility. To some extent they were forced to do this by circumstances, but always the missionaries felt their standards were too low. If this was so, my belief is that it was because the *education of experience* in the *middle posts* of the Church had continually been denied to Solomon Islanders through all the formative years.

ROMAN CATHOLIC METHODS

The period during which the Methodist work was being brought under control from New Zealand, during the twenties and thirties, was one of open doors in Choiseul, Bougainville and Buin. In Bougainville especially the growth should have been more rapid, but the cry was always one of shortage of staff. It was a period of active competition from the Roman Catholics and something of their methods can be seen in an interesting collection of private letters written by one of their men, Father McHardy, without any idea of publication.[38]

Despite the economic depression, the low price of copra and the continual complaint of shortages of staff, this mission was relatively strong with fifteen stations, all with resident priests and seven of them with convents. Some nine or ten officials lived at Kieta, their seat of administration. The priests itinerated continually, crossing the interior from coast to coast if need be.[39] McHardy opened a new station at Tunuru in June 1929 and after eight months had commenced a catechist's school. The scholars could read an English primer and were working at a catechism by June, 1931, by which time he had obtained lay assistance for the school. The lay assistance was specifically provided so that the school need not interfere with the priest's itineration.[40] So the two preliminary drives were raising catechists locally and maintaining itineration.

As might be expected, the letters show a continual emphasis on the virtue of baptism and the importance of having the rite performed before death. McHardy baptized hundreds of infants, with the consent of pagan parents. This gave him the right to enter the village and return again.[41] Also, he gave injections and medical treatment which gained him sympathy. Subsequently the baptized children were taught and brought to confirmation.[42] Careful records of all these baptisms and confirmations were kept and McHardy found the clerical work a burden, but the statistics were demanded by headquarters.[43] Conditional baptisms were given for eleventh hour conversions.[44] In cases of regular adult conversions, baptism was delayed until after an intensive period of instruction and testing. Much preparatory instruction was done by the indigenous catechists.[45] The priests itinerated to test the knowledge of these candidates for baptism and to perform the rite.

Selected students from four different linguistic areas were taught in McHardy's school. Courses in English and theology prepared them for the role of catechist, after which they returned to their own areas.[46] The important thing is the use of young converts as frontier evangelists, bringing adults up to a state of knowledge considered adequate for baptism. This was possible because the priests never flouted the authority of the elders but sought parental permission before baptizing a child or young person.

In page after page McHardy reveals his awareness of the great open doors in Bougainville.[47] In most places he was well received. People accepted medical treatment and often brought their infants for baptism. Everywhere he was entertained and escorted from village to village.

Once people accepted his form of Christianity he found them anxious to have it passed on to their more distant relatives, so kin structure soon came into play.[48] When normally rival villages were converted, they tried to outdo each óther in the new faith. During the three years covered by this collection of letters the Roman Catholic numerical strength rose from 10,000 to 14,000 in this region.[49]

Converts were educated from the beginning in the festivals of the Christian Year, in the Litany, Holy Communion and Confession. Duties were divided, the catechists giving basic instruction and the priests itinerating for the pastoral office. The Roman Catholics thus had a locally controlled organization penetrating into the mountain areas along lines of kin contact and the exchange markets along the trade routes. The Methodists in this extensive area were still organically under the control of Roviana—remote control. The priests used pidgin English and one or two local languages, but they had the help of the catechists who were appointed to their own people.

McHardy's letters show an awareness of ethnic units. He named three large villages in his area, whose people differed from their immediate neighbours. They represented a tribe ready to receive instruction *as a total unit*.[50] In another place, beyond his own linguistic area he discovered that some of his trainees had personal contacts. They served as intermediaries for the introduction of his religion.[51] He made use of the coast–mountain trade exchange pattern, not only for school food supplies, but also for evangelical contact.[52] Thus he writes:

". . . thousands more, so ready and willing to enter the Church"

and again

"The people are ready, almost waiting for the faith"

and again

"A fair percentage of them are not baptized, but are heading that way."[53]

Whatever onc may feel about Roman Catholic theology, this data is not cited to that end, but rather to show their awareness of the open doors in Bougainville at the time, their real concern to bring folk out of paganism, and a readiness to follow every line of the ethnic or social configurations. It shows that the people themselves were disposed to accept Christianity and that the Methodists were not alone in the field.

The Methodists also were careful not to neglect their itineration, although they were not equipped with the lay staff to free them from station administration like the priests. Their pastoral programme and mobility were frequently curtailed by the compound duties they had to carry. *The Open Door* contains a number of interesting accounts of the Methodist itinerations over this period, and these can be followed on a good map. If less frequent they were no less arduous and no less effective.

INDUSTRIAL MISSIONS

The Methodist Mission in the Western Solomons came into being at a time when the concept of *industrial missions* was being advocated, though not by any means unchallenged. The pattern required the acquisition of tracts of land large enough for the establishment of plantations and technical and industrial institutions, which were supposed to demonstrate the importance of industry and the reward of honest labour, and in so doing to bring people under the influence of the gospel. For the Methodists this was a significant shift from their earlier policy in Oceania, as for instance in Tonga and Fiji; but the policy was approved by the Mission Board and the home Church.

After about six years, when the doors began to open in various parts of the area under Roviana domination, requests began coming in to the station for Christian teachers. The missionaries were hard-pressed to find them and often released students as helpers. But from about 1908 these requests were persistent and came from as far as 100 miles. The missionary was liable to be confronted by a frustrated chief, who had built a church and long since prepared his group for the reception of a teacher. None having been sent, he was now asking whether he was to have the teacher or burn down the church. Doors open and close like that in pioneering periods.

Yet from the very same report that records that case, one also reads:

> The plantation at Roviana adds to the cares of the Superintendent. Land has been cleared and planted and in addition to the planting of coconut trees, about 7,000 sisal hemp plants have been planted, which in a couple of years will yield good returns. The supervision of this work taxes the energies of the strongest.[54]

One may well ask where the priorities lie in this kind of a mission station, when for want of teachers chiefs were destroying the churches they had built in hope. Two months later the official missionary journal reported a growing feeling in official circles that the Mission must face the demands of industrial mission work—new and better systems of agriculture, house and boat-building, to reduce mission expenditure and provide ways and means for young individuals to become independent.[55] Shortly afterwards this was supported by an article on Industrial Missions in Rhodesia, which argued that self-support must be seen as economic and the system should aim at supplying better returns and more skilled workmen.[56]

The Chairman justified his involvement in the cultivation of sisal hemp because of the value it had in bringing people to Christ, and because of the satisfactory conversions among labour, though he adds another and less worthy motive "if we do not improve our mission lands we shall lose them".[57] After about a decade of mission activity in the Solomons the missionaries were of one mind in supporting these priorities. One of them stressed that:

> the mission must educate the natives to profitably cultivate their own lands.

Another said that the conditions prevailing in the area

> make it imperative we develop our work on industrial lines. Within ten years this will be the only method open to us.

At the same time the Chairman said:

> I am more than ever convinced that the future of our missions will depend on teaching the people some form of industry.[58]

Now it is highly probable that every one of those missionaries would dispute the idea that there was a priority of industrialism over evangelism. They would probably argue that one was the approach to the other. Yet the facts are undeniable from the archival records they themselves have created, that at every point of time when doors for evangelism opened they were hindered by the administrative burdens of the stations. A continuous dichotomy runs through the records. They were continually being forced to make choices. One of the two had to have a priority.

When the young people's movement was spreading round the Lagoon among the Roviana teenagers, they were encouraged to visit the central station and find their interests there. About a hundred assembled there to clear land for a cricket field. The form of Christianity, even in its entertainment, was one which extracted them from village life and its social round. The new festivities were station-centred. The mission was a model for industry and recreation. The church which emerged had its centre in the station rather than the village. The events of the Christian year, more particularly Christmas and Easter, became festival occasions which provided monster rallies at the stations. When the pagan festivals finally disappeared there were no village substitutes, there was no substituting village Christian structure. The general idea was that all that was traditional had to go, and the Christian looked to the nearest station for his satisfactions. There was no careful appraisal to ascertain what traditional elements were worthy of preservation or open for Christianization. It was assumed that the new day required interests that were entirely new. In reality that meant foreign. On the stations one could participate in boat-building, carpentry, saw-milling, or the cultivation of plantations; one had access to medical services and education, to recreation and religion.

When the gospel began spreading beyond the stations, more and more personnel were required for effective follow-up of the large intake from paganism. Normally one would think of this as the major priority of Christian missions; but when this was a crying need in New Georgia, the item claiming the most official recognition was the development of a new plantation project of a thousand acres at Banga. The character of this type of Christian witness must have puzzled the indigenes, unless they associated it with the general colonialism of the white man.

The son of a leading Roviana chief went to the station for a teacher, but the Chairman had none to send. One had long been promised. The man declined to return without anyone and took one of the students. "A promise is one thing," he said, "a live man another." Without the persistence of the chief's son, that long-open door would have closed. Many areas marked today by Roman Catholic and Seventh Day Adventist stations were first opened to the Methodists.

In 1916 the General Secretary visited the Solomons and wrote:

> Undoubtedly God has given to our Church a unique opportunity in Bougainville. The door stands wide open to us. The people's hearts have been prepared to receive us. They wait eagerly for the message we have . . .

Side by side with this we read of extensive plantations—splendid freehold property, comprised of about 2,000 acres of excellent land, which was partly cultivated and should become a great revenue-producer, as he says of one of them. But when it comes to some concrete proposal of missionary action for these two situations, it is the latter which receives the priority:

> The time has come when the Board should raise, on the security of such valuable properties as the . . . Banga plantation, funds sufficient for the development and upkeep of those properties instead of making such expense a charge on the annual income of the Society.[59]

Meantime let it be noted that by the time the Methodists really became active in the evangelism of Bougainville and Buka, they were no longer the only Mission interested in the area and its opportunity.

In 1921, when the district was handed over to the New Zealand Church for missionary support, the writers of the long report on the Mission presented to Conference were well aware of the openings for evangelism in Choiseul and Bougainville and reported also the commencement of both Roman Catholic and Seventh Day Adventist activities in the area. The report recognized that:

> a determined effort must be made to carry the gospel to all the remaining heathen people of the Western Solomons

and admitted the time for this "has arrived" and was "long overdue", and that many requests for teachers had to be declined. The role of the home Church was seen in the provision of extra missionaries for the training of the indigenous agents for evangelistic extension.

The same report outlines the plantations, technical and industrial projects, the need for administrative consolidation of them all, enlargement of the central stations, improvement of machinery and equipment, printing press, a faster boat, saw-mill and so on. The functions of these institutions were said to be to produce full-orbed men—physically, mentally, morally and spiritually, and to teach them to work their lands and to develop industrious characters. Whether we agree with this concept of mission or not, the one thing that stands out clearly from the records the missionaries themselves wrote is this dichotomy—opportunities for evangelism in unoccupied areas and the station-centred industrial mission method, the latter receiving the priority. This situation was carried over from the Australian into the

New Zealand period. The closing section of the long report looked into the future in terms of the establishment of trusts, land titles and insurances.[60]

This concept of trainîng full-orbed men was western and it was rationalization. The concept of conceiving wholeness as a complex of compartments—physical, social, mental, moral, religious and so on—is western. People coming out of animistic philosophy regard religion as the integrator of life, not a mere compartment. When you change a man's religion, you change the whole man—because the religion integrates the whole man. There is a strong reason therefore for converting the man first and then allowing his new religion to make its impact on the whole life. But turning first to develop industrious characters, agricultural competence and religion as compartments of life, one finds that these do not develop at a uniform rate. Furthermore, personnel resources were frequently inadequate and choices had to be made between one compartment and another; as things turned out, the station-centred Mission quite clearly demanded first the protection and development of the vested interests. The missionaries' lives were weighed down by administration.

The emphasis on industry was furthermore within the colonial frame of reference, with the white master and the brown servant. This was felt in all compartments including that of religion. Holy Communion was denied to most of the converts, and even when it was opened to Solomon Islanders there was not always intercommunion between island teachers and European missionaries.[61] Instruction in religion from teacher to student was given but facilities for private devotion were poorly provided. It took over fifty years to get the New Testament translated into Roviana—extremely slow by Methodist standards.[62] Baptisms were delayed. Appointment to Christian office was held up till high standards were attained. Yet in secular compartments men were pushed into action. The denying of religious privilege to the brown man and driving him in industry is a strange way of developing the full-orbed man.

When the sons of chiefs came for teachers to tell them the way of life, and found highly developed stations with islanders maintaining plantations and industry, yet no one available for explaining the new religion to them, with promises made but not kept, they would form their own ideas as to where the priorities lay. They must have seen it this way, although I believe every missionary on the field would have denied that his first priority was to achieve anything but bring men to Christ. They rationalized that industrial missions were the best way of bringing men to Christ—one of them said the "only" way.

THE 1928 REPORT
AND THE DECADE BEFORE THE PACIFIC WAR[63]

The 1928 Report was prepared by an official of the Church in New Zealand for the guidance of the Mission Board. It comprised eleven pages of single-spaced foolscap typescript, 45 per cent of which was devoted to the narrative of the visit, with descriptions of stations, plants, plantations, technicians, engineers and so on. Another 14 per cent was devoted to hospitals, medical supplies and such health matters as village sanitation, houses, clothing and betel-nut chewing. Village teachers, general needs, education for girls. political relations with New Guinea, the need for introducing teachers from New Guinea, literature and printing, divided the remainder into roughly equal sections. Although the report ended by claiming as a general aim "the evangelization of the people of the Solomons", I found only one reference to evangelical openings, and for this New Britain teachers were being sought instead of Solomon Islanders.

The report recognized the need for producing more Solomon Island teachers and agreed that the days of the use of Fijians and Tongans should be limited. Yet side by side with this, more were asked from New Britain. Manifestly the preference was either economic or political, as they were required in Bougainville. This really begs the question, which in reality is one of spiritual maturity and organic church growth.

A most disconcerting paragraph in the report urges the use of the Lord's Supper in the native church. It is fantastic to think that we have here a Methodist cause with 10,000 adherents and 5,000 of them members, without having had them introduced to the sacrament of the Lord's Supper.

Once again we find the concentration of missionary work in sedentary stations. One cannot dispute the devoted service of the missionary staff, or the high quality of the work in the schools, hospitals and other institutions; but there is no doubt that by 1928 everything had become excessively centralized and enclosed. There was much talk about "model villages" and "model plantations", but these models were far from pilot projects, because they were built on resources of men, money and material not available to normal villages that might be expected to emulate them. A true model village is one which, while remaining itself an island village with its own resources to draw on, can yet be an example to others. Mission stations are never model villages. They are concentrations of the resources of an overseas helping Church and they do not necessarily bring about the development of village maturity and independence, unless they specifically work to this end.

The 1928 Report stated eight urgent needs for the Board's consideration: a fourth missionary for Bougainville, the appointment of mission sisters for Siwai, a technical instructor for Kokeqolo, an additional teacher for the same place, a new sister's house for Babatana, the building of a hospital, the provision and equipment of a hospital launch, and sufficient funds to put the medical work on a surer foundation. Now I raise no objection to any of these worthy items, but if the situation is to be properly appraised I must point out that all these recommendations are for *help from outside*. All are concentrated on the European stations. There is not a single guarantee that any one of them will actually deal with the doors open for evangelism, which the report suggested existed in the mountain districts.

Quite apart from these recommendations many of the requests

presented to the enquiring official while he was on the field were station-centred. Bilua wanted a Fijian or Tongan who could teach music. One plantation asked for modern copra driers and trucks. The work of another station "was healthy and the singing was particularly good", another was a "model", another had "fine buildings on the hilltop with a flight of 200 steps, and a coconut plantation of 80 acres". This is how industrial missions worked out after a quarter-century. The writer of the report did *a tour of mission stations*—he saw nothing of village religion, and thus his descriptions and the needs he reported to the Board were concerned with the stations. No doubt he did what he thought the Board wanted.

A diachronic study of the records shows what happened. Stations became larger and larger, with more and more activities and increased administrative duties. Whether the missionaries liked it or not, they were becoming more and more station managers and less and less itinerant missionaries. Time after time in their meetings and private correspondence they complained of this weakness in their system. At one stage one of them was actually managing plantation business for an Australian company.

The very next Synod after the appearance of the 1928 Report, the staff on the field recorded that "it views with concern many features of our mission work" and the Synod resolved:

> Synod feels that a forward evangelical movement is necessary, and believes the time is opportune for a complete review of mission policy, and requests the Board to consider whether we are not overburdened by the plantation and commercial side of our work.

The Board took them up on this and when it became a case of specifying which of their centralized responsibilities could be dispensed with, the Synod did not have the courage for a bold restatement of strategy and became self-defensive. The missionaries now claimed they did recognize the priority of evangelism and under pressure a plain statement of truth became a mere pious resolution. They wanted to have a spiritual priority without changing too much the situation itself. They specified that their duties were in the pastorate, they reiterated the importance of itineration, the inspection of the work of the village teachers, they stated some basic principles of discipline, asserted the priority of the spiritual needs of the islander over the social, commercial and political; and they declared their disapproval of normal secular trading by Missions—with a careful rider to safeguard their technical institutions, and avoidance of all reference to plantations.

In other words, the 1929 resolution, which came from their own frustrations at station entanglements, when put to the acid test of implementation, came to nothing. The men were not prepared to cut their plantation and station responsibilities. Thereafter year after year throughout the thirties the Synod resolutions reveal a self-defensive sensitivity. They report the gospel spreading in the villages under a general resolution for all the Western Solomons without reference to localities. One circuit presented the same figure of 2,500 from 1929 to

1936 without change: obviously at best an estimate. In another area there were losses through a nativistic movement. In 1930 the total figure fell by 300, despite growth in Bougainville. In 1940 the parent circuit itself, Roviana, suffered a statistical drop of 150. Indeed from 1929 to the beginning of the Pacific War, though the number of church adherents had increased by 6,662, far more than half of these had come from one area; in other areas it is doubtful if the figures kept pace with population growth.

In 1937 two stimuli were introduced into the church year and both became permanent annual events. May 23 is the anniversary of the landing of the first mission party (1902) and the following day was the date of Wesley's experience of the *warmed heart*. A great commemoration was organized for the bicentenary of this in 1937.

The Synod procedure was to hear reports from the circuits (actually from the stations) and to pass a general resolution to record gratitude for growth. There was a general growth on the membership level—i.e., adherents coming on trial as members—internal quality growth; but if the Bougainville figures be excluded, the number of adherents in all the Western Solomon circuits actually dropped by five that year. However, although statistically the growth did not keep pace with population growth, there were some healthy signs within—more particularly a new concern for bringing mere adherents on into more definite membership commitment. Quality growth can be fairly claimed. Synod also claimed improved educational standards and a deepening experience in the teachers' villages. This latter claim would be hard to measure, but it was a sensitive Synod and each department of the work received its due commendation.

In 1938 some statistical effect was seen in the quality growth of the Church; there was also some intake from the pagan world. Looking back in perspective the bicentenary does seem to have stimulated some new life in the Church. Synod was convinced of this and said so in 1938.

At this time also Synod gave some thought to the matter of self-support. It was stated that station training should produce men to go out and found a self-supporting island community. The records do not indicate how this was to be achieved, nor do they show how a new type of village teacher could acquire the kind of authority necessary to convince the village elders that they should be self-supporting when they had learned to be thoroughly dependent. It would involve villages rethinking their attitudes to the Mission—as it still does.

By 1939 the burst of new growth had slowed down again, although a further resolution of satisfaction was passed. Each year recorded the *urgent need* for evangelists in Bougainville and Buka. Each year Synod looked to New Britain for help rather than to her own resources. It was at this point that the battle for self-support might have been won. The Solomons ought to have had an indigenous ministry emerging by this time, but the barriers were against opening the Christian ministry to those who could not reach certain intellectual and educational standards. Yet if the central station education was as good as the reports claimed, a ministry should have been possible. The secretary of Synod, while admitting that worthy men should be given encouragement, added that

> we feel that the entrance to the native ministry should be jealously guarded.

And there, I believe we have the answer. No ministry emerged and the organic growth of the Church was obstructed.

In 1940 some areas declined despite a further resolution of satisfaction with spiritual affairs. Roviana dropped considerably, Vella Lavella and Choiseul were static, and apart from the graduation of some from junior to senior membership the membership figures for the Western Solomons as a whole were static. There was growth in Buka and Bougainville, but nothing like the potential within the situation there.

One factor which caused me some concern as I went through the official records of this decade was the complete absence of references to the spiritual obstructions which I know existed: for instance, certain nativistic cults which did much harm to the Church in the period. One would expect to find a record of concern. The missionaries knew of these. On the circuit levels they were dealt with, yet in the district records they have no mention in the resolutions on the spiritual state of the work. But a line graph of church growth reveals the telltale irregularities which are the statistical effect of intake and exodus going on at the same time—the stimulus of the Wesley Bicentenary and the growth in Bougainville on the one hand and the losses through nativistic movements like that of Pokokoqoro on the other. (See graphs, pp. 210, 213.) The roots of Etoism go back to this period, as also the Chair and Rule movement in the eastern islands. The current importance of Etoism demands our present scrutiny of this pre-war decade.

On the surface the Church seemed to be growing and the missionaries believed that this was so. It is clear that things were thriving on the stations and standards were rising. But the official figures seem healthy only when taken whole. When broken down into circuit sections one discovers the situation was uneven. Because of Etoism as a current problem, we are particularly interested in Roviana.

The Roviana figures show that between 1929 and 1940 the preaching power of this head circuit dropped and there was no growth in the number of class leaders. The Roviana drop in local preachers from sixty-eight to sixty, and the static class leaders' figure at fifty-four, have to be set against a general rise of preachers from ninety-eight to 155 and of class leaders from 116 to 143 for all the Western Solomons. If changed into percentages the situation is that over this decade Roviana dropped from having 69 per cent of the Methodist preaching strength (1929) to 39 per cent (1940). This is one way of viewing the unevenness of the spiritual state of the district during these years.

For some time the growth of Bougainville and Buka Christianity was handicapped by being administered from Roviana. In 1931

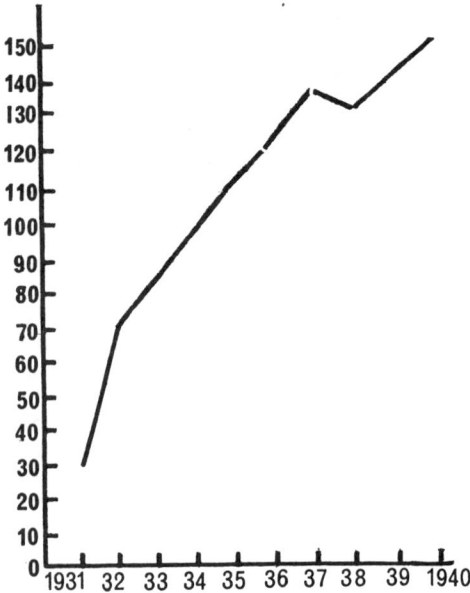

*Until 1931 this
huge area was under
the control of the
head station at
Roviana and many
opportunities for
growth were lost.*

*The creation of a
new circuit for this
area was followed by
a period of great
growth with the
planting of 118 new
churches in the
decade.*

*POLICY OF
DECENTRAL-
IZATION*

*The policy of de-
centralization has
been continued since
the war. the area has
been formed into
four circuits since
1953—Buka, Teop,
Buin and Kieta.
Despite the loss of
several whole con-
gregations to the
Hahalis Movement,
full members have
grown by 37%. The
increase of 106% in
the youth roll shows
internal growth
keeping pace with the
population. The
statistical reduction
of nominals suggest
some quality growth.*

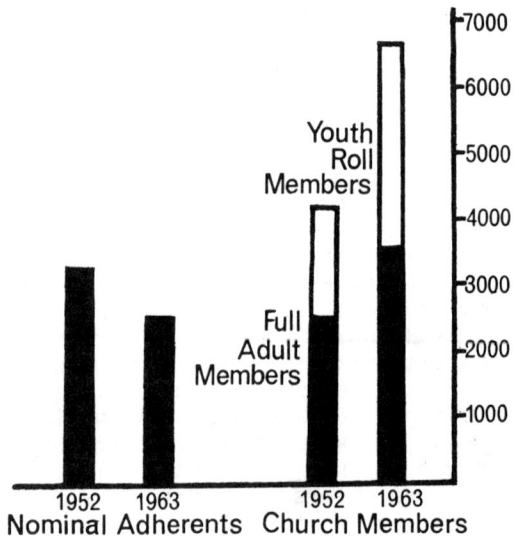

Bougainville and Buka became a separated circuit and growth there became more rapid. After this separation Roviana membership strength stood at 3,214. By 1940 it had dropped to 2,522. A drop like this on the level of preachers and members (not merely the adherents on the fringe) is a serious quality decline.

If we look at the level of adherents for the whole of the Western Solomons immediately prior to the war, we find 17,189 Methodists recorded. They were distributed over the islands in village congregations that averaged sixty-six persons each, yet the church had only one lay preacher for every 111 church-goers. There were over a hundred villages in which the pastor-teacher had no local preacher or class leader to help him. It must be admitted that by the Methodists' own criteria in other parts of Oceania, this was an extremely slow rate of quality and organic growth for four decades of missionary work.

It shows the type of church that was emerging—congregations depending on the pastor-teacher and making no effort to develop local leadership among themselves. Synod felt that the road to indigeneity lay in raising the standards of the pastor-teachers. In point of fact Melanesian development to indigeneity comes faster and more soundly by the development of facilities for local participation. The higher the pastor-teacher stands above the level of the congregation, the less the congregation will participate and the more dependent they will become. At the level of administration, it is dependence on the missionary: at the level of the congregation, dependence on the pastor-teacher supplied by the Mission. Evidence of this is still seen in Roviana villages, and this was one factor which made them vulnerable to Etoism.

Junior membership, which has always been a strong feature of Methodism, was not taken seriously until 1936. Sunday schools were mostly confined to the stations or villages that could be serviced from the stations. Holy Communion, as we have seen, was virtually denied to the island converts. Day schools taught the people to read but the Bible was not translated for them to use. By 1940 221 Methodist villages which had day schools were still without Sunday schools. This was certainly not the normal Methodist pattern, but its mark is felt to this day in the Western Solomons for the simple reason that if the pastor-teacher (who is teaching at day school all the week) does not take the initiative to establish a Sunday school, the local congregation will not do so. They will neither run the school nor teach in it.

There had been conversion growth from paganism over these forty years and a great many churches had been planted, but the internal quality growth on the levels of maturity were retarded. Stations became more and more efficient and the people became more and more dependent. The festivals stressed—Christmas and Easter—were *station* festivals, when huge crowds came from far-distant villages rather than developing their own festivities at the villages. Now the day of big gatherings has gone, for economic reasons, and no village festivals have been created in Christian times. Etoism was a reaction against this change.

The blame for this must not be held against the missionaries of the thirties, who did make some attempt to correct this emphasis of earlier policy. They certainly stepped up the training of teachers and catechists during the decade, so that their numbers rose from 124 (1929) to 273 (1940). This was an institutional achievement. Had it been done in the second decade instead of the fourth, it would have made a world of difference. Certainly the Church had enjoyed a considerable growth from paganism over the four decades, although this might have been much greater had all the opportunities been taken up. However, right through to the Pacific War, the members of Synod remained convinced that the hundreds of open doors could really be handled only by more highly trained men. In other Oceanic areas, where raw converts were sent out into frontier situations, to tell what great things the Lord had done for them, there was phenomenal growth—conversion, quality and organic—and some of these areas are today among the strongest churches of the Pacific.

Part Three

PROBLEMS OF MISSIONARY ATTITUDE AND THEORY

Introductory Note

6 Problems of Theory and Practice
    The Solomon Island Situation
    Static and Dynamic Thinking
    The Advocate, the Acceptor and the Innovation
    Paternalism and Melanesian Capacity for Organization
    Mission and Indigenous Church
    Unity among the Churches

7 Problems of Encounter
    Mana and Taboo
    Power Encounter in Conversion
    Opinion Groups and Pressure

8 Problems of Institutions and Education
    The Church's Role in Education
    Criteria for a Mission Institution
    The Role of Education in the Church
    Mission Institutionalism and the Emergence of the Church

INTRODUCTORY NOTE

THE PROBLEMS of the evangel and pastorate in Melanesia differ from those of the western world, not because of differences of intellect and personality, but because the new religion (like the new health programme, education and economic patterns) is in confrontation with a Melanesian orientation to life. The encounter between light and darkness is simple and clear but its outworkings in conversion, sanctification and discipline may be quite complex. The purpose of this section is to bring some of these problems before the reader, before we turn to a detailed examination of the current situation.

The idea of a 'Solomon Island situation' itself presents a problem. Is there such a thing ethnically as "The Solomon Islands" or must each locality be treated as unique? Were the villages we selected for studies in depth typical? To what extent may our observations be treated as safe generalization for Melanesia?

There is the important question of the Mission and the local Church, which has bearing on so many other issues; the degree of paternalism of the former and the degree of capacity of the latter; the clash between Mission and people in nativistic movements and the schismatic Etoism in particular.

There is the matter of the rationale of conversion experiences and patterns of growth in grace, the differences in western and Melanesian logic and philosophy, problems of sorcery, magic and taboo. Are these issues to be faced in western psychological dimensions or in terms of Melanesian dynamic encounter? Have *mana, taboo* and *magic* (as distinct from sorcery) moral qualities? Are they good, or evil, or open for either good or evil use? To what extent is the motivation of the activator involved? Is the concept of *mana* to be cast aside as heathen, or can it be won for Christ and sanctified?

There is the problem of whether or not the Melanesian, as a person who lives close to the soil like the Hebrew, should make greater use of the Old Testament than the western Christian does. Is the Old Testament relevant to the cycle of Melanesian harvests and seasons? Should men like Abraham, Daniel and David be presented as prototypes for faith, piety and repentance? How can this be done without a vernacular Old Testament? What priority has sculpture translation for congregational education over the administrative burdens of mission stations and plantations? To what extent should the Old Testament power demonstrations like those between Elijah and the prophets of Baal be regarded as prototypes for Christian evangelization of animist areas?

Have the narratives of the exorcisms of Jesus any relevance for the Melanesian demon-possessed, or should the missionary resort to education in psychology and physiology? Is victory to be dynamic

and spontaneous, or a slow educative process over three or four generations? In either case, what problems emerge with the second generation?
Perhaps 10 or 12 per cent of the old unadulterated animism still
remains. How may this best be won for Christ? However, a great deal
of the population which has turned to Christianity is still only superficially Christian. Much of the second generation has had no real spiritual
experience of Christ. The pastoral perfecting that remains to be done is
tremendous. Within itself the Church is confronted with a new
formalism which could itself become a new form of animism. A priestly
type of religion needs the infusion of something prophetic.

Although we must admit there have been many cases of splendid
growth, the progress of the gospel has certainly been uneven. The
Church has grown in sharp bursts, usually on people-movement
patterns, alternated by static periods. In some places Christians and
pagans have existed side by side and apparently become satisfied with
this co-existence. Paganism has adapted itself to new laws and
administration regardless of religion. In some places pagans are slowly
graduating into Christianity by a process of exhaustion and without
dynamic experience. The old traditional world dies slowly. These
situations are often far-removed from the mission stations. What is the
responsibility of the nearby local Christian congregation?

Different again are the problems of the emerging town. Honiara is
a post-war creation and is growing at a great pace. The older settlements of Gizo and Auki may also grow. The development of townships
has changed mission attitudes, and comity agreements are more
difficult to observe. The emergence of new classes—labouring, clerical
and professional—and of an intermediate stratum of Fijians, are formative factors in the growth of the new Solomon Islands town. These
classes have influenced living standards and have widened the Solomon
Island outlook and pastimes. Increasingly the township irritates the
denominational problem. Individualism increases among islanders
away from the village, but communal awareness, though more tenuous,
still exerts a moral force in decision-making patterns in the labour
concentrations. The danger of materialism increases and foreign values
are idealized. New types of living conditions for islanders emerge. The
army hut survivals from the war threaten to become permanent,
though newer housing projects are of cement block. To what extent is
the Church aware of this new atmosphere and who are *the Church*
within this situation? What patterns of Christian faith and practice
meet these needs?

More developed towns in other parts of the Pacific, like Suva in
Fiji, for example, suggest that in the next generation, when those
born in the town have grown up, two types of islander will be apparent
—townsman and countryman. We can only hope that the Church
that grows with them will produce the men to deal with that situation
when it comes. For the time being, we think the Solomon Island
situation in the town is still primarily a rural orientation. The encounter with fear, sorcery and animism is still the stronger. That with
materialism is not yet far advanced.

Now, Part III has been included in this book because it is quite manifest that missionary thinking on all these matters varies considerably, which means that hope for united action is slight. Often the missionaries' attitudes are conditioned by the requirements of the particular post they happen to occupy. Their stations are widely scattered. Their united assemblies are not very frequent. Much missionary action is from the top level, and the indigenous staff on the village level frequently pleads ignorance of missionary action from above. The appreciation of church growth theory and basic missionary technique is very uneven among the missionaries, and the same may be said of their knowledge of anthropology. Some missionaries are unaware of the importance of allowing for cross-cultural variations and values. Probably this reflects weaknesses in the basic missionary training itself, but, be that as it may, the wide range of opinions and the difficulty of getting together for discussion both militate against speedy and effective action. If this is difficult on the missionary level it is even more so on the level of the indigenous Church. Yet action is urgent. Of course synods are held and both Anglican and Methodist indigenous leaders have their conferences, though their powers are very limited.

The three chapters in this part of the book attempt to organize some of these problems into categories of what might be called *areas of missionary disagreement.* I try to bring these into focus, so that at least, whether the reader agrees with me or not, we may understand what are the issues calling for thought, prayer and decision in our time. It seems to me that these areas are those of basic missionary theory, of direct encounter with the non-Christian (animist and secular) world, and of the nature and function of mission institutions.

CHAPTER 6

Problems of Theory and Practice

THE SOLOMON ISLAND SITUATION

THE PRELIMINARY research documents for this survey led me to put my project in terms of a single question—what does it mean to a Solomon Islander to be a practising Christian within the Solomon Island situation? Before long in confrontation with the field situation I began to doubt if there was such a person as a Solomon Islander, or such a thing as the Solomon Island situation or way of life.

Methodist Synod resolutions frequently complained of "artificial political boundaries" across territory "geographically and ethnically" one. Even so, one is confronted with a wide range of customary and linguistic differences. Even in material culture the area displays great variety. When one comes to reduce the similarities to a common core, one finds that most of it has affinities with New Guinea in the north, with the New Hebrides and New Caledonia in the south, and with Fiji in the east. One thus arrives at the conclusion that the common elements in the Solomon Islands as a whole may be put down to the general Melanesian characteristics.[1]

The localities I studied in the Solomons were so radically different, both in their *situations* and their *reactions*, that they might have been different countries. The four nativistic movements which receive consideration in this book all had regional limits. Marching Rule did not survive beyond Malaita and within Malaita its goal was a vision with Malaita limits. The Hahalis movement has no outreach beyond its Buka cultural limits. The outreach of Etoism to Guadalcanal is largely confined to New Georgia migrants. It was rejected in Malaita. Moral patterns, especially with respect to sex, may be classified according to localities. The Administration strives to achieve a pan-Solomon concept with only very limited success. The Malaita entity means far more in Malaita than any entity of the Protectorate. The Melanesian Mission structural involvement with the New Hebrides in the southeast, and the Methodist involvement with part of the Territory of Papua and New Guinea in the north-west do not help the Solomon Islands concept.

Yet even the large islands like New Georgia, Guadalcanal and Malaita are not themselves entities. They have their distinct linguistic areas, and always the salt-water and bush people dichotomy.

As I gather together the results of my few depth studies, no one realizes more than I do the shortcomings of this research. My samples are all too few. They are probably far from typical. One runs the risk of conceptualizing a general situation on a basis of two or three non-typical cases. I am therefore the first to admit that there is no Solomon Island situation, and no typical village. Every local situation has its own character and its own problems. What I have put forward as general findings are therefore presented with this qualification. Of one thing I am certain—the solution of each unique situation must be found within the situation itself, by the local community of Christians which is the Church in that locality. A Mission cannot do this. It requires an indigenous Church.

STATIC AND DYNAMIC THINKING

A dramatic change of atmosphere has taken place in many old colonial lands since the war. Older missionaries who remember pre-war conditions have felt it strongly. In the Solomons the Chair and Rule Movement, Marching Rule, the Hahalis Welfare Movement and Etoism have been the *manifest* evidence of something *latent*. This force has not been confined to young nations moving into selfhood or national entity. It is evident also in many long-established nations which are moving now to international entity among thinkers who seek one world in political, social and religious dimensions. It may be said that there has been a shift from *static* to *dynamic* thinking.

The political scientist, Gunnar Myrdal, demonstrates this in a discussion on the word *integration*, a term which cultural anthropology has used to describe the cohesion of the group and the interrelation of its parts, the stability of fixed *mores* and established functions, by means of which the continuity of society is achieved.[2] Despite the value of this concept, it had a pre-war *static bias*. It dwelt on the stability, balance, integration of society. Any social change or serious disturbance was spoken of as 'disequilibrium', 'maladjustment', 'crisis' or 'disorganization'. Since the war, the word *integration* has emerged with a new connotation that opposes the cultural isolation of communities and sees them as becoming integrated in larger units. Formerly there were passive races. Now there are rising demands for equality and participation in the modern world. This demand for integration in the larger world is a *dynamic* concept, a programmed activity directed towards a goal.[3] Perhaps I can represent this changed attitude schematically thus:

| Socially Static | ———> | Socially Dynamic |

On the national level the same process goes on also with young nations emerging into selfhood. Excessive concentration of effort on the national level may hold up integration on the international level, but until a nation realizes itself it cannot fully participate in international integration. Here the changed attitude may be represented in the modification of old terminology:

```
┌──────────────┐                    ┌──────────────────┐
│  Backward    │      ────────>     │  Underdeveloped  │
│  Regions     │                    │  Countries       │
└──────────────┘                    └──────────────────┘
```

The pre-war term was static; the post-war term implies something to be actively corrected, so that national selfhood may be achieved. When Myrdal uses such terms as *economic integration* and speaks of the economic development of *underdeveloped countries*, he insists that these are more than mere terms: they "symbolize interests, ideals, aspirations and visions"[4] which are new on the international scene since the war. He is writing of economics and political science, but his insight has a wider validity. He could be writing of the emergence of young Churches and a world Church. In actual cases where the recognition of underdevelopment becomes a matter of specific policy change manifested in remedial action, the term *underdeveloped countries* is sometimes dropped for the more positive reference *developing countries*. In any case the post-war temper is dynamic rather than static, either latent or manifest, as the case may be.

The post-war passage from static to dynamic thinking has important consequences for the Church. There is a currently critical mood to discard policies and methods that have not produced the anticipated fruit. Times are propitious for change. We are in days of acceptance and rejection (which will be discussed in a moment). Second generation Christians in great numbers in the Solomons have rejected the traditional form of Christianity. Migration to towns and plantations has revealed the cleavages of denominationalism to people who hitherto knew only one form of Christianity. The possibilities of new projects in evangelism, group activities, lay participation and many other Christian innovations are open today as never before. The attractions of the materialistic west are represented on all sides and the material prosperity of the secular majority of the white residents is quite apparent. The fiasco of the Liquor Bill indicates the pressures at work in the Protectorate. It is a world fraught with great dangers for the Church, but also with glorious possibilities. The day of static thinking is dying. The coming dawn is dynamic.

An emerging indigenous Church in any land has to integrate itself and achieve its own selfhood before it can take its place in the movements of the wider world. The achievement of this entity is organizational, financial and spiritual. Sometimes these do not proceed at an even rate. We are confronted with such a situation in the Eastern Solomons, where the Church is organizationally well developed but financially static. Schematically we may represent the required change thus:

```
┌──────────────────┐                    ┌──────────────┐
│  Station-centred │      ──────── ->    │  Indigenous  │
│  Missions        │                    │  Churches    │
└──────────────────┘                    └──────────────┘
```

or in terms of descriptive adjectives as:

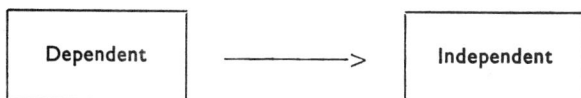

```
┌──────────────┐                    ┌──────────────┐
│              │                    │              │
│  Dependent   │   ─────────>       │  Independent │
│              │                    │              │
└──────────────┘                    └──────────────┘
```

This process is uneven throughout the world: i.e. it proceeds at different rates. The purpose of this study is to ascertain the degree to which the process has taken place, if at all, in the Solomon Islands. Therefore when I write of *Mission* or of dependence, I am thinking of something foreign, paternalistic or static, and imply an unduly long survival of pre-war thinking. When I write of *indigenous Churches* and *independence*, I am implying involvement in a dynamic situation.

An unduly long continuation of static thinking in the Church, especially at the village level, is dangerous with Melanesia in its present mood. Dynamic thinking has of course its dangers (one of which is rejection of the Church by second generation Christians), but it is the only way of survival in the modern world. For this reason I have paid particular attention to the study of Etoism. I lived for a period in a village which had rejected Etoism. In economics it was a village of dynamic thinking, but religiously it was thoroughly static. The congregation of this village has capacity for great organic growth in the Church, but it was thoroughly resigned to dependence. Three courses might be open to these people. They might suddenly become aware of the religious independence of Etoism and break away from the Church. Secondly, they might, because of the satisfactions of their economic development, transfer this to religion and begin to think independently about the Church. The third possibility is of their economic solidarity becoming the major concern of life and the congregational life showing a drift to religious marginality and mere nominality and irrelevance. Any of these could happen. In the circumstances, perhaps the first is unlikely; but unless some effort is made to channel this congregation into the second course, it will probably be the third which eventuates. The Mission can bluff itself into thinking that this congregation is strong because it has resisted Etoism. In the matter of faith this may be true, but in its view of the Church its thinking is dangerously static.

In fairness I must return once more to Myrdal before leaving this theoretical unit. The emerging nation concept is not represented as a mere westernization of the young nation for a place in a world that has come from western civilization. He saw the problem thus:

> How to direct planned policy, so that institutions, patterns and mores are adjusted to avoid cultural impoverishment and social chasms.[5]

He recognizes the necessity for drastic change, but through it a cultural continuity must be retained because of the danger of 'social chasms'. In my own writing I have used the term 'cultural voids',[6] when cultural institutions are abandoned without any functional substitutes being supplied. Thus an *emptiness* becomes part of the new pattern, and against this the New Testament rightly warns us (Luke 11: 24–26). Although Myrdal advocates social and economic change, he does not disregard the old traditions from which the young nation is emerging.

> Anthropologists are also right in warning us against Western ethno-centricism: there are social values in these cultures very much worth preserving, and there are impediments to change, which, in the interests of preserving those values and avoiding cultural breakdowns, should be circumvented and not brutally overcome.[7]

One question we must probe is whether or not the voids which Etoism sought to satisfy were not caused in the first place by evangelical negativism.

THE ADVOCATE, THE ACCEPTOR AND THE INNOVATION

The Department of Agriculture has stated its basic aims and principles as (1) strengthening the economy,[8] (2) raising the level of subsistence in rural areas,[9] (3) ensuring the best use of land, (4) identifying and combating disease, (5) encouraging technical training and a new outlook, and (6) improving methods of agriculture. This is very much an *ideal* policy. It bears the weakness of many theoretical ideals—*there is no guarantee of acceptance of any of these innovations on the popular level.* In the final analysis the Department is no more than the *advocate*—the people alone can be the real innovators.

In the same way the medical and health policy is stated as (1) concentrating on preventive medicine and health education, (2) a malaria eradication project, (3) development of rural health services, (4) improved sanitation, and (5) maintenance of existing hospital services.[10] The malaria project has been prosecuted with authority in some areas, although the officials were expelled in one area. Otherwise these principles and aims have the same features as those of the agricultural policy. I saw free medical services made available in certain villages, and yet only indifferently used by the public. Many of the ideals of health education and sanitation, although well known, are not applied. When a medical officer arrives to give injections to all the members of the village, in the final analysis he can treat only those who trouble themselves to come for treatment. The medical White Paper recognizes the Department's dependence on "adequate legislation" and the "strengthening of the inspectorate" to carry out its programme of public health. The need for such pressure indicates their awareness of the advocating-accepting problem.

In one of my village studies I saw that simply providing a school building and a teacher was not enough to ensure the education of the children. If the children are not disposed to attend school, or the parents to see that they attend, the Church which supplies the facilities will be inevitably disappointed. If the mothers desire their daughters to absent themselves from school for domestic service, the advocacy of education for girls is futile. In the final analysis, salvation lies in the local situation itself. The people themselves are the acceptors or rejectors of the advocated innovation, whether it be a co-operative society, a pattern of agriculture, a medical service, education or a religious institution.

Our problem therefore is not necessarily the excellence or otherwise of the innovation advocated, but rather the pattern of communication that will most readily ensure acceptance.

Quite often the ultimate acceptance depends on some factors that did not occur to the administrative or missionary advocate—sociological, economic, cultural or orientational factors perhaps. In any given situation across cultural lines we are liable to find a single complex of orientational ramifications influencing towards the acceptance or rejection of educational, medical, agricultural and religious innovations. Sometimes then the acceptance of one may provide a clue to the acceptance of the others; although normally the Administration, commerce and the Church would not use identical forms of advocacy.

At other times the general idea of an advocated innovation may be accepted but modified by the acceptors to suit their own ends. Here we see clearly that the converts and not the missionaries are the real innovators. From our point of view this may be good or bad, desirable or undesirable. For example, a missionary offers Christianity to an animist community. The offer probably has some foreign elements. The occasion is propitious for innovation. The community is disposed to accept the new faith; but what is ultimately introduced is not exactly what the western missionary envisaged. If that variation is merely the innovation of a real Christianity within indigenous forms, then the modification is good and desirable, because an indigenous Church will eventually emerge. But there is always the possibility of the emergence of a Christopaganism where the names and forms are Christian but the motives and beliefs are magical. This is a recurring problem in missions. In the course of our investigation we shall apply tests at this point to Etoism, for instance, when we ask what are its pagan associations.

Despite the impressive "Aims and Purposes" stated in the White Papers, the social and economic life of the Solomons is poorly developed. When the Department of Agriculture states that its priorities are copra, cocoa and rice, we need to remember that there is as yet virtually no cocoa yield. It is second priority only because it "offers most chance of success". Rice is third, not because of any worthwhile production, but because the country imports 2,500 tons a year for local consumption in the industrial and town areas, and so there is a local market for any rice that might be produced. Clearly the Protectorate has a vulnerable single-crop economy. Much that is written about this and the other crops is something planned and hoped for in the future. Only 40 per cent of the small revenue for official spending (£A2,835,000 in 1964) was locally raised, for the Protectorate is 60 per cent dependent on foreign aid. Yet for seventy years the Government has been advocating patterns of agricultural production.

The dependent character of the Protectorate's finances reflects a still deeper dependence. Qualified agricultural officers are mostly recruited from overseas. Qualified Solomon Island replacements are not likely to be found "for some years to come", though training to this end has begun. Visitors to the Protectorate are astonished by the impressive role of Fijian and other island medical workers in the Group—and one might add clerks, teachers and engineers. There is quite a community of these people in Honiara and the smaller townships, in government and clerical posts that should be occupied by Solomon Islanders helping their country on the road to selfhood. Exactly the same applies to the Church in the Western Solomons. Many of the plantation yields are decreasing and there is urgent need for replanting. Higher overhead costs today restrict the commercial plantations[11] and the future seems to depend on indigenous replanting programmes. Aware of this, the Department tries to stimulate action by spending 30 per cent of its budget on extension services, and to raise the quality of copra by a system of differential prices. It organizes displays at public gatherings (I saw one myself) to strengthen its advocacy of these innovations. Here again action must take place on the local level. The White Paper propositions are theoretically sound, but somewhere along the line the proposals are not sufficiently orientated to sociological and cultural factors to ensure acceptance. Awareness of this failure is indicated by the Department's decision to restrict cocoa extension services to "areas where farmers are receptive to advice", and staffing priorities to areas producing results.

On the level of the village living and farming conditions, the Government advocates all kinds of worthy innovations to raise levels and increase comforts, but only here and there do they meet with acceptance. Projects of sanitation, food supply, leprosy eradication, maintenance of schools and co-operative marketing facilities are continually placed before the people. Medical facilities only have to be asked for. There is much good in all these proposals, but what I saw of them was a painfully disappointing acceptance. Perhaps the present Government has to fight against an inbuilt attitude against the white man, a distrust that has grown over a century during which he has been seen as a kidnapper, an exploiter and a tax-collector.[12] The Missions, on the other hand, have built in an attitude of paternalism, so that the people are reluctant to do things for themselves. The effect is the same—it is hard to stir up village action. But in social, economic and religious life there can be no renewal unless the people themselves are ready to "work our their own salvation". What *movements* we have seen have been indigenous innovations, breakaways from those proposals advocated by the foreigner. In all aspects of life indigeneity involves action on the village level. It is only here that innovations are accepted.

PATERNALISM AND THE MELANESIAN
CAPACITY FOR ORGANIZATION

Some missionaries and administrators have felt that the Melanesians have no capacity for organization: that there must be Europeans in charge, directing procedures and organizing whatever is desirable for the good of the people. They say Melanesians can do things well provided they are directed from above. This pernicious doctrine fits both mission paternalism and commercial colonialism, prolongs the dependence of the islander, and generally retards progress because all decisions are made *for* the people instead of *by* the people.

A Church ruled from Mission stations, with attractive properties, efficient hospitals and high-grade schools, may seem to be a 'going concern', yet because everything is directed from the stations may never emerge into selfhood at all. Until each congregation becomes a decision-making body, there is no indigenous Church at all but merely a community under mission paternalism. There are many Christian villages which are quite content to remain thus.

It is possible for missionaries to talk *indigeneity* in their committees and to desire it, to change their mission terminology to church terminology, and yet get no nearer to indigeneity—because the committee members are not prepared to take the leap or risk of faith required to make either the total church organization or the village congregations autonomous. Until these central committees which make the vital decisions have an indigenous majority, there is no indigenous Church, and not until the local groups carry their own organizational loads can they be called indigenous. That means housing and providing for the pastor, organizing, collecting and dispensing their own finances, supplying their Sunday school and church groups with leaders, and so on. We shall return to this in the next unit. At the present moment we are discussing the question of whether or not the Melanesian has the capacity for this.

In my own missionary experience I saw a Melanesian Church take this step of faith at the end of the war. It entrusted the village congregational finances to village congregational committees, eliminated a European Synod, and gave the remaining Synod an indigenous majority—a very considerable majority. It even placed the stationing of missionaries in the hands of that indigenous majority. From that moment that Church which had been static for decades began to develop new forms of spiritual growth, and though one would not claim it as any paragon of perfection, it is today as virile a young Church as there is in the Pacific. It took a real act of faith on the part of those missionaries to sign away their ruling powers and to turn over the finances to village committees. Yet once the step was taken, in spite of the few mistakes that have been made, no one would ever think of going back to the old paternalism. These Melanesians proved their capacity for organization.

This capacity for organization is apparent in Melanesian life, social structure and even children's games. No feature of Rarumana life was more open to our observation than the behaviour of the children, since our house was situated next to the school. We heard their lessons and saw them at play. Their capacity for communal projects and team games was impressive. At playtime they poured out of the building and organized themselves into teams with alacrity, and played to win the game as a team.[13] Everybody participated and everybody enjoyed it to the full. Capacity for organization was natural even in the children.

In a less happy dimension, the movements of Marching Rule and Etoism have disproved once and for all that Melanesians have no capacity for organization. One of the current views of Etoism is that it was possible only because of the emergence of one strong character who demonstrated this capacity; that he is unique, and without him there could have been no Etoism. He was not unique—Eto and John Frum and scores of others were identical types. Their movements differ mainly because of the different circumstances that surrounded their respective emergences. Although Etoism has this one half-prophetic, half-deified figure, there is a widespread organization which carries on by itself, whether Eto be present or not. There is effective local organization in each of its twenty to thirty village communities. There are thoroughly organized patterns of worship and enthusiasm among both adults and children. My question then is: If the people of the Roviana and Kusage villages were capable of this spontaneous reorganization of their lives and their worship patterns into what they now call the Christian Fellowship Church, why has it not been possible for an indigenous Church to emerge under missionary guidance? It is not a matter of capacity. We are now ready to take a deeper look at this matter of Mission and Indigenous Church, which has become to us so great a problem.

MISSION AND INDIGENOUS CHURCH

The *ideal* of establishing an indigenous Church has for long occupied the missionary thinking of both Anglicans and Methodists in the Solomons. It was firmly established among the former by the first Bishop Selwyn and his successor, Bishop Patteson, who was actually the first Bishop of Melanesia. Amongst the Methodist archival material one finds many references to their hopes for a "self-governing, self-supporting and self-propagating Church".[14] No one could ever say these ideals have not been the desire of the missionaries. In the face of this, then, we must ask why after so many decades of missionary activity, during which time the numerical growth of Christians has been considerable, these ideals are still unrealized in many ways. The question of the emergence of the Church is possibly our major problem.

The Anglicans have measured indigeneity in terms of an indigenous clergy and indigenous worship patterns, architecture and so on. Progress was slow to the end of the century, for reasons we have already discussed, but speeded up by Bishop Wilson, who made the preparation of an indigenous clergy one of his major interests. Today, the Diocese of Melanesia, 78 per cent of whose members are in the Solomon Islands, has a strong indigenous clergy of 100, with seventy-eight brothers and 900 catechists.[15] On the level of the higher clergy, two Melanesians are now Assistant Bishops. This is a considerable accomplishment. However, the same degree of indigeneity is by no means apparent in financial matters. The lack of a dimension reaching towards self-support keeps the Church bound to the mission financial

organization, to foreign aid, and prevents the development of stewardship on the village level. The Christian service rendered by the Anglican
Church to the community in the Solomons, which is quite considerable,
is rendered by the Mission and from overseas funds, rather than by the
local Church. The expenditure of overseas money is enormous. On the
village level the people are spiritually well fed by their priests and
catechists, but there is little personal exploration of their religion
outside the church building, and very little application of the faith
in the social situation that surrounds them. One can certainly speak of
an indigenous clergy but this is only one step towards an indigenous
Church.

The Methodists have virtually no indigenous ministry, although
they are well off for pastor-teachers and catechists. The door to the
ministry has been jealously guarded, and the 'perfectionism' demanded
in this respect has discounted their expressed desires. At two points of
time when an indigenous ministry was most needed, when the work
was being handed over to the New Zealand Church and at the time of
the 1928 Report, when the *ideals* were being stated most, the 'screws'
of this 'perfectionism' were most forcefully applied and they were not
relaxed up to the time of the Pacific War.[16] The same reluctance to
share ministerial status with indigenes we have already also seen with
respect to the Lord's Supper. On the financial level, the obligations for
self-support were lessened by incoming revenue from plantations.
From my own observations I can say that the contributions from
Christian households are far less than they ought to be according to their
economic position. The general religious participation could also be
much more than it is. They view their activities as those things "which
the missionary decided they should do". Except for those villages
which have cast off the Mission, I think this resignation to paternalism
is fairly widespread. Since the war the missionaries have tried to
stimulate church-thinking. They now speak of the total organization
as a Church District rather than a Mission. My feeling was that the
missionaries genuinely desired an indigenous Church, but quite often at
'grass-roots' there was no awareness of the issue. The people still
'think mission' and see everything in terms of what the Mission does
or does not do for them. One has real sympathy for the brethren who
now have this problem to face and solve, for it is not of their devising—
it is an unhappy inheritance of past policy. The tragedy of it all is
that the *ideal was perceived in the past but never acted upon.*

There never was a time when these islands needed a strong indigenous
ministry with pastoral insights as they do now. Such a ministry is not
raised in a day. More effort is at present being made in this direction
than was made in the past, but the principle of sound growth is surely
that *the indigenous ministry should grow at a rate relative to the intake
of converts.* The strength or weakness of a Church in this respect may
be measured by examining the *minister: adherent ratio.*

The Anglicans slowed down evangelism to maintain the pastorate
and the Methodists pushed evangelism but failed to develop the
pastorate. One lost conversion growth, the other lost quality growth.

One allowed others to reap much of the harvest, the other opened the way for Etoism. The basic cause in each case was a reluctance to trust and act on the indigenous experience, a fear that indigenous standards might fall short of the ethical and theological requirements of western Christianity. For this reason the General Secretary writes:

> The ideal is a self-governing, self-supporting, and self-propagating native church

but then he adds a rider—

> This, of course, is a long way off.[17]

Missionaries and Mission Boards have to learn the risk of faith. Until they are prepared to act on their ideals, the indigenous Church will not truly emerge. The present Lord Bishop made this very point in his last Synod charge, when he pressed his men "to take risks for the extension of Christ's Kingdom" with their minds on "the ultimate end" of the work.[18]

The reticence to trust the ethical and theological strength of converts has also been reflected in a doubt about their capacity to handle finances. This is a widespread attitude not confined to the Church, a feeling that the island people are not yet ready for responsibility. Only a decade ago a research economist wrote, generalizing for the South Pacific at large:

> In conformity with the generally accepted view that the indigenous people of the South Pacific are not yet ready to become trading bank customers, the commercial banks of the South Pacific make no special efforts to provide banking facilities for these people. Legal limitations to islanders discourage the practice of granting overdraft accommodation . . . Similarly the communal ownership of native land precludes the mortgaging or charging of land for security purposes. . . .[19]

If this applies to Pacific Islands economically far in advance of the Solomons, showing that commercial and legal opinion presupposes that someday they may be ready, but certainly not yet; then we realize that we are not facing an obstruction from missionaries alone. This is something inherent in the thinking of white men in the Pacific. Paternalism is characteristic of the white race.

Now, I am well aware that it is one thing to point out the weaknesses of an existing pattern, and quite another to suggest ways and means of adjustment. The Solomons need a Church which is indigenous in ministry, organization, worship patterns, stewardship and financial controls, but how to reach this goal from the present position is a serious problem.

Missionary theory has long been aware of this problem, although it was lost sight of during the last war. Sidney J. W. Clark[20] developed a theoretical differentiation between *Construction* and *Reconstruction*, using the former to describe church-planting on lines that were indigenous from the outset,[21] and the latter for the work of correcting the shortcomings of dependent 'churches'. The simplicity of the former and the complexity of the latter were recognized. The concepts are too valuable to be lost.

Clark approached the task of reconstruction from three angles:

1. Scrapping things that are wrong or useless or have served their purpose.
2. Reshaping features which still have some power for service.
3. Adding such new features as are required to bring renewal and life to the Church and make it adequate for the needs and purposes of today.

This is at least a valid frame of reference for planning correction. It provides a mechanism for thinking out a situation and fixing on a corrective programme; but the actual thinking and implementation of reforms must come from within the situation itself. This should be effective in any case in which the local people realize the weakness of their cause and desire to correct it. My one fear for the Solomons is that the local village congregations are unaware of, and unconcerned for their shortcomings, and will first need to be convinced that the current pattern is in need of adjustment. This is a very serious problem indeed. The Roviana segment of what is now Etoism was lost partly because the post-war missionaries modified pre-war policies and some of the important elders resented the change. I am well aware that too much pressure from the top for village communities to be more self-determinative and more involved in activity and financial responsibility, might well bring a further exodus. The changes therefore should not have any appearance of an imposition from above.

Possibly group dynamics has something to offer here. Would it be possible to persuade one progressive community to experiment with self-support, financially and organizationally, giving them in return special representation in Synod and a vote; so that the community becomes a pilot project? Where this has been tried elsewhere in Melanesia, before long other communities have begun clamouring for similar rights, and thus a new *mental set* or disposal towards indigeneity has been built up on the local level. There may be other and better methods, but once again we return to the position that the battle for the emergence of an indigenous Church has to be won on the level of the village congregation.

UNITY AMONG THE CHURCHES

Although the purpose of this study is to discover what it means to be a Solomon Island Christian in the Solomon Island situation, any study of an emerging Church must ask how that Church perceives its own role within the universal Church of Jesus Christ, which is bigger than its own denominational entity. I have included this unit among the Problems of Attitude and Theory, because in this present case that is where it belongs. The villages are largely unaware of any Church bigger than their own denomination—except where the concepts of *organic union* and the *World Council of Churches* have been injected *as problems*, with foreign overtones of western theological disputation by a few missionaries who are personally opposed to both. Otherwise there are no ecumenical perspectives in this village Christianity.

Yet there are two specific factors within the Solomon Island environment that make a discussion of this kind pertinent in our times. I do not mean that there necessarily ought to be organic union of Churches in the Solomons; but there should at least be a drawing together of such a character that the spiritual oneness they are supposed to have is more apparent. Let us examine these two factors:

(1) Town and plantation are both centres for labour concentration where people from all parts of the Solomons are brought together— not merely Christians and pagans, but Christians of all denominational persuasions. These people are now more aware of denominationalism than ever before. Although the historic origins of these divisions are of no consequence to the islander, he is now aware of the divisions within Christianity. These denominations mystify him in that they draw quite different teachings from the one sacred book, and reinforce different beliefs and practices, generating a good deal of heat and rivalry in the process. The history of the Church in Oceania shows that time and time again this realization has opened the way for some neo-pagan resurgence, with a syncretism of Christian forms and allegorical interpretations of Christian scriptures in line with traditional beliefs. The reasoning has always been the same—if Anglican, Roman Catholic, Methodist and Seventh Day Adventist can all interpret the word of God in their own way, then why can we not have a Polynesian or Melanesian interpretation linking it up with our own mythology and way of life?

This same factor—awareness of denominationalism—has reduced the *authority* of religion, *per se*. Pre-Christian religion, as we have seen, was the integrator of society. Christianity was taken over communally as a basis of faith for life and action, and for the first generation was counted as something which could be taken for certain. The observation of comity helped to preserve this to some extent; but comity is no longer a fact. The awareness of denominationalism has confronted the second generation with a choice—not a simple choice between Christianity and paganism, but a host of choices with bewildering differentiation. Uncertainty takes the place of certainty. In most villages the people were united, even if a different denomination existed along the coast a mile or so. Now, one rubs shoulders with Christians of quite different form and faith in the same set of buildings. The social stability of life has vanished: religion, once the integrator, now becomes the cause of segmentation. This process from fusion to fission is creating a situation that demands investigation. The oneness of the Church is suddenly a relevant issue.

(2) The town and plantation have also shown the Solomon Islander that a very great many Europeans have virtually no religion at all; that prosperity, status and wealth may all be achieved without religion. Religion thus becomes dispensable in the very same places which might well become the centres of diffusion of religious ideas, pagan and Christian. The more people dispute about their denom-

inational viewpoints, the more confused they become and the more vulnerable all religion becomes. So men begin to set their hearts on purely material comforts and are open to non-religious ideological substitutes for religion.

One young Anglican catechist told me that the hosts of young men absent from their villages on the plantations in Russell Islands and Guadalcanal, have taken "money as their God" (his expression). Much of the trouble in the areas of the nativistic movements examined in the anthropological section of this book has grown from envy of the white man's riches, especially his capacity to make money quickly. This was so in Buka, which conceptualized its 'salvation' not in religious terms but as a *welfare society*. If ever the Solomons needed a united Christian witness, it is today—the apostolic "singleness of heart". The Churches ought to draw together as *the* Church. If not organic, it ought at least to have the spiritual unity that makes it recognizable as the one Church of Jesus Christ in the Solomons, not this or that denominational mission.

Not with the Solomons in mind, but generalizing for the mission of the Church everywhere, the Ghana Statement put it thus:

> The mission to which they [the Churches] are called is not *their* mission; it is Christ's mission. . . . To seek first to safeguard the interests, the activities, the sphere of influence of our Church, our mission, our confessional body is in the end a denial of mission, a refusal to be a servant. . . . We must ask of any proposal for new work, new developments, new patterns of co-operation, not 'How will this affect us?', but 'What is God's will in this situation?'[22]

The very presence of town and plantation situations in the Solomons, with firstly the process from fusion to fission in religion, and secondly the awareness of the dispensability of religion, prompts this very question: What is God's will in this situation? The Churches should be meeting more together to discuss this, to discover God's will, and to deal with the situation, not as denominations, but as *the* Church.

I make no suggestions about organic union. Among the missionaries at the top level some thought has been given to the matter but the situation is complex. From the Anglican side I obtained a clear expression of possible drawing together on a basis something like the union in South India, and I met no vocal opposition to this from the Methodist men, although they were thinking in another direction. The scheme would have the advantage of preserving any ethnic entity the Solomons might have, but of course the island Churches themselves would need their own organic entity to emerge before they could unite. They would need independence first from their supporting home churches, so once more we come back to the major issue of the emergence of the indigenous churches.

There are bodies of opinion among both Anglicans and Methodists seeking organic consolidation of their own respective denominations for all Melanesia, and then after that perhaps discussions between the Churches. The Methodists have already formed a United Synod linking their work in the Solomons with that in the Territory of Papua and

New Guinea; but this has all been done at the administrative level and the indigenous people know very little about it.

In the Territory of Papua and New Guinea the Methodists are already negotiating with other bodies, one Congregational and the other an organization known as Kwato, for organic union. This movement grew out of the Samoa Conference and has its own Continuation Committee. Its motivation springs from the same kind of situation outlined at the beginning of this unit, as it applies to Port Moresby and Rabaul. Viewing the situation from a distance, the proposal would appear to be quite relevant for those two towns, although these two towns cannot represent the whole situation that will be involved. Nor can I evaluate its effect on the Solomons situation. I would imagine that the Methodists would be moving away from any union with the Anglicans in the Solomons by this move, especially as the United Synod already ties them to the Territory. It would also greatly complicate relations between Church and State in the Solomons. My impression was that the missionaries involved were more concerned with pressing their own solutions than in exploring all possible solutions.

The most serious danger of all seemed to me to be that, whatever the move, it was likely to be a *mission-decision* rather than a *church-decision*. The mission leadership might well arrive at a right decision, but is it the right way? Among the islanders whom I thought would have definite ideas on this matter, there was a haziness about the facts, and an attitude that it was all being decided at the top anyway. Furthermore the same islanders were more disposed to see the importance of union with Ysabel and Guadalcanal than with New Guinea and Papua. It would be a tragedy to see any move for organic union cut across lines of ethnic solidarity. It is bad enough having political lines doing this. It would be to found a united Church on theoretical principles that do not allow for all the ethnic dimensions of the situation. The only way of avoiding this is to start discussions from the village level—which brings us back again to the need for that indigenous self-expressing Church in the villages.

One would hope that, if a true Solomon Islands indigenous and united Church were to come into being, it would also include the other large evangelical church of the eastern islands. It has many affinities with the Methodists, even though its attitude is against Anglican formalism and emphasis on Church tradition. Its spiritual emphasis could give much of great value to such a union; but it is opposed to the principle of organic union, *per se*. Even so, the three churches should be able to work more together in united Christian witness.

I have left the question of organic union as a mere statement of the situation as I saw it. Ideas in this direction were not well developed and I had the impression that answers to my questions were often guarded and circuitous. But there is scope for united Christian action, and this is urgent.

Anglicans and Methodists have much to give each other, even without any thought of union. They could meet for the sharing of ideas, discussion of mutual problems and for fellowship. This could be done on all levels of leadership, especially indigenous leadership. Congregational units could be brought together in the towns. In worship, the Anglicans have much to give with respect to the Christian Year, preparation for and emphasis on Holy Communion, and a planned lectionary; the Methodists, in their personal exploration of the scriptures and in Christian hymnody. The Methodists could learn much from the forms of Anglican prayer patterns, catechism and liturgy, but teach a new dimension to the Anglicans in personal and extempore prayer. The Anglicans could demonstrate the importance of the total scope of Christian doctrine, and learn from the Methodists in the dimension of application of faith in good works. Both already make considerable use of each other's hymns.

In women's work, the Anglicans have a fine organized prayer network with an Anglican ecumenical perspective in the Mothers' Union,[23] from which the Methodists could learn something; but they in turn have other dimensions in their Methodist Women's Fellowship to offer the Anglicans, especially with respect to stewardship.[24]

None of these things are contradictory, nor would any infringe against the beliefs of the other denomination. It is just that they have explored different aspects of a common faith and practice, so that each has something to offer to the totality of the other.

I saw a little of theological training at both Siota and Banga. Perhaps some intercommunion could be introduced at this level. Could the young men who are to form the ministry of tomorrow meet for retreats and discuss matters of worship and Christian practice, and above all form friendships to be retained throughout their ministries? They are all Solomon Islanders, or at least islanders serving in the same political region. At Siota I found a great interest among the students in the activities of other branches of the Christian Church in other parts of Melanesia—Fiji in particular, as they knew I came from that area— and in the World Council of Churches because of my project among them. They were specially interested in anything related to the indigenous Church and the training of the ministry. I had a feeling that here, at least, was one place where young men, the hope of tomorrow, could be brought together with similar men from Banga, to share something of their preaching, village itinerations, confrontations with pagan survivals and other aspects of their mutual concern. If an awareness of the oneness of Christ's Church could be established here, it would soon be inevitably transmitted to the village level by indigenous means.

The transmission of ideas about church union to the village level was evident only in villages of the South Seas Evangelical Church. This was because some missionaries had itinerated with a hostile negative polemic against both church union and the W.C.C. This negative polemic had achieved the opposite of its intention, in that it had made the people curious to know what it was all about. They ask any European they meet—traveller, anthropologist, or members of denominations other than their own. This was specially so in Malaita, where the value of unity had been demonstrated in

Marching Rule, in which South Sea Evangelicals played a far from insignificant role.

In the same island the issue of unity had been injected into the same denominational community by the Baha'i movement, which stems from a certain trader in Honiara and has now quite a community of members round Hauhui in Malaita. It began there through a South Sea Evangelical who had been disciplined. After a decade the Baha'i now claim about 800 adherents in five assemblies, one at Honiara, one of considerable strength at Auki, and the others round Hauhui. These people have a natural urge for unity, which attracted them to Baha'i in the first place. With religious and political movements in this direction and the widespread attitude of enquiry, one is led to feel that the time is ripe for innovation along the lines of unification movements. Anything could happen, good or bad, given the right stimulus and some prophetic figure capable of utilizing it. It could be an opportunity for the Church or for some other movement.

One of the great hindrances to unity lies in the variant patterns of church discipline. This is a bone of contention among the adherents of different denominations congregated in the labour concentrations. But it is not merely the different moral perspectives of the denominations; for even within one denomination people from different communities have different moral perceptions. Even if the churches could agree on a common policy or attitude to such questions as marriage, liquor, betel-nut chewing, magic, sex, sorcery and so on, unanimity would be unlikely for cultural reasons. The social relations between male and female in, say, the Shortlands are so completely different in structure from those in Malaita that their perspectives of offence and justice are bound to differ. The economic values of the family units of Rarumana, a settled community, and those of the migrating labourers of the Tai Lagoon region, are so different that one given regulation might well work out with a quite different moral significance in each case. The abandonment of the traditional patterns of 'bride price' in one island may be desirable and lead to progress; but in another it could mean economic and social disaster, and obligate the manufacturers of shell-money to seek a completely new means of livelihood, which in all probability would bring them into competition with their present trade exchange partners with whom they have hitherto had a symbiotic relationship. Government laws aiming at unifying the whole group may well benefit one segment of the community and injure another. These problems of a highly segmented island Group make unity movements difficult in both Church and State.

Here we are faced with a most serious problem—the right of the small cultural unit to be what it wants to be. Do such communities (and there are scores of them in the Solomons) have to sacrifice their individuality and be absorbed in the total unity? Is it to their advantage to conform to the uniformity of Church and State? Their loss of communal entity is a tragedy of the first order to them: is there compensation in being part of the larger and stronger union? Before giving a quick answer to that, let us ask if it is practicable for the small island community of say 400 persons, many miles off the regular trade route, to draw the educational, medical and commercial benefits to which it is entitled? In the Solomons, with its great distances and limited resources this question will not stand examination. This is a complex problem with no easy answer. It may well be that these isolated units should work out their own salvation within their own patterns. There is always a danger of imposing on the smaller segments, in the name of unity and progress, western concepts of law and ethics, denominational patterns of discipline, and the political policies of the total Group.

Yet the growth of plantations and towns has made this Group part of the modern world. There is interaction and cross-fertilization of culture, whether people like it or not. More and more, politically, socially and commercially, forces for unification are going to be pressed on all the cultural segments of these islands. Is it perhaps not time that the denominational and regional leaders got together, to set in motion a process of helping Christians to know one another? Is it not perhaps in this way that men may discover that there is in life something greater even than society and culture—and what it means that all things are to be summed up in Christ?

CHAPTER 7

Problems of Encounter

MANA AND TABOO

A MISSIONARY from the area narrates a series of events associated with the cutting down of a taboo banyan tree. Tradition held that any person breaking this taboo would surely die. A Christian teacher with about thirty axemen set about removing the forbidden monster after public declaration of their intention to engage in this encounter. A great crowd assembled in an atmosphere of tension. "They will die! They will die!" some cried. "Let me be the first to die then!" the teacher declared, driving his axe first into the tree. Some hid their faces in their hands, but the tree was cut down, though a week was required to reduce it to firewood. The teacher and his friends suffered no harm. They erected a cross on the sacred place and held a Christian worship service there. For a long time a few diehards refused to go near the terrible place, but for the majority of the people it lost its fears.

Every reader of Church history is familiar with this type of incident, and no one can dispute that the Church grew mightily in this manner. However, those who know the facts are by no means of one mind in their interpretation of them. The missionary in question writes:

> I personally was delighted to hear that the banyan tree was going to be chopped down. When the natives responsible for its felling suffered no ill effects, the villagers would have to accept the evidence of their own eyes. The pernicious doctrine of *tapu* would be revealed in all its stupidity. Unscrupulous witch-doctors would no longer be able to terrify the credulous native with such flagrant absurdity. If men could ignore the formidable *tapu* of the banyan tree and still live, then all other *tapus* were demonstrably innocuous.

And again—

> The evil symbol was methodically razed to the ground, but nobody was bewitched and nobody died as a result. The *tapu* was a fake.

Whether one agrees or not with the personal opinion of this missionary, whose name I withhold, is not the point so much as the bunch of fallacies in its logic, and its failure to allow for Melanesian logic. The doctrine of *tapu* or taboo[1] is prejudged as pernicious—a generalization which will not stand testing, because many taboos in Melanesia are protective and operate as a form of law to protect personal and communal rights, persons and property. The 'witch-doctors' are prejudged as unscrupulous, although the term is not defined and the missionary concerned does not distinguish between sorcerers and medicine-men.

Terms like "all its stupidity" and "such flagrant absurdity" reveal a personal disposition to impatience on the part of the missionary which will not help in understanding the basic problems. That all taboos are "demonstrably innocuous" because one is found false does not follow, even in western logic. The assumption that the deliberate breaking of a taboo would cause one to be bewitched shows a misunderstanding of terms and processes. Finally, because a taboo fails, it does not necessarily mean it was a fake. It may be so but it is not proved.

This raises a great many problems which are basic to any appreciation of Melanesian thought and action. The missionary tells us the taboo was created so long ago that no one really knew much about it. A powerful chief had put the taboo on the tree but the circumstances regarding the inauguration of the prohibition were forgotten. We do not appear to be concerned with sorcerers and medicine-men. The tree is sacred because of its *mana*. It is the *mana* which kills. The taboo is the prohibition. *Mana* is quantitative. Its supply has been built up. There are many ways of doing this. Sometimes skulls were placed in banyan trees. Sacrifices were made at banyan trees. Often snake cults were associated with them. All through Melanesia from New Guinea to Fiji we meet this kind of thing. Quite apart from the fact that banyan trees themselves are widely regarded as sacred, *mana* was accumulated by associated rites. This accumulation of *mana* by means of sacred rituals is a basic presupposition for animists.

The incident under discussion would not be taken to mean the taboo was a fake. The taboo failed because the *mana* had failed, just as with us a law of prohibition fails when the police cannot enforce it. The Melanesian would ask why had the *mana* failed, and to this question he would find one of two answers. Either

(1) The sacred tree had lost its *mana* because, for a long time, the rites had been neglected, no sacrificial rituals had been performed, and the traditions had become vague and half forgotten, or

(2) The *mana* of the sacred tree had been overcome by a greater *mana*. The teacher and the young axemen would in this case be seen by the animists to possess a Christian *mana* that was all-powerful. Two things ought to be noted: (a) they claimed victory in the name of Christ, and (b) they erected a cross, which, in the eyes of the villagers became a functional substitute for the tree, the symbol of a power which claimed their allegiance.

Whether or not the western missionary personally rejects this philosophy is to beg the question. He is working in a Melanesian world, facing a Melanesian philosophy, and will have to learn to understand Melanesian thought forms, and fight for Christianity on Melanesian levels. Actually this is a relevant encounter and a real victory, with many scriptural precedents. Western missions might do well to face up to the statistical evidence that animists are being won today by a Bible of power encounter, not a demythologized edition. I am not introducing the rights and wrongs of the latter, but merely the statistical facts of conversion figures.

To return to the quotation—the "evil symbol" of the taboo was said to be able to "bewitch" the axemen. We ought to clarify our concepts. A taboo is a prohibition, sacred or legal, valid only if it has enough *mana* behind it to enforce it. The *mana* is quiescent as long as people observe the taboo. The *mana* is activated by the offender himself who voluntarily or involuntarily stimulates it. Sorcery is activated by another party with malignant intent, to cause sickness, death or some other harm. The missionary cited did not distinguish between a penalty brought on oneself by breaking a prohibition and a sickness caused by a malevolent second party. The missionary needs to be aware of these distinctions because of the differences in communal attitude towards these various forces. If he fails to appreciate the attitudes and motivation in the Melanesian power complex, he will certainly not understand Melanesian reactions to victory in Christ, which are matters of real encounter, not merely a proof that one Melanesian institution was a fake.

If the missionary is to be effective across cultural barriers, he must transmit an atmosphere of sympathy, even of empathy. To make pre-judgements that things are absurdities and fakes is not the way to win converts. If a mission operates in an atmosphere of *mana* and taboo, the missionary should at least be aware that his gospel will have some different implications in this mental climate from those with which he is familiar in the west.

POWER ENCOUNTER IN CONVERSION

In conversion, power encounter and people-movements go together. I purpose recording as cases two movements described originally by persons who were involved in them, and using these as a basis for discussion. We will take the case of Florida, which was recorded at length by Alfred Penny,[2] the missionary who baptized hundreds of the converts; and the case of Ulawa as recorded by Clement Marau,[3] the Melanesian teacher involved in the movement.

Case Study One: *Florida (Gaeta)*

The growth of the Church in Florida began with Charles Sapibuana, whom Bishop Patteson had taken to Norfolk Island as a boy of twelve. In 1877, at twenty-three, he settled on his own island at Gaeta, as a Christian teacher, against considerable opposition. Working within the kin-structure he first won his own family, then that of his brother, and then the relatives of his brother's wife. These were baptized as a group in 1878 and marked the beginning of the Church. Sapibuana established classes for Christian instruction.

The witness and stability of this group led to many enquiries, and within a year the classes for enquirers were crowded with persons who had virtually resolved to give up heathenism. Penny, who knew them, said:

> They let go their old superstition, and faced danger in the strength of a new religion, refusing to attend sacrifices, treading on forbidden ground where sickness once was found through fear, and doing things which once brought death.[4]

There is no reason to doubt the contemporary vigour of the heathenism of Florida, as the *Sandfly* murders of that time show. By 1882 Penny had 100 adult baptisms, and Sapibuana was ordained as a deacon.

In the following year Florida witnessed a *débâcle* among the spirit-shrines (*tindalo*)[5] It began at Gaeta, when chief Kalekona (who had been obstructive hitherto) and some of his people suddenly appeared at Sapibuana's school one evening and announced that they had destroyed their charms and relics and now wished to be taught. By this time about 250 adults had been baptized on Florida, all having registered their decision for Christ by giving up their *tindalo* and their paraphernalia. These events had led to much discussion in the chiefly and priestly circles, and Kalekona had now made his own decision. News of his rejection of his *tindalo* spread rapidly and, as usual, all forms of calamity were predicted, but nothing happened. Heathen opinion began to swing to the view that the new religion at Gaeta was one of great power. The heathen argued that this power was confined to Gaeta, but let Kalekona come outside its orbit and see what his new power stood for outside !

This opinion led Kalekona to undertake an encounter with Rogani, who owed him a debt and apparently had no intention of adjusting his accounts. Custom provided a legitimate mechanism known as *dunning* for the recovery of debt. Kalekona, acting within his just rights, dunned the debt, making sure that the pigs he seized in settlement were actually taboo pigs, and at the same time smashing the *tindalo*. None of his party suffered any ill-effects through this venturesome act.

As a result of this general deflation of *tindalo mana*, much sacred ground was now thrown open for garden use, taboo anchorages were opened to the public, sacrifices were dropped, sacred objects were either destroyed, or given to the missionary, or traded as curios, and many pagan priests either retired or began enquiring about Christianity.

The *tindalo* which lost their power in this movement comprised ancient war-clubs, clam-shell rings up to nine inches in diameter, and armlets made from stalactites from a sacred cave. Hitherto all had been concealed within taboo houses. There was also prehistoric taboo money kept in sacred baskets, each new basket made receiving the remains of its predecessor so that no human hands need touch the sacred money. The remains of twenty-five baskets in one case suggested this particular *tindalo* had been served for two to three hundred years. Kalekona's own tutelary *tindalo* was a lemon-shaped stone with a rude human face. To this he had prayed regularly for a personal supply of *mana*. He alone knew its secret place, which had been revealed to him by his father.

This movement expanded into an almost complete conquest, with but a few limits. In some localities intimidation and fear remained to oppose the new religion. Any accident or misfortune to a Christian was declared to be the work of some offended *tindalo*, but such reactions were brief and soon gave way to Christian advance. The Gaeta movement required about three years for the intake of converts. Each convert was given about a year of instruction before baptism, and Penny recorded adult baptisms as about 200 in the first year, 200 more in the second, and 283 in the third. No infants were baptized until after their parents. This represented the winning of a total social unit, and was typical of the movement which continued spreading through Florida.

In his last year in the Solomons, Penny saw a similar "spiritual upheaval" at Honga. It began with the baptism of twenty adults with "the same tokens of power working in the hearts of the people in a remarkable manner". He described the changed character of the chief, Tambukoru, who was afterwards baptized with fifty-six others by the bishop. Actually this movement at Honga was a *planned* evangelistic thrust organized from Gaeta. The new Christian community had developed a concept of outreach from the start.

Case Study Two: *Ulawa*

Clement Marau was sent to Ulawa. It was not his own home and he had no kin-connections there. He had met Ulawa boys at Norfolk Island but had yet to learn their language. After three years of failure he asked the bishop to remove him. The bishop prayed with him and left him for another year. Marau worked on a young man of his own age, convinced him of the truth of Christianity and sent him to win his parents. The youth met with hot opposition, but Marau followed up his work. He started a little class for gospel narratives. Before long the mother of the youth came to the class and in time the father also. They were the first couple in Ulawa to "put on the cloth" as the symbol of changed hearts. As a family they met with much opposition, but they stood together as a family and endured. Their nearest neighbour was impressed by their witness and changed lives, and shortly he and his family joined the group. Marau himself had convinced another youthful neighbour, and together these comprised a Christian cell of eight persons on a basis of locality and two family units. They formed a compact unit, building each other up in prayer and faith in face of persecution.

The question now arose in their discussions: could the cell remain firm if Marau were taken away from them? Although they had formed a real bond of fellowship, yet Marau knew that there were still things in their houses that would undermine their strength in the face of danger. He felt the time had come to challenge them on the point. "If you are sincere, let me see a proof in you!" he demanded, and went on to speak of "things belonging to deceiving spirits—holy stones and money sacred to deceiving spirits, and things used in sacrifices". They accepted this challenge and handed over the sacred paraphernalia to Marau. Together they took them out to sea and formally threw them overboard. This was a regular Melanesian pattern for disposing of things supposedly charged with *mana*, salt-water being as effective as fire or burial. As sacred objects they no longer existed. The Christian cell had rejected its ancient traditions.

There was at Ulawa, near their locality, a sacred grove. A revengeful snake, supposed to dwell there, afflicted men with ulcers. The Christian group now decided on a bold stroke. Their iconoclasm up to this time had applied only to their personal and household fetishes. They now determined to involve the non-Christian community and made a public challenge. It was a wedding occasion when folk had gathered from far and wide. They declared they would burn the grove and destroy it to prove that they no longer had fear of the spirits, and to demonstrate the power of the True Spirit.

As good as their boast, the father of the first family cut the sacred vines and together they pulled down the fence. They took the holy stone from its place of honour and set it in the path to be trodden on by men. They took females of the group to the place which was forbidden to their sex. They did away with the skulls and bones venerated there for ages. They cooked and ate the sacred yams which were for the spirits alone, and transformed the sacred enclosure into a food garden. The astonished pagans adopted a "wait and see" attitude, predicting calamity. The spirits were powerless and the pagans now declared that the missionary ship had driven away the *mana* of the place.[6] In time, some were angry and wanted to kill the Christians, but the latter were not intimidated. They felt that things in Ulawa would never be happy until all the people came to the truth and took the same stand. After a long description of these events Clement Marau added:

> This was the beginning made in their new religion . . . when I sought a proof whether they would let it slip or not. . . . Now there are already sixty-two of us. When anyone wishes to enter the school he asks that he may be thought of in prayer; and on the day that he comes in as a hearer he declares that he entirely gives up all that he has to do with ghosts of the dead or the spirits that he has worshipped. . . . He begs me to teach him a little prayer, that he may pray to God to protect him from the anger of those spirits . . . he prays and he has no more fears.

For a time the movement in Ulawa had a family structure, passing in small units from family to family. Eventually it became a full-scale people–movement on a community level. In the centre of the island was a large public building where dwelt the ghost of greatest power and where arms and war regalia were deposited. Groups from all round Ulawa sacrificed here where a regular priesthood was established. Marau won the priest in charge for Christ.

It was now incumbent on the priestly convert to demonstrate the sincerity of his decision. He issued a public statement that he was about to be baptized as a Christian, that all his life he had been concerned with holy things, but that he was now turning from the ancient forms of holiness to Him who was the Holy One, who gave him power to overcome the spirits which had hitherto impoverished him. Having made this announcement in terms appropriate to their thinking, he set to work destroying the sacred place of his old faith. As a result of this demonstration a new public attitude emerged, for this priest, Marita, now knew the True Spirit. Was he not there, with his son and heir, smashing the skulls and bones they had all feared for generations?

They knew he had the truth. Perhaps Cardinal Newman would have spoken of this as one of those *convergences* of history.

Clement Marau gave himself for Ulawa, ministering there until his death. He married a girl of the island, built a church of coral blocks, and gave his son to enter the Christian priesthood.

Discussion

Christian missions have been criticized for their iconoclasm, especially by the salvage anthropologists. The criticisms have been mainly against two points: the loss of material of cultural and archaeological value, and the imposition of one religion on the people of another by force rather than reason. Neither criticism is quite fair, because missions and missionaries have very seldom done this. Of the hundreds of cases I have investigated, I know only two (possibly three) in which a missionary was foolish enough to initiate any iconoclasm, though objects were frequently handed over to missionaries for disposal. There is logic in this. Iconoclasm was the indigenous symbol of the rejection of a *mana* repository. Throughout Polynesia and Melanesia this is the indigenous conceptualization of power encounter. I remember once seeing a fine Melanesian spear dance which ended with every dancer shouting and smashing his spear across his knee. This was a great loss of cultural material and a waste of fine craftsmanship; but the termination of the dance was a symbolic act representing the end of war and the beginning of a new day of change. It was thoroughly meaningful and appreciated by the large audience. So the iconoclasm must be seen for what it is—a cultural mechanism within a social pattern, the proof of sincerity in a time of major decision-making. Again, it was always a voluntary act undertaken by the approved authority within the structure, or a challenge of proof by contest within a specific frame of reference. When done by a large group it was preceded by much discussion and agreement—i.e. by multi-individual decision— the approved authority of the group thereafter taking the initiative with the support of the group.

To pass from these generalizations to specific points in the two cases outlined, one of the first things which strikes me is *the place of the social structure in power encounter.* The patterns of this type of movement are not uniform everywhere but the differences can often be accounted for by social structure. In the case of Sapibuana, the man was set down within his own kin-unit, but in the face of communal opposition. He wisely set out to win first the nuclear family to which he belonged, and then the extended family followed by those related by marriage. It was out of this that the Church grew. He started with the smallest cohesive group, expanding until their very solidarity began to win folk from the wider community.

In the case of Marau, who had no kin-connections and had inadequate language for proper communication, the evangelist was faced with a more serious barrier. But Marau was a shrewd observer and had the courage to discard any method which did not work. As he said afterwards, he made the mistake of speaking to the pagan community at large. Considerable crowds gave him a hearing but there was no response. Fortunately he recorded his reason for changing his tactics. He had observed that the cohesive units of pre-Christian religious life in Ulawa were the independent families:

> these Ulawa people, *every family*, having its own spirit, every man sacrificing without fail, and sacrificing without exception about everything . . . in every place there is a place or object of sacrifice, *according to the family*. . . . *In every family* a pig is set apart for the spirit and kept so. . . .

It is a long passage and Marau went on to ponder the phases of family life to which these sacrifices applied.

With this in mind Marau strove to win his friends—the appeal of youth to youth—and through him, his family. Each family was urged to seek to win its neighbour. This was possible because the families were independent decision-making units. Marau had, by his own testimony, found his prototype for family action in the Old Testament Hebrews, and he himself conceptualized his task as leading them from their family sacrifices to the One True Sacrifice. He was impressed by the place of sacrificing and praying in their lives, and felt that if only they could come to know the Scriptures they would attain to a superior knowledge in these things.

By the time a number of families had become Christian, Marau considered the wider community with the same astuteness. He identified the key figure of communal affairs in the chief priest of the central shrine, and directed his attention to this person. This man, more than any other, could have been his enemy and obstructor. Marau, having won him for Christ, demanded evidence of his sincerity, and the resultant demonstration, devised by the priest himself, became itself the stimulus of a community movement. Marau might have won scores of lesser persons, priests among them; but nothing was as effective as winning the competent authority for affairs at the central grove. It was an important victory. The public statement made by Marita shows how deeply Marau's teaching had gone and how clearly Marita himself had thought out the consequences of his symbolic actions.

Another form of public encounter set out above is *encounter by challenge*. This was often used by island evangelists who found it difficult to break through social obstructions. Its biblical prototype was the contest between Elijah and Baal on Mount Carmel; and as with all societies which employ mechanisms of contest for proof or ordeal, it is assumed that the result is not merely the personal strengths of the contestants but the power of the God or spirit on whom the contestants call. "The God who answers by fire, let him be God!" (1 Kings 18:24).

When a chief came with a group of people and announced that they had destroyed their paraphernalia and were ready for instruction, as Kalekona did, it may be quite certain that a long period of discussion had preceded this act. Some missionaries avoid this kind of behaviour, wrongly considering it mass action without individual conviction. Invariably it is the result of long debate and often complete unanimity

is required before any group action. When Dr. Welchman ascended
1,800 feet to Juleka to start a Christian cause there and gave a brief
exposition of the faith to those who gathered to meet him, he asked for
assurance that they were definite about wanting to be Christian. Two
or three said together, "If we had not made up our minds, should we
have been here today?" It had been well discussed. Frequently the
multi-individual decision included not only the decision to become
Christian but also the specific ocular demonstration to be employed as
a power encounter to prove the validity of the new faith.

One question which arises from this is whether or not such a demonstration is adequate proof of faith to permit baptism or whether
further instruction should be demanded. The question is whether a
man should be *baptized on the basis of an act of faith* or *an understanding
of the faith*. Baulee, an old high-priest and a powerful magic-man of the
Belaga district, forced this issue. He wanted baptism there and then
without any delay of a year. He pointed out that he had let go his hold
on all those resources of power on which he had relied all his life, and he
wanted the full resources of the new life. His old sacrificial role had been
completely discarded, and he now wanted to partake of the means of
grace of Christian fellowship. Confronted with a definite conviction and
demand, missionary Penny felt constrained to grant his wish and
baptized him immediately on this expression of faith.[7] But not all the
missionaries would have agreed with him. On what basis is a man
baptized when he comes out of paganism—an act of faith or on knowledge of the faith?[8] In the eyes of the Melanesian the symbolic act is
conclusive.

There is another reason for pressing for some ocular demonstration
of effective encounter. A second generation Christian who knows his
New Testament might put it thus: You cannot escape from Satan; he
will never leave you alone; you can only deal with him by facing him
and defeating him. Penny felt that few, if any, Melanesians came to
understand that those spirit forces in which they had once believed
never really existed at all. They were powers which had been defeated
in Christ, and would still hold people who were not Christ's. That this
dynamic experience should be conceptualized in terms of personalized
or spiritualized encounter, is perhaps a better way of formulating these
vital and determinative experiences, than our modern, sophisticated,
disbelieving explanations in terms of chemicals, mathematics and
gastric juices—which, be it well noted, in the final analysis have to be
described in symbols themselves. In simplest terms we are confronted
with changed lives—in mental set, in behaviour patterns and in spiritual satisfactions. It is a change from fear to triumph. If the Melanesian
chooses to demonstrate this by dismembering or burning his *tindalo*
or *tigono-na*, or burying the skull of his ancestor, we ought to accept this
at its face value—an act of faith and a symbol of victory. Whether we
ourselves believe those ghostly forces were real or not, for this convert
from animism they were real. He has met the ghost face to face and defeated him. He has struggled with Satan and won. If he does not have this
victory, then Satan is bound to return. First generation Christians who

lapsed back into paganism were very few, but in those cases where evidence is available they usually seem to be people, who, for some reason or other, failed to demonstrate their faith by an act of power encounter. I have never found a case of pagan resurgence—individual, family or community—without an accompanying recovery of the spirit shrine, or a rebuilding of the altar, or a restoration of the sacred grove. If the shrine had actually been destroyed, a new symbol or fetish would have to be created. We need not wonder at this—it was the regular pattern in pre-captivity times in the Old Testament. (In a third or fourth generation, more remote from the animistic original state, there can be a lapse into materialism under the influence of acculturation, but we are not discussing that here.)

With people who have just come out of animism there is a *continuity of temptation when paraphernalia are not destroyed*. This is demonstrated by the case of a shaman, Siama, of Barasaka, who had given up his practice and for some time had been attending Christian prayers. He had, however, made no public demonstration of his apparently quite genuine change of heart. In the end he went to Dr. Welchman for baptism and took his paraphernalia with him—a bag of leaf prepared in scented oil (*manuni*) and a tin box with some scented beans. He confessed that though he had been attending prayers and this was well known, and he had not performed his rituals for some time, yet people continued plaguing him to perform them on behalf of their sick. Because he only did good in trying to help the sick. and because he made no sacrifices to ghosts, he had apparently avoided any demonstration of encounter. But not until he made his confession and handed over his equipment to the missionary and accepted baptism did the community accept his devotions as sincere and stop plaguing him for his shamanistic services.[9]

If the act of destruction is not a public challenge or ordeal, it is expected that it *be performed by the approved authority*—the individual himself for a personal charm, the head of the family for some family relic, and a priest if the sacred object has wider significance. It must be the priest of that particular shrine. This is another reason why the mission should not be the perpetrator of the act. An indigenous preacher can also run into trouble at this point unless his act is accepted by the public as a challenge or ordeal. Abraham Faidangi allowed his Christian enthusiasm to run away with him in San Cristoval. He collected the carved sharks of Lomahui, which were skull repositories, and threw them away as if they were nothing. Abraham found that heathen authority still counted for something and he was compelled to replace them in the devil-house. In time, however, his work was effective and the same elders determined to become Christian, whereupon they themselves discarded the skulls and sacred paraphernalia.[10]

The right of disposal could be transferred by a timid authority provided he himself took the responsibility of giving it away. This was interpreted as regarding it now as a mere thing of no value, despised like the houshold gods of Laban that could be hidden by a woman sitting upon them (Gen. 31: 34). In the museum at Munda is a piece of prehistoric clam-shell filigree work (*barava*) carved from material extracted from an uplifted reef by some obsolete technique. The little figures of dancing men and rings are supposedly the work of the gods. This sacred object brought death to a Lauru bushman, and the people, terrified by its *mana*, wanted to dispose of it. By community decision two Christians, Simon Peter and Mulakana, were allowed to take it away and present it to the missionary. The approval was legitimate, the Christians took the risk, and the actual disposal was left to the missionary. This was frequent in the Western Solomons, effective but not nearly as realistic. Goldie wrote in 1917:

> Our mission house verandah is lumbered up with gods – gods of all shapes and sizes – the one-time objects of veneration and worship of our people, who offered sacrifices and prayers to them continually.[11]

With the South Sea Evangelicals also the onus for destruction and disposal was often left to the missionary. In *Dr. Deck's Letter* in 1914 is given an account of the opening of the church at Tanaha. The people asked him to remove their *adaros*. Deck and his party dismantled the charms and sacred objects, took them away and cast them into the sea. If the people were not even prepared to dismantle the sacred objects themselves and bring them to the missionary, their Christian commitment was not very deep.

In the case of the filigree removed by the two Christians, the people of the village concerned were still heathen, and were afraid of the sacred object because it had killed a man. The two Christians gained very much respect for their bravery, and as a result gained a hearing. We are not surprised then that before long they were able to bring the whole group into Christianity. This Christian fearlessness of sacred objects and taboos was part of the power encounter complex. Sometimes a taboo, such as a prohibition against climbing a sacred mountain, would be discussed in a village. Such conversations were frequently a source of inspiration to dynamic Christians open for challenge. Solomon Damusoe was one such who accepted a challenge at Zonga to climb Mount Sambe, which rises from the lagoon by dangerous precipices. The climb was quite a physical test in any case and local tradition declared that anyone attempting it should surely die. Damusoe and a small party of Christians accomplished the feat without fear or ill-effects. The achievement gave Damusoe a hearing and shortly afterwards as a result of his advocacy the Zonga people accepted Christianity.[12]

All the cases cited in this unit on power encounter are fairly typical. Many others could be narrated but they would be redundant. The unit shows *the importance of specific decision in coming to Christ and the public demonstration of that decision* within the thought-forms and behavioural-forms of the cultural structure. The power encounter for the new convert is both a symbolic act and a step of faith. It represents what Emil Brunner described as a step of faith into the unknown.

However, this is not the end of the road, but rather the beginning. A growth in faith and knowledge and grace has to follow. The power

encounter experience has to be consummated. Evangelism always requires effective follow-up. Conversion growth requires consolidation in quality growth. McGavran speaks of these two processes as *discipling* and *perfecting*—the former the rejection of the pagan gods and spirits and the enthronement of Christ, making disciples, and the latter "teaching them to observe all things I have commanded".[13]
I realize that some readers may not accept the intellectual orientation of this unit on power-encounter, but I must insist on two things: (1) unless they are aware of it, they cannot *think Melanesian* and (2) unless they can put themselves in this position, at least conceptually, any acceptance of the gospel they achieve will have a different meaning to the acceptors from what they intend.

OPINION GROUPS AND PRESSURE

To pass from the purely Melanesian atmosphere of animist communal society to the feelings and pressures of a town like Honiara requires some reorientation. This is not because the Melanesian way of thinking is absent. On the contrary it is well represented; but in Honiara the Melanesian counts for little, he has no prestige and no wealth, and not nearly as many rights as he should have. Honiara is a foreign town with opinion groups and pressures of its own. Encounter here is in a quite different frame of reference from that of communal society. In this unit I purpose examining four things—first, the opinion groups involved in the encounter, with a simple classification; second, the rather delicate question of indigenous feelings; and then the liquor question as an example of encounter as it works out in this setting; and finally and very briefly, the question of free speech.

1. *Opinion Groups*

We are interested in opinion groups, not a mere catalogue of opinions. I am not concerned with the fact that an important citizen, Mr. A, says that $x = y$, and that Mr. B says the opposite. We are dealing with a social situation and are concerned only with the fact that a body of persons exists who believe that $x = y$. I recognize that in reality x may or may not equal y. What is important to us in evaluating the Honiara situation is really that there is a corpus of public opinion that believes this.
I thought I detected five clear opinion groups in Honiara, for which I suggest the following typology, based on an analysis of opinions expressed, behaviour observed and things noted during my short time in the town with an admittedly limited number of interviews. I did not structure this typology as a hypothesis for testing; it seemed to me to reveal itself as the natural classification of my collected data.

A. *The Official Corpus*

There are two sub-groups in this category:
(a) The Government official majority, all of whom are expected to support official views and policies, and to vote officially. I can see here no freedom of political opinion.

E

(b) Subordinate to these, we have the employees of Government, whose jobs and means of revenue depend on loyalty to official policy. One would expect that they too probably are not free.

This is common to colonial structures and even in the most progressive colonies has been a hindrance to the free expression of opinion, public debate and general progress.

B. *The Christian Corpus*

Here again there are three sub-groups:

(a) Mission administrators and missionaries, who have spiritual convictions and have voluntarily subjected themselves to church policy where they believe moral and spiritual issues are at stake. In other matters they are free and represent a wide range of opinion. When policy has to be fixed they usually do so by discussion.

(b) Indigenous Christians, who often have their own committees and bodies for discussion. Their convictions are fairly similar to those of the missionaries, possibly because of training, and they have similar freedom of opinion except where the Church legislates on a matter. Those who do not wish to bind themselves to full support and loyalty may still be loosely attached to this corpus of opinion. One church provides a level at which folk may be classified as adherents rather than members, but this level is unstable and tends to fluctuate in opinion, though it does allow for freedom.

(c) Christian laymen, both European and other non-Solomon Islanders, who have moral and spiritual convictions and take a voluntary stand with the Church. This is a small group but includes some important persons and some in Government service.

There was a tendency of one portion of the European community to say that the Christian corpus (a) exerted some compulsion on sub-group (b). This was said in the case of the recent liquor bill, the group (b) having petitioned against the bill. The idea that there was pressure from (a) on (b) was in my opinion quite untrue. I was there at the time and made enquiries on this point, but the fact remains that this thrust was used by certain persons at the psychological moment to discredit the petition. What has to be remembered about the Christian corpus is that it is voluntary. Any man is free to be involved or silent, to be inside or to withdraw. There is much more freedom here than on the official level, but the cohesion is strong because of the moral and spiritual convictions.

C. *The Materialistic Corpus*

This also includes three sub-groups:

(a) Europeans, without any Christian convictions, who by their lives and choices, voluntarily set private standards that operate against Christian action[14].

(b) Interracial and island groups in the town for economic reasons, who are not interested in religion or its ethical outworkings. Mainly they are concerned with getting regular income and finding regular means of spending.

(c) Young men serving as labour, who have not affiliated with any town church group, and are largely absent from home, either to avoid communal duties, to escape prosecution or with a desire to 'walkabout'.

This corpus does not tie itself down to principles, is more free than any other, the most outspoken in its own interests—claiming all the freedom possible within the law. Some will ignore the law if possible to do so without being caught. When the law is involved in public discussion, this group tends to support the relaxing of legal controls. In this respect it is the most predictable of all groups.

D. *The District Representative Corpus*

These are the district representatives who come to Honiara for official occasions, such as the meeting of the Legislative Council, and are supposedly representing their respective districts. They are, however, an uncertain group, and represent their districts in a remarkable way. One has a strong impression that they operate rather as private individuals than as district representatives, and perhaps under pressure at times. The district councils are a most important set of opinions outside the town—perhaps the most important in all the Protectorate. Their declared opinions on the liquor bill were certainly not reflected in the voting of their representatives.

The above is not the only possible schematization of opinion groups, neither are they exclusively watertight. They represent the situation as I saw it, and though based on objective observations, they should be regarded only as the opinion of the researcher.

Viewing the matter from another angle one could well speak of an *Indigenous Corpus*. This would comprise some from each A(b), B(b), C(b), C(c) and D. There is in Honiara a strong representative body of indigenous opinion of this composition, based on tradition, with a strong conviction that the Solomon Islander is the underdog in his own islands. This view includes persons of all denominational groups, and also materialists and pagans as well as Christians. This view is not without some justification; so much so that we will now pay some attention to it.

2. *Indigenous Feelings*

I had a strong impression of a deep and widespread unrest in the feelings and opinions of the indigenous corpus. Beside this may be set the opinion of a good many responsible Europeans who feel concerned at the Melanesian's lack of legal advice at many points where the members of other races have an advantage of wider experience and a readiness to exploit their greater knowledge of legal devices. A Melanesian killed a European and was treated as a murderer. A European killed a Melanesian, whether intentionally or not is not the point: his case was taken out of the country and he was declared insane. When the leaders of Marching Rule were fighting for political rights, they sought permission to bring a defending counsel from Sydney, but their request was not allowed.[15]

A case of falsification of copra weights put two Melanesians in prison. The Chinese dealers involved were tried in Fiji and the case deferred. It is now said that they have been acquitted. These are circulating reports. I am not concerned whether they are true or not and have not sought to verify them. My concern is that a very large body of opinion believes them to be true, and there is a deep discontent about it. The general feeling is that the smart foreigner, who has either the money or the 'know-how', can escape justice and leave the Melanesian to pay. Ultimately, this widespread impression must lead to serious trouble, unless the Melanesian can be convinced by ocular demonstration that he has equal rights in mode of trial and availability of legal services.

This is not the only way in which indigenous feelings express themselves against western legal patterns. Many offences, as conceptualized by social tradition, called for a death penalty. Many of these traditional penalties have been eliminated by western law and order, making the country safer for foreign settlers. However, traditional verdicts and justice differ from their western counterparts, and western justice may not satisfy traditional verdicts. As a result many Melanesians resort to secret adjustments, especially forms of sorcery, which, though generally deplored by society, are nevertheless accepted as a necessary corrective to western injustices. Melanesian concentrations in town and on plantations greatly facilitate the exchange of sorcery patterns from all parts of the Group. Frequently it is easier to obtain justice through the use of sorcery than by the mysterious and expensive mechanisms of civilized law. Both in town and country sorcery is currently on the increase. Even when tried by an indigenous president of a native court, cases against sorcery are ineffective, because the evidential procedure is western. One such official told me that sorcery cases were being brought less and less to court. He now had only about one case a session. He admitted the problem was a matter of evidence. Sorcerers work in secret, so that though people may know the process is being practised they cannot testify that they have seen it being done. In the second place, even those who could testify are frequently afraid of the powers of the sorcerer or unready to make an enemy of him, because the law gives them no real protection against him. In the locality from which my informant came, the sorcerer must go to the grave of his victim and pierce the dead body with a spear, lest the evil of the sorcery rebound on him. When I asked this magistrate what evidence he would demand in a case of sorcery, he said he would ask who had seen the accused thrust in the spear. Then he added that as this would be done perhaps at 2 a.m., obviously no one would see him unless he had lain in wait for the purpose, though everyone would see the spear in the grave the next day. In other words, another case of sorcery was proved but not the identity of the sorcerer.

When the Melanesian discovers that western legal patterns fail to give satisfactory verdicts or justice he returns to his own patterns of justice. Divination is used to discover the sorcerer and counter-sorcery is applied against him. Or a new form of counter-sorcery is created on which the name of the victim is unstated. The justice of the ghost or spirit through whom the sorcery is worked is expected to deal with the original offender.

These indigenous feelings then represent two strong tendencies: first, the belief that they receive little justice from western law and procedure, which rather serves the foreigner and the man with money; and second, a tendency to retire to their own patterns of justice. This is not a healthy situation and could well lead to trouble in the future.

3. *The Liquor Question, Opinion and Pressure*

During my time in the Solomons public interest fell on the liquor question, in which the Church fought a losing battle. There are two aspects of this problem. In both, the initiative comes from the towns though much of the effect is felt in the villages, especially the villages which supply the migrating community.

The more vicious aspect of the trade may be summed up in this illustration, which came to me from a reputable European informant, not a missionary, and one whose personal attitude to drink I do not know. A Chinese merchant trades in the outer islands of the Group. He supplied methylated spirits by the four-gallon tin to folk of one small island with a population of about 400 people. When the official representative of the Church, at a very great shipping cost, visited this island on one occasion he found the entire population completely drunk and was unable even to hold a worship service. This is one aspect. In areas where the Church has responsible Melanesians in charge of local situations, things are more under control, but always there has to be continual vigilance. In one Anglican area where I worked, the Melanesian priest, who had a strong sense of responsibility, kept things under control especially for the sake of the women and children; but even here, as one of his parishioners told me, "the men who go away as labour are hard to handle when they come home".

The second aspect is more 'respectable' and subtle. It concerns the free right of Melanesians to drink and has been pressed under the cry of racial equality: that every man, regardless of race, should determine for himself what he may and may not do. It was at this level that the recent liquor bill was presented.

The general rural attitude as expressed in the district councils was against the bill, yet their representatives voted for it. A number of statements I heard made in Honiara suggested, at least to me, that pressures were at work on the representatives with the second reading of the bill. One Melanesian, of his own volition, told me he was very disturbed about the accessibility of gin and spirits to Solomon Islanders, though I had not asked a question about it. Shortly afterwards he voted for the bill. As an objective observer I was concerned, not so much with the liquor issue itself, as with local opinions about it. Of one thing I am strongly convinced—that the Melanesians were not impressed with any argument about racial equality.

In an interesting interview with a Solomon Island president of a native court, who openly stated his liking for his glass, and his agreement with the policy of opening liquor supplies to all people on a principle of equality, I was surprised to hear him add to this testimony that, of course, the argument counted for nothing! In the final analysis drinking liquor is not a matter of race but of class. He put it like this:

> The High Commissioner said 'Why shouldn't we all be one people? You drink beer. We drink spirits. Let us all be the same.' How can we all be the same in our present relationships? Spirits are £1 5s. a bottle. I can only drink when it is given to me.

This Melanesian was aware of the inconsistencies of any argument based on race, presented by foreigners who were not prepared to equalize class and economic opportunities. My feeling was that he might well be the mouthpiece of a fairly large body of opinion. On the whole, over the last seventy years neither the Administration nor commerce has done very much for the Solomon Islands. This is painfully apparent to the Solomon Islander himself, when he sees what other Melanesians, the Fijians for example, can do and earn in his (the Solomon Islander's) own land.

The liquor issue was relevant to me as an indicator of opinions and pressures within society. Some of these 'still streams' run deep. My feeling was that the districts must have adequate representation, not individuals subject to town pressures. There are good reasons for this. On the whole the islander thinks of himself as more of Roviana, or Lauru or Mala, than as a Solomon Islander. In each island group there is a tendency to think in terms of its own entity and interests, as for example, a reluctance in Mala to have its tax revenue spent outside the island itself. Right or wrong, the body of local opinion, especially after it has been formulated in council discussion, should be communicated to the other groups if there is ever to be a Protectorate entity. Furthermore if the local people become convinced that their local councils are dead ends, especially if the obstructing force is a foreign economic one in the town, this will lead to another build-up of tension that could have serious results. It is not so much the particular issue that is being debated—taxation, liquor, land registration or anything else—but the feeling of frustration, of being the underdog, of having no access to the 'know-how', or the wealth to pay for it. Local opinion-groups can be forced to withdraw within themselves. The local segmentation of the Protectorate is vulnerable at this point and the general situation is more dangerous than is often imagined.

One should not completely by-pass the moral issue of the liquor question. In the villages where I lived, reasonable control was exercised and the people in general were temperate, though some of the community held permits. In Anglican areas, control depended on the wisdom and personality of the priest, which, in my limited range for observation, was adequate. The Methodists consider drinking to be not reconcilable to their *call to holiness*. The Anglicans seek to protect women and children and to preserve concord. The Methodists refuse any church office to drinkers or permit-holders, and urge all members to refrain from drinking, though they are not excluded from membership on this account.[16] On the whole the villages seem to be quiet, except when labourers return from town and plantation.

From what I saw, the more objectionable intoxication was a town phenomenon. Drinking and gambling often go together. We may fairly bracket them. I slept one night at the wharf in Gizo beside a Chinese store and had ample evidence of this unholy combination. Most village disturbances can be traced to town contacts—returning labourers, especially at festival and holiday seasons; an occasional farmer who has disposed of his produce in the town and returns intoxicated; and the occasional visit of a trading launch. The moral issue is always one which needs watching, but I thought the Church was alert at the point.

4. *Free Speech*

An interesting opinion group exists with strong feelings on free speech. I do not think this group has any moral or sociological structure, except that it comprises thinking people. It includes both Christian and materialist. They share a deep concern because there is no mechanism in the Protectorate for the expression of opinion on public matters, no medium through which ideas may be put forward and discussed. This is especially so when ideas are in opposition to Government policy. One most responsible person, who is himself rendering a significant service to the Solomon Islands today, put it:

> We have no free press. If a paper criticizes the Government over any policy or decision, that paper is accused of being anti-government.

I met with this opinion among responsible Europeans both in and out of Honiara.

Certainly the Group needs a local newspaper, and a radical one would not be a bad thing. It is psychologically bad for an emerging country to be denied the institutions and devices for expressing their feelings and 'tossing about' ideas, which might very well be germinal and to the benefit of the country. After all, many of these thinking people are permanent figures in the scene, whereas administrative officials are here today and gone tomorrow. Furthermore, many of these observant and thinking Europeans could often present a position for the Melanesian interest, if a free press were available.

The Churches ought to support a free press and be ready to partake in controversy through its columns, presenting the Christian point of view on public issues. The Churches owe this to the Melanesians in the face of the materialism of the rank and file of the resident Europeans.

One government official estimated the white population as 5 per cent Christian.

Thus there exists a strong opinion group of differently motivated people, who feel the country needs an instrument for expressing public opinion if the place is to progress.

CHAPTER 8

Problems of Institutions and Education

THE QUESTION of education in the Solomon Islands needs examination by a small team of experts, with education *per se* represented, but not dominating. Education bristles with problems, many of which threaten to become permanently built into the Solomon Island situation. I am not an educationalist and am not proposing educational reforms. Nor is this book anything but a study of church growth and obstructions to growth. Yet problems of education and problems created by education of course impinge on my subject at many points. Sooner or later Government and Mission will have to face these problems squarely, if these islands are ever to be raised from their present underdeveloped state.

One difficulty arises from the fact that the supposed political entity known as the Solomon Islands is not a real entity to either of the Missions we are studying. One domain extends into Australian Trust Territory and the other into the New Hebrides. Each Mission deals with two different Administrations, and the three of them represent three different types of administration. Policies may proceed at different rates and in different directions.

The problems go deeper still. There is the problem of the Church's role in education. There is the matter of this huge build-up of educational and other institutions, which an emerging indigenous Church can never hope to take over from the Mission. There are the problems of the character of education within the Church. We may well ask— education for what? In this chapter we examine these problems, more particularly as they relate to the purpose of mission.

THE CHURCH'S ROLE IN EDUCATION

Some definite and critical attention needs to be paid to the basic theory of this problem. For years the Government left the entire burden of education to Christian Missions. In spite of the fact that this has been beyond the financial capacity of the Missions, the Government allows this state of affairs to continue.[1] This effort has absorbed huge resources in personnel, equipment, labour and funds given to the Missions by overseas supporters for the spread of the Church. From the point of view of investments the spiritual dividends have been small. As a substitute for Government social services, the Church has been unable to render much more than a token service, village schools are not of a high level and central institutions are inadequate for the Protectorate if it is to develop as it should. Both private industry and Government have introduced an intermediate class of persons from other parts of Oceania—engineers, clerks, medical workers—to carry loads for which Solomon Islanders should have been trained long ago. No one disputes that within their resources the Missions have rendered a fine service to education; but there is considerable doubt whether Missions should carry the role of secular education in a Protectorate. The Missions appear to have accepted this role.

It may be that education should be regarded as a just burden of the Church in its service to the community, in which case it is part of the outworking of the gospel, the fruit of the tree, as it were. What value education has rendered to the growth of the Church has been on the level of post-conversion quality growth—the training of leaders, some of whom have become effective evangelists; but except for persons isolated from their social contexts and converted in a more or less western pattern, educational institutions have not been effective evangelistic agencies making impact on paganism within its own social structure. Relatively few of the thousands who came over to Christianity were actually won for Christ by education. The value of education has been basically post-conversion. Even this has not been as productive as was hoped. Only recently a high official of the Church expressed his disappointment that the schools were not supplying men for the Catechist Schools, neither were educated men offering for the Brotherhood.[2] Furthermore, the educational work, which has taught people to read, has often been rendered ineffective by a failure to supply literature for reading.

The hope was expressed by some educationalists, who had worked with considerable patience and devotion over the years, "confident that a sufficient education would give ultimate victory, and that other things would follow slowly over a period of time because the child was father of the man". This was a common view:

> We simply worked on the principle that girls trained at our mission schools would certainly raise the standard of village life and in their own islands by passing on whatever information they had accumulated. It was an admirable system which paid good dividends.

I must confess that nothing disappointed me more than the state of the Christian villages in an area served by the very school referred to in that quotation. I saw no evidence whatsoever of sanitation, domestic hygiene or general good living conditions. One cannot expect a school, even now at its greatest strength perhaps 130 strong, to make a major impact on a community of some 50,000 persons. Any outstanding girls would probably go into nursing or teaching and be located at educational institutions. Few would return to the villages.

We are up against Melanesian thinking and logic if we dig deeply into this. My wife reminded me of this Melanesian conception when we were discussing this problem in a village. The Melanesian villager explains his position like this:

> When we live on the mission station we live by the white man's customs, because this is his way of belief, he is our teacher, and the station is his area of control, and he insists on our doing things his way. But when we

return to the village, we live by our own way of life, as our fathers did before us.

In my own missionary experience I met this philosophy. The missionary teaches the young men to contour the hillside when planting, but is subsequently disgusted to see his graduates on return to the village digging the old type of drains that carry the top-soil directly down into the already-soured valleys. The offender will say:

My fathers did it this way and they were good gardeners. The white man may grow things better in his own land but our own ways are best here.

This psychological attitude strikes many social workers when they move out from their institutional centres into the villages. I met a European agricultural officer who was quite depressed over this very point, and I was amused to meet Fijians at Gizo who had become equally discouraged because the Solomon Islanders would not take their advice on the best methods of cultivating sweet potatoes.[3]

Perhaps we may raise the question of whether or not the centralized sedentary type of organization can ever really bring about village reforms. I am not suggesting the disposal of all such institutions, which seem to me to be essential for leadership training and organic growth, but we certainly have a great deal yet to learn about how knowledge may be transmitted from central institutions to local situations. If the policies of institutional missions have failed it is at this point—they are out of touch, foreign, isolated. Their ideals may be excellent, but they fail to transmit them to the village situation. Their graduates tend either to drift back into the village ways and forget what they have learned, or (if what they learned became meaningful to them) to become little replicas of the dogmatic white man, and say their piece but fail to transmit.

In medical work the Missions also have been carrying the Government load. Some mission hospitals send out nurses on village rounds, others do not. Those who do, make the greater impact on village life. They are getting people accustomed to inspections, injections and health procedure, and in time a good roll-call responds to visits *if they are regularly carried out*. The justification of this policy is to me that it transmits something to the village level. One wonders whether this should be a Government or Mission role. If the Church was committed to a healing ministry by our Lord, then these visits should be accompanied by prayers, as He showed Himself in the days of His flesh. Some missionary itinerants commence and conclude their medical routine with brief prayers. Others insist the visit is purely medical. The people, however, are religiously disposed. The healing of the sick, to pagan or Christian, was always a matter for prayer as well as medicine, and prayers, when offered, are always appreciated. Regular itineration of a missionary medical worker, provided he insists that he is a servant of the Church, by adding prayer to his medical skill, is bound to contribute something to quality growth on the local level, though we cannot measure it. This will certainly count for far more than by isolating

all the workers at a central hospital, without any direct contact with
the villages of the surrounding area.

Supporters of Christian missions and missionaries on the field often
fail to distinguish between education and an educational institution.
The educational report of a mission district is often merely a report of
mission institutions located at sedentary stations. In reality (except
for the training of leaders for specific roles) the vital education is what
goes on in the village situations all over the Group. One combs over
reams of paper in the archives to discover what is really going on at
'grass roots' level. Is the Church growing (either in size or in quality)
at the village level? Is the educational process being felt in the village
church? The official reports are reports of station activities and institutions, and even when supposedly applied to a circuit or parish or
district, they are at best perspectives from the stations. It is because
of this 'remote view' of the archival records that depth studies of the
type of Part VI of this book are a necessary corrective to the official
picture of the emerging Church. Education is often equated with
educational institutions.

There are also educational institutions in the villages. It would be
dangerous for me to generalize at this point. In one village I lived
beside the school run by the pastor-teacher paid by the Mission. This
school was well supported by the village elders, and although the
teacher was hopelessly overloaded, by any standards, his teaching was
good and all the eligible children of the village went to school. Sessions
opened daily with devotions and new religious music was taught to
supplement secular studies. I wish I could think this was typical.

In another place there was no public interest in education. People
begrudged a five-shilling fee for a child's schooling and only 20 per cent
of the eligible children attended school at all. The school had an
efficient and adequate staff supplied by the Mission concerned, but
they were not appreciated. Education for girls was not generally felt
to be necessary, even by the more enlightened families. Nearby at
another location, a fine school property, well laid out with extensive
buildings, had been abandoned and had fallen into disrepair. When
I visited the place two highly competent teachers were struggling to
rehabilitate it. One of them was depressed by the manner in which the
people would start such a project and then drop it, leaving it without
support. He saw the village level as uncertain and unstable. Yet it is
at this level that any real growth in knowledge or devotional life must
be established. This particular area settled down twenty years ago
to a state of Christian-pagan passive co-existence. When the Church
lost the evangel, its education began to stagnate.

Confronted by these quite different situations the reader will agree
it is unsafe to generalize. The variability of local situations is a feature
of the Solomons. However if there is to be organic growth of an indigenous Church, there will need to be conversion growth from paganism in one place, the revival of nominals in another, and quality
growth everywhere. The Missions depend on education for at least
part of this. The question might well be asked: What is this mission-

controlled education actually accomplishing? What secular and religious achievements has it to show?

The Government relies for the time being upon the present pattern of Mission involvement in education. Is it entitled to assume this should continue? When the Missions give way to the local church, whose responsibility will the village education be? These are formative days when the emergence of the indigenous Church should be pushed and the Missions as such should be withdrawing. The question of what is the Mission role in education should be a short-term one. It now becomes—what is the role of the local church in education? In the light of this shift, the issue which has to be carefully and prayerfully resolved is whether or not the local church ought to be saddled with secular education as the Missions have been. Quite apart from what the Government may think of this, there is here a serious problem of missionary strategy. And let us understand clearly, that whatever reasons may be advanced for the Church's role in secular education, and however good it may be, there is no scriptural mandate for it.

One often sees missionary promotional material in terms such as, Our Commission: to preach, to teach and to heal. That is not exactly what the commission says at all. The commission to teach is not an open order, it is to teach "those things" which the Lord Himself revealed to the twelve. This is a spiritual education, just as the preaching and healing have their spiritual dimensions—and we might add a systematic programme of exorcizing demons. It may well be that there are good reasons for the Church being involved in secular education, but any such policy must stand on its own merits. It has no scriptural mandate. It may be a necessary form of Christian application, but if so let it be declared so. This brings us back to the question of the responsibility of the emerging Church—is it to be saddled with secular education? It seems unwise to think any longer in terms of Mission education. The Church must act for herself within a decade—fifteen years is risky, twenty positively dangerous.

Is it time perhaps that secular education in the villages was handed over to the Government? The mission teachers are very much needed for graded religious education within the village congregations, with youth groups, classes and Sunday schools, all of which are tragically underdeveloped. I realize that handing over secular education to the Government would have to be a gradual process. However, it would promise a more permanent solution, raise the status of the village teacher, provide him with more material resources and with a firmer authority, and in time produce better schools. It would free the mission agent in the village of some of his impossible load, his dual role of being both material and spiritual educator, and allow him to deal with pastoral duties that are at present beyond his physical strength because of this load. It seems to be as urgent for the village congregations to improve religious education as it is for secular education to be improved. There can be no adequate progress in either one while a single person has to shoulder the two burdens and, in a sense, serve two masters. From the standpoint of this book—viz., that of the growth of the

Church—I trust that, whether this argument be accepted or rejected, the local leaders will consider and restate their attitudes to the educational role of the Church. The organic and quality growth of the emerging Church demands it. *The basis of the dilemmas in Solomon Islands Christianity is a conflict between the theory of the Church's role in education and the theory of the growth of an indigenous Church.*

A well-informed Anglican observer has pointed out that at the present rate of progress it will take at least twenty years to provide even a primary education for all the children of the Solomons, and he rightly adds that we can hardly afford to wait so long. He feels that Government policy has stimulated interest in education and pressures for education will increase, that these will be beyond Government resources, and that Missions may be faced with suddenly increased burdens.[4] I should hope that, before any increase of foreign allocations was made for Mission expenditure, the theoretical and practical consequences of such a step would be fully explored. It would greatly delay the growth of the local Church organically and tend to increase the existing paternalism.

However, I am glad to have this observer's word for progress, because he inspected an area I was unable to visit and was impressed. On a neighbouring island I was unimpressed, for schools were suffering from a lack of parental interest. Both these localities were in the same region and served by the same Mission. It shows again how uneven the situation is. Exactly the same contrasts exist under the other Mission at the other end of the Group. Thus in one area Church Associations, Village Unions, District Councils and the schools they serve, all operate with enthusiasm and insight; but a few miles across the water, these organizations limp along indifferently. This has nothing to do with the comparative merits of the faithful servants of the Church who carry on through "the heat and burden of the toilsome day". There is something inherently different in the two local situations: something that has been formed by the cultural processes of the years. In local situations of this kind the local Church has to be relevant. The future surely lies, not with the Mission, but with the local Church, and especially the Church at the village level. What kind of education must the Church provide at this level? It seems to me there are four possibilities:

1. The Church may act on the scriptural mandate alone, and provide education in those things which the Lord taught to his disciples. This is the policy of one church but it does not satisfy its adherents.
2. The Church may accept secular education as her legitimate role, as applied Christianity in confrontation with the needs of the local social situation.
3. In desperation the Church may say "If the Government will not carry the burden, then we shall have to do so".
4. The other possibility is that Church and Mission become permanently co-existent, that education remains a burden on overseas support, and the state of dependence becomes perpetuated in the Solomon Island situation.

CRITERIA FOR A MISSION INSTITUTION

If the theory of the emergence of an indigenous Church be carried
to its logical conclusion, the Mission must disappear and the Church
take over. Missionaries may perhaps remain as fraternal workers, or
better as servants of the indigenous Church. The process may perhaps
be most safely carried through in stages, but ultimately the Mission
as an authority must vanish altogether. We cannot rightly speak of
the Church as indigenous until the mission authority and administration have completely gone. Clark's test for indigeneity was: can the
Church carry on if all the missionaries are taken away? The greatest
obstruction to this process is undoubtedly the administrative and
financial burden of large institutions—educational, industrial, medical,
as well as commercial ventures. All such institutions should be critically
appraised today and graded along a dispensable-indispensable polarity
axis. It is quite manifest that some institutions, like training centres
for catechists and clergy, are essential; but the same cannot necessarily
be said for time-consuming plantation systems, the disposal of which
might well provide the necessary funds for inaugurating an indigenous
Church with a reduced administrative burden.

I believe there are four criteria by which institutions may be tested
and graded on a dispensable–indispensable axis. I think of these administrative reductions, not as retrenchment, but as simplifications that
will help the emergence of an indigenous Church. There is also another
value—funds and personnel concentrated on dispensable institutions
can be deployed to others which have greater priority. Theological
education for a better indigenous ministry, for example, is a high
priority if there is to be quality growth of the Church; but even here
the criteria should apply.

(i) *The function of a mission institution is to provide in some way for
the growth and strengthening of the local Church.* To put this negatively—
the role of a mission institution is not to provide a class of collar-and-
tie persons for Government and commercial positions. It may happen
to provide a number of such persons, but this is not its purpose. In
any case such persons from a mission institution should be leading
Christian laymen helping the growth of the local Church. Going to a
mission school to get a Government job is a poor motive.[5] One would
expect that at least the mission schools would supply an adequate
number of candidates for church leadership, catechists and clergy in
particular. The organic growth of the Church depends on this, as also
does the prayer life and instruction in the faith in the villages.[6] The
fact that government and commercial positions are more remunerative
and less arduous may attract the graduates of mission schools. If this is
so, then perhaps the Churches should investigate the economic position
of catechists and clergy; but the fact remains that many who enter
these more remunerative positions do not qualify as 'leading Christian
laymen'. The first criterion for a mission institution, then, is a measure
of its results, its graduates and its contribution, not merely to the
country, but to the Christian witness in the country. This of course is
the witness of the indigenous 'fruits', not the institution itself.

(ii) *A mission institution should provide a course or programme relevant to the local situation where its graduates will live, and to the Christian encounter in that situation.* Whether the course is purely religious and theological, or commercial or cultural, it should (in this case) be relevant to the Pacific world and the Solomon Island scene in particular. Graduates should go into their respective situations ready to meet the problems and needs of life with physical equipment within the range of economic possibility, and a faith adequate to the progress demanded by their own changing world, rather than equipment and faith for a foreign world beyond the seas. On several occasions I shot a direct question at a missionary—Do you think the courses offered (and the text-books used) are relevant to the local village situation? Usually after some hesitation, a negative admission was received. In fairness I should add, however, that at one institution I was impressed with the efforts made to discover the real needs of the villages, by sending students out on brief visits with specific methods and directions, and having them report back with their responses. This was good. It was a real practical attempt at bringing an institution into line with the demands of the criterion of relevance.

(iii) *A mission institution should train its graduates to operate as catalysts in the local congregations.* Most graduates from mission institutions go away with a clear understanding of the difference between right and wrong and the basic principles of the Christian faith. These concepts may nevertheless remain only in the background of their thinking and judgements, and lie dormant. One of the main findings of my depth studies is the need for dynamic action in the local congregations. The congregations seldom burst forth in spontaneous action. The capacity of the congregation is largely dormant. Usually there has to be some go-ahead person who 'sparks off' the enthusiasm, or, to change the figure, who serves as a catalyst. Catalysts are needed in the Solomon Island congregations to precipitate congregational action. Mission school graduates should see themselves in this role, as being responsible for keeping their local groups active. It is not enough to hope that graduates will do this. They should be systematically imbued during their courses with the idea that they are being actually trained for this role. A mission school does not exist as an end in itself, or to give a diploma. It is supported by missionary contributions from overseas to carry out the Great Commission—that the Church may grow. If the vital need for today is a local Church which comes to grips with uncommitted nominalism or with paganism at its door, and catalysts are needed to precipitate such action, then a mission institution should exist for this very purpose of producing that kind of person. This is the criterion of congregational leadership. We are not thinking here of catechists, clergy and public figures, who were mentioned under the criterion of indigenous Church growth, but we are asking if an institution produces graduates who will maintain dynamic action in the local congregations at the village level. It will be quite evident that a large centralized institution with a routine quite foreign to the village way of life, and an academic programme, may have no bearing whatever on the village congregations around it. Yet in all probability the reports on missionary activity for the region will emanate from that institution. However, if the missionaries in the institution are diligent in their own village itinerations and make use of them properly the danger may be avoided. This should be planned and regular.[7] An institutional missionary must establish and maintain his identification with the village situation. If the missionary is out of touch, the institution will fail also by this criterion.

(iv) *A mission institution should be one which can be taken over by the indigenous Church.* By 'take over' I mean in both finance and administration, and also that it should produce graduates who can ultimately assume leadership in the institution. After studying the emergence of many young churches and the factors which obstruct them, I am constrained to state this criterion firmly, though I know many will disagree with me.

What distresses me about the Missions in the Solomons is the massive institutional administration, the burdensome stations, the huge plantations, extensive plants and machinery, equipment, schools, hospitals and fleets of ships. I cannot see how any indigenous Church can ever take all this over. How can it become independent? How can it realize its own selfhood? Can the Missions ever be eliminated from the situation? True these have been used in the Lord's work; but are they all essential? Perhaps the time has come to ask of every one of them, is it dispensable or indispensable? How many of them have evolved because of the very backwardness of the country itself, the failure of the Government to provide essential services in the pre-war years? To what extent has mission shipping activity itself prevented the emergence of commercial shipping facilities? Has the organic growth of the indigenous Church reached a point where drastic pruning of the Mission secondary pursuits, and competition with private enterprise, are required, in order to permit the local Church to emerge?

Let me put the matter in another way. Time after time in Honiara I found Europeans outside the Church speaking and thinking in terms of "big Missions" and "powerful Missions", but never of a local Church. They were seen as plantation owners, shipowners and engineers, as the main educational and medical servants of the Government. They were conceptualized as commercial and political powers—and, though perhaps unwittingly, the Missions have really built up this image themselves. Yet the Missions must decrease if the Church is to emerge. A cataclysmic termination of the Mission would create many social and political problems, but there should certainly be some careful and systematic planning in this direction. As things stand at present, the very image of the Christian Missions is a major obstruction to the organic growth of a young Church.

The four criteria may be more briefly stated thus: (1) Does this institution help the Church to grow? (2) Is it relevant to the local situational encounters? (3) Does it raise people to deal with those encounters within the situations? (4) Does it permit or obstruct the emerging of the Church, as regards allowing the young Church to take it over? These criteria are 'good questions', I offer them as suitable testing points which help us to evaluate institutions, and permit us to grade them along a dispensable–indispensable polarity axis. This is not for retrenchment, I reiterate, but to discover what can be weeded out, to permit the free emergence of a truly indigenous Church and a deployment of funds to bring the emphasis on the true priorities of the Christian mission.

I have dealt with this under the head of problems because I recognize that there are no easy solutions. Personally I feel the Missions must decrease and disappear, and some of the institutions with them, that the administrative burden could be drastically reduced, and the commercial activities and plantations handed over to private enterprise. On the other hand, personnel and funds could be deployed to such projects as theological training. The degree to which the mission medical and educational institutions are doing the work of the Government needs critical examination. What medical and educational institutions are retained should be the responsibility of the Church, not the Mission.[8] There may be other and better solutions, but I think this warrants serious consideration because it is based on a theory of church growth which I believe to be unassailable. Whether the leaders of the Missions, who know the situation from the inside better than I do, agree with me or not, they cannot afford to ignore the fact that, in the eyes of outside observers, Christian Missions have assumed a specific image as a commercial and power factor in the Solomon Islands scene. The outsider cannot see the Church for Missions.

In this chapter we have discussed the role of the Church in education and have tried to establish some kind of criteria for testing institutions, relating them in some way to the growth of the Church. We must now raise the question of the role of education in the Church—a very different matter from the role of the Church in education. This is surely the teaching our Lord had in mind in the Great Commission, and has direct bearing on the quality growth inside the Church.

THE ROLE OF EDUCATION IN THE CHURCH

The anthropologist, F. E. Williams, shows the inevitability of change in island culture patterns and discusses the justification for an Administration or Mission directing such changes by means of education. He saw the error of trying to preserve the ancient culture when it was impotent to deal with newly emerged life situations. He also saw the opposite error of sheer Europeanization. He sought his ideal education in a blending of cultures, a control of culture change by means of education, preserving the good of the indigenous tradition and rejecting its evil, making such modifications as seemed necessary to keep the general pattern adequate for the daily life of the people who live it. Thus he came to express the task of education in terms of three basic functions:

Maintenance —	preserving the good of the past.
Expurgation —	removing evil and useless elements.
Expansion or *Incorporation* —	innovating positive contributions to meet the emerging situations.

He speaks of renovating an old building, where the basic structure is sound, but where weak and dangerous portions need removing and new features have to be added to meet a new situation. Then he adds the qualification, that of course we are dealing with a living organism not a house. He then develops the above threefold programme.[9]

The three tasks of education apply equally to secular education for general progress and to the internal religious education for growth within the Church itself. We have traditions to maintain, weaknesses to eliminate, and new ideas to introduce to meet the changing situations in which we live. If the role of the Church in education has been overdone in the Solomons, the opposite certainly applies to the role of education in the Church. It is true that in the eastern islands there has been careful instruction in the Creed, basic doctrine and worship patterns. It is also true that everywhere in the Solomons Christians have an appreciation of church music, but there is much room for systematic education at many other points. Let me enumerate a few:

(i) There is the place of the Bible itself. It is not a well-known book, and is very little read by Christians in many areas. Although in the western islands members recite selected passages every Sunday night, the passages are removed from context and not very well selected. The biblical narrative, especially that of the Old Testament, is not well known. The record of how God guided His people, Israel, by His mighty arm, the series of dynamic incidents showing a God who acts in history, has never been seriously taught. Abraham, Moses, David and Elijah are mere names. In one part of the Solomons an Old Testament passage has to be read in a New Hebridean language and in another part in English. I found it extremely difficult to strike up a discussion on the Bible, even with leaders in the village church. This is the very opposite of my experience in other parts of Melanesia. It came to me as a shock.

(ii) Where the whole Bible has still not been translated into the vernacular, it is all the more necessary that the Sunday school functions regularly. Yet, except in the town or on mission stations, I never once met an organized Sunday school. I know they do exist in some parts, but a careful examination of what statistical records I could obtain showed that even these were largely a post-war development. There is far more readiness to gather young people together to learn to sing a new hymn tune than to meet systematically for Bible study. This applies on all levels, for I do not confine Sunday schools to children. There is a crying need for the religious education of the congregation on some graded basis; for what Gorald Lansley called a "fundamental policy of progressive Christian education and evangelism from childhood to maturity".[10]

(iii) Pastors, lay preachers, prayer leaders and members of the village congregations do little, if any, reading. They could do more. Some of the leaders are self-defensive and object to paying two shillings for a guide to Bible study. Some go so far as to say that if the Mission expects them to read, they should supply the reading material free. Yet many of these men have been able to buy wrist-watches, pipes, radios, outboard motors and other prestige symbols from the western world. The secular and mission shops of the Solomons are deplorably lacking in stocks of reading material. Probably there is no demand, but there does not appear to have been any education for a demand. One would expect that so long a period of missionary activity would have produced at least a basic vernacular library—a *Life of Christ*, a *Journeys of Paul*, some simple exegetical studies, an exposition of Creed and Catechism, a book of Bible stories for children, and a few Christian classics like *Pilgrim's Progress*.[11] One would also expect a vernacular devotional paper with a village level circulation. These are a minimum. After sixty years a developing Church should have more than this, even allowing for possible losses during the war.

Some argue the difficulty of a multiplicity of dialects. Others say the ravages of insects and climate on book stocks prevent any serious programme. These are to beg the question, for even the abundant English material available has not been explored. This could have been obtained in small quantities at a time and is written simply. The fact of the matter is that the education of the Church in Christian reading has never had a priority. Missionaries have been energetic persons and competent linguists, but voluntarily or involuntarily they have been bound by their administrative burdens and compound duties. Competent linguistic work has certainly been done in the east, in the preparation of dictionaries and the translation of prayer books and a few other aids to worship; a good deal of fine literary work has come from the Group, much of it missionary promotional material for the home Church, and experiences for the secular press; yet there has been no vernacular literature established progressively over the years. I think only one language has a full Bible, though one more is promised shortly.

The question that arises now is: why is it necessary for Christian villages to have schools and to teach reading, if the Church supplies nothing for them to read? Is competency in reading merely a status symbol? Surely if this is the business of the Church, it is to permit education within the Church through which the quality growth of its members may be achieved.

(iv) There is also scope in the Church for more education in the nature of the Church itself, the character of and need for its organic growth, so that definite effort may be made towards this end. One of the real problems of the passage from mission control to Church is the unreadiness of many island communities to accept release from mission paternalism. Quite often the reason for this is an unwillingness to assume responsibility in the activities and the stewardship it will involve. Perceptions of a congregation with respect to its stewardship obligations can come only by education of the congregation. This does not come by synod decision. It cannot be imposed or directed from above. It has to be perceived and accepted from the level of the village congregation, and this requires effective education on that level.

The indigenous Church will come more easily in the east than in the west because there has been more education for the indigenous Church there, and the education has been at the 'grass-roots' level, not from the committee level as in the west. In the east the Melanesian character of the Church has always been emphasized, but even here there is room for more education in self-support. The whole question of self-support is urgent everywhere in the Solomons today, although some areas like Ysabel appear to be moving along satisfactorily. It is not easy to persuade an island community that they ought to be carrying a heavier financial load. It cannot be imposed by a decision from outside. It has to be accepted from within, and this needs education that will prepare the congregation for that psychological moment when they themselves will reach forward in acceptance. Group dynamics have much to teach us here.[12] Perhaps the more progressive villages may be used as pilot projects.

(v) There is also scope in the Solomons today for educating village congregations in ecumenical horizons. The increased mobility of the post-war period makes this important. All the mission churches reflect strongly the characteristics of the sending churches that have sponsored the missions. The island Christians are more and more coming face to face with these denominational differences. A form of education is needed within the Churches to help the members to appreciate the essential unity of denominations that have so many formal differences, and to perceive that each has something to give to and something to receive from the other. Denominationalism threatens to become a major problem. The need of today is education in the essential unity of Christianity in the face of other religions and ideologies. Town and plantation communities could do good service by occasionally having inter-denominational worship; but unless something educative is planned, denominational clash will be the major result.

These are a few ways in which the role of education in the Church may be conceived. This is part of organic and quality growth. The list can be expanded considerably. I merely suggest enough to indicate the differentiation between the role of the Church in education and the role of education in the Church. It is high time we made the distinction.

MISSION INSTITUTIONALISM AND THE EMERGENCE OF THE CHURCH

A Mission Secretary analysed the question of evangelism by means of schools in China and advocated drastic policy changes.[13] Some of his contemporaries were exploring the area of education within the Church on local indigenous levels.[14] This promising research and its practical results were interrupted by the war and post-war political changes. Similar feelings had been expressed by missionaries in Korea,[15] and another missionary in South America was pressing similar ideas from a biblical basis.[16] Much data of this type was collected by the missionary strategist, Clark, before his death.[17] Possibly his insights both stimulated and were stimulated by Roland Allen.[18] A whole corpus of church growth writing was emerging, but the war brought new crises, new streams of thought, and new personalities on to the scene. These valuable church growth insights were submerged. Three decades have gone by—decades riddled with nativistic movements and missionary losses from Oceania to Africa.

My own research in the Solomons drove me back to the thirties for
the root causes of Roviana nativism. The 1928 Report, to which I
devoted a unit of chapter two, could well have been cited with its
contemporary writing from China. The culture patterns were quite
different but the missionary policy was remarkably similar at many
points.

Another approach to the matter of education and evangelism was
pressed by Blamires,[19] who defined education as "the whole process
of leading life to its real fulfilment . . . a life-long process, and in it God
and man are partners". He was concerned with organic and quality
growth and the conversion of the generation growing up within the
Church, rather than conversion from paganism or the world. His work
is relevant because he differentiated between education and an educational institution. He saw education in worship, in preaching, in instruction, and in social service—in the active life of the Church. In agricultural imagery he described the ploughing and cultivation that had to
precede the harvest. To translate this into terms relevant for the young
Churches, we would need to ask if the local congregations are providing
the education within their own organization to ensure organic and
quality growth, and bringing those born within its ranks to the conversion experience. The drift from marginality to nominality, as shown
by my study in depth, would suggest a negative answer. Blamires was
perturbed by the British statistics, which showed discrepancies between
population growth and internal church growth—that is, the 'fall-out'
alarmed him. His problem was how to save those born in the Church,
and bring them to a participating adult membership. This is also a
major problem in the Solomon Islands. His emphasis on the continuity
of education within the Church for every age group at every point of
Christian faith and practice has certainly something pertinent to say
to the second and third generation Solomon Island churches. But
Blamire's outreach into the pagan and secular world is inadequate.

The outreach of the Church is part of its totality. A Church without
intake is just as vulnerable as one without inner quality growth. Again,
a Church that attends to education within, at the expense of outreach,
is open to what is known in church growth writing as the *fallacy of
consolidation*, a concept stressed by Clark, and in more recent times by
McGavran. It is easy for a Church to excuse herself from outreach
because of the 'necessity' for 'consolidation', but if intake is stopped in
order to consolidate, this tends to lead to introversion rather than
consolidation. Thus we have a fallacy.[20] Furthermore, the Great
Commission commits us to outreach. The remarkable thing is that
where the Church is alive to its responsibility for outreach, it is usually
also found to be alive to the responsibility for inner quality growth.

The danger with centralized institutional emphasis lies in the ease
with which its missionaries can slip into the fallacy of consolidation,
claiming they are building a strong Church by sound scholarship, high
moral tone and discipline—what they call 'quality' when in reality it
may well be introversion. Administrative burdens increase and itinerations through the villages decrease. The institutions receive the atten-

tion, outreach is lost sight of, and with it the missionary identification with the village situation. The kind of quality growth that is achieved may well tend to become foreign and academic, remote from the intellectual and cultural level of the village community. This is a real danger. Every large institutional mission should probe honestly into these possibilities among its shortcomings, because institutional introversion both slows down the physical growth of the Church and hinders its organic emergence.

The missionary theory of the emergence of the indigenous Church may be widely accepted and yet be in practice obstructed. Such obstructions come from three directions: (1) some leaders of the sending Church and Mission Boards who are concerned for the capital investments in missions; (2) certain missionaries on the field—ministers, teachers and doctors—who are obsessed with western academic or disciplinary standards; and (3) some mission institution graduates who are themselves dependent on the system. These persons can be real obstructions and much grace is required if policies are to be effectively changed. The writer is familiar with one case in the islands, but not in the Solomons, where it was determined, after some decades of failure to evangelize by means of education from central stations, to change the methods to rural evangelism through farming families. Obstructions were considerable and many hard feelings made change of method difficult. But once the change was made the Church began to grow. In this case the obstructions came from the types (2) and (3) above. Many missionaries have resisted the ordination of islanders for fear that western standards of theology and morals might not be maintained. This has obstructed organic growth. Sometimes indigenous servants of the Church, who have been admitted to office after a long period of trial, have safeguarded their own status by demanding excessive standards before the admission of other fellow-countrymen. Thus they have reinforced the missionary obstructions. Indigenous staff paid by foreign resources tend to be similarly obstructive to moves for self-support.[21] These are obstructive individuals.

I have already suggested that the institutions themselves (as distinct from individual obstructors) can be obstructions to the emergence of the Church. I mean the very fact that the parent missions are ship-owners, engineers, plantation owners, and administrators of large hospitals and schools (demanding commercial and government dealings and agreements and the operation of elaborate budgets) creates an impression that the complexity and burden of it all is something to which the indigenous Church can never aspire. The Government attitude does not help.

The Government has resigned itself to an inability to carry its own financial responsibility and has accepted a position of dependence on Missions, though it hopes the Missions will recognize the authority of Government Departments. It makes its programmes for five-year terms on the assumption that Mission contributions will remain constant. The Missions have thus allowed their personnel and revenue to become part of the configuration of Government policy. The earmarking of

Mission resources for five-year periods is certainly risky, as Mission revenue operates only on an annual basis.[22] Both the medical and educational systems, it must be admitted, though present relationships appear to be happy, are open to the possibility of two-master problems. The pattern does not promise well either for stable development or for control by an indigenous Church.

Social services, including medicine and education, should be developing towards indigeneity parallel with the Church, each developing organically with its indigenous officers at each level. The same retarded growth is apparent in all cases, and the complexity of mission administration because of added social loads reinforces the Mission image of social indispensability. Development of the indigenous potential of education, for example, would bring the local councils more into action. It would be here in such community service that the Christian laymen of the local congregations could render their Christian witness. But on the whole the village communities expect the Missions to carry on, and they themselves are not prepared to make an effort. At least this was so in the localities I visited. As Father Huddleston said of a quite different situation in South Africa, the Church is facing a challenge which cannot be met with official pronouncements alone, and only the ordinary lay folk who are the Church can meet it—but I do not believe they are doing so.[23] Ultimately the village congregations must assume the responsibility for the emergence of the indigenous Church.

One of the main hindrances to this is the villagers' own image of the Mission, with its social, institutional, commercial and administrative complexity. True, this is seen as foreign, but it is also seen as indispensable. Its disappearance in favour of a self-supporting indigenous Church is unthinkable. Any pressure from the Mission, either through its missionaries or its official pronouncements, towards this end, any official reduction of paternalism, is regarded as evidence that (and I use a common claim of my informants) "The Mission no longer loves us". The danger of this attitude is that when such a group does decide that the Mission is dispensable, instead of emerging as a self-supporting Church, it breaks away into some form of nativistic movement. It reinforces itself against the Mission at certain points—moral standards, theological concepts, magical forms—by means of revivals from pre-Christian Melanesian society. The result is an enthusiastic syncretism. Meantime those villages which remain 'loyalist' continue to insist on Mission paternalism, and have no disposition to develop as a self-supporting Church. This is the problem as I observed it. Here is the very situation which Clark said called for *reconstruction* (see p. 92). The problem is clearly the result of a prolonged period during which the Mission was unready to act on its ideals of organic growth (see pp. 91–92). The only solution I can see to this problem is the possibility of pilot projects and group dynamics (see p. 93 and fn. 12, p. 363).

There is one more argument against excessive mission institutionalism which should be mentioned, though space does not permit developing it. A research economist who visited various island groups pointed out that population was increasing more rapidly than production, because of the manner in which social services were developing "in a somewhat philanthropic manner". Education was biased *away from* production towards "white-collar jobs", and was not raising the economy or greatly improving social conditions, because social services were largely *dependent* for their extension and/or maintenance on grants-in-aid or revenue from copra. The revenue from Britain, from mission plantations and from overseas missionary support represents an enormous percentage of what is spent on social services in the islands in general. One effect of this philanthropic approach is to place its physical and financial costs beyond "the capacity of the indigenous people".[24] This is another way of saying that a state of dependence obstructs the emergence of indigeneity—it applies to both country and Church. The missionary movement ought at times to test its institutions and policies, to be sure that its ideals and good motives are not perhaps obstructing the very ends it desires.[25]

Part Four

THE RELEVANCE OF ANTHROPOLOGICAL DIMENSIONS

9 The Transmission and Control of Authority and Leadership

10 The Head-hunting and Slavery Complex and Socio-religious Change
   Roviana–Simbo Head-hunting and Slavery as a Working Process
   Changes brought by the White Man
   Effect of the Suppression of Head-hunting by the Administration
   Roviana Colonizing
   Effect on the Planting and Growth of the Church

11 How Village Structure Reflects Christian Patterns
   The Village of Rarumana
   The Village of Fouia
   The Village of Sulufou

12 Exchange Economy and Christian Innovation
   Concepts of Wealth
   Some Economic Dimensions of Custom
   Village Absenteeism and Communal Responsibility
   Socio-economic Organization in the Villages
   Religio-Economic Organization
   Trade Networks and Conversion Growth

13 Feud and Reconciliation
   The Feud
     Chronology and Distribution
     The Mechanisms Involved
     The Bearing of these Events on Church Planting

The Procedure and Ceremonial of Reconciliation
The Role of the Go-between
The Symbol of the Overthrow of Enmity
The Peace-making Ceremony

14 Comparative Analysis of Nativistic Movements
The Pokokoqoro Cult
Marching Rule
The Hahalis Welfare Society
Etoism

CHAPTER 9

The Transmission and Control of Authority
and Leadership

IN THIS short chapter we are to consider a number of matters related
to leadership, the descent of the chieftaincy, the degree to which it may
be controlled by public opinion, and the public attitude towards the
discipline of a person with authority. Some missionaries are convinced
of the rottenness of the chiefly system and blame this for the power Silas
Eto has over his people, as will be discussed in the study of his schism in
Part V of this book. Is a democratic missionary entitled to assume the
rottenness of the chiefly system? Or has the traditional pattern of authority something to show us with respect to possible leadership patterns for use in the Church in the Solomons? Or are there dangers of
the emergence of an ecclesiastical aristocracy if the indigenous pattern
is given too great a place?

To study the transmission and control of authority I shall use a
Roviana genealogical table. I have tabulated the relevant portion of
the lineage of Gove. Gove himself traced his ancestors back through a
long line, but too great an extension of the tree would only reveal the
same principles and complicate the tool. In the same way I have not
shown the present generation of children, being satisfied merely with
the use of an asterisk to show who is married and has children living in
the village. They are, of course, very numerous. The table could also
have been extended by showing the descendants of the other sons and
the daughter of Gove, but I was unable to pursue this investigation in
the time at my disposal. This table shows the descendants of Gove
through his eldest son, Pequ Vovoso.

Pequ Vovoso had two wives, Ani Mali who came from Marovo and
Mere from Vuragare, the people who traditionally own the chain of
islands of which Wanawana is a part. Pequ Vovoso's mother came from
Kazukuru, from the line of the chief of Toa Lavata, Kidu, where part
of the lineage is still resident. Pequ Vovoso's descendants through his
first wife, Ani Mali, have migrated over a period of about sixty years to
Nusa Qele, to Mabura and eventually settled at Madou on the island of
Wanawana about 1921 or 1922, and have since remaind there. The line
which descended through the second wife, Mere, has remained at Munda
and represents both a resident community and a lineage.

When the gospel arrived in the Western Solomons, Iqava was the
paramount chief. As we have already seen, he opposed the introduction
of Christianity. He was an old man at the time. Gemu and Gumi,
grandsons of Pequ Vovoso, figured prominently in the spread of the
Church. They were both figures of high prestige and authority in the

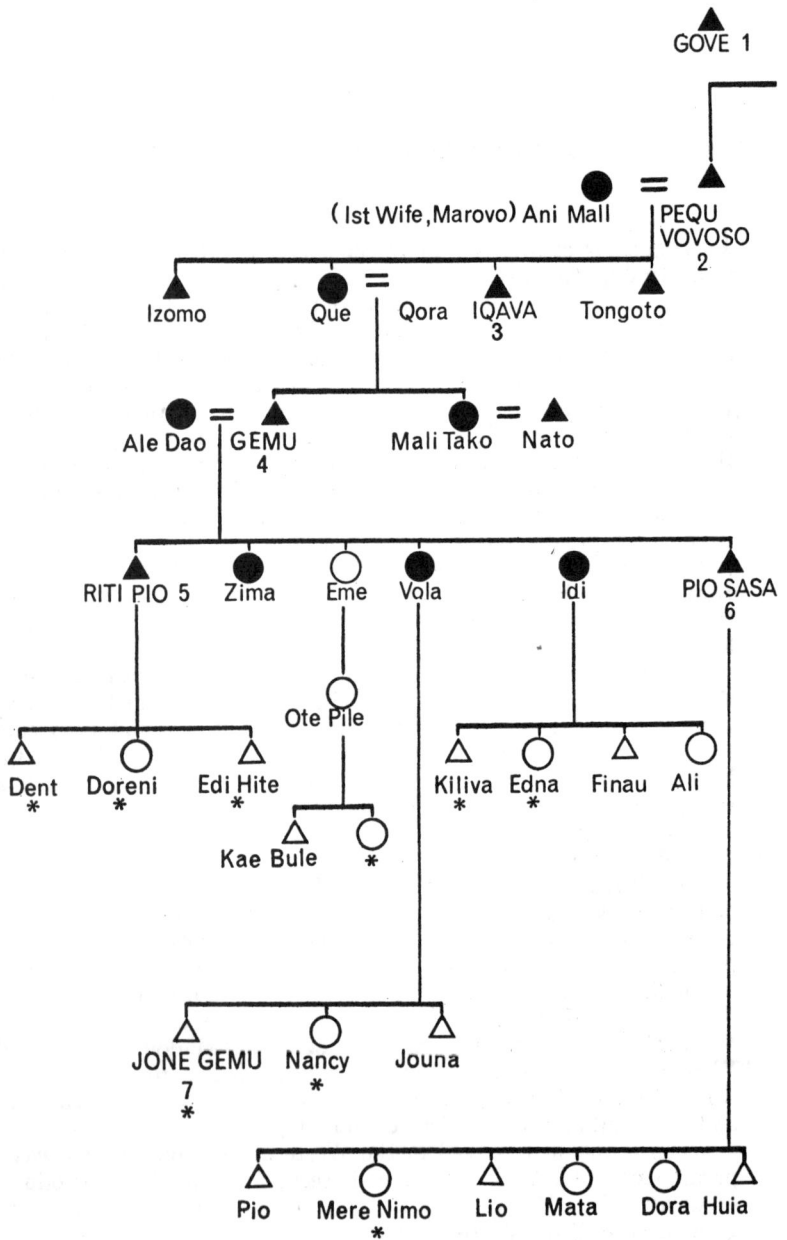

THE LINEAGE OF GOV

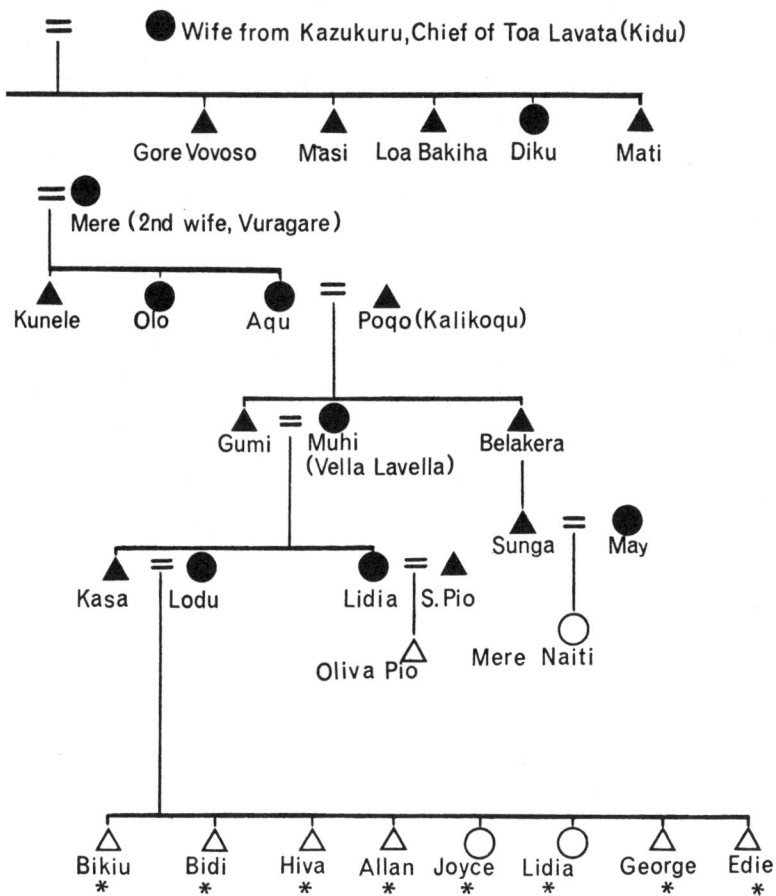

Wife from Kazukuru, Chief of Toa Lavata (Kidu)

Gore Vovoso   Masi   Loa Bakiha   Diku   Mati

Mere (2nd wife, Vuragare)

Kunele   Olo   Aqu   Poqo (Kalikoqu)

Gumi   Muhi (Vella Lavella)   Belakera

Kasa   Lodu   Lidia   S. Pio   Sunga   May

Oliva Pio   Mere   Naiti

Bikiu   Bidi   Hiva   Allan   Joyce   Lidia   George   Edie
  *   *   *   *   *   *   *   *

Legend

Numbers indicate the line of the chieftaincy.
* *These are married and now have children.*

THROUGH PEQU VOVOSO

first decade of this century. Their own generation and that of their children were those who rejected paganism and accepted Christianity. Authority today lies with their grandsons, who were born within Christianity and did not personally have to make a dramatic choice between animism and Christianity. They are now adults and another generation of children is coming along. The names of Gemu and Gumi are still honoured names in the history of the Church in the Western Solomons and their own lines are now resident at Madou and Munda. Both these groups had come out squarely for Christianity against paganism in their day.

However, the two segments of the lineage have been segregated by the Etoist schism. The common bond which existed between Gemu and Gumi has been lost. Despite the fact that both segments had a common ancestor less than a century ago, and despite the strong ceremonial pledges of Gemi and Gumi to each other, the two segments will now have virtually nothing to do with each other. With the exception of two children of Kasa (who have married back into villages that are now Etoist, and have been pressured into Etoism) the division is clear-cut and on a basis of social structure. It shows how, even after sixty years of Christian instruction and example, decision-making in communal societies still tends to be made along lines of social or kin structure. It shows how a group movement can occur, moving out of the Church along kin lines if conditions within the Church do not give general satisfaction.

In discussing Etoism with a prominent Solomon Islander in Honiara, I found him bitter about it, not so much on theological grounds, but because it had split his lineage into two smaller kin segments. This to him was a tragic thing.

According to Goldie[1] the authority pattern which operated in the west in pre-Christian times recognized three types of official. The village headman was known as *Palabatu* (a word also used for husband). The villages were divided into sub-groups each with a chief known as *Bagara*, who frequently held more actual power than the village headman. Over a large region or district, perhaps a large island or a number of islands, was a principal chief, known as *Gati-Bagara*. *Gati* means 'stem' or 'trunk'. This is the real hereditary chief. Ingava was such a regional chief.

Another observation worth recording about this lineage table is the way it shows the descent of the chieftaincy. Observe its passage through the family of Pequ Vovoso's first wife, Ani Mali. Although Pequ himself was the eldest son, the chieftaincy did not go to his eldest son, Izomo, but to Ingava, his third child. The next in the line of chieftaincy was the son of neither Izomo nor Ingava; but Gemu, the son of Que, daughter of Pequ. After Gemu, Riti Pio, his first son, became chief; but because the group considered his behaviour unworthy of the office, he was relieved of it. His younger brother, Pio Sasa, took office while the demoted Riti Pio was still alive. However, although both Riti Pio and Pio Sasa had sons, none of them assumed the chieftaincy in the following generation. It went to Jone Gemu, who is currently chief, eldest son of Volo, daughter and fourth child of Gemu. By this time there were nine males eligible for the office.

This very clearly demonstrates that the descent of the Roviana chieftaincy, although hereditary, was not a hide-bound line, as for example through the eldest son. It allowed for some individualism and selection within certain limits. In the early days of the Methodist work, Goldie was struck by the fact that the authority pattern did permit a man of character and initiative to rise and assume more power if the chief turned out to be a weakling or a man of no influence. This applied to Palabatu and Bagara as well as the paramount chief. In these cases of the lesser chiefs, a more suitable leader, though not actually usurping the office, and not always recognized by the dishonoured chief, was nevertheless looked on as leader by the common people. This same principle applied in some parts of the Solomons with respect to the line of the priesthood. If the eldest son turned out to be unsuitable in some parts of Malaita, a second son or even a 'brother' in the extended family concept could be chosen.[2] There was thus a widespread concept in the Solomons which recognized the capacity for leadership as an important factor in the selection of leaders, either chiefs or priests; and this provided an escape mechanism for dealing with a chief whose behaviour did not please the group. Some old narratives I heard rather suggested that, for some tribes at least, the origin of this policy of selectivity lay in the head-hunting days, when capacity for leadership was a matter of life and death.

In the Christian Church it simplified the matter of disciplining an official, even if he had chiefly status, if he failed to measure up to Christian standards. It was for this reason that many of the Solomon Island Christians thought Silas Eto should have been disciplined long before his movement came to a crisis. One of my best informants kept returning in every conversation to the thing which mystified him most about the whole business: "I cannot understand why the Mission let it go so long, and why Silas was not disciplined." Roviana social structure and status-determining mechanisms have the germ of *no respect for persons*, that make Christian discipline acceptable. The range of selectivity for substitutes is not particularly narrow. Eto's self-assertion and theology had long made him unsuitable as a catechist, and local opinion is that he should have been dismissed long before the crisis. It is not for me to decide whether the Church courts were right or wrong in their reluctance to act against Eto; I merely point out as an observer that the local indigenous view is that if disciplinary measures had been applied, the situation would not have developed as it did. The discipline would have been meaningful and acceptable as a means of handling the problem. Having said this, however, I am obliged to add that although this might have held off the crisis, it would still not have dealt with the local situation which made the whole schism possible. It may well have dealt with Eto, but the problem of the religious matrix in which Etoism flourished would have remained—as it still remains—unsolved.

Our genealogical table, then, illuminates two points. (1) Even after

F

two generations of Christianity it is possible for large social segments to cut themselves off from the Church. When they do so they tend to be structured sub-groups of the lineage, and in the eyes of an islander a division of the lineage is a major calamity which generates strong feeling. (2) The patterns for selection of persons in authority are rather elastic and tend to lead to the choice of men of character and initiative and natural capacity. Unsuitablity for office or unworthiness is adequate reason for discipline.

This orientation to the chieftaincy, which some missionaries of recent times have not understood (as their correspondence shows), applies to other forms of status and office, such as posts in the Government and Church. It is expected that an unsuitable person will be removed from office, because the *work* of the office, being for the good of the whole community, is more important than the *person* of the individual selected. This is a widespread attitude in Melanesia. The principle was well stated by Moses for Israel in Deuteronomy 1: 13–17, but this passage of Scripture has not yet been printed in the Roviana language.

The first of the above observations shows how Eto was able to establish his cause in complete village units—for each village is virtually a kin segment of some larger lineage. It was in this way that the subject Kusage people were able to split the more powerful Roviana overlords into kin sub-groups. The second explains why many of the island 'loyalists' disagreed with the slow policy of Mission non-intervention in the hope that Eto would think matters over and return to the fold.

To this point in our study of the transmission and control of authority we have worked from Roviana data, because of its bearing on Etoism. However, Roviana is not necessarily typical of all the Solomons. Ingava was perhaps the greatest of the regional chiefs; an alternative selection, however, might well have been Gorai of the Bougainville Straits, of whom Guppy wrote so much,[3] but I did not visit that area and had no means of reconstructing his lineage. Allen has pointed out that these politically and socially significant families, which established themselves on their prowess as head-hunters, were confined to the Western Solomons.[4] Although this is by no means proved, I think we may generalize for the Solomons on one point—that Solomon Island societies probably all had social mechanisms for varying the transmission of authority if necessary. Everywhere the chief seems to have been forced to maintain his reputation in order to retain his office. He had to maintain the cohesion and the stability of the group over which he exercised his authority. In all parts of Melanesia which I have studied this has been so. The appraisal of a chief by the populace has always been by this norm. Various mechanisms like patricide, fratricide, ostracism and the functional sub-division of roles have been used to vary the transmission of the chieftaincy for the common good. There are usually several possible alternative choices for the office. Infanticide may be used if a weakling is born in the priority line for the chieftaincy. Or if two have equal claim, an ordeal or contest may be employed.

In many parts of the Solomons, authority or leadership does not depend on heredity at all, but on personal qualities, initiative, generosity and competence. Such a leader has to establish himself through social responsibility, organization of food production, and provision of feasts and entertainments. He has to prove his ability, win public favour and maintain it. He can never live on his laurels. Such a man is accepted as leader, maintains law, punishes offenders and negotiates reconciliations. In return for this service, his family is elaborately celebrated at times of life crisis, a marriage in his family especially being a public festivity.[5] This acquisition of authority is quite a different pattern from that of Roviana because birth is of no consequence whatever, but the high value placed on capacity for good leadership is the same. In both places the leader must maintain the cohesion and stability of the society where he exercises his authority.

This represents an indigenous *mental set*. In itself it is neither pagan nor Christian. It is an indigenous cultural value. The Church might well take note of this. Indigenous leaders in the Church should not be appointed on a basis of western norms of training, theological knowledge and western morals, though these may all be useful. In the eyes of the rank and file of the local congregation, the ultimate measure of a good leader will be based on his capacity to maintain the integration and enthusiasm of the congregation in worship which satisfies the spiritual and physical needs of the group. Those needs are culturally conceived. The congregation desire prayers in their own thought-forms and sermons relevant to the daily life they know—to the fears and problems of the Melanesian way of life—rather than theological and moral abstractions. They need something in which they can participate wholeheartedly. They need mechanisms whereby they can themselves have a say in policy and the choice of their own leaders. This goes for the country as well as the Church. In political realms the headmen selected by administrators on a basis of their knowledge of English have frequently not been acceptable to the people and have created much discord. I make that statement on a basis of indigenous testimonies. In the Western Solomons in particular I often wondered if the failure to develop real leadership at the village level had been due to (1) the desire to measure a leader by European values and (2) the failure to allow the indigenous congregations more voice and vote in the Church decision-making councils.

On the other hand, in the east where the Church has opened the way more for the development of indigenous leadership, I had strong feelings in several places (and I am not alone in this feeling) that these leaders were carving out for themselves an ecclesiastical aristocracy with a monopoly of wealth, status and decision-making that was not confined to spiritual matters. In one village I found a priest, choir-master, leaders of the women's group, medical dresser, school teacher and village head-man all within one kin sub-group—and it was a composite village where numerous lineages were represented. In another village not far from this place, but served by a different mission, which did not co-operate with this survey, the Church is a prestige-creating body, the elders owning the hill-top lands and pushing the ideas of the missionaries against the feelings of the common people. They not only hold the best land, but they hold most of the wealth; in trade they grossly exploit the rank and file, far more than any foreigners in the land—having money, economic advantages of hawkers' licences, and asking up to 200 per cent profit. They support the mission demand for no smoking and betel-nut chewing by themselves drinking tea on their hill-tops, and deny betel-nut to the poor who economically have no other indulgence. I am not speaking of the right and wrong of betel-nut, but of the wrong of the economic exploitation of the poor by the elders of the Church. This particular village is in danger of a serious split, in spite of the fact that the church is alive and active in many ways. Membership is poorly developed because of the exclusiveness and prohibitions pressed by the elders. Three-quarters of the group consider themselves Christians but are not baptized.

One informant told me that in older days people lived in smaller sub-groups, and if dissatisfied with their leadership they could either change their leader or remove to another hamlet. During this century the escape mechanisms are being lost and the villages are larger, so that migration merely takes one to another similar situation. Social structure is changing and, under this mission policy of barriers against baptism, a class division is arising, with the Christian leaders powerful, wealthy and aristocratic. This is new. Traditionally leaders were individuals of outstanding merit, subject to approval or rejection by the rank and file. The corrective voice of the populace (or congregation) has been lost.

Leadership, based on a social class, whether political or religious, is difficult to dislodge. Island society has no mechanisms for dealing with the problem except by internal strife. The old pattern of leadership by outstanding individuals who had to maintain their office by competence at serving the common good was more satisfactory, and certainly approximated more to the norms of Scripture. If an indigenous Church is to emerge, care should be taken as to the kind of Church it is to be. Not all patterns borrowed from the west represent *progress*.

CHAPTER 10

The Head-hunting and Slavery Complex and Socio-religious Change

In this chapter I wish to take one cultural configuration and show its social, political, economic and religious ramifications in pre-Christian times, and then trace the changes caused by acculturation and Christian contact. I shall also deal with those aspects of this configuration that left the way open for the acceptance of Christianity.

Head-hunting and slaving raids were a dominant feature of Solomon Island life both for perpetrators and for victims. One of the most vicious of these networks operated in the Western Solomons from Roviana, in New Georgia, and Simbo a little to the south.[1] The outreaches were so widespread that other communities borrowed Roviana patterns although often to satisfy different needs and purposes.[2] Raids were for heads, or for slaves, or for both, depending on the needs at Roviana. Usually the raids were accompanied by cannibalism, frequently but not always ceremonial.

The wide area covered by Roviana and Simbo raiding led to the emergence of many protective innovations among the potential victims, especially architectural and defence mechanisms. Penny, who had personal experience of these raids, claims that the Ysabel tree-houses were devised for this purpose. They were comfortable and thoroughly effective and one of the best architectural achievements in these islands.[3] Life continually formed its patterns about the reality of raiding. It was a period of innovation. There was nothing static about this way of life. On the one hand it was open for the introduction of destructive western features, like the use of tomahawk heads and firearms, and on the other to protective devices like forts and tree-houses. The fact that the whole complex was open to innovation and not static had important consequences for traders and missionaries. It will therefore be necessary for us first to reconstruct the configuration as it was before culture contact.

ROVIANA–SIMBO HEAD-HUNTING AND SLAVERY
AS A WORKING PROCESS

The influence of this pattern was felt for 300 miles from the centre—Choiseul, Ysabel, Florida, Guadalcanal and Buin were in the regular orbit. On occasions the raiders travelled as far as New Britain. Large-scale raiding goes back as far as our records permit investigation. The slaving system was noted by Surville's expedition in 1769.[4] In 1844 Captain Cheyne met with an expedition returning to Roviana with ninety-three heads.[5] Woodford described another about 1886 with thirty-one heads.[6] Every village had its heap of skulls for which special houses were built. In Simbo in 1901, Brown recorded twenty to thirty skulls at each repository.[7] According to Knibbs the Roviana head-hunters caught so many victims that they decapitated them, for the sake of a cargo of heads, which they eventually stripped, cleaned and ornamented before hanging them in the taboo house or the men's meeting-house.[8] The procedure was well established and ritualized for a multitude of ceremonial occasions.

It is frequently supposed that one of the features of political change during the last century was the emergence of *master tribes*. Each of the major island Groups seems to have had one or two groups fighting for the hegemony of the area. The Roviana people, with their Simbo allies, had certainly established some such paramountcy and were well on the way to establishing it in other regions. Even where they had not established direct rule they were universally feared, and they had done some colonizing. This widespread prestige of Roviana and the fear of her head-hunting propensity was reinforced further by her slaving patterns.

Psychologically the slaving established a distinction between the Roviana people and others. The slaves were captured from other islands whenever needed. They were often high-born persons taken in infancy or adolescence, so that they were usually detribalized and lived in sodalities rather than kin units. Servitude in the slave community was not oppressive but there was never any doubt about their lowly status. They had to eat their food among themselves, or at least segregated from the Roviana people.[9] Their life was uncertain, for they might be called on at any time for some sacrificial purposes.[10] Neverthe-less they had some degree of security, in that an economic role was assigned to them, and proficiency in craftsmanship was a reasonable guarantee against a slave's becoming a sacrificial victim. The slave com-munity had little cohesion because the members came from widely scat-tered localities, spoke different languages and had no ties of kinship. They had to acquire the language of their masters and had no escape from the slave status. A slave's hope of survival depended on his personal capacity to make himself a useful member of society. Furthermore they were, as Guppy pointed out, "marketable commodities".

Slave traffic and head-hunting were thus both 'recognized systems' and raids might be for either one or both purposes. The political and military status of Roviana and her prestige among the tribes depended on the effectiveness and regularity of these raids. Her economic stability and religious ceremonial also depended on the availability of heads and slaves for many occasions. The presence of so many slaves in Roviana and their exemption from kin involvements had important consequen-ces for the introduction of Christianity, which certainly infiltrated through this slave community of detribalized persons.

The main business of life in Roviana was war—that is, raiding. Craftwork centred in the manufacture of those magnificent sewn-plank war canoes. Effective raiding required huge flotillas, with a force of warriors capable of dealing with whole villages.[11] However, raiding and

HOW AN INCREASE OF HEAD-HUNTING AND SLAVE-RAIDING MAINTAINS ITS OWN EQUILIBRIUM

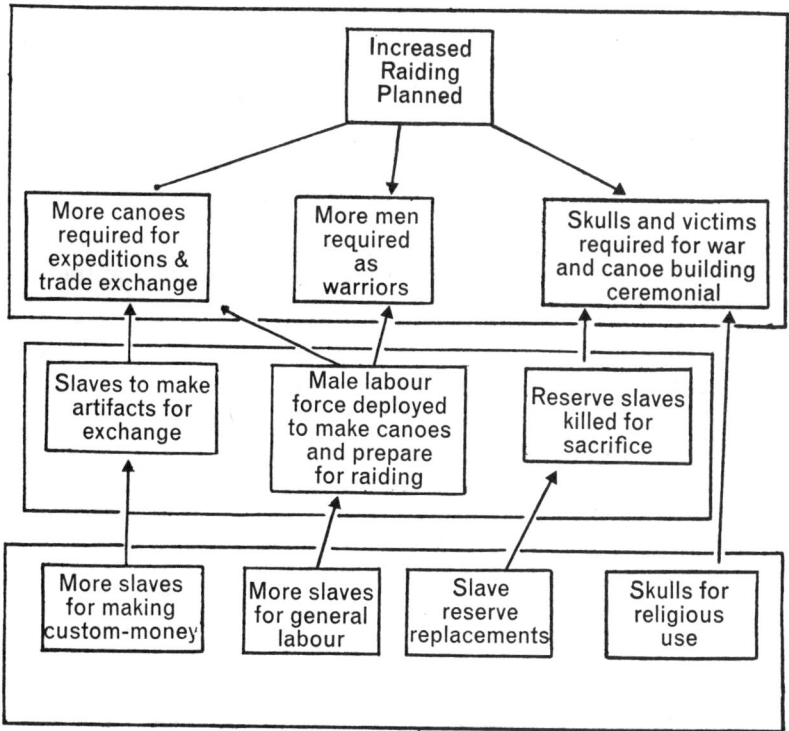

```
                          ┌──────────────┐
                          │  Increased   │
                          │   Raiding    │
                          │   Planned    │
                          └──────────────┘
        ┌──────────────────────┼──────────────────────┐
┌──────────────┐      ┌──────────────┐      ┌──────────────────┐
│ More canoes  │      │   More men   │      │ Skulls and victims│
│ required for │      │  required    │      │ required for war  │
│ expeditions &│      │     as       │      │ and canoe building│
│trade exchange│      │   warriors   │      │   ceremonial      │
└──────────────┘      └──────────────┘      └──────────────────┘

┌──────────────┐      ┌──────────────┐      ┌──────────────────┐
│Slaves to make│      │ Male labour  │      │  Reserve slaves  │
│ artifacts for│      │force deployed│      │   killed for     │
│   exchange   │      │to make canoes│      │   sacrifice      │
│              │      │ and prepare  │      │                  │
│              │      │  for raiding │      │                  │
└──────────────┘      └──────────────┘      └──────────────────┘

┌──────────────┐ ┌──────────────┐ ┌──────────────┐ ┌──────────────┐
│ More slaves  │ │ More slaves  │ │    Slave     │ │  Skulls for  │
│ for making   │ │ for general  │ │   reserve    │ │  religious   │
│custom-money  │ │   labour     │ │replacements  │ │    use       │
└──────────────┘ └──────────────┘ └──────────────┘ └──────────────┘
```

canoe-building accounted for so great a percentage of Roviana time and labour that it was imperative other economic connections be established. Roviana was by no means self-sufficient. The same applied to Simbo. In this way there evolved a system of symbiotic relationships between Roviana and a number of communities of little political consequence. Trade with Roviana gave them some recognition, but more important it freed them from the danger of head-hunting and enslavement.

Although Roviana engaged in plunder and raiding in Choiseul (and one informant told me of 200 taken there in one raid) there were localities where the Roviana people went for trade—for gold-lipped shells, pigs, *ngali* nuts and turtles. Sometimes they exchanged canoes. Roviana also sought certain ornaments from Choiseul. These were not coastal productions, so that Choiseul trade networks were involved. Some of the Roviana symbiotic trade was with New Georgia communities— shell ornaments from the island of Bili, basket shields from Pondokono (which held a monopoly of this), black dye from the head of the Omba

River, which shows Roviana also had inland contacts, to mention a few. Other items, like the red and yellow plaited work on combs, spears and other artifacts, though common in Roviana, were not of New Georgia manufacture.[12]

The inclusion of *ngali* nuts in the above list raises the matter of trade in food. Roviana acquired further supplies from Simbo via Wanawana.[13] They were a highly desirable exchange commodity. Simbo, however, had to supplement her food supplies with *taro* which she needed for her ceremonial feasting patterns.[14]

Like Roviana, Simbo needed a regular supply of artifacts, especially weapons. She obtained her war bows from Alu, her wicker-work shields from Kusage, via Roviana, and her reed shields and turtles from Choiseul. Later on when head-hunting was prohibited by the Government, Simbo tried to maintain her slavery configuration by trading for slaves with Choiseul.[15]

Although Roviana had to maintain these trade connections, the slave community was organized to serve as a corrective to her economic vulnerability. A good deal of craftwork and the manufacture of domestic artifacts was assigned to the slaves. Any surplus they produced was disposed of in the trade exchanges. It might even be used in the purchase of more slaves from some friendly chief who had been recently successful in his own raiding. But the most important of all the slave productions at Roviana was shell-money, which had a universal exchange demand and value. This task was delegated to slaves from Ysabel and Choiseul. They also manufactured the highly ornamental clam-shell symbols worn by the Roviana chiefs, a craft which has vanished since the coming of Christianity. Every Roviana village had its strangers' house, where the war canoe was kept and communal gatherings were held. In times of peace it was here that the Choiseul and Ysabel slaves were employed in making money and shell products.

The prospects for a female slave varied. On the one hand, there were the grim possibilities of being accused of sorcery because of the death of some person in the village, or being killed as a sacrifice, or being used by the male population for the satisfaction of their sex instincts; but, on the other hand, there was the possibility of being chosen by a master as his wife, or being sold by him to some other man for this purpose. In such a case she had good hope of escaping a sacrificial death as long as she was faithful and obedient.[16]

To turn from the socio-economic to the religious aspect of slavery, slaves were held, as we have seen, against the requirement of human sacrifice. Death might come without warning at any moment. Sometimes a body was required, or a skull, or a live sacrifice. Some of these ceremonial deaths were extremely gruesome—live sacrifices buried in post-holes of sacred houses, launching of great canoes over the bodies of human beings, to mention two.[17] In all these things ceremonial requirements had to be met.[18] Skulls were required for sacred places and taboo houses, for funerary rites, for atonements and for retaliation in feuds. Certain types of accident demanded human sacrifice to correct the misfortune.[19]

As we have already seen, behind all sacrifices was the concept of ghost worship. The ancestor had to be satisfied, in order that atonements and restitutions should be effective. For sacred houses and war canoes to be effective the sacrifices had to be adequate. The more blood spilt, the more potent the offering. This was the grim reality confronting every slave, no matter how he might have won his way into the affections of his master. His best security was to be an industrious and skilled technician.

The other religious feature of head-hunting was the acquisition of *mana*. Heads, as we have already seen, were repositories of *mana*. The number of heads held, said Penny, were "the measure of a chief's power".[20] We have also seen that any conversion required some practical demonstration such as the burial of one's accumulation of skulls. Wherever I went in Malaita, when looking at the burial grounds I was always shown the tomb without a cross where the pre-Christian skulls were buried.

Human sacrifice and skull collection represented two forms of heathen worship, two different approaches to the ghosts. The interinvolvements were so complex and the slave's fortunes were so uncertain, that his competence as a craftsman might save him one day to decorate a new war-canoe, and the launching of the canoe claim him as a sacrifice on the next, or perhaps claim his head to adorn the canoe house. He may have been the son of a chief back in Choiseul or Ysabel, or he may have been bought by means of shell-money made by other slaves from among his own kinsmen. By such patterns the ghosts of Roviana preserved prestige, solidarity and superiority for the living members of the tribe and kept the lesser people in subjection. Then the white man came.

CHANGES BROUGHT BY THE WHITE MAN

White men entered the scene seeking bêche-de-mer and sandalwood, and later kidnapping islanders. They bought what they required with tomahawk heads, arms and ammunition. They found it most satisfactory to establish their trade connections through the regional chiefs who controlled the slaving circuits. Thus quite often these chiefs had to open new exchange contacts of their own to acquire stocks of material for the white trader, otherwise the tomahawks and arms would have fallen into the hands of lesser men. Thus the head-hunters of Simbo had to procure supplies of bêche-de-mer, ginger and sandalwood from New Georgia for the white traders or lose the trade in arms.[21] The same pattern was reported from Buin.[22] Alu and Mono obtained smoke-dried copra from Siwai to supply to white traders for calico, axes and adzes [23] It is interesting to note that this new trade, which developed after 1880, followed the lines of the earlier trade in slaves. Alu and Mono obtained men and women captured by Siwai people to serve as working slaves, prostitutes and sacrifices.

Even after controls were established to restrict the trade in arms, they were circumvented by showing arms on the ships' manifests as axes.[24] Under the influence of this trade the character of raiding changed. Men could be killed from under cover and from a safe distance and heads were easier to obtain. With the increase of firearms the manufac-

ture of island weapons began to decline and some of the symbiotic contacts became dispensable. Hitherto protected localities were now exposed
to raiding, and some of these places near to Roviana were completely
depopulated when symbiosis was no longer required by Roviana and
Simbo. Wanawana, Kiso, Tetipari and much of Kolobagara and
Marova were laid waste by the headhunters of Roviana, Simbo and
Redova. Some eastern head-hunters had penetrated into the mountains
of Vangunu with the aid of western arms, and the slaves exported from
Siwai to the Shortlands were increasing in great numbers. The emerging
master tribes were achieving their prowess by means of western arms.

In 1891 Commander Davis of H.M.S. *Royalist* sacked and burned
Roviana and destroyed the accumulation of skulls. As a result Ingava
spent the next decade replenishing his stock. He exhausted his regular
slaving grounds and launched a large-scale invasion on Ysabel. He used
two English-built boats, hunted with 500 men, between 300 and 400 of
whom had rifles, and 9,000 rounds of ammunition. The fruit of this
expedition was seen by the writer of my primary source—rows and
rows of skulls, newly decorated and stacked round the leading canoe
of the expedition.[25] The Captain of the *Royalist* not only failed in his
purpose but stimulated an increase of the very thing he sought to
correct.

This type of punitive action only made things more dangerous for
the honest trader and missionary. Skulls of white men were very much
in demand. Over sixty were obtained in Roviana within a few years of
the arrival of the missionaries.[26] In discussing *mana* I have already
shown the *mana* scale of skulls that emerged in this period: a pig, a
woman, a man, a warrior, a chief, a white man.[27] Thus was the white
man himself incorporated into the structure of the configuration. It
also explains why certain traders were able to exert so obstructive an
influence against the Missions.

EFFECT OF THE SUPPRESSION OF HEAD-HUNTING BY THE
ADMINISTRATION

The pattern of punitive action employed by the naval commanders
was continued by the Administration after the establishment of the
Protectorate. Periodically a naval vessel visited the islands and accounts
were 'settled'. The abolition of the institution of head-hunting was
effected by Government decree because it offended the ideals of civilized
people. Traders, planters, officials and missionaries alike were glad
enough to see it go for humane and social reasons. Having said that,
however, one must add that it left a *void* in life because of the countless
social, economic and religious involvements that were disorganized by
its prohibition.

The anthropologist, Rivers, related the depopulation of the area to
the termination of head-hunting, because it led to a *loss of interest in life*.
In a careful analysis of this he took specific cases of head-hunting to
illustrate his argument. Dealing with the factors influencing the death
and birth rates at Simbo, where he worked out a number of genealogies
over three generations, he found a decreasing number of marriages, a

decreasing birth-rate, a smaller number of children per marriage and an increase of childless marriages, as well as an increasing death-rate. Tabulating his statistics, he compared them with another Solomon Island locality with somewhat similar general characteristics. In these localities the usually admitted reasons for depopulation were absent. There were no severe epidemics, no white residents, no missionaries, no changes of native dress or structural changes in dwelling-houses, alcohol was hardly known, and there had been no kidnapping or exodus of labour force for indenture.[28]

Rivers attributed their dying out to this psychological factor, the loss of interest or zest in life. He argued that the basic cause was the suppression of head-hunting, because the whole pattern of organized life surrounded this. The Simbo and Roviana patterns were very similar. The sacrificial system, acquisition of *mana*, serving the ancestral ghosts, the ceremonials of house-building, a whole year's activities round the building of war-canoes, feasts, trade exchanges, funerary rites and many craft activities were all involved. Although head-hunting expeditions lasted only a few weeks, with but a few hours of actual fighting, these were the culmination of a long period of communal activity. The canoes for the expedition had to be new and involved elaborate labour and craft organization and a series of ceremonial feasts, which as social occasions with specific patterns stimulated horticulture, pig-breeding and the acquisition of important food through trade circuits and travel. So the abolition of head-hunting also meant the abolition of a great many social functions, economic activities and the disappearance of various crafts. These were social, religious and ceremonial, and did represent a great deal of interest in life.[29]

There is a good deal to be said for the case presented by Rivers. All these multitudinous activities were undoubtedly tied together in a configuration, and the loss of the central feature did cause disintegration of the way of life. Undoubtedly this left what I have elsewhere called a *void*. The problem of the void arises when reformers—administrators, missionaries, teachers, doctors or agriculturalists—remove or prohibit cultural institutions without considering the total context. Of course, head-hunting had to go. The problem was how to dispose of a bad custom without injuring the whole structure of labour, craftwork, horticulture, animal husbandry and trade, together with their communal values and social occasions.

From this point Rivers became more theoretical, and considered the *functional substitutes* (as they are now called) that might have been tried to provide motives for the manufacture of new canoes, craft industry and festival occasions. It is true, of course, that the construction of the splendid sewn-plank canoes did die out with head-hunting. He imagined a pattern of canoe racing linked with ceremonial, fishing and trade. He was aware that the European boat might replace the island canoe, and hoped that indigenous craftsmanship and labour could be attached to this trade. The essential thing was for changes to grow naturally out of native institutions and to maintain interest.[30] In this his reasoning was good. Among the ex-Roviana people now living at Rarumana on the island of Wanawana, this is what has happened by the initiative of the people themselves. Canoe-building, though greatly modified, has survived. The canoes are smaller domestic craft, dugouts not plank-sewn, but suitable to the new needs of the community. I counted seventy canoes in this spread-out village. Every household has one or more. Six households had outboard motors for use with them. The craft were built locally with tools structured as of old (i.e. adzes) but with plane blades replacing the stone heads. Local labour was used and was often available for hire. The modifications fitted the social changes of the area. Gizo has developed as a trading centre twenty miles off. Copra and other produce may be sold there for cash and trade goods bought. The small canoe with the outboard motor meets this requirement. In this village family individualism has replaced the extensive communal activity and trade exchanges. There is still an interest in life, though it has shifted from the community to the family. The modifications have come of their own accord from within the situation itself.

It may be difficult at first to see individuals making small domestic dugout canoes as a functional substitute for the communally organized production of a magnificent sewn-plank war-canoe. Yet it may be claimed to be so because it keeps alive many of the same elements— a round of craftwork, the building of canoes that facilitate the exchange of goods, planned labour with some ceremonial affiliations—and above all it retains an interest in life and gives some satisfaction for its creativity. The foreign innovations—outboard motor, plane-blade adze, trade-goods from the store—are not impositions but have been naturally incorporated into the pattern. All is within the range of practicability and meets the needs of the new situation. In this community the current tendency is for communal activity to give way to family activity. It is therefore natural for the communal ownership of two or three large canoes to give way to the private ownership of seventy. It shows that change need not necessarily upset satisfactions and create voids. Even a major cultural institution like head-hunting can be discarded without leaving a void. This can be so, as Rarumana shows, but unfortunately this is by no means typical. Furthermore the head-hunting configuration was so complex that it was possible to meet the economic needs and yet leave voids on the religious level. We shall return to this when we deal with the Western Solomons Schism.

ROVIANA COLONIZING

Any study of these political outreaches of Roviana in the other islands of the Solomons would be incomplete without reference to her colonizing. To examine this we shall take the case of colonizing in Buin, because this has been carefully investigated and recorded by an anthropologist who visited the area twice and was able to observe the changes that took place in the interim. We are also interested in Buin because of its proximity to another strong trade and slaving circuit centred in the Shortlands. It says something for Roviana military strength and prestige that it could establish this colony 160 miles from home.

Connections between Roviana and Buin were social, economic and political. They involved head-hunting and slaving, the Roviana shell-money trade and colonization mechanisms.

The tall black element in the Buin racial stratification can be traced to Roviana, whose pirate head-hunters settled in this area, taking local women for wives like the Spanish in Latin America, and introduced many cultural features quite different from those of the aboriginal people. Those colonizers who married local women of rank became the aristocrats of Buin society. They were spoken of as *mumira* with awe. Others married the daughters of bondsmen and were known as *minei*. They retained some status by claiming succession by patrilineal descent and also because their capacity for trade made them rich. The bondsmen were known as *kitere*. This stratification was quite stable when the white man arrived, and it was still so when Thurnwald made his first observations in 1908.[31]

Roviana influence was evident in many features of the life of this colony, especially in their ceremonial feasting and its excesses, in the head-hunting patterns and the slave raiding and trading, and in the ritual of sacrificing to ghosts. Much of this is reflected in the secular songs of the period.[32] One chief might sell a bondsman to another for 100 fathoms of ordinary shell-money, knowing that he made a worthy sacrifice. The victim would be killed after the Roviana manner, so that his head might adorn the chief's house. The ghosts of these victims were said to be ghost slaves, to serve the chief's personal war-demon.[33] The personal war-demon (as distinct from the ghost of one's ancestor) is a Bougainville concept; so we see here a capacity for syncretism before the coming of the white man.

Among the more valuable trade brought into Buin from Roviana through this colony was that in precious necklaces (*mimici*) made of red *spondylus* shell. The shell was dived for, and the necklaces manufactured by the slave community at Roviana. The value was much higher in Buin than at Roviana, one fathom being worth twenty fathoms of ordinary shell-money. These items were not used for ordinary trade or passed about in light flirtations but were reserved for marriage patterns.[34] Even ordinary shell-money was of economic importance in Buin, especially as exchange for pigs, which were required for feasts, which in turn were essential for the maintenance of prestige. In Buin one could enjoy the luxuries of life if he could exchange one form of wealth for another—shell-money for pigs, for example.[35]

When the anthropologist returned to the area twenty-five years later he found that the Administration had effected major interferences in the status pattern. A new class of chief (*kukurai*) had appeared, appointed by the Government, on the basis of supposed merit, usually from the *minei*, but some even from the *kitere*. The old hamlets where the people dwelt before had been replaced largely by 'lines', to simplify tax collection. This had been destructive to social taboos and made it possible for the *kitere* to look on the wife and daughter of the *mumira*. Head-hunting had been suppressed, ceremonial feasting had ceased as the aristocracy no longer had incentive to provide it—the 'spice' had gone out of life in many ways. In 1920 some police 'boys' had been sent in to enforce the new patterns and had been killed by the aristocrats for their interference with the established way of life. The Administration executed some of the aristocrats and those who remained saw the futility of resisting the white man.

This social upheaval terminated the old head-hunting and slaving patterns and the rule of the Roviana aristocracy, and set an international political barrier between Roviana and Buin. It also permitted the rise of a new class comprising any who could exploit the situation. It was a time propitious for innovation. The mental set of the people changed. Thurnwald detected the changes in the popular songs he collected at the time—a shift from the wonders of nature, life, men and women, to the miracles of the white man's devices and an accompanying disbelief in the old way, which now became criminal.[36]

Although their tendency was now to follow the white man's way and seek his prosperity, even by using *imitative magic* to this end, this new mental set provided a readiness at least to hear the message the missionaries brought. The Church became one means of access to the white man's devices. Doors for evangelism opened.

EFFECT ON THE PLANTING AND GROWTH OF THE CHURCH

Social factors within the head-hunting and slavery configuration influenced the character of the conversion growth of the Church at several points, both aiding and obstructing it.

1. As inhuman and unchristian customs, the missionaries were opposed to both head-hunting and slavery. This put the chiefs, priests and warriors against them. We have already seen that the doors were not open in the Western Solomons when the Mission began work there. The Methodists selected Roviana deliberately and the Anglican bishop was surprised at the selection. The missionaries set out to undermine these customs and their supporting religion. All this was against the likelihood of conversions. The place was not interested in the gospel. The missionary faith was in terms of the challenge of the greatest needs, not the existence of open doors. Their motive was high. Their courage was great. Their faith was strong. But their strategy is to be questioned.

It is to be questioned, in that the field was far from ripe unto harvest. They were correct in the assumption that Roviana was the key to a larger area—although Roviana was not loved over that area. Socially and religiously Roviana was a dominant influence over the whole of the Western Solomons, where the ghost worship and skull cults were remarkably similar.

2. Roviana was the key to a wide area because of the head-hunting and slavery configuration. Her men were good navigators and knew their way about the islands. Having enslaved folk from all parts, they had some familiarity with many dialects and customs. Because of their symbiotic trade connections they had friendly contacts with many remote places, and ways and means of communicating. In their slave community they had many bilingual people who were available for service as interpreters. Many of the Roviana people were themselves

bilingual. Roviana was certainly a key for communication. Even so, capacity to communicate does not necessarily mean acceptance. The widespread fear of Roviana was against their becoming good advocates for the new religion.

3. We have already seen that people-movements within the kin structure were slow in coming. Even after the chiefs had become resigned to the presence of the missionaries in their land, and had become superficially friendly, the regular patterns of Melanesian conversion were still slow in coming. The story is vastly different from that of Ysabel and Florida twenty years earlier. We have seen that when the conversions began to come in Roviana and the islands under Roviana influence, they were of sodalities on the mission compounds, of persons separated from the village structure, whose conversion well-nigh wrecked the whole Christian enterprise because of the offence it gave to the tribal elders. Though these converts rendered great service thereafter, we have seen that a large percentage of them were detribalized persons, orphans, refugees and slaves. This fact undoubtedly influenced the slave community at Roviana, though it slowed down the conversion of kin groups. There were no people-movements among the slaves, because they had no family or lineage cohesion, and furthermore conversion of a village slave was a quick way of asking to be selected for the next sacrifice.

4. However once Roviana did become Christian, the slave community immediately became a significant group for the wide communication of Christianity. Many converts returned to their own localities after manumission. Their very deliverance was itself a remarkable tale to tell.

5. With the breakdown of the authority of the Roviana aristocracy in Buin, and the general readiness there to experiment in the new ways of the white man, the Church had her opportunity. Methodist influence certainly spread in South Bougainville during this period. The first enquiries from the area led to an inspection by an island teacher and preaching began there in 1917. There were some young men from this area among the converts at Roviana, so the Mission was able to pioneer the place with its own people. They were mostly *kitere*, but the decline of the aristocrats and the rise of men of merit, regardless of status, provided an opening. One of these men pioneered church planting in twenty villages, and by 1933 almost three thousand people were at Methodist worship regularly, and education was being provided at forty-four day schools staffed by men trained at Roviana. Although the Roviana aristocracy had lost its status in Buin, the Roviana–Buin connections still provided both the men and the opportunities for planting the Church.

6. One question remains to be asked and answered. How do we account for the fact that slaves were able to introduce a new religion into animistic society, especially a dominant society with a head-hunting configuration? How were they able to act as individuals? When this angered the elders, how were they able to escape with their lives? This is really one question, which I shall try to answer from the case of Simbo, since it can be documented well.

In such areas the chiefs and elders were disposed to leave much of the specifically religious activity to selected slaves, because it saved them from the risk of breaking taboos. A slave who showed signs of magical or religious capacity was more likely to be assigned to magical responsibilities than to be used as a sacrificial victim. Both Munda and Simbo were centres for the distribution of incantations, charms and other magical devices. Ysabel charms and medicines were in great demand and also divination processes. When Hocart recorded a medicine he appended a note on its origin and purchase price, thus:—

Suna of Karivara taught Nina a headache prayer for a fee of four arm-rings.

Njukili paid Matemata of Ranonga one large ring and one arm-ring for the treatment and prayer to cure a stomach complaint, *tagosoro*.

Taravai bought a Vella Lavella cure for this same complaint for one arm-ring.[37]

Panda paid twelve rings for a war-charm.[38]

This desirable market was not without considerable risk and it suited the elders to keep suitable slaves to take these risks and to treat them well. The capture of slaves from a Christianized area would, to the animist head-hunters, present possibilities in this direction. The elders would proceed at least with caution, and would regard any Christian worship patterns with respect. Christian hymns were treated as *mana* repositories.

In his study of the Cult of the Dead at Simbo, Hocart discussed the role of the mortuary priests of the skull-houses. They built and consecrated these structures on behalf of the chiefs. Although the mortuary priest belonged to the chief, the latter was very much dependent on the priest, whose post was remunerative. Of the four principal mortuaries in Simbo at the time, it is noteworthy that three were tended by foreigners. Nubui and Soge at Narovo, and Lepo at Karivara were men of Ysabel, and Rona at Ove was a native of Vella Lavella. Pero and Maro, famous Simbo magic-men, were both Ysabel slaves. This shows how captive slaves who demonstrated religious propensity could establish themselves as individuals. These men brought *mana* and magical methods from Ysabel and Vella Lavella. If they did anything wrong in their rituals, they themselves ran the risk rather than the elders. To escape the dangers of foreign magic the elders were prepared to grant them status and wealth. At the same time they hoped to draw benefit from the magic. The mortuary priest wore a special protective girdle, handled the taboo skulls and other taboo paraphernalia. Any ordinary slave with knowledge of magical formulae could market these at Simbo and thereby derive enough respect to ensure his own survival. Pepele of Ysabel established himself thus and it was from him that the Simbo magic-man, Erovo, learned his arts.[39]

This readiness for cultural borrowing and innovation within the dimension of Roviana-Simbo magico-religion, the respect for religious foreigners, and the tendency to assign roles of religious risk to slaves, enabled the Christians to escape from the wrath of the elders and warriors. Because one more deity might even bring more *mana* to the community, which was polytheistic in any case, it was possible for individual Christians to worship and survive the period of persecution. It was Christian exclusiveness and the rejection of traditional religion which involved them in the greatest danger. But even then as religious persons they were treated with some respect. It is clear that the slaving patterns did contribute towards the eventual spread of Christianity. Unfortunately we have no way of measuring the influence of the Christian slaves, of whom there were a great many from Ysabel.

CHAPTER 11

How Village Structure Reflects Christian Patterns

MANY OF the coastal villages of the Solomon Islands have come into existence in Christian times. They have evolved over a period of time and lack evidence of serious planning. Missionaries who preferred to do their itinerations by boat sometimes persuaded mountain folk to come to the coast to settle. Evangelization tended to follow the coasts and this is why many pagan pockets remain in the mountains. Quite often the structure of a village tells its own story and illustrates some peculiarity of local behaviour patterns. In post-war times, villages have sprung into being along army roads and on the old camp sites of the war. Much army equipment is evident in some of the un-Melanesian constructions which have emerged. The town of Honiara and the labour settlements of its environs show army designs and material built into its very structure, quite apart from the wreckage of ships, planes and tanks around Iron Bottom Sound (so called because of the ships sunk there during the war). The war and its impact is a key to many features of that town.

But there is always something for a careful observer to learn from a village structure. I purpose taking three quite different villages of which I have personal knowledge as short case studies for this chapter. They differ in character, and have emerged from different causative factors, two of them in Christian times and the third greatly modified in Christian times. Their respective structures reflect psychological and religious factors in the different situations. At the same time the range of difference made apparent by the comparison should warn us against speaking of any village as typical.

THE VILLAGE OF RARUMANA
ISLAND OF WANAWANA (NEW GEORGIA GROUP)

Rarumana, with a population of about 200 people, is the largest village in Wanawana. It sprawls out along a narrow strip of land for a mile or so between the coastal hills and the beach, but the habitations are not continuous. They form a chain of residential segments separated by patches of forest or coconut plantations, and linked by a well-made and beautifully kept path. Each residential segment is known as a *vasina* and comprises a cluster of houses, homes of nuclear families, so that the total cluster often represents an extended family. There are about thirty independent households (*tatamana*) distributed over nine *vasina*, named on the accompanying sketch-map. The whole village community comprises the larger part of a lineage, the remainder of which is on the island of Nusa Roviana, the original home whence these Rarumana people migrated.

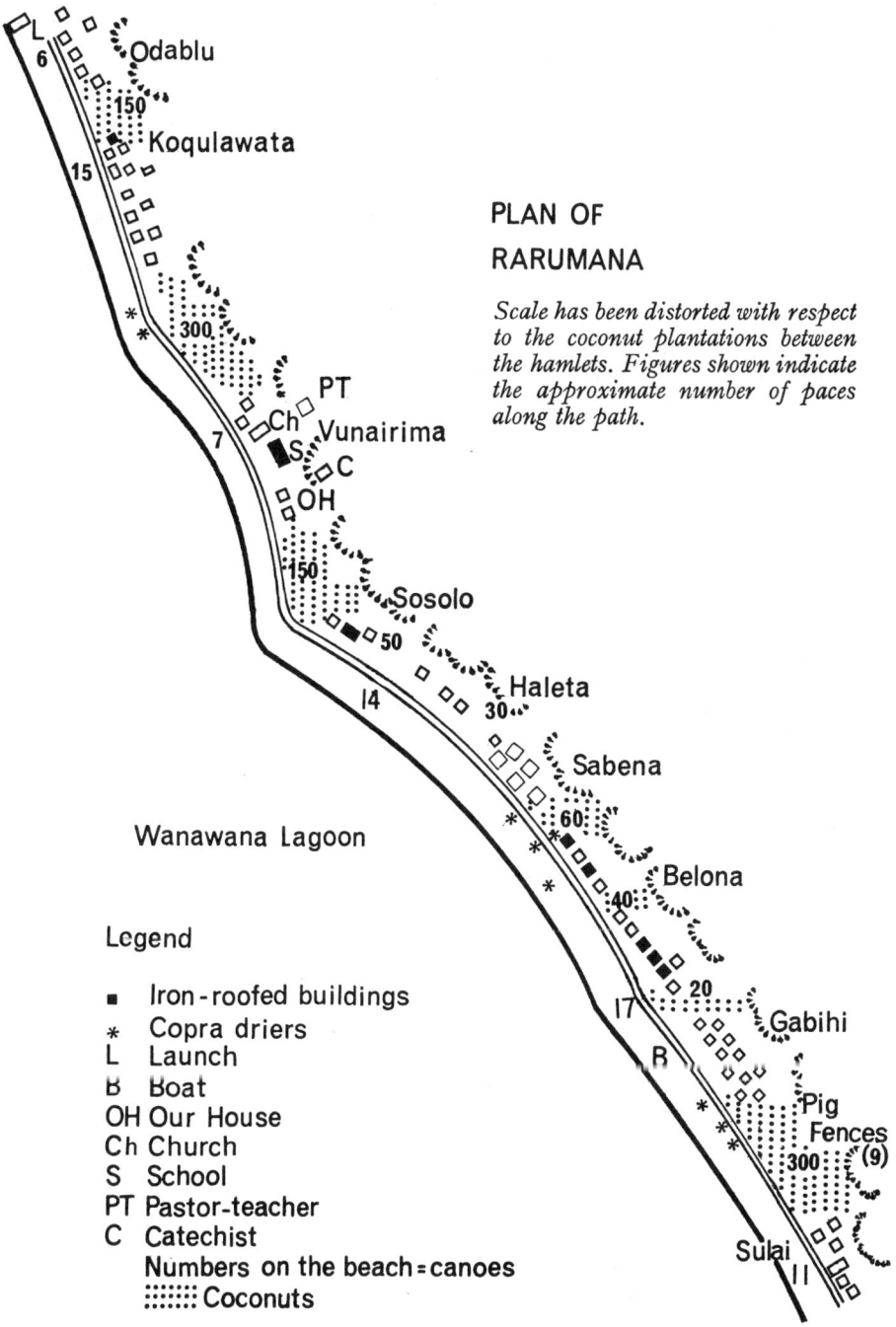

L
6
Odablu
150
15
Koqulawata
300
PT
7
Ch
S Vunairima
C
OH

PLAN OF
RARUMANA

Scale has been distorted with respect to the coconut plantations between the hamlets. Figures shown indicate the approximate number of paces along the path.

150
Sosolo
50
14
30 Haleta
Sabena
60
Wanawana Lagoon
Belona
40
20
Legend
17
Gabihi
■ Iron-roofed buildings
B
* Copra driers
L Launch
Pig
B Boat
Fences
OH Our House
300
(9)
Ch Church
S School
PT Pastor-teacher
C Catechist
Sulai
Numbers on the beach = canoes
11
:::::: Coconuts

The *vasina*, Vunairima, is the communal place where the catechist and the pastor-teacher live and the school and the church are situated. There also is the open space where town meetings are held and where most of the communal projects are carried out. Medical inspections, marketing cocoa, local elections, children's sport, women's gatherings and public working bees are held here. As our house was at this *vasina*, we were in a good position to observe all communal activities. The catechist and pastor-teacher lived on the hill-side. Our house and that of our neighbour were by the school near the water-front.

Beyond the coastal hills, a little inland, were the extensive gardens of each family and one communal garden run by the women's group for church purposes.

This structure reflects the character of the village itself, which operates on a delicate balance between communalism and individualism. Sosolo and Haleta were the first sites occupied in 1916, when Sasa, the oldest inhabitant, came from Nusa-Roviana and established his individual home with his wife and family. Then Koqulawata was established, sufficiently distant to allow for the central communal *vasina*, though at this time this was still part of the land claimed by Sasa. Subsequent growth has extended along the coast in each direction as the topography of the land has permitted. Clearing the coastal forest must have been back-breaking work and the whole village is a model of industry.

The various *vasina* rival each other for progress and tidiness. The sketch-map shows the distribution of copra driers which are individually owned by the domestic segments. Most of the segments have one or more houses with an iron roof—which means a water catchment. I counted seventy canoes, fairly evenly distributed and privately owned, a launch, a boat, and six outboard motors. Three canoes were being built while we were there. The pigs were correctly fenced in one part of the forest well away from human habitation. The gardens, like the *vasina*, were individually worked by the domestic units and each marketed its own copra and cocoa. No individual unit had enough cocoa to warrant the building of a private drier and therefore the community had decided to build a communal one, this being the more economic policy.

This is a good example of how a village structure can reflect character. Nor are we surprised to find that problems in the church life at Rarumana often tend to arise from the balance of the communal sense and individual interests. At present there is a clear drift from corporate responsibility towards personal interests. Yet both are recognized. About 50 per cent of the available adult male labour force would turn out for all communal duties. The church and school are focal points for the group solidarity, but an increasing drift from marginality to nominality in church loyalty is reflected in the drift of the social segments towards individualism.

In a later chapter an attempt will be made to measure the piety of the congregation of this village, and the 'struggle' between individual interests and group responsibility will be manifest. The physical structure of the village and the spiritual structure of its congregation seem to reflect each other. It also explains how a few strong individuals were able to keep the cult of Etoism out of Rarumana. Affairs in the village, the school and the church are largely controlled by the same small group of progressive individuals from the various segments. The pastor has a strong voice but he has to carry this group of individuals before he can make any innovations. In reality the people are the policy makers. In one sense this is good, but it can be frustrating to a pastor who desires to make reforms in the congregational patterns and practices.

THE VILLAGE OF FOUIA
TAI LAGOON, ISLAND OF MALAITA

By way of complete contrast the village of Fouia stretches along a headland between a bay and a tidal creek, rising from the sea (where the first houses are built over the water) up to a height of perhaps a hundred feet. The houses are cramped along both sides of a rough and poorly cared-for path that ascends to the top of the ridge where the path and houses improve a little.

Partway up the ascent is the Church of St John the Baptist, the centre and focal point of the village. Although at first sight the houses are so close together and arranged without apparent planning, there are nevertheless two clear structural segments among this community of about 140 residents. Those living between the water-front and the church are salt-water people. Those living above the church are the bush people. It is below the church, for instance, that one will see men making fishing nets and find most of the canoe owners. All the leading people of the church life and village affairs are salt-water people and related.

In pre-Christian times the salt-water and bush people were enemies, even though they met for trade exchange and had some other trade connections. The former had built the artificial islands largely as a defence from raiding bushmen. Half a dozen of these islands can be seen from Fouia. The first salt-water people to receive the gospel found the persecution on their islands so difficult that they left and established themselves on the mainland. In the same way a few bush people with whom they had marriage connections and also leanings towards Christianity came and joined them. It was natural for the salt-water folk to cling to the shore and the bush people to build on the higher ground. It was natural for the church, which was both their meeting place and the factor which brought them together, to be centrally placed between them.

Although the village is not nearly as clean or progressive as Rarumana, the Church is the biggest thing in Fouia life. Everything revolves about it. Folk are diligent in prayer. The choir may practise three times a week. Holy Communion is regular and well attended. The school, on the other hand, is on the fringe of the community and poorly supported. It serves other villages as well as Fouia and is supposed to have eighty children, only a small percentage of those eligible. When I visited the school, there was nothing like this number present—I counted fifty-

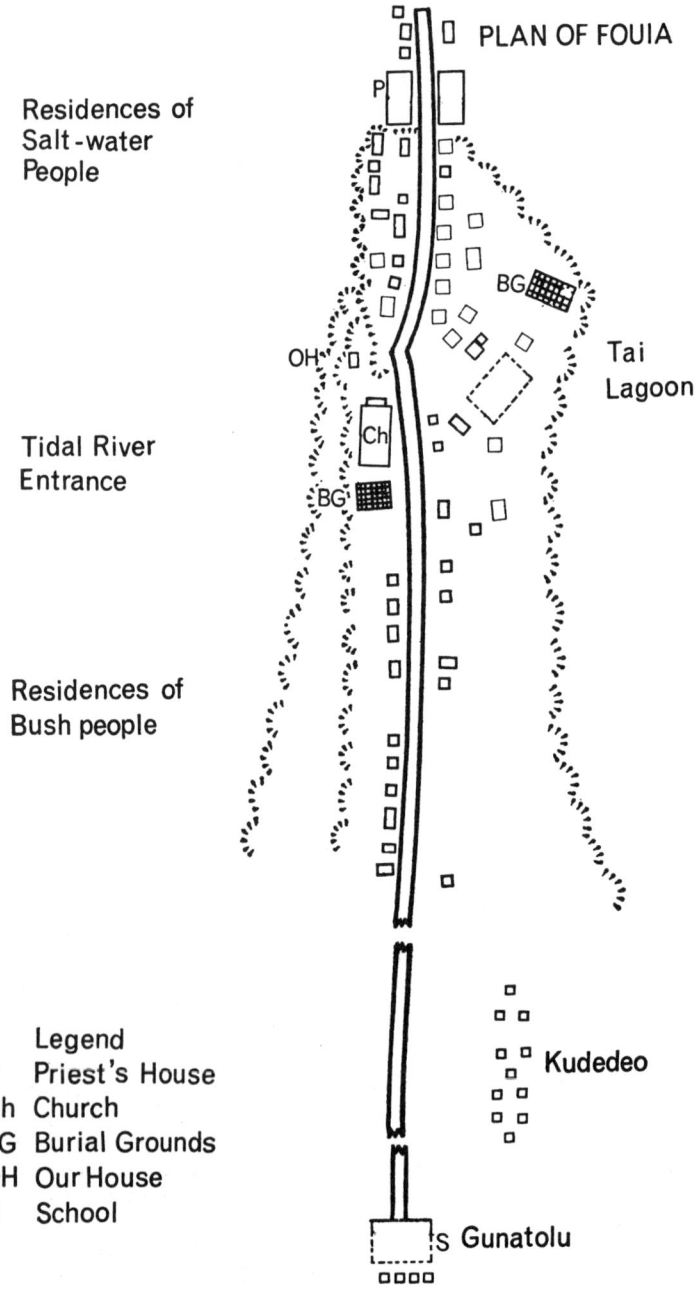

PLAN OF FOUIA

Residences of
Salt-water
People

Tai
Lagoon

OH

Tidal River
Entrance

BG

Residences of
Bush people

Legend
P   Priest's House
Ch   Church
BG   Burial Grounds
OH   Our House
S   School

Kudedeo

S Gunatolu

three. Many of the children who should have been present played in the village. With parents and children, education was only a fringe interest. This was all in direct contrast with Rarumana, where the school was centrally placed both in village thinking and in the physical structure.

Although the Fouia people were ready to turn anything at all into cash, they had very few true economic insights. They were not interested in planting coconuts or cocoa because so long a time would have to pass before income could be derived from the venture. They preferred to go away and labour for ready cash—which they soon used. Although each man built his own house and cared for his own garden as an individual, few had long-range vision. The houses clung closely together without much pattern. No one showed any pride in his property. Most of the houses were dirty and in need of repair. I was astonished at the way in which the people drank coconuts at any hour of the day or night and ate their planting nuts, when they so badly needed a constructive planting programme. So they lived from day to day, making the best of what was at hand, and getting a cash return if possible. They made no coconut oil and took little care of their bodies, which were badly infected with ringworm and other skin complaints. Their personal habits were irregular. They observed no really regular times for meals. What was once a well-built hospital was out in the forest, beyond the school, the football field, the river bathing place, near the village burial ground beside what was once the local taboo place. The hospital was no longer used. It had fallen into a sad state of disrepair. The bottles of medicine were still stacked there as if forgotten. The building probably belonged to a period when a European lived in the vicinity. There was a dresser resident in the village, to whom the people went freely for plaster for their cuts; but they seemed to be unconcerned about their skin complaints, for which free medicine was available.

The village lacked social organization. Many, who were deeply pious and loyal in religion, were unwilling to pay the five shillings required for educating their child; ready to pray for the officially appointed evangelists but blind to the evangelism needed at their door. I was not surprised to find the Church Association and Village Unions, so strong in the nearby island of Ysabel, poorly supported in Malaita. One Malaita priest put it loyally, "Malaita is weak in organization but strong in faith". Yet anyone who has studied Marching Rule cannot see why Malaita should be weak in organization. However, the priest was right. Nothing constructive is done to organize the village life and hygiene. There is no drainage. Pigs wander about the village at will. A pack of dogs prowls the area at night. One sees children, who should be at school, lounging about and delousing themselves daily—something I never saw once in Rarumana. The question which persistently kept returning to me while I lived in this village was: Has the Church which is so central and deeply valued in the lives of these people nothing to say with respect to their living conditions?

Just before the war one of the great missionary conferences of the

Church did have something to say about this very situation. It claimed
that in places where the Church experienced what were then called
'mass-movements', the converts should be led to see the local responsibility and involvement of the Christian family, with a concern for
health as an outworking of care for others in Christian love. It was
stated that it is not enough for a Mission to supply a health service
from foreign resources—the emerging Church has to see its obligations
for serving within its own community.[1]

I have sketched brief portraits of two Solomon Island Christian
villages, the first basically matrilineal and matrilocal, the second
patrilineal and patrilocal; one progressive in a social sense, the other
static; so different that the reader will understand why I hesitate to
speak of typical villages. Each situation is unique. I have also tried
to show that psychological and religious attitudes are often reflected
in the social structure of a village, especially with respect to the
structural location of church and school buildings. Each of these
villages had its problems. The common point is that each of these
villages had evolved in Christian times and the physical structure might
perhaps be the evidence of the basic attitudes. In both cases the current
problems are of the second generation of Christians, so we are concerned
with quality growth and the application of Christianity in the local
situation. Both these communities have had about sixty years' contact
with Christian missionary effort—long enough for us to be justified in
asking such questions as these. What difference does the profession
of Christianity make to the structure of social life? How does a Church
grow in piety yet neglect the physical well-being of the group?

SULUFOU, A VILLAGE ON AN ARTIFICIAL ISLAND
TAI LAGOON, MALAITA

We now turn to another type of situation, where the people, though
confronted with the Christian challenge for an equally long period,
accepted the gospel only twenty years ago. By way of complete contrast from the other two cases, the physical structure of this village
shows specific planning and architectural achievement. The sketch
plan demonstrates how physical structure is influenced by environ-
mental conditions. This island is entirely man-made and is thought of
as such, being known as *Fera i asi*, not *'Au'au'a* (a natural island).
These *Fera i asi* are built with tremendous effort by transporting
countless loads of coral rock from the reef and building up the foundation, surfacing it with fine coral, gravel and sand until perfectly flat.
The process was used in pre-Christian times by the salt-water people
for defence purposes. As the salt-water people owned all the canoes,
the defence measure was effective. The bush people, on the other hand,
had to fortify their villages with stone walls and keep continual watch.

With the passage of the old war period some island people came to
dwell at different locations on the mainland opposite these islands.
Although this gave them the advantage of garden land and fresh water
for bathing and drinking, the move has not been widely acceptable.
Even since the last war a large part of the village of Ngorifou has

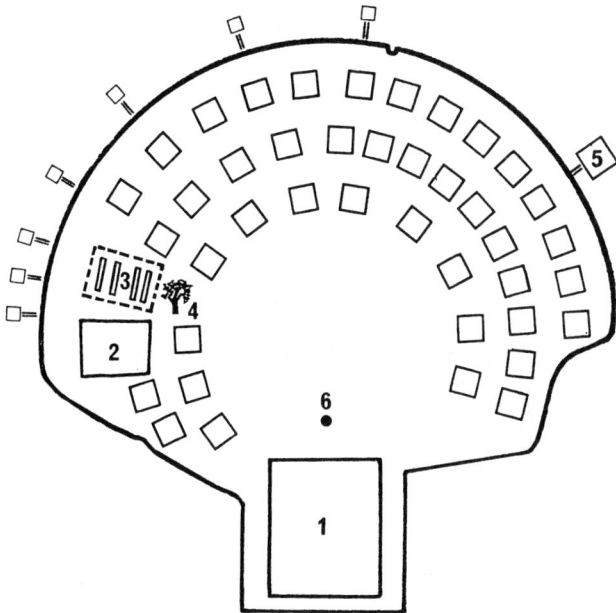

Legend
1 Church
2 Net making House
3 Graves
4 Ancient Tree
5 Single Men's House
6 Flag Pole

PLAN OF SULUFOU

constructed a new artificial island (Ngoleana) and returned to the sea environment. They have to visit the mainland for garden food, and carry their firewood, water and building materials, but they prefer this to the sandflies on the mainland.

The physical effort required for building or enlarging an artificial island sets the value of space at a premium. This is apparent in the sketch-plan which shows how a maximum number of persons is crowded into a small space. Sulufou literally swarms with people. It is probably the most overcrowded area in all the Solomons. Yet the crowding does not destroy the possibility of social life and they have still managed to preserve the central public area, which is absent from many Solomon Island villages. The streets are arranged as crescents and the houses are all double: two families living in an edifice, back to back with front doors at the ends opening on to different streets. One might call them apartment-dwellers. The same element of economizing on space preserves the institution of the young men's house, a large building built out over the water and occupied by the marriageable but unmarried men. The other buildings out over the water are toilets and pig-pens.

Co-operative tasks are performed in the large building, a kind of canoe house. When I visited this place a team of men was engaged in the manufacture of fishing nets and the place was a hive of industry.

The houses are built on, not above the ground, and each has its own fireplace. The women had devised special methods of their own for cooking root foods under cramped conditions. There is probably more original innovation in one artificial island than in all the remainder of the Group. The island had a small store, a tailor, a baker and a radio. In this respect it was more progressive than the villages on the mainland. We ourselves had to send across to this place from Fouia if we wanted bread. Yet, as with all overcrowded areas, the people lived in slum conditions. All I can say is that the Christian islands were less dirty than the pagan, and Sulufou one of the cleaner of the former. In one I saw a pig in the human living quarters.

The village structure of Sulufou after twenty years of Christianity shows the huge church as central. This is the cleanest and most spacious part, and is a real credit to the people. It shows that when they accepted Christ they were ready to make him pre-eminent, and whole-heartedly enlarged their island so that the Lord's 'acre' did not need to suffer from the overcrowding they all felt pressing upon them, and this enlargement was a tremendous demand on their time and labour.

Living so close together, there is a better co-operative spirit here than in the mainland villages. They co-operate to make their nets, the very net itself being an instrument that requires a group to operate. They engage in regular fishing drives. It is team work. We counted forty-two canoes engaged in one of these co-operative projects one day.

The best chapels we saw in Malaita were the buildings on these artificial islands, where every inch of space had to be given at the cost of hours of human labour and effort. In all cases local artists had either painted or inlaid the decorative work of the sanctuary, altar, lectern and baptismal font. Though a westerner might think some of this grotesque, it represents the dedication of the best artistic talent of the island to the glory of God. To these buildings each morning and evening the community retires for prayers every day of their lives. In many of these chapels in the artificial islands I saw offerings of first-fruits before the altar.

The physical structure of Sulufou reflects the character of the people, industrious and co-operative, forced to economize at every point on their own account, but generous in their gift of time, labour and resources to God.

This appraisal is supported by the record of the building of the Sulufou church, a superb example of planned co-operation, based on the same principle of distributed time and service that David used in biblical times for strengthening the defence of Israel. The entire labour force of the island contributed to the project, being divided into relay teams of the most efficient size for handling their equipment. They worked in relays of a week in turn and continued thus until the work was completed. The work involved enlarging the coral rock foundations of the island, constructing rafts for transporting the rock and other building materials, making coral lime, building and furnishing the church, and it continued week after week for eighteen months, by which time every labourer had served quite a number of full weeks. No one suffered from this generosity, for the remainder, who were not in the work team of any given week, farmed out among them the private responsibilities of each man who was thus working for God. They took care of his garden, carted his firewood and water, saw to the preparation of meals, and provided for any other necessities. One would go a long way in this selfish world of today before finding a better example of consecrated co-operation. This is all the more surprising when we remember that about one hundred of the adult male labour force of this island are always away on plantation work or in Honiara.

There is an interesting historical link between the two Tai Lagoon villages of Fouia and Sulufou. Jack Taloifuila, later known as Father Jack, the founder of Fouia, was a Sulufou man. He had contracted under Queensland indentured labour and had been converted in that country. Upon his return, the social solidarity of Sulufou was such that they would have nothing to do with his new religion. A Christian in their midst was a threat to ethnic cohesion and defence security, so Jack had to choose between his home and his new faith. Thus he went to Fouia and established himself as a lone Christian. Yet his new life and witness did have some effect on at least some of his kinsmen, and as time went on others joined him. For forty years Sulufou held out in opposition to the new religion and any who became Christian had to separate themselves from the large island village. Two men, Beni Wako and Robert Suli, moved from their domestic units in Sulufou and took up residence at Fouia. The present salt-water people now at Fouia are related to this Sulufou lineage but they are the descendants of the early group who separated themselves in this way.

The cohesiveness of the main body of Sulufou people has remained throughout. When the time came, after forty years of resistance to Christianity, and they were at last convinced of its truth, they debated the matter at length, made their decision, and acted as a united body. They have been Christians now for twenty years and have in all things demonstrated a remarkable unity, as we have seen in their church building project.

Fouia, on the other hand, was built up of small domestic units, who came from paganism and settled round the dynamic person of Father Jack. Although all the salt-water people of Fouia are of one lineage either through a male or female line, there were also bush people who joined Father Jack in the same way and with the same motives. As we have seen, they settled on the upper side of the church so that the two types of people remain as discrete units in the structure of the village. These bush people came from Angia and Aina'alu, both of the

Baigu district. They came out from their social cohesive units and sought the protection of Father Jack's growing community.[2]

The church building stood between the two different kinds of people, a symbol of the new faith which made them one. But these bush people had no bargaining power. Cut off from their fortified villages they were glad of any protection available. They retain their elders to this day as distinct from the salt-water elders, but they count for little. In civil and church affairs the salt-water elders and their wives make the decisions. Through the female line we have the present priest and the medical dresser; through the male line and Father Jack, we have two teachers, the catechist and choirmaster. The old man who determined the village work belongs to this lineage.

As yet the Christians have never been able to convert the pagan residue in Angia and Aina-alu, and for some reason I never understood the usually most helpful priest was unwilling to take me to those two villages. The gathered settlement of Fouia has a dominant clan and the subordinate position of the bush people there within the Church has not helped the evangelistic outreach among their pagan relations. The lack of structural planning in Fouia stands in contrast with the co-operative solidarity of Sulufou.

CHAPTER 12

Exchange Economy and Christian Innovation

THE PURPOSE of this chapter is to investigate some of the social depths of the exchange economy and their bearing on the acceptance or rejection of Christian innovations. In this sense innovation may mean Christianity itself as a new religion (conversion growth) or Christian organizations and mechanisms aimed at producing organic and quality growth.

Belshaw described the Melanesian society of the Solomons, New Caledonia and the New Hebrides as "society at the primitive colonial stage, at which the Governments concerned have made little attempt to develop the inherent possibilities of advancing the commercial status of the indigenous people".[1] He was writing a decade after the war, and though some effort has been made by the authorities since then, the place is still painfully backward. The Government's inaction over the years has meant that many changes have come about of their own accord as indigenous acceptances, not directed by any official policy.

However, when we speak of people living under an exchange economy as *backward*, we are taking a western view. The exchange economy is by no means a backward system. Within its own world it was ceremonially and elaborately organized, highly efficient and certainly not static. The trouble came with the great changes that have taken place in the social matrix where it operated, acculturative factors that have demanded dramatic innovation. The kidnapping trade followed by indenture, the establishment of plantations, the arrival of white traders and missionaries, the introduction of minted coin, arms and ammunition, punitive expeditions, administrative law and order, and so on *ad infinitum*, have drastically changed the environment, and the old has been faced with adjustment or extermination. Some of these changes have involved essential needs, some have changed both the supply and demand of raw materials, some have led to the disappearance of industry (the substitution of axes and guns for indigenous weapons, for instance, robbed one class of craftsmen of its means of livelihood), and some have greatly influenced the supply of essential goods (thus, for example, the European offer of tobacco, axes, guns and cloth for shell-money, since in New Guinea they could buy gold-dust with the latter, led to the scarcity of shell-money in some parts of the Solomons, causing in turn a reduction of the marriage rate). Many changes had *chain effects* in social, technical and professional life; yet, in spite of all this, the exchange economy still operates and serves its social purposes.

This capacity for survival is significant for our study because the economic dimensions of custom relate to basic social attitudes, and these in turn affect decision-making, either for the acceptance or rejection of innovations. The innovation advocated may be a co-operative society, a church organization, village education or even Christianity itself. In one locality there is ready acceptance, in another resistance. These acceptances or rejections by group decision can frequently be traced to common sets of basic attitudes. Even acceptance does not mean that the values or motivation of the acceptors are the same as those of the advocates. Quite often administrators, social workers and missionaries are mystified at the acceptance of their ideas in one community and their rejection in the next. This is the greatest practical problem obstructing the organic emergence of an indigenous Church, because the organizational structure acceptable, say, in Ysabel may not be at all acceptable in Malaita. It raises the very awkward question whether it might not be more suitable to work for the emergence of a Ysabel Church and a Malaita Church, rather than a Solomon Islands Church. Because I believe that there is much to be discovered in the economic factors which bear on decision-making, I propose to deal with this subject at length.

CONCEPTS OF WEALTH

"Wealth", says Belshaw, "is a social concept. Gold, nickel and chrome were present in early Melanesia as they are today, but these metals were not related in any way to the wants of the communities and therefore were not wealth."[2] According to this definition he listed their wealth as agricultural land, food plants, stones and flints, industrial plants (for cordage, resin, thatch and timber), fish, pigs, shells, birds, opossums, flying-foxes and handcraft products. The latter would presumably include everything from domestic utensils to weapons of war, from houses to canoes. Many of these goods were made for, or acquired by, exchange. Specialization in craft production is highly developed. Trade exchanges were and still are highly organized as focal points of social life. Ivens has argued that the primary motive for the building of the artificial islands along the coast of Malaita was a desire for effective trade exchanges.[3]

Labour. Many of these forms of wealth were acquired by personal effort, and there is some justification in classifying labour itself as a form of wealth, because it could be given in exchange for goods. A strong man, or a capable one, could demand a higher return in goods. His labour had greater bargaining power. However, concepts of labour differ in different parts of the Solomons. In one place labour is for the acquisition of personal and communal wealth, and in another it is itself a commodity for exchange either individually or communally. The contrasting attitudes to labour in Rarumana and Sulufou again remind us of the danger of generalizations. These economic attitudes account for basic social differences and varied conceptualizations of progress and prosperity.

Personal capacity and *specialist knowledge:* These also have some equation or affiliation with wealth. A man charged with *mana* could acquire material property merely by the offer of his powers and prestige to some particular end. Specialist knowledge of songs, dances, chants, charms, forest lore, medicinal plants, fishing techniques and various ceremonial procedures had an economic value, much as the westerner had to pay goodwill when buying a successful business. Chiefs, warriors, priests, skilled craftsmen, hunters and fishermen had this *mana* from the ghosts and their personal technical proficiency to exchange for more tangible forms of wealth. At many points Christianity came into actual conflict with this intangible wealth. One of the major objections to the new religion was the undeniable fact that it deprived the celebrated warrior and the pagan priest of their buying-power. It threatened their intangible wealth. Our Lord himself met with this form of opposition when the spirits he had exorcized entered the pigs with economic loss to their Gadara owners (Mark 5: 17). Paul met the same thing at Ephesus (Acts 19: 24–28) and Philippi (Acts 16: 19). Economic loss may often be the basic attitude behind the rejection of worthy innovations, including Christianity itself.

On the other hand, if there are certain pagan professions which the Church sets her face against, such as head-hunting and forest medicine, is she obligated to provide some other avenue of income? Should she give thought to legitimate substitutes for such roles? Would this strengthen her advocacy of Christianity? Both documentary research and personal observation have satisfied me of one important fact—that, when converted, pagan priests tend to make superb Christian pastors. Frequently the missionary and the pagan priest become bitterly antagonistic, for religious reasons to the missionary and for economic reasons to the priest, who fears the loss of wealth and prestige. This is quite different from the face to face religious encounter of the *challenge* or *ordeal* type. But when one is religious and the other economic, the two never really come face to face and the priest tends to become a long-term obstructor to the group acceptance of Christianity. Therefore many priests feel they must hold on to their rights and prestige as pagans, yet allow their sons to have Christian training to protect them from similar insecurity. Quite a number of these normally hereditary successors to the pagan priesthood in Melanesia have become effective catechists and clergy. Often the long years of obstruction by the pagan priest could have been avoided if the missionary (either foreign or indigenous) had approached the priest sympathetically with a practical solution for his economic problem, and a recognition of his leadership in the community at large. Many a good missionary has disarmed his opponent by recognizing the man's prestige and cultural knowledge, even using him as an adviser in secular matters, and at the same time presenting his gospel claim. This is no universal solution but it does have something important to say to the situation.

SOME ECONOMIC DIMENSIONS OF CUSTOM

Nearer to the western concept of money is a group of commodities known as *custom-money*. In themselves they have no utilitarian value except for exchange, or for gaining prestige by a display of wealth.

They can be acquired and stored without deterioration for some future occasion when major social transactions are anticipated. They have a specific value that does not fluctuate like the majority of market goods. In the market exchanges procedure varies, but usually there is some bargaining. This is not so with custom-money. Its value is fixed and nowadays can be stated in terms of cash.[4] It approximates the western concept of money in these respects, and since it is manufactured by a special group of persons approved by the community at large as the source of supply, we could perhaps speak of this as 'minting' the money. Beyond this, however, it serves its own functions peculiar to the island way of life. It is used only for special types of purchase—more particularly for brides, canoes, offerings to ghosts, festal pigs and fees for men's clubs.[5] These uses are all ceremonial. In another part of this study I have mentioned how a nephew was 'bought back' for the priestly succession after the death of the priest. A thousand porpoise teeth and thirty fathoms of red shell-money were paid to the mother's locality for this redemption. Custom-money is used for customary transactions—marriage, feasting, peace ceremonial, and in the old days for war agreements and official assassinations. Today it can be acquired for cash at a fixed rate. This means that a man can exchange his labour for cash, the cash for custom money, storing the latter until such time as he should desire to marry and then buy his bride. The process may be symbolized thus:

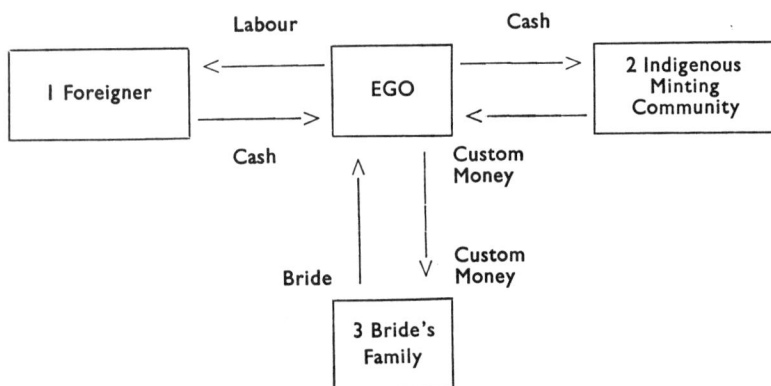

In this complex of exchanges Ego makes use of the foreigner, trader or plantation, where he worked, and also the western money earned in cash, and innovates these features into the traditional economy pattern. They are functional substitutes for the various ways of obtaining money in the old days—military action, magical performance, professional entertainment, pig breeding or professional murdering. Custom-money is still required for the continuity of social life, and still must be acquired by personal effort. Brides still have to be bought. Custom money is still worn on festival occasions to gain the prestige that is attached to any display of stored wealth. The only major change, apart from the above innovations, was a rise in the price of brides when the facilities for acquiring western money increased early in the century.[6] This particular pattern is based on observations made in Malaita and may differ from those of other parts. I have made this choice because I think it explains how the Malaitaman accepted the plantation system; not through any love for colonial machinery or western commercial patterns, but because it offered a means of preserving customary procedure *in spite of* changing economic conditions caused by culture contact.

Why was it necessary to retain the customary pattern? Why not simply take the western money and buy brides for cash—a more obvious simplification? The answer is found in the whole character of the minting pattern itself.

The minting of Malaita shell-money was big business long before the coming of Christianity. Its commercial outreach, described eighty years ago by Penny,[7] provided large quantities of money for the islands of Ysabel and Florida, involving the construction of sea-going canoes of considerable size, adequate for the return transport of yams, nuts and pigs up to two or three tons in weight. This was a regular trade before shell-money had any fixed cash value owing to culture contact. There were fixed prices in terms of yams and nuts, and only when pigs varied in size was there any bargaining.[8]

However, it was not merely the interinsular trade which made the minting of custom money so important. Its significance ramified through all Malaita, along the coast and into the mountains. The Malaita mints were found in a number of artificial islands, more particularly Alite, Langalanga and Auki on the southwest coast.[9] For the manufacture of shell-money red, white and black shells are required.[10] In division of labour it was women's work to dive for the shell and men's to make the money.[11] However, the manufacturers are unable to obtain adequate supplies of the three kinds of shells in their own waters, so this involves them in trade at the coastal markets buying at so much a basketful. This involves the minters in much travel and many trade contacts with all parts of Malaita.[12] The manufacture is a highly developed process, as demonstrated by its technical terminology,[13] the complexity of which shows that the minting of shell-money is a highly developed communal craft—what Firth would call the *inflorescence* of this culture, the most central element determining life of the community, the most specialized feature of life. The manufacture of a highly precious length of red money, for which a *romu* shell might yield only one disc of sufficient colour, may take two years of selection and labour to produce.

Not only do the makers of shell-money visit distant markets for suitable shell but they visit specific markets for material for the manufacture of their tools of trade. They obtain their grinding stone from the market at Fiu, and the stone from which the drill is made comes from the Malaita bushmen. The minting trade is therefore important also to the vendors of shell, grinding stone and drill stone,

G

and the pattern is seen be to complex and interdependent. Because of this the customary marriage pattern must be seen, not as an independent institution, that can be retained or dispensed with on its own merits alone, but as something which both reinforces and is reinforced by the economic trade network. To discard the custom of bride purchase would mean destroying an established means of livelihood for hundreds of people.[14] This explains why, though the Malaitamen have no particular love for the plantation system, yet they will accept it into their patterns because they can use it to serve their own ends. Labour for cash fits comfortably into the structure of their own pattern of life. With the passing of many pagan means of acquiring custom-money because of Government prohibitions and Mission standards, a substitute had to be found.

This also illustrates how advocates and acceptors may have completely different motivation. It shows furthermore that economic factors may be *latent*, and operate as either aids or obstructions to the acceptance of new ideas—including Christianity.

In Malaita the Anglican Church has accepted the economic structure of traditional marriage, modifying only the religious ceremonial. This has been an acceptable adjustment and the pagan elements have been effectively eliminated without social disturbance. This has not been so on every mission-field. It is not infrequent that some missionary claims that some customary procedure (not necessarily marriage) has pagan associations and therefore he will have no dealings at all with it. If this be done without consideration of the social or economic involvement, that mission may well be faced with the charge of having removed an element basic to social stability and of jeopardizing the livelihood of its converts. Marriage patterns are but one example of this principle. It applies also to entertainments, for example.

The picture of the custom-money complex I have given here has been from the orientation of Malaita, and must not be generalized· In the last study we saw a different pattern of shell-money minting by the Roviana slave community. I was concerned there with the acceptance of Christianity by detribalized persons and by the potential for communication through trade and slaving contacts. In this case also I could have developed further the economic significance. There is another shell-money complex that works its way down through the Group from New Guinea. It is strongest in Bougainville but reaches the central islands. In this case also, like Malaita, there is a clear distinction between normal commodities for exchange on the regular market days and the restricted special functions and regulations associated with custom-money.[15] From Taunita, where Metcalfe was shown a great quantity of shell-money, he recorded:

> They get it from the Konua side of Bougainville, probably Buruata, which indicates frequent communications between Taunita and Konua. I was assured there was a good track.[16]

Still another circuit has its origins in antiquity and its centre of activity in Choiseul.[17] The Hounihu community in San Cristoval was another.

It broke down with the acceptance of Christianity, because its work was done under pagan ritual. According to Belshaw the people now say they cannot get the chalcedony to break correctly for the tips of their pump-drills because they have forgotten their charms. They no longer have faith in their own ability.[18] There may be others also, but I have chosen Malaita, partly because it is better documented and partly because I made personal observations in that area—also because one has to think in terms of money whenever one looks at the cultural inflorescence of Malaita, and because the money complex has survived there best. Money is a deep factor in the attitudes and decisions of these people.

VILLAGE ABSENTEEISM AND COMMUNAL RESPONSIBILITY

The acceptance of the plantation system, though it met one need in the Malaita way of life, created some serious problems for village solidarity and the maintenance of quality growth in the Church. Village travel to and from markets had confined and specific limits. The only travelling beyond this was for war expeditions and this also had its routine patterns. On those journeys the young men had the opportunity of gaining prestige as travellers and warriors. After the establishment of British controls, the old kidnapping trade assumed the more 'respectable' form of indentured labour. Many things passed under the guise of legality and the argument commonly given in favour of this doubtful business was that many labourers signed on for a second term. The argument was an empty one. The islander accepted the idea of indenture because it offered scope for travel and prestige, gave him a little cash for spending, and the opportunity of owning a gun and buying a wife. Indenture to Queensland was terminated by the establishment of the White Australia Policy, and that to Fiji gave way before the large-scale Indian indenture to that country. The only labour openings thereafter were those offering within the Solomons in the plantations and more recently in Honiara. The economic gains of the labourer are slight. He could make much more money by cultivating his own garden and nuts at home. The advantages of his cash remuneration are grossly overrated. He does however gain prestige as a traveller and a labourer beyond the confines of the village. A few odd individuals, who have the art of husbanding their resources, have something to show for it, but on the whole little economic gain is apparent.

On the other hand, the losses to the community are considerable and the stability of the village is certainly threatened by the excessive absenteeism. The loss of adult male labour force to the village throws an increased load of communal responsibility on the remainder, so that if things are to be done the children and the aged are much overloaded. One is confronted with an unhealthy state of social unbalance in these areas of labour recruiting. The shortage of mature labour is evident from the state of the villages, paths, sanitation and houses.[19] Although the religious life of some villages is strong, at periods when the absentee labour returns home there is excessive drinking and gambling and a quality decline in social and religious life. I came to the conclusion that Malaita badly needed a system of revenue production at home. The Church needs it. The villages need it. The families need it. This Malaita absenteeism has been a continuous feature over the years. Forty years ago some 4,000 absentees were reported from this island alone.[20] It creates an attitude of economic individualism within the most physically able age-group and therefore greatly increases the communal load carried by the less physically able. This plays into the hands of any radical element, who are bound by public opinion to their communal service if they remain at home. Thus though all members of the village were expected to carry their load, many did not do so. In Fouia, for instance, attendance at communal work on Fridays varied considerably. Usually the bell had to be rung several times before there was any response, and then if any work was done at all, those who came were the physically disabled, the elderly and a few girls who had been denied the opportunities of attending school. The greatest number I saw was twenty. Sometimes none came at all. They would clear the grass round the church and along the village path and perhaps drift away within a half-hour or so. It required some speech-making by the head man and the catechist at church to get the men along. Twice in the six weeks I was there they worked on renewing church seats that had been damaged by white ants. Nine men came each time and worked for five hours. The chief of the bush people always came to village work, and strutted about to give the occasion his blessing, but I never saw him do any work or touch a tool. All this was in contrast with things in Rarumana, where absenteeism was at a minimum and where some specific programme of work was handled by both the men and women each week, where the communal areas and public paths were well kept, public buildings cared for, and private houses and gardens a credit to the people.

Even so, although the percentage response to communal work was statistically more than twice as good at Rarumana, I thought I was able to detect some common features. I checked on twenty-two men working on the school windows at Rarumana and found them almost all devoted churchmen. Furthermore, week after week nearly all the lay preachers and prayer leaders were present for communal work. The much smaller group of men who worked twice on church repairs in six weeks at Fouia were also regular attenders at morning and evening prayers. The same applied to the women. But in each case there was some relationship between those who, though present in the village, absented themselves from village work, and the casual attenders at church or non-attenders. A great many in each case who went to church only once a week avoided their communal duties.

The much smaller number of public-minded citizens at Fouia may perhaps be accounted for by the general spread of this type of individualism, stimulated by long absences from the communal scene. Absenteeism tends to make them forget their responsibility to the village, the home and the church. The Rarumana people are far more prosperous, having learned to derive their income on a family basis within the village rather than by personal individualism outside. Those who avoid communal responsibility among the latter are often the most prosperous, who have allowed material prosperity to become their greatest desire. Thus absenteeism in one case and material prosperity in the other can both lead to the avoidance of communal duty. They are two forms of selfishness. Both injure the village cohesion, the family solidarity and the quality growth within the church. Occasionally an absentee meets Christ on his travels. Some link up with the Church in Honiara or on the plantation; and such usually return home to be responsible citizens, but on the whole absenteeism is a major cause for *shrinkage* in church attendance.

One of the problems in Oceanic societies is the need for pressing individualism and initiative for the sake of progress, but doing so without injuring the communal sense and the responsibility of the group. Some aspects of the growing individualism have a perilous similarity with the western philosophy of "each man for himself and the Devil take the hindmost". The pre-Christian economic system was symbiotic, and symbiosis is a principle the Creator wove into nature to ensure its survival. The same interdependence is seen in the interrelated parts of the body, to which Paul likened the Church itself. If individualism is necessary for progress, co-operation is necessary for survival. These two extremes should always be kept in a state of balance.

It is my considered opinion that prolonged absenteeism for individuals, and the continuity of the state of absenteeism as a factor of village life, are injurious to the solidarity of the villages supplying the labour, to the normal development of their families, and to the quality growth of the village church. To talk of social reforms on the plantations, to improve labour conditions there and to raise wages, may indeed be necessary, but at this point it is to beg the question—the deserted villages are threatened by social, psychological and religious decay. Professor Elkin has said:

> Whatever may be the results of this system, do not let us beguile our consciences into thinking we are doing more than protecting the native from a form of serfdom. Although we say it is good for him to learn to work regularly, and even though the regular life and food are of physical benefit to him, our motive is to use his labour, and then turn him adrift—in his village—after the appointed period. We are *not working out a positive plan for his life* as an individual or as a people. . . . The system leads nowhere worthwhile for the native people; it is only a paternally-controlled method of obtaining labour for ourselves in an uncomfortable environment. For this reason it stands condemned—not because of injustices, but because it fails to ensure for the natives economic adjustment and social security.[21]

Elkin goes on to show that after a period of plantation life many a man returns to his village a social misfit and a discontented person. I may add that this is a reason for his unreadiness to share the communal load. On the village level Elkin blames indenture for increasing child delinquency and causing social disintegration. He advocated the abolishment of the indenture system by some form of compensation, unless its characteristics could be so drastically changed as to ensure "economic adjustment and social security *for life*".

Elkin was concerned with personal and village levels. I believe we may fairly add religious levels—personal, family and community. Quality growth in the Church is obstructed by both the absenteeism itself and the disequilibrium after return. The biblical concept of the Church as a fellowship of people with a kindred spirit of devotion is weakened. One should also point out that the migration of labour to Honiara, though not indenture, has some of the same effects back in the village. Our problem is not the plantation or the town but village absenteeism and subsequent readjustment. The building of housing settlements to accommodate families in Honiara may solve the problem of divided families and be realistic in the face of the inevitability of urbanization; but it aggravates even more the disintegration of the village and militates against the improvement of village standards of sanitation, family life and religion. We shall now turn to see how the Government tries to meet this problem of absenteeism.

SOCIO-ECONOMIC ORGANIZATION IN THE VILLAGES

Co-operative societies have been advocated in the islands for the very reason that they approximate to communal patterns of organization. An economic survey in 1954, covering most areas where co-operatives were reasonably successful, stated the principle thus:

> It would be unrealistic to promote economic development among these people through methods and facilities that have been developed to meet the needs of metropolitan and other environments where 'individualism' is the rule and not the exception. Hence the value of village co-operatives which modify and rationalize but do not discard the basic elements of the traditional communal methods of organizing production in the Pacific islands.[22]

The present Government tries to stimulate interest in co-operatives, but development is slow, in Malaita painfully slow.[23] Officials have visited various localities and explained the virtues of the movement. I have had discussions afterwards with those who attended some of these sessions. There is no room for doubt—the explanations were fully and clearly understood. There is also a general agreement about their economic soundness. But understanding and appreciating do not necessarily mean acceptance. Advocates of the co-operative movement are often mystified by prolonged non-acceptance. In Malaita, whenever I discussed this movement, my informants invariably raised the case of a precedent where the experiment had been tried and failed. A general attitude of scepticism had to be broken down before there could be any hope of acceptance, even though they seemed to be quite aware of the reason for the failure. I also had a feeling sometimes that they still needed convincing that the white man wanted to help and not to exploit the Solomon Islander. This is an effect of some generations of seeing Government officials as taxation officers.

During my residence in a Malaita village I felt aware of two deep-seated problems that militated against the acceptance of co-operatives.

They cannot be described in terms of traditions, customs and needs. I can think of them only as attitudes of the Malaita (or perhaps the Fouia) way of life. Although the ultimate goal of the co-operative is perhaps a village store or a boat for trade, it is to begin with the preparation and sale of existing nuts. The initial returns will be slight but will increase as time goes on.

In point of fact, there are not a great many nuts in these villages. Co-operatives based on coconuts can have no significance for the bushmen in the interior or for the dwellers on the artificial islands. At best it can only hope to help those who dwell along the mainland coastline. Very few of these villages have what could be called plantations. The limited number of trees that exist are used daily for food and drink. Meal habits are quite irregular, families seldom sit down together, and the pattern of daily life depends on the possibility of acquiring nuts at any time of day to supplement the sweet potato that is eaten whenever a person feels hungry. Even where nuts were placed under a taboo (I presume with the idea of supporting the co-operative proposal), it made no difference. They were consumed daily, and there was no authority to enforce the taboo. The whole food pattern would need to be drastically changed to make the co-operative scheme practicable. A strong headman with the necessary power to enforce his authority might make a difference, but I cannot envisage the voluntary acceptance of the innovation otherwise.

Nor do I think the proposal allows for the Malaitaman's love of money in the form of immediate cash return when the job is done. The idea of planting nuts and cocoa for a steady return five, six, or ten years hence has no appeal for him. He will make no attempt to dispute the wisdom and virtue of such an idea,[24] but he will not be moved to do anything about it. The modifications that would be required in the daily routine would be a burden to him. This all 'boils down' to the fact that he is satisfied to leave conditions as they are. The only thing he is likely to be agitated about is to cry out for higher wages for his labour.

Co-operatives have been more acceptable in the central and western districts, but a number of the experiments have failed.[25] This has often been cited as evidence of the Melanesian's lack of a capacity for organization. But one of the finest examples of all Melanesian movements, Marching Rule, had its organizational centre in the area of greatest failure with co-operatives. When an idea captivates a Melanesian group there is no difficulty about organization—but the idea must captivate the group. We have here a clear example of how an organization may be seen as good and useful, and yet be rejected, because it runs counter to latent psychological and economic factors in existing patterns, which people feel are not convenient to change.

What has happened in some places with co-operatives can happen also to church organizations like the Methodist Boys' Brigade, and the Anglican Village Union and Church Association. Theoretically they may meet the situation perfectly, yet they may meet with rejection, leaving their advocates mystified. We are shortly to examine some of these religio-economic innovations aimed at stimulating organic growth.

The recent Department of Agriculture White Paper supplies a good statement of the helpful role co-operatives could play in the development of agriculture. It correctly sees this need for development at the village level. It is, however, an ideal picture and must stand or fall, not by its theoretical merits, but by the readiness of the village community to accept it and act upon it.[26] The anthropologist, Belshaw, claimed that

> Melanesian organizations . . . are built upon satisfactions effective in Melanesian society, and therefore extremely valuable pointers as to the way in which collective activity can be organized.

But to this he added

> . . . traditional forms of co-operation could be used a great deal more widely than at present, though their nature must be examined carefully before their possibilities can be understood.[27]

Probably acting on this opinion the Administration has pressed co-operatives since about the date that was written. In 1957 there were only five societies in all the Solomons, with a membership of 195. The statistics have shown steady improvement so that by 1962, 3,365 members belonged to forty-seven societies.[28] The tabular arrangement of these statistics suggests rapid and effective growth, but a detailed analysis will disclose that acceptance of this innovation has been good within restricted localities, but in other areas there has been virtually complete rejection—still another evidence of the regional segmentation of the Solomons.[29] Belshaw was right at both points—co-operation could be more used, but careful examination of the different situations was needed for understanding. In any event 3,365 looks an impressive figure as growth from 195, but in reality it is a small membership for a region with a population of 125,000.

We must now turn from the area of socio-economic innovation to the religio-economic counterpart and see whether the factors of acceptance and rejection in each have any similarities.

RELIGIO-ECONOMIC ORGANIZATION

Religio-economic organization overlaps with what I have chosen to call the organic growth of the Church. The common area comprises those organizations by means of which the Church is achieving its own selfhood within the local situation. A good deal of experimentation has taken place since the war—with some acceptance and some rejection.

The Methodists have pressed hard with an organization known as the Boys' Brigade, but I had no opportunity of studying it at depth. It did not operate in the village where I lived for a period of time, although the situation there called for drastic action in the interests of the age group for which this movement caters. Psychologically the movement aims at meeting the needs of young people on the fringe of church membership, who need some form of activity or participation to make them feel a place in both the Church and community. There were young men in the village who understood the workings of this movement. They were not devoid of initiative in other respects but they were not active advocates of the Boys' Brigade idea. My impression from a distance was that the movement represented too much of a tie with New Zealand and lacked indigeneity. An official from New Zealand visited the islands, and indigenous leaders have been set aside for specialist organization of this programme and there must be some areas of acceptance, but there are also areas of rejection and complete indifference. The movement, together with its counterpart for girls, the Girls' Life Brigade, touch about one seventh of the members of the Church's youth roll, according to the 1963 official statistics. It would have been revealing, had I set out to obtain the figure at the time, to know what percentage of that one seventh is station orientated.

The Village Union and Church Association are ideas which have sprung from Melanesian ingenuity itself, within the Anglican Church, like the Melanesian Brotherhood, their evangelistic spearhead. They are largely confined to the Eastern and Central Solomons, yet despite their indigenous origin and manifest suitability to the island way of life, they have met with a varied reception—almost total acceptance in one area and virtual rejection in another.

The Church Association aims at strengthening the Church organically through the financial support of schools and medical work and the improvement of gardening and farming. It operates a system of raising money that is indigenously orientated[30] without interfering with existing collections and Government tax payments. It has a spiritual quality of stewardship and is stated with a biblical basis related to the New Testament Church. Though it has far deeper spiritual depths than the Co-operative Movement, it employs many of the same principles and has also met with a wide range of acceptance and rejection in a pattern not dissimilar.

The Village Union is a stewardship project in terms of labour rather than money. It recognizes the responsibility of every member to contribute service and time to the needs of the Church. The pattern is borrowed from concepts of community service in social life. It provides a voluntary labour force for clearing bushland, preparing new gardens, working on plantations and other projects. The work is done by volunteers under group organization, without the expectation of personal remuneration, but one pound a day is paid by the beneficiary to the Union for the group labour irrespective of the number employed. The revenue goes to the Church Association and the work assists the general development of the local community. It also gives incentive to any man disposed to open new gardening areas. As a voluntary co-operative project it is a demonstration of true brotherhood. Yet despite the good of the scheme and its official approval it has not been accepted over all areas. Even where the organization exists it is not always active. Highly acceptable in Ysabel, it lags in Malaita. No mechanism of pressure, except public opinion itself, is brought to bear on those who abstain from membership. Inasmuch as I was able to form an opinion, it seemed to me there was again some relation between the awareness of social and religious responsibility. Where village communal work was poorly supported the same seemed to apply to the Village Union. This, however, was not always related to Christian devotion, for some pious communities were neglectful of the practical demonstration of their faith in service. Only the real inner core of pious persons seemed to have a sense of service responsibility.

But this is not the whole story. It is perhaps hardly fair to contrast Ysabel and Malaita in this matter because other factors operate. Ysabel is almost entirely Anglican, has a tight social structure with some 8,000 people, divided into social segments under strong and loyal headmen, and the Assistant Bishop for that area is himself in the true line of the paramount traditional authority. Malaita has a population of some 50,000, only half of them Anglicans and the remainder Roman Catholics, South Sea Evangelicals, Seventh Day Adventists and pagans—not to mention small groups like Baha'i and Jehovah's Witnesses. The segmentation of Malaita is social and political as well as religious. What unity there is in Malaita has been achieved by revolutionary means through the Marching Rule Movement after a long and unsettled history. Ysabel has had other advantages. Few places have had a more fortunate run of long-term missionary guidance, competent linguists and effective follow-up of the original people-movements from paganism. Here the people came into the Church as a body in a short period when ripe fields were harvested without any denominational competition. The winning of Malaita, still incomplete, had been a long and fragmentary process with all kinds of complications and rival methods of evangelism.

It is very difficult to compare the Church in one island with that in another. Each has its own historical background, social peculiarities, economic orientation and conversion patterns. We would need to derive some complex of all these dimensions to explain their bearing on the various types of church growth—conversion, quality and organic. Then, if we could measure the intensity of each of these dimensions in the total complex, we would be nearer to understanding the true character of organic growth in an emerging island Church. Many of these factors have bearing on the ripening of situations which are propitious for spiritual innovation—communal acceptance of the gospel (for conversion growth), new forms of programmed education in the faith and knowledge of the Word (for quality growth) or organization for participation in and the functioning of the young Church (for organic growth).

Economic factors can condition people for group decision, either for acceptance or rejection. To put this in religious terms—the way for the operation of the Spirit in the various forms of church growth may be opened or obstructed by latent economic factors. In that economic factors can create a rebellious or resistant spirit in man, they can become obstructions to church growth at all levels. The Scriptures are quite clear about this possibility of the human spirit of rejection obstructing or quenching the Spirit.[31]

Because economic factors can be obstructive to growth the missionary should pay attention to cultural economics. The growth of a young

Church should be orientated to the economic pattern, not planned on a basis of western economy. It should be locally relevant, i.e. meet local needs and draw on local resources. This principle should be applied immediately the converts come out from paganism. The teaching of stewardship after a generation of converts has learned to become dependent on external mission revenue and the profits of centrally administered plantations is a problem of the first order. This is the Solomon Island problem. The problem of paternalism is as much economic as it is theological. If self-support is presented as part of the follow-up of the conversion experience, within the orbit of cultural practicability this problem never arises. But when the idea of self-support is presented to a second generation, it is received as the advocacy of an innovation with serious economic dimensions. At heart a large percentage of the local communities are mission-minded rather than church-minded, and many innovations proposed are rejected, either actively or passively, because of years of economic paternalism.

In a rather well-to-do village where I lived, the contributions of the various extended families comprised one bag of copra per family. They regarded this as a duty, but compared with their income and relative comfort it was a meagre offering to the Lord. They continued to think in terms of what the Mission ought to do for them. This orientation is naturally disposed against innovations of stewardship, and the organic growth of the Church is thereby obstructed.

TRADE NETWORKS AND CONVERSION GROWTH

At various points in this book I have mentioned markets where salt-water or coastal folk met and exchanged goods with bush people. Frequently these were hostile to each other and while the women exchanged their wares the men would stand guard, armed with axes, guns or spears. Yet these were vital contacts and the paths followed by these folk to market were the very routes along which the gospel frequently penetrated into the mountains. This is a safe generalization for most of the Solomons, though only one of many factors involved. Just as the gospel spread along the Roman roads in New Testament times because of the continual travelling of armies and merchants, so reports about Christianity and then its advocates followed these island trade routes.

These trade connections reached from coast to interior, followed the coastline and crossed straits from island to island. I have already mentioned the voyaging of the minters of shell-money to obtain raw material for money and tools. I attended one trade exchange market near the island of Adagege. It was mainly a simple direct exchange of sea produce for forest produce, but some cash did change hands and a Solomon Island storekeeper was present with a suitcase of trade goods, soap and tinned meat. Thus I as a foreigner was able to buy bananas from a bush woman, who shortly disposed of the coin for trade goods. Some of the trade networks are far more elaborate than this and sometimes a village community has the role of an entre-

preneur. Exchange is at least two-directional and every community
has contact with more than one market. We are not dealing with a huge
two-directional circuit like the *kula* ring of Papua. Each community
had its own circuit or circuits. These had evolved to solve problems
of supply and demand. I now cite an example of the type of economic
problem confronted by such a community and how the problem was
met by a circuit of journeys and exchanges. To get away from Malaita,
I turn to the extreme north-west of our area of study.

Problem: The people of Lontis desire shell-money for ceremonial
purposes. This can be bought only with pigs, but Lontis has no
pigs.

Exchange Circuit: The ultimate purpose of the exchange circuit is to
obtain pigs, which can be obtained from the distant island of
Nissan in exchange for pots, but Lontis has no pots. Lontis has
taro in abundance and this can be disposed of to Petats, which
trades in women's hoods. Pots may be had from Malasang, and
Malasang is ready to trade their pots for women's hoods. The
resultant exchange circuit involves four journeys and four different
exchanges, but it leaves all parties satisfied. It permits each area
to use its natural resources and to engage in specialization.
The situation before exchange is therefore:

Malasang makes pots	Petats makes hoods	Lontis grows taro	Nissan raises pigs

The resultant trade exchange may be schematized thus:

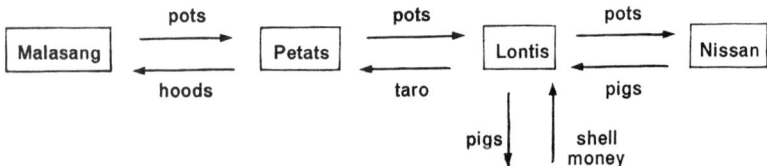

Three different trade transactions have been required to get
the pots from Malasang to Nissan. The latter is a remote island
involving a long voyage by sea-going canoes. Lontis is well
equipped with such canoes. Having acquired her pigs, Lontis is
now supplied with the buying power of shell-money—a ceremonial
trade not a bargaining market. This was a typical trade exchange

pattern operating in the Buka–Bougainville locality at the time when the doors opened for the spread of the gospel.

These exchange circuits, and there are indeed a great many of them,[32] help us to understand why large areas often come open for the acceptance of Christianity at one period of time. The conversion of one community is bound to have repercussions on all others with whom it has symbiotic trade relations. I do not say these trade circuits are the cause of conversion, but they are certainly the lines of indigenous communication along which news of the gospel spreads. A missionary well acquainted with the trade routes of his region should be able to plan his evangelistic itinerary to move from one responsive area to another.

One is amazed at the distance travelled and the regularity of some of these circuits. Blackwood[33] took a count of fish-taro exchanges between the Petats people and certain Buka hill tribes. In October 1929, when the gospel was beginning to penetrate into these regions, exchanges took place on the following dates of that month: 4, 7, 9, 11, 12, 14, 15, 19 and 23. These were nine exchanges in the three weeks of the sample. Sometimes the bush people added opossums to the trade. The meetings were arranged by exchanging pieces of string, knotted to indicate the market days, and cut off as the exchanges took place.

The bush people of Kunua came down to the west coast to trade with the coastal people who had come under the influence of Christianity. These contacts are mentioned in both the Roman Catholic and Methodist writings of the period. Both denominations were aware of the openings for church planting.

In this region the bargaining was less than in some other parts of the Solomons. Prestige factors were involved in value fixing for certain commodities, but the variety of exchange was great—loin-cloths, hoods, pots, tobacco, pipes, taro and taro-tops, food-trays, fish, sweet potatoes, red and black paint, pigs, putty nuts and canoes. The missionaries of both denominations and also their island teachers and catechists itinerated along these same routes. One of my Fijian acquaintances, who had retired and returned to his own land, described to me his journeys into the hill country behind Teop, and one of the European missionaries of these pioneering days narrated how whenever he arrived at Kieta, where the Roman Catholics had a central station, they rushed their agents into the back-country villages to warn the people against Methodism. He found it necessary to enter the mountains along the more remote trade routes and to come down on Kieta from the hills. His long account of these travels appeared in *The Open Door*[34] and the route can be reconstructed with a good map. In doing this one is reconstructing both the trade route and the course of the spread of the gospel.

Even so, the opportunities were greater than either mission was able to handle. Missionary Cropp complained of openings along the Kunua coast over a long period of time and for which he was unable to supply teachers. Though he itinerated regularly he knew that opportunities were being lost. The area was densely populated and he recorded the nature of many of these trade exchanges, of excursions to distant Nissan for pigs, and trade in pots and cloth. He established Methodist agents at Tanamal and Lontis and visited these localities regularly. He put a schoolboy from Skotolan into another place and found spontaneous growth under the lad's ministry.[35]

A record of similar experiences has been left in Father Emmet McHardy's letters, which were discussed in Part II of this book. He has a dozen references to open doors along these lines of contact.[36] The Methodist missionary, Voyce, after a long itinerary in the interior, which occupied five weeks, was able to establish certain localities like Teobuhin Vainana as *keys to the back country* (his own term, which he repeated). He emphasized these in his writing at the time to show that doors were opening.[37]

Farther down towards the south-east of Bougainville, the trade networks, though quite different circuits, were similar in pattern. The people of Siwai exchanged pigs, taro, smoked 'almonds', pottery and decorated spears for shell-money, fish and lime. After the coming of the white traders they added smoke-dried copra for calico, axes and adzes. The latter trade was organized through middle-men at Mono and Alu. They also supplied slaves for service, prostitution or sacrifice.[38] Some of these who survived their enslavement eventually returned as Christian teachers. In this particular complex some special relationships exist between the trade partners (*taovu*) whose exchange has a different character from normal barter. This exchange (*oourumum*) forbids the bargaining and argument of normal trade (*puunum*), reciprocation is generous, each rather trying to outdo the other.[39] The early requests for Christian teachers came to the Methodists through these trade partnerships.

There was also one other type of economic contact in this area. Unlike Malaita, the islands of Bougainville and Buka were dotted with European plantations. Planters meant culture contact. From these plantations money and trade goods began to appear in the trade exchange circuits. Islanders began accepting employment on the plantations. Missionaries Cropp and Voyce visited these places and made contact with the labourers, who eventually returned to their various localities with some idea of what Christianity was. This often led to enquiry later.

Thus we see that economic patterns and especially the trade exchanges were major instruments for the communication of the gospel and many of the Christian innovations that accompanied it. To a large extent a flow chart of church planting would also be a map of trade circuits. Both the Roman Catholics and the Methodists achieved growth in the western islands along these lines of contact. It is further interesting to note in passing that while both of these missionary causes were growing in the Bougainville–Buka region, they were static in other areas where they were under the same respective administrations. One area was a field ripe unto harvest. The others were not.

·   ·   ·   ·   ·

We have been examining the place of factors of an exchange economy in the acceptance and rejection of Christian innovation. We may perhaps sum it up thus:

1. Economic dimensions of custom determine attitudes that influence the acceptance or rejection of proposed innovations. Acceptance in one area and rejection in another may be accounted for by variations in these economic dimensions of custom.
2. Patterns of labour supply which lead to village absenteeism may satisfy one felt need and therefore be acceptable, but on the other hand absenteeism hinders social and family life and obstructs the quality growth of the Church in the villages concerned.
3. Religio-economic organizations aiming at developing organic church growth to indigeneity may be influenced by local economic factors, leading to acceptance in one place and rejection in another. The same applies to socio-economic innovations.
4. An ingrained acceptance of economic paternalism by a village congregation obstructs the organic growth of the Church.
5. Trade exchange circuits have opened the way for church planting and conversion growth from paganism. The Church has often spread along the trade exchange routes.

CHAPTER 13

Feud and Reconciliation

THE AIM of the Church was to bring feuds to a point of reconciliation. Reconciliation is easier to describe than feuding, because it merely involves outlining the role of mediators and the symbolic ceremonial of reconciliation and peace-making. This dramatic and emotional crisis offers itself for straightforward description. The analysis of a feud, on the other hand, demands a diachronic treatment. It is only in a study *through* time that one can examine enough cases of retaliation in their respective contexts to reconstruct the network and the social mechanisms brought into play. Furthermore, as some of these feuds continued for years, a considerable amount of documentation is required and this is not always available.

One of the best examples in Melanesia that can be documented was the Senga–Vurulata feud on Lauru (Choiseul), which lasted for twenty years. In this chapter I propose taking that feud as a type,[1] reconstructing a summary of the main events and giving the names of persons, clans and villages[2] involved. The episodes will be numbered for purpose of comment. Following that I shall discuss briefly the social mechanisms employed by the parties involved and tell something of the manner in which they operated. Then we shall investigate how the feud held up church planting, but eventually provided the ways and means for the entrance of Christianity and opportunity for reconciliation and peace-making, and how this determined the particular pattern of Christianity advocated and accepted, in which the Church is conceptualized as Peacemaker. Finally, I shall describe the roles and ceremonial of the reconciliation and peace-making and show the effect on the Church's conversion growth in the area concerned.

THE FEUD

(a) *Chronology and Distribution of the Senga–Vurulata Feud.* In the following table the arrows indicate the direction of action, from the activator(s) to the victim(s). This feud accounted for over 140 known deaths, on the principle of 'a life for a life' as indicated by the alternating arrows of retaliation. When raids on a village lead to the taking of a greater number of lives the process 'snowballs'. In the end a large part of Lauru was involved in this particular case.

(b) *The Mechanisms Involved.* This particular case shows a number of the pre-Christian destructive mechanisms at work. In the first episode the activator was a sorcerer using his own weapon, *taravalu*. Once this guilt was established, the kinsman of the victim was obligated to deal with the sorcerer or one of his family. In all probability had he killed the sorcerer only, the matter would have ended there, as sorcerers were

Senga-Vurulata Feud

Episode	Senga			Vurulata	Dates

1 — Gnu, sorcerer of Kuboro Clan ——— killed ——→ Kumbala of Selavaqa Clan   1901-02

2 — Gnu and two children ←——— killed ——— Semoto

3 — Dorovoqa and party ——— attack ——→ Village of Gugua, behind Paqoe. Neqobangara and two women killed

4 — Dorovoqa ◄—killed— Aranai —hired — Victims' kinsmen

5 — Penjaeqole of Boeboe section of clan ——— killed ——→ Qalonioro

6 — Parasusu ←——— killed ——— Lalaku of Banganoe

7 — Kinsmen of Parasusu —hired→ Aranai —shot→ Qalaboe

8 — Dalapa ←killed Aranai ←hired Roke

9 — Pondekana, Aranai and Vaivo —reported to→ District Officer —P.E.*→ against Parava-vosa, inland Silavaqa village near Gagara 7 men killed

(a) — also killed ↘

(b) — Vaikumu Kodosiko

10 — White police officer ←—shot (wounded)— Pakivai

11 — Kin of Aranai and Podekana (Number not known) ←killed Nodoro and Daleale of Boe ←hired Ngavala   1010

12 — Takokolo ——— killed ——→ 2 daughters of Jipe, Vurulata

*P.E. - punitive expedition.

Senga-Vurulata Feud— Continued

Episode	Senga		Vurulata	Date
13	Lipa and others including Ngalatoti	← killed — Buki and party ← hired	Liliboe	
14	Takokolo, who fled to Guadalcanal	← sought to kill	Jipe, on Ngalatoti's account	
15	Paruku and Vuvulenga of Senga	attacked →	Raqe, west of Mt. Matambe, Liliboe's locality. 2 men 20 others killed	
16	Konjo (south of Ruiana, East Coast) Lekezoto killed and 30 others	← attacked	Liliboe and party	
16 (a)		counter attacked →	Jipe killed and 5 others	
17	Papaqui and Ngalarusa with 100 warriors from Senga, Varese and Ririo	attacked →	Pakisake village 40 persons killed, 11 women captured	1916
18	Jijipili village. Attack beaten off but 5 warriors killed	← attacked	Liliboe and party	
18a	Some Jijipili women	found →	Liliboe wounded in the bush and killed him	
19	Kinsmen of Jijipili victims	→ paid shell-money → Taveqa → betrayed →	Biliki	
20	Pabulu	← killed — Karoso using Didimari as decoy ← hired	Tabipuda brother of Biliki	
21	Police	hanged →	Koroso	
21a		imprisoned →	Tabipuda	1921

(Note: In this table 'd' has the value of English 'nd', 'b' of 'mb' and 'q' of 'ngg').

regarded as anti-social. However, by taking three lives he involved the kin community and the feud developed. Sorcery was often a mechanism used in feuds, but it was not so in this case. The common method of killing individuals was by means of a spear, and regular war parties were used for raiding villages after the feud became a large-scale war. It is interesting to note the part played by foreign innovations, which were always acceptable if they fitted the island way of life. The women despatched the wounded Liliboe (18a) with a tomahawk, and western arms and ammunition were conspicuous in several episodes— the shooting of Qalaboe (7) by Aranai and the wounding of the white policeman by Pakivai (10), for instance. Evidence of culture clash and misunderstanding in the punitive expedition (9), which only confused the issue, was not based on justice, and solved no problems. It brought a retaliatory shot at the white officer, but did not in any way discount the tribal retaliations demanded by the pattern of the feud. The administration of western justice in the last episodes—hanging and imprisonment—well-nigh wrecked the whole of the peace proposals which were being brought about by negotiation.

Quite conspicuous in this table of episodes is the role of the professional murderer(s) available for hire, like Nodoro and Daleale of Boe (11), Buki and party (13), Aranai (4, 7 and 8) and Koroso (20). These men were bound to no loyalties. They killed for business and Aranai's record shows he made profit from the feud by letting out his services to either side, and even figured in the false representations of the deputation to the District Officer (9). In the end Ngavala (11) employed other professional murderers to deal with him.[3] These men differed from Taveqa (19), who by treachery for shell-money betrayed his ally, Biliki, brother of Tabipuda. He was not a professional murderer, living by the business of killing, but the incident shows that even pledged allies were not above the temptation of wealth and could be bought over. Didimari also showed another from of treachery when he decoyed Pabulu by innocently calling him to help him to beach his canoe, so that the assassin, Koroso, could catch him unawares. For this he received a fee of a shell arm ring. Not all professional murderers used help of decoys. They were left to their own methods and well paid. In San Cristoval (to leave Choiseul for a moment), if a chief wanted a man killed he would display a length of money. There was nothing secret about this. His people might even add something to the offer. An adventurer or professional murderer would accept the challenge by biting the length of money in two. Thereupon the chief would build a platform on which gifts for the murderer would be placed. According to Fox, the authority on San Cristoval, some of these men killed hundreds of victims, using all manner of treachery. They were bold and astute, feared and hated—but society accepted them.[4]

The chronological table shows something of the network of obligatory involvements. Many of the retaliatory acts were initiated by the next of kin to the most recent victim. Thus Tokakolo was involved on Podekana's account (11 and 12) on one side of the feud, and Ngavala on Vaikumu's on the other side (9b and 11). Tabipuda had to do something about the murder of his brother, Biliki. Although Vaikumu was killed by the punitive expedition, his kinsmen held Aranai and Pode-kana responsible, because by their reporting they had brought the expedition against them.

When the nearest kinsman was unable personally to exact a requital, he might employ a professional murderer or call in the chief of his group. Or the chief could take up the feud on his account. Liliboe did this (13) when the daughters of Jipe (a member of his Vurulata tribe) were murdered by Takokolo (12). When the party of professional murderers under Buki got out of hand (one of Buki's relations, married into the opposite camp, being killed by a member of his party), Jipe held the Kerepaqara Clan (Takokolo's) responsible. Takokolo found the burden of obligatory involvements too heavy and dangerous, and, betraying his responsibility, fled from Lauru even as far as Guadalcanal. This made it virtually impossible for him to return home again and so he settled and married in voluntary exile. Thus were Paruku and Vuvuleqa of Senga obliged to preserve the honour of the total group by taking up the responsibilities avoided by Takokolo's flight. Liliboe had to be dealt with.

In 1901 it began with a disagreement over sorcery involving two individuals. Soon it became a feud between the Kuboro and Selavaqa clans. The death of Dorovoqa (4) brought in the Boeboe section of the tribe (5) because Dorovoqa had been the leading chief. The activities of this group involved Lalaku of Banganoe, and the feud spread to Babatana (6). Roke was involved as a pledged ally of the Selavaqa clan. The punitive expedition only aggravated the situation, and by 1910 it had developed into a regular struggle between Varesē, Rereo and Senga districts on the north coast, and Babatana and Vurulata on the south. There were no signs of settlement. The feud had become war. Villages were fortified. It was only because of this that Jijipili was able to beat off Liliboe's attack (18). Counter attacks of the same engagement did not count as retaliation. Thus, though the people of Konjo (16 a and b) had killed six of the enemy in defensive action, they had lost thirty and retaliated on the principle of a warrior for a warrior and a village for a village. The resultant act of retaliation was a thoroughly organized expedition against Pakisake in 1916 (17). The feud dragged on over this wide area for another five years, a large part of Lauru being involved and perhaps with other episodes we cannot now document.[5]

As it happened, the Jijipili people were thoroughly tired of war, and, though they might well have pursued the war because of the death of Pabulu, were open for peace because Pabulu himself was very little loss to society. Amos Tozaka, the Christian teacher, who had long been striving for a reconciliation, seized this opportunity to negotiate for peace. The arrest of Koroso by the police and the official verdict almost destroyed the effect of his negotiations. Koroso insisted he was only the hired murderer, that Tabipuda was the guilty party. Foreign justice hung the hired assassin and imprisoned the perpetrator of the act. But it was the Christian mediation and not the foreign justice which

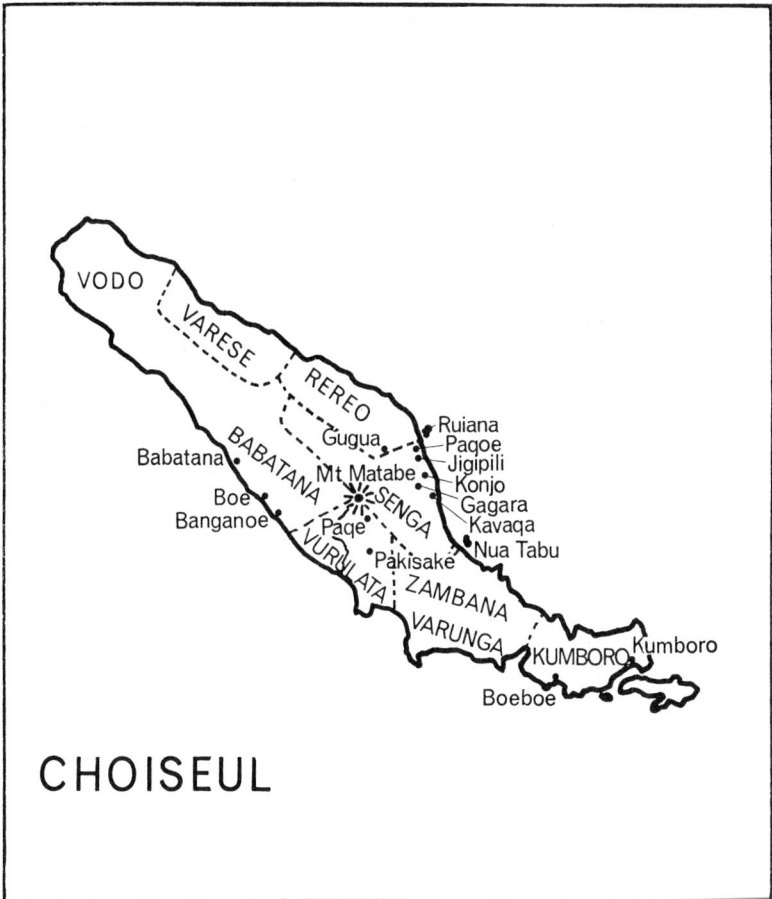

CHOISEUL
showing the districts and villages involved in the feud

eventually won through and brought the feud to an end after two decades of unrest.

(c) *The Bearing of these Events on Church Planting.* Before we turn to the procedure and ceremonial of reconciliation and peace-making, we ought to note the bearing of the feud on church planting, because it provides some valid points for observation. They may be summarized thus:

1. During the period of the feud the gospel was spreading slowly through Lauru, and strangely enough the network of connections which facilitated the feud also led to the spread of information

about Christianity. Christian teachers were already resident in a number of the villages concerned. They had the courage to go and come along the same paths as the hired assassins.

2. The utterly foolish punitive expeditions delayed the solution of problems and were neither just nor sympathetic. The fact that the Christian party was opposed to punitive expeditions and offered another way—that of negotiation within the structure of indigenous mediation patterns—gave Christianity a good hearing, especially when the feud dragged on so long and both parties were tired of war.

3. The courage and concern of the Christian teachers for the termination of the feud, their readiness to make long and dangerous journeys, and their skill at getting through enemy watches, gained them respect and a hearing. The readiness of the missionaries to take similar risks and to provide facilities for peace-making ceremonies, with or without the acceptance of Christianity, made quite an impression. Many accepted peace long before they accepted Christianity.

4. The case for peace pressed by the Christian teachers and missionaries determined to a large extent the form of presentation of the gospel—namely, Christ as Prince of Peace and the gospel as a way of reconciliation.

5. The feud itself undoubtedly hindered the growth of the Church. Christians were suspect as underminers of the warrior way of life. However, in the face of the unreasonableness of the way of punitive expeditions, the Christian way of mediation was at least meaningful; and when it became quite apparent that the life of war, feuding and head-hunting was to be stamped out by the Administration in any event, many turned to the Church and asked for teachers. The indigenous attitudes towards the indigenous Christian teacher were infinitely better than those towards the island police.

6. The Church achieved the peace. Immediately the wound that had been open for twenty years was healed, the growth of the Church accelerated and spread along those very lines of hitherto bitter rivalry. Either for war or peace those lines of contact operated. One by one the mechanisms of murder—sorcery, treachery, spearing, shooting, professional murder and retaliatory raiding—became things of the past. Preachers itinerated where assassins had previously crept stealthily. Travellers greeted one another on the mountain paths instead of taking cover till the other had gone by.

This change of attitude of man to man was either directly or indirectly the result of the gospel of reconciliation. The reduction of anarchy in Lauru, like the spread of education and medicine, was the work of the Methodist Church.[6] I have used Lauru only as a type. It might have been an area where the Melanesian Mission had done the pioneering.[7]

THE PROCEDURE AND CEREMONIAL OF RECONCILIATION

Feuds had to be settled on two levels—that of negotiation and reparation, and that of symbolic acceptance of peace. The Christian Church played a notable role on both these levels, so much so that the Administration even sought her aid when civil persuasion had failed. Peace-making proved a good advocacy for the gospel and the resultant growth, as I have already said, was considerable. The more I think over this, the more convinced I am that the Methodist missionaries and teachers were well fitted for this task because of their doctrinal position. They saw the life of man as a struggle in which the only satisfactory goal was reconciliation. When a man made his peace with God, an intelligent decision was demanded, his sins had to be confessed, restitution to be made if sins were against other men, and some public demonstration of his decision was expected. The pastor saw his role as bringing people to this position where man was one again with God and fellow-man. This theology certainly fitted the procedure and ceremonial of reconciliation in Lauru society, to which we now pay attention.

1. *The Role of the Go-between.* Although the mechanisms for peace-making existed in pre-Christian times, they were infrequently used. Feuds lasted for decades and often ended in the extermination or enslavement of one party. However, sometimes peace was restored when both parties were confronted by a mutual enemy, or when the social and economic state was too difficult for both. In any event, unless the situation produced an acceptable go-between, no peace was likely to result. Within the social group, only the strongest chief or some important priest was suitable for this role. Negotiation of peace called for powerful advocacy and considerable courage. Many of the early Christian teachers possessed these qualities and did not hesitate to use them in the cause of peace. In Lauru they won great respect.[8]

In the Senga–Vurulata feud Amos Tozaka was such an intermediary. He was, like Liliboe, one of the Vurulata tribe, but was stationed as the Christian teacher at Varese. Thus he had some contact with both sides and this made a suitable go-between. He and a companion crossed the island and followed the coast for thirty miles as unarmed mediators. They were shown a string of knots—sixty in all, each representing a 'kill' which had to be avenged. The companion string showed that only half had actually been avenged. Therefore he was told there could be no peace. Shortly afterwards, when Vurulata had secured another head, Amos tried again. Alone, by night, he visited the Vurulata barricaded stronghold, avoided the pits and stakes of its outer defences, bowed in prayer, climbed the barricade and reached the centre of the well-defended village without being discovered, to the great astonishment of the guards. They felt that Amos's God must have powerful *mana* so to hide him from their sight. Again he pressed his claim for peace. For three days and nights they debated the case and eventually threw the responsibility back on Amos—if he could persuade Senga, then they would consider terms for peace. Amos covered 100 miles in three days and went to the Senga canoe-house where the elders were assembled.

With a cold muzzle against his heart he asked for Joni Hopi, the Christian teacher in this locality. Between them they debated the issue until some terms for peace were acceptable and a date was fixed. In that canoe-house these intermediaries had bargained for the terms of a reparations agreement. They had to secure terms adequate and worthy to both sides and many journeys backwards and forwards had to be made before both sides had agreed.[9]

Missionary Binet had much the same experience when negotiating the settlement between the Kamunga and Vurulata people, in a case which took him 100 weeks with perhaps 100 interviews and 1,000 miles of travelling. The reparations demand had been inordinately high and Government mediation had been rejected. The settlement was also hindered by the French Roman Catholic fathers, who urged Vuruleke to demand higher terms, justifying their case on the French demands from Germany at that same time. In this case the go-between was shown, not knotted strings, but notched sticks, on which the tally was recorded by the number of points between the notches. Knotted strings or notched sticks, there was a primitive justice in this system which was recorded with strict accuracy. The system also provided something constructive to function as a basis for reparation discussions. Serving in this capacity, Binet learned much about the dimensions of quality and quantity of Lauruan custom-money,[10] and this knowledge helped him secure an 'adequate' and 'worthy' settlement. Although he had to make a contribution from his own treasured collection of 'curios' in the end, he gained great respect by his negotiations, and shortly afterwards the Kamunga people, who were pagans when they accepted his mediation, asked for a Christian teacher to come among them.

2. *The Symbol of the Overthrow of Enmity.* The ceremonies of reconciliation had to symbolize in the first place the overthrow of enmity. Restoration of friendship had to offer facilities for gathering together, for feasting and for dancing. This was symbolized in a demonstration known as the *felling of the suqu.* The *suqu* was a huge mushroom-shaped basket of food, held in position by supports. In the case of the Senga–Vurulata feud, which we have been discussing, the carved heads of the former enemies Jipe and Liliboe were at the base of the great basket. The enclosing basket-work signified the barrier between the clans, which prevented the two hostile parties from sharing food together. Before this basket the unreconciled parties assembled, everyone in full regalia all armed. The celebrations began with a sham fight, symbolizing the state of war and an early morning attack on a village. Then the reparation money was exchanged with due ceremony, followed by the peace-making ceremony to which we shall pay attention in a moment. In the heathen pattern the final act was the cutting of the supports of the *suqu,* so that the huge basket came crashing down before the skulls of the two rival ghosts. The food from the broken basket was distributed and feasting and dancing followed.[11]

With the use of Christian go-betweens, as we would expect, some Christian features were added to the ceremonies, but no significant changes were made to the symbolism of the indigenous pattern itself, which, as a symbol of reconciliation, already had a dimension that reached out towards Christianity.

3. *The Peace-making Ceremony.* When all the negotiations had been completed and the compensations actually made and accepted, but before the feasting and restored fellowship could be enjoyed, there had to be a face to face encounter between the two groups, in which the peace was accepted by ocular demonstration.

For this the two war parties lined up facing each other. It was a tense moment, for both parties were fully armed and facing their life-long enemies. Peace was established by the exchange of armlets, so the leaders placed their armlets on the ground, crunching them into the sand, symbolizing the burial of ill-will and past antagonisms. Then they picked up the armlets and exchanged them and thereafter were at peace. It was thus in the Senga–Vurulata reconciliation.[12] In the case of the Kamunga–Vuruleke ceremony, when the armlets were placed on the ground each chief touched the armlet of his opponent with his big toe, to signify that he was reaching out for friendship rather than war. Subsequently in each case, handshaking (a Christian feature) was included. When possible a Christian party also lined up for the occasion, mission people dressed in white singlets and loin-cloths with red sashes. When the armlets were exchanged, the Christians would sing some suitable hymn like "All hail the power of Jesu's name". Perhaps there would be a little speech-making by the go-between or the missionary; in the Kamunga–Vuruleke case, since it took place on a Sunday, a religious service followed. The reconciled parties, after some hesitation, stacked their arms outside and went into the church, listened to the hymns and a sermon on Psalm 46: 9: "He maketh wars to cease."[13]

Both these reconciliations in Choiseul were effective, and the Government officially expressed appreciation of the mediatorial work of the Church. The work of reconciliation was continued by the teachers and missionaries, their follow-up taking the form of efforts at effecting the manumission of slaves. In some areas they were immediately successful, but in others it took considerable time.[14]

The termination of these two feuds removed much obstruction to the growth of the Church. The next decade saw some 2,000 pagans come over as adherents to the Christian Church, and more than half of these demonstrated the quality growth demanded to bring them into full membership. These were organized into thirty congregations and produced thirty indigenous lay preachers. It seems obvious that feuds would hold up the growth of the Church, and that their termination would open the way for growth; but what we may easily overlook is that the very social lines (military, economic and political) which spread the poison of hate, now became channels of His grace, and Lauru is possibly the strongest Methodist area today.

.   .   .   .   .

Nevertheless, though this is a true account which can be fully documented, the chapter cannot be ended without pointing out its consequences, for the current situation is far from satisfactory.

The pattern of vengeance and feud served a social function in pre-Christian times for all within the network of kinship ties and the inter-clan supporting loyalties. Their pre-western ceremonial exchanges and also the structure of and supplies for feasting involved organized co-operation for self-defence and general security. This also determined their concepts of wealth and provided for the creation of *big men*, who gave the social units in the co-operative pattern their cohesion and strength. If they were to resist their opponents effectively, they required efficient leadership. The vengeance pattern of feuds both called forth the natural leaders and provided the facilities for their capacities of leadership to develop. Competence in war was only one of the characteristics required, but the loss of the feuding pattern deprived the Choiseul people of both leaders and the means for training leaders. The seriousness of this problem in Choiseul society today has been discussed by Scheffler—

> It is now virtually impossible for a man to acquire power through any source other than the missions or the government. The Choiseulese are quite aware of and disconcerted by these facts; they see that one of their major problems is that everyone is a big man and that consequently no-one is . . .

and again

> The Choiseulese today have little to unite them, either as individuals or as groups, into a larger society. They remain, instead, associated by little more than the fact that they live together, though hardly 'united' on an island. They feel deprived of leadership. . . .[15]

In several other sections of my report on the Western Solomons I have mentioned other cultural features, removed by commerce, mission or administration, only to leave cultural voids. Yet blame for this is not because the old patterns have been discarded—for these most certainly had to go. Furthermore, the islanders saw that this was so. When both Government and mission began encouraging coastal settlements and coconut plantations, a more peaceful state of affairs was required. The fault did not lie in the changes themselves, but in the fact that the changes deprived the people of activities and interactions and offered no functional substitutes for producing and developing leaders among the indigenous people. Both government and mission were thoroughly colonial and paternal.

Of course the vengeance system had to go. The missionaries *won* this phase of the struggle with great honour and established belief in the Prince of Peace and Reconciler of Men. However they *lost* the 'follow-up', by failing to realize that the things discarded, though admittedly bad, did nevertheless serve social functions. Legitimate functional substitutes should have been provided. The domination of affairs from Roviana was paternalistic. The system of plantations did not help matters, because its control was foreign and it called folk away from village life.

CHAPTER 14

Comparative Analysis of Nativistic Movements

NUMEROUS MOVEMENTS of political and religious consequence have emerged in the Solomon Islands during the last forty years. In this chapter a brief comparative analysis is made of four, emanating from different localities in our area of study. The Pokokoqoro Cult flourished in Choiseul shortly before the war. Marching Rule had its most extreme form in Malaita immediately after the war, and more recently Etoism has appeared in New Georgia and the Hahalis Welfare Movement in Buka. In structure and operation they differ considerably, but they have a number of common points.

All these movements have been thoroughly Melanesian, with an anti-Government feeling, though the manifestations of this have not been equally aggressive. They were all movements for Melanesian independence led by Melanesians. Where individuals have stood out as leaders, they have usually been from the social classes which have come into being under acculturation—school teachers, mission agents, or policemen—persons who have been associated with European authority, discipline and privileges. For example, Eto was a mission catechist, Paukubatu was a disgruntled teacher, Teosin trained but failed at the Government Teachers' College, Pokokoqoro was a discharged policeman, and Timothy George had witnessed the great Sydney dock strike of 1913.

All four movements emerged more or less suddenly and spread spontaneously and enthusiastically over confined areas with some basis of social structure. Each demonstrated competence in organization. Each drew in some ways on Melanesian traditions and patterns, but not all the same traits. Each had a strong economic dimension in its aims and programme. Each had some clear roots in the pre-war state of affairs. Belshaw[1] has raised the question of 'mystical significance' in cults of this kind. He considers it common to them all—the mysteries of the circulation of money, the European reverence for flags and flagpoles, for towns and houses rather than villages, and for the drilling of soldiers (which must be mystical because it has no other value). This may have something to do with the common manifest forms of the movements.

So many common points would seem to justify the inclusion of this chapter applying the comparative method to several specific cases. One (Etoism) will be treated fully later but any one of these movements could really demand a book for itself. The Pokokoqoro Cult was a pre-war movement, and died on the eve of the war by a *challenge* and *encounter*, in which a Christian party overpowered a group of Pokokoqoro's followers, who were each supposed to have 'the strength of ten' from magical preparations. Its importance to us lies not only in this method of dealing with the problem but also because it was a fully fledged cargo cult that existed before the war. Its influence is seen in the Church statistics and it shows that, although the war did *stimulate* such movements, it did not *cause* them. The causative factors must be sought in the pre-war period.

All the areas concerned saw the Japanese occupation and the American invasion. The American influence is strongly marked in Marching Rule and to a lesser extent in Etoism. Marching Rule was the most highly developed politically and was not anti-Christian, Christians (especially evangelicals) and pagans alike being involved. Etoism is the most important theologically and seems likely to gain the most permanent recognition, although the Buka movement is giving the Administration the most concern at present. The most singular feature of the latter is the moral aspect of its *baby garden*, which is clearly anti-Christian and a direct challenge to the missions. Both Etoism and the Hahalis movement have been responsible for major exodus from the Church.

It would seem then that the religious, moral and political features of these movements have differed widely, but all of them have promised a coming period of prosperity, a plenteous food supply, and a Melanesian renaissance under Melanesian control. They were all movements towards social and economic independence. Let us now examine them one by one:

1. *Pokokoqoro Cult*

This cargo cult was established by a policeman, Pokokoqoro, banished from the Force in 1921 for blackmail, but reinstated to participate in the Malaita Expedition in 1926. He left a bad record in Malaita, where he obtained magical processes, medicinal formulae and incantations.

Obtaining a pedlar's licence and a launch, he settled in the Tabataba district of Choiseul. He set up his movement on the small island of Vasu, a regular cargo cult promising a glorious prosperity in the near future, complete with a steamer bringing its cargo of rice, tinned foods and other forms of wealth in abundance. He persuaded the local people to invest in his project sums of £10, £20 and £30, and thus he managed to maintain a show of affluence for a time. He had a ready supply of labour among his supporters. They cleared the small island of its casuarina forest and built houses to store the supplies to be brought by the anticipated steamer. He sent occasional gifts of rice and biscuits to the mission pastor-teachers to gain their friendship. He fed the members of his cult on rice and tinned meat. When no steamer arrived and funds began to run out, he removed to Varesē, where he was joined by an assistant, Paukubatu, a competent but disgruntled teacher.

The Mission now took a stand against his cult and activities. He was denounced at the church quarterly meeting and his gifts to pastor-teachers were criticized. When the Church declared its mind on these matters, his creditors became alarmed. Pokokoqoro and his colleague now removed to a tract of land with a Mission plantation. The land was tribal but the Mission owned the trees by traditional ownership pattern, i.e. a mission teacher had planted them. Pokokoqoro could not be expelled from the land, neither could the Mission police the collection of its nuts. Pokokoqoro lived on these Mission resources and intimidated the neighbourhood until 1940.

A group of men who had defected from Christianity—six Roman Catholics and six Methodists—were provided with a secret Malaita magical preparation by Pokokoqoro. This was the *samuka* which gave each man 'the strength of ten'. Thereafter this gang roved the countryside terrorizing those who remained true to the Churches. Eventually a small group of Christians took up this challenge and gave them a sound thrashing. One of these was a Methodist teacher, who had suffered from paralysis, and whose body bore the marks of this complaint. In the fight he pinned one of those with 'the strength of ten' with a painful armlock so that the latter began crying for mercy. The crowd, which had gathered to witness the contest, shouted "The *samuka* has lost its power". On the beach an act of Christian worship was held. God was thanked for strengthening the teacher, the twelve promised to behave themselves, and cut their losses—each had paid Pokokoqoro £5 for the *samuka*. Paukubatu also wrote off the £14 he had handed to Pokokoqoro and the prophet was now left high and dry. Thus ended an organized movement which had lasted for a number of years and had done much economic, social and religious harm.

In passing we should note that the Christians—and they were young Christians who had not travelled far in the faith—did not assert that the *samuka* was a fake. They accepted it at its face value. They knew Pokokoqoro had been to Malaita and had left a very bad record there, that he dealt in magical traffic, and they knew him as something of a prophetic figure. The Christian pastor-teacher, on the other hand, was known to them as physically weak because of his paralysis. What man of this kind could master the 'strength of ten' and have his victim crying for mercy, unless he were one who had some still greater power than the *samuka*? It was regarded as a power encounter. It was therefore natural that the struggle should terminate in an act of Christian worship on the beach. Thus the Pokokoqoro Cult was effectively dealt with by indigenous action within an indigenous frame of reference.

Our data on this movement comes from letters written between 1936 and 1941.[2] It is important to have these primary sources stating this idea of steamers bringing cargo for the benefit of Melanesian communities and the dream of prosperity 'just round the corner'. The American transports and war supplies are frequently blamed for this Melanesian concept. No doubt they stimulated it, but letters dated before the war show they did not originate it. A tendency towards the millenarianism of Melanesian cargo cults was in the pre-war situation, and this is why the pre-war decade is so important to this book as a whole, and why so much space was devoted in Part II to the policies and procedures of that period.

2. Marching Rule

Marching Rule did not originate as a single movement from a single prophet, but sprang from a number of competent leaders in different localities. Some were pagan and others Christians. Religion was not a basic drive in this movement. Worsley insists this movement was "not a cult but a political party" and points out that their demand for equal wages, for improved education and social services, for independence and self-rule and for national self-expression is the ordinary stuff of world politics.[3]

Masinga Lo and *Masinga Rulu* were new terms, attractively mysterious, with no local meaning. Europeans interpreted them as Marching Rule, because of the militant aspect of the movement; but Fox presses the view that they represent Marx's Law or Marx's Rule. Undoubtedly the influence of American communists, critical of British colonialism, was strongly felt in this movement. The Americans are said to have left $200,000 in Malaita. Fees for entrance into the movement were in dollars. British money was not acceptable. The prototype for the observation towers in the Marching Rule villages was the American customs house at Tulagi. They called their towers "custom houses".[4] Allen insists that *Masinga* has no connection with Communism, but is a South Malaita word for *brotherhood*.[5]

In any event the desire for American goods was passionate. Many American soldiers assured them that after the war America would see they got independence from Britain. The idea of communal farms was tried under Marching Rule, but failed because the people were traditionally individual farmers. There is no doubt these plans were formulated during the period of American occupation.

Yet this could not have happened without something in the situation itself on which to build. The cry was for no taxation, no obedience to the Government, no labour for the white man (i.e. the foreign profiteer).[6]

The economic situation was aggravated by the fact that 3,000 Malaita men in the Volunteer Labour Corps, serving under ex-planter officers, were receiving £1 per month as pay, as against £14 being earned by free labourers. The latter also had profitable side-lines in island curios and fresh food supplies for the Americans.[7]

The amazing organization of the movement surprised everyone, for Malaita had always been a very much divided island and not much loved by the surrounding people, many of whom came in with the movement for a time. Government and Church had tried in vain to secure this unity. Another surprising fact was the spontaneity of the explosion and the wide range of its rapid spread. The secrecy maintained against the European was perfect.

The movement sought economic betterment and believed in a paradise to come when the big ships returned from America after the war. Any desire for return to an old Melanesian way of life was on the part of the younger members who did not remember the horrors and ceremonial inhumanity of the old way, but who felt that under acculturation something of the past had been lost. They wanted to attain to the advantages of civilization and its wealth, and had learned a new, but not completely meaningful cry for 'freedom'. Where Marching Rule was in control, life was strongly regimented— it wasn't free at all.[8]

The organizers divided Malaita into nine districts, under head chiefs, and towns with sub-chiefs. New towns were laid out like army camps and built along the coast. Towns were picketed, communal duties and labour were supervised, security forces were drilled, a body of clerks drew up lists of members and operated under the routine of a typical army camp. Legal procedure, based on customary law, was established with courts and gaols. The codification of customary law had been denied hitherto, and the failure of the Administration to understand or consider custom had long been a 'bone of contention'. The movement symbolized its entity and loyalties by means of a flag.

The Government attitude fluctuated and this is variously inter-preted. Officially it is said that from 1945–47 the Government respected the movement and tried to turn it into productive channels, but action had to be taken on numerous reports of intimidation and false imprisonment by the Marching Rule leaders. The leaders were arrested and dealt with before the High Commissioner's Court. When the Government made this stand, many of the non-Malaita adherents left the movement and turned to economic pursuits recommended by the Government. Malaita was passively non-co-operative, to such an extent that 2,000 passively went to gaol and remained there for some time. A hard core of resistance remained in Central Malaita, even after the nine leaders were released from prison in 1950 on a promise of co-operation.[9]

After release they changed their tactics and sought to use a con-stitutional resistance by setting up a Federal Council independent of the Administration in 1951. In 1952 the Government offered Malaita an Island Council but the Federal Council ordered boycott. In September of that year the High Commissioner visited Malaita and offered them a Malaita Council, with its own President chosen by the delegates, if they would recognize Government authority and district officers and obey laws.

The official attitude was that only economic prosperity could solve the problem. The Government claimed that local native authorities had been set up before Marching Rule and policy had been to channel the initiative of Marching Rule into this con-stitutional machinery. But the Malaita people wanted their own forms. The Government was annoyed at their attitude to labour supply, and blamed the movement for holding up rehabilitation after the war, when the economy required rapid restoration of plantation production. Marching Rule supposedly prevented the development of co-operatives and census-taking. Later the Government reported that Marching Rule was breaking down because of increasing economic prosperity in the Group.[10]

The movement is now quiescent.

Outside Malaita the movement had strong origins in Guadalcanal, where it had first begun under Vouza, a war-hero, who holds both the George Medal and the American Silver Star. The Government frowned on his political activities and gave him a course in local government, which was the best way of handling the problem.[11]

Brown Julamana, a Melanesian Mission teacher, involved in Vouza's movement, had previously worked with a missionary connected with an earlier movement known as Chair and Rule. This teacher circulated a story that the missionary (who had been sent away from the Protectorate, though much respected by his followers) was back in Guadalcanal in an American military hideout. Julamana opposed farming, diving for shell, preparing copra, or working in any other way for the white man.[12] The Chair and Rule Movement operated in Savo, Gela and Ysabel and agitated for a seat on the Advisory Council.[13]

Another Guadalcanal offshoot of Marching Rule was known as Freedom Movement and was led by a Roman Catholic catechist. It was based on the U.N.O. Charter of Rights, the Atlantic Charter, Scripture, Churchill's famous speech after Dunkirk, and borrowed also from Marching Rule and the cargo myth.[14]

The official position does not allow for some of the major factors, especially with respect to Malaita. The Government claim that it had been working on Native Courts and Councils before Marching Rule depends on where the origins of the movement are placed. The Government had been forced into this by the Chair and Rule Movement.[15] We shall have to pay some attention to this point. One wonders if the Administration would have made any of these moves for indigenous development without these movements goading them into it. The official reports suggest a greater concern for supplies of cheap labour, as the means for restoring plantation production, than for the real progress of the island people.[16]

The official position is perhaps what might be expected from a central body, which very much desired a unified Protectorate controlled from a central station. But this is certainly not where the Solomon Islands stand today in their political evolution. They are still in the transitional stage of achieving their passage to insular unity from a multiplicity of warring tribal units. The salt-water man and the bushman have still not fully realized that they are both Malaitamen —let alone Solomon Islanders. The big forward drive in Malaita is to achieve the unity of their island. This was a major feature of Marching Rule there, and, let it be admitted, a progressive forward move.

I had a long and profitable interview with an interesting Malaitaman, a man of some civil status and one not afraid to express his opinion. He declared that Marching Rule was one of the best things that had happened in Malaita and that most of the things they had fought for they had won. I asked him there and then to specify them. As good as his boast he immediately ticked off five points on his fingers. He said:

1. We wanted the unity of all Malaita with a president or a paramount chief. We now have this.
2. We wanted a council under that president, where affairs of concern to all Malaita could be discussed. Now we have it.
3. We wanted representatives from all the different areas of Malaita, so discussions could be effective. We now have this.
4. We wanted Solomon Island magistrates to try local cases, and not Europeans who knew nothing of customary law. We now have them.
5. If Malaita was to be taxed at all, we wanted that revenue expended on the development of Malaita. This is now being done.

My informant was convinced that without Marching Rule none of these things would have been achieved. He put his finger on three important problems—the unity of Malaita, the unfamiliarity of white officials with customary law and attitudes, and the distribution of revenue derived from taxation. These have been points of distrust with Administrative policy over the years: administration from outside, judgements from outside, and expenditure of local revenue outside. They represent three passionate cries—the cry for entity, the cry for justice, and the cry for development. The Government could well argue that these were its own motives. True, but they were differently conceptualized. It is just that difference which is all-important to the Malaita people, who see progress in terms of the unification of one large island, hitherto much segmented, rather than in terms of a Protectorate which is far from being an ethnic entity at all. Whether my informant's claim was right or wrong, he was convinced of its truth and he represents a large body of opinion. One could never convince the Malaita people that they had held up progress. They had to give way on the matter of labouring for the white man, but they achieved their purposes everywhere else. The fact that they did not win the labour issue means that it has still to be faced at some future date.

The plantation labour problem emerged as a problem in the days of the economic depression of the early thirties. European commercial interests were alarmed at the depopulation and blamed this for the difficulty with which they obtained labour supply. They agitated for Indian indenture but the Advisory Council rejected it.[17] They were badly hit by the low price of copra and pressed for aid in various forms, including the discontinuation of tobacco rations to labour and reduction of their wages and extension of indenture terms.[18] While it is true that there was a widespread belief that Oceania would be completely depopulated ultimately unless Asian labour was introduced,[19] the remedies pressed by the commercial interests meant a gross injustice to the Melanesian labourers. There are two fallacies in the viewpoint of the commercial interests. One is the supposition that

H

a sound economic structure and happy society can be built on cheap labour. The second is the assumption that such establishments require white men to rule, administer and control, while it is the duty of the brown man to do the manual labour—that they were each born to these stations of master and servant.

It is significant that at the very time we are discussing—the thirties—the earlier labour agitation was coming from the Melanesians. The Chair and Rule Movement, which accepted the chair and rule as symbols of leadership and constitutional procedure, agitated not only for representation but also for increased wages. Some of the Marching Rule leaders came from that movement. Once again we find the roots in the pre-war decade. In this case, as we have seen, they were economic not religious, but more than this the real issue is the respective status of white and brown, the right of one to rule and the duty of the other to labour, the high wage to one and the low to the other. Even more than all this, it is the matter of the foreign master and the indigenous labourer in the homeland of the latter. This problem still remains to be answered.

The question of tax appears to be settled for the time being. The test will come when the Government begins to use some of the Malaita revenue for wider Protectorate burdens or central costs. For many years government officials were seen as tax collectors only. It was this issue (together with the calling in of rifles legitimately bought from traders) which led to the Bell murder and the accompanying massacre in 1926. Though this was a local affair only, the Administration called in warships, some forty persons died and another twenty were hanged. It has been described as a "Gilbert and Sullivan expedition" of planters and traders who went to Malaita to restore order, well paid in liquor and rations, and entirely colonialist. The attitudes of the people which made Marching Rule possible had been built up over many years of taxation, western justice and colonial authority patterns. Without this background the American anti-imperialists would never have received a hearing.

In addition to the war and the American influence, Allen attributed Marching Rule to the following factors: the long contact with the labour traffic and indenture, the failure of the Government in matters of education, the Administration's disregard of custom, the interlocking of taxation and indenture, cultural fatigue, the domination of Government headmen by the South Seas Evangelical Mission teachers, the influenza epidemic before the war, the Chair and Rule Movement and the fundamentalist dogma of the Mission mentioned.[20] I leave Allen to defend all these claims for himself, but I certainly agree at two points—the general complexity of the causative factors, and the fact that the roots lie in the pre-war situations and policies.[21]

The Australian Board of Missions issued an official statement in 1952 and interpreted the situation in the following way. Marching Rule is linked with other movements in other islands that were not purely economic and political. Everywhere the Church is confronted by organizations of Communism or Nationalism, it being the latter in

Melanesia. Their common point is said to be freedom from oppression; the basic cause, resentment of inequality between islanders and white men. Missions, Governments and war have all given hope, but none has been fulfilled—hence the resultant resentment. The Board sees the only possible solution in bringing the island people to understand that wealth and prosperity can only come by hard work. Meantime missions are faced by many problems—poor equipment, a demand for education they cannot finance, the meagre support from the home Church, and on the mission field itself the obstructive influence of agnostic Europeans.[22] One may agree with all this but even so it is to 'beg the question'. In the last analysis such problems are not solved by equipment and foreign funds, or by hard work by the people themselves. If human relationships are wrong, and attitudes are wrong, and situations of wrong relationships have been built up through misunderstandings over a period of years, the only ultimate solution is the correction of these relationships, attitudes and misunderstandings themselves.

I have not seen any statement on this matter from the evangelicals, although their indigenous teachers are supposed to have provided 15 per cent of the leaders of the movement.[23] This Mission has lost standing since the war and has handed affairs over to a South Seas Evangelical Church. It is interesting to note that one of the first basic statements in their *Association Guide Book* for the use of the emerging Church was:

> Christians willingly obey the laws of the Government in all matters except those to do with religion (worship). The laws of the country are good for the people.[24]

It would appear that the Mission and Church did not quite see eye to eye on the matter of Marching Rule. The assumption that the laws of the country "are good for the people" would not be appreciated by the 15 per cent who were leaders in Marching Rule, nor is it necessarily true, if it means what it says.

3. The Hahalis Welfare Society

Buka has been subject to movements of this kind ever since the place came under culture contact. A new form appears roughly every decade. The Lontis Cult of 1913 emerged under German Administration and numerous arrests were made at the time.[25] After the war, when the territory had passed under Australian influence, there were disturbances in 1920.[26] A further revival came in 1932–33, a regular cargo cult proclaiming the coming of a steamer with goods and a unified rule of all Buka from Lontis. The adherents built a store for the expected goods, abandoned gardening and prepared to resist any police interference.[27] The leaders were imprisoned but the cult continued. It revived again in 1942–43 under the belief that the arrival of the Japanese heralded the long-promised millennium. It was a distinctly military form that the movement took, and cultural borrowings included the Japanese ceremonial bow and elements of their ancestor cult. The Japanese, however, became

INSTABILITY AND IRREGULARITY IN CHURCH GROWTH
DUE TO NATIVISTIC MOVEMENTS
Based on Methodist Statistics for the Western Solomons

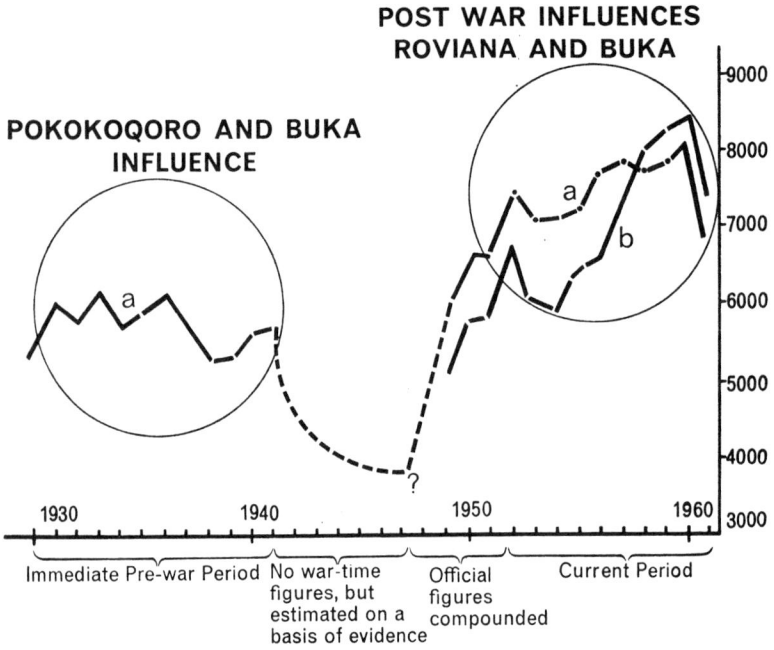

a. Full church membership   b. Youth roll membership (post-war)

Note the zigzag statistical effect of movements of growth and loss going on
at the same time. These are district statistics. A breakdown into localities
is needed to discover the real situation.

alarmed at the organization of the movement and arrested the
leaders.[28] The dates given in this paragraph are by no means clear-
cut. It could be argued, as Worsley does, that Buka reveals a "continuity of cults"—certainly the basic beliefs were continuous.

The movement in its current form broke out in 1957 in the village
of Hahalis and three subsidiary hamlets. It spread along the east
coast and occupied the land area of Hahahakalan, the leadership
running through one kin lineage, but the adherents coming from
three different linguistic areas. At its maximum strength nearly
10,000 people were influenced. Opposition was met from some west
coast units and from Tanamalo and some inland people. The movement reacted with hostility to this opposition.

In character the Hahalis movement is strongly political, anti-
Government and anti-Christian. Its economic pressure was for

common ownership. The name *Hahalis Welfare Society* was adopted, and the officials include *Spokesmen*, who stir up enthusiasm by magical rites, and *Party Whips*, who use intimidation if necessary. The movement has a total disregard for any outside authority and is thoroughly belligerent. There is resistance to the payment of tax, resistance to enforcement of the law by armed police, and up to five hundred have been gaoled at one time according to the press.[29]

The movement borrowed Christian hymn tunes for paraphrases, established ceremonies for dressing graves and supplying food for ghosts, holds a nightly indoctrination gathering known as *kivung*, followed by the pairing off of partners for sexual relationships.

The unique feature of the movement is its *Baby Garden*, based on a perverted interpretation of the Virgin Mary and Jesus Christ. This open prostitution expresses a desire for children in great numbers, as a sign of prosperity. It is highly organized. All girls are available to any men of the Society. Marriage counts for nothing and wife-exchange is openly practised. This is one expression of resistance to Christianity.

Roman Catholics, who have been hit badly by this movement, are hostile and offenders are excommunicated. The verbal hostility of Seventh Day Adventist preaching has led to their expulsion from some areas. Methodists have rejected the movement, but have maintained their work wherever possible, leaving the way open for any to return who repent and accept the Methodist position. Some have 'returned to the fold' but the movement is still strong and appears to have settled at a strength of about 6,000 persons.

The Government attitude of "Crush Teosin!" (the leader) aggravated the situation. The people refused to pay tax. Four hundred police crushed riots and 200 people were injured. Some high officials visited the area and made promises which have not materialized. As a result, under Roman Catholic pressure, a Government station was then built at Buka, but the only material achievement has been the expenditure of £60,000 on a Government road, for which the Society had asked. The Methodists also urged the appointment of Teosin to the Bougainville district council.[30] There is now a Buka local council but the Society refuses to have anything to do with it. At present the Government is making use of an intermediary to try to remedy this situation.[31]

This movement differs from the others mostly in its moral attitude towards marriage and sex and the family. Here it has departed from both its own traditions and the Christian position. Both Roman Catholics and Methodists have admitted concern at the number of mere nominals in this area. A Methodist missionary thought this probably applied to 50 per cent of the people before the breakaway. A Roman Catholic missionary thought this applied to 75 per cent of his. The lapse into immorality is clearly an anti-Mission gesture. It was a thorough-going rejection, and I have more unpleasant data about this which it seems unnecessary to disclose.

The Society reflects many of the personal attitudes of Teosin, one of the leaders responsible for introducing some of the unique features. He had attended both Methodist and Roman Catholic institutions, and had some teacher training, but had achieved nothing and was disgruntled. The Missions had promised eternal life but had not supplied it. Education got them nowhere, and more and more English was being demanded. Teosin saw that Australian wealth came from gambling, and so he studied arithmetic to learn how to manipulate numbers, but his efforts failed and the Missions opposed gambling anyway. The Government demanded tax, promising to develop the country—but in seventy years there had been no development, only trade for the white man's profit.[32] So let us go our own way, Teosin urged, because Missions, Government, education, hospitals, co-operatives and development programmes have all made promises and have all come to nought. This was his declared attitude.[33] If he was representative of the group, this explains a good deal.

One question I asked of this movement was whether it preached a messiah or had anything messianic about it. My principal informant gave me a negative reply. Another informant, however, whom I questioned in the Solomons, said that one of the stated motives of the brothels in the Hahalis villages was that some day they believed there would emerge from one of these a Melanesian messiah. This testimony has now been confirmed. This is just the type of concept which becomes enshrined in a myth and gives a movement 'staying-power'. Sooner or later some child of a Hahalis 'baby garden' is bound to make that claim. All he needs is some prophetic characteristic and the movement will be revitalized on a large scale. There is perpetual danger in this area unless the whole place is swept by a strong evangelical revival with a demonstrative power encounter.

4. Etoism

Etoism is examined in greater detail in Part V—"The Western Solomons Schism". I include here only enough information to permit comparison with the other movements.

Etoism arose in the Kusage area of New Georgia and spread rapidly through Roviana and some of the smaller islands nearby, along lines of social structure. It met with strong opposition from Seventh Day Adventist and some Methodist villages. After a crisis the movement broke away from the Church and made the claim of being itself the true Church—the Christian Fellowship Church or the C.F.C.

This movement has good organization and leadership based on Christian patterns. The central figure is a prophet, who now claims a place in the Godhead. The theology is highly developed and may be studied from their extensive collection of Eto hymns. It is thoroughly syncretistic and incorporates both Roman Catholic and Methodist beliefs and practices with pre-Christian magical rites, behaviour and belief.

Etoism has a specific structure, attempts to fill some of the voids

EFFECT OF NATIVISTIC MOVEMENTS ON THE GROWTH
OF CONGREGATIONS

This graph depicts the growth of churches (congregations) in the Western Solomons in the post-war period showing how the tendency to grow by people-movement is obstructed by people-movement defections in the areas that have been long evangelized, but where no indigenous church has been developed.

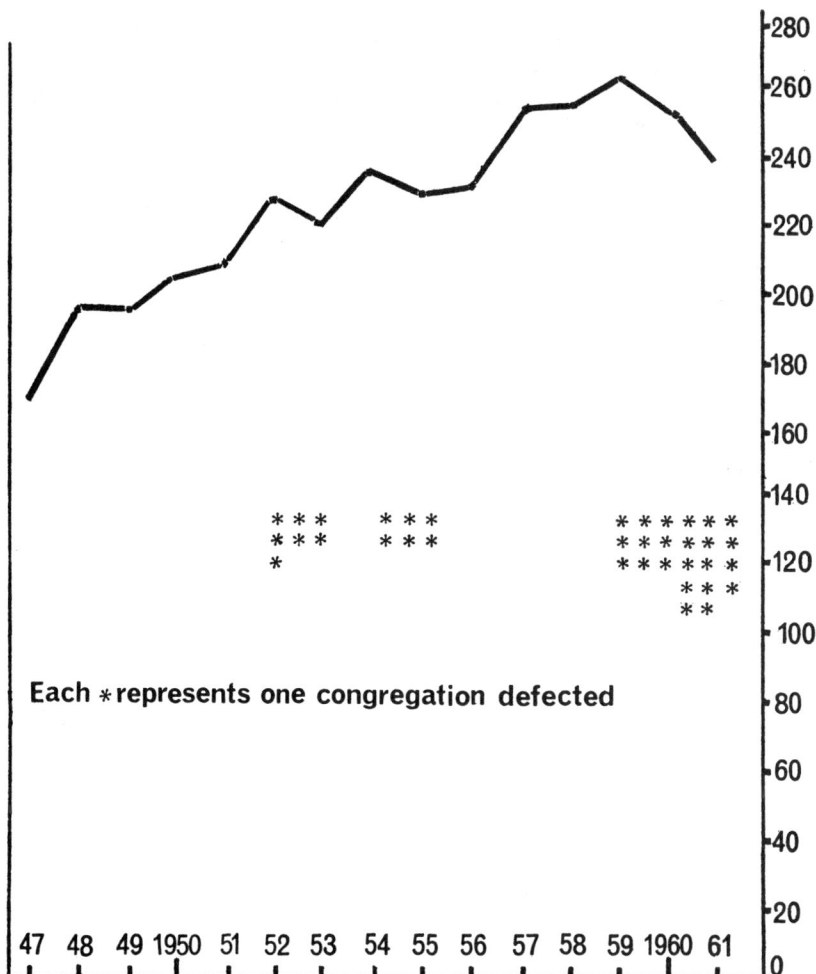

Each * represents one congregation defected

left by Christian negativism, has a system of mass rallies, and a highly developed and stimulated *enthusiasm*, supposedly the work of the Holy Spirit.

The movement has strong economic organization and some accumulated funds, from which the leaders draw more benefit than the rank and file. It has a strong awareness of its own entity. It is anti-foreign and resists authority in many ways (church committees, medical services, mosquito control) but has not had an open rift with the Government. It does not appear to be in any way militaristic. The marching and demonstrating is not military but enthusiastic, i.e. designed to create a particular emotional state.

Civil authority and planters tried to persuade the Church to act against the movement, but the Mission policy was one of 'wait and see'. The movement has its own social segments, which, though currently cohesive, could break apart. The children are subject to intense indoctrination. The movement is at present in the process of establishing itself as a 'church', and is seeking a legal constitution.

Etoism had its roots in the pre-war period. Long before the war the case of Etoism had been discussed in the church meetings, and on one occasion a deputation had been appointed to investigate Eto's activities, especially among the children. The children of his group at that time are now the adult members of his fully developed movement.

Eto personally was displeased with the post-war policy changes in the Mission. He claimed special lines of inspiration from the founder of the Church in the Western Solomons (Goldie) and from John Wesley, accused the missionaries of hiding the true doctrines of Wesley, and insisted that he was always under the guidance of the Holy Spirit.

Quite manifestly this is a religious movement. Even its economic organization has borrowed from the church organizational structure. The worship patterns are central and intense. The beliefs have much more theological (if heretical) depth. Eto himself itinerates regularly for mass rallies, but not so frequently that these will become commonplace. He remains on his lofty height as Holy Father. He draws the movement's capacity for organization from a social unit other than his own. This coalition is a great achievement. The movement appears to be stable.

.   .   .   .   .

Of these four movements with so many points in common, the Pokokoqoro Cult is dead as a result of direct encounter with Christian Melanesians, the Marching Rule is dormant and there is currently some constitutional development which will probably prevent its being revived, but the other two seem to be establishing themselves and claiming recognition, one in the Protectorate and the other in the Territory.

The question which now confronts the Methodist Church is whether these two organizations, one with a completely un-Christian morality and the other completely heretical in the eyes of orthodox Christians, are to be received in co-existence. Or are they to be fields for evangelism? A policy of just "leaving the door open for repentance and return" will mean the former. If they are to be re-won for Christianity, it is doubtful whether the white missionaries should activate that evangelism. It seems rather a role for the indigenous Church itself, though strangely enough in both cases there has been more opposition to the secessionists from the indigenous pastors than from the missionaries. It is difficult to see through this problem confronting the Church, but it will have to be faced sooner or later.

There can be little doubt that in those areas where movements of this kind have assumed moral and religious dimensions, the Christians involved have been largely nominal. In both areas they were resisted by Christians of a more solid experience, and in Buka we know that many Christians died for their faith during the Japanese occupation. Yet my feeling is that even in the stronger Christian Solomon Island villages there are a significant number of merely nominal Christians. This will be demonstrated shortly in piety curves. In this event one has a strong feeling that the Church should organize a planned drive for revival and rededication within the remaining congregations, and then with the resultant new life, press on in congregational outreach to those who have defected in these movements. This ought to be planned and prayed for. I do not see how the outreach can be effective unless there is first some real revitalization within. This would be very much easier if there were less Mission and more Church in the Western Solomons.

Once more I pause to underline that last sentence. A Mission that fails to produce an indigenous Church within three or four decades from its large accessions from paganism is almost certain to experience this kind of movement. Where the indigeneity is defective on the level of the pastorate, the movement tends to be theologically or morally neo-pagan syncretism; where the indigeneity fails on the level of stewardship, the movement tends to assume political and economic proportions. In Malaita the pastorate is well developed, but the stewardship is sadly lacking. I think this accounts for the absence of neo-pagan theological dimensions in Marching Rule. It would be interesting to know if this is true for such areas as Africa.

Linton,[34] who pioneered the study of this type of movement, claimed that:

> Nativistic movements tend to arise only when the members of the subject society find that their assumption of the culture of the dominant group is being effectively opposed by it, or that it is not improving their social position.

Perhaps we may even go a step further than this. The distinctive features of the movement will suggest those aspects of the culture contact in which the frustrations are most keenly felt—social, economic, political or religious. It therefore follows that the same distinctive features will also suggest the area in which effective remedy must be found for the situation. The most important bearing of this truth for this present volume is that a failure to develop an indigenous Church within five or six decades (or say four decades of the people-movements from paganism) is itself a major cause of any nativistic movement with strong religious dimensions. It is for this reason that Part V of this book is devoted to a careful theological and structural analysis of Etoism.

I also feel it incumbent upon me to stress for missionary readers that basic features of these movements do tend to persist. They do not disappear with the failure of some prophecy, or the exile or imprisonment of the leader—or even with his death, for resurrections are common in nativistic movements. Failures can be explained away by Melanesian logic, and even these very explanations reinforce the faith on the vision, the millennium, the messiah or the doctrine. Worsley calls this *the continuity of the cults*, and he superbly illustrates this from the case of Buka from 1913 down to the end of the Pacific War.[35] Even while his work was in the hands of the publisher, the movement was breaking out again. After half a century of German, British, Japanese, American and Australian influence, the basic issues are still alive and unresolved, as the daily paper has reminded me only this week. The issues are still the same egalitarianism—a simple communism, abandonment of taboos, resistance of status levels, antagonism against foreign rule, demand for an equal share in the prosperity and the financial returns of the white man. So in Buka it takes the form of a Welfare Society with a 'free' life (even though that 'freedom' be established by intimidation), and a hope that some day a messiah will arise from the progeny of the 'baby garden'. The continuity can be broken only when the sources of social discontent are met squarely and the community desires are satisfied—political in Malaita, social in Buka, or religious in New Georgia.

Part Five

THE WESTERN SOLOMONS SCHISM

15 The Prophet and the Situation
    The problem
    Historical sequences
    The prophet's dreams and personal claims
    The Fraternal Investigator's Report
    Diffusion

16 The Group Experiences of Etoism
    The behaviour of the group
    Enthusiasm and encounter with sin
    "Battle for the Mind"
    Wesley and enthusiasm
    The dynamics of the emergence ofEtoism

17 Theological Analysis of Etoism
    Pagan associations
    Analysis of Etoist hymns

    Concluding Summary for Part Five

CHAPTER 15

The Prophet and the Situation

THE PROBLEM

THE METHODIST line-graph of growth for the Western Solomons during the post-war years shows a common statistical effect of two compensating forces in competition. Such graphs need regional break-down. In Bougainville there was considerable growth but the Roviana figures reveal a real landslide. In this chapter we are to survey briefly the character of an exodus of some 3,000 persons from the Church, involving some twenty or more villages. The movement is known as Etoism. Aiming at establishing themselves as a 'church', the adherents now speak of themselves as the *Christian Fellowship Church*, although one more frequently finds them saying the *C.F.C.* They have not yet been so constituted, though the matter is in hand.

Almost all the European missionary informants begin by saying that Silas Eto always was a peculiar person and a problem to those who knew him best—in other words, the man is usually blamed for the movement. Most informants have reached a few general conclusions to explain the catastrophe. None of these is completely satisfactory. My very first European informant, for example, was satisfied that there were four main factors which stimulated Etoism:

1. Eto learned many of his eccentricities long ago from a certain mission sister, who used to climb under the house and hang at prayer like a bat.
2. One of the missionaries laboured his Second Coming preaching and spoke of a great revival that was about to sweep the land.
3. The Mission leaders ignored the movement. This *laissez faire* policy permitted Etoism to get established.
4. The influences of the war were important, especially that of the American Negroes and the book, *Battle for the Mind*,[1] which brought the movement to a head.

Some informants, unlike this missionary layman,[2] were not ready to express opinions as to causes, but were ready enough to report facts and events. Fortunately there is an abundance of evidence as to what happened, both with respect to the character and sequence of events. However, the general feeling of both missionaries and people was to blame Eto for everything. This is a *negative* view—a direct loss of some 3,000 adherents due to a person, a *coup d'état* at the expense of the Church, a calamity which fell unexpectedly on a well-established missionary work.

Now I submit that no spontaneous movement of this kind, which undoes half a century of missionary labour in a few weeks, can ever be regarded as purely negative—a direct loss due to a person. A *positive acceptance* is required. To leave Eto as alone responsible will never do. Of course he is the key figure, the advocate of the innovation, but the *act of acceptance* of both Eto and Etoism was a communal movement on a large scale, and this is *positive*, not negative. The people were the acceptors, the innovators, Etoism studied as a movement of acceptance seems to offer a more hopeful line for investigation. I therefore ask the reader to keep this in mind as we proceed: What were they seeking? What were the primary needs which Solomon Island Methodism was not supplying? When the years of crisis came and the cost of separation from the mother Church was brought home to them, they could still put their positive hopes in Eto and Etoism, and expect the prophet to bring them through—what were these hopes? We are to treat Etoism in a positive way, because the acceptors were more concerned with what they were gaining than with what they were discarding.

When the High Commissioner rebuked the Etoists, saying that they had turned from the Society which had done most for their physical health, their educational growth and spiritual outlook, he was viewing the matter negatively. Such an approach merely leaves us mystified at the folly of the whole movement. It disgusts us. But it brings us no nearer to an understanding of the people and their problems.

If this book is a study of church growth and obstruction to that growth, it is incumbent on me to examine Etoism against a background of Roviana Christianity, which it sought to displace. Does this examination disclose to us the shortcomings of Roviana Christianity, its voids, its growth or non-growth at the quality level? Ultimately we shall have to determine whether or not any shortcomings still apply in the residue of Roviana Christianity. Has the situation passed, or could there be another outburst?

We shall now proceed to outline the course of the movement, to provide a general perspective. Following this, we shall examine the prophet himself, his dreams and his personal claims; and after that, the effort at solving the problem through the fraternal delegation; finally, I shall attempt to chart the current regional distribution of the movement.

THE HISTORICAL SEQUENCES

The associations of Silas Eto with the eccentric sister of some forty years ago are fairly well established. I cannot verify that she prayed "like a bat" under the house, but it fits the reputation she still has locally. She claimed the gift of tongues and retired to the bush with Eto to pray in her own way. Her official record shows an arrogance towards the chairman, whom she frequently corrected, claiming she was doing so under the guidance of the Holy Spirit. It is interesting to note that Eto faced the crisis of his conflict with authority with the same attitude and claim. He was a disobedient catechist and it is surprising he managed to be so disobedient for so long without discipline.

At the close of his schooling Eto was accepted as a teacher and appointed by Goldie (contrary to his normal practice) back to his own village, where he also had some chiefly rank. For some time his moral influence there was good and the combination of civil and religious office made him an important person. Financially his contributions to the Church were good, and he sent many students for training to the central institution.

Eto was a great admirer of John Wesley. He himself had painted a portrait of Wesley, which had a prominent position in his house. He had translated Wesley's *Twelve Rules of a Helper* into the Roviana language; and the handsome church he built in his village, like Wesley's, had a special prayer room. Eto was a man of spiritual convictions and had a definite capacity for mysticism. He tended to respond to persons who could share this experience. His church was highly ornamented in Melanesian fashion, and inside was his own declaration of faith:

> Let us shelter beneath the cross of the Lord Jesus Christ, which is for the blotting out of our sins and the salvation of men who seek God by faith and in truth.

Some of the men who knew him well in those days thought him "distinctly original in thought and artistic temperament" rather than "peculiar", and I can document missionary opinion to this effect as late as 1949.

However, before that date he made a number of innovations in his worship patterns. He set a large Melanesian crucifix in the porch of his church. It was a crucifix, not the Methodist empty cross, symbol of the risen Lord. This was quite a departure from Methodist custom. Worshippers would enter church on the march, and instead of bowing to the crucifix would salute in military fashion and say "Good morning, Jesus!" It was apparently purely an act of worship. There was no breakaway movement, nothing anti-Mission, anti-white or unpatriotic. In fact, another innovation was the regular singing of the National Anthem as a prayer.

Some time before the war, questions were raised in the central Church meetings about some of the worship patterns Eto was using, and in particular his use of rhythm, stick-tapping, flag-waving and marching. The quarterly meeting at Pativa sent a deputation of one European and three Solomon Islanders to Menakasapa, his village, to look into the matter. Silas defended himself on the score of congregational joy and participation, especially for the children. He cited Psalm 47: 1:

> O clap your hands, all ye people;
> Shout unto God with the voice of triumph.

Apparently his explanations were accepted. From time to time there was some disapproval of Eto's individualism. He became irregular in his attendance at the routine meetings of the district, and kept himself largely to his own pastorate, doing things in his own way, always claiming it as under the guidance of the Spirit.

In 1942 the area of his influence, Kolobagia, Keru and Burongo

Island, threatened to break away from the controls of the Morovo area. The matter required careful handling but the incident passed. The first sign of real disagreement with a missionary came when the congregation applauded after a baptismal service. After the sermon the missionary objected. The congregation agreed to refrain from applause if the missionary did not desire it, but they assured him they liked it that way and would continue the practice as it warmed their hearts.

For some time after the war Eto was still looking for *something* in Solomon Island Methodism, before he began experiencing his dreams and visions and proclaiming his prophetic revelations. In 1949 he felt constrained to set down his feelings in writing. He felt the Solomon Island situation showed four serious dangers:

1. The lack of unity because of denominational jealousy. (He had seen both the Roman Catholics and the Seventh Day Adventists enter the area.)
2. Lack of unity because of commercial competition.
3. Lack of unity because Government and Mission so often seemed to be pulling in opposite directions.
4. The unwillingness of his own people to stick at a job long enough to make a success of it.

Together with this appraisal of the situation as he saw it, Eto saw fit to advocate the following solutions:

1. Union of all the Churches into a single denomination.
2. Only one trading company to operate in the islands, so that buyer and trader would be forced to help one another.
3. Better Mission–Government co-operation.
4. Stimulus to make islanders more dependable in their jobs.

Without any attempt to expound these solutions further, he appended the following prayer:

> God of my heart, bless the Church in New Zealand, Australia, England and America, that it may o'ershadow Thy Church (still a child) in the Solomon Islands.[3]

These were Eto's thought-out opinions in 1949, when the local headline news was *Marching Rule*, which threatened to unite the eastern islands against the white man. It was about a decade before the western crisis. Eto was still a loyal Methodist and an appointed catechist. He showed a genuine concern for the future of the Solomons at large, and saw the need for unity based on religion. From the Mission documents it is also apparent that he was long dissatisfied with the disunity of the district and area meetings of the Church.

Ten years later he had abandoned this paternalistic prayer, lost his faith in the Mission, refused to listen to the peacemakers sent by the New Zealand Church, and had set up a schismatic 'church' against them. In order to do this he had abandoned his orthodox theological position, probably by 1959, and declared himself as part of the Godhead. Nor is there any reasonable doubt that at one time Eto envisaged his movement as uniting all the Solomons. One of my best Solomon

Island informants is dogmatic about this, and there are also suggestions of it in the hymns of the movement.

During the war years the area had been overrun first by Japanese and then by Americans. Eto drew much from the latter, for whom he provided swimming facilities and other conveniences. These soldiers appear to have introduced him to Mormonism, Jehovah's Witnesses, Oral Roberts and several others from whom regular supplies of literature have continued pouring into these islands to the present day. These influences were more indirect than is generally believed. Their importance lies in the fact that through them Eto discovered the multiplicity of 'Christian' sects, and the many possible interpretations of Scripture. He also discovered something of the wide range of spiritual phenomena attributed by 'Christians' to the Holy Spirit. *Battle for the Mind* had not then come his way, but his own mind was certainly being prepared for it.

The fifties were frustrating years for the would-be reformer but when, towards the end of that period, Eto obtained a copy of Sargant's book, it supplied the piece that fitted the 'jig-saw' and the crisis came suddenly. *Battle for the Mind* did not mean to Eto what it meant to the writer. It permitted him to link with other types of spirit phenomena discussed and illustrated in Sargant's book his own claim that he was in the true Wesley tradition and his doctrine of the Holy Spirit. This was about 1959. From this point of time he appears to have projected himself back 'in the Spirit' to 1952, to the jubilee celebrations of the Church, and to have perceived himself receiving his prophetic commission from Goldie and from God. (Eto could never give up the Goldie tradition. He used to call himself "son of Mr. Goldie" and went into mourning for a year upon his death.) He now revealed his visions and called upon the people to follow him. He held meetings for the "warmed heart" experience (Wesley terminology), and these were so effective that worshippers began climbing the church walls, flinging themselves to the floor, drumming with sticks, and passing into such a state of ecstasy that they completely lost control of themselves.

During the crisis—1959-61—these excesses increased.[4] Several missionaries were directly involved, their preaching was rejected, and doors were closed against them. The direct break came when some of the missionaries expressed the opinion that Eto was serving some evil spirit. Eto insisted it was the Holy Spirit and he left Methodism with his followers. The missionaries disagreed about how the situation should be handled and virtually let things take their own course, hoping the offenders would repent and return sensibly to the fold. This they did not do.

Some of the missionaries disbelieved that the movement was heretical, as claimed by the indigenous loyalists, and this also delayed action. When the crisis came, some of them shifted their positions. Many of the Solomon Island loyalists are still mystified by the attitudes of the European missionaries and are critical about it. They feel that had Eto been disciplined, the matter would have ended there.

The Chairman's correspondence at the time shows his deep concern over the spiritual state of the Church in Roviana. He felt the people had lost the drive of their early conversion period and that there were resurgences of the use of charms and spells and many references to death by 'poison' (sorcery). He was distressed that so many of the leaders of the new movement were men who had trained in the District Theological Institution, and raised the question whether the training that had been given was soundly rooted in the life of the people.

Nor was he the only missionary who reflected disquiet in his correspondence at the time. Some of these men did their thinking in their correspondence and I respect its privacy. It must suffice to say that the files reveal their changing attitudes as the truth of the theological significance of Etoism dawned on them. There was also deep concern over the discord of their quarterly meetings after the war, and the failure of Roviana men to offer for the work of the Church, but rather to seek remunerative positions. On a personal level they were disturbed at their own personal involvement with business, organization, buildings and properties, rather than with the pastoral office. As all my own investigations pointed to these facts without the evidence of the files, which were generously opened to me, I merely say that these are among the supporting evidence. It seems fair, however, to point out that the missionaries were aware of this state of affairs and were concerned about it. It was not their personal fault, but the weakness of the system under which they laboured.

Groups of men sent for training by Eto to Goldie College commenced bush prayer meetings. The Principal told them the chapel was available for that purpose and regarded the continuation of bush meetings as an act of disobedience. The Chairman was called in to support him but the party insisted on doing things Eto-wise. For the Europeans the questions of authority, obedience, and legal procedure were important.

In September 1960, immediately prior to a conference at which the Kusage people split from Methodism, the Chairman had sent two Fijian ministers on a round of visitation through the Roviana Lagoon and Rendova. They found some of the villages defecting, some loyal and some divided. Everywhere there was a general feeling that since the war they had been neglected. They had carried on and kept things going during the war, and even given their thank-offerings, but now they seemed to count for little.

The Fijians were not impressed with what they called the "foolish spirit", and were convinced it was not the Holy Spirit. They listed the non-Methodist forms being used, disapproved the damage done to buildings, and detected some theologically pre-Christian ideas and millenarianism based on the assumption of the close proximity of the Day of Judgement.

They made four recommendations, two theological and two practical. They felt that more adequate instruction was badly needed on the nature and use of prayer and on the true work of the Holy Spirit. They pointed out the need for more ministerial itineration in the area and recommended that help be found for the Chairman in this respect because of his involvements in district business.

For a three-day investigation, which involved a good deal of travelling, they had made some shrewd observations, but their visitation was
too late to be of any material value.[5] They found anti-European feeling
high and in some places they were themselves rejected. As the millenarianism has not continued as a major feature of the belief of the movement, it is interesting to have evidence of its place in the actual crisis.
The villages of Kusage and Kolobagia left Methodism in September
1960. The villages of the Roviana Lagoon followed in April 1961. In the
interim the New Zealand Mission board had sent a fraternal visitor to
enquire into the situation. The report of this enquiry was not satisfactory to the schismatics. It was western in character and sought to
explain problems in terms of modern psychology, which was to beg the
question.

When I came to investigate Etoism, it was fairly firmly established
over western New Georgia and the surrounding islands, and was operating with an organization being spoken of as a 'church'. The movement
was seeking a legal constitution, held extensive funds, and was holding
periodic rallies at key places. The prophet was itinerating and continuing to hold his people effectively. The regional limits appeared to have
become stable. The movement had a fairly strong body of leaders, most
of whom had had a good training in the Church they had left, but it
seemed to me that the prophet rather than the leaders held the movement together. The ultimate stability of Etoism probably depends on
the effectiveness of the establishment of the constitution, although it
could well be determined by the personal fortunes of the prophet himself, or by the duration for which the two quite different social segments
of the movement can remain cohesive. At present the man Eto counts
for more than his doctrine.

I interviewed two persons at Munda, one a Kidu leader of the movement, and the other a Methodist somewhat embittered because Etoism
had divided his family. The former was more of the pacifist type of
Etoist, who seemed to be trying to retain friendships in both camps, as
if he still hoped for some reconciliation. He was inclined to play down
the differences, possibly because the proximity of his village to the
Mission and hospital made their associations inevitable. He told me
their noisy meetings were only occasional and usually preliminary to a
big gathering, and that except for the marching of the children the
demonstrations were no longer used. This was very different from the
report of the other informant, who described the *round* and the closure
of doors after entry as the regular pattern. What we heard from the
mission house that night confirmed that there was still much noise and
nothing restrained.

These C.F.C. people of Kidu wear a flower in the hair whenever they
leave the village and seem determined to declare their identity. Yet I
felt that this could be one place that could some day return to the fold
if ever Eto loses his grip. The Kidu people have lost educationally,
socially and economically by the separation and they are aware of it.
Though a large village, and centrally placed in the regional distribution
of Etoism, they are no strategic centre for the movement. The strong-

hold for this area is Madou on the island of Wanawana. Only Standard I children attend school at Kidu. Standards II to IV go to Madou, where their indoctrination is solid. At Kidu, the more pacifist leader maintains a moderate position and avoids encounter. He avoided all attempts on my part to discover what he actually believes, and all I learned was that the Eto hymns were composed by a number of different persons, mostly of Kusage.

THE PROPHET'S DREAMS AND PERSONAL CLAIMS

Silas Eto claims that in 1952 at the Jubilee of the Church John F. Goldie, founder of the Misson, handed him a box which contained the instructions he should follow in restoring the life of the Church in the Solomons. Does Eto claim this to have been an actual event, or was it a dream experience? Eto told one of my informants personally that he had dreamed of going to heaven and meeting Goldie there and getting the box. The curtain between the real and dream experiences of Eto seems to be very thin. Eto's vital experience came in the late fifties some time after the Jubilee. His purpose seems to have been to establish himself as the legitimate successor of Goldie. He also tried to retain some of the features of Goldie's pre-war patterns, in particular the large rallies. Preparations were being made for one at Madou on Wanawana at the time we left that island.

In his dream visit to heaven Eto discussed matters with God, "an old man now", whose work in creation had finished and who was prepared to leave things on earth in the control of the Holy Spirit and Silas Eto, who now assumed the name *Holy Mama* (Holy Father).

Another of Eto's visions took place at the top of a mango tree where he met an angel. The mango tree revelation is symbolically featured today by one member of the assembly dressing in angelic robes and climbing to the tree-top. He sits there for the duration of the regular worship service as a reminder of the revelation. This is spoken of as *Batu Rereke* (lit. the mango-tree head). Here we have the Etoist counterpart of the New Testament transfiguration. There are many such counterparts in Etoism, which thus becomes a revelationary religion claiming two sources of inspiration—the Godhead (either God Himself or the Holy Spirit, direct or through the medium of an angel) and the ghost or transfiguration of Goldie, who is seen in the line of spiritual descent from Wesley.

How many of the claims made by this movement come from Eto himself would be hard to establish, because his utterances and pronouncements have been made in the form of sermons, delivered in select gatherings, often behind closed doors; but it is not difficult to find witnesses who declare that Eto claimed both these sources of inspiration. Furthermore, in this type of experience a dream meeting counts as a real one. One of my European informants sought to demonstrate Eto was a fake by showing that he claimed to go off to heaven, but was later discovered in the bush by a team of pig-hunters. This is no argument. If Eto had gone off into the bush to seek, what is often called, a *Vision*

Quest, this would count as, and be spoken of as, a real experience. Even so in the period of crisis some of Eto's followers did make fantastic claims and Eto disowned some of them. At one time the momentum threatened to get beyond his control, and he brought the situation under control by a declaration that what he taught was to be regarded as secret for the faithful and not disclosed to any Europeans, especially missionaries. From this point meetings were held behind closed doors, which served to establish a secret Melanesian character and also had magical significance.

Eto's claim as being himself part of the Godhead is a firm tenet of the movement and is clearly developed in their hymns, both in the terminological changes they made to Methodist hymns (in which Eto was often substituted for Christ) and in their own original hymns. Most of these hymns were not composed by Eto himself, but as he leads the movement and approves the singing of the hymns he personally must be held responsible for the teaching. The precise contents of these hymns will shortly be examined (Chapter 17).

THE FRATERNAL INVESTIGATOR'S REPORT

During the crisis some of the missionaries had been subjected to most humiliating experiences. They witnessed spiritual *enthusiasm* and have described it in their reports. They were spiritually rejected before the doors were physically closed against them. The Church in New Zealand sent a Fraternal Delegation to enquire into the state of affairs. As an attempt at mediation the move was good, but it failed to effect any reconciliation. The report of the findings was multigraphed as *Report on the New Way of Worship, 10 February, 1961*.[6] It attempted to steer a middle course, setting out the good points of the movement as against the bad, but was satisfactory to neither the Etoists nor the loyalists. One or two of its findings, frankly, amaze me. It reported that the new way was specially concerned with the Holy Spirit but was not opposed to any other doctrine. On the contrary Etoism departed considerably from the orthodox position on the whole nature of the Godhead. On the level of theological practice it was thoroughly Eto-centric, the Holy Spirit bearing witnesses to Eto, not to Christ. I do not know how the delegation enquired into this theological aspect, but there is an abundance of evidence of Eto's theological departures from the Methodist position, and I am forced to the conclusion that the Etoists revealed only what suited them to the delegation. One Solomon Island informant told me that at the time there was a widespread belief that the fraternal delegate was looking into the situation prior to his taking over the chairmanship, and that had it not been for the possibility of Mission policy changes, the delegation would not have received a hearing from the Etoists at all.

In dealing with the enthusiasm, or manifestations of excitement (*taturu*), said to be irresistible because their "hearts were hot" and because "the Holy Spirit came upon them", the report adopted a paternalistic attitude, which sealed its rejection before it was fully read:

We white people have a great deal of medical knowledge and much of it is about the mind. We call it Psychology. We know many things about the mind that you have not yet begun to learn.

Such an approach to a discussion of what the report called *mass religious hysteria* was a dismal failure as a method of reconciliation. The report argued against the reality of evil spirits and spirit forces, by attributing all these things to the work of *one's own mind*. Right or wrong scientifically, this was certainly the wrong approach to reconciliation— acceptable neither to schismatic nor to loyalist. The useful comments in the report that suggested ways and means for improvement of the mission were lost sight of because of its basic paternalism and its attitude of 'scientific' disbelief, which discredited the whole report as western in the eyes of the Solomon Islanders.

The report also indicated that the greatest need was for a second missionary in the Roviana Circuit, either to itinerate through the villages or to assist at the head station, to teach new games and entertainments and to free the chairman from some of his administrative duties for travel. This was good, in that it recognized the need for pastoral oversight and more group participation, which were two real factors in the situation. However, this solution had the serious short-coming of introducing further paternalism from outside—an extra missionary, at Board expense. The causes were all within the situation itself, and the solution also should have been found there. Without coming into encounter with the root causes within, there could be no *real* solution at all. The report failed to see that the whole trouble of inadequate pastoral oversight was not a need that could be met by another servant of the Board from New Zealand, but that over half a century of quite successful intake from paganism had failed to produce an indigenous ministry. Most of the pastor-teachers were more teachers, with pastoral care as an adjunct, than real pastors. The follow-up of conversion had been more station-centred than orientated to village life, religious education in the villages had been inadequate, and the changes of the post-war situation revealed the poverty of village Christianity. If the victory was to be won on this level, it had to be something positive from within the situation—not merely an additional Board appointment. So the delegation neither brought a reconciliation nor solved the basic problems.

If the delegation was denied the relevant data, of course, this would be reflected in its findings, but I cannot answer for this. In one sense it comforted the missionaries to be able to share their problems, and, even though the report failed to come to grips with the situation, it satisfied the conscience of the Church that some specific attempt at reconciliation had been made. I must nevertheless confess that my impressions were that it was an eleventh hour attempt to regain unity and forbearance for the Jubilee Year, rather than a solution of the problems within the situation. Some of the missionaries felt the report ignored the personality of the prophet, Eto, together with his messianism and message. They also felt it failed to allow for the Melanesians' own cultural attitudes towards Eto's social behaviour, especially with respect to his female assistants. In other words, the missionaries themselves felt the report went too far in its outreach to reconcile the schismatics. Bringing them back to the fold was more important than correcting their error. They themselves felt Eto was "the villain of the piece"; they were deeply grieved with him, and felt that had there been no Eto there would have been no Etoism. So the report was unsatisfactory to them.

Although they had every reason to be offended with Eto, I feel they failed to appreciate the degree to which Eto capitalized an actual situation. Had there been no Eto, sooner or later there would have been another like him. Another movement might have differed in some ways, but the inner life of Roviana was in such a state that something like this was bound to happen. Some of the missionaries felt Eto was unique. I cannot agree. He is very like John Frum—not so very far away from the Solomons.

The emergence of Etoism was what Elkin calls *a return to faith*, new in that it was syncretistic, but nevertheless an "awakening to self-consciousness . . . brought about by disillusionment with the white man and a realization that the native is not getting anywhere by aping or living under the shadow of the white man. He must express his personality and the genius of his race in his own way." This is "the process of the 'return to faith' ".[7] In some of its forms and ideas Etoism returned to the pre-Christian. It tried to reinterpret experiences it took to be Wesleyan, but denied to the Solomon Islanders by the missionaries. It attempted to retain some elements of Goldie's pattern discarded by the post-war leaders. I do not think this aspect of Melanesian psychology and the situation which brought it into emergence were adequately examined by the delegation. Indeed, the psychology of the delegation was distinctly western.

THE DIFFUSION OF ETOISM

The accompanying map shows something of the geographical distribution of Etoism. A few places I have been unable to locate, and I know that the movement extends beyond the limits of the map as far as Choiseul and Guadalcanal. At one time Eto made a move to send his advocates to Malaita but nothing came of it.

In view of the fact that the movement did not spread into certain Adventist villages, where there were strong lines of kin connection, because the people recognized it as theologically pagan, we may well ask along what kind of lines the movement did spread. Did it have any sociological base? One hears a good deal about the unhappiness it caused by dividing families, but the term 'family' is carelessly used, meaning a different thing to European and Melanesian. It is rare to meet a divided nuclear family unless the family already had divided residence—i.e. one member living away from home. Some single men were caught up into the movement in this way. There were two such in one place I knew. Sometimes a man personally loyal to the Church was threatened by the probable disloyalty of his wife. In such cases the man was usually in some occupation which separated him regionally from his home group. Perhaps he has married into her family

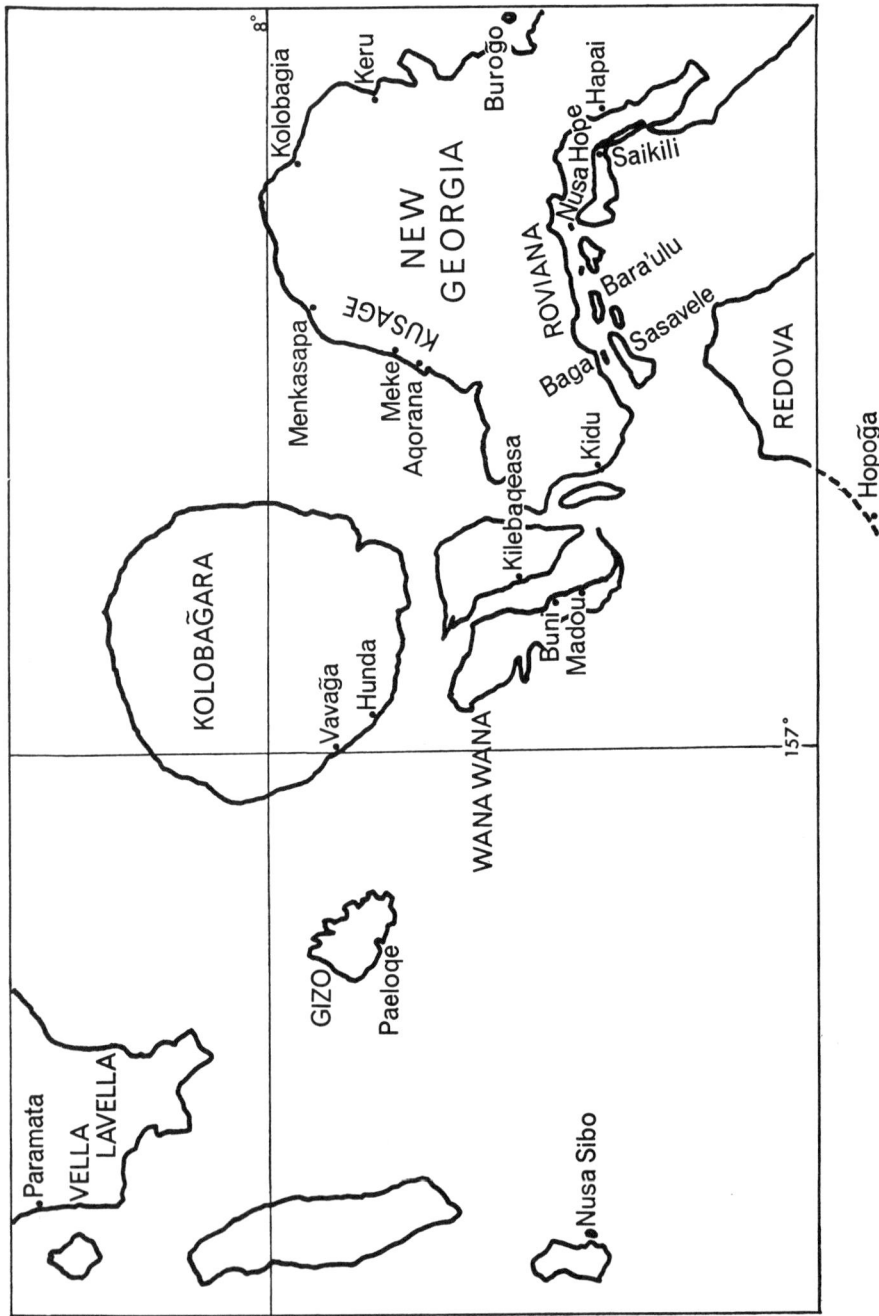

Paramata
VELLA
LAVELLA

KOLOBAG̃ARA

Vavag̃a
Hunda

GIZO
Paeloqe

Nusa Sibo

WANA WANA

Buni
Madou

Kilebaqeasa

Kidu

Baga
Sasavele

Bara'ulu

Meke
Aqorana

KUSAGE

ROVIANA

Nusa Hope
Saikili

Hapai

Burog̃o

NEW
GEORGIA

Menkasapa

Kolobagia

Keru

8°

157°

REDOVA

Hopog̃a

(matrilocally) and her family had become Etoist. The few cases of divided nuclear families that came under my notice had some such explanation—itself sociologically conditioned. When the man concerned was a church agent, this could be serious for him.[8] These cases were not numerous. So when we speak of families divided by Etoism we are not speaking of nuclear families, but of *extended families* or *lineages*. As much as I was able to investigate this matter, it seemed to me the divisions were extended families or other segments within the lineage. It was the lineage cohesion, not that of the family, which tended to break. Quite often these segments worked out also on a basis of locality. Thus it is common to find Eto villages and Methodist villages. Divided villages are few, and the divisions appear to have been sociologically based, as with denominationally divided villages in general throughout Melanesia.

To a Melanesian in olden times a divided lineage was threatened with extinction. Tribal solidarity was essential for survival. With the rise of individualism something has certainly been lost, but the Melanesian still feels the importance of the social solidarity of his group. There are many Melanesians (and some of the best educated among them) who are opposed to Etoism because it divides their lineage, though they never think for a moment of the theological division.

How did Etoism spread so rapidly through so many Methodist villages? The spiritual state of the area was ripe for change. It might have been an evangelical revival that spread, but the Church had virtually given up this approach, and it was left for Eto to capture the situation. Throughout the area of Kusage the villages had kin connections and accepted the chiefly authority of Eto, who had proved a good leader throughout the years and now promised them something essentially their own. Some of those a little farther afield, though not related, were impressed and accepted the movement and its authority because it offered an indigenous answer to their felt needs.

The movement was taken to the island of Wanawana and later to Nabusasa (Choiseul) by one of the affected graduates of Goldie College. He was one of Eto's own men, sent in by him for training and officially appointed by the Church.

Along the islands of the Roviana Lagoon, where people considered themselves socially above the Kusage, across the water to Nusa Simbo, and even as far as Paramata in Vella Lavella, the movement spread spontaneously. In each case the people of the locality concerned had heard about the movement, and their chiefs either went or sent representatives to interview Eto and to see personally how his organization worked. In each case they were convinced of the effectiveness of the movement and took it home to their own locality of their own accord. In each case the response was spontaneous and reached by group decision after deliberation. Obviously the general state of affairs was ripe for change. The door was open. It might have been used for second-generation evangelism, but Etoism captured the situation.

CHAPTER 16

The Group Experiences of Etoism

THE BEHAVIOUR OF THE GROUP

ETOISM IS a boisterous business. During the years 1959 to 1961, when the movement was establishing itself on the basis of its eccentric enthusiasm, this was particularly so. The missionaries, who have left a number of written descriptions of the pandemonium they witnessed, classified it as *Pentecostalism*, a popular but unfortunate term for this phenomenon. Today the pattern has established itself more definitely and the total construct claims the name of *Christian Fellowship Church*. Despite this title it is still a noisy form of 'worship'.

Ceremonies are held on the beach when any visitors arrive. They include prayer charms and sacred words, such as *Worship, Honour, Power* and *Salvation*, borrowed from the *Book of Revelation* and shouted enthusiastically by the crowd. Then begins a form of military display, of marching round the church with flags and other paraphernalia, and the rhythmic beating of sticks and hand-clapping. Eto had learned semaphore in his mission days and used a signal system to accompany the sacred words. The behaviour was not meaningless. The march is known as the *round* and ends with the whole assembly entering the church building and closing the doors behind them. The clapping and stick-tapping continues and may produce a rhythmic trance, supposed speaking in tongues, many people gabbling incoherently together, and some before long falling on the floor in a state of exhaustion. In the more violent period some climbed the church walls and destroyed parts of the building, and it was not unusual to see a heap of writhing people on the floor in a state of ecstasy or collapse. This was interpreted cathartically as the Holy Spirit striving with the sin in their hearts. It was counted as good and highly desired because it was the process of purification.

This performance, though less violent today, has been incorporated in the permanent pattern of the movement. The elaborate carving of some of the tapping sticks shows their sacredness and permanence. The *round* and the stick-tapping can be observed by passers-by and are regular features of every meeting. The state of excitement increases when Eto himself visits a locality.

A good deal of the missionary attack fell on the nature of this phenomenon of enthusiasm and missed the theological significance of what was really happening. Attempts were made to explain the behaviour in terms of psychological processes, although the loyal Solomon Island Christians explained them in terms of dynamic encounter; as one of them said to me "our European friends would not believe this". The Fraternal Investigator's Report is a good expression of this western attitude. I found my Solomon Island informants had done much thinking about the nature of this group behaviour, and particularly with respect to Eto's own role in it. Whether the Europeans were prepared to believe or not, they should have taken more cognizance of the views of the loyal islanders, whose attitudes were at least more biblical than their own. I heard one Rarumana layman give a morning devotional on "The Spirit of Christ and the Spirit of Anti-Christ" (1 John 4: 1–6). He spoke of the *encounter of faith*. "We ourselves have seen what can happen when a false prophet comes into our midst," he declared. He was not concerned with "processes in the mind" which led to "mass hysteria". He saw life as a spiritual encounter on the level of faith, and he knew where he himself stood. We shall look more into this in the next unit of this chapter.

A more pietistic and less boisterous aspect of Eto group behaviour is apparent in their pattern of building up merit by a tally of short prayers. Each individual keeps his own tally and each family and at the end of the week the whole village totals up its score, which will run into thousands. The tallies are kept with little mid-ribs of the palm leaf, as a Roman Catholic ticks off his rosary beads. This is not the only evidence of Eto's outreach towards the Roman Catholics, probably as part of his drive for unity. The missionaries dealt with this matter under the category of "vain repetitions" and branded it as Pharisaical. But this begged the question because it never considered the motive. These short prayers, or *qetuqetu*, about which more will be said in the theological analysis to follow, were expressions of joy and praise. They were aimed at fixing the minds of the worshippers on the cardinal points of their new faith—whether those points were right or wrong to our way of thinking. The motive was to drive home the need for joy and praise, and the tally was to satisfy the leaders that every member was attending to this matter. It was, in point of fact, a way of relating private devotions in the total group. The error was not in the method but in the doctrinal content which glorified Holy Mama as one of the Godhead.

ENTHUSIASM AND ENCOUNTER WITH SIN

We have seen that the Etoist interpretation of the writhing, fainting and excesses of the experience of enthusiasm was in terms of catharsis. It was conceptualized as the struggle of the Holy Spirit with sin (or the sinful spirit) within the victim. Sometimes it was seen as an act of exorcism. John Wesley could preach a sermon on "Satan's Devices", showing first how Satan tried to destroy the work of God in the human soul, and then how this activity should be resisted. It was a thoroughly biblical sermon about personal encounters and suited the Melanesian, because it was in imagery that was real to him. Yet this imagery was more vocal in the eastern Solomons than in the Methodist area, where the teaching emphasis was more strongly foreign and moralist. Our village studies revealed this. I am of the opinion that the experience of enthusiasm satisfied something that was missing from the lives of

the Roviana Christians, and tentatively I put it down to an over-
emphasis on moral requirements presented didactically as a demand
on human effort, rather than a victory over sin through Christ or the
Holy Spirit. This is not characteristic of Methodist missionary areas
known to me and therefore it struck me all the more forcefully.

Because Eto offered this demonstration of struggle with and victory
over sin in the name of the Holy Spirit, and thereby satisfied a felt
need, he received a good hearing in the Roviana area.

It is interesting to note that in the east where the Chair and Rule
Movement had operated and where Marching Rule held sway, and where
Eto might well have expected a hearing, his advocates were rejected.
It is quite impossible to be dogmatic as to why; but we note that all
the missions in the area had a strong doctrine of the struggle with
Satan in terms of personal encounter. The South Sea Evangelical
position will be examined when I deal with their image of the Bible;
but I believe they would accept the statements set out in the Roman
Catholic *Faith and Fact Book* on this subject.[1] The argument for their
position has been stated in purely biblical terms, and its expositor does
not depend in any of his arguments on the tradition of the Church.
I take this then to be in harmony with the belief they transmit through
the catechism and other aids for instruction.

The same theological position is met in the Anglican villages. It was
the basis of encouragement offered to folk going to the priest for
confession and was implied in many of the prayers. The Anglican
priests practised exorcism in line with the apostolic commission. This
power encounter is implied in two petitions and responses in the Litany,
which is used every week, and two of Bishop Patteson's prayers (for
Sunday and Wednesday) in the Brotherhood Book. The hymn used for
Compline is a prayer for victory over "our ghostly foe", the prayer
Anima Christi requests defence from the "malicious enemy", the
Litany for Missions asks for salvation from "the deceits of the devil",
and a Rogationtide prayer seeks to "drive from this place the snares
of the enemy". In Baptism and Confirmation the candidate answers
the question:

> Do ye here, in the presence of God, and of this congregation, renounce
> the devil and all his works . . .?

The power encounter between Christ and Satan and the Christian's
personal involvement in the encounter are continually brought before
the Anglican people.[2] One has no hesitation in saying that the three
denominations on Malaita are united at this point.

The same claim cannot be made so definitely in the western islands,
although it is found in Wesleyan theology and hymns.[3] The doctrine
of personal encounter has been 'watered down', presumably to allow
for those who no longer believe in a personal devil and the existence
of evil spirits, but if this was meant to make the current Methodist
Book of Offices relevant for western cultural perspectives, it certainly
has its limits for people emerging from animism. I think it probable
(though this is tentative because one could not actually prove it) that

the weakening of the concept of personal involvement in a conflict of power encounter, and the substitution of an emphasis on moral demands *per se* (which our depth studies did indicate), created a spiritual need which Etoist enthusiasm was able to make claims at satisfying.

Eto was dogmatic that the Methodist missionaries had withheld some of the true Wesleyanism from the Melanesians. He had long maintained this, but was firmly convinced when *Battle for the Mind* came his way. Though it is unlikely he understood the thesis of this book, even when translated for him by a friendly planter, it led him to see white Pentecostalism and Wesleyan revivals and enthusiasm in the same category as African and South American drumming and spiritism. We are not concerned with the rightness or wrongness of this association, but that Eto saw the connection this way. In the enthusiasm of his own movement he saw the individual's desperate encounter with the personal devil and his victory over sin. The extreme emotionalism was certainly cathartic. Was this a reaction against largely moralist teaching? It would be hard to prove, but it fits the facts.

BATTLE FOR THE MIND[4]

Our purpose is not to evaluate the book *Battle for the Mind* but to determine the part it played in stimulating Eto and his followers; not *what* it contains, but *how* its contents reinforced the schismatics. Eto's English was inadequate for an understanding of the book, nor do I think he mastered it in a translated form although a planter is said to have helped him in this. The physiological and psychological theory would have been lost on him. The descriptive passages, however, were quite another matter. Sargant's data, without his theory, meant quite a lot to Eto. I read the book while I was in the area and discussed it with my island friends and informants, and as a result I feel the following observations are legitimate:

1. The illustrations feature African drumming, rhythmic dancing, hand-clapping, the ecstatic state of participants, the role of priests in whipping up excitement, cases of Brazilian and Balinese possession; the same features in snake cults and other ecstatic experiences among white Americans; the use of music to stimulate religious excitement; penitent form responses to gospel appeals, including pictures of converts in a state of collapse. These alone, without any accompanying text, would have a dramatic effect on any Melanesians with a tendency towards enthusiasm. Several of these features were known in pre-Christian Solomon Island religion, snake cults and trances especially. Realization of the existence of this phenomena among white 'Christians' is an important factor in the present case. The persistent rejoinder during the crisis period was, "There are many kinds of *Lotu* (Christianity)!" One of the photographs in the book illustrates a snake cult performance. A notice reads quite clearly "The Dooley Ponds Church of God—with signs following". The description beneath the illustration spoke of signs, trance and possession used "by certain Christian groups". This discovery of the variety in Christianity permitted the

Etoists to insist that their behaviour was still Christian and to call
themselves a Church.

2. In the text of Sargant's book immediately adjoining the illustrated
section[5] is a study of the *trembling, weeping and swooning of the Wesleyan
Revival*. This permitted an unfortunate identification of the Wesleyan
Revival with certain other movements with which Wesley had no
dealings and about which he was quite outspoken. I will deal with this
in the next unit of this chapter. In the decade before the Pacific War
the missionaries in the Solomons were commemorating Wesley's
experience of the "warmed heart". They pushed the matter to the
utmost and the islanders within range of the stations were quite
Wesley-conscious. These identifications enabled Eto to press his claim
that the missionaries had not revealed the full practices of Wesley to
the Solomon Islanders, but had withheld the deepest part for their
own exclusive use. Either this—or they never had it at all. Thereupon
Eto declared that Solomon Island Methodism was like a can of meat—
the Mission had the can but Eto had the meat. Incidentally, one
loyalist of Rarumana admitted to me quite frankly that many of the
church people had "the body but not the heart". He was bitterly
anti-Etoist but he had used very much the same figure to describe what
he observed. The second rejoinder of the Etoists, then, was that the
true Wesleyanism had hitherto been hidden from the Solomon Islanders,
but now it had been revealed to Silas Eto.

3. *Battle for the Mind* associates Christian sects with African possession and Voodooism, thus confusing evil spirit possession with the
work of the Holy Spirit. They are offered as alternative 'interpretations'
of allied phenomena. The effect of this was complex. Many Christian
antagonists of Eto accused him of practising spirit-possession. When
Eto was accused of serving an evil spirit his reaction was hostile. It
was for this very reason that he ultimately severed all connections
with the Church[6]—that they accused him of dealing with evil spirits.
He insisted throughout that everything he did was inspired by the
Holy Spirit. Yet his antagonists were not without evidence, and he is
certainly suspect for having made use of pre-Christian Melanesian
possession techniques. Some of the basic contradictions within Etoism
lie at this point. I think the book did make this equation for Eto, consciously or unconsciously. He might have been quite honest in believing
he was dealing with the Holy Spirit, yet his methods and techniques
were pagan and had been rejected by Christianity. In the section on
Eto's sacred and secret place I will say more about this. If this appraisal
is correct Eto's error was something like that of Simon Magus (Acts 8:
18 ff.), because he sought through the Spirit not monetary profit, but
his own personal aggrandizement. He has certainly manipulated the
theology of the Holy Spirit to this end. In the hymns of Etoism his
own role is clearly developed.

4. The book would also have introduced Eto to Sundkler's *Bantu
Prophets in South Africa*, from which it cites a section on how Bantu
Christian pastors stimulated stereotyped dreams of an apocalyptic
character, featuring Jesus or angels, from whom God's revelation was

received.[7] Here again we have identification of this behaviour with Christianity. Eto's religion was revelationary. He had been to heaven, had met Jesus and God and Goldie. From Jesus he is supposed to have received authority to carry on his work; from God he learned of His retirement from active work also; and from Goldie he received specific instructions about what should be done for the good of the Solomon Islands. If this section was translated for Eto by the planter, it would have included these words:

> In the name of "the freedom of the Holy Spirit" the sect thus exercises a totalitarian control over the individual, which does not even shun the hidden depths of the people's sub-conscious mind. The individual is malleable and the sect is moulding him into a standard type.

Now I doubt if Eto would fully understand that, even in a translated form. Nor would he understand Sargant's use of it. He would, however, most certainly understand that there were Bantu groups, claiming to be Christian, who had cut themselves off from white Christianity, having dreams and revelations in the name of "the freedom of the Holy Spirit". This "freedom of the Holy Spirit" became the theme song of Etoism. Eto and his assistants certainly moulded the rank and file into a standard type.

After the description of an emotional incident observed by a doctor and cited from Wesley's *Journal*, Sargant says[8] that Wesley and his followers attributed the matter to the intervention of the Holy Ghost— "It is the Lord's doing and it is wonderful in our eyes". Sargant is contrasting this with a different interpretation of what he considers "the same phenomena", but Eto would hit on any passage about Wesley. It suited his mood and plans and he could use it in the local situation. If the snake cults illustrated could be ascribed to the Holy Spirit, and the ecstatic behaviour of the Wesleyan Revival likewise, then he too, in his Melanesian fashion, could have the "freedom of the Spirit".

5. As to the methods by which his followers were to be welded together as a body, Sargant's book certainly brought before Eto the idea of rhythmic drumming, dancing, marching and hand-clapping. Eto had been using this long before he found this book. Twenty years earlier he had defended himself on the score that it provided facilities for congregational participation and had cited scripture. The investigating committee had questioned it but, unable to counter it, had let it pass. Now here in this book these ideas were developed and illustrated by a foreign scholar. He realized they were distributed through time and space. Did Eto get his peculiar slant on catharsis from this book?[9] Sargant tells of continued rhythmic drumming and dancing leading to emotional collapse, which brings a feeling of freedom from sin. He says that belief in divine possession and mystical trances are common at such times. In Voodoo possession the divinity may be an African god or a Roman Catholic saint—called by the same term (*loa*) in each case.[10] In his comments on the Mau Mau he tells of prisoners condemned to die, yet filling the prison with their songs of joy. Sargant

equates this with the Hallelujahs of Wesley's converts in Newgate Prison.[11] Such a book might well have had a profound effect in the days of crisis, especially if Eto had access to a translator. Analysis of the chronology shows the crisis came very soon after the availability of the book.

6. The book has a section on the effect of drugs. I hesitate to suggest this played any part in Eto's thinking. However, Eto certainly did have pre-Christian medicinal plants in his secret place. How he used them in his private ceremonials I cannot say. Some of his accusers say he uses hypnotism. But these things would be hard to prove.

Battle for the Mind appeared in 1957. The Eto movement had been simmering for some time before that date, but the real crisis came in 1960. There can be no reasonable doubt, if Silas Eto had access to this book, which both missionaries and indigenous informants assure me was so, that it would help him to organize his ideas and reinforce his convictions that he had discovered how the Europeans monopolized the power that rightly belonged to the Melanesians. It certainly provided the rejoinder—"There are many kinds of *Lotu*". It also provided the basis for the Eto contention that they were the true followers of Wesley, that the missionaries had either hidden the enthusiasm or had never had it.

The period of crisis passed and Etoism is settling down to organize itself into a type of 'Christian' community. This is not new. Many nativistic movements have eventually emerged as churches. Sargant wrote of the Quakers, who had once "trembled at the word of God":

> The Quakers later settled down to become rich and respectable, abandoning the means by which they had built up their early spiritual strength. It is the fate of new religious sects to lose the dynamism of their 'enthusiastic' founders; later leaders may improve their organization, but the original conversion techniques are often tacitly repudiated.[12]

Sargant sees this in the Welsh chapels, the Salvation Army and the Methodists. If that was translated for Eto he would have said that the later missionaries were not like Goldie, they had improved the organization perhaps, but had not the dynamism; they had the can but not the meat. Eto did say this but I cannot say whether the idea was his own or borrowed. Eto certainly had a strong attachment for Goldie, and there was certainly a great difference between Goldie and the later missionaries. However, there is no evidence that Goldie could be categorized as a founder with the dynamism of enthusiasm. His authoritarianism was colonialist, his missionary theory was industrial and his evangelism was rationally systematic. His theology was Wesleyan but he kept emotion to a minimum. He sought decision for Christ, but he liked folk to be quiet and sober when they made it. It is possible the book may have reminded Eto that later missionaries were bound to differ from their founders. He himself had been attracted to Goldie's pattern of large central rallies, and to the drilling, the band and the signalling with flags, which had been given to them at Roviana by Mr. Waterhouse. He mourned the loss of these activities, and has tried to recapture them in his own movement. However, apart from perhaps reminding him that later missionaries do change the policies of their founders, *Battle for the Mind* would not have been important at this point. He already knew these things.

The importance of Sargant's book lies in the fact that it helped Eto organize the basic philosophy of his movement—the claim that the demonstrations of enthusiasm were the work of the Holy Spirit, were acceptable as 'Christian', were cathartic in function, were identifiable with both the Wesleyan Revival and with African and South American forms of expression. Eto had long been looking for some way of identifying his development of emotion by means of rhythm with some Christian doctrine. He was now provided with "the freedom of the Holy Spirit" which the eccentric sister had pressed many years earlier— a doctrine of some importance in Methodism, though for some reason or other not well developed in their religious instruction in the Solomons, as the two Fijian ministers had pointed out and as my own depth studies revealed.

WESLEY AND ENTHUSIASM

I feel constrained to include this small unit on Wesley and enthusiasm for the following reasons:

1. The movement of Etoism has hit the Methodist Church, and therefore I desire that my analysis and suggestions should be measured by Methodist criteria.
2. Eto himself believed he was in the Wesley line of tradition and he must be appraised by Wesley criteria.
3. The Bicentenary of Wesley's Conversion was highlighted in Roviana Christianity, and what Wesley said and did was current conversation with Methodist village congregations.
4. The missionaries who had to deal with the schism continually referred back to Wesley's doctrine.
5. *Battle for the Mind* involved Wesley, the Wesleyan Revival, its behaviour patterns and belief.

Wesley is so involved in the total situation that his criteria should be stated, especially for the benefit of any non-Methodist readers.

In his sermon on "The Nature of Enthusiasm"[13] Wesley discusses the word *enthusiasm,* distinguishing between the good type which is approved and expected of Christians and the various unfortunate types, which he classifies. Finally, he directs his advice to his people. How would Wesley himself have applied his tests of genuineness to Eto and Etoism?

Wesley recognized that

> there is a real influence of the Spirit of God, and there is also an imaginary one: and many there are who mistake the one for the other.

Clearly then he would have set out to appraise the man and his movement—is it of God, or not? He speaks of those "who imagine they have gifts from God", especially those who seek *extraordinary* demonstrations

I

(italics his), particularly "visions, dreams and sudden impulses". Although he does not deny that God uses these, he disapproves of "waiting for supernatural dreams". I think this suggests that Wesley would have suspected Eto's departure into the forest for anything like a *vision quest*. God might call a prophet by means of a vision that is unexpected. This is different from seeking or inducing a vision by one's own desire, and perhaps gaining prestige, power and authority thereby. This is the difference between a true prophet and a shaman. The Bible is vocal on the point. Most biblical prophets were unwilling men who had to be convinced that God wanted them for this role (Jeremiah 1: 5–7; Amos 7: 14–15; Isaiah 6: 5–8; cf. Peter's experience, Acts 11: 5–17), and there are New Testament episodes which show the wrongness of thinking shamanistically about the Spirit of God (Acts 8: 18–23; 19: 13–17).

Having recognized this distinction, Wesley's criterion was always to test by Scripture. This was his "general method of knowing what is holy and acceptable to the will of God". Wesley discussed the type of enthusiasm whose initiates "expect to understand the holy Scriptures without reading them and meditating on them". Eto's own declaration on the nature and function of Scripture, and the equation of biblical references to Jesus with Holy Mama, would for Wesley roundly condemn Etoist enthusiasm.

Wesley says of the enthusiast who imagines himself "the particular favourite of heaven" that this produces "dreadful effects", including "pride" and an "unadvisable and inconvincible spirit". By imagining that he is "led by a higher guide . . . he grows in pride . . . unadvisableness and stubbornness . . . attached to his own judgement and his own will, till he is altogether fixed and immovable". Spiritually this is getting near home. Wesley continues:

> Being thus fortified against the grace of God, and against the advice and help of man, he is wholly left to the guidance of his own heart, and the king of the children of pride.

These are strong words, but I feel sure that the first thing Wesley would have observed would have been the extreme arrogance of the island prophet. Wesley left other teachings also on pride and humility.[14]

His sermon on the "Nature of Enthusiasm" concludes with a warning to the congregation against the error of fancying they have remarkable gifts, which in reality they do not have, of trusting in visions and dreams which do not line up with the plain rule of Scripture, through which we know the true guidance of the Spirit operates. In view of Sargant's interpretation of Wesleyan revivals and Eto's use of Sargant, I thought it fair to state Wesley's own declared criteria. The missionaries would have been familiar with this sermon, no doubt, and had their Bibles to make the tests. A pastoral letter of the chairman was circulated in July 1960 and attempted to deal with the practices of Etoism—character of the worship, gifts of the Spirit, and so on—by appeal to Scripture.[15] It may have been this which led Eto to make his declaration on the use of Scripture, though I cannot be sure of this.

On the other hand, to be fair all round, for half a century while the Roviana Church was growing and being consolidated, the people had been given no Bible, nor even a New Testament, to apply the tests. Time after time we come back to this as a basic cause of current problems. It was extremely fortunate that the Roviana New Testament appeared at the time Etoism was beginning to take shape. It was Etoism that drove many of the loyalists to explore their newly acquired treasure, but for hundreds the habit had not been acquired and Etoism sought to cultivate other forms of piety.

THE DYNAMICS OF THE EMERGENCE OF ETOISM

Any attempt to analyse a movement like Etoism must allow for the fact that we are not dealing with personalities or situations, but with personalities within situations. In this research I have thrown a good deal of emphasis on the situation which made the movement possible; this is firstly because I am studying the Church, its growth and the obstructions to its growth; and secondly because I found so many who blamed Eto personally for everything, and felt that without Eto there would have been no Etoism. I have already pointed out that the real innovators were the *acceptors* not the *advocate*. The achievement of the advocate was, in this case, the effective communication of his ideas that ensured acceptance by the group.

To accomplish this, he himself had to undergo a change from a low-status church agent (a catechist) to a prophet with direct revelation from God. Without this he could not act in defiance of Mission authority.[16] The prophet also had to understand the local situation, its needs and dissatisfactions, and offer a constructive programme for its alleviation. This programme had to be communicated to the groups he sought to win, and accepted by them. Failure at any of these points would have left him the low-status church agent. It was the group acceptance that actually created the prophet.

One common feature of all movements of this type is the eventual confluence of these two streams of human personality at some point in time and space—a situation felt by a group, and an individual who recognizes it and can capitalize on it and perhaps actually make the felt situation articulate. The situation of the group and the personality of the prophet, though both influenced by many common factors, may be the result of two completely different streams of influence. I have tried to demonstrate this by means of diagrams, one showing the influences which appear to have worked on the prophet himself and the other showing the dynamics of advocacy and acceptance with the emergence of his movement.

A prophet may come from inside or outside the local situation but it is in that situation that he must demonstrate the relevance of his claims. It is therefore important that we recognize that the prophet and the situation are different 'constellations', and there is possibly only one point of time in our period of history when the two 'orbits' come near enough to interact. A prophet may have to wait for years for his psychological moment. If he lets it go by, the opportunity may

FROM CHURCH AGENT TO NATIVISTIC PROPHET

Influences at work   **Stages of Development**

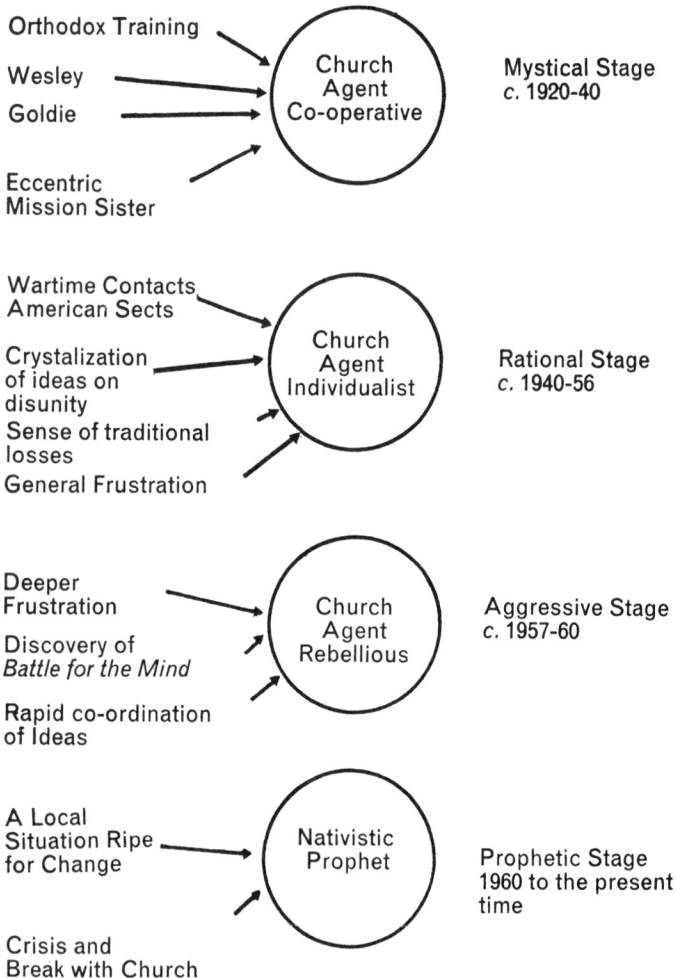

Orthodox Training

Wesley

Goldie

Eccentric
Mission Sister

> Church
> Agent
> Co-operative

Mystical Stage
c. 1920-40

Wartime Contacts
American Sects

Crystalization
of ideas on
disunity

Sense of traditional
losses

General Frustration

> Church
> Agent
> Individualist

Rational Stage
c. 1940-56

Deeper
Frustration

Discovery of
Battle for the Mind

Rapid co-ordination
of Ideas

> Church
> Agent
> Rebellious

Aggressive Stage
c. 1957-60

A Local
Situation Ripe
for Change

Crisis and
Break with Church

> Nativistic
> Prophet

Prophetic Stage
1960 to the present
time

Schematization of developing mental processes and external influences that serves as a key to the personality of the emerging prophet. All the statements and actions of Eto must be evaluated in their historic dimension. The Prophetic Stage is beginning to pass into the Messianic.

be lost for ever. If he strikes a moment too soon, he himself is lost. Silas Eto showed shrewd insight, both in 1960 and 1961 with the Kusage and the Roviana Lagoon situations, and he won them both. This was not mere diffusion of the movement. They were two clear cónquests.

The relevance of this observation for church growth is that the situation which Eto capitalized was one which called for dramatic change: a complex of dissatisfactions and social boredom. As the Church was still the recognized authority in control, the change could have been stimulated from within. The second generation of Christians of the whole area needed (and still need) personal confrontation with the gospel and a religious programme for better participation on the local level. They needed religious leadership, action and new life. The Church was a dying cause in need of a transfusion of life. The Church needed growth at the quality level. There is no doubt whatever that during the fifties the situation was ripe for revival. But the missionaries were tied up with post-war rehabilitation and the administration of the stations. They had trained virtually no indigenous ministry and infused no techniques of evangelism within their lower-level agents, who were mostly concerned with day-school teaching at a low level.

As the situation became more and more acute, the Church's hold grew weaker and the prophet's hour drew near. He showed masterly judgement in selecting his moment. During the crisis, anti-European feeling was high and the Europeans could do little about it. We cannot blame the missionaries for the manner in which they handled the crisis itself. Their hour had passed—others were in control.

The Kusage people, long before, had been persuaded to come down to the coast to settle. They ran into epidemics and other problems of adjustment and acclimatization, and their fortunes had dropped in Christian times. They had been despised by the Roviana aristocrats. Eto himself had been personally victimized by Roviana church leaders, and in the opinion of many unfairly gaoled by the Administration. Their loss of security was accompanied by general dissatisfactions after the war. The great traditions of the past 'melted away'. The Church had brought no lovely substitutes and the Government had imposed law but provided no real evidence of progress. Civilization, high-lighted by the American occupation, was desirable but quite out of reach, as one Eto hymn puts it. In the heart of it all was a frustrating void of hopelessness.

For twenty years Eto had served as church agent and chief at Kusage. It was quite apparent that the efficiency of his church organization and worship patterns was his own original contribution, and that authority tended to frown on it. His church life differed from that of all others, and his chiefly authority and personal originality were held in high respect by the people of Kusage. At one time his settlement had been visited by an overseas educationalist who suggested it might be taken as a model village, and trainees taken from the mission station to see how the place was run. Twenty years is a long time in the life of a community. The children whom Eto taught to participate in flag-waving and stick-tapping twenty years before were adults when the crisis came. In all my enquiries no informant pointed this out—that the adult congregations which led the break-away in the Kusage area were Eto's stick-tappers when the first enquiry was made into his behaviour in 1942. At the present time Etoism has a strong indoctrination programme for children. Even if the current movement should collapse, the potential for some future renaissance is in the rising generation.

So Eto already had some claim on the situation at Kusage when he began having his dreams and visions, proclaimed his prophetic call, and announced his revealed commission to take over things in Goldie's succession. He had been articulate as early as 1949 in matters of unity and reform. He now offered them unity and some recovery of their losses, a place of respect and leadership in the Solomons, and at least an elevation above the Roviana people. He offered them a Melanesian structure under a Melanesian prophet, a revival of craft and sculptured art forms for which New Georgia had once been famous, and new indigenous rhythms and thought-forms to compensate for cultural losses due to the white man. Once he was able to establish from *Battle for the Mind* that the Holy Spirit could be claimed to operate through possession phenomena, the die was cast. In September 1960, Kusage cut itself off from the Church.

All this can be understood. It was a natural enough sequence of events. But Eto's great triumph was his capture of the Roviana Lagoon situation about six months later. Though the two situations had much in common, there were some important differences. Roviana had not suffered a series of calamities and humiliation. The Roviana people were the rulers and had been accepted as such by the Mission. Their linguistic forms had been used for translation. Their status had never been questioned. They had a good percentage of the limited number of trained indigenous leaders. Furthermore, during his most frustrating days Silas Eto had been continually opposed and kept in check by these very Roviana leaders who now came over to his side. He had not even enticed them. They actually sent representatives to inspect Eto's worship patterns and asked him to take over. All Eto had to do was to convince them he had "the freedom of the Holy Spirit".

There were two ingredients in the Roviana Lagoon situation which opened that area to Etoism. The mission system, strongly station-centred, had its headquarters in the Roviana area. No people drew more from the great central rallies than the folk of the Roviana Lagoon. Not only had they chiefly rank, but they also provided a number of church leaders, who drew a great deal of personal prestige from these rallies. After the war, because of changes due to acculturation and new economic demands, and also to some extent through mission policy change, the large centralized gatherings came to an end. As no local festivals had been developed, the disappearance of the rallies left a void in the Solomon Island life, and those who held the prestige positions under the former missionaries felt that their own positions had slipped. To them, the Church was on the decline and the Goldie régime had ended. In the second place they were grieved because of what they regarded as pastoral neglect in the post-war period. Mission administration had increased, post-war rehabilitation had been time-consuming, missionaries had been engaged in rebuilding stations, and during the fifties itinerations were less frequent. Two of the Roviana leaders who had been strong opponents of Eto now became his supporters. They felt the Mission had rejected them, though they had maintained the work during the war. They were deeply grieved.

Eto had the public eye. He had effectively defied the Mission. He offered a programme that was Melanesian, and despite the humiliation for Roviana to have to dance to the tune of Kusage, the people of the Lagoon were attracted by the possession phenomena, the excitement, and the prospect of continued big rallies for which Eto was disposed to itinerate.

The reconciliation of Eto and the Roviana Lagoon leaders had important consequences. Eto badly needed a few key men to serve as his deputies or subordinate commanders. One of these was elevated to the position of President. This permitted Eto to ascend above the routine organization. The steps of the mysterious prophet led to messiahship. He would emerge here and there at great rallies and would itinerate, so as to be always within reach but never too familiar. His subordinates could maintain the organization. By surrendering their Methodist theology they could regain their prestige and draw from the economic resources of the movement. (They now have better salaries than they had from the Mission and special grants are possible at times.) Within their limited horizons they had now re-established their status.

As might be expected, the period of change-over was a time when they justified their actions by stimulated bitter anti-white feeling on the score of pastoral neglect.[17] The two Fijian missionaries recommended another missionary appointment to the station to relieve this neglect. By the time of their visit the resentment had become vocal. It was too late. The Church was not cultivating conversion growth among its second generation Christians, or quality growth by pastoral nurture, or organic growth by developing an indigenous ministry. Because its policy was heavily administrative and based on commercial, industrial, educational and medical administration at the expense of this growth, the village church was in a state of serious decline with a tragic void at the centre.

Although at present the Kusage and Roviana segments of Etoism are working in unison, it needs to be remembered that they are segments with different interests and have sociological lines of possible cleavage. The death of any of the leaders could effect a major change. This danger will be reduced if they succeed in obtaining their legal constitution, without which they can have no real recognition in the country.

Meantime the Church should strive to improve the quality growth of the village congregations in the loyalist parts of the Roviana area. If the dominant control of Etoism should pass from Kusage to Roviana there could well be more dynamic adjustments. It could mean a division

THE DYNAMICS OF THE EMERGENCE OF ETOISM

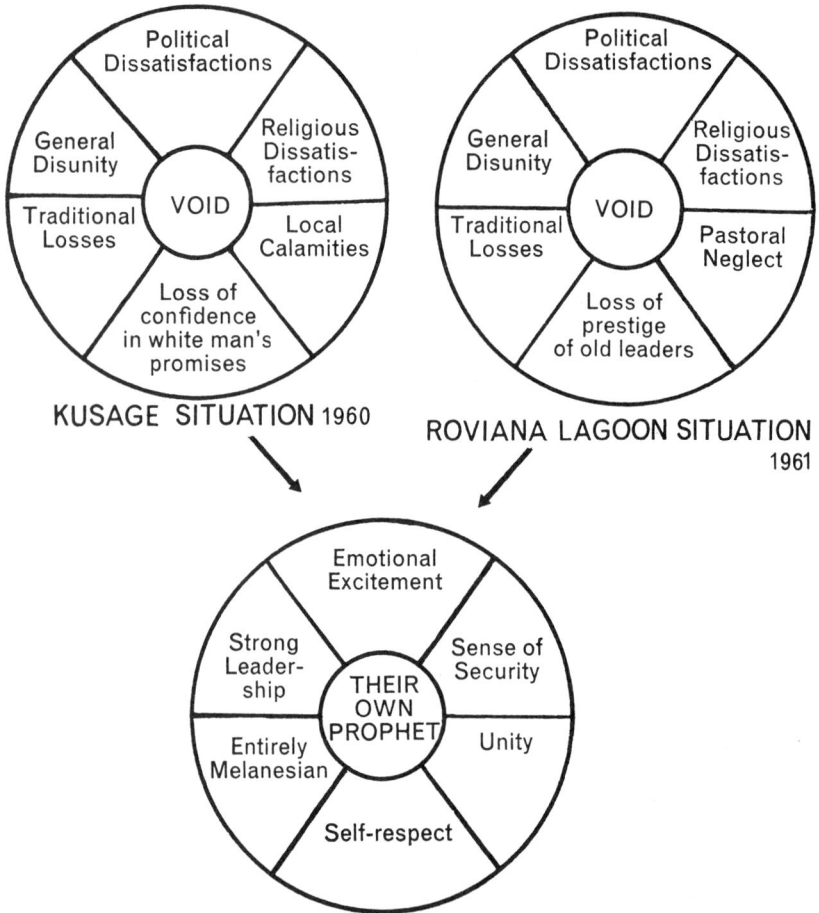

KUSAGE SITUATION 1960

Political Dissatisfactions / General Disunity / Religious Dissatisfactions / Traditional Losses / VOID / Local Calamities / Loss of confidence in white man's promises

ROVIANA LAGOON SITUATION 1961

Political Dissatisfactions / General Disunity / Religious Dissatisfactions / Traditional Losses / VOID / Pastoral Neglect / Loss of prestige of old leaders

Emotional Excitement / Strong Leadership / Sense of Security / Entirely Melanesian / THEIR OWN PROPHET / Unity / Self-respect

How Silas Eto was able to capitalize on two similar but not identical situations, one in 1960 and the other in 1961. Both were ripe for change. Both were group-movement rejections of the Church in favour of the nativistic movement.

of Etoism or, on the other hand, a reconciliation of the lineages of Gumi and Gemu, for example, moving either one way or the other. A segment could return to the Methodist fold, or another segment could be lost and join the C.F.C. The sociological possibilities in the situation are numerous. At present it seems a stable situation but its permanence is based on a purely personal coalition of the Roviana organizational leaders and the prophet. This is a symbiotic relationship in a current situation, which may be of limited duration. It has to remain sufficiently strong to exist in the face of segmented lineages or 'divided families'. I shall shortly show how this can continue for years in pagan-Christian encounter, but often with the death of the strongest resister, chief or priest, the family suddenly unites again.

The sociological possibilities because of the present equilibrium within Etoism and the Roviana divided lineages suggest impermanence. The main characters in the drama are all advanced in years. I think the Methodist Church would be well-advised to do her utmost to stimulate real indigenous development in the loyalist congregations, while it is still within her power.

Josué Danho[18] attributed the revivals of pre-Christian and magical forms in Africa to the process of Africa gaining her freedom. If this be so with Etoism, we should not overlook the fact that the loyalist villages may have clung to the Mission because of their refusal to abandon their dependence on mission paternalism. If this be so, we may not yet have seen the end of the movement.

Christianity in the Western Solomons was certainly strongly alien and anti-traditional. Few, if any, of the traditional features were considered worth saving. Customs, instead of having been won for Christ, have 'melted away'. New alien forms have not always given satisfaction. Some, like the Holy Communion, have been withheld. Resultant voids have caused dissatisfaction, and those who have felt this have been ready to put their trust in a Melanesian prophet who could recapture some of the lost magic of their ancestors—which, from a distance, seemed to have some glamour. In the next chapter we shall examine the degree of recapture of pre-Christian belief and form by Etoism.

CHAPTER 17

Theological Analysis of Etoism

In this chapter Etoism will be examined as a system of thought and practice from two perspectives. Firstly we shall try to determine what features may be classed as its pagan associations, or in other words, how much of this syncretism is pagan resurgence. The second part of the chapter will be devoted to a brief systematic reconstruction of its basic theology. The only written sources for the actual beliefs and teachings of Etoism are the hymns of the movement, of which I think I have a fairly complete collection as at the end of 1964.

THE PAGAN ASSOCIATIONS

Eto's grandfather, Mapuro, was a celebrated magic-man. He demonstrated his magical powers in many ways with a sacred stick. He could make a drinking-nut fall from a coconut tree by pointing the stick at it. Many of the older folk still remember Mapuro and his magic. One of the Vella Lavella mission teachers, who served at Marovo for a time, saw Mapuro at work with his famous stick. He used to take it everywhere just as Silas Eto, his grandson, does with his sticks today. A Fijian at Gizo challenged Eto about the two sticks he carries. The former is reported to have received the reply that the Spirit operates through them whenever Eto wants a group response from the crowd. Eto, no doubt, would have justified himself from such Scripture as Acts 19: 12, had he been familiar with it, but my strong impression is that he had incorporated the old Melanesian magical practice into his cult.

A Marovo man, who has married a girl from one of the Eto villages and has lived with her people according to the matrilocal pattern, has adopted the Eto worship for the sake of expediency. He reports two things about Eto. There was certainly a general fear in which Eto was held by everyone. As an example, he told how Eto had set a taboo on the village coconuts, so that the revenue from copra could be set aside for the general fund, which was a normal Melanesian pattern of money-raising. There was a general fear to disobey Eto, but for one man who cut his copra as usual. Shortly afterwards that man's child died, which was widely interpreted as the result of breaking Eto's taboo. The second thing which had impressed the Marovo man was that, though the people put a good deal of money into the movement, they were paying dearly for their excitement and the benefits of the investment were drawn only by the leaders. He felt the people were held by fear and unable to do anything about it.

This is the opinion of one with only a fringe involvement in the

248

movement. One of my best informants confirms these points. He says Eto has tremendous *drawing power*, but that he also secures some stability for his movement by economic pressures. His group collects money three times a year for the fund. It is a considerable fund and my informant named several persons who had drawn from it, one for an outboard motor, another in Honiara had drawn £300 towards the cost of his car. People who become economically involved in this manner are likely to be loyal to the movement. But Eto is no fool, they are also persons needed by the movement. Then my informant added significantly—but for the rank and file he has other means.

Pursuing further the matter of Eto's *drawing power* we discussed the prophet's 'angels', girls dressed like the people of Palestine, who accompany him wherever he goes and who stand beside him when he preaches. He always had a tribe of women following him, and all kinds of reports circulated about it, which may or may not be true. The Solomon Islanders believe that he holds his power over them by the process known as *vinaroro*, a sexual charm operated with a torch or with tobacco. The general opinion is that Eto uses this with its normal sex intent. The girls are powerless to resist once they know *vinaroro* has been applied against them. Whether this be true or not, the subject of *vinaroro* and belief in its efficacy has been very much revived through this behaviour of Eto with respect to his 'angels'. The missionaries themselves were dissatisfied with the fraternal investigator's apparent by-passing of this matter.

The same informant told me there were two other practices which people fear Silas Eto may use against them. One is *pele*, the 'evil eye', which will kill them. The other is *doma*, which "makes one know nothing", so that the victim would blindly do what was commanded of him without being aware of it. One of Eto's followers from a New Georgia village admitted to a relative, "We know that this is no good, but we cannot free ourselves from it. We are afraid of Eto and of *doma*."

A general fear on the part of many of Eto's followers is well established; but this in itself does not establish that Eto actually uses these practices. In point of fact, there is a verse in one Eto hymn which speaks against these very things. If Eto does use these particular processes, then we must class him as a sorcerer, but I am not at all confident he belongs in this category. However, we can be sure of three things: (1) There is a strong body of indigenous opinion against him. (2) Many of his followers do fear him on this account. (3) There has been a revival of belief in the power of those things.

On the other hand, I have no doubt that Eto does practise many of the arts of the magic-man. I mean that it seems to me he does use white magic if he does not use black. His methods of worship and general procedure have strongly magical structures.

On two occasions I was told of an episode supposed to have taken place at his home village, when his taboo room was sprayed by the malarial control officer against his wish. Subsequently I believe he successfully prevented any further spraying, as he has prevented medical inspections, injections and other official programmes. In the former case, the officer responsible found the regular paraphernalia of an ordinary ghost-cult taboo place: (1) male and female figures, (2) skulls, and (3) dracaena plants. The male image had his eyes covered. The female was looking heavenwards, with arms outstretched, receiving the Spirit. Such images were certainly used in pre-Christian Roviana religion, though they were not universal throughout the Solomons. Elsewhere I have described how some of these figures were not destroyed in Eto's area, so that the dynamic encounter had been defective there in the initial conversion movements from paganism.

The skulls, on the other hand, were a universal feature for the Solomons in their pre-Christian state. My informant was of the firm opinion that Eto would have collected his own family skulls. He would know where they were buried and could get them with little trouble. Especially as Mapuro was a great magic-man in his day, this would be important to Eto's purpose. However, the whole area was overrun by Japanese and Americans during the war and there may still be remains in the forest. The mere presence of skulls in Eto's secret place does not establish their identity. It is convincing evidence, however, against the form of his 'Christianity', because the Church has adopted a strong attitude to the burial of skulls.

The dracaena plants also are highly suspect. They were used for all forms of protective and counter magic, medicine and exorcism. To a magic-man they were indispensable.[1]

What is more important still than any one of these things is the significant combination of the three in a sacred place. If we can rely on this report,[2] the place was set up exactly as would be expected if Eto was calling on the ghost of Mapuro, his ancestor and a celebrated magic-man in living memory. As we have seen, this was the pre-Christian pattern. This would mean that Eto was practising, not sorcery, but the ghost-cult. It would also classify Etoism as a Christo-pagan religious syncretism, in line with many other Oceanic cults. When Wesley met this kind of thing in England two centuries ago, he described it as "an awkward mixture of real Heathenism and imaginary Christianity". For Eto it marked a tragic departure from his position as a Christian catechist. On the other hand Eto has made no personal confession of this. Outwardly he has insisted that he is dealing only with the Holy Spirit.

The charm-prayers, stick-tapping and sacred words at the beach on the arrival of visitors, the *round*, hand-clapping, flag-waving, or waving of dracaena leaves, followed by procession into church and the closing of doors are all the regular protective and exorcist techniques of old pagan Roviana, which were then done in the name of the ancestral ghost. Whether these Etoist rituals are to be regarded as pagan or Christian will depend on what they signify to the participants. Whatever they may mean to Eto himself, it is clear that to many of the participants, as also to many of the loyalist observers, they have magical significance.

The spirit-possession and the enthusiasm of Etoist meetings also followed patterns used by Roviana before the coming of the gospel, according to the evidence of old men who remember the former times. One of Eto's own relations, now an Adventist pastor, has said many times that the ecstatic dancing and weeping is no new thing and that the Kusage people were noted for it in olden times. Still another informant claims that this aspect of Etoism is identical with a heathen practice known as *sabusabukae*.

I made enquiries as to why Etoism did not spread to certain Adventist villages where I know there were lines of kinship along which one might have expected some transmission. I was told that these folk took a definite stand at this very point—that Eto was using pagan procedures, which they had rejected when they became Christian. My informant in this case was a Methodist loyalist, not an Adventist, and he added that if the Methodist Mission had taken some stand from the start, one man would have been disciplined but there would have been no schism. In passing, note also how he expected the Mission to make the decision and take the action.

To the question "Are pagan rites being used by Eto?", I can only say that it looks very much that way, though only Eto's own confession or exposure in the act could prove it, at least to the westerner. The rites to be pagan would have to be secret. The fact that Eto maintains his secret place and performs some kind of private rites is well known, and to the Melanesian rank and file has only one meaning. To many of his followers the prophet draws on resources of power polytheistically from both Christianity and old Melanesia. and this accounts for the awe in which he is held by many. It also throws a spotlight on the ineffectiveness of quality growth in the village churches that were won over to Etoism. The technique of building up an atmosphere of mystery round the personality of a human being who comes as an intermediary between the people and the "powers that be" was a powerful instrument of the pre-Christian priests. Eto hymns are used to this very end, as were the pre-Christian chants. Whether conceptualized as a prophet, priest or saviour, Eto is central in everything. His followers think this way and I believe that much of it has been stimulated by Eto himself. In any case he has permitted their expression and gloried in it. It is hard to free him from the responsibility.

All these possible pagan associations are highly suspect, especially when seen as cumulative evidence and in the light of Eto's avowed doctrine of God, which is none other than pre-Christian Roviana theology. It shows the uneven state of Christian belief in the area when Etoism burst upon it. As one Rarumana Christian put it: "These people do not know the Christian encounter with fear and evil in which they have victory through Christ. They have no fellowship with Christ. Therefore they resort to preventive magic to deal with their fear." He knew the Etoist leaders saw the manifestations of enthusiasm as cathartic, but he himself considered it magical.

I came upon several cases of Etoist use of holy water and was interested because this is a departure from Methodist practice. It is nevertheless a good example of the complexity of the problem we have to resolve.

Holy water is used in the Christian Church in two branches which are strong in the Solomons, and one must therefore ask if this is part of Eto's outreach to other denominations in his desire for one universal Church for the Solomons. On the other hand, holy water also figured in pagan ritual, and if Eto was reviving the practices of his grandfather he would certainly use this device. Water was regarded as a *mana* repository and its symbolic relation to *life* in Scripture would appeal to any Melanesian disposed towards syncretism.

One missionary in another part of the Solomons had investigated a case of a parishoner who was apprehensive because he had accidentally emptied a bottle of Etoist holy water. He had come upon the idea that a prayer is directed to God, asking that He *enter* the bowl of water. This would make the bowl of water a shrine or vehicle of God. We have already seen that this is a widespread Melanesian concept, and a long way from the Christian position, and especially the Methodist position.

It is true that in the Eastern Solomons the Anglicans use holy water in their rite of exorcism; but the water is, I believe, symbolically used and not a divine shrine or vehicle.

The last-mentioned missionary had also picked up a story of the eccentric mission sister who influenced Eto in his early days, saying her prayers before a bowl of water. Perhaps she saw it as the symbol of the water of life, but this is to speculate. We can prove little by these reports, except that the very fact of their circulation suggests their feasibility. Tentatively we may perhaps consider the Eto use of holy water as syncretistic.

One European informant declared the anti-malarial sprayers had killed a snake kept by Eto, who supposedly likened himself to Moses. This would not be inconsistent with other Eto equations with scriptural persons and episodes. Ancient snake cults were known in Melanesia and I have myself done some work on this subject. Dr. Fox has done it in the Eastern Solomons. Snake cults were also mentioned in *Battle for the Mind*, but I have no evidence for assuming any pagan associations in Eto's activities at this point. Of course, if he did keep a snake with his religious paraphernalia, then the matter is certainly open for investigation.

I leave it for the reader to determine for himself whether or not Silas Eto was reviving magical practices for his peculiar form of 'Christianity'. I have stated the evidence objectively. All the informants I have cited are, I believe, reliable persons. I doubt if a western court of law would condemn him, but a Melanesian court most certainly would.

This unit has been confined to the forms and behaviour of Etoism and the belief they involve. We must now turn to the hymns of the movement. Here we have concrete evidence which should satisfy any westerner, though it will lead to a charge of heresy rather than magic. Nevertheless, I trust the reader will keep in his mind the early chapter on "Pre-Christian Religion", because the pagan associations are not confined to forms and rites. Many of the theological divergences are evidence of pre-Christian pagan belief, none more significantly than the doctrine of God.

ANALYSIS OF ETOIST HYMNS

Silas Eto himself and his leaders, having cut themselves off from orthodoxy, and having closed the doors of their churches to all but their own adherents, have posed a problem for the investigator. How can one discover exactly what they teach if they operate as a secret body? When cornered the Etoist will declare that he believes the Scripture "as taught by Silas Eto", though he cannot or will not expound this further. Most of Eto's doctrine is an oral tradition. I was able to locate only a couple of documents actually written by Eto. For the rank and file there was an ecstatic experience which purported to cleanse them from sin by the Holy Spirit in an act of possession. This was an exciting event witnessed and experienced, and this was its own verification and validation. Beyond this it was extremely difficult to get any clear statement of belief. There seemed to me to be contradictions in the popular testimony, as for instance with respect to the role of Eto himself in the Godhead.

Eventually I was able to borrow a collection of Etoist hymns and anthems, and on the assumption that what the Etoists believe they also sing about, I have attempted the following brief systematic theology of the movement. This required a great deal of time and I was helped in the translation work by Joeli Zio, a loyal Methodist, who also pointed out to me the symbolic significance of many phrases that would undoubtedly have eluded me otherwise. Only one of these hymns appears to be Eto's own composition. So we have here the beliefs of Etoist followers and I can only assume that they have Eto's personal approval in that he allows them to be used at his meetings. Without this collection of hymns a systematic statement of belief would have been impossible. However, with its aid I discovered that my impression of contradiction was confirmed, and I was able to examine this more carefully from evidence that had been prepared for actual worship and not for any investigator like myself. I think the explanation of this lies in the fact that Etoism has evolved as the role of Eto has itself evolved. It is probable therefore that the hymns have a significant chronological sequence, although it may be that different composers have different ideas. In any case they show Etoism as dynamic, not static.

The most striking impression of the whole hymn collection is the centrality of the personality of Eto. He really assumes the role of Christ in that all things, including the Holy Spirit, testify of him. He goes by the name of *Holy Mama*, and even the earliest hymns appear to be solely for his glorification. If this sect survives it will probably deify Eto, according to the well-known Melanesian pattern—unless it breaks up owing to sociological factors.

One informant told me that at first the regular Methodist hymns were used, the Etoists changing certain words and phrases to transfer the devotion from Christ to Eto. This enraged the loyalists and generated a good deal of heat on the purely indigenous level of the Church. There are no Methodist hymns in the collection I used, with the exception of one in English, which I shall mention in its appropriate place.

Although many of the hymns have retained a *tone* of worship, their *Mama*-centricity is obviously aimed at one end—reinforcing the personal authority of Holy Mama, establishing this title, and enshrining him with an aura of glory. I now analyse what seem to me to be the significant features.

1. *Eto's Personal Call and Dedication*

One hymn, supposedly by Holy Mama himself, could be regarded as his prophetic call and dedication. In this he calls on Jesus to stand by him in the house that he builds, that it may be on the rock and not on the sand, and that the Holy Spirit may not judge him in the Day of Judgement. Much could pass for orthodox if it stood alone. He calls on the Holy Spirit to "creep over his life" so that "God, His Son and Mama" may be "one only". He vaguely incorporates himself into the Trinity, as it were, and addresses himself to Jesus, who has disclosed to him that:

> My day is passed away
> The time belongs to the Holy Spirit

His life now is transformed by the Holy Spirit, and he dedicates himself to the holy life. This hymn speaks of "my new teaching, through the Holy Spirit".

The earliest Etoist hymn I have contains no violent heresy. Although he is called Holy Mama, he is the servant of Christ and seeks to build up the hearts of the congregation into a house for the Holy Spirit. As time went on Eto departed from this position—not by contradiction, but by the incorporation of new ideas, which gradually assumed the dominant doctrinal position. More and more the hymns became Mama-centric, and even when he was not mentioned in the text, the hymns were given a title dedicating them to him. The welcome hymn calling the folk together for worship could be translated thus

> We welcome you Holy Mama.
> The Church gives
> Our fellowship greeting
> In the Holy Spirit

> This is our happiness
> Holy Mama.
> Joy, joy, joy, joy, Holy Mama!
> This is Holy Mama.

> 'Good-day, Holy Mama,'
> Comes from our hearts.
> Look! Your Church
> Waits to welcome you.

This very long hymn has some political overtones. It dates from the period when the movement had incorporated four localities and aspired to win all the Solomons. After greeting Holy Mama, these four geographical areas are greeted thus:

> Good-day, Kolo side, (i.e. toward Keru)
> Happy to meet you.

Let us rejoice together
Through Holy Mama.

Good-day, Kusage side,
Happy to greet you.
Let us rejoice together
Through Holy Mama.

Good-day, other side of the Lagoon. (Roviana)
Happy to meet you.
Let us rejoice together
Through Holy Mama.

Good-day, Solomon Islands,
Happy to meet you.
Let us rejoice together
Through Holy Mama.   (Each time with the chorus)

There is something of a folk atmosphere about this. One can almost see
the groups bowing to each other.

A similar idea is expressed in what I take to be a dismissal hymn.
Holy Mama is addressing the congregation or church, with each verse
beginning "Farewell to you Church." The hymn contains the lines—

Hip, Hip, Hurrah! Solomon Islands,
Hip, Hip, Hurrah! Beyond the Lagoon,
Hip, Hip, Hurrah! Top of the Mango Tree,
Jesus holds you in his hands.

Phrases like "Good-day!" and "Hip, Hip, Hurrah!" are inserted in
English, although the hymns are otherwise in the vernacular. The "top
of the mango tree" is a frequent reference to one of the revelations to
Holy Mama.

Farewell to you, Church!
You see me at the top of the mango tree,
You see me with the Son,
I stay with him.

To this point it could well be that Holy Mama was a particularly
favoured prophet, who had personal interviews and fellowship with
the Godhead and with political aspirations for uniting the Solomons.
There is a tendency for him to take the place of Christ, however; for
instance, it is Holy Mama's church, not Christ's. Even at this early
stage the way is open for his incorporation into the Trinity.

2. *The Person of Holy Mama*

To all appearances Holy Mama is deified, but there are contradictions, either because the hymns are not from a single pen, or because
the conceptualizing of his personality is evolving. From time to time
Holy Mama is equated with God, or the Son or the Holy Spirit. The
words of Jesus are cited to serve the Eto purpose, without any apparent
awareness that, after all, the words are Christ's and not Eto's. Whether
used by Jesus or by Eto the words are said to come from the Holy

Spirit, and these personalities seem to be used interchangeably, as Christians interchange the Holy Spirit and the Living Christ today.

If questioned on this matter, the Etoist will reply that the work of Christ is finished, and Holy Mama's has now begun. The words of the former prepare the way for the work of the latter and the words of Jesus can therefore be applied to Holy Mama. This is the key to many of the hymns, and much biblical illustration is used in this way.

Thus in a hymn the dominant motif of which is to show the work of the Holy Spirit through Mama, his work is equated with that of Jesus:

> I am the way and the greatest life,
> As Jesus said to the Church

after which the chorus comes in:

> Holy Word of revelation to us,
> Holy Mama lives with us.

In another verse Holy Mama is equated with God:

> God certainly is our Leader,
> Holy Mama certainly is our Leader.
>
> Holy Word of revelation to us,
> Holy Mama lives with us.

In another hymn the theme is "Salt is important". The scriptural idea of the salt of the earth is adapted to Eto's purposes and the verses following the structure of Hebrew (and biblical) parallelism run like this:

> Salt is important like God in my life.
> Salt is important like Jesus Christ.
> Salt is important like the Holy Spirit.
> Salt is important like Holy Mama.

The chorus runs—

> Take care of Holy Mama,
> Don't let your heart be empty.

From Moses' experience of God on the mountain top Holy Mama seems to have borrowed something for his own experience—

> I stand on the top of the mountain of Israel
> Belonging to the Christian people,
> I laid its foundations,
> The pillar of the Holy Spirit.
>
> The Holy Spirit is in front of me:
> The Holy Spirit is behind me:
> The Holy Spirit is round about me:
> At the top of the mountain of Israel.

Israel is likened to an egg. Jesus Christ gave it life and the Holy Spirit hatched it for Holy Mama. Holy Mama claims to have met Jesus personally, as one hymn declares:

I have already seen Jesus
In my own life.

As most of these hymns are supposed to have been composed in Kusage, we may perhaps assume that they do contain a body of Eto's personal claims, otherwise it is difficult to understand how so many are in the first person.

Now what do these hymns actually say of Holy Mama's precise relation to the Godhead? It was at this point the orthodox Christians clashed violently with the Etoists and where the more stable congregations rejected the movement. But let it first be well noted that trinitarian theology is not clearly understood in the Western Solomons. The very fact that the people are confused allowed Eto to tamper with the doctrine. The ambiguity of the commonly used benediction confuses God (*Tamasa*) and the Father (*Tamana*). The concept of God, as Father, Son and Spirit, is interpreted and translated as God, Son and Spirit, which destroys the unity of the Godhead and leaves us with three Gods. I do not desire to enter into a trinitarian discussion, I merely state the observation I made in the Western Solomons that the majority of Christians think, not of a Godhead but of three Gods. This permitted Eto to give them temporal limits.

The Etoists think themselves through this problem in two ways, which, to the westerner, are in conflict. Nevertheless they are both well established in the Eto hymns.

(*a*) In some references we find God eliminated as an old man, who finished his work long ago and retired. Christ also is relegated to the past because he finished his work when he died on the cross. Any current revelation must belong to some living agent. This, of course, is Holy Mama. The continuous element in all these passages is the Holy Spirit. It was operating through God the old man and creator, and through his Son in the time of his revelation, as it does now through Holy Mama.

(*b*) Some hymn writers treat Holy Mama as a fourth person of the Godhead, insisting that the four are "one only", so that the Trinity becomes a Quadity, as it were.

The first of these is expressed in one hymn as the "three fruits of the Holy Spirit in God, His Son, and Holy Mama". These are thus the three chronologically arranged historic agents of the Spirit's activity—God the creator, now retired; His Son who more recently died to show the seriousness of sin and the way of love, which revelation has been made and is also finished with; and thirdly, Holy Mama, the current instrument for bringing the promises of Jesus to pass and opening eternal life to the faithful. This picture of God is, as we have seen, thoroughly Melanesian; as also is the demand for a living shrine or incarnation of the Spirit for today.

The four-part Godhead which appears to contradict this is common in doxologies, choruses and parts of anthems. One frequently meets it in parallelism—

Hallelujah God!
Hallelujah Christ!
Hallelujah Holy Spirit!
Hallelujah Holy Mama!

Or it may be expressed like this—

Salt is important like Mama in the Church.
Your words and your admonition
Taste good in my heart.
God, the Holy Spirit, Christ and Holy Mama,
These four distribute the words of life.

3. *The Role of Holy Mama as Life-giver*

The last verse cited will serve as a bridge from the person to the work of Holy Mama. It is at this point where he is so often equated with the second Person of the Trinity. In a number of hymns Holy Mama is substituted for Christ and does the work of Christ. In one hymn each of the first four stanzas begins by declaring Holy Mama is the "light of Christ", meaning the lamp to interpret Christ to a new day, or the 'Christ' of this new day.

I lighted the way that Christ may walk,
Jesus and I live in men's hearts

and again

Mama lives in men's hearts

without any reference to Christ at all, but doing his work. He is the light

Mama is the light of Christian fellowship

or again

Mama is the light of the hearts of the people,
Mama embraces God and His Son,
Mama embraces the Holy Spirit,
This is his fatherhood: Mama is the Christ.

Another hymn is addressed to

Father God, Mama,
Father of the Church

A ten-verse hymn devoted to the theme of Mama as the Light, shows him as both mediating the light of Christ and as himself the Light. He becomes the light in the hearts of the people and he is the light of the Church.

Mama is not only the light-bringer; he is also life-bringer. Another hymn declares:

Holy Mama gives us life,
To aspire to the greatest life.
Holy Word of revelation to us,
Holy Mama lives with us.

> Behold now the Church reveals her fruit
> That we may live together in peace.
> Holy Word of revelation to us,
> Holy Mama lives with us.

Still another assures us that "peace in this life comes through Mama" and yet another says:

> Behold the picture drawn of Mama
> To transform the life of the people.
> Peace, love and spiritual life.
> Holy Mama alone is its measure
> Within his New Church.

The hymn "Isireli" announces:

> My work is only one—
> To save the souls of men.

Bezili's Hymn declares:

> Not my wisdom alone,
> Mama is my wisdom
> In the new day
> God . . . Christ . . .
> Holy Spirit . . . Holy Mama . . .
> Hallelujah!

It would seem from these typical examples that Holy Mama, the living agent for the work of the Holy Spirit, has taken over the role of Jesus Christ as Light, Life-giver, Root-cause of peace and love among men. My anti-Etoist informants had been most critical of this aspect of his theological claims, because he "takes unto himself the glory that belongs only to Christ". Eto was apparently offering a living incarnation to replace a dead and buried Christ.

4. *Messianism*

The existence of any eschatological messianism in Etoism was disputed by some missionaries. It certainly is not a pronounced doctrine, but neither is it absent. Given a different political set of circumstances, I feel sure it would have been more vocal. I have already cited one hymn which declares "Mama is the Christ". We have seen Eto interpreted in terms of Scripture, and the promises of Jesus being applied to him. One of his roles is to bring about peace, and a state of bliss. Heaven and Paradise are prominent in his hymns. His villages have all been renamed with biblical names, and his rebuilt model village was given the name Paradise. One hymn begins—

> Paradise, country of the blessed,
> Joyful land of Christian people

and goes on to explain how human aspirations to this happy place are realized through Holy Mama:

> Holy Mama opens here
> Entrance to the realm of Heaven.

The term 'realm of Heaven' (*sa popoa Mañauru*) appears in numerous hymns. The witness of Scripture, the words of God, of Christ, of the prophets and of John (because of his vision of Heaven in the Apocalypse) in one hymn are interpreted by Holy Mama alone:

> Your words Holy Mama
> Are revealed to Christian people,
> The Holy Spirit is your witness.

One anthem opens:

> The entrance is opened:
> The key to the Kingdom of Heaven:

and goes on to declare that "Holy Mama is the entrance" and "the Holy Spirit is the key". This anthem is essentially messianic in its imagery and invites believers to enter Heaven, which is both a Kingdom (*butubutu*) and a land (*pepeso*). Still another hymn of this type speaks of Holy Mama as "the leader of our life" and as "the path" to Heaven. Heaven here is a locality (*vasina*) and a land (*pepeso*) or country (*popoa*). There is plenty of scope here for an earthly messianic millenium, had the external conditions been ripe for it. The hymn finishes with hallelujahs to Holy Mama and calls on the angels of Heaven to rejoice.

The concept of *Glory* figures conspicuously in these hymns. A hymn of desire is addressed to Holy Mama. A man needs a helper on his way to Heaven. Mama only is "the way and the life" through whom Paradise is gained. Heaven is described as "the land of the new life", to which men need "helping" or "leading". It has to be "revealed" or "seen". This is all specific terminology.

Therefore, although one does not say the movement was actually messianic, it did have all the 'tinder' for it, had the political obstructions been there to spark it. The Administration was concerned about Etoism but was even more reluctant to act than was the Mission.

5. *The Concept of the Church*

The only serious obstructions against Etoism came from the Church and these were formative in helping the schismatics to conceptualize their own entity. It is interesting that when the loyalist villages clung to the long-established Mission paternalism, the schismatics realized that they had to establish a new entity of their own to stand over against the Mission concept. They saw themselves as a New Church (*Ekelesia Vaqurana*) as the hymns put it, but which the fraternal delegate conveniently spoke of as the *New Way*. The term *New Church* fits their rejoinder "There are many kinds of Lotu". It is capitalized in the hymn manuscripts. The fact that they were able to establish their own organization shows that an indigenous Church could have been cultivated after the war, had the Mission worked to this end.

Now, however, the New Church is described as "a tree, whose glory is Mama". This gathering of "those who rejoice in new life", who know "the glory of Heaven" and "the peace of that country", is itself the creation of Holy Mama.

> Father God, Mama,
> Father of the Church.
> And Mama is its prize.

In the chorus of this hymn the church is referred to as "Your New Church", i.e. Mama's, a transfer from Christ. It is described as a "worthy" community, marked by "fellowship", "goodness" and "peace", and is called to demonstrate its "life" with "good works". We have here a well-formed doctrine of the "marks of the Church". What is missing is Christ, the Head of the Church, whose position has been usurped throughout by Holy Mama.

The Etoist hymns occasionally have a 'dig' at the Methodists who resisted them. They are conceptualized as "disbelievers" and as "critics".

> He that knows me
> But follows his own wish,
> He will never test me
> Through the Holy Spirit

for the Spirit witnesses only to Holy Mama.

> People who are really not happy with Jesus,
> Those who cannot see where Jesus lives,
> Miss both seeing Christ
> And the eternal rejoicing.

"Seeing Jesus", in the chorus of this hymn, is bringing people together through Holy Mama, for "Jesus is in me (i.e. Holy Mama)". These lines are occasionally thrown at the loyalists.

6. The Pattern of Etoist Piety

The formulae known as *Qetuqetu* are ritual prayers for daily recitation, counted with the ribs of coconut leaves, like the "Hail Mary" is counted on a rosary. A daily count of these acts of devotion is kept by each individual, and the household totals are added up and reported each week to the village group. A great deal of virtue and merit is built up by such devotion, and the total congregational counts become almost astronomonical. This is a strong departure from Methodist practice and tradition and shows the dramatic swing to the Roman position. Was it another of Eto's out-reaches for a universal Church with a greater emphasis on form? The missionaries resisted this as "vain repetitions".[3]

Each *qetuqetu* is addressed twice to the angels. They feature the Holy Spirit, the Church, Heaven and Holy Mama, together with numerous hallelujahs. They express the desire to live in peace and praise and to aspire to Heaven. They give thanks for the revelation of Holy Mama and call on the angels to rejoice.

The collection I obtained contained ten *qetuqetu*, and I note the adherent whose copy it was had recorded a tally of from three to nine rounds daily. His record covered thirty-six days, during which he had presumably counted off 183 rounds of ten prayers, with the aid of the coconut ribs. This is an actual figure, but it may not be typical. I am told many are more pious than this. At one period the ribs placed in the hair of the person concerned helped to mark him as a "praying man", which accounts for the missionary criticisms of this Pharisaism. In the period of crisis this form of religious participation played an important part in giving the movement its sense of entity.

7. *Political Overtones*

Has the theology of these hymns any political overtones? There is an anthem the Etoists sing, with all parts coming in like a regular oratorio, which is pathetic evidence of some of the deeper feeling which made the movement possible. It is called *Independence*, and contains many English words and phrases. It illustrates the effect of the acculturation process, the Solomon Islanders' unrealized aspirations, and their ultimate rejection of the very Church which brought them out of their old paganism of head-hunting and slavery. Their verdict in favour of a Melanesian half-Christian and half-pagan pattern is a sorrowful cry of failure that ascends to Holy Mama in the vain hope that herein might freedom be found. He promises them freedom from within their own indigenous life and tells them to stand alone on their own feet. The parts in the first person are sung as a solo.

> I am in a hurry for civilization
> But I cannot attain unto it.
> Civilization I desire but I cannot reach it.
> Independence I desire, but I cannot reach it.
> Independence I desire.
>
> > Civilize! Civilize! Independence!
> > Civilization! Civilization!
> > Civilize! Civilize! Independence!
> > I am unable to attain to civilization.
>
> I am sorry, Mama! I am sorry, Mama!
> I cannot reach civilization. I am sorry, Mama!
>
> The Holy Ghost reveals alone to Holy Mama.
> Indigenous! Standing alone.
> We attain freedom.
> We stand alone, indigenous, Holy Spirit.
> Indigenous! Indigenous! Holy Spirit!
>
> > Standing alone! Standing alone!
> > We stand alone.
>
> Hip, Hip, Hurrah! We attain freedom.
> Hallelujah, Holy Mama!

8. *The Holy Spirit*

Apart from the central role of Holy Mama himself, the Holy Spirit is the dominant doctrine of Etoism. He is the source and inspiration of every action of Holy Mama, as he was of God in creation and of Jesus in his day. The justification of every decision or statement of Eto, and therefore the source of his authority, is said to be the Holy

Spirit who reveals all things. Thus when some anti-Etoist suggests that Eto may be dealing with some other spirit, even an evil spirit, it struck deep into the heart of Etoism and brought the most hostile action from Eto himself.

One of the hymns conceives of Holy Mama as the Light, by means of which the Holy Spirit discovers the cause of trouble, so that it may be corrected. The figure used is a daring one: viz., that of a magic-man, whose spirit goes forth to discover the cause of sickness or sorcery. The person who composed this hymn was familiar with shamanistic thinking, which is pre-Christian. It shows how, even after people have been Christian for a generation, pagan thought-forms may survive in their conceptualizations unless they are actually defeated.

But the use of such a figure also raises again the possibility of Eto having used pre-Christian preventive, protective and medicinal magic. His hostility to black magic is stated in the hymn purporting to be his own. He names certain types of sorcery as things to be stamped out; but the idea of the Holy Spirit going forth to discover their cause and deal with them aligns Eto's Holy Spirit with the divination and corrective magic of the pre-Christian magic-man. If this was really Eto's hymn, he is thinking ghost-worship into his doctrine of the Holy Spirit.

There is no doubt the Etoists have used the doctrine of the Holy Spirit to justify all their activities. Everything is by revelation from the Spirit through Holy Mama. Scripture means what the Holy Spirit reveals it to mean to Mama. The hymn collection bears this out. The answer of the orthodox Christian was expressed by a preacher in a morning devotional at Rarumana, "The true Spirit testifies of Christ". This is scriptural. "A spirit which glorifies anyone else," he said, "is the spirit of Antichrist." He then discussed the prophet who had come into their midst.

.   .   .   .   .

The hymns of Etoism leave no room for doubt as to the doctrinal eccentricities of the movement. The orthodox Christians were disturbed above all by the way Mama himself usurped the place of Christ. Mama interprets the Scriptures, he mediates the Holy Spirit to men, in him alone can men find peace and wisdom and freedom.

> Mama is the only way to life
> By which we reach
> The Paradise of God.

Eto himself was frequently discomfited by the missionaries citing Scripture against him. Thus at the time of the crisis he had to establish his attitude to the Bible. He knew he was no match for them in ex-position, and he knew the Bible was their norm and authority. He declared that the Bible was like a dictionary or an A B C, to be used only for reference. It should never be read as a book, for this would lead only to confusion. It was written by fallible men, he declared, as some American soldiers had told him. In reality, the Kusage people have no need of it, for they have the Holy Spirit and the new life, and to this there is nothing the Bible can add. If they do need it, Holy Mama can interpret it for them.

Once Eto and his followers had severed their connections from the Mission, its discipline and aids to worship, they were thrown back on their own resources. Not only did Eto claim the right to interpret Scripture in his own way, but he tended to line both belief and practice with his old traditional heritage—his doctrine of the retired God, the shamanistic role of the Holy Spirit, the magical paraphernalia of his secret sacred place, and his rituals of protective magic. The theology of Etoism has been a progressive drift away from orthodoxy to Solomon Island neo-paganism.

It calls to mind something said of the Independent Church in South Africa by Sundkler—

> isolated from effective Christian teaching, (it) is in the long run defence-less against the forces of old African heritage.[4]

Concluding Summary to Part Five

1. The Western Solomons Schism had its roots in the spiritual state of the Roviana Church. The spontaneous expansion of Etoism shows a hunger for something the Church was not providing. This pastoral starvation was the result of a long policy of industrial missions at the expense of the pastorate.

2. The gradual development of Etoism from a harmless demonstration to a radical heresy, and the phenomenon of possession over a period of twenty years, show that the unsatisfactory state of Christianity was a continuous matter.

3. The shortcomings of the Church's doctrinal instruction may be judged by the comparative ease with which Eto tampered with essential Methodist doctrine, especially the nature of each Person of the Godhead.

4. The official policy of *laissez faire*, for a decade or more after the war, permitted the movement to organize itself and to establish its roots. (In fairness to the missionaries of the time, it is pointed out (i) that this resulted from long-term station-centred policy, and (ii) it was Methodist procedure to give the accused the benefit of the doubt until his error was completely proved. Eto played on this.)

5. The fact that the patterns of Eto's worship, whether magical or not, followed so closely those of Roviana ghost-worship, suggests that Christianity had removed features of the old religion without providing functional substitutes.

6. Etoism is a typically nativistic cult, with a prophet-saviour and a message of revelation, incorporating both biblical and old traditional concepts, the latter gradually assuming dominance.

7. The prophet himself passed through a series of intellectual changes from a somewhat mystical Wesleyan piety to dramatic self-glorification. He originated the system of Etoism, capturing a local situation which was ripe for change or revival. The personality of the prophet is still the main element holding the movement together, but he is dependent on leaders from the Roviana Lagoon segment.

8. Overseas religious literature and identification with certain sects, mostly American, permitted the identification of the emotional crisis with Christianity and the supposed work of the Holy Spirit. As the Church had supplied virtually no literature to its adherents over the years, they were vulnerable at this point.

9. The pagan associations of the movement were acceptable to the Etoists because they were thoroughly Melanesian in character. The Church, on the other hand, was foreign and had eliminated much of the traditional culture.

10. The eccentric group behaviour, which was taken by the missionaries as the focal point, was an expression of something deeper—an awareness of spiritual need, a craving for cleansing and renewal. The prophet was able to provide a dramatic experience of supposed release and of new life.
11. The attempt to explain these experiences away in terms of western psychology was unacceptable to the Melanesians, who were concerned with dynamic encounter. It convinced both the schismatics and loyalists that the Europeans did not understand the Melanesian position and had no real solution to offer to meet their needs.
12. The explosion of Etoism temporarily relieved the pressure and has eliminated the weakest localities of the Methodist work, but the theological causes within the situation have not yet been eliminated by any means. It could well be that other prophets will arise.

.   .   .   .   .

I am well aware that it is one thing to point out causes of trouble and quite another to suggest a remedy, but because this affects a Methodist area, I make these suggestions within the patterns of Methodist action:

1. The Church needs planned second-generation evangelism. Even a penitent-form evangelism would still be acceptable, in view of the manifest need for cathartic experience.
2. The Church needs pastoral nurture through graded age-groups.
3. The Church needs more facilities for indigenous participation in both worship and applied Christianity.
4. The whole Bible in the vernacular is needed (it is shortly to be provided), also extensive provision of scriptural aids for lay preachers and prayer leaders.
5. Well-organized and regular village Sunday schools are badly needed.
6. Better and systematic instruction in basic belief is required.
7. The Holy Communion should be celebrated regularly.
8. The indigenous ministry should be rapidly expanded, and the village congregations should be developed towards selfhood.

This is entirely Methodist. Nothing new is suggested here. I believe Methodism has the capacity to deal with the situation.

Part Six

THEOLOGICAL DEPTHS OF THE CURRENT SITUATION

18 The Process from Animist to Christian Forms
    Functional Substitutes
    Changed Perspectives
    Christianization of Vocabulary
    Confession
    Symbolism
    Are these Forms and Symbols adequate for the Second
        Generation?
    Animistic Revivals in Second Generation Christianity

19 Hymns as a Theological Index
    Hymn Selection Sampling in a Methodist Village
    Hymn Selection Sampling in an Anglican Village

20 The Bible in the Village Situation
    Scripture Selection Sampling in a Methodist Village
    The Use of Scripture in an Anglican Village

21 Measuring Congregational Piety by Curves
    Explanation of the Tool and its Use
    Application in a Methodist Village
    Application in an Anglican Village

22 Half-Christian Half-Pagan Villages
    Co-existence and Missionary Obligation
    Modified Paganism
    Conversion and Obstructions
    Sociological Aspects

23   Urban and Industrial Situations
    The Urban Situation
      Migration Growth and Innovation
      Rural Roots in Urban Society
      Honiara 'Collective Man'
      Diffusion of Religion and Morals
      Analysis of Marginality
    The Plantation Christianity

CHAPTER 18

The Process from Animist to Christian Forms

THE ESTABLISHMENT of worship patterns is a major feature of the church planting process. Given a movement out of animism, with a clear encounter and faith in the power of Christ over that of all other spirits, what form of worship pattern is to be established for that generation coming out of animism? Bishops Selwyn and Patteson and their successors insisted that the Church which was to emerge was to be thoroughly Melanesian. The passage from animism to Christianity was to be comprehensible to those involved in it.

In the study of magico-religious practices we observed the use of prayers, invocations, incantations, symbols and ritual charms. These were not purely magical acts with a potency of their own, so much as potent because they were done in the name, or with the *mana*, of some significant ghost. They represented ritual forms of approach and appeal from man on earth to beings in the spirit world. Did these mechanisms offer or suggest ways for achieving a meaningful passage from animism to Christian worship for first generation converts?

FUNCTIONAL SUBSTITUTES

Clearly a complete rejection of all these forms without any functional substitutes would leave cultural voids. Christian worship had not only to supply forms that were culturally appreciated, but also to fulfil certain social functions as the pre-Christian forms had supposedly done.

Let us take, for example, the rituals associated with planting and fishing, the serious business of life—food supply. What involved more time or labour? Although perhaps the Christian Church did not develop all the forms she might have initiated at this point, it was not neglected, at least by the Anglicans. Rogationtide has been worked into the Christian calendar as an occasion for special celebration. The Melanesian Mission Rogationtide prayers have been included in the Brotherhood Book, which means they are used throughout the year. In the village where I lived, they were used every week, in some weeks several times. This simple but effective liturgical unit is a natural step from animist food-production and fishing ritual to its higher Christian counterpart founded on the belief that "This is my Father's world". Let us recall the unit.

Let us pray for God's blessing on the fruits of the earth and the labours of men.

The eyes of all wait upon Thee, O Lord!

And Thou givest them their food in its proper time.

Bless, we pray Thee, O Lord, all those who work in the gardens or fish in the sea, that we may safely gather in the crops of the earth and the food of the waters; and grant to all planters and traders, and to all who sail in the ships and work on plantations, that they may receive a fair reward of their work, and may praise Thee by living according to Thy will; through Jesus Christ our Lord. *Amen.*

Here is a unit of Christian liturgy in a set *form*, serving as a *functional substitute* for pre-Christian incantations and charms, that called on some ghostly aid to make the labour expended in the fields and at sea effective. It is a substitute because it satisfies a felt need; but it is more than a substitute because it brings about a deeper congregational involvement in participation in the act of worship itself. In pre-Christian days either the priest would have performed the rite in secret, or if the group was present they would have joined only in the "Mana!" (cf. "Amen!"). In point of fact the Christian act of worship is more than an invocation, it is a confession of faith in God as Provider. Both the priest and people make their affirmations of faith before the actual prayer is offered. Thus a Christian innovation is introduced within a familiar structural form and the people are led into a deeper realm of faith.

The psychological and spiritual need for such functional substitutes is schematized in the diagrams opposite. Figure 1 represents an actual case reconstructed from a Malaita community. Two types of power were sought, one from ghosts and the other from spirits; the former was required for both food supply and war, the latter for war only. With the disappearance of the war situation, under Government and Christian influence, the second need has been eliminated but the food supply need is continuous. With the passing of the old way, a mission has to determine whether or not substitutions will be employed or whether a convert's devotional life is left to him as an individual. Some missionaries think that everything associated with the pre-Christian way of life is pagan and should be discarded. There are cases where this led to the abandonment of porpoise fishing and the isolation of Christians from local economic pursuits. In other cases the failure to supply recognizable religious substitutes has led to the complete secularization of the business of procuring food and livelihood. The rightness of the use of the functional substitute is that (1) it retains the relevance of religion in daily life, and (2) it meets the inherent and felt needs and creates no cultural void. The substitute should be as near as possible to the indigenous form to simplify the process from the lower to the higher faith. These alternatives discussed are reduced opposite (Figures 2–4) to the same structural scheme.

Not so very long ago an Anglican Melanesian pastor became involved in the issue of Christian substitutes at a very practical level. He began life by a remarkable escape from infanticide and believed God had saved him to a purpose,[2] and had become an aggressive and powerful man of faith working among the islands of Christian–pagan co-existence

THE SPIRITUAL IMPORTANCE OF FUNCTIONAL SUBSTITUTES

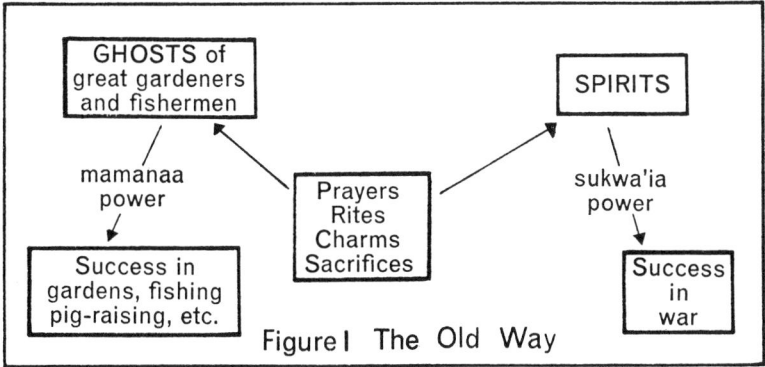

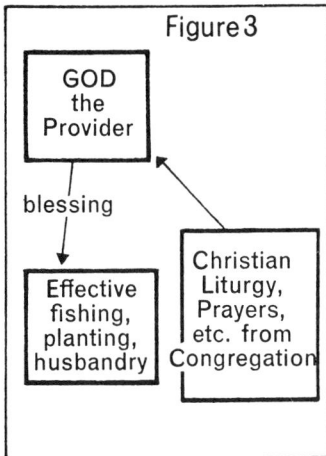

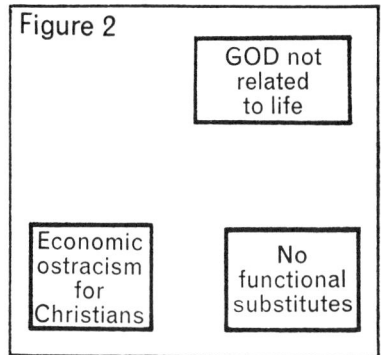

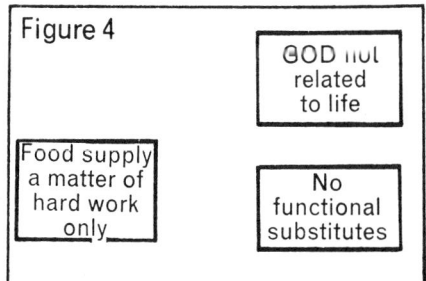

Figure I   The Old Way

GHOSTS of great gardeners and fishermen
mamanaa power
Success in gardens, fishing pig-raising, etc.
Prayers Rites Charms Sacrifices
SPIRITS
sukwa'ia power
Success in war

Figure 3

GOD the Provider
blessing
Effective fishing, planting, husbandry
Christian Liturgy, Prayers, etc. from Congregation

Figure 2

GOD not related to life
Economic ostracism for Christians
No functional substitutes

Figure 4

GOD not related to life
Food supply a matter of hard work only
No functional substitutes

New Ways

Figures 2 and 4 show how the failure to supply functional substitutes create religious voids.

K

off Malaita. When the porpoise fleet was preparing for its seasonal drive, he organized Christian prayers for the success of the expedition, although it was a communal project in an area of co-existence. The heathen had always performed their rites but for the Christians it had become secularized. When the pastor determined that the project needed the Lord's blessing, the pagans were annoyed and declared there would be no catch. Each day they went out and for five days there was no catch, and the heathen jeered more and more for their failure. On the sixth day they caught 200 porpoise and more still on the following day, so that today they still talk of it as the "biggest season ever". This priest believes in prayer, not merely because he thinks God answers it, but because the earth is the Lord's and the fulness thereof, and man should commit himself to God in his labours on earth and at sea.

One comes across many narratives of this kind both in conversation and in the records. Deck records one of Rennel Island, a Polynesian outlier in the Solomons. When the people rejected their *atua* worship, they put aside their shark-fishing with it, because their mechanisms for discovering the whereabouts of the sharks was an act of worshipping the *atua*. But the people felt this economic loss and after a time went to their pastor, who determined that now they knew God they could pray to Him as Creator and Provider, and a Christian prayer pattern was introduced for their shark-fishing. They had highly successful fishing thereafter. These folk are attached to the South Seas Evangelical Mission, but in both cases I have cited the decisions were made by indigenous pastors, not by missionaries.

At the level of the individual farmer, all through the Anglican area I found that each gardener religiously brought the first produce of a new crop and presented it to the Lord by placing it before the altar. For us to see a heap of sweet potatoes in the church when we went to evensong was a regular event.

The Anglican Prayer Book is well organized to serve the Melanesian converts. In the Book of Common Prayer as authorized for use in the Diocese, the section of assorted prayers and thanksgivings provides for numerous occasions. They meet many of the felt needs of the people. Each is arranged with a response of faith from the participants before the prayer is offered. There is the prayer for the place itself where the worshippers live, the prayer for travellers, the prayer for seasonable weather, the prayer for the sick and suffering, and many others. These were the motives behind the pre-Christian prayers, and there was no difficulty of transition from the old day to the new at this point. They were real functional substitutes, but reached a higher level by providing for participant group confession of faith.

CHANGED PERSPECTIVES

There were some aspects of daily life in which Christianity demanded a complete change—in attitude to war, for example. In such cases the substitutions were direct opposites. War prayers were changed to specific positive prayers for peace. The worship pattern was the same but was reorientated to a new desire. Another significant shift is seen in the widening of the range of petition, as for instance by including specific prayers for one's enemies and for the heathen. The prayers of this type I found regularly used. It represents a real advance in religious experience and the application of New Testament standards. On the other hand, one may find occasionally what one anthropologist called 'Christian sorcery'. He refers to a prayer asking God to deal with some person, known or unknown, who has done him harm. The fact that these extremes of the forgiving and revengeful prayers are found in the same congregation indicates the wide range of transition from animism to Christianity. Old Testament and New Testament characters worship together and create a problem in quality growth for the pastor.

Let it not be imagined, however, that these two extreme types represent sincere and superficial Christianity. It may well be that the revengeful person is actually the more positive and more intense in his religion. In our own society sometimes the folk who feel the deepest about their religion are the most unbending and hostile to those whom they imagine to be their enemies. The crux of the matter in the Solomon Island situation is not that the seemingly Old Testament Christians are vindictive, but that they are expressive of a deep cry for justice in island society today. When western law gives no satisfaction, fails to right wrongs, and makes no recompense to injured parties, their cry goes up to a God whom they believe is just, and who will see that sin does not go unpunished. The anthropologist who accused them of sorcery, might better have said 'counter-sorcery' and thus differentiated between the functional and motivational aspects of the two. The Government has classed them both as sorcery and forbidden them, but one is the vehicle of jealousy and the other of justice. The island philosophy regards the former as wrong and the latter as right, and because western law has failed to right the wrongs he often retains his cultural orientation. The interesting thing about the transitional and the fully-developed Christian is that each will defend his respective position by citing the same words of Scripture:

> Vengeance is mine,
> I will repay, saith the Lord.

The transitional Christian underscores *repay*, for He is a just God who will not allow sin to go unpunished, since society can be happy only when wrongs are righted. For all its shortcomings, this is a considerable improvement on the old way, when he was committed to take the law into his own hands. But the more fully-developed Christian will underscore the pronouns and quote the passage in full and do positive good to his enemies. It is not his affair to ask for any requital. God Himself is the best judge of that need or otherwise.

The average island Christian does not see these issues in the abstract or as general principles. He sees them working in concrete situations— a sin has been committed, a social structure has been threatened, the cohesion of a kin unit is jeopardized, western law gives no settlement

and injured parties have to bear their suffering alone.[3] The young
convert has to practise his Christianity in this setting. Once he would
have employed his counter-sorcery in a sense of duty akin to that of the
Old Testament avenger of blood. Now he turns to God and says, "O
Lord, grave injustice has been done, wilt Thou deal with the offender
that we may have peace again." If he still has much of his Christian
pilgrimage before him, he has at least travelled some distance along
the way.

The Anglican set prayers have a positive approach to these problems
of daily life. There is a strong emphasis on prayers to God as the Great
Protector of man in the dangers of life. There are prayers for health
and for recovery from sickness, prayers for defence from evil, for the
preservation of concord in household and community, prayers that
this day we fall into no evil or danger:

Visit this place and drive from it all the snares of the enemy.

There are prayers for protection from temptation, and prayers that
men receive a fair return for labour and produce. Those who love and
use their prayer book—and a great many of them most certainly do—
have placed their lives in the hands of God in *certain* faith. God to them
is just and faithful. This fine collection of prayers for protection was
perfectly meaningful to converts from animism, and satisfied a deep
sense of need. My impression was also that where the prayer was
habitually used there was little or no Christian 'counter-sorcery', but
"being defended from the fear of [their] enemies" they were more able
to find "rest and quietness".

The strong emphasis on Holy Communion and the General Confession
are safeguards against self-righteousness. The Christian is called to
"live in love and charity with his neighbours" and to love his neighbour
as himself—terms which recur continually in village worship. Rather
than asking for punishment on their adversaries, these people have
been taught to pray:

That it may please Thee to bring back into the way of truth all whom
Satan has led away

and again

to lift them that fall

and again

That it may please Thee to forgive our enemies, and those who hurt us
by word and deed, and to turn their hearts.

These are all from the Litany, and the people respond in unison:

We beseech Thee to hear us, good Lord.

Computation for a year on the basis of the figures I kept in Fouia would
suggest the Litany is used about sixty times a year in an Anglican
village. I felt it was a good aid for bringing folk effectively from
animism to New Testament Christianity. It is meaningful and relevant
and a corrective to any Christian 'counter-sorcery', which has been

reported from areas where no prayer book is used but where Marching
Rule pressed strongly for justice in a political manner. The Litany is
also a fine instrument for congregational participation in worship.
Christian liturgy therefore reveals two dimensions of the passage
from animism to Christianity. Firstly, it was a natural step based on
that aspect of the pre-Christian religious life which was its finest and
best, and which seemed to reach out to something more noble. In spite
of the pagan cruelty and dynamic evil against which Christianity set
its face, there was in its essential worship-patterns something with
Christian potential, if it could be transformed by deeper insights and
higher faith. The Melanesian had a natural capacity for Christian
liturgy. In the second place, with respect to the elements of pre-
Christian religion that demanded rejection, Christian liturgy was
directly corrective—prayers for peace took the place of war prayers,
one prayed for one's enemy and for the heathen. The worship forms
were retained but the spiritual *set* was reversed. Pre-Christian forms
were won for Christ and sanctified to higher motives. The Anglican
Prayer Book was ideal for this situation.

Although the Prayer Book is an aid for Christian practice, it also
has an educative value. In this respect it is accompanied by Creed and
Catechism. In each case we see that education in the faith is an effective
barrier against syncretism, which is always possible during the follow-up
period after large intakes of converts from paganism, or when isolated
converts are settled in pagan surroundings without a Christian teacher
or congregation.

One missionary reported in 'Island Voyage' an account of a man who
had been influenced by Roman Catholicism in Fiji, and on his return
attached himself to a sorcerer in South Mala. Their resultant religious
pattern was quite syncretistic. They used a form of baptism by affusion,
observed fasts on Wednesdays and Sundays, and rested three days a
week, men and women alternately so that communal activity did not
cease.[4] This cultural borrowing indicates a society receptive to new
ideas. It might well have been won for the gospel by a Christian who
knew his Creed and Catechism. It is amazing how much one Christian
can communicate if his belief is structured. The communication of the
Lord's Prayer has been most effective in preparing the way for a
Christian teacher in many parts of the Pacific. It is a simple and
structured statement of the relevance of religion in daily life and it
meets the felt needs.

CHRISTIANIZATION OF VOCABULARY

In the Anglican area where I worked for a time, the Church had
taken over the pre-Christian prayer vocabulary and Christianized it.
Thus prayer patterns were presented in their own linguistic thought-
forms. There was nothing foreign about it, except for the word *God*.
The root of the unit of prayer terms is *foo*, literally 'to bind', so that
prayer is a binding of man with a spiritual being. *Foota* is a bundle tied
together, and *foosila*, the act of worship, is a binding together. In
pre-Christian patterns, an incantation appealing to a ghost was *foo*

ngwane, and *foosi* was to pray to a ghost. This concept of prayer, as an appeal to a spiritual being or source of power from without, was a concept worth winning for Christ, and as a result we have a number of elaborations of the same root—*fooa, fofo'oa* and *fooala'a*—to cover the Christian dimensions of prayer and worship.

In the Methodist area, *varavara*, the current Roviana word for Christian prayer, used also in nearby islands like Simbo, is borrowed by Christianity from pagan medicine.[5] It was originally used in removing a taboo or treating a patient, and has to be distinguished from another word, *pito*, a simple prayer request. The choice between the two was apparently made because of their physical differences. *Varavara* was formal and lengthy, figuratively expressed, and the form was memorized and perpetuated. *Pito*, on the other hand, was impromptu and the form was not important. It is interesting the Methodists should make the choice of *varavara*, because their prayers are actually *pito*, extempore and not set in form. The word *pito* has now dropped from use. However, although Methodist prayers are not set down in printed form, and are extempore, they are quite formal nevertheless, and quite figurative and very long. It is probable that when the enquiries were first made for the required word, the missionary concerned used as his illustratiom a case of prayer for recovery in sickness, and was thus given the word *varavara*. In this case prayer was encounter. The pray-er was calling on one spiritual being to deal with sickness imposed by another spiritual being, and I am not at all sure that missionary and convert would give the same meaning to the word they used. It shows how care must be taken in the selection of key words for translation. In time the word acquired its own Christian meaning. Even so, it is a pity the word *pito* was lost. The two words might well have been preserved and Christianized as formal and extempore prayer.

CONFESSION

The confession of sin is a strongly developed trait in the Christianity of the eastern islands, but underdeveloped in the west. In the Anglican Church, the sinner makes his or her confession to the priest, often in the church after the morning or evening devotions. Other worshippers may still be in the building and be aware of what is taking place though not themselves participant. To all intents and purposes it is a private confession, though there are few secrets in the village. At certain seasons of the year, particularly Lent and Advent, it is considered right to pay special attention to setting one's spiritual affairs in order, with self-examination and confession.

In the South Sea Evangelical churches the sinner makes his confession before the congregation, whereupon the members offer prayers for the sinner's forgiveness. Both these patterns serve the same basic purpose of relieving the sinner's burden and giving him an opportunity of demonstrating his real desire to get right with God again. The shame involved by open confession requires a degree of sincerity and humility for most people, but it can be abused. Hogbin narrates a bogus confession which appears to have been designed to give the person concerned a reputation as a lover. It is also true that public confession sometimes stimulates an amount of gossip.[6] On such occasions it may defeat its purpose, but the important thing in both patterns is that for the majority of persons the confession leads to a sense of forgiveness and a restoration of the broken divine-human relationship. The Christian assumes on the promise of Scripture (1 John 1: 9) that a genuine confession from man brings a genuine forgiveness from God. In each of these patterns a human intercessor (the priest in one case, the congregation in the other) supports the request of the sinner for forgiveness.

Multi-individual confession by the whole congregation is important in the Anglican pattern, as is manifest in the frequent use of the General Confession. The emphasis placed on the centrality of the Holy Communion also stresses this congregational confession and desire for forgiveness.

In contradistinction, confession is underdeveloped in the western part of the group, where the public statements of individuals before the group are either scripture verses cited from memory or occasional testimonies of faith by recognized leaders, and hortative rather than confessional. Confession of sin is rare, either from the individual or congregation. Incidentally, the cathartic enthusiasm of Etoism came in this region. Was it a reaction against a neglect of confession?

We saw in the study of pre-Christian religion that society had numerous mechanisms for effecting reconciliation. Most of them demanded some form of confession and usually a public act. This was so natural a stepping-stone to Christianity that any neglect of the Christian dimension of confession would be bound to create a spiritual void.

SYMBOLISM

The Anglicans have also made good use of symbolism, not only in vestments and religious paraphernalia, which appeal to the Melanesians, but also in the use of symbolic acts. I noticed how carefully the village folk followed such things as the lectionary instructions for the altar colours. They were changed on the correct day and the floral decorations were brought as much as possible into line with the prescribed colour—frangipane with the white cloth, ixora with the red, leaves or ferns with the green and so on. The symbolism of religious behaviour in church, the use of vestments appropriate to the function of the particular act of worship, and the rhythm and sequences of procession were always done in the approved manner. Undoubtedly this would satisfy the Melanesian requirement of correct procedure for all religious acts. The people had accepted the new religious forms naturally and they seemed to have become deeply part of the Christian way of worship.

However, this very strength can also be its weakness. The danger is always a drift into formalism. If the worshippers see beyond the symbolism and concentrate on the participant confessions and prayers, and if the symbolism is occasionally explained by the priest, it has some wonderful depths for the Melanesian people, who think naturally in analogies and symbols. But without this appreciation, the forms can easily become things valued for their own sake rather than for what they say, and religion can drift back into a pre-Christian, or at least sub-Christian, state as 'magical'. Perhaps with some this has happened. I felt, when reading a collection of Roman Catholic letters from one area, that the virtue assigned to Christian ritual for its own sake was highly questionable. At several points where I tested my Anglican Melanesian friends with respect to the symbolism they were using, I was satisfied that there was depth in their worship.

Discussing the Communion Service I asked one Melanesian what the use of incense signified to him. He did not give me a textbook answer but it was spontaneous. To him it was symbolic of the communal prayers of the congregation ascending to God. His thinking was a coherent complex that fell in line with the scriptural picture in Revelation 8: 3–4 of the prayers of the saints before the altar. I am sure that for him there was nothing magical about it. The ritual act was a reminder of the importance of prayer and the great privilege of having access to God. For someone else it may have been a symbol of purification, but for this man it symbolized prayer and meant a great deal to him.

On another occasion I was discussing the types of sorcery found in the locality with a Melanesian Christian. He was describing the insertion of some object belonging to the intended victim in a bamboo tube by the sorcerer. He suggested that the decomposition of the object would symbolize the wasting away of the body of the victim, for it was this type of sorcery. I asked him how such a victim could be saved. How, for instance would a Christian priest deal with this problem? He assured me that only an act of faith in Christ could do that, and that the victim might have this faith the priest would pray to this end over the sick man, but it would also help his faith if the priest himself made use of some symbolic act, such as taking the bamboo tube, sprinkling it with holy water and destroying it. I asked him where the efficacy lay. He was quite definite—it lay in the man's faith in the power of Christ. The symbol merely reinforces his knowledge that the *mana* of any sorcery is less than the *mana* or power of Christ. The ocular demonstration of the destruction of the symbol of the evil power would be followed by direct prayer in the name of Christ. The faith of the victim is strengthened by the action and faith of his intercessor, but the saving power comes from Christ alone. I pursued this discussion at some length and I think I am right in saying that this Christian viewed the act of sorcery itself as symbolic for drawing on powers for evil, and that symbolism should be countered with symbolism and power with power. The priest in this area has been effective in handling this kind of problem and I believe his procedure is in line with the Lord's gift to the apostles—*power (exousia) over all the power (dunamis) of the enemy* (Luke 10: 19). I am sure there was nothing 'magical' about the use of holy water. One should not generalize, of course, from a few isolated cases, but at the points I probed in

Malaita I found a clear differentiation of the symbolism from the faith, and an appreciation of the former as a reminder and strengthener of the latter. Symbolism and environment have been taken into consideration in organizing Anglican baptismal services in a pagan locality. Let us say that a chief and his extended family are to be received as Christian. A new church has been built in the village. From this the procession leaves and calls on the chief, who with his wife joins the procession, then the eldest son and his wife followed by the rest of the catechumens of all ages. The procession continues to the mountain stream which services the village with its water supply, and all those not yet baptized cross to the other side opposite the village and church. The bishop or priest who is to perform the rite stands in midstream. The catechumens now come, one by one (for though a communal act it is also individual) from the heathen side of the stream, meeting the bishop in midstream, where they are each baptized by affusion in three movements. They then pass on to join the Christian group waiting on the church side.[7]

I am assured that this is not a heathen custom that has been Christianized. It is nevertheless thoroughly meaningful to the Melanesians. The pagans and Christians are on opposite banks separated by the stream. The pagan can join the Christian, but it means an act of decision on his part. He must cross the stream. He must reject his paganism. In crossing he makes a confession and pledge and is symbolically received in a rite, which has been carefully explained to him. Coming up from the stream on the other side he is received into the fellowship. This is an act of acceptance by the congregation. It is deeply significant because it appeals to that strong Melanesian sense of *belonging* to a group. The ceremony brings together in symbolic acts the essential truths of conversion from paganism to Christianity—decision, rejection, the step of faith, confession, pledge, divine blessing, incorporation into the fellowship. For people coming out of animism this is deeply meaningful.

ARE THESE FORMS AND SYMBOLS ADEQUATE FOR THE SECOND GENERATION?

These forms and symbols have served an important function in bringing the first generation of converts from animism into a meaningful Christianity. The question now arises—are they equally adequate for a second generation of persons born within the Church? It is here that the Church is confronted by the dangers of formalism. The problem is further complicated by the fact that folk are still being won from paganism, so that the Church of today has to provide meaningful forms for both first and second generation Christians together. I do not feel competent to answer this question, certainly not as competent as the missionaries living continuously in the area, but I can give some reasons why it ought to be faced squarely.

The Solomon Islands very much need a sense of entity. Political, social and religious progress calls for it. The basic faith of Anglican and Methodist (and we can add the South Sea Evangelicals) is very much the same. They worship the same Lord, offer the same plan of salvation, use scores of the same hymns, accept the same Bible as their norm for life, and their concepts of social and moral evil to be resisted are not in very serious conflict. Their forms and practices, however, are very different. Because of this they are a divided witness in a day when Christianity should be presenting a united front to a materialistic and pagan world.

The Methodist worship patterns in the west have their strength, but they have neglected the liturgical forms, to their own loss. The Lord's Prayer and the Benediction are their only universals, although new members now recite the Creed when they are received. A musical introit, the *Gloria* and the practice of reading a psalm responsively are used in a few places. The Creed, the Ten Commandments, the General Confession and some other items have been translated, but in my experience were seldom used in public worship. In 128 consecutive acts of worship I attended in a Methodist village of 200 persons, these forms were not once used, nor was the Holy Communion celebrated. By way of contrast in an Anglican village, of slightly smaller size, I attended ninety-five consecutive acts of public worship, during which eight different specified forms of service were used. At these the *Magnificat* was used thirty-five times, the *Nunc Dimittis* forty, the *Jubilate* eight, the *Venite* eleven, the Creed and General Confession every day and Holy Communion almost every Sunday. The communal participation was of a high order. I do not imagine that this is typical of every Anglican village. A Melanesian priest was resident in this one, but he itinerated also to see that other villages received the Holy Communion regularly. Frequently some fifty or sixty would come from smaller villages on Sunday for the sole reason of receiving Communion.

Although the Methodists in the west have lost much by their neglect of these forms (which were all provided for in Wesley's pattern), they have other strengths. Their worship patterns are more extempore, and this certainly leads to a greater exploratory use of what aids to worship they have, especially the hymn-book and New Testament. Prayer also is extempore, more personal and less formal. At this point they have something to offer the Anglicans, as I think they also have with respect to their exposition of the Word. At the same time this pattern must have been very much less attractive to the first generation Christians coming out of a highly ceremonial and symbolic paganism. It was a foreign form of religion, and possibly the forms and symbols of Etoism were a reaction against it. Even so at the level of exploring the depths of Bible study and private prayer it has something to give to Solomon Island worship at large and especially for the second generation.

In our study of primitive religion we saw that divination was highly important for discovering the mind or will of the ghost. Before a journey was undertaken, for instance, a rite would be performed to see if the ghost approved. An unfavourable result would mean a change of plans. The same was done with planting, fishing and many aspects of daily life. In a pagan way, religion was relevant to daily life. When a pagan who has learned to act on the disclosure of the mind of his paternal friendly ghost becomes a Christian, what is the Christian counterpart for this dimension of his cultural outlook on life? Surely it must be to discover the will of God, the Father. It is here that the Methodists have something worthwhile to offer those for whom the Bible is only read from the lectern. The island Methodists do explore their New Testament, assuming it to be the word of God, and therefore expressive of the will of God.

On the Methodist stations, Bible-study, preaching the word and hymn-singing were stressed as explorations of the faith. The men trained on the stations went forth with an exploratory faith rather than a structured creedal faith. Unfortunately, the lag in scripture translation and publication did not assist the villagers to advance with the same degree of exploratory faith. Even so the Methodist pastor-teachers have played a formative role, and there is a characteristic Methodist pattern in the western islands.

Surely then, each Church has grasped something vital. Each Church also needs to develop more the insights of the other. The Anglicans need the exploratory dimension to safeguard against formalism in the second generation, and the Methodists need a structured faith to protect them from heresy, voids and loss of symbolism, which could be helped by a greater use of liturgy and especially the Holy Communion. All the Churches have something to give and something to get by drawing nearer together, at least on the level of devotionals and worship. The towns and plantations are bringing folk of the different denominations together. Civil administration is striving to make the Solomons a single entity. More and more the religious, cultural and social barriers between the western and eastern islands are disappearing. Does not this social process itself indicate the situation in which the second generation Church must exist and exist relevantly? Socially and politically the Solomons are coming slowly into a new day of the cross-fertilization of ideas. Because this will involve religion, whether the Church desires it or not, should not the Church be examining its worship forms, its symbolism and patterns? The faith of the Church continues from age to age, the forms must meet the changes of each generation. As an outside observer, it seems to me that a cross-fertilization of Christian practice would be a great thing for the Church at large in the Solomons.

ANIMISTIC REVIVALS
IN SECOND GENERATION CHRISTIANITY

Another question which arises in any discussion of the passage from animism to Christianity, one which troubles Christian missions and young churches, is that of the animistic resurgence which sometimes comes with a second generation. I am not thinking only of nativistic movements, such as those discussed in Chapter 14, which involved a whole complex of social and political factors. I am thinking of the revival of this or that magical form, or of sorcery; perhaps the

lapsing of some person supposed to have been Christian for years.
From observations over an area much wider than the Solomons, I believe that such resurgences are mainly among individuals whom we have termed *nominals* in this report. The more nominal Christians there are in a village, the more vulnerable is that village to animistic revivals. Occasionally a Christian leader does fall from grace, but usually there is evidence of frustrations and psychological factors which have undermined his confidence in the Church itself—or the Mission. Such persons tend to become leaders of break-away movements, which will include a great body of nominals, some of whom may subsequently become quite enthusiastic. But mostly our problem cases are nominals or perhaps a few marginals.

A cultural issue is involved here. In western society, when a man gives up his Church he may fall into agnosticism or immorality or alcoholism or into sheer secularism—there are regular patterns and every pastor has to face such disappointments. What happens when a second generation Christian .from an animist background falls from grace? Clearly the most natural thing is for him to return to his former state, or to as much of it as he can reconstruct, or to one strong feature of it which satisfies his desires. He may seek to bring together some of the things he imagines he has lost and some of the features of Christianity he ha.: appreciated—creating a Christopagan syncretism.

This may apply to individuals or to multi-individual groups, but in either case there are a number of possible causes. Let us look at a few of them.

Animistic resurgences can occur in either the first or second generation *when the follow-up after conversion has been ineffective*. Conversion is the doorway into the Church: it is not an end in itself. It gives a numerical growth of adherents, but requires a consummating growth in grace—quality growth, as I have called it. Unless this is carefully attended to with good instruction, opportunity for participation, facilities for sharing fellowship, and ways of applying Christianity in daily life, conversion becomes an end in itself and leads nowhere. Without adequate instruction after incorporation into the group, the faith which brought the convert in can be founded on error, without participation it becomes merely formal, without fellowship it becomes introvert, and without application it becomes irrelevant. The faith that brought about the initial decision has to be consummated in all these ways. It must grow and blossom as *experience*, not mere formal achievement. If this follow-up is ineffectively achieved, religion gives no real satisfaction, and it is always possible the unsatisfied convert will return to experiences he feels he has lost.

A second cause can be found in cases where missionary work has been successful in achieving wide-scale conversions throughout the villages *but the efforts at instruction have been station-centred*. The areas I know which have had the most effective quality growth have been those where missionaries, in addition to itinerating regularly themselves, have had the indigenous agents (catechists, pastors, teachers or exhorters) in all the converted villages as residents. The effectiveness of their work did not depend on their intellectual ability but on the changed character of their lives and the reality of their faith. Where it has been possible for these agents to visit the station weekly or monthly, for sharing their own experiences and spiritual refreshment, this has been a great stimulus to their village ministries and preaching, and an aid to both quality and organic growth. But where a limited number of select converts have been isolated for separate training on a station, their Christianity has become theoretical and foreign rather than being worked out within the village life. Mission stations tend to create sedentary situations, involved in commerce, plantations, administration and institutions. Agents who come in for a year or two, for training in this isolation, often go out to become little replicas of the missionaries. They control their village church life 'from the table' and become themselves figure-heads and deprive the congregation of real participation. Growth potential is reduced. In this type of 'one-man situation', marginals instead of being brought in to the core tend to drift to mere nominality, and in time old animistic experiments are undertaken, not because they are desirable, but rather to relieve the boredom.

A third cause for revivals of animism can safely be put down to the fact that *the second generation is not always brought to the conversion experience for itself.* One generation may borrow from its predecessor in many ways but it lives on its own experience. Young people growing up in the Church, being accepted without making a decision for themselves, offered very little opportunity for participation, and still less for expressing their opinion, being subjected to heavy moralist sermons, are liable to grow tired of this religion that their fathers accepted. Again in boredom they may experiment in the things their fathers rejected. Somewhere along the line the Church should have presented a personal challenge to this second generation to take its stand with Christ, and having done so, opened to them a way of practising the new experience of faith in service and fellowship.

Still another possible cause lies in *a reaction of resentment against the foreign controls imposed upon them.* When a Mission fails to give way to an emerging indigenous Church and the times are psychologically ripe for it, Christianity may indeed find itself facing rejection by many persons because it is foreign and imposed. People in this atmosphere of resentment are extremely vulnerable to animistic resurgences which they identify psychologically with the things they feel they have lost, though these voids might not have worried them had their indigenous development been cultivated. It is a reaction of resentment.

These are only some of the cause of animistic revivals. Sometimes one may operate alone, sometimes the situation is complex; sometimes isolated individuals are affected, sometimes whole communities. In any case, returns to animism are pointers—*something is wrong within.* A healthy church should grow *organically, quantitatively* and *qualitatively.* It should be culturally relevant, and bringing its younger members into a vital experience. Such a church is not likely to have revivals of animism.

However, a church that has been won out of animism should not forget the possibility of a renaissance of animism within the first few generations. Many things may be lying dormant under the surface, as regards the more nominal portion of the group. Social and political factors may activate them again. The obvious solution to this problem is a continual and unrelenting drive by the Christian group itself to bring any marginals and nominals into the core of the Christian life. Nominals endanger the Church in any culture.

To leave these generalizations and come to the case of the Church in the Solomons. If this matter has to be watched for two or three generations, one would expect adequate coverage in the Church's laws and discipline. The Anglican position is clear. The Christian must make a complete break with heathenism and the local Melanesian priest can pronounce the sentence of lesser excommunication on any guilty Christian.[8] The relevant laws read:

> Any baptized person who shall have in his or her possession or make use of any harmful heathen charm, or shall invoke heathen spirits, or shall be known to reverence heathen powers or places, shall be liable to the lesser excommunication.

> Any baptized person having in his or her possession or making use of any charm intended to cause death or grievous bodily or mental harm shall be treated as though he or she had actually committed the crime, which the charm is intended to accomplish.

> Any baptized person who is accessory to the use of such a charm by any other person shall be liable to the lesser excommunication.

This is perfectly clear, and avoids the shortcomings of having "actually to see the spear thrust into the grave by the sorcerer" which enables so many to escape the civil justice. The Melanesian priest of the area would act on these laws.[9]

The Methodist discipline does not allow for such specific action. The current handbook, in thirty-seven pages of single-spaced typing, has not a single reference to any pagan customs. There are questions under which paganism could probably be discussed but there is no law as to how it should be dealt with, and if the offender had status or prestige in a village it could be difficult to deal with him at all.[10] It was much easier for Silas Eto to emerge in the Methodist area than the Anglican. Once it was reported that he had a taboo room with images, skulls and dracaenas, the Melanesian priest would have acted, as many indigenous Methodist leaders wanted to act. The current handbook was prepared in 1963 from resolutions passed up to that date. Etoism is covered under a special resolution passed after the break. They are not now recognized as Methodists, but no reasons are given.

I have no doubt the Methodists would quickly discipline any proved offenders, though they might argue at length about the proof; but it is surprising that their handbook should seem so unconcerned about magical survivals and revivals—*so unaware of the possibility*. It is aware of liquor and immorality. It recommends wedding rings for marriages. It covers properties, statistics, allowances, conduct of meetings, order of business, and the practical machinery for the running of the church. Yet it is unaware of *pele*, *vinaroro* and *doma*. It seems to regard this as past and forgotten. I picked up references here and there to spirit-possession, preventing magic against evil spirits, satisfying lust by magical enticements, and other signs of boredom with traditional Christianity. I do not think these are more numerous in the west than the east, but the latter has the legal mechanism for the Christian priest to act: if the paraphernalia is there, he can act.

In either case, the fact that these pagan forms do reappear calls for continual spiritual revival within the Church on the level of the local congregations.

In this chapter I have traced something of the process from animistic to Christian forms. Much of this transition has been thoroughly effective, more especially in the east, but not for several generations can the Church afford to relax her safeguards against the possibility of individuals and groups backsliding into animism. The possibility will eventually decrease with acculturation, but that day is some distance ahead.

CHAPTER 19

Hymns as a Theological Index

THE METHODIST CHURCH in the Western Solomons has provided its adherents with a large and representative collection of hymns and tunes. They figured prominently in the original evangelization of New Georgia. Yet we have also seen that the same Church neglected to give the local converts a whole Bible or even a completed New Testament in the first fifty years. An early catechism, published in 1912, was a poor affair, and as far as I have been able to ascertain, was the only one ever produced in the Roviana language. It was reproduced as an appendix to subsequent hymn-books but is now out of print. In the absence of Bible, prayer-book and an adequate catechism, it was natural for the hymns to serve as the theological frame of reference for the belief and practice of the emerging church.

It is also significant that when the schismatic movement of Silas Eto came into being, it should use the Bible only in such a way as would suit its own end of making *Holy Mama* himself its final revelation. The Bible was purely anticipatory of the *New Ecclesia*. Without a systematic biblical theology and a good scripture catechism, orthodox theology, as we have already seen, was roughly handled.

The stress on hymnody had penetrated so deeply into Melanesian Christianity in the western islands, that the new heretical movement felt it essential to provide a functional substitute. Some forty odd Etoist hymns were analysed in Chapter 17. They are truly Melanesian in that they depend on rhythm and ignore rhyme, but are western in their structure for antiphonal participation and the provision for the soprano, alto, tenor and bass units of the congregation. We have already seen that the desire for congregational participation was a strong point with Eto. We also noted that rousing hymns were regarded as effective *mana* repositories in the earliest days of Christian acceptance round the Roviana Lagoon. In still another place I noted that a capacity to teach hymn-singing was specifically required of Tongan and Fijian teachers for station posts. It is my very carefully considered opinion that in the Methodist area the Christian hymns have been the dominant formative for popular belief. This was not so in the Anglican area, where prayer-book canticles for chanting were far more developed.

The Roviana hymn-book is well organized on a theological basis today. It has a selection of hymns of praise, but, let it be honestly admitted, it is not a widely used section nor are the Roviana Christians jubilant or radiant by other Melanesian standards. There is reason to believe that Etoism, with its boisterous and eccentric enthusiasm, may well have expressed a reaction against a religion that, though very practical, was 'proper' and joyless.

The Etoist doctrine with the most daring development and originality was that of the Holy Spirit—the weakest section in the Roviana collection. The commemorative drive with respect to Wesley's conversion and the arrival of the first mission party with Goldie have been so stressed in the Roviana Christian year as to eclipse Pentecost.

Because of the formative role of hymnody in Roviana Christianity, some attention has to be paid to the hymn-book itself and its evolution over the sixty odd years of mission history.

The original hymns were taught without a book; however, by the end of the first decade a book of 39 suitable hymns had been published, mostly the work of Helena Goldie, all but four of which have been retained in subsequent editions. The second hymn-book with 152 hymns appeared in 1918, and a supplement of another 24 of Mrs. Goldie's hymns was printed in 1920. Four years later a new edition was produced with 176 hymns. A post-war edition, dated 1949 brought the hymn total to 251, and in the current edition (1963) one finds 287. This will serve to show how the hymn collection has evolved, with new editions and revisions in 1912, 1918, 1920, 1924, 1949 and 1963. Each represented a considerable increase in the number of hymns and shows this to have been a strong emphasis in mission activity and priority. This in itself is highly commendable—except when we consider it against the slowness of the same Mission to get on with the job of translating the Bible.

The 1912 catechism was never revised and was a miserable effort. Five of its fifteen pages were devoted to a mere list of biblical names: Who was Adam? Who was Eve? Who was Cain? Who was Abel, Enoch, Noah, Abraham, Isaac, Jacob, Joseph and so on? Nor were the answers very informative about why these characters are in the Bible. Thus the hymn collection tended to become the theological frame of reference for this emerging Christian community.

However, it was not until the 1963 edition in the sixty-first year of the Mission, when an attempt was made to organize the hymn arrangement upon a theological structure, that the full devotional and instructional value of the collection could be appreciated. This is surprising because Wesley established this tradition firmly, and most Methodist hymn collections have retained his scheme, or at least his classificatory method. This rather suggests that the Solomon Island collection just grew without any planning. I have been through the various editions and feel that this must have been so. My analysis suggests that the early hymns were probably the favourites of Mrs. Goldie. They fitted her own personal spiritual experience and were her special gift to the emerging Church. I do not think she ever intended them to become the systematic framework of belief.

Using the classification of the current hymn-book as the norm, the hymns in the original book were 20 per cent concerned with the Person and Work of Christ and the Gospel Call, and over 40 per cent with Christian life and service. God the Creator and Provider, Praise and Adoration, and the Holy Spirit were not represented. Any systematic planning for a Melanesian community would most certainly have had a strong section on God as Provider and Preserver.

By the post-war (1949) edition, a constructive attempt seems to have been made, not only to enlarge the collection, but to widen the scope. Praise and Adoration, the Trinity, God as Creator and Preserver had 6 per cent. The present collection has 9 per cent covering these aspects. Christological hymns on the Person and Work of Christ and the Gospel Call, sixty-five in the 1949, have been increased to eighty-four in the current classified volume. The Christian Life having already seventy-eight was increased by only four new hymns in 1963, reducing its percentage from 31 per cent to 28 per cent. The theological distribution is certainly most balanced in the current edition, but it is still miserably weak in hymns on the Holy Spirit, there being only five in the whole collection. Up to 1963 there was only one hymn on the Holy Spirit. The failure to develop this section of Methodist hymnody undoubtedly left the Church exposed to Etoism.

The strong theological weightage for Christian life and practice in the early selections continued in the 1920 edition supplement, 54 per cent of the new compositions falling within this category of the Christian Life, applied Christianity, good works and moralist hymns. These were undoubtedly formative during the twenties and thirties and have an emphasis remarkably similar to that of the hymn and Bible reading selections in present-day Rarumana, the village in the Roviana area in which we did our sampling. These observations strongly suggest the importance of hymn translation as a formative theological factor, not only with the original, but also in the succeeding generation.

The greatest period of hymn translation appears to have been during and immediately after the Great War, but these hymns were entirely missionary compositions. No indigenous hymns, either original or translations, appeared during the first sixty years, and this reflects the paternal character of the Mission. Mrs. Goldie continued producing hymns after 1920 and thus she herself assisted in adjusting the theological balance. Of the current collection, 48 per cent are her compositions: a great contribution to the growth of the Church.

The new hymns of the 1963 collection have yet to establish themselves. In the eight weeks sample of hymn selection we took at Rarumana, involving over 300 selections, four of the new hymns were sung, so there was no obstruction to their use. The school teacher was teaching them to the children in the school, though they were not often selected by the village prayer leaders. Twenty-eight of the new hymns were composed by Solomon Islanders—the first evidence of indigenous self-expression. But before these hymns were included in the Methodist hymnal, the Etoist schismatics had produced twice as many heretical hymns to glorify Holy Mama. Neither is it without significance that eight of the new indigenous compositions were added to the section on Praise and Providence and two to that on the Holy Spirit. Certainly the deeper religious thinkers among the island Christians were aware of these deficiencies.

Taking the new classified collection of 287 hymns as a working tool, we recorded all the voluntary hymn selections at the Rarumana public meetings, morning and evening daily devotionals and all Sunday meetings for a sample period of eight weeks, with some interesting results which we shall now examine.

RARUMANA HYMN SELECTION SAMPLING

This is an attempt at measurement. It is not easy to measure the things of the Spirit, but something can be done within certain limits. Because these villagers make use of this wide collection of hymns, theologically classified, and because their regular worship patterns provide for hymn selection by purely indigenous leaders, it was possible for us to make a completely objective statistical analysis of their hymn selection range without their being aware that such a record was being made. We believe that our presence did not in any way affect the result.

The village of Rarumana has one of the stronger congregations in the Roviana area. Morning and evening prayers are held daily and four meetings on Sunday. During our sample period, one evening devotional lapsed owing to a tropical rainstorm. The congregation was served by a catechist, who also had responsibility for other near-by villages, and a pastor-teacher, who ran the village day school. There are also a number of lay preachers and prayer leaders. The devotionals are farmed out among these folk, the heaviest loads being carried by the catechist and pastor-teacher. Some of the prayer leaders, three of whom were women, had one assignment weekly. Fourteen different persons shared these responsibilities (indicating a congregation of more than average strength and capable of greater independence than it really manifested), and four preachers or students came from other villages, each for one of the Sunday services. These eighteen persons, all islanders, selected 333 hymns for congregational singing in ninety-five week-day devotionals and thirty-two Sunday meetings, with the following results:

1. *The Primary Sample*

As we had no idea of what kind of a result we might expect, we took a primary sample of two weeks and analysed the results, making these results an hypothesis for testing in the subsequent weeks. The scheme was most fruitful in that each of the four fortnights showed much the same pattern, although we were amazed at the wide range of hymns that were selected.

The leaders made eighty-two selections in the two weeks of the primary sample, using sixty-three different hymns and tunes. This suggested a good appreciation of the hymn-book, despite the fact that the euphony of the language and the rhythm of the English tunes did not always synchronize. Forty-eight hymns were used once, eleven twice and four three times. These four were translations of well-known English hymns that might have scored similarly in any western congregation. Ten of the selected hymns concerned the Person and the life of Christ, and seven His work and the gospel call; but thirty-seven of the eighty-two related to the Christian life and the moralist aspect. We noted that Christian ethics was receiving emphasis in other ways also.

Negatively the primary sample suggested gaps. Out of the eighty-two selections only three had been hymns of praise and adoration, and hymns on God as Creator and Provider were not used at all. We particularly noted this, as fourteen of the meetings had been early morning devotionals when such selections might well have been expecpected. One hymn on the Holy Spirit was used. We were to find that, though the term *Holy Spirit* figured prominently in prayers and preaching, it was formally used, almost as preachers' jargon and often in the trinitarian formula. The doctrine of the Person and work of the Holy Spirit was not developed at all. We observed that this was a shortcoming of the hymn-book selection itself, and realized we would eventually have to make comparison of the selection for use in worship against the hymn-book selection. We have compared these two measurables in the tables at the end of this unit.

2. *Subsequent Weekly Samples*

Examination of the tables will further show how the subsequent samples, which have been arranged week by week, and how the total figures also have supported these primary observations.

(i) Each week showed both a wide range of hymn selection, including a number of new hymns. By the eighth week, 133 different hymns had been used and there was no evidence of tailing off. A little further on we shall graph this against the comparative figures of our Anglican village sampling. We had heard new hymns being taught in the school each week, some from other hymn-books, and others in the regular hymn-book but not selected in our statistical samples. In other words, we know the eight weeks did not exhaust their repertoire. In any case there were seasonal hymns, like those of Christmas and Easter, which would certainly be used for their respective occasions. As it was, 46 per cent of the total hymn-book range of nearly 300 was used in eight normal weeks. This wide range of appreciation of a hymn book still amazes me. One can understand its importance as a devotional and theological frame of reference.

(ii) The local selections did reflect something of the character of the hymn-book itself. The norm (i.e. the hymn-book) showed 30 per cent of hymns on the Person and Work of Christ and the Gospel Call, as against the figure of a 20 per cent selection for the eight weeks. Praise and Adoration and God as Creator, Preserver and Provider, with a norm of 9 per cent registered a score of 7 per cent. Hymns on the Church were 8 per cent in both the sample and norm. The norm showed the low percentage of 1.5 per cent for hymns on the Holy Spirit with the selection score of 1 per cent, and that 1 per cent was scored by repeat selections of only one hymn. As the selections were completely voluntary, we may assume that the range of the hymn-book has been formative.

(iii) The most notable variant concerned the hymns on the morals and practice of the Christian life, which comprises 28 per cent in the norm. Our samples each week showed something like half the hymns being selected from this category—46 per cent for the full eight weeks. This is an unduly strong deviant from the norm. However, it can be explained by the analysis of the previous hymn-books, the weightage of which it certainly reflects.

(iv) The most used hymn of the whole selection was the translation of one demanding loyalty and service—"A charge to keep I have". Following very closely on this was "Go, labour on; spend, and be spent". But the hymns of encounter like "All hail the power of Jesu's name" and "Jesus the Name high over all" before whom "devils fear and fly" were never used. This is very un-Melanesian.

This rather suggests a second or third generation congregation, which sees its faith in terms of fathful service and continued effort, rather than the dynamic encounter with evil or with paganism.

The ideal theological distribution is a matter of opinion; but if (as we are dealing here with a Methodist community) we compare the Rarumana statistics with general Methodist patterns, it is overweighted on the moral and ethical fruit of Christianity and weak in the doctrines of the Holy Spirit and the Church. The latter may be accounted for by the paternalism of the Mission. But how, one may ask, are Christians to produce the moral and ethical fruits expected without a clear appreciation of the work of the Holy Spirit in man? I hesitate to make comparisions with Methodist hymnals of a thousand hymns, because the larger the hymn-book the more it tends to complexity, with hymns for special occasions, but I do point out that the Methodist book I know best has some thirty vital hymns on the Holy Spirit, which were available for translation, had anyone felt disposed to do this. The understanding of the term was taken for granted, and the lack of instruction or hymns about the Spirit and his work left the way open for the Etoists to develop their new doctrine in the area.

VARIETY IN HYMN SELECTION—RARUMANA

	Total Number of Hymns Sung	Weekly Range of Selection	Progressive Total Range
Primary Sample			
2 weeks	85	63	63
3rd week	43	38	84
4th week	43	41	102
5th week	39	35	111
6th week	43	37	115
7th week	38	38	124
8th week	42	37	133

Total Range of Hymn-book	287
Total number of hymns used in 8 weeks	333
Number of different hymns used	133

The evidence of hymn selection does not stand alone. It must be considered beside that of scripture selection, to which we shall turn shortly. Meantime we record that hymn collections are so formative in developing the character of an emerging Christian community that they should be systematically planned from the start and not grow haphazardly. They are a quantitative mechanism and to some extent usage will reflect the numerical distribution. We ought also to see that, when a Mission enters the stage of translation work, hymn translation is not allowed to take actual priority over scripture translation. Both are certainly needed and they should reinforce each other, but a fine collection of hymns is no substitute for the Bible, especially when it evolves without specific planning and structure and some key aspects of the faith are over-looked.

RARUMANA HYMN SELECTION RANGE
Showing Theological Strength and Weakness

	A	B	C	D	E	F	G	H
Primary Sample								
2 weeks	3	3	10	7	37	2	7	16
3rd week	2	0	7	5	21	0	0	8
4th week	2	2	2	2	23	0	4	8
5th week	1	1	7	1	18	0	6	5
6th week	2	0	3	4	21	0	5	8
7th week	3	0	8	2	15	1	3	6
8th week	3	2	7	2	20	0	2	6
	16	8	44	23	155	3	27	57

RARUMANA HYMN SELECTION
Comparison with the Norm in Percentage

	A	B	C	D	E	F	G	H
Primary Sample								
2 weeks	3·5	3·5	12	8	43·5	2·5	8	19
3rd week	5	0	17	12	51	0	0	15
4th week	5	5	5	5	56	0	10	14
5th week	2·5	2·5	19	2·5	49	0	16	8·5
6th week	5	0	7	10	51	0	12	15
7th week	8	0	22	6	42	3	8	11
8th week	7	4·6	17	4·6	48	0	4·6	14
Total Sample	5	2·5	13	7	46·5	1	8	17
Norm Hymn-book	5	4	23	7	28	1·5	8	23·5

Legend: Categories of Theological Classification based on Hymn-book

A Praise and Adoration   E The Christian Life
B God, Creator and Provider   F The Holy Spirit
C Jesus Christ—Person   G The Church
D Work of Christ: Salvation   H Other sections—Life beyond, seasonal,
                                  national, children's hymns, introits, morn-
                                  ing and evening, etc.

HYMN SELECTION SAMPLING IN AN ANGLICAN VILLAGE

Fouia did not offer anything like the quantitative data for the study of hymn selection that we met at Rarumana, but the facts brought to light are no less significant. It is important because hymn selection is one of the few elements where there is free choice in Anglican devotional pattern and worship service, where the local leaders can reveal their own preferences and biases, either consciously or unconsciously. These people have access to three hymn collections, one in the vernacular comprising 107 hymns, one in simplified English with forty-nine hymns, and also the large *English Hymnal*. A large percentage of the congregation had all three. Others had laboriously copied out the words of the most used hymns into note-books, which in itself suggested a limited range of selection with much repetition. In all, they had a possible range of about 700 hymns, but of course they could not be expected to know a great many from the *English Hymnal*.

The Anglican hymn arrangement is not based on a theological classification like the Methodist. It is essentially practical and based on the Church's Year, the Christian rites and seasons, processions and occasions when the hymns might best be used. The 150 odd "General Hymns" scatter over a wide range of theology. The English book contains perhaps nearly two hundred Christological hymns scattered throughout the Christian Year from Advent to Ascensiontide and in the section for use at the Holy Communion. This is a convenient mechanism, which exerts a partial remote control over the selection of hymns, and guarantees that they are appropriate to the occasion. This would make virtually impossible the situation I met in one Melanesian village outside this area of study, in which the choir leader selected as the marriage hymn —

Onward Christian soldiers
Marching as to war.

The guarantee of a balance in the theology of the Anglican hymn-book selection is that the Christian Year is itself theologically balanced. Yet, in spite of this safeguard, one had a strong feeling of biases in the village hymn selection at Fouia, even before the time came for us to take stock of the figures we assembled over a six-week sample, which was taken after Trinity in the season just before the beginning of Advent, when there should have been a good selection of the "General Hymns".

The statistics revealed a wide selection of two types of hymns at the expense of all others:

(i) Hymns specially designed for use at the break and close of day.
(ii) Soteriological hymns relating to the atoning death of Christ for sinners.

These accounted for 31.5 per cent and 24 per cent respectively, well over half the hymns selected. One can easily understand the regular selection of morning and evening hymns, but over a period of time the figure should even out more with other selections. The total sample covered eighty-four different meetings and if the sample was an average one, the computation for a year would reveal that hymns like "Now that the daylight fills the sky" (the most popular), "The day Thou gavest, Lord, is ended" and the hymn of adoration "All people that on earth do dwell'', would be used from thirty to sixty times each during the year. Where the hymn selections are limited to only fifteen per week, as against forty at Rarumana, making less than 800 selections for the year, that over 250 should be morning and evening hymns does suggest a failure to explore the range of available hymns. The 25 per cent selection of soteriological hymns was aided by the strong emphasis on the Holy Communion. It may also be partly accounted for by the people coming from a strongly sacrificial pre-Christian orientation. The atoning death of Christ meets an inherent sense of need among these people. Usually where the atoning death of Christ is emphasized, there is an accompanying evangelistic drive. But this certainly does not apply with respect to the winning of the pagan pockets near-by, so that I am inclined to think the strong preference for this type of hymn springs from the cultural orientation of the people who feel the basic need for sacrifice. They identify themselves in a real way with the Holy Communion—preparation, confession, participation, It has to them a cleansing effect. Let us note in passing that in the west, where Etoism saw the experience of enthusiasm as a cleansing from sin, the Holy Communion had been largely withheld from the people.

Another surprising fact that is apparent from examining the figures over the total eighty-four meetings, is that 49 per cent of the total hymn selection is confined to repetitions of twelve hymns. It is hard to account for such a limited repertoire. The choir does a great deal of practice, but most of this is directed towards special features of the Christian Year, which call for special music from outside the regular hymn-books. They were practising Christmas singing while we were there, and one is led to the conclusion that they must make a great festival of such occasions. This is in line with the Melanesian cultural orientation of high-lighting certain occasions during an otherwise routine way of life. The choir will prepare special music and gay costumes. The preparations themselves are exciting and enliven the otherwise routine periods. By comparative Solomon Island standards— village, not station standards—their singing was good and the result of hard work, though their range was so limited.

Their limited repertoire is also indicated by the fact that the sixth week of our sample recorded no new hymn to the range of selection. The weekly analysis over the six weeks shows the following position:

	Number of hymns selection	Number of new hymns used
1st week	13	12
2nd week	17	14
3rd week	15	10
4th week	18	4
5th week	14	2
6th week	16	0

The majority of hymns selected were used within a period of three weeks. Of the forty-eight hymns selected in the following three weeks,

RANGE OF HYMN USAGE

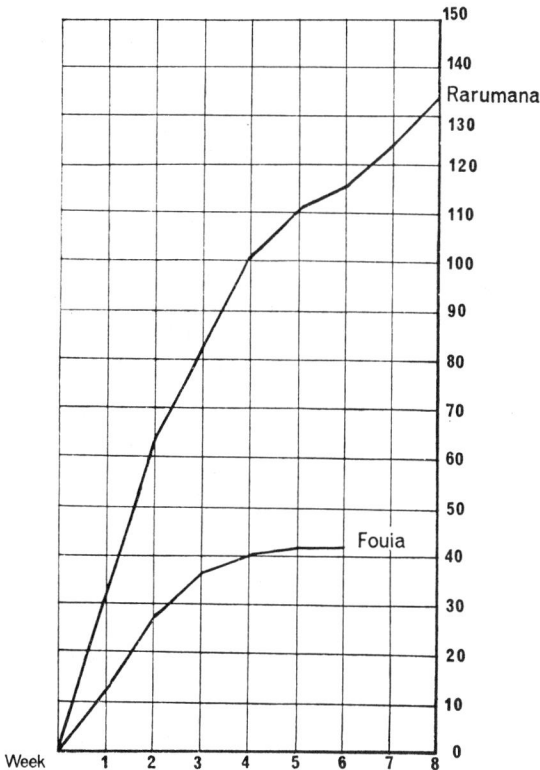

The line-graphs show the progressive range of different hymns used over the period of sampling in two villages.

all but six were repetitions of hymns sung in the prior three weeks. Even in the eighth week at Rarumana there had been no sign of such a tailing off. The contrast may be seen by the graph above. The fact that hymns are not used does not necessarily mean they are not known, and there may be no more need than to point out the fact, but I felt there were possible reasons for the tailing off. I doubt if the great teaching and devotional value of a good hymn selection was really appreciated. Undoubtedly also the hymn singing was subordinated to the chanting.

Chanting was highly developed in Fouia—and quite well done. My first impression was of a foreign innovation, for it was thoroughly Anglican. However, a little more thought led me to believe that it was probably received as a functional substitute for the Melanesian chants, which were structurally not dissimilar from the Christian. The four principal scriptural chants, the *Magnificat*, the *Nunc Dimittis*, the *Jubilate* and the *Venite*, by computation from our samples would take the place of some 815 hymns a year for a Methodist pattern. If we take the four most popular Methodist hymns from our sample, they would not account for a quarter of this number. These chants do actually take the place of hymn-singing and thereby lose the freshness of variety and restrict the devotional and doctrinal instruction possible through music. They are well chanted but one wonders how they can do other than lead to formalism.

The repetitions of the General Confession, the Creed, the Gloria, responsive sentences, the Lord's Prayer and the Benediction, do not take the place of hymns, but the chants do. As the danger of formalism is real, one is disposed to suggest a little less frequent use of the four chants by the substitution of different psalms or hymns. I think it would have a freshening effect and perhaps the chants themselves would be more appreciated.

The main difference between the Methodist and Anglican hymn selection patterns was that the type of hymn most frequently selected in the Methodist west was hardly ever used in the east—hymns concerned with the Christian Life and in particular its practical application. We only recorded six hymns in this category all the time we were at Fouia. Charles Wesley's hymn "A charge to keep I have", the Rarumana favourite, is not in the Anglican selection, though many Wesley hymns are. Bonar's "Go, labour on", which was also popular in the west, though in the Anglican book was not used. It occurs to me (and I noted this before I left the village) that these people, though they have a deep appreciation of salvation and a trust in Christ, still have a long way to go with respect to the 'working out' of that salvation in life around them. They make no apparent effort to share that salvation with their pagan relations near by ; there is no evidence of a belief that "cleanliness is next to godliness", and no real husbanding of time; nor is there any practical demonstration of concern for the physical and mental advance of the village children. Of the practical and ethical out-workings of the gospel in the village life, they seemed to be unaware. In the light of this it was interesting to note that the hymn selections showed no real perspective of service. In Fouia the stress was on *faith*. In Rarumana it had been on *works*. If the latter needed an emphasis of Paul's preaching on faith, the former needed a word from James.

The reader has been warned against taking these as typical villages. Above all they are not to be taken as typical of Anglican and Methodist villages. At the same time there may be many other villages which do present these features—either congregations with a highly developed faith but without Christian application, or with practical and ethical demonstrations yet without real spiritual commitment. Furthermore, these general impressions of congregations should not be taken as typical of all individuals within those congregations, for each had a good (if numerically small), solid Christian core.

CHAPTER 20

The Bible in the Village Situation

IN A paper entitled *The Bible in the Missionary Situation*,[1] G. H. Wolfensberger raises such questions as: What image do people have of the Bible? What authority has it? How is it used in the village situation? Is it merely a church book or is it a book for the contemporary world? In a moment I shall attempt to deal with some of these questions in actual situations in an Anglican and a Methodist village, in both of which I lived as a participant observer. However, I wish first to examine the image of the Bible in a certain community served by the South Seas Evangelical Mission, and attempt to relate it to the other denominations in a general manner.

I should say at the outset that this mission did not desire any representative of the World Council of Churches to enter its churches, so that I was forced to learn what I could from the outside, from their publications, from the work of anthropologists, by observations on occasional visits to their villages, and from a few informants whom I met unofficially but with whom I had good interviews.

Dr. Hogbin once interrogated a member of this Church and checked his testimony against that of other persons of the same denomination. Although I do not agree with all Hogbin's arguments and his personal theology, at this point I am satisfied with the accuracy of his observations. His enquiry was directed at the man's basic beliefs rather than at his knowledge of the Bible, though the two synchronized well. His belief was a summary statement of the biblical narrative, though certain features were emphasized to a degree which many modern biblical scholars would consider out of balance. We reserve judgement at this point, because it can be well argued that these emphases were relevant in the Melanesian scene.

The informant stressed the primal fall of man and Satan's subsequent struggle with God for mansoul. This was told within the cultural construct of Malaita imagery. Both God and Satan were anthropomorphized in terms of the Malaita chiefly structure and its personal rivalries. The vocabulary, thought-forms, personal relationships and psychological motivations given to the biblical figures were thoroughly indigenous. Satan's envy and desire to establish himself, and God's way of dealing with him indirectly, first through Michael and subsequently through His Son, were indigenously conceptualized. Satan's mode of tempting Eve was part of his strategy against God. The incident of the serpent (and there were spirits which supposedly appeared as snakes in the Eastern Solomons) is said to be treated like a real island myth—a tale explaining existing conditions—why a snake crawls on its belly and why man is burdened with work. Man can reinstate himself with God by obedience and sacrifice, although Satan continues trying to destroy God's handiwork until in the end God sends His Son, who Himself becomes a perfect and final sacrifice. Ordinary sacrifices are no longer required and man must take his stand now on one side or the other. He will spend eternity with God or Satan in heaven or hell as the case may be. The sacrifice of Christ is remembered in the Holy Communion, the most important rite of the Church, which is regarded by these Malaitamen as a functional substitute for their old sacrificial rituals.[2]

That such a Christian statement of belief should be enshrined in Melanesian thought-forms is not surprising. It had given meaningful roots to the new religion. As a summary, based on Scripture narrative, it retains four important features: (1) its biblical perspective is whole, (2) the struggle of Satan against God, with its focus on the fate of mansoul, is the theological frame of reference within which man lives, (3) man's fate depends, on the human side, on his own personal decision whether he stands with God or Satan, and (4) on the divine side, on God's action, through His Son, who is offered as a perfect sacrifice to atone for sinful man. If the South Seas Evangelical Mission teachers succeeded in implanting this basic biblical outline across the cultural barriers of Malaita, this was no mean achievement, whatever an anthropologist may think of it.

Their faith is based on an image of the Bible which sees it as a narrative of divine action, an offer of a gospel of salvation for man, and a demand of personal decision from him. We can go further than this. Such a Bible has become for them the word of God and the norm for daily life. It has authority and determines whether the acts of daily life are right or wrong. These people reveal a capacity for citing Scripture, often with chapter and verse. I have heard this, but have not had the opportunity to test them as to their knowledge of the contexts from which they cite. Not having lived in these villages, I cannot say whether they read their Bibles constructively. If those whom I met were typical, I am inclined to think they use the Scripture for proof-text purposes rather than solid devotional study, but this is only an impression from a few cases.

Strange as it may seem to many evangelicals, the Roman Catholic *Fact and Faith Book*, which deals with the power encounter of Satan against God, is very much in harmony with the 'fundamentalist' position.[3] This is because both have teaching based on literal interpretations of the same passages of Scripture. However there are two important differences. For the Roman Catholics this is only one of many features of the Faith, but for the South Sea Evangelicals it is the frame of reference in which everything else is set. The other difference is that the evangelicals have their own Bibles, read and interpret them for themselves. The Roman Catholics obtain their knowledge through the Church, and the people themselves have little way of distinguishing between which teaching given to them is biblical and which is church tradition. The Bible here is more likely to be conceptualized as a sacred or taboo object, which is best left for the priest to handle. Thus the image of the Bible with each of the two denominations is diametrically opposite.

The third strong denomination in Malaita is the Anglican, whose image of the Bible is quite different from either. We have already seen that the conflict between Satan and God is continually presented in prayers and rituals. Biblically based, it is not however a direct biblical emphasis but comes from worship patterns. The Bible has a place that is both conspicuous and inconspicuous in the Anglican pattern. It is always on the lectern and always read. It is available to the people and used by them, but is a church book and not a family one. The word is not personally explored, but distributed in the correct manner and at the correct time. I heard about a hundred Bible readings in Anglican village meetings, but it was never expounded.

At the western end of the Group, the Methodist prayer leaders frequently 'pin-point' some of the main teachings of the passage read in their meetings. They also engage in much more preaching, and some sermons are expositions of the word. Their image of the Bible approximates more to that of the South Sea Evangelicals, in that the people use the book freely, read it for themselves and learn many verses by memory. However, as they have only a vernacular New Testament, their knowledge of the Old Testament narrative is poor. They exhibit a great preference for moralist teaching, and view the Bible more as a norm for living than as an aid to devotion. This struck me as being somewhat un-Melanesian. There was almost an *avoidance* of dynamic passages and a *passion* for the didactic.

In no part of the Solomons do I think that the authority of the Bible as the word of God would be questioned among Christian people. Even among the Etoists who were influenced by American soldiers, some of whom pointed out to Eto its human and composite authorship, there has not been a rejection of the book. Eto has reinterpreted it as a reference book, not to be used by ordinary people, but interpreted by himself in the light of his own revelation. When he cites it, he, makes it testify to himself, but he always claims its authority from the Holy Spirit.

Undoubtedly in the places of theological training the young leaders learn something of what biblical criticism is, and are aware of its problems. However, the issues stemming from the question, "What kind of a book is the Bible?", which disturb Christian communities in western society, are not apparent in these islands. The divisive feature which denominationalism has introduced into the islands is not the authority of the Bible, but, *Who* has the authority to interpret it?

We shall now take two village situations for examination at greater depth, using the same Methodist and Anglican villages as we used for the study of hymn selection in the last chapter.

SCRIPTURE SELECTION SAMPLING
IN A METHODIST VILLAGE

The occasions which provided facilities for our recording statistics of hymn selection at Rarumana provided the same facilities for Scripture selection. We had before us 127 passages selected for reading in the public devotionals and services during our total eight weeks sample. We had again taken the first two weeks as a primary sample, and noted certain similarities between the two. On most occasions the selected passage was expounded by the preacher or prayer leader. The primary sample covered a range of thirty-two lessons and expositions, again with a strong emphasis on Christian morals and the life of service, although throughout Christ Himself was certainly central. Fifty per cent of the lessons expounded were didactic passages from the epistles, usually with a moral but sometimes with a theological content. Sixty-two per cent of the passages selected from the four gospels were also didactic. One lesson came from the Acts of the Apostles and one other from the Book of Samuel, the latter read in English.

Negatively, we were again struck by the lack of praise and adoration. The prophetic note, so strong in most Melanesian preaching, was entirely absent. As the selection seemed to relate itself to the hymn selection, we determined to test these observations in the subsequent sampling.

The people had had access to the complete New Testament in their own language for about a decade only, so we must keep in mind the unhappy fact that for the first fifty years of their Christian pilgrimage they had had to be satisfied with selected passages and single books that had been translated. Having come from a part of Melanesia where the whole Bible had been available in the vernacular from an early date, and where the prophetic passages of the Old Testament had been deeply appreciated, I was struck by the contrast of the two situations.

Some fifty-four of the psalms were translated and published in the back of the now obsolete hymn-books, and most of the prayer leaders possessed torn copies of these old volumes. Subsequent experience showed that frequently when a leader was called on unexpectedly, through the sickness or absence of the appointed leader, he fell back on these psalms. I do not know whether these would have been selected had the leader done his preparation at home. The interesting thing, however, is that of the twelve readings selected from these psalms in the total of 127 readings, they were usually not psalms of praise, but used for their teaching rather than inspirational or devotional value.

The Christian expression of these people has certainly suffered from the deprival of the rich resources of the prophetic literature. Their admittedly high moral teaching needed something of the spiritual quality of Jeremiah. When I questioned them on the matter of Scriptural 'holiness', I had a strong feeling that they saw it in terms of ethical perfection rather than spiritual experience, which is the Methodist position.[4] They needed the prophetic voice that speaks God's word to the current situation. After having listened to scores of Melanesian preachers for over twenty years, I missed the dramatic encounters of the Bible. The Melanesian way from animism to the gospel makes good use of Old Testament stepping-stones. While I admired the strong moral sense of this community, I felt that the dramatic experience of God in action was missing. Had they been given the whole Bible at an early date, things might have been quite different. The fact that the Mission recently seconded a missionary for this purpose is irrelevant—the Mission has six decades of history behind it, priorities were given to plantations and industrial projects, people were taught to read and write, yet given virtually nothing to read. I wish it were possible to make some statistical measurement of the problems these people confront through having been denied a Bible or even a full New Testament for half a century.

Another factor which was demonstrated by the sampling over the total eight weeks was that even the New Testament within their present reach was not being *fully* explored. The prayer leaders had a definite 'taste' in their selection. I found it strange that the most frequently used books for reading and exposition were James, Hebrews, Romans and Corinthians—all teaching passages, whether moral or theological, and very few of them easy. When the gospels were used, they were again mostly teaching passages. The failure to draw from the narratives and miracles of our Lord, the preference for his own formal teaching over his parabolic presentation of it, and the by-passing of the dynamic experiences of the early Church in the Acts of the Apostles, all struck me as strange. Furthermore, all these neglected aspects had so very, very much to say to the Roviana situation itself.[5]

A few scripture selections had been printed in earlier hymn-books, and our records show that twenty-nine of the 127 selections in our eight weeks' sample had come from those which had previously appeared in the hymn-books (23 per cent), and some of these had been chosen several times, like Proverbs 24: 30-34, passages from the Sermon on the Mount and from the Book of James. When a Church relies on a limited range of Scripture translation, the limits of that selection tend to be perpetuated even after the whole New Testament has been available for a decade. This effect can be statistically recognized in the sampling.

Furthermore, as these passages were dominantly didactic, this characteristic has been transmitted to the subsequent generation, which persistently selects this type of passage in spite of the much wider range now available. In the Scripture selections in earlier hymn-books, thirteen out of nineteen passages from the gospels were teaching units. Apart from two miracles and three parables, only eight narrative units appeared in the thirty-eight selections from outside the Psalms.

This characteristic is reflected in our Rarumana sample in the following way for the thirty-one readings taken from the Synoptic Gospels:

Miracles	5
Other Narratives	4
Parables	6
Abstract Teaching	16
	31 gospel selections

If we exclude the parables, 101 of the total 127 Scripture selections were didactic—either moral or theological. The weak representation of parables, and the avoidance of the Lord's miracles, of the dynamism of Mark, of the encounter of Jesus with sin, sickness and demons, and of the dramatic action of the early Church, are all remarkable for a Melanesian Church. The writings ascribed to Paul, James, Peter and John claimed 55 per cent of the lessons selected. Even without counting parables as teaching, we have the overall result showing 80 per cent of selected readings as teaching passages. Here is a *specific characteristic*, and it fits in with the emphasis on Christian morals and service in the hymn selection sampling.

A few tentative conclusions may be suggested. The limited number of Scripture passages translated and printed in different earlier hymn-books were missionary selections, and probably reflect their teaching emphasis. Their stress on diligence and hard work lines up with the policy of industrial missions. There was no wholeness or balance about the selections. They probably grew in the same manner as the hymn collection. I am quite confident that no missionary, knowing he could only translate forty passages for a people without a Bible, would have made this particular selection as representative of the whole. I believe they produced translations as situations demanded—hence the imbalance and the striking omissions.

The selections of our sample must be seen as the selections of the eighteen persons who led devotionals and other meetings in Rarumana —that is, of the leading persons of the village, the core of the Church. They are not necessarily the selections the rank and file of the congregation would have made, but they do represent the emphasis of the indigenous leaders of the congregation. It may be well to point out that although all the village leaders were not in this core, all of those in the core were leaders also in social life, and the preaching of industry, morals and service was to their advantage.

One is not able to assess the degree to which this kind of preaching became tiring to the congregation, but I felt it was making no contact with the children and young people, although they were not in any way disobedient. The leaders kept a strong hand and occasionally served out a disciplinary lecture, if there was any sign of over-exuberance among them. One wonders if this continual ethical exhortation partly accounts for the drift from marginality to nominality, which will be discussed in the next chapter.

Finally, if this characteristic was common to Roviana Christianity five or six years ago, does it account for the rejection of the Mission by the Etoists? A spontaneous outburst of enthusiasm under an indigenous prophet might well have been a natural reaction to a continuous emphasis on morals and service. If this be so, then the reason for the failure in Rarumana of Eto's movement was the existence of a strong nucleus of characters who played a major role in both civil and church affairs and kept the situation in control. I am told from some informants that this was so. They told me which leaders took action, and what they said and did. In other places, where the leaders of the people had drifted to religious marginality or nominality, Etoism had a better hearing. Hard work has done much for Rarumana. Its prosperity gives emphasis to the biblical warnings against the slothful man. This gospel has given them self-respect, and good standing in the eyes of the Administration. The people do read their Bibles, but they tend to select this kind of passage.

THE USE OF SCRIPTURE
IN AN ANGLICAN VILLAGE

The people of Fouia are entirely Anglican. They were first confronted with the gospel about sixty years ago, when Father Jack settled on the spot and gradually collected Christian sympathizers about him, as described in our study on village structure. Actually their exposure to Christianity has been of roughly equal duration with that of the Rarumana people, though the latter have migrated more recently to their present locality. With respect to their use of Scripture, one major difference prevented our employment of identical procedures. The prayer leaders in the Anglican village had no freedom in Scripture selection, everything being laid down in their lectionary,[6] issued annually by the Diocese of Melanesia.

Like the Methodists in Rarumana, the Anglicans in Fouia had no vernacular Old Testament. The Lauan New Testament was used, but when an Old Testament reading was prescribed it had either to be read in English, or (the more normal procedure) in the language of Mota, which, according to the priest, was understood by some of the congregation. Checking on this from the catechist, I found that the few who could understand were older folk with mission training. The young folk did not know it, and these lessons were just not understood by the congregation in the main. Such Old Testament readings were mostly confined to Sunday services, and when they fell in the Communion Service they were intoned.

Some of the Psalms were used for chanting and others for responsive reading, but the selection in the vernacular was limited. About a third of the Psalms had been translated. Once again the great passages of dynamic encounter, of God in action, and of the prophetic experiences were not frequently given to the people.

By following the lectionary, however, the New Testament was being systematically read to the people at public worship, and those who attended regularly both morning and evening prayers could follow the sequence. During our period in Fouia, the congregation was being taken through the narrative of the emergence of the early Church in the Acts of the Apostles. This was something we missed at Rarumana and it served to remind us that by following a carefully prepared lectionary, the personal preferences and idiosyncrasies of the readers are eliminated by the sequence and totality of the lectionary. Although we were saved from having one type of selection persistently set before us at the expense of all others, we lost our research capacity for testing those preferences.

L

The lectionary serves its protective purposes well, and has the additional advantage of corporateness, for the whole Church in the diocese is studying the same Scripture. This does give the folk a feeling of belonging to something bigger than the village.[7] The Methodist preachers had access to the lectionary and expository notes of one of the Bible reading associations, but it was not used "because it had to be paid for". The advantage of free selection, on the other hand, is that readers select passages which mean something to them personally, and they probably read them more expressively. The Methodists did read their Bibles with more feeling and power.

In Fouia the reading, both in the morning and evening, was read in a standard manner without explanation. The Bible was left to make its own appeal and to be its own interpreter—all the more reason why it should have been well read. The Methodist readers felt obliged to point out the relevance of the passage. Worshipping in each pattern for a period, and always having my own English Bible with me (since I always tried to be a participant as well as an observer), I found blessing in each, and I felt that each congregation received some real spiritual satisfaction, though in neither case did I feel the full potential was realized.

How do the people of Fouia regard the Bible? They certainly regard it as an essential part of worship, and come to hear it read each morning and evening, but after making enquiry I was assured they do not read it or ponder it for themselves. Many of them have the Lauan New Testament and follow the reading in church, but mostly these books are not taken home. Many of the folk have made for themselves little cloth bags which pull on string at the necks for protecting their books and keeping them together—prayer-book, hymn-book and Bible—but they leave them in the church. I doubt if there were more than three or four English Bibles in the village, though there would be a few more English prayer-books. Many of the people know the creeds and liturgies in English and equate them with their Lauan Counterparts, but their comprehension of English is slender and they do not understand the English Bible when read. Sometimes one of the young men who would like to become a catechist or a brother will try to read a lesson in English,[8] but except for the priest and one catechist, all who read the Bible at Fouia were poor readers in any language. The Psalms are often used on Sundays. The Ten Commandments, though in both Methodist and Anglican books, and used in confirmation classes by the latter, do not appear to be used in public worship. We did not hear them once in from 200 to 300 meetings.

The use of the Psalms calls for special comment, for the two churches use them in different ways and derive different satisfactions from them. In the Anglican prayer services, Psalms 95 and 100 are the most commonly used. Both are chanted at least once every week. The range of psalms translated into Lauan and published in the prayer-book was sixty-one, a little more than a third of the Book of Psalms, as against a now out-of-print Methodist list of fifty-four,[9] twenty-six of them being common to the two lists, so their range for selection was roughly the same, though their availability was not equal. Seventeen of the Anglican list were assigned for special use on specific occasions of the Christian year. The Methodists had no 'sense' of a Christian year, and their range of worship suffered because of it. Other psalms were used at Fouia for congregational responsive readings at a rate of four in six weeks. If there were no duplication, the greater part of the collection would be used in a year. One wonders why they have not been given the whole Book of Psalms in Lauan, especially for Sunday worship, in view of their disposition to use them.

Fifteen years ago one of the Anglican missionaries wrote about this to a colleague. He felt that translation was being very much neglected.[10] In the meantime, the same man has prepared a version of the Book of Psalms in simplified English, which he thinks the people could understand. I believe they need it in the vernacular, and they have Melanesians who could translate it.

Like the Hebrews, the Anglicans use the Psalms mainly for public worship. The Rarumana Methodists very seldom used them for congregational participation (though the responsive reading of psalms is common Methodist practice elsewhere), but their prayer leaders are interested in the psalms as meditations of men of God. They frequently cite a verse "as David said", and apply it to their Christian life and practice. Here again we have the basic differences; to one group the psalms were aids to public worship, to the other their use was for exploration, exposition and application. Each has something worthwhile, but neither had a full appreciation of the potential.

There are other scriptural passages, particularly the lyrical songs of Mary and Simeon, which have been woven into Anglican worship. Computation on the basis of our sample of eighty-four acts of worship at Fouia, would suggest that the *Magnificat* and *Nunc Dimittis* are used 303 and 347 times respectively each year. This seems to be overdone, and must tend towards formalism. Though I think the Methodists could profit by using these occasionally as chants, their present attitude would be to treat them as Scripture for reading and exposition—likely passages for selection at Christmas time. Again each has something to offer the other.

In the Holy Communion the priest intoned the gospel and epistle, and thus again they were absorbed into the worship and did not figure prominently as when read from the lectern. The Methodist preachers and prayer-leaders never intoned their Bible readings. Some of them read badly, but on the whole they were reasonable and clear readers.

Confronted by the fact that the people of Fouia did not read their New Testaments very much, if at all, in private, I found one fundamental difference between the members of the two denominations. When it came to meeting the problems of daily life and the local situation, the Methodists would turn to "search the Scriptures" for some guidance and then to extempore prayer. Faced with similar problems, the Anglicans would turn to their priest for personal counsel and to formal printed prayers from a very fine collection. In these village situations, the Methodists have never learned to understand the value of pastoral counselling and the prayer book, nor the Anglicans the value of "searching the Scriptures" and extempore prayer.

Preaching, in Fouia, was reduced to a minimum. Normally only the priest ever preached, and this he confined to Holy Communion. There was no pulpit. He spoke from the sanctuary. His sermons were short, fatherly chats, not expositions of the word. Though the Anglicans have opened many more positions in church leadership to Melanesians than have the Methodists, they have not encouraged them to expound the word with anything like the same freedom. Something has clearly been lost thereby. They have good safeguards in creed, prayer-book and catechism. One hopes that the young men now in training will make more of scriptural exposition.

Where there are no creeds, prayer-books or catechisms to serve as a theological frame of reference, there may well be dangers of too much freedom in exposition. The Methodists discovered this with Silas Eto. However, their system cannot be judged by one failure; furthermore, they have a theological frame of reference by which Eto could have been disciplined.

Quite a different danger is seen in the case of the South Sea Evangelicals, who appear to press the view that the Bible is its own interpreter, and the final authority for everything in one's daily life. Exploration of the Bible by each individual is a richly rewarding experience, but without a frame of reference like the creed, as Eto observed, the Bible is full of difficult passages which can be very confusing. Without some frame of reference, the myserious figures of some books lend themselves to all forms of allegorical interpretation, a practice to which the Melanesian interpreter is naturally disposed. The Bible without any aids to worship and interpretation is vulnerable to any nativistic philosophy, or to any peculiar religious sect, which can, like Shakespeare's Shylock "quote Scripture to his purpose". Members of the body known as Jehovah's Witnesses, a well-known sub-Christian sect, have recently invaded Malaita and gained some hearing in evangelical villages. Their 'happy hunting ground' has always been among people without creeds, and to these they cite Scripture *ad infinitum*. No matter how badly they maul their exegesis and extract verses from their true context, they throw one verse upon another in a sequence of argument full of fallacies, moving on rapidly before the poor Melanesian can detect the error. He believes the Bible, and recognizes the passages as Scripture, and is thereby persuaded.[11] It is in this situation that a creed and catechism stand by the victim and at least make him cautious. It is just at this very point where the Anglicans in Malaita are proving their solidarity. A religious teacher of this type was in Fouia when we were there, but he obtained no hearing. The Fouia Christians know their basic belief. Their aids to faith stand by them well, for these have come down through history and have their roots in the Bible itself. In view of this solidarity and general structural knowledge of the faith, one would like to see it developed more in the exposition of the word.

Soteriologically, the Evangelical faith is similar to that of the

Anglicans. They have developed much more the joy of "searching the Scriptures", but their very strength has made them vulnerable to Jehovah's Witnesses. Here again both the Christian denominations have something to offer each other.

The problem of biblical interpretation is very real in Oceania. For over a century now prophets have arisen, like Silas Eto, accepting the Bible as the inspired word of God and using it to reinforce non-Christian traditions, Christopaganism and schism. Each Mission, each nativistic movement, each sub-Christian sect claims the guidance of the Holy Spirit as its interpreter. They come up with vastly different interpretations. How can these be tested? Is it not high time for a denominational *get-together* on this matter?

CHAPTER 21

Measuring Congregational Piety by Curves

WHEN A careful record is kept of church attendance over a period of time in a single congregation, some specific categories are usually observable. On the assumption that diligence in church attendance is one form of piety, I shall attempt to show by means of curves how such statistical records can indicate attitudes and throw light on a situation.

EXPLANATION OF THE TOOL AND ITS USE

This tool is used in cases where a village population virtually all belongs to a single denomination, so that the denominational constituency and population each represent 100 per cent. Within this, the individuals are classified into categories, A, B, C, D and E according to their piety or diligence in church attendance, ranging from the highest intensity in "A" to indifferent nominalism in "E". The actual delineation of these categories is by the patterns of the denomination or situation. Categories are set out in sequence as segments or columns on the base of a graph. The statistical score of each category is plotted vertically at mid-point of each column in percentage, and the resultant curve is completed.

The effect may be observed in Figures 1, 2 and 3, hypothetical cases which may be taken as norms. Figure 1 represents a weak congregation with a small nucleus of pious persons and a great deal of indifference among the majority. Two types of situation can produce this kind of curve. It could be either (a) a young cause just emerging in a pagan village, or (b) in the case of a second generation Christian village, a static cause in which the congregation has become enclosed or sealed off from the unconverted remainder of the village. In the former, the category "E" represents the pagan reservoir or residue, and this represents an open door for evangelism, so that although the Christian cause is statistically weak, the situation is dynamic. In the latter, the cause is static and new spiritual insights are required by the nucleus. The field for evangelism is still there, although it may well have hardened and become more resistant. Both these types appear to exist in the Solomon Island scene, and could be studied by persons prepared to collect six or eight week samples of statistics for examination.

Figure 2 represents an average village congregation, where about a third of the people attend church regularly twice a Sunday, with greater piety and greater laxity spreading on each side. This is a theoretical or statistical average for the islands, where facilities for piety in worship are provided for morning and evening for every day of the week, and where economic and social attractions do not compete with the church as in western society. It is my tentative opinion that this is a very common pattern in the Solomons among the second generation Christian villages. It suggests a need for quality growth within. Thirty-three per cent is too large for "C" to be healthy. Some effort is called for, some special programme within the congregation, to push the bulk from "C" towards "B" or even to "A". This must be worked for, because otherwise there is a natural tendency to drift in the opposite direction, average folk tend to become marginal and the marginal merely nominal. Only conscious effort at achieving deeper spirituality and increasing personal responsibility and participation can correct this matter.

Figure 3 represents the curve of a strong cause. In reality there may be no actual congregation as strong as this hypothetical case. It is therefore perhaps the curve of a practical ideal towards which congregations should be working. Once such a state is achieved, this strong congregation should be vigorously and creatively exploring every opportunity for evangelism beyond its own locality.

The tool thus indicates important principles of church growth, even though it is only a statistical measure on a basis of attendance. Attendance does reflect something of attitudes. If the indicator of this tool points at the percentage-strength, a church that is growing, either quantitatively or qualitatively, should be pushing that indicator of percentage-strength towards the left—from "E" to "A". Another important principle is indicated by the percentage-strength at "E". A high score here indicates the need for local evangelism, either the Christian nominals or any pagan residue. On the other hand, if "E" is at a minimum score, then the congregation should be pushing out into other areas in evangelism.

We must move now from the hypothetical and theoretical to actual village situations, for which we recorded the attendance statistics for

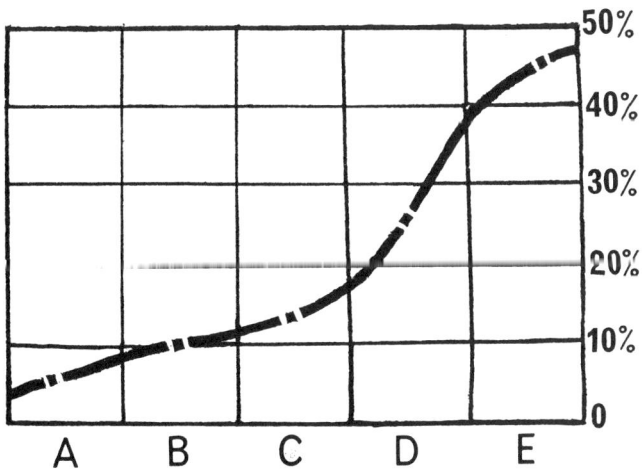

Fig. 1. Piety Curve of a Weak Congregation

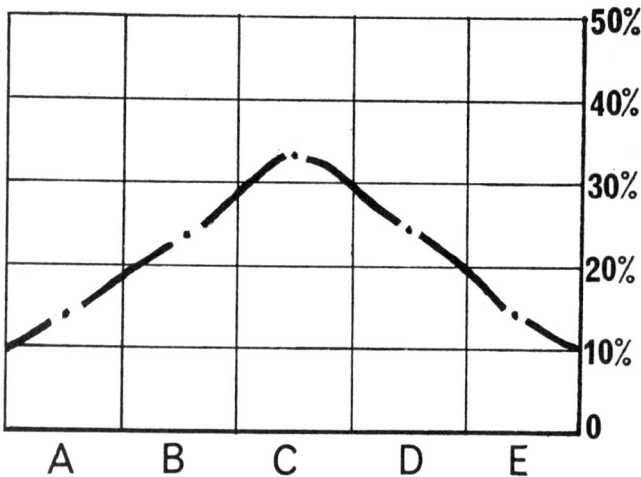

Fig. 2. Piety Curve of an Average Congregation

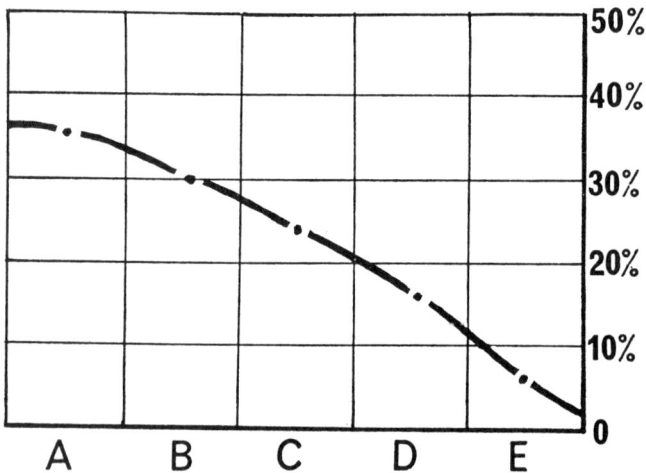

Fig. 3. Piety Curve of a Strong Congregation

every religious meeting in the same places and over the same periods as our hymn selection sampling and scripture reading.

APPLICATION OF THE TOOL TO THE RARUMANA SITUATION

In the village of Rarumana on the island of Wanawana we recorded the attendance figures over a period of eight weeks. Four public gatherings were held each Sunday. For statistical purposes I am operating with the figure of 191 for the total population.[1] The actual attendance figures have been broken down into categories and calculated in percentages. Those in category "A" gave themselves entirely to every means of grace offered on the Lord's Day. This came to 30 per cent, a fairly high figure of piety, as far as this can be marked by attendance. That this congregation has some spiritual dimension is also supported by the fact that one of their number has been sent away for theological training and another is performing missionary service among the Gilbertese migrants near Gizo.

Those classified in category "B" attended three of the four Sunday meetings, and those in category "C" twice. Those whom we registered under "D" were satisfied with going to church once a week, and those listed under "E" statistically did not bother about going to church at all, although they considered themselves Christians.[2]

The unexpected feature of this case study is revealed by the curve depicted in Figure 4. I had been told before going to Rarumana that the place had a reputation for piety, but I did not anticipate such a clear bi-modal curve, setting off a segment of pathetic indifference over against the pious core. What does this bi-modalism indicate?

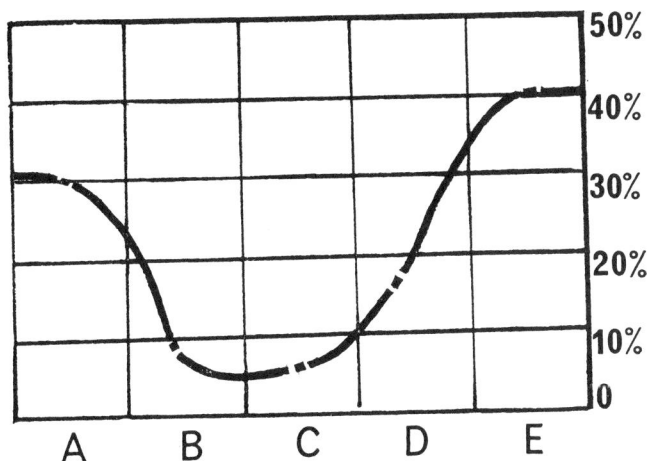

Fig. 4. Piety Curve at Rarumana

It indicates that this second generation Christian village, though highly moral and pious in many ways, has (perhaps over a fairly long period) experienced a quality decline. Folk who were average Christians (C) have become more and more marginal (D) and ultimately merely nominal (E). I think it can be demonstrated that this drift is currently active, but before we look into that, let it be said that were this curve test applied to many of the supposedly strong causes of Melanesia's second and third generation Christians, we would find these bi-modal drifts a widespread reality. In villages which have responded to the gospel *in toto* as a result of a dynamic encounter, but where the follow-up or Christian nurture has been poorly attended to, these curves are to be expected. In second generation causes where the subsequent generation has not itself felt the same spiritual rebirth as the first, we may expect the same pattern.

One of the weakest points in the Melanesian Christian armour is the assumption that a person is a Christian because a generation or two ago his fathers rejected paganism and became Christian, that he is a Christian by birth, regardless of whether he be nuclear or nominal or has made a personal decision or not. Although church attendance is no ultimate criterion for depth of religious experience, it does indicate attitudes, and at least at the negative pole, we can assume that people who do not bother to go to church at all are not committed Christians. This assumption that a man is a Christian because he is not a pagan is the most vulnerable point in Melanesian second-generation Christianity.

In the case of this Western Solomons sample, this misconception is aggravated by the Mission's departure from its original theological base for church membership. Merely to graduate young people from a youth roll to full membership at the age of sixteen (with some extra instruction, if the persons concerned happen to be on a mission station) is a policy fraught with dangers.[3]

The figures of the curves illustrated are of course only statistical patterns, but the attitudes of piety and/or indifference which they reflect, are quite obvious, once one's attention has been directed to them by the figures. If a two month sample could be taken in the same village at, say, two yearly intervals, at the same season of the year, I venture to suggest that many villages would reveal their percentage strength sliding slowly along towards the pole of indifference, even though the pious segment remained constant. Bi-modal curves are curves of active drift—with a pious segment sealing itself off from the village, and more and more of the marginals dropping out as mere nominals. The more secularized they become, the harder it will be to win them back.

We have already seen something of the character of preaching in this village. It revealed a strong bias towards Christian ethics and service, but neglected praise[4] and the Holy Spirit and the spiritual experience itself. It advocated service in the name of Christ, but did not first set out to bring folk into an experience of Christ from which such service might emanate. Confession was entirely absent.[5] To put it statistically: when the village is served with 50 per cent of its preaching on the fruit of salvation—i.e. works and service—salvation itself is bound to get a very small percentage of the remainder, which has to be divided among many aspects of the faith. The more moralist the preaching becomes, the less will the marginals feel disposed to come and hear it, unless at some point of time they are brought face to face with the dynamic of the gospel itself. There may be a whole complex of reasons for this drift, but I feel quite sure that this is at least one of them.

Our data permit a more refined analysis of the figures on which the marginal (D) and nominal (E) computations were based in the Rarumana curve, for the application of another technique. Over the eight weeks it was found that an average of 116 persons attended the biggest service each Sunday. Many of these attended other services as well, but the average of the best-attended service each Sunday was 116. This, however, was the average of a wide range of variation, fluctuating from 89 to 145. The averages of the second, third and fourth Sunday meetings showed nothing like the same degree of fluctuation. The averages for the four services were 116, 86, 74 and 57. The difference between the first two figures shows that some 30 persons attended church *only* once a week (116 − 86 = 30). This again is an average figure with a huge fluctuation from 3 to 59.

The relevance of this statistical observation is that there is more or less stability at the pole of piety, and considerable fluctuation at the pole of nominality and marginality. In point of actual fact, only three or four marginals did attend once a week. The average of thirty was achieved because another fourteen or fifteen more attended only once every three weeks, and still another fifteen more only once in the eight weeks. Thus, though the marginals averaged statistically at thirty, there were actually fifty-nine persons involved, but some had drifted so far towards nominality that they attended only once in eight weeks. A sample over twelve months would probably reveal others who attend once or twice a year—say at Christmas and Easter. A good pastor should observe this marginal-nominal drift and try to counter it by pastoral visitation and personal work. Attendance fluctuations invariably indicate drift, and by the time a curve presents this clear bi-modalism, the drift has well advanced.

In the case of Rarumana, the pious core of nuclear Christians happens to include most of the leaders of village and communal work, and the church has not suffered for the want of competent men as leaders. Neither has there been any organized or active opposition among the mere nominals. Thus the drift has been quiet and perhaps unnoticed.

Marginality is a great danger to any Christian cause. The villages which swung away to Etoism appear to have had congregations dominantly marginal, and often the village leaders were only marginal in the church. Their theological *débâcle* shows that they were theologically marginal, and I feel sure that had statistical returns been kept, they would have manifested this same marginality in attendance at church. Marginality means vulnerability. When a prophet can win village leaders and heads of families because they are marginals and perhaps bored with Christian traditional religion, anything might happen. The whole region was apparently ripe for revival in 1959–60. The Church was not equal to the opportunity and the initiative was taken by Silas Eto, who had been moving in this direction for nearly twenty years. In those villages where there was a strong stable core of responsible leaders, like those at Rarumana, his movement was rejected. His two advocates in that village have been well and truly kept in their place. Yet, even so, I would be neglecting my duty if I failed to point out that some areas that stood against Etoism may still have dangerously large numbers of marginal members. I reiterate, marginality is vulnerability.

Some years ago Bishop Montgomery, writing of the Eastern Solomons, raised this question of second generation Christianity.

> As the Church in Melanesia becomes a settled Church, and thousands of children of Christian parents are baptized into it, how shall the indifference of universal Christianity be overcome? This evil must be faced, for history is full of the special dangers of the second stages of a Christian mission.[6]

A more refined analysis is also possible at the opposite pole, where we are dealing with the pious nuclear core of the Church. At Rarumana this was 30 per cent of the community, and these persons, as we have seen, entirely give themselves to every means of grace offered on Sundays. An even more intensive analysis may be made by examining the statistics of the weekday morning and evening devotionals, which are attended throughout (i.e. for an additional twelve meetings per week) by 42·5 persons. This represents twenty-two of the 30 per cent of nuclear Christians, and gives us the figure of the *communal weekday piety*.

The following table gives the weekly average attendance over the twelve weekday devotionals for the eight successive weeks in Rarumana. The high figure for the first week we attribute to the novelty of our presence in the village—perhaps the stimulus of inspection. The drops in the fifth and seventh weeks were due to very inclement weather, an undue amount of sickness and travelling (a number of leaders being absent at church meetings for a large part of the seventh week). Apart from these, the nucleus was remarkably constant throughout.

1st week	61
2nd week	45
3rd week	40
4th week	41
5th week	35
6th week	41
7th week	30
8th week	47
Average over 8 weeks	42·5

This 22 per cent of the total population, I have called the measure of *communal weekday piety*. The word 'communal' is used deliberately, because the figure does not measure those who maintain domestic devotions in individual households in the evening, instead of going to church. A number do this, but I had no means of measuring that number or their regularity. It might be fairly close to the possible 8 per cent.

APPLICATION OF THE TOOL TO THE FOUIA SITUATION

Figure 5 is the curve produced by the Fouia church attendance statistics. It should not be compared point by point with the Rarumana curve, because the actual categories are determined independently within the respective situations. The two situations do not provide identical programmes for the faithful. Therefore each takes its measure from its own pattern and creates its own norm. Interpretation therefore is as follows: Figure 4 represents the attendance curve of a Methodist village according to the Methodist norms, and Figure 5 represents the attendance curve of an Anglican village according to Anglican norms. The general effect of the curves may be compared. The categories "B" *Steady* and "C" *Average* are not absolutely identical, because the two devotional structures which provided the statistical data differed slightly. Fortunately the real focal points "A" *Nuclear*, "D" *Marginal* and "E" *Nominal* do coincide exactly in their scales of measurement. In each case, for example, "A" represents those who attend every means of grace available, and these *Nuclear Christians*, the real core of the Church, number roughly a third of the community in each case.

In both cases the results were similar for the total community (including children), and for adults only. Curves taken for children and adults would have been almost identical. The village children virtually reflected the adult attitudes. In each case there was a nuclear core of really devout children who were always present and were ready to recite texts, sing a hymn or participate if given the opportunity (Rarumana), and make full use of the prayer book and other aids (Fouia). The only difference I detected between the child and adult attendances was that at Rarumana a few more children would classify as "D" and a few less as "E". They had not yet drifted from marginality to nominality. This falls in line with my impression that the drift takes place with the later teen-agers and young adults.

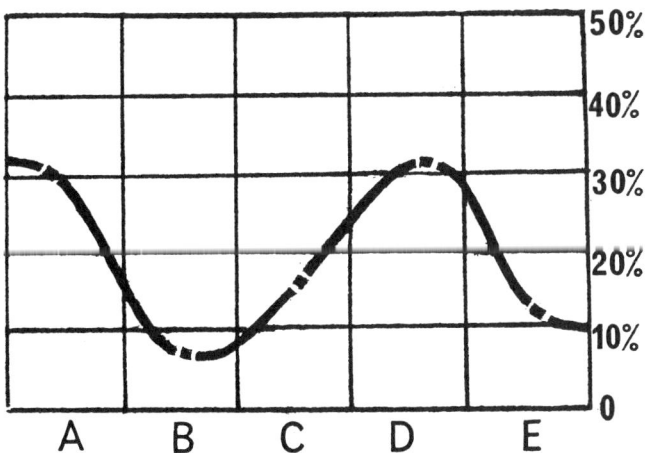

Fig. 5. Piety Curve at Fouia

When we compare the curves of Rarumana and Fouia we are struck by their bi-modal similarity and departure from the hypothetical norms. We are also attracted by the similar distribution of strength and weakness. There is, however, one significant difference. The percentage strength among the Nominals at Rarumana is found among the Marginals at Fouia. There are several possible explanations. It may mean that the Anglicans have avoided the drift. It may mean that the drift has just gone further at Rarumana.

There is little doubt that the Anglican pattern has been less subject to drift than the Methodist—remembering that the two groups have had a roughly equal time of exposure to Christianity, and have both emerged as Christian villages away from their traditional localities. The Methodists explore their religion much better, but this very fact means they have need for guides and aids. Unfortunately they have only very few and they do not make good use of these. Their religion is less organized, with no dramatic focal points, and many loyal Christians feel that they have been deprived of something from their past. The Anglican pattern is built round the Holy Communion, which in Fouia is almost a weekly service. It is significant that the marginal Christians who attend no more meetings than one service a Sunday, choose the Holy Communion. I have no doubt that for Fouia this high moment is an effective instrument operating against the marginal-nominal drift.[7]

Even so, there is real danger that the Fouia marginal will convince himself that as long as he attends Holy Communion, other things do not matter very much. It is not from statistical evidence alone that I point out this danger. For instance, there is a danger that springs from the Melanesian background, orientated as it is towards sacred objects and magical rituals. At several points I had a strong fear that some of these marginal Christians saw the Holy Communion as essential because they viewed it almost magically, and attended because their 'good fortune' in daily life depended on it. Some of them still think of religion negatively as a means of avoiding fears and calamity. It is quite true that *attendance piety*, while it reflects the disposition of people to worship and attend the means of grace, does not necessarily imply a real depth or quality, or indicate whether the motive for worship is positive or negative. The importance of the piety curve is that it raises questions for investigation. At this point, for instance, it asks—Why do so many marginals attend Holy Communion, but ignore all other Sunday and weekday worship? And arising from this another—What does the Holy Communion really mean to them?

Another feature of the Fouia situation should be noted. If the figures given me by the priest are correct, an inordinately large percentage of the adult male labour force is absent from the village in employment elsewhere—in Honiara, in Gizo, and on plantations in the Russell Islands and Guadalcanal. If all the folk belonging to the two villages we observed were living at home, they would be roughly the same size, but Fouia has three times as many absentees. Two informants among the younger men at Fouia told me that many of those absentees do not go to church at all. They are so widely scattered that this could not be checked. Were it possible to check this, we might find a considerable marginal-nominal drift among this group.

Having made these allowances, however, we are still impressed with the fact that the Anglican residents within this village have, despite their heavy marginality, avoided the problem of nominality. Any nominality not recorded is due to exterior factors (the labour system). The people have not been attracted to any neo-pagan movements, and have not responded to the Watchtower advocates. Their basic theology has been determined by prayer-books with a wide range,[8] and their hymn-singing has been strongly soteriological. They are diligent in bringing folk on to confirmation, and regular in their use of the means of grace. These have led to a fairly strong solidarity within the village. Those who seek more exciting and remunerative employment on plantations and in the town, especially when confronted by people of other denominations, pagans and materialists, may not be quite so stable, as their religion of set forms has not taught them to explore for themselves. There probably is drift at this level.

As to the measure of *communal weekly piety*, we found that our personal presence in the village had no statistical effect. In Fouia the presence or absence of the priest counted for more than our own. He was absent for a fortnight at a conference, and during this period the attendance figures at morning and evening prayers showed an average drop of 14 per cent. On the whole the weekday attendance was evenly distributed, being very slightly larger at the evening meetings. Over all weekday meetings an average of 30 per cent was recorded, and this was slightly higher than at Rarumana. In Fouia the weekday piety was all communal. I did not find any evidence of domestic piety in the way of household devotions, so the piety figures may have been fairly close.

We observed a slight 'communal versus family' tension at Rarumana. In Fouia, although there were several kin segments, the nuclear family had very little entity. The members even ate at irregular times, each one as he felt the need during the day, or at night after fishing or catching crabs. Small groups of children would spend the evenings seeking seafoods along the shore by torchlight, cook and eat their catches as sodality age-groups, rather than as families in their 'homes'. Each household has its pot of sweet potato, but the members usually took a piece or two, and ate as they went to work or as they sat outside talking. Such irregularity militates against family corporateness. I found no evidence of family devotions, Bible reading or grace before meals, except when we sat down to a specific meal with the priest in his home. He had been much more in contact with white people, had a better house, more personal possessions, and his was not in any way a typical household. I do not mean that the folk were not devoted to their children—they certainly were. The old men in particular were frequently seen with the one- and two-year-olds. But the nuclear family was less real in Fouia than in other villages I had seen. The children would play about in the village at night, without any apparent parental concern. Several times they had to be broken up and sent home, but it was neither the parents nor the elders who took the necessary action. It was usually a young single catechist.

On the other hand, the church life was perfectly orderly in every way and quite regular. The procedure laid down in the *Kalendar and Lectionary* was followed on all occasions. They were much more careful about observing time than in most Melanesian villages. Choir practice on a week-night always ended with Compline. My impression was that religion was associated with the church building, which was always there for anyone to use and was regarded as sacred. Pipes, knives and other secular things were never taken inside and put in the pocket or under the seat. They were left outside. One by one they would take a last draw from the pipe, then set it in the fork of a tree or in a cleft in the rock, and go on into church. The 'home' was quite a different matter—a place for preparing food and sleeping. The *Companions* and the *Mothers' Union* were additional prayer organizations, which functioned regularly by a set pattern with a set programme of prayer for missions covering a full calendar year—but these again were associated with the church building, and as I have already pointed out, the Bibles and prayer-books were left in the church where they belonged.

I felt that a simple but specific programme of "Religion for the Home" might help the situation at Fouia, and bring some of the many marginals into a more real experience of religion. Before anything really effective can be done in this direction, a sociological issue has to be faced—the village first needs *an awareness of the idea of home*. The church building is the focal point of the village. Awareness of the Church is good. The danger is that religion becomes confined to the buildings and fails to ramify through the homes and lives of people.

CHAPTER 22

Half-Christian Half-Pagan Villages

ONE OF the puzzling problems of the Solomon Islands scene is the existence of villages which are half-Christian and half-pagan. My observations were made in Malaita, but I am told the situation is also found in Guadalcanal and Bougainville.

CO-EXISTENCE AND MISSIONARY OBLIGATION

It is now over a century since the Church began trying to win Malaita for Christ, and for the last sixty years a strong Christian cause has been established in many parts of the island, and over that period liturgical and other worship patterns have been consolidated. Along the north coast the mission station phase has long vanished and the region is organized under Melanesian priests, who, as far as I was able to decide, are true fathers of their people. A second generation of adult Christians has now grown up in the village where I lived. It is entirely Christian, yet visible from my house was another village half-Christian and half-pagan. I heard nothing and saw nothing to suggest any real concern on the part of the established Christian congregation for the winning of the pagan units. Even in the villages which were so divided, the Christians seemed to have become resigned to an indifferent co-existence. I visited several of them and had the feeling that both parties were satisfied with things as they are.

Yet all these Christian congregations have a strong missionary interest. The *Companions of the Brotherhood* do actually meet and pray daily for the Brothers and their mission to the heathen. I have heard them day after day and been impressed with their devotion. Then, confronted by these pagan groups at their very door, one has the impression that they have compartmentalized their missionary obligations, assigning the task of evangelism to the Brotherhood and confining their own to devout but inactive prayer. The pagan situation in their midst appears to have no personal relevance to them. They feel no obligations to be missionaries themselves, nor were there any Brothers working in these communities. On a morning which followed a day I had spent in these villages with the priest, I noticed he read the prayers for the heathen from the Brothers' Book, so that at least he was not unaware of the situation. Perhaps my questioning had stimulated him to prayer—I do not know—but there was certainly no indication that the Christian congregation as a whole was aware of its responsibility for winning these neighbours.

MODIFIED PAGANISM

Malaita villages have come into Christianity over a period of time. A number came over from paganism to Christianity about the time of the Great War. Others took the step during and after the last war in a considerable people-movement which has run out with the winning of numerous complete segments of society. Some bush villages are in the process of coming over at present under the efforts of the Brothers. However, pagans are in the minority today, and pagan villages are not what they used to be. The old patterns of war and murder have gone, and the defences. Pagan society is as disrupted as Christian society. These people have been adjusting themselves to change for sixty years and more. They have learned to live as pagans among Christians, and, we may say, in spite of Christianity. This is not the old type of confrontation with animism reinforced by pagan war and ceremonial cannibalism. It is a modified animism which had adjusted itself to a 'Christianized' milieu. This is a new type of confrontation for the island Church. The tragedy is that the majority of Christians do not see it as a confrontation at all.

This present-day pagan community, facing the same social and economic changes as the Christian community, apart from being a little dirtier and a little less clad (though this is not always so), is different only on the level of religion. I have seen the pagan meeting the Christian for trade exchange at a forest market locality, and although it was quite simple to distinguish the bush people from the salt-water people, it was impossible to distinguish the pagan from the Christian. On the level of religion they took each other for granted.

The half-pagan, half-Christian village may have a church and a pagan sacred place within sight of each other; or if the pagan group is small, it may have a shrine or sacred room, in a house. There one still finds an ancestral skull,[1] which is the dwelling-place of his ghost or at least the place the ghost will visit. Offerings are placed there and also relics. Although war and murder, slavery and cannibalism have gone, their worship is just as before, and the relics repose still in bamboo containers or hang in a sacred basket. And so things will remain until these relics have been taken down, the skull buried, and other paraphernalia burned upon the acceptance of Christianity.

In the olden days, facing a pagan majority, it was dangerous to reject the worship of one's ancestors. One lost one's social status in the tribe, brought upon oneself the displeasure of one's family, or maybe lost one's life. There is no persecution today. A man is free to be pagan or Christian and no one will stop him, yet many prefer to face the new age as pagans.

CONVERSION AND OBSTRUCTIONS

Asking a Melanesian Christian leader of the area how he accounted for this preference for paganism in the present situation, he assured me that there were still two strong obstructions to conversion, despite the fact that persecution had vanished and times were more Christianized. They still have a genuine fear of hostile forces in the forest and at sea, of evil spirits, of sorcery, of unknown dangers, of sickness, and of things that go wrong and cannot be explained. They have learned to trust their family ghosts, partly because having lived on earth themselves, they understand the human problems of their descendants and have sympathy for them, and partly lest they be angered by rejection (which acceptance of Christianity demands) and bring calamity on the living. This is an important testimony, because it shows that the power encounter with animism is still a live issue in the Malaita scene. Although pagan life has been humanized, philosophically it is still thoroughly animist.

In the particular case we were discussing, the second obstruction was the heathen priest who was personally responsible for preserving these animistic dimensions in popular thinking. My informant asserted that as long as these people had a priest to sacrifice a pig for them, there would be resistance to conversion.[2] As long as the priest is there, they will rely on him in their fears. If he should die, their fear will increase because they will regard themselves as vulnerable. This is one point of time when people are sometimes specially open for conversion. The motive is expediency, because it is a terrible thing to be without a priest in an animistic world. People who turn to Christianity under these circumstances are due for a long period of instruction before baptism, but even so it does require an act of no little faith to bury the ancestral skull and burn the sacred paraphernalia, and this they must do before baptism.

However, this is not the only conversion pattern in Malaita. There are some who lose faith in their ancestral spirits and their power to save them from evil. Still confronted with evil about them, they turn to Christ for power. For these, conversion is a real *power encounter*. Christ is sovereign Lord with power. This is a positive experience, and may be either individual or shared by a multi-individual group.

Then there are others who, as individuals, have become personally convinced in the rightness of Christianity as a way of life, and turn to it with *intellectual conviction*. Sometimes such an individual becomes vocal in a small cultural unit in which he is respected, and may convince the whole group of his personal conviction, and they may become Christian as a group.

These three forms of conversion were outlined to me by a Malaita Christian. We note that they are all cases of prevenient grace—i.e. the Spirit of God seems to have been working *among the pagans themselves*. My informant did not mention any missionary action, witness or evangelism, although the Brothers are winning people to Christ in other parts of Malaita. In this region of half-pagan half-Christian villages, conversions may come through expediency, power encounter or intellectual conviction. This makes it all the more difficult to understand why there is no specific evangelistic approach to them by the existing Christians. No informant was able to tell me of any cases.

When doors began to open in Malaita earlier in the century, there were Christian advocates, men who had met Christ in Fiji and in Queensland, who were prepared to risk their lives urging their fellow-countrymen to accept Christ. This positive evangel on the part of the existing Christian is not apparent today, although they will pray diligently for their officially appointed evangelists at work further from home. In fishing, trade exchanges, and communal projects, they are continually in contact with pagans, yet appear to have resigned themselves to a state of co-existence.

One is well aware that this may be said of many places in the western world also, but my concern in this Malaita situation is not merely that the church is static, but that it is static where it could be growing.

SOCIOLOGICAL ASPECTS

The problem also appears to have sociological aspects, though one would have to establish the genealogical evidence for a number of specific cases to be dogmatic about it. I am assured by reliable informants that frequently the half-pagan half-Christian division is on a basis of kin segments. The Christian-pagan cleavage, if it is part of the kin structure, may well have long-standing personal family rivalries within it. This is a common problem met in many parts of Oceania.[3] It often ends with some other denominational mission coming in and winning the second segment, and much of the denominational rivalry which inevitably follows is a fire fanned by kin jealousies. Frequently when a Melanesian community ripens for conversion, all segments can be harvested at one time, so that two competitive missions may meet the unhappy 'requirements' of the situation of kin competition. The danger of the Malaita situation is that these pagan segments are an open invitation to any other mission if the Anglicans do not make some special effort to win them. Time and opportunity did not permit a full enough investigation for me to be dogmatic about the depth of rivalries in these situations, but the division has been a long-standing pattern and it has a social structure. Furthermore, this society had its pre-Christian facilities for effecting reconciliations. I had a strong feeling that a constructive preaching of reconciliation and the unity of the group might have proved an effective stepping-stone to a total acceptance of Christianity.

However, it is not safe to generalize. One case, which I investigated as far as one could do so in a single visit, revealed the ridiculous situation of an island with all its full-grown men pagans, while the women and children were Christians. The only religious facilities on this island were pagan, and the women had to visit a neighbouring island for any Christian worship. The latter island was small and not populous, and had to provide a church building very much larger than its own requirements to meet the needs of the women from the pagan island. I asked the highly intelligent Christian teacher on the smaller island how he accounted for this situation. He said the men were awaiting the death of their priest, and then they would become Christian as a group. Apparently the matter has been discussed, but it will be a formal and superficial kind of conversion and will require careful and thorough teaching in its follow-up. Clearly if there were any conviction about it, the men would not be hindered by the old priest.

At the same time it does throw light on a number of important factors. Firstly, it confirms the claim that a priest can obstruct conversion. Secondly, it shows the strength of customary ties, this priest having been brought in twenty years ago, and established ceremonially, so that the men still felt honour-bound to respect the contract by which they had 'bought' his services. At the same time, the adult men were not prepared to bind their sons to this contract and were allowing them to be raised as Christians. They recognized that the future might be with Christianity, but it was not with paganism. Pagan loyalty to customary contract for the generation that makes it, is much stronger than the average westerner realizes, and this seems to be the crux of the matter. If the priest would not free them from their contract, it was this customary contract rather than the priest which was the obstruction.

Of the thirty-three artificial islands distributed along the coast of northern Malaita, with populations varying from one family to perhaps seven hundred persons,[4] twelve have been totally converted to the Anglican form of Christianity, one small island is totally Roman Catholic, and one with perhaps 200 persons is now Seventh Day Adventist. One small island is served by the South Seas Evangelical Church, five are still totally pagan, and two are now empty. One small island is occupied by an advocate of the Jehovah's Witnesses movement. Nine islands are part-Anglican and part-heathen, one is part-S.D.A. and part-heathen, another is divided into three segments between Anglicans, S.D.A. and pagans. This illustrates the scope of the problem in the artificial islands of the salt-water people along the Malaita coast in the districts of Ata, Kwarade, Tai and Makwanu. This is not the only region where we meet this problem.

We had opportunity to reconstruct something of the historical dynamics of one specific case, and have set this out in the diagram. The localities are represented by the dotted rectangles and the original male characters by triangles. The descending lines indicate the origin of the present populations of the respective localities. We are dealing with the lineage of the man "A" who lived in the island of "W". He had four sons, "B", "C", "D" and "E". As these grew to manhood and produced families, "B", "D" and "E" migrated to the localities "X", "Y" and "Z". "C" remained in their home locality to carry on the place developed by "A". The island "X" was in another district, and likewise "Z" a much smaller island. The island "Y" was a new island built by "D" and his family not very far from "W" their homeland. Thus the lineage is divided today with two extended families in the original district and two in another. Over a period of time they multiplied, especially those resident at "W" and "X", whose descendants now number hundreds. Down to the time of the last war, the whole lineage resisted all attempts at evangelization. They were not always hostile to it but preferred to remain pagan, though some of their children had been allowed to go away from their respective islands to Christian schools, and had indeed become Christian and had not returned to their island homes. Others had also accepted Christianity by migrating away from the pagan islands and settling with some

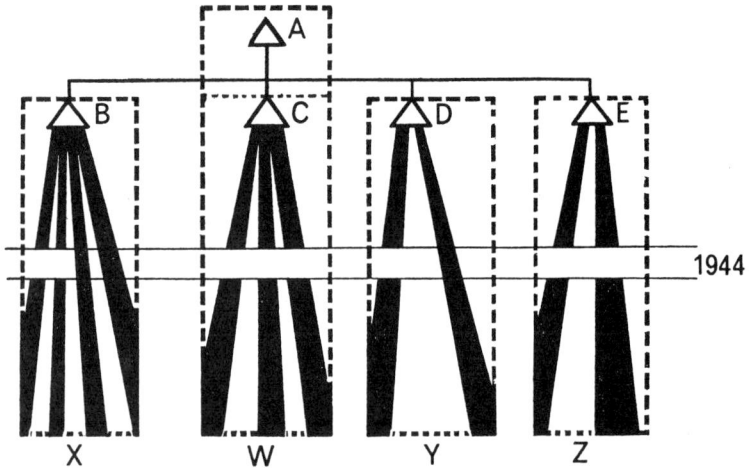

Illustrating how the death of the pagan high priest in 1944 opened the way for the acceptance of Christianity in four of the artificial island communities (represented by the rectangles W, X, Y, Z), peopled by the descendants of four brothers, B, C, D and E, sons of A.
Segments in X and Y rejected the advocacy of Christianity and remained pagan. The narrative in the text describes the method by which a new pagan priest was appointed when none was provided for by the normal succession: a good example of cultural adaptation to a crisis situation.

Christian community on the mainland near by. Individuals were free to do this, but there were no Christians in any of the four pagan islands.

This large community in four localities was served by a high priest who was ready to sacrifice a pig to the ghost of "A" at any time. As long as he lived there, the four communities remained totally pagan. About 1944 the high priest died. Observing the direction of the changes through acculturation, the priest had allowed his son to have a Christian education away from the locality. The lad, who was heir to the priesthood, had become Christian and entered Christian employment away from the district. Upon the death of the high priest in 1944, many of the people were ready to become Christian because of their own convictions; others were ready to try Christianity as an expedient because they were left without a priest and without a successor. Thus four islands were suddenly open for evangelization because of the removal of one obstruction. As a result the whole of the island "W" and the smaller community "Z" became Christian, disposing of their religious paraphernalia in the approved manner. All the ancestral skulls of the community were buried in a common grave under a simple cement slab, without any symbolic cross like they use on the Christian graves.

A large number of the descendants of "B" at "X" and some of the descendants of "D" at "Y" for the same reasons and at the same time became Christian. About fifty persons at "X" and a couple of nuclear families at "Y" determined to remain pagan. These two groups, although in different districts, felt they had to act together as they served the ghost of their common ancestor. A new priest had to be found, but the only eligible one was a Christian.

They determined to introduce a new priest from outside—to 'buy' one. The deceased high priest had a sister who had married into a village of the bushmen. They decided to 'buy back' her son, bringing him back into the tribe from which his mother had been 'bought' after the customary manner. The transaction of 'buying back' the priest cost them a thousand porpoise teeth and thirty fathoms of red shell money. This priest still serves the pagan remnants in "X" and "Y", though they are in different districts, and this accounts for two of the nine islands that are part-Anglican and part-pagan today. In this particular case I have no evidence of why the two smaller segments refused to move with the majority in 1944, but it is fairly clear that they still feel they have to honour the 'buying back' of the priest. They have lived through another twenty years of paganism rather than break that customary contract.

The pagan group at "X" includes some of the most influential elders of the community. Perhaps their traditional pride prevents their surrender now. But this very possibility shows how vulnerable they are, if some sub-Christian sect or another mission should display interest in them. How easy a way of becoming 'Christian' without the humiliating admission that they have been so wrong for so long. I do not say this is likely to happen in this case; but it has happened in scores of similar situations in Oceania, and I merely point out how vulnerable they are.

If this situation is based on a clear structural division in the kin sub-divisions of the lineage, there is only one solution to this problem—it requires *an act of reconciliation* pressed *within the lineage* in the name of lineage cohesion. This could well be done in the name of Christ and a ceremonial compensation be made to the priest to terminate the old contract, a new generation having emerged since it was made.

The presence of numerous *completely isolated* Christian units belonging to three other missions in otherwise strongly entrenched Anglican areas (both bush and coastal areas) rather suggests a vulnerability of some such type as this. Any isolated village or social unit of any denomination must suffer pastorally from its isolation. I don't see how any of them can be properly nurtured.

In pagan times religion was the strength of the lineage, and one of its major functions was the maintenance of the cohesion of the total group. As long as there are denominations in an island community, it is difficult for Christianity to fulfil this important function. The sub-divisions of a social structure were intended for decision-making and social controls, so that the solidarity of the whole could be preserved in the interests of all. In olden times the isolation of one of these sub-divisions meant the danger of exposure to the enemy. The community did not rest until reconciliation had been effected and this was achieved on a basis of religion. Christianity has the finest capacity of all religions for reconciliation; yet the Christian community settled down to a state of resignation to Christian-pagan co-existence and unconcern.

These structural sub-divisions exist in all Melanesian societies, although there are many different patterns. The two areas where most of our depth studies were done were quite different, for example, one being matrilineal and the other patrilineal. To the westerner, who lives his life mainly within the confines of a nuclear family, the cohesion of kin segments within communal society often seems a mystery and is often regarded as undesirable. Yet these sub-divisions are so important for decision-making and communal behaviour that the westerner working among these people must try to master the pattern and to do his work within its configurations. To the missionary trying to win people and groups it is important that he should see which people are the key to the groups and how the groups are constituted. Let us take a specific case, the salt-water people of Malaita, with whom we have been dealing in this chapter, and let us examine their concept of the *family* itself. The family is conceptualized on three levels, which I have reduced to diagrams in the familiar kin symbols, as illustrated. A man speaks of *bara gami*, our family, and means the nuclear family comprising his wife and their children as the westerner would mean. Many of the personal and petty things of life are wrapped up in this small unit, but the really important things of life belong to the larger concepts of family. In pre-Christian days this small unit would have a sacred place with a basket of sacred objects and perhaps a skull or some less significant relic. The diagrams have been reduced to a minimum, showing one male and one female child to each marriage. In reality, each nuclear family might be two or three times as large.

However, the family is more commonly conceived in its wider sense. When a man speaks of *'ae bara*, he adds to his wife, himself and their children, his brothers and sisters and their children, but does not include his brother-in-law and sister-in-law. Thus other nuclear families are partly within and partly outside his extended family. This is a real family, related by blood. His sons and daughters and also the sons and daughters of his brothers are all spoken of by the same term—his children (*ngwela*). This being a patrilineal society there is a distinction made between these children and those of his sister, who are spoken of as *ko'o*. Although these are differentiated from a man's children, they are objects of his special affection and have a right to claim his help on many occasions. Thus the *'ae bara* family has a cohesion of its own, with a specific network of relationships and obligations within it.

The family concept has a further extension in what is known as the *gule bara*, which includes all the blood relations on both sides in a bilateral grouping, as illustrated in the third diagram opposite. With these diagrams reduced to their simplest form, it will be readily seen that if husbands and wives had seven or eight children, the *gule bara*

THE CONCEPT OF FAMILY AMONG THE SALT-WATER PEOPLE OF MALAITA

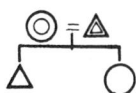

First Concept
BARA GAMI
(Our Family)

Second Concept
'AE BARA
One's immediate
family circle.

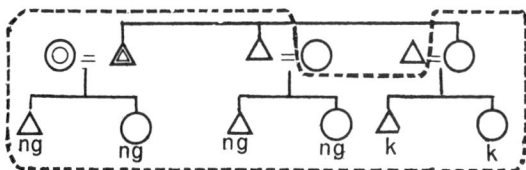

Third Concept GULE BARA   The limits of the family concept

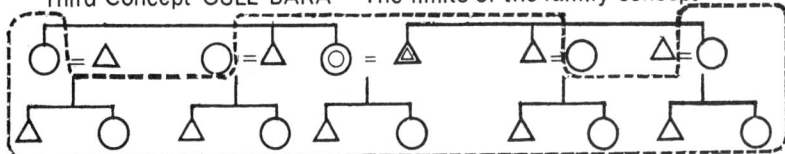

The family is bilateral, but based on ties of blood, not marriage. The dotted lines indicate who is inside and who is outside the true family.
The symbols 'ng' and 'k' indicate the relationship of children in 'ae bara to the father. ng = ngwela (sometimes written simply wela). k = ko'o. Note that nephew and niece by a brother stand in the same relationship as one's true son and daughter, but those by a sister are differentiated.

could be a very large community of people. It bears the same structural characteristics as the *'ae bara*, being confined to those related by blood, and excluding those who are entered on the diagram by marriage only. The dotted lines indicate the family limits. The key to this conceptualization is thus seen to be blood, not marriage.

The *gule bara* is the limit of the family concept. It is a useful unit for major decision-making and co-operative work programmes—enlarging island foundations, church building, fishing drives and so on. It is frequently the instrument of group action and would be the group most likely to take action in the rejection of paganism and acceptance of Christianity. It has to be seen by the evangelist as a winnable group. In the community at large the *gule bara* are important pressure groups. On the whole they can boast fairly solid cohesion; but their ties are not quite as strong as those of the *'ae bara*, and when a community of this kind divides on an issue, a programme or a public decision, it is frequently a case of the *'ae bara* within the *gule bara*. I believe that this potential cleavage may often account for both pagan-Christian segmentation and denominational segmentation. I am sorry I had not more time to investigate this more fully.

In that each man who marries establishes a new nuclear family in which two parties are involved, it might seem that each nuclear family is the centre of two *gule bara*. This may be argued theoretically, but in point of fact the matter is determined by "belonging to the island" (*'aei fera*). A bushman marrying an island woman, or a bushwoman marrying an islander, even though becoming resident of the island is not *'aei fera*, because he or she is not *too futa*—viz., "identified with the ancestral religion". It is here that we see the important role of the ancestral cult in the decision-making of these people. The children born to the outsider who has married into the group are born *too futa*, so that there is a process of absorption that takes a generation to be consummated. The person marrying-in counts for very little, and this relieves the tension of any potential rivalry from strong personalities marrying-in.

This unfortunate, who seems to have been cut out of the family, retains blood contact with his or her own family back in the bush, and this may mean an important political or economic contact for the family, but he cannot become vitally identified with the ancestral cult, which gives cohesion to the communal decision-making.

In the planting of Christianity it should therefore be clear that the winning of such individuals for the Church is of little strategic value to the group, their individual decision being more likely to stir up active opposition of all the *too futa*, and especially that of the ancestral priest. On the other hand, the winning of the priest is an important step in bringing the Christian advocacy into the group discussions of the *gule bara*, where the group's multi-individual decision is actually made. Wherever a pagan priest allowed his son to have a Christian training, it was in one sense an important individual pre-decision, that was bound to be significant when the multi-individual decision of the group was eventually made.

Now, in the light of this picture of family structure, let us glance again at the incident of the 'buying back' of the priest. We saw that the old priest had no sons (*ngwela*) for the priesthood. There was no succession in the nuclear family. Neither could his brothers supply a *ngwela*. However there was a *ko'o*, a son of his sister, who was within the *'ae bara*, and although born to a man of the mountains, and born in the bush, was nevertheless *too futa*—identified with the ancestral religion of the island group. This explains how the island people *'aei fera* could bring back this man to perform the priestly office. It was a binding contract on a tie of blood and family. This does not necessarily explain the motives for this decision, but it does show the structure of the cultural mechanism within which the decision was made, and why its character was so binding. The priest has been obligated by the contract to maintain traditional paganism. The family has been obligated to support the priest. From the limited amount of information I was able to collect in the time, I suspect the structure of this division to be an *'ae bara* within a *gule bara*.

We have been examining the sociological roots of the Christian–pagan co-existence in these islands. Surely the Pauline concept of the unity of the Body is relevant here. It is not difficult for these people to understand that a house divided against itself may come to nought, yet they have become unconcerned at a point which in pre-Christian times would have been vital to them. It should be possible to tackle this problem within their own thought-forms. The concern of the group for its own totality is the element that has vanished from their life—and it is a serious loss.

It is interesting that both in the Anglican east and Methodist west we should meet different forms of what is basically the same problem— viz., the responsibility for the Christian segment to win the unchurched segment at their door. In the more primitive Malaita situation, the task of evangelizing pagans has virtually come to an end and left numerous segments still in darkness. In the more sophisticated western village, a less cohesive segment has drifted from marginality to nominality and stopped going to church at all. In neither case did the Christian core appear to realize that the task of doing something about correcting the respective situations was its own responsibility.

CHAPTER 23

Urban and Industrial Situations

THE NEW TESTAMENT congregation at imperial Rome emerged as a result of migration growth, without any evangelistic mission or missionary visit. Many folk mentioned in Paul's letter were known personally to him and had worshipped in congregations farther east. There they had learned the interdependence within the fellowship, and having migrated to the capital they sought each other out and the Church emerged spontaneously. Before long it was reaching out even into "Caesar's household". Statistically, migration or transfer growth is not growth at all, but in the formation of a new congregation there is always organic growth, and such a new cell should achieve numerical growth by its outreach within the new environment. When we consider the Roman Church as against those of Greece, we realize the biblical precedents offer us more than one pattern of church planting.

The New Testament situation in Rome has something to say to Honiara, the only place in the Solomon Islands which can really be called a town. Clearly Honiara, more than any other place in the Solomons, is open for new ideas and experiments. In one sense it is the centre of diffusion and therefore the key to the Solomons, but this statement needs considerable qualification. The popular idea that roads and other communications, laws based on official enactments, officials implementing them, and many other forces radiate over the rural areas from the capital, is a matter for debate. Strong evidence exists for centripetal rather centrifugal forces being dominant. It is certain that the movement of people is more *to* the town than *from* it. For missionary policy and technique, the important question is whether the town is key to the country or the country is key to the town. The Roman Christian community had its roots in the outposts of the empire and their deaconess was sent from Greece (Rom. 16: 1). However, that young Church was operating on principles of self-determination and self-propagation, reaching out into places where civil authority ruled.

Missionary theory in this area was developed some forty years ago by Clark, who based his research mainly on Asia, North China in particular. Unfortunately the war and subsequent events of a political character have changed the face of China, but his research is still relevant. He also told of an Anglican bishop pointing out to him that whereas 80 per cent of the people of India were living in the country, 80 per cent of the missionaries were resident in the cities. He was investigating the comparative merits of city and country as strategic points for church growth, and was impressed by the fact that city converts did not plant churches in the country but that many city churches were built of communicants who had been converted in the rural areas. In my own experience of over twenty years in Melanesia, I must admit that this is undeniable. Clark traced the dissemination of Christianity to rural focal points, especially the hundreds of rural market centres, the regular meeting places of rural folk. He devoted years of study to village situations where doors were open for evangelism.[1] Those areas where missionaries acted on his proposals soon had very encouraging results to report.

Dr. Peill, a medical missionary, took up the same theme and reached very much the same conclusions, developing the significance of migrations *to* rather than *from* the cities. Those who sought employment became permanent city-dwellers, returning to the country only for the Chinese New Year. Those who obtained their education *away from* the villages, lost their sympathy for them and cared even less for village betterment than the foreigners. Peill believed that far more flowed from the villages into the cities than vice versa, and thereafter concerned himself with developing techniques of village church-planting.[2]

Rowlands applied Clark's methods in Siaochang with good results. He concentrated on the rural markets rather than the towns, and planted simple self-supporting churches which certainly produced some spontaneous growth.[3] Peill and Rowlands worked in an area where nine million people lived in 11,400 villages. Each of the rural markets served as the meeting place for folk of some twenty to thirty villages. Clark's theory is founded on a solid body of objective data, and the truth these men established is too valuable to be allowed to perish because Communism has changed the situation. If anything, the fact that it involved the last pre-Communist research makes it all the more important as valid for other areas not yet under Communist domination.

While it is true that some ideas do become diffused from an administrative centre in all directions, we must not overlook the importance of movements in the opposite direction. If we are to understand the Honiara situation, or a plantation situation, we must first master those elements, characteristics, beliefs and practices from the scores of rural areas which are being thrown together as the constituents of the Honiara and the plantation situations.

THE HONIARA SITUATION

(i) *Migration Growth and Innovation*

The churches grow in Honiara, but I cannot answer for their degree of conversion growth from the world or from paganism. It is largely migration growth at the expense of the villages. The Anglican cause in Honiara is composed mainly of folk from the Eastern and Central Solomons and Polynesian outliers. The Methodists come from New Georgia and Choiseul. By agreement with the London Missionary Society, they are trying to incorporate the Gilbertese. The Fijians also are Methodists in the main, and some of the local initiative, as for example in the choir work, comes from this direction. The Roman Catholic, Seventh Day and South Sea Evangelical causes in Honiara are all found to have strongly regional bases for their respective congregations. In this way the denominations of Honiara reflect the country from which their adherents have migrated.

The New Testament congregation in Rome produced a spontaneous expansion in the imperial capital, so much so that before long Nero had to do something about it. There was, of course, no foreign mission organization in Rome to take them under its paternal (or maternal) wing, no organization which could supply a chaplain. If they were to emerge at all, they had to do it of their own accord, and of course they did. The missions are very busy in Honiara. They have numerous projects in the settlements that are springing up like mushrooms about the town. The missionaries are trying to bring these groups to self-support and one can honestly say that much good work is being done. The official Methodist policy conceives their work as that of a chaplaincy caring for "our people who have migrated to the capital". This grows from a long policy of comity. The post-war capital has been established in an Anglican comity area. This confinement is admittedly honourable but it in no way lines up with the New Testament concept of a church, having no outreach. It will never win "saints in Caesar's household". It will become enclosed—sealed off from the world in which it is called to witness. There is a real dilemma here. It is an issue in all the emerging towns of Oceania. I see no justification for establishing chaplaincies to circumvent comity agreements, because we are called to plant *churches* and churches are called to outreach. Comity agreements were made in the Pacific to avoid denominationalism and maintain Christian unity within regions. If in our post-war world these comity regions are no longer discrete, then the comity pattern has become obsolete.[4] If obsolete it becomes an obstruction. Whether the time has come for interdenominational co-operation in joint projects or for organic union, I am not sure, but of one thing I am quite certain—chaplaincies to care for "our people who have migrated" are spiritually wrong if they are to be denied outreach. Enclosed congregations are not only static but they exert a negative witness in the community, because they advertise Christianity as enclosure. I trust that what I have said will not be taken as a criticism of the missionaries personally—I am criticizing the policy under which they have to labour. Neither are the Methodists the only folk who have chaplaincies in other comity areas.

This policy may seem the easy way out, but it is thoroughly paternal and inhibitory to spontaneous indigenous growth. Honiara, and to a lesser extent Gizo and Auki, are new situations which call for vital church-planting free from enclosure and colonialism. Paternalism and colonialism go together. The whole orientation and terminology of the Europeans of Honiara is colonial—and it has not many years left for peaceful change.[5]

Although the growth of the town brings new forms of materialism and social problems, these need not necessarily be bad for the Church— if for instance they provide stimuli for an emerging Church to struggle towards its own entity as a relevant organism within the changing scene. It is true that folk who have drifted from their villages have great adjustments to make. They receive many shocks. Their lives are suddenly opened for re-evaluation. Thousands of innovations are thrust before them for acceptance or rejection. The town also has opened their eyes to denominationalism. Many of them have come from areas where there was little competition. They have insular perspectives, controlled by linguistic and cultural differences and possibly reinforced by denominationalism. It operates against the unification of the Solomons as a country and against the united witness of the Christian Church in the face of the materialism of the capital. Yet a real indigenous Church can emerge in this very type of situation, if it can free itself from paternal controls and be allowed to struggle for its selfhood.

The town is a loosely held agglomeration. It has not the social solidarity and structural cohesion of a village. Religion is no longer the integrator of society. If there is any integrator at all, it is the economic concept of 'work for wages'. Materialism and money usurp the place of religion. I have pointed out that the church communities comprise migrants from rural areas, but many migrants are lost altogether to the Church. Folk from dependent communities are not always able to stand alone when they reach the temptations of the town. So there is disequilibrium and change everywhere. The new class structure of Honiara is beginning to take shape on a thoroughly colonial pattern, but it could be subjected to a major social upheaval of a formative character before the pattern becomes stable. Times of migration and the emergence of towns are propitious for innovation. This means that religion itself comes up for re-evaluation—for reacceptance, for adjustment, or for rejection. The churches of Honiara are therefore faced with specific problems of advocacy. What do they offer or advocate in their programmes? Do they offer the same paternalistic patterns of the last generation missions, or is the programme modified? If modified, how is it modified? Is it 'modernized' to bring it into line with changes in the western patterns of the home church of the missionaries, or is the modification rooted in the soil of the Solomons? Is it still colonial with the white man running the affairs of the Church and making the decisions, or is it so geared that the missionaries could hand over entirely to an indigenous Church without injury? Who actually runs the age-group activities, the women's groups, the work projects? Who makes the announcements in church—the indigenous laymen and women, or the white missionary?

Times of migration from village to town, I have said, are propitious for innovation. The day which offers regular wages, materialism and escape from church-going to the young islander who migrates to town, also offers to the Church an opportunity to modify her advocacy and swing from paternalism to indigeneity. The urgency of the situation lies in the fact that almost every boat entering the port of Honiara from the other islands brings persons who will personally re-evaluate religion as they have known it—either for escape from it or loyalty to it

(ii) *Rural Roots in Urban Society*

The situation at Honiara, or Kukum, or on any large plantation, is very different from the emerging town or industrial area in western society. Despite its modern aspects, materialism, money, gambling, liquor, hours of labour, facility for spending and being entertained, and so on, the situation remains *a Solomon Island situation* and must not be appraised by western industrial criteria. It is just here that administrators, educationalists, social workers and missionaries can go wrong. It does not follow that an organization effective in New Zealand will be effective in the Solomons, or that a western health policy will be acceptable to the islanders. Neither does it follow that a young islander sent overseas to study youth work, social work, or some other branch of learning and practice, will be able to handle the island situation upon his return. The town and industrial situations in the islands are built up, as we have seen, by hundreds of individuals who have been plucked out of rural configurations. Some of them are second generation Christians and some are pagans.[6] For many of them the socio-religious background is a Christian–pagan co-existence. The issue of magic versus sorcery, the prestige of an accumulation of shell-money, the traditional method of obtaining a wife, together with the numerous ties and responsibilities within the kinship organization, are the big factors which still determine their principal decisions. This is another way in which the village is the key to the town rather than vice versa.

No one will deny that the town situation has features of its own not common to the rural area, and these have to be faced. However, it is often better to allow the indigenous leaders in the complex itself to evolve their own solutions, with just a little inconspicuous guidance, than to equate these situations with overseas 'counterparts', which on the surface seem to be similar because they are urban and industrial. These new features of the town are still innovations being advocated— not yet fully accepted. The really abiding features of the new town way of life may well turn out to be matters of rural orientation which the migrants have brought with them.

It is sometimes thought that an islander with an overseas education is a natural choice for handling a town or industrial situation. This does not necessarily follow. He may be the right man, but the overseas education may be the very thing that disqualifies him for the role. Every group has its natural leader. It may be more profitable to take the natural leader, with or without education, and give him opportunity to lead, the missionary keeping in the background.[7] Natural leadership and acceptance by the group is something overseas training cannot provide. It is easy to hold up growth by overlooking natural leaders because they do not measure up to required academic standards. This means that leadership is being determined by foreign rather than indigenous criteria. If new indigenous labour groups are emerging in urban and plantation situations, we may be quite certain that those groups will stabilize only as the natural leaders emerge. Writing of the rural region Clark said:

> Leaders exist in every community. To find, help and get out of the way of these is one of the best pieces of work to which missionaries can address themselves. Abundant proofs can be found of the capacity of

these leaders to do the work required. . . . The most difficult task before the missionary is perhaps to get out of the way. . . .

and again

To be able to distinguish natural leaders, to give them the fullest opportunity to lead, to encourage and support them in their leadership, is one of the chief services a missionary can render.[8]

The concentrations of labourers in the town and on the plantations are groups of villagers, not westerners, and they retain the orientation of the rural world from which they have migrated for at least one generation. Their children, born in the town, will present a different situation, but when they mature it is hoped that that generation will produce leaders from its own numbers. Any growing church should supply its own leadership, commensurate with its social and academic levels at any given point of time.[9] If a congregation fails to produce leaders, then the fault must lie with its own methods of organization for growth. I do not know any group of islanders in sport, labour or social life, in country or town, that has not sought out some natural leader around whom the group stabilizes itself. No church needs to be built round a missionary. The role of the missionary is to recognize the natural leader, open facilities to him and support him.

A good example of the power of a natural leader to consolidate a new situation may be seen in the village of Roroni in Guadalcanal. This village has social units from very different regions and people of three different denominations. Their social stability has been established round a natural leader, a strong personality who sees that each social segment, while maintaining its own domestic unit, does so in an orderly and tidy manner. The village is a credit to its purely indigenous leadership.[10] While it is true that every group does not produce a leader of this calibre, every group does produce a leader. This is a profound fact which assures any emerging group or church of indigenous capacity. With respect to the town situation, we need to realize that it is a composite pattern of emerging groups, each group with its natural leaders. The Church must seek out those leaders, win them if they are not Christian, and give them scope for leadership in spiritual matters, so that the groups that are forming may have Christian orientation. The criteria for selection of leaders will be indigenous, and missionaries must not try to force this in other directions. If the members of the group come from one cultural or linguistic region the rural criteria of that locality will most certainly apply in the choice of leaders. If it is a work group from different cultural and linguistic areas, the group may work out new criteria, but we can be certain they will have Melanesian rather than western dimensions. Here again the key to the town situation is in the rural areas.

But the folk in the town are more open for innovation than their relations back in the village, and in this respect the town is to some extent the key to innovation and experiment. Innovations that are acceptable in the town may be expected soon to be diffused throughout the country. I said, '*acceptable*'. It is not right to assume that things

M

advocated in the town will spread to the country; but if they are *accepted* by the rural migrants to the town we may anticipate diffusion. Here again there is a relation between town and country.[11] The fact that radical behaviour in the town (like marriage outside a kin pattern) brings a violent reaction when the news reaches the village, shows that migration to the town does not mean separation from ethnic responsibilities and perceptions. Furthermore, migration involves the town-dwellers in continuous hospitality obligations for any casual visitors from the village. In many ways a community of Solomon Islanders in the town is still essentially an island community. It may in time achieve a greater degree of education and sophistication but it will take more than one generation to change its basic orientation.

(iii) *Honiara 'Collective Man'*

Much of what has been written of rural work in this study is valid also for the town congregations. However, the town environment is certainly different, congregations are not ethnic units, are interracial, and worship may be in English. Social outworkings of the faith in service will certainly differ. In either case the Church must demonstrate that it is a community mediating Christ's programme to all within its reach in its own specific situation. In both cases Christ depends on the Church to win those who are not religiously committed to him. However, the two entirely different environments—one rural, subsistent and ethnic, the other urban, commercial and interracial—cause us to ask whether they require entirely different approaches and methods of evangelism. We may ask, for instance, if town-dwellers are now individualists who can be dealt with outside the group. This assumption is common among missionaries working in many cities. It has made some very lonely Christians. My experience is that the islander finds isolation difficult. Even though he never returns to his village, the ties hold fast. In the city he seeks out some other group, even though it be some loosely held sodality that meets for gambling in a Chinese café, some group to serve as a substitute for that which he knows he has lost by migrating to the town. For good or bad, he transfers his loyalties to this adopted group. Basically man is a gregarious creature and the Melanesian is no exception.

In bringing people to Christ, we are not asked to isolate them as individuals, but to see them incorporated into a group, a *fellowship*, as the apostle called it (1 John 1: 3). There is something to be said for winning groups whole, and this means winning also industrial groups for Christ, *as groups*—even in modern western society there is something to be said for this. The evangelist, Bryan Green, has raised this very point, asking whether the missionary experience of the winning of whole communities for Christ (which he admits removes many of the problems faced by the isolated convert) has not after all something to offer in respect of methods of evangelizing "the more sophisticated collective of the industrial man. Should the evangelistic approach here too," he asks, "be to win the group over into baptism, and then individuals into personal conversion?"[12] He leaves the question unanswered. I react in two ways to this suggestion. He does not allow for the fact that these great movements require a period of (to use his own term) *pre-evangelism*, which brings the individuals who comprise the group to unanimity and thus permits the *manifest* collective action. However, he certainly had a point in finding some similarity between the two *collective man* situations. Both groups will have a cohesion derived from structure, loyalties and leadership, from which both security and satisfactions are derived. In one case they are based on personal qualities alone, and in the other cultural and kin factors may also be involved. Nevertheless they are similarly structured. In the case of the groups in Honiara and on the Solomon Island plantations, the labour having been gathered from communal societies, the solidarity of the group is more or less assumed. The labourer expects that there will be a cohesive group, and even if it be a purely work group he transfers his normal loyalties to the new group. The ties are less strong in that he knows he can break with them at will, but as long as he remains with the group he submits to its cohesive discipline.

For residence he will attach himself to a household that has previously migrated to the town from his own island and there he remains within the kin cohesion. Thus he compartmentalizes his life and divides his time between a work sodality and a kin unit. He finds no difficulty in being loyal to both, because he lives one life at a time. He thinks of both collectively and acts with the group after having had his say in the discussions that ultimately determine the group action.

It is therefore hoped that the role of the group will not be overlooked by the Church as it deals with the migrants to the town. The fact that islanders have demonstrated a readiness to transfer loyalty to a town group which offers leadership, cohesion and satisfaction, surely offers opportunity to bring the pagan migrants into a Christian experience in the town. Can they be brought to see in the Christian fellowship such a group as meets their needs? There are certainly opportunities for church growth on the plantations and in the town.

On the other hand, this dualism of loyalty to work group and kin group may well cut across the Christian connections. What happens when a young Christian takes up residence with pagan relations, or works with a group that is purely materialistic?

In Honiara the growth or non-growth of the Church lies with the congregations themselves. If the indigenous Christians set out to win others and to incorporate them into the group, there are certainly opportunities for growth. If, on the other hand, the Christian groups are enclosed, and if the Christians in the social and industrial groups do not stir themselves into action, the town has overwhelming dangers and the ever-increasing migration to the town will usually mean secularization. So once again, as we found in the village studies, the emphasis falls on the role of the local congregation. Can the Church in the town become a self-propagating community? The door is certainly open if Christian migrants retain their allegiance and town Christians have the *will* to evangelize. A foreign mission has little hope; an indigenous Church has great opportunity.

(iv) *Diffusion of Religion and Morals*

In the earlier units of this report we saw that much of the magico-religion and sorcery of Roviana and Simbo had been imported from Ysabel, Vella Lavella and Choiseul. Hogbin reported that the Kaoka people of Guadalcanal, with whom he lived, had also imported much from outside, from Florida, Marau and San Cristoval. In our study of the nativistic movements we saw how Pokokoqoro obtained his *samuka* from Malaita, and how Marching Rule borrowed some of its ideals and methods from the Chair and Rule Movement. In connection with the latter we saw something of its inter-island communication. Within historic times, no matter how strongly these islands have fought to retain their independent entities, there has nevertheless been a widespread diffusion of indigenous concepts, both religious and political. The medium of such diffusion was once the head-hunting and slavery configuration. In more recent days the instrument of diffusion of political ideas has usually been the labour system, either for commerce or for war.

Since the disappearance of the head-hunting and slavery complex, the diffusion of magico-religion and sorcery has been transferred to the labour system of recruitment and employment. As long as labour recruitment is pursued among the pagan communities, the purely *nominal* Christians (and a large percentage of nominals are interested in the proposition of labour for wages), who live and work with them in the labour concentrations on plantations and in towns, will be tempted to explore again the lost mysteries of their ancestors.

If the majority of labourers recruited were *nuclear* Christians, the diffusion of religion would no doubt be a more healthy one in the opposite direction. We seem to have here a kind of spiritual 'osmosis'— a nuclear Christian tends to draw the pagan to conversion; but in the case of a mere nominal the attraction is reversed, as the root draws water into itself, or has its water withdrawn if the salts outside are too strong.

Christian witness in the labour concentrations is further weakened by its denominational division. It lacks a united front and is therefore inclined to be argumentative and is confusing to the pagan who might be attracted to it otherwise. It is difficult to suggest a solution for this problem. To encourage the enlistment of nuclear Christians, or even to present the plantation as an opportunity for evangelism would hardly meet the need, for denominationalism would continue and the village congregations would be considerably weakened. The only real solution is a drive to reduce the number of marginal and nominal Christians in the villages, so that whoever signs on for labour, his witness will be true. Time after time we are brought back to this fundamental issue— the need for deepening the spiritual life of the local congregations.

The important fact that we have established is that Honiara and the smaller towns, and also the plantations, are the 'clearing-houses' for trade in all kinds of magico-religious formulae and rites, for sorcery and for sexual experiments. The origin is back in the still pagan villages. The market exists because of the marginality and nominality of many of the Christians who sign up as labour. If the town and plantation patterns are new, the patterns of the magico-religious trade are survivals from the past. The only safe cure I can see is a revival of true religion in the second-generation Christian villages which supply labour for these concentrations.

Hogbin, the anthropologist, found the plantations a focal point for the increase of homosexual practices. He correctly pointed out that there was no standard sex pattern for the young man of the Solomon Islands, that each locality had its own peculiar moral orientation. To take three adjacent islands as examples. There was chastity in Malaita (which accounts for their hostile reactions to a sex offence), considerable freedom in San Cristoval, and instituted prostitution in Guadalcanal. When labourers from such different orientations meet and live together for a prolonged period, there is naturally some resultant cross-fertilization of ideas. One of these effects has been a lessening of sex controls when a group of young Malaita-men return home from service.[13] This is deeply resented at home and often leads to bloodshed. The problem of welding the Solomon Islands into a political and social entity is an extremely complex one.

(v) *Analysis of Marginality*

For some time there has been an awareness in Sociology of Religion of the problem of marginality. Among the numerous research projects in this matter, one Roman Catholic study known as the *Southern Parish* seems to offer something for setting over against the Honiara situation.[14] The community investigated was analysed in four categories, which the sociologist, Fichter, has called, *nuclear* (active participants and faithful believers), *modal* (normal practising Roman Catholics), *marginal* (conforming to a bare arbitrary minimum of expected patterns) and *dormant* (those who had given up Catholicism but had not joined any other denomination). The study was scientifically computed on a basis of specific questions and answers in three southern urban localities for persons over the age of seven years, who numbered 14,838 baptized people. Of these, 5,786 were recorded as *dormant* and were eliminated from the study. Of the 9,052 remaining, 11 per cent were recorded as nuclear, 68 per cent modal and 21 per cent marginal. To include the dormant as I have done in my piety curves for Rarumana and Fouia ("E"), rough computation would give us the following percentages:

nuclear	7
modal	42
marginal	12
dormant	39
	100%[15]

In spite of the important facts that these figures are Roman Catholic and not Protestant, western and not Oceanic, urban and not rural, yet they present some similar features. From my personal observations (but without any statistical analysis), I imagine this would approximate fairly closely to the overall strength and weakness of collective Christianity in Honiara. When we study constituencies whole, i.e. including my nominals or Fichter's dormants, it would seem that bi-modal curves are a feature of our age. Fichter is right in focusing on the marginals, for these are the most unstable category. They are still in the Church but have negative attitudes to religious obligation and are the most vulnerable.

This sociologist put forward four generalizations as reasons for the instability of this segment of marginals. He admitted these factors work on all Catholics, but that the effect was least on the nuclear and increased as it moved to the dormant end of the scale.

The first he calls *contrasting assumptions*, the problem of reconciling patterns of conduct with religious values that are contradictory. The second is a *relative morality*, acceptance of the idea that the Church's position is right, but that it does not allow for 'my' particular case. God, of course, would understand 'my' special circumstances. The third is *anti-authoritarianism*, because of the ideal of personal independence. The fourth is the *dysfunctional parish*, the fact that the social structure and values of urban society have interfered with the parish as a *community of persons*.[16] These are important insights and are not confined to Roman Catholics or to western society. In these respects the urban life of Honiara has similarities with urban life of the west. I do not think they exhaust the kinds of pressure felt by Christians in urban society, nor do I think that ours is the first generation to have felt them, but they are useful concepts for self-examination and offer a suitable frame of reference for studying the problem of marginality. They could be used by missionaries who minister within the Honiara environment, as a tool for analysing their situation.

It must be pointed out that these are general principles. The mode of their outworkings will differ in each type of urban society. For the Melanesians in Honiara we must remember that they are migrants from communal units—different types of communal units, with different patterns of authority, status, prestige and responsibility. They come from subsistence economy into a western money economy, from technological specialization for exchange trade into labour for a foreigner for weekly wages. They come from a society in which they had the choice between paganism and one form of Christianity to a confrontation with a host of Christian denominations, on one hand, and agnosticism and materialism on the other. These are all new experiences. Fichter's generalizations may be applied to any urban society, but where an urban community is emerging because of migration from communal villages, each one of those generalizations is immensely complicated by the factor of *acculturation*.

However, it is one thing to discover the reasons for marginality and the drift of marginals into nominality, and it is quite another thing to discover how to deal with it. We know the process goes on. We know that any form of migration permits people to slip from the marginal status to the nominal or dormant almost unnoticed—what missionary Miller of Korea used to call the problem of *shrinkage* in church membership. Perhaps methods and approaches can be modified to keep in step with the changes on the cultural scene, but in the final analysis it comes back to a matter of personal decision and the acceptance of a relevant faith for life. Each generation in the Church has to come to this for itself. Is the Church to modify itself to fit the changing environment, or is it to press its own claims as a factor causing change in the environment? Is the Church to adjust itself to new secular values, or is it to strive to ensure that the new values have spiritual dimensions? Can the encounter with the world ever be avoided? Why must Christian relevance be found *within* the secular world, unless for the very purpose of winning that world?

To classify marginals into categories should tell us much about why they are marginals; but nothing other than direct confrontation with Christ will bring the transformation which the Church must continually strive to achieve.

The Church's problem in Honiara and the plantations has been accentuated by the fact that the labourers have not constituted a representative cross-section of village Christian community, but have largely comprised marginals and nominals. The character and standards of such groups do not line up with those of the villages. A great many indeed just stop going to church at all. The only effective counter to this lies with the better type of migrant who does link up with the Church in town—he should be impressed with the urgency of being a missionary to his own marginals and nominals.

PLANTATION CHRISTIANITY

At many points in this report the plantation and town have been mentioned together because the two situations have much in common. They are both artificial situations, they both draw from all Christian denominations as well as pagan communities, they are the two types of community where the greatest amount of cross-fertilization of culture takes place, and they are the places where the Melanesians are experimenting with new ideas, both foreign and neo-pagan. I am not speaking of mission plantations, which have different controls, and I confess that I was unable to do more than pay a visit to a non-mission plantation. But this aspect of Solomon Island life cannot possibly be omitted from this survey. I am indebted to Robert H. Black for the factual and statistical material in this unit. He has discussed Christianity's role in such a plantation and published his findings in an important article.[17] I use his data, but do not hold him responsible for the manner in which I use it.

These observations were recorded in the Russell Islands between New Georgia and Guadalcanal, where people from five different Christian denominations are employed, together with a number of heathen. From among these, nine Solomon Islanders were regarded as *élite* by the plantation management. These were recorded as Church of England (3), South Seas Evangelical Mission (2), Seventh Day Adventist (2), Roman Catholic (1) and heathen (1). The other Christian denomination was Methodist, whose people Black described as quiet, keeping to themselves, and recognizable by the fact that they used bed-sheets, pillows and pillow-cases! One of the Church of England *élite* was the Assistant Medical Officer (A.M.O.), a lay reader in the Church. Another of the *élite* was the official Seventh Day representative for the area. The A.M.O. worked with six dressers, three of his own denomination and three Adventists, though his native language was different from that spoken by each of the others.

The residential households were not all established on the same basis, which might be religious, linguistic or occupational. One case is recorded of nine Anglicans living together. They all came from the eastern islands but represented three different language groups and five different occupations. In the next house, however, the basis was occupational, the inmates comprising fourteen carpenters, twelve of whom were Church of England, but among them they spoke five different languages.

The men of the cattle scheme were supposedly the 'misfits'— twenty-eight in all, twenty of whom were Roman Catholics under a spiritual leader who ran a few 'side-lines' like 'rain-making' and 'curing the sick'. As a group they spoke seven different languages. The European management had excluded the one Jehovah's Witness, to prevent industrial strife.

In sport, the local football team comprised ten Anglicans, one Evangelical, one Adventist and two Roman Catholics. They were all from Malaita, but from three different linguistic areas. When they met the Yandina Police, they were confronted by a team of seven Anglicans, two Evangelicals, one Methodist and some Polynesians. The Melanesians were from nine language areas. The Church of England weightage may be accounted for by the instruction given in football in Anglican schools.

One is not surprised at this denominational mixture, which Black reports, having seen the Russell Island recruiters at work in Malaita, going from one locality to another. Let me reiterate that this denominational mixture, however, is only one element of the complex, which is also occupational, regional, linguistic and customary. We must not overlook the fact that these areas have widely different traditional behaviour.

Sometimes a cross-linguistic quarrel within one denomination could cause a whole segment to change its denomination. It was such a quarrel which permitted the entrance of Adventists into Ysabel. Labour from Marovo was mainly Adventist, and their choir competed keenly with the Malaita Anglicans at Christmas time; but the former would not incorporate any Malaita Adventists, nor did any Melanesian Adventist group receive or fraternize with their Bellona co-religionists. These observations of Black line up with much of my own material collected in other places. Regional sub-structural entity is strong and is a hindrance to the unification of the Protectorate in many ways.

Church attendance is noticeably highest at Christmas and Easter, and for weddings and for the re-incorporation rites for women after child-birth, when feasts are held. All this suggests a strong representation of Christian marginals and nominals on the plantations.

Black took a check on a sample of fifty marriages—fifteen of them were cross-linguistic, but nine were in the same denomination. It was noticeable, however, that there were no cross-denominational marriages from the same linguistic area; this rather suggests that such people living so far from home are yet not beyond the perspectives and tensions of their home community. Although the plantation offers every opportunity for escaping these restrictions, once again the village feeling is the key to the plantation behaviour.

Up to this point we have been concerned with the encounter of Christians of different denominations and linguistic groups. Now what of the Christian-heathen engagement? Many disputes arise, but mostly they are caused by the failure of Christians to observe heathen taboos. This especially applies to Christian women who ignore the fact that heathen people have made certain localities sacred for the purpose of pagan rites. The Christians no longer fear them and therefore it is easy for them to be 'polluted' by the women. However, although the labourers from the Christianized areas consider themselves Christian, the form of their Christian practice can at times be somewhat syncretistic. They are certainly open to experiment in heathen magical rites and customs.

The Adventist member of the *élite* took a woman of his own denomination to live with him, trying to pass it off as a *custom marriage*. Only a "barrage of persuasion" led him to marry the woman before the child was born. The younger men will laugh at 'rain-making', but "the mention of *vele*", says Black, "brings a sudden hush". Except for the very old men the old clan totems have been well-nigh forgotten among the Christians, but there are surviving elements, such as people believing they will become ill by eating certain animal foods. There is still a widespread fear of sorcery, apparently with some justification.

The explanation is not far to seek. The *élite* and those who are advancing along the road to economic prosperity are mainly Christians. They have had some education, and understand better some of the traps of the western money economy, and particularly its temptations. The heathen recognize this manifest superiority, and have no way of holding their own in this competitive world except by magical means. It is to be noted that the speeding up of economic opportunity for individual success since the war has been accompanied by an increase of sorcery.

What is of the greatest significance to us in this report is how the Christian deals with this. The A.M.O. reported that many cases were brought to him too late, after *customary* cures had been tried and failed. One "custom sickness foreman" is a carpenter by trade, married to an Anglican woman of another linguistic group, and he himself goes to church and reads his Bible. He has his own classification of disease: (*a*) that which can be cured by the white man's medicine, and (*b*) custom-sickness, about which the white man knows nothing. This requires a protective procedure to counter the sorcery, certain vegetable concoctions, manipulations and ritual prayers. With these he also makes use of the Lord's Prayer and a Christian collect. This is a syncretism of Christianity and the ancient protective magic, and the form in which Christo-paganism is currently spread through the Solomons by the Christian marginals and nominals. This also shows that the present generation has not been brought face to face with the Christ, who said, "All power is given unto me". The fathers of many of these so-called Christians had this experience, but somehow the churches have not transmitted it effectively to the second generation.

As I see the plantation situation, we are confronted with a clear complex, involving the interaction of three parties—progressive individuals, heathen, and Christo-pagan curers. The former are the subject of the envy of the heathen, who maintain their own prestige by hostile magic or sorcery. The progressive individuals have acquired some degree of wealth, and because of their ability to pay they are subject to exploitation by the Christo-pagan curers, who deal with the custom-sickness by counter-magic. This complex shows a thoroughly pre-Christian economic and status structure, and is still another example of how the village provides the key to the plantation. The complex may be schematized thus:

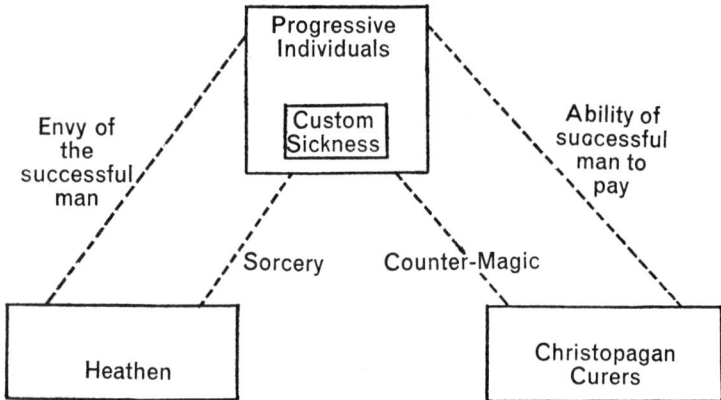

This is the pagan magico-economic configuration, with the Christopagan curer being substituted for the priest of the ancestral ghost. A progressive chief always had to establish himself by merit and to maintain his position against his rivals. He usually did this by falling back on counter-magic, worked by another party. With the re-establishment of this pattern, much of the fear and tension has returned, perhaps to a lesser degree than in pagan times, but none the less real. The Church needs to watch this situation, lest it find itself exchanging one form of animism for another.

On the other hand, plantation Christianity seems to be largely marginal and therefore not typical in the sense of being representative.

What it does reveal, however, is what happens to a marginal island-Christian when he falls from grace. He does not tend to become materialist or agnostic, but to drift back into a modified animism—a syncretism of animistic concepts and Christian forms. Because of this the battle for quality growth must be unceasing.

CONCLUSION

Solomon Islands Christianity

The use of the term *the Solomon Island situation* was questioned at the outset. The pattern—if it has a pattern—is complex. Its many local units all have their configurations and can be analysed, but one hesitates to describe anything as *Solomon Island*. The awareness of the Solomon Islands entity is imperfectly developed. A man is a Malaita man rather than a Solomon Islander—indeed he may even prefer to think of himself as of Sa'a or Tai than of Malaita.

In addition to this geographical segmentation we have met with linguistic and cultural entities of widely divergent patterns. Christian denominationalism has imposed still another form of segmentation on the situation. Mission and political boundaries have separated areas of long-standing ethnic contact and have brought together other areas of no cultural or linguistic affinity. All this complicates the subject before us—Solomon Islands Christianity: a study in growth and obstruction.

Mission Achievements

If Solomon Islands Christianity is hard to define and analyse, there can be no doubt of its existence, because of the impact it has made. Christianity has brought about great changes and the lot of the people is infinitely superior to that of their forefathers. The missions have done much constructive and effective work and Christianity has enjoyed considerable growth. It would be easy in a critical and problem-orientated study of this kind to create the impression that the missions had failed. This would be unfortunate and untrue.

If one recalls the study of the head-hunting and slavery configuration, the analysis of a pre-Christian feud, which documented some twenty odd retaliations, and the statement on ceremonial inhumanity, no further argument will be needed to show that the missions have brought these people out of a vicious way of life. Both the foreign missionaries and the indigenous agents of the Church have distinguished themselves in courage and devotion to their Christian call. The personal failures among them have been very few indeed. As I look back over what has been written, I realize I could have written more about them, but they have been remembered in the writings of the missionaries—Fox, Armstrong, Hopkins, Nicholson, Rycroft, Codrington, Luxton and others. This is a critical survey by its terms of reference. This does not mean that I am either unaware of or unappreciative of the splendid work that has been and is being done.

346

The Growth of the Church

The most effective aspect of the work done has been seen in what I have called *conversion growth* from paganism, although this has not been confined to any one pattern, either in the east or in the west. However the missions have not been nearly as effective in bringing the second generation of Christians face to face with Christ, and this is a basic weakness reflected in the current situation.

In some areas there has been good *quality growth*, but this also is uneven. The best quality growth has been mostly manifested on isolated stations, i.e. in artificial situations. Village Christianity lags badly.

The *organic growth* of a Solomon Island Church has been slow—especially so in the west. The Melanesian Mission, after a century of devoted effort, has produced an indigenous clergy in the east. The Methodist ministry is only beginning to emerge. The concept of local stewardship is poorly developed in all the Solomons, with the possible exception of Ysabel. The people in many localities have convinced themselves of the rightness of mission paternalism and expect the missions to nurse them rather than that they should act for themselves. On the other hand, in other areas there has been a reaction against this. The high financial commitments of the missions for education, medicine and shipping involve huge sums of foreign money and are out of all proportion. The readiness of the Administration to accept this situation and allow for it in Five-year Plans in White Papers reflects the instability of the whole economy of the Protectorate. It may be that this major expenditure of mission resources is for the immediate good of the country at large, but I fail to see how it can do anything but perpetuate paternalism and hinder the emergence of indigeneity, whether social, economic or religious. Clearly the economic and social involvements of missions in the Solomons have obstructed the organic growth of the Church.

Theoretical Problems

A number of matters were grouped together because of their more or less theoretical nature. The reader may disagree with the position taken by the writer, but each one is relevant and warrants serious examination. Some of them are matters of attitude and others are of practical urgency. The Solomons are too slow in emerging from the pre-war static thinking into the dynamic post-war world. Many of the missionaries are aware of the importance of change but are unable to transmit their changed thinking to the local situations. This is not their fault. After all, the innovations are determined not by the advocates (missionaries) but by the acceptors (local people). The local people are often the victims of decades of mission paternalism. However, paternalism still does exist in high places. The Melanesian capacity for organization is still doubted, despite evidence to the contrary. Solomon Island Christianity is still a missions situation rather than that of a Young Church. Changing terminology will not create a Church without the acceptance of the idea at the village level.

Missionary attitudes to cross-cultural situations have varied greatly through the years. Some have manifested deep understanding of island life and thought, but others, through their western outlook, have caused both misunderstandings and cultural losses. The voids so created have caused many of the nationalist and neo-pagan clashes of recent times. Basically the Melanesian situation has always been one of *encounter*. It is through encounter leading to victory that confidence and the sense of security are achieved. This life orientation has to be won for Christ in terms of the victory of *exousia* over the *dunamis* of the enemy (Luke 10: 19). The basic problem for second-generation Christians is that for so many there has been no face to face encounter with sin, no personal experience of victory in Christ.[1] So much of the situation in the Solomons comes back to this fact—the need for a revitalization within the village congregations.

Education and medicine need careful investigation. Their centralized institutionalism is too top-heavy to allow the emergence of the Church. They are foreign and dependent on foreign funds. One wonders whether these institutions exist to 'minister' or to be 'ministered to'. Criteria for testing their validity have been suggested in Chapter 8. This is only a suggestion. It is, however, of great importance that some criteria be established and the whole pattern be tested.

The role of education within the Church (as distinct from the role of the Church in education) needs a great deal of development. This should be done within the structure and perceptions of the Melanesian way of life, not foreign innovations. I do not think that a Church will emerge by attempts to identify it with foreign home–church organizational patterns. Something active needs to be provided for each age-group in the local congregation, and especially is something needed to pilot teen-agers into a maturer appreciation of the fellowship itself.

The scars of culture contact are still evident. It is high time that European conversation abandoned the terminology and attitudes of colonialism. This is necessary for the good of both the Church and the Protectorate. Progress is also delayed by the absence of any organ for vocal expression of critical opinion on public issues. New concepts of justice for the Melanesian badly need development. The point to be considered is perhaps to what extent should the Church *actively* set out to correct these evidences of the survival of pre-war static thinking and colonialism?

The Melanesian Way of Life

The unit on anthropological dimensions was limited to six elements. It could have been much longer. These are not to be generalized. Each is a specific study of one theme in one locality, deliberately selected from different regions in order to distribute the research. Five of these deal with the island *way of life*—the transmission and control of authority, socio-religious interrelations, village structure and the place of the church, the exchange economy, and the loss and restoration of social cohesion (all of which are still relevant for an understanding of island life); the sixth is a study of head-hunting and slavery and the analysis of a feud (which show the changes made in island life by the acceptance of Christianity). Any of these studies may be taken as an entity by itself, but cumulatively their presence in this research was demanded by my terms of reference: what does it mean to be a Solomon Island Christian? They illuminate the difference between cross-cultural situations and the evangelistic and pastoral ministry in western culture. They indicate why every missionary, especially pioneering missionaries, should be trained in anthropology.

Nationalist and Neo-pagan Movements

The comparative analysis of nativistic movements in the Solomons should warn us against imagining that all such movements are identical, despite their many common points. Each must be appraised on its own merits. The study of Etoism was a special aspect set before me for investigation. I hope that my criticisms will not be regarded as unkind. As David Paton said of his critical analysis of the situation in China:

When a disaster has occurred, nothing is really wise, or even kind, save ruthless examination of the causes.[2]

The section devoted to this has its own set of conclusions and these are offered to the Methodists in terms of Methodist belief and practice, partly because they have to deal with the problem and partly because Wesley figured so prominently in Eto's personal claims. Unlike the Marching Rule, Etoism is found to be a religious movement.

Theological Dimensions

Many of the problems of Solomon Islands Christianity have theological roots. Some attempt was made to measure these dimensions in the village congregation by hymn selection sampling, Scripture reading selection and piety curves for church attendance, an Anglican and a Methodist village having been selected for the purpose. None of these tests stands alone, but each is in itself a measurable part of the total village religious situation. The various tests were found to reinforce each other in numerous ways and I consider their cumulative evidence more important than the mere sum of the units. They show the doctrinal strengths and weaknesses in both situations, have a good comparative value, and, I think, offer a methodology which could be used by missionaries to test their own situations.

The chapters which cover this aspect of the study show that the denominations have much both to give to and to learn from each other. They also show the formative importance of hymn and scripture translation, and the need for a planned programme in this direction, and the danger of the evolution of a collection of hymns and scripture passages without any total theological structuring, and the importance of getting the whole Bible into the vernacular as soon as possible.

Christian–pagan Co-existence

One of the serious problems of the Eastern Solomons is the manner in which many local congregations have settled down to a state of Christian–pagan co-existence at home, while they satisfy their missionary urge by enthusiastically supporting in prayer the work of missions further afield. This strange anomaly is a side-stepping of responsibility, for not only is it to see the distant opportunity and to be blind to the local one, but it is to assign the confrontation to the Brothers and to confine themselves to prayer. This is an unfortunate compartmentaliza-tion which divides the totality of the Christian personality. While it is true that the members of the Church, or Body, have not all the same office, and the *Brotherhood* and the *Companions* do represent function-ally two different organs, yet the missionary Brothers dare not neglect their prayer life, and the praying Companions ought also to be missionaries to the unconverted at their door.

Marginal–Nominal Drift

The drift from marginality to nominality in the second-generation churches is a matter for urgent attention. This drift, which was detected statistically in the piety curves, is not without evidence in spiritual matters, according to the testimony of many informants. Quite often the village congregations have settled down to a state of being led by the mission agent, a pastor-teacher or catechist, who supplies all their needs and around whom the church organization and worship gathers. He is central and is the symbol of the missionary above him, who is in turn symbol of the mission. This state operates against wide participant interaction in the local congregation and tends to reinforce the basic paternalism. Instead of local leaders being stimulated by the local needs, they would ask the mission for "an additional teacher" if the need was pointed out. Interest within the congregation flags. While the small core of nuclear Christians remains loyal, the drift of the less conspicuous members moves from average to marginal and eventually to nominal only. Some educational and evangelistic programme of revitalization within the village congrega-tions is urgently needed to counter the boredom which is behind the drift.

Christo-paganism

The main centres for the diffusion. of Christo-paganism—i.e. a neo-pagan syncretism of pagan magical beliefs with some Christian forms—are the plantation situations. The Christians who are found in these locations are mostly from the marginal and nominal groups. Their lack of Christian depth means they are not well equipped to stand firm in confrontation with their pagan fellow-labourers. They tend to resort to pre-Christian solutions for their problems, especially the problem of sorcery. Some of these nominals set up as 'curers'. The more educated and more prosperous of them, the victims of the pagan sorcery, acquiesce in the general pattern by employing the Christo-pagan curers. The situation calls for a first-generation type of evangel-ism, by encounter with "the Name high over all", before whom "devils fear and fly". As the plantations provide every facility for the diffusion of ideas and for the trade in magical rites and concoctions, the spread of Christo-paganism is considerable. This is another reason why the

Church should not rest until she has cleaned up all those pagan pockets in Malaita and Guadalcanal. It is also apparent that a reduction of marginals and nominals in the villages would lead to a better type of Christian labourer.

Urban 'Collective Man'

Honiara is a post-war town. The cross-fertilization of culture is considerable, pressure groups are active, and Christians are brought together with pagan and materialistic concepts. The town and its environs represent a conglomeration of small residential entities, the key (for the greater part) being mostly back in the villages from which they migrate. They are served by missionaries or chaplains, the majority of whom are Europeans. Mission churches in the town are active and many folk from very many widely scattered areas do go to church. Many more, however, do not go at all, although if challenged they would claim to be Christians. Attempts to enter the *collective man* situations in the industrial areas need to make allowance for the emerging cultural structures of these new entities. Hitherto they have been on the old denominational lines. I see no hope for this policy. Denominationalism is being sorely tested in Honiara, but even the Baha'i which aims specially at winning those who seek unity in religion, is itself only yet another divisive unit within an already divided situation. Meantime pagan ideas, especially sorcery, protective counter-magic and medicinal concoctions are all *commodities* traded in the town and widely diffused like many of the unfortunate innovations brought by the white foreigner.

In this situation the Church has an opportunity. It is perhaps here that missionary leadership can be felt in the face of secular pressures, but the greatest opportunities lie with the town congregations themselves, to win their pagan and nominal countrymen to a vital experience. An urban situation which facilitates the diffusion of neo-paganism is also winnable by Christian evangelism, because they are just opposite answers to the same psychological conditions.

Denominationalism

It must be admitted that, to people who have become as mobile as these islanders, denominationalism is a personal problem and a hindrance to their Christian witness. When they came to Christianity in their different localities, they obtained a clear faith which spoke with authority to them against the pagan way of life. Now they are confronted by confusion. The Christian way is uncertain and debated. This does not help the stand against paganism and secularism. Secularism in the Solomons comes in a subtle guise today, in terms of commercial prosperity and things that are only just within the law. These times call for a united Christian witness.

I am not advocating *organic union*, which calls for years of fraternal discussion, congregational education, and examination of union in other parts of the world, in order to relate them to the local situation, and especially with other movements and discussions in other parts of

Melanesia. Much groundwork would have to be done for any meaningful organic union. Nevertheless there ought to be stresses on the essential *unity* of the Churches and some practical demonstrations of the fact that they are spiritually of one faith. If they serve the same Lord and stand on the same norm of Scripture, they ought to say so and demonstrate it. There ought to be active co-operation and congregational inter-communion.

Revitalization of Local Congregations

The one thing which cries aloud from every chapter of this survey is that Christianity of the second and third generations certainly needs an experience of renewal and revitalization, but though this may indeed be helped or hindered by mission policy and missionary attitudes, the renewal itself must take place *on the village congregational level*. It is there that men and women have to be brought face to face with Christ, where fellowship must be developed, and facilities for better participation explored by every age-group. It is within the village situation that the congregation must emerge as *the Church* in that locality. It is at this 'grass-roots' level that the drift from marginality to nominality among second-generation Christians must be stopped, and where Christians must work out their own personal obligations to the Great Commission, in the face of current Christian–pagan co-existence. The key to the Christo-paganism and morality of the plantation and the town lies here in the village congregation, which supplies the majority of the migrating people from among its marginal and nominal elements. I do not mean that the plantation and town situations are of secondary importance. As centres of diffusion they are of tremendous importance. Nevertheless, we underrate this very factor if we fail to allow for the truth that marginals and nominals, when isolated from the nuclear core of a congregation, are disposed to compromise with aggressive paganism. The diffusion from these plantation and town situations is therefore dominantly pagan. With a revitalization of village congregations, the character of this diffusion might well be reversed.

Clearly, then, the battle must be won in the local village congregation. Spiritual reform cannot be imposed from without, least of all by legislation. Only a numerical reduction of marginals and nominals, and a corresponding increase of nuclear Christians, in these new collective situations can effectively deal with paganism—and this calls for revival in the village churches from which the labourers are recruited.

Perceptions of a young Church growing organically also must be developed at this level. It is here that people have to overcome their inhibitions due to a belief that they are under the 'wing' of the Mission. Here they must discover the local situation as their own confrontation with the world and their opportunity as *the Church*. Here the local congregation must also discover its responsibility for cultivating its own *quality growth*, and for finding within its own membership such individuals as the situation demands. It is here at the level of the local congregation that a Church grows—or where its growth is obstructed.

NOTES

INTRODUCTION

1. Goldie: "Chairman's Report", 1945–46.
2. Politically, Buin and Bougainville belong to the Australian Trust Territory of Papua and New Guinea, but it is impossible to separate their missionary history or their cultural and economic connections from those of the Western Solomons.
3. The resettlement of non-Melanesians in Melanesian areas is receiving considerable attention from American anthropologists. A church survey by a Polynesian or Micronesian scholar should be valuable.
4. I received an official letter asking me to enter none of their churches. The President of this Church was touring at the time and lecturing on "Why we cannot join with the W.C.C." (Reported in *Not In Vain*.)
5. *Synod Proceedings, p.* 16.

CHAPTER 1. PRE-CHRISTIAN RELIGION

1. Goldie wrote impersonally of this deity and gave no name, yet the name Bañara was well known to him, for he selected it for use as 'Lord' in Scripture. The same name, however, was used for the village sub-group head-man. The concept of a 'retired' deity still survives. (Goldie: 1908, p. 30.)
2. Oliver (1955, p. 42) says this is a "transparent Christian innovation", because the people have no sky concept. It is possible that in the process of time the myth has borrowed from Christianity, but I find it difficult to imagine an Oceanic people without a sky concept. Oliver may be right but this is surprising.
3. A good leader among the Siwai, according to Oliver (ibid., pp. 43–44), is more concerned with his own strong personal demon (*horomorum*). These folk think of spirits in general as dangerous and of ghosts as fickle. Success depends on the personal demon, and these are more relevant in daily life than the creator gods of the origin myths.
4. I am treating *mana* as a universal in this study, although I know there are areas where it does not exist as a word (Hogbin: 1936). Capell says the concept is found even though some other word be used (1938, p. 93). Many terms show a common origin—*mamana'a, mena, mamana, namana* and *nanamanga*—to name some from our area of study. But I found the word *mana* understood everywhere I went. The ceremonial use in invocations and such concepts as the building up of reserves of *mana* as power for magical purposes were widespread. In some Christianized areas the word has passed into Christianity to supply the complexes of thought-forms for *power* and *blessing*. In Roviana, the translator of the hymn "Holy! Holy! Holy!" chose to use this word, *Mana!* As an adjective it now means *potent* or *effectual*, as a noun (with an infix) *minana* it currently means *blessing*, and with a prefix *ta* we have *blessed* (*tamanai*) for which there is also a noun form, *tinamanai*. Melanesian religion, as Codrington pointed out (1891), involved a man in acquiring *mana* for himself or in getting it used for his benefit. The theory of *mana* was developed by Marett (1909), largely based on material supplied by Codrington from the area of our present study.
5. Williamson: 1914, pp. 71–72.
6. Forde: 1948, p. 203.
7. Tippett: 1960, pp. 416–17. Another aspect of this problem has been raised by Welbourn (1963), where we are confronted with the hypothesis that as long as the patient believes in ghosts and witchcraft, the doctor has to make the same assumption.

354 SOLOMON ISLANDS CHRISTIANITY

8. Some missionaries fail to recognize this positive side of animism. They see every man for himself, and every neighbour as his enemy. His acquisition of *mana* is always for his individualist ends. This is very much less than a half-truth and partly explains the individualism of many mission conversions—station conversions as distinct from communal conversions.
9. Words which have the dual meaning include *urar* (Bougainville), *adaro* (San Cristoval), *akalo* and *agalo* (Malaita) and *tindalo* (Florida). However, Bogesi (1948: p. 327) says that at Ysabel *tidatho* were spirits and ghosts were *tarunga*.
10. *pinari, tatapiok, turkis, kirin, kakamora*, etc.
11. Raucaz: 1928, pp. 64–65.
12. Confirmed with much wider documentation by Moss: 1925.
13. B. Gina.
14. These were described and illustrated in *Man* v. 4, pp. 129–31, together with a Roviana mortuary hut. In both cases the ghost of the ancestor is said to inhabit the skull.
15. *The Open Door* xvi, Leadley: 1937.
16. Even so, there are many accounts of cannibal feasts left by early travellers. Sometimes as many as twenty bodies were dressed whole (Guppy: 1887 pp. 35–39). The experiences of Father Verguet leave little room for doubt that cannibalism was enjoyed for its own sake, and this by persons of all ages (Piolet: 1902 pp. 347–48).
17. Hopkins: 1928, p. 203.
18. Piolet: 1902, p. 347.
19. Raucaz: 1928, pp 64–65. The abode of ghosts from Gela, Bugotu and Savo, however, was a different place altogether—Moumolo (Bogesi: 1948, p. 209).
20. Raucaz: 1928, p. 59.
21. Parrinder: 1958. He distinguishes between good and bad magic, equating the latter with sorcery; but he also distinguishes the sorcerer from the witch. The sorcerer works with deliberate intention to do harm and may even drop poison into the cooking-pot. The witch performs no rite, uses no spell and possesses no medicines. It is a psychic act. At night she leaves her body and joins an assembly of other witches. She preys on her victim, causing his body to waste away, though she may not be aware of this until identified by a witch-finder. (Pp. 11–12, 133, 161.)
22. The distinction between religion and magic is a purely theoretical problem. It may have some value for classifying observations, but it is not conceptually indigenous. The Melanesian does distinguish, however, between his personal and technical skill and the *mana* he acquires from the ghost to make his competence more effective.
23. A soul was partly stolen when a disease was located within only one part of the body, such as, say, a paralysed leg.
24. Wilson, E.: 1935, pp. 95–97.
25. Woodford: 1890, pp. 150–52.
26. Hocart: 1925, pp. 229.
27. Hogbin: 1935, pp. 31–32.
28. Hocart: 1938, pp. 156–57.
29. Ivens: 1927, pp. 190–91.

CHAPTER 2. EARLY CULTURE CONTACT

1. Canasius–Dept. of State, U.S. Nat. Archives, R.G. 84.
2. Guppy: 1887, p. 27.
3. Brown: 1908, p. 517.
4. Piolet: 1902, pp. 352 ff.
5. Under the nom-de-plume *Outis* in a series of nine long articles in the *Daily Telegraph*, 1873, and under his own name. See also Dunbabbin, 1935.
6. Frater: 1947.
7. Fox: 1958, p. 141.
8. Armstrong: 1937, p. 191.
9. Brown: 1908, p. 520.
10. Lambert: 1946, p. 115.

11. Guppy: 1887, pp. 17,21, 26, 54.
12. Luxton: 1955, pp. 28, 47, 52, 74, 95, 105.
13. Ibid., pp. 95 ff., 74, 47.
14. Nicholson: 1924, pp. 45 ff.; Luxton: 1955, pp. 95 ff. and also the files of official district correspondence.
15. Especially Goldie–Danks Mar. 11, 1910, in M.O.M. Archives, Sydney.
16. Goldie–Danks Apr. 20, 1910, in M.O.M. Archives, Sydney.
17. Durrad: 1922, p. 23.
18. Luxton: 1955, pp. 108 ff.
19. Ibid., pp. 118–19.
20. Goldie: 1908, pp. 24–25.
21. Rivers: 1922.
22. Ibid., p. 107.

CHAPTER 3. LEVELS FOR STUDYING CHURCH GROWTH

1. How is the shepherd of the flock to know that one is missing if he does not know that the numerical count of the flock is a hundred? One is appalled at the rough estimates in round hundreds or thousands in some mission statistics. At least the editor of one official record in Melanesia had the conscience to footnote it, "Many will testify that these figures are not entirely accurate".

CHAPTER 4. THE GROWTH OF THE CHURCH IN THE EASTERN SOLOMONS

1. Statistics: South Solomons Vicariate.
2. Artless: 1937, p. 5.
3. Much missionary money was wasted by the great societies, through trying to distribute their activity too widely over all continents, involving long lines of communication.
4. This is why the practice of comparing the wages paid by different missions to their agents is an unsound criterion.
5. Belshaw: 1954, p. 51.
6. On his first voyage Selwyn met an English trader, Captain Paddon, whom he thereafter called his tutor. He traded in sandalwood and boasted that by fair dealing he had maintained his trade for years with perfect understanding. Although his record was not as good as his boast, Selwyn was impressed, and felt that what Paddon could do for gain, he himself could do in the service of God.
7. A good account of this trade is given in *Journal of Mission Voyage*, 1866. It tells how "the missionaries become yam and pig dealers for a time" hanging a steelyard on a branch and giving a hatchet for 70 or 80 lb. of yams (p. 5). The bishop regarded the "redemption of the barbarism of barter" as a "necessary step to a more perfect acquaintance" (p. 7).
8. This is Patteson speaking but he uses the pattern laid down by Selwyn. Ibid., pp. 18–19.
9. Two charges have been made against this policy. Dishonest traders and kidnappers used this mission policy as a cloak for their exploitation, declaring that they were doing no more than the Mission. It also exposed the Mission to slavery charges, for they were buying people. It was well known, for instance, that the bishop bought fourteen girls on one voyage, as brides for his 'sons'. If this was legitimate within Melanesian patterns for him, could the Mission oppose renegade sailors buying themselves 'wives' for the voyage? (See Armstrong: 1937, pp. 107–08, 233.)
10. Armstrong: 1937, p. 9.
11. Fox: 1958, p. 2.
12. This term is used by David Hilliard, who is engaged in historical research on the Solomons at the National University, Canberra.
13. The mission historians have recognized the importance of the pioneering work of these men. The training expanded in the following manner. In August 1849 the bishop collected five young men, restored them in 1850 (May), collected four more in December and returned them the following

July. More came in 1851. Over four years he visited fifty islands and collected forty boys, speaking ten different languages. By 1852 four had been baptized. In 1856 he brought back fourteen more, seven of them from the Solomons. Five, who had been baptized, became communicants in 1856. This was a slow but steady process of graduating into Christianity. In November 1857 the bishop called at sixty-six islands, made eighty-one landings and collected thirty-one men for his institution, mostly from the Solomons. There were forty-five in 1858 and this time some women, and thirty-nine more in 1859 (Armstrong: 1937, pp. 13, 14, 18, 19, 21, 23, 30, 46, 48; Penny: 1888, pp. 5–6). Even so, after a successful trip in 1866, after seventeen years Bishop Patteson admitted that "there was nothing (humanly speaking) to encourage us to look for any rapid or widely spread acceptance of the gospel".

14. Patteson served as Selwyn's chaplain from 1854, was at St John's and St Andrew's schools and proved himself competent at handling the Melanesian students, although apparently he was surprised at being chosen as Bishop of Melanesia.

15. He developed this idea in an address at St Mary's, Belmain, Sydney, in 1864. He did not stress the moral depravity of the Melanesians, but their capacity for being removed from that state to one of holiness. God made men of all nations of one blood and gives His blessings to "mankind collectively" when Christ becomes man.

16. Page: n.d., pp. 119–20.

17. "Abstract of Expenditure for 1868", *Island Mission*: 1869, p. 300.

18. Fox: 1958, p. 45.

19. Banks Islanders went out to Anudha, Motlav, Savo and Santa Maria (Armstrong: 1937, p. 114). Ara had only a hundred people but sent men to Vanua Lava, Ureparapara and Merelava (p. 193). Motlav, says Fox (1958, pp. 45–46) was the Iona of Melanesia, fifty missionaries going out in one year from a population of a thousand.

20. This is common in missions of many denominations. The most common reason assigned is a demand for standards. Quite often missionaries fear to trust a convert from animism to too responsible an office in the Church, lest he fail in the test and do harm to the Mission. Yet even Paul had his Demas (2 Tim. 4: 10), Hymenaeus and Alexander (I Tim. 1: 19–20). But all missions have also had their glorious successes and these have by far outnumbered the failures. A long training may improve an indigenous pastor's knowledge and his capacity to reason with unbelievers, but it does not necessarily improve his spiritual strength. The longer he is out of his society in an institution, the more remote his ministry is likely to be from the rank and file he has to serve. The issue for a community emerging from animism really is—what kind of a ministry does such an emerging church need? I ask this of the pioneering period. Of course a second generation church will need a better educated pastor, but in neither case should the pastor's academic level be too far above the people. To demand western levels before ordination is to hold up the organic growth of the church.

21. In 1849 Selwyn exposed himself at this point by severely criticizing other Pacific missions which used indigenous agents as their evangelistic spearhead. He claimed that sending them into danger in this way was to treat them as lower level missionaries. He was wrong. The motive was the opposite. It was a recognition of their superiority as front-line evangelists. As an anthropologist I have never been able to reconcile these criticisms of Selwyn with his own policy of extracting men from their social and cultural matrix, converting them under cover, and sending them back as isolated Christians to win their own pagan kin for whom communal cohesion alone meant survival.

22. *Journal of Mission Voyage*: 1866, p. 21.

23. This is not reconstructed from isolated references. Selwyn's colleague at St John's, Abraham (later Bishop) has left a written statement of this, and the phrases in my text are his. He sought to justify his position by allegorical reasoning from the Holy Communion being possible by a combination of divine grace and human labour. The availability of bread, he argued, required farming and industry. The availability of wine required commerce. Abraham's

statement has been preserved by J. R. Selwyn, to whom it was written. (J. R. Selwyn: 1897, pp. 123–25.)

24. To cite one example: In 1883 two Solomon Island chiefs were at work in Guadalcanal setting up Christian schools when "a murdering raider from Savo came across and set them against the 'good teaching'. Neither would have any more to say to it, nor allow [his] lads to go to Norfolk Island." This kind of problem was also met by the Methodists in the west, and indeed it extended through Melanesia to Fiji. (Armstrong: 1937, p. 235.)

25. In 1890 in Florida slavers emptied the schools (including adult schools), 175 were kidnapped by one ship visiting Santa Cruz in 1883. The population of Santa Maria by three thousand. (Armstrong: 137, pp. 233, 280, etc. Fox, 1958: p. 235.) See also Rivers: 1922.

26. Armstrong: 1937, pp. 165, 169, 186, 197, 233, 193.

27. Ibid., pp. 301, 308, 327, 331, 316.

28. Ibid., pp. 220, 259, 279.

29. Ibid., pp. 97–98; Fox: 1958, pp. 133, 145.

30. Wilson, E.: 1935.

31. At that time the Melanesian Mission had four hundred Melanesian teachers but only two priests and seven deacons. Surely with so many teachers, more could have been raised to the priesthood. Currently there are 292 teachers, 80 evangelists, 820 catechists, 22 deacons, 79 priests and 2 assistant bishops. This shows the very considerable organic growth in the period which commenced with Bishop Wilson.

32. *Proc. 1962 Synod.* The statistics show 47,500 Anglicans in these particular islands, 60,610 in the whole Diocese, p. 82.

33. In March 1904 there were 8,557 Melanesian labourers in Queensland, about two-thirds of them from the Solomons. (B.S.I.P. Report 1 April 1903–March 31, 1905.)

34. The rules had to be modified because the Church was unable to find enough teachers. (Steward 1939 "The Brothers" p. 113.)

35. *Proc. 1962 Synod.* p. 15.

36. Official Statistics, Vicariate of the South Solomons.

37. Wilson: 1907 Report.

38. Coaldrake: n.d., p. 46.

39. Fox: 1962, p. 75.

40. The rules of the Melanesian Brotherhood, the office for admitting a brother, and Ini Kopuria's vow are found in an appendix in Fox: 1958. The same writer has provided a more personal account of the Brotherhood at work in his autobiography (Fox: 1962). Two other published accounts are available, one a paper "The Brothers" by Bishop Steward (Newbolt: 1939) and the other a small unit in Coaldrake's more recent report of his visit to the islands.

41. The rules, order of admission, and office of this group have been published (Melanesian Mission: 1963). This little volume also includes the vow, the daily prayer, and a special liturgy for every Friday, when the brothers and all their mission fields are specifically remembered.

42. *Proc. 1962 Synod*, p. 69.

43. A good example is related by Fox (1962, p. 72). Two brothers found a lad crippled by ulcers. The father had tried every cure to no effect, and agreed that the brothers take him to their household. They carried him from the interior to the coast on their backs, and in two months took him home restored to health. The village was impressed with this devotion and asked as a group for Christian instruction.

44. Coaldrake: n.d., p. 48.

CHAPTER 5. THE GROWTH OF THE CHURCH IN THE WESTERN SOLOMONS

1. At that point of time the Melanesian Mission work in Fiji was confined to Suva and Levuka. Floyd ministered to fifty Solomon Islanders at Levuka, and Montgomery found 150 at a school under Jones. He confirmed eighty-three who had awaited the bishop for a year. These were town communities. They had no plantation outreach. (Montgomery: 1896, pp. 185–87.)

2. Goldie: 1914, p. 566.
3. The Wesleyan Church became involved in Methodist Union soon after the turn of the century. It was the new Methodist Church which opened the Solomon Islands Mission.
4. Beauclerc did much for the social and religious life of Fiji over this difficult period, especially for foreign labour. He served as Protector of Immigrants and visited the Solomons. He ran an interracial school in Suva and worked for the establishment of the Indian Mission.
5. He did so twice—Apr. 23, 1896, and Sept. 22, 1896, M.O.M. Archives, Sydney, 165: 36.
6. Danks: 1901.
7. Published in *Aust. Methodist Missionary Review*, Dec. 1901.
8. Brown: 1908, also Jul. 1901. In earlier correspondence Wilson intimated his readiness to receive the Methodist Solomon Islanders if they would be confirmed as Anglicans. Brown thought they would agree, but apparently they did not.
9. Wilson: 1907. There were some subsequent misunderstandings about Choiseul, which Brown understood to be in the Methodist area. The Anglicans subsequently questioned this, but Fox admits Anglicans were withdrawn from Choiseul (1958, p. 45).
10. Samuela Angarau, who had spent 27 years in Fiji, was converted there and volunteered to go with the Solomon Islands Missions. In education he was inferior to the other members of the party but as a Solomon Islander he had advantages and rendered a long and useful service. (Goldie: 1914: pp. 506, 568, 572; Luxton: 1955, p. 63.)
11. Angarau came from Rewa, the same part of Fiji as the two Guadalcanal Roman Catholic families through whom that work was introduced into Guadalcanal (Raucaz: 1928). The New Hebridean was Ulu. The personnel of the party was strongly associated with the Fijian labour fields. Rooney also was the son of a Fijian missionary. See "Teachers for the Solomon Islands", *Aust. Meth. Miss. Review*, May 1902.
12. According to Dr. Brown, whose address at the Foreign Mission Public Meeting, 1901, was published in *ibid*. Apr. 1901.
13. These reasons were stated in the Abstract of the Annual Meeting Report, Feb. 1902 in *ibid*. Mar. 1902. The reference to Protestants indicates that Roman Catholics had already moved in to the area. Beckett, who accompanied Brown, says they had; *ibid*., April 1901. This fact may have influenced Wilson's agreement to allow the Methodists in. (See *ibid*. Sept. 1901.)
14. Especially Frank Wickham and Norman Wheatley, mentioned often in official reports. Commissioner Woodford and Asst. Commissioner Mahaffy also co-operated. Several other planters opened copra sheds for meetings. One of these was Benskin of Simbo, where chief Belangana was a violent head-hunter. Incidentally some of the same parties also invited the Roman Catholics and Seventh Day missionaries.
15. Brown: Jul., Sept., Oct. 1901, also 1914, p. 520.
16. Brown: Jul. 1901.
17. Brown: 1914, p. 515.
18. Ibid., pp. 516–18.
19. Woodford informed Brown, who wrote twice to the missionaries about this. Brown objected that the folk in Fiji and Samoa would be dissatisfied with this station employment when they had been sent as evangelists (Brown–Goldie Feb. 27, 1903; Aug. 29, 1903. M.O.M. Archives Letter Book.)
20. Luxton:1955, pp. 30, 34–35, 40–42.
21. Ibid., pp. 44–45.
22. Ibid., p. 46.
23. Ibid., pp. 42–43.
24. Ibid., p. 69.
25. Missionary Correspondence released to Sydney *Morning Herald*, 1912.
26. Luxton: 1955, pp. 72–75, 77.
27. Report for 1911, p. 127 (Nat. Library Canberra).
28. Metcalfe documents.

29. His life story is told in Nicholson: 1924. Another is David Vule, whose biography is also in print (Rycroft: 1926).
30. Luxton: 1955, pp. 99–100.
31. In some two hundred pages of correspondence on business matters, movements and health of the staff, engines, boats, mission buildings, behaviour of island agents, budgets, supplies, problems with the Government over punitive expeditions and so on, I located two references to the growth of the Church. At the head station many of the best young men were taking their stand for Christ. "One feature was the total absence of any excitement, but a quiet determination to follow Christ" (Goldie–Danks Mar. 3, 1910). A month later the work is still going on. He calls it a "time of harvest" and mentions "the strength of purpose and devotion of the young converts" (Goldie–Danks Apr. 6, 1910), and then silence for a year and a half. In August 1911 when reporting the baptism of a group of twenty on the island of Wanawana and conversions at Simbo and Vangunu, he adds almost casually that the movement at Roviana is still continuing (Goldie–Danks Aug. 1, 1911). This is all that was recorded. Events in the villages were even more briefly reported, and yet statistics show they were taking place. It was a period of growth.
32. Goldie–Danks, Sept. 19, 1911.
33. Goldie: 1914, p. 574.
34. Rooney. *Aust. Meth. Miss. Review*, Correspondence Aug. 13, 1913.
35. "New Venture in Evangelism" 1933, Luxton: 1955, pp. 116, 86, 106, 147–51, 213; Metcalfe "Two Friends", Interview Mrs. Voyce, for the cases cited in this paragraph.
36. Goldie: 1914, p. 576.
37. From Shakespeare, *Julius Caesar*, Act 4, Sc. 3.
38. Published under the title *Blazing the Trail*, 1935.
39. Ibid., pp. 158–63.
40. Ibid., pp. 88, 153, 173.
41. Ibid., pp. 34, 79, 85.
42. Ibid., p. 47.
43. Ibid., pp. 42, 117, 123, 152.
44. Ibid., pp. 35, 90, 96.
45. Ibid., pp. 29, 32, 49, 117.
46. Ibid., pp. 24, 28, 89.
47. Ibid., pp. 36, 38, 48, 50, 115, 121, 136 175, 184.
48. Ibid., pp. 83, 160.
49. Ibid., pp. 61, 184.
50. Ibid., p. 70.
51. Ibid., pp. 82, 161.
52. Ibid., p. 129.
53. Ibid., pp. 184, 121 and 175 respectively.
54. Abstract of Report 1908 in *Aust. Meth. Miss. Review* Mar., 1908.
55. Ibid., May 1908.
56. Ibid., Aug. 1809.
57. "Report on Solomons" in ibid., Mar. 1910.
58. These three statements from Messrs Rooney, Nicholson and Goldie all appeared in that same number, Mar. 1911. The same number also reported open doors in the villages served by each area.
59. Report to the Board, 10 Nov. 1910.
60. New Zealand Methodist Conference Minutes, 1921.
61. Bensley, 1933.
62. *The Gospel of Mark* appeared in Rovianan after fifteen years of missionary activity. Mrs. Goldie prepared a simple *Life of Christ* in manuscript but would not attempt the Scripture. She translated some Old Testament history (published 1918) and some *Tales from Shakespeare* and *Pilgrim's Progress* By 1927, after a quarter of a century, the Board was urging the translation of the New Testament, but it took more than half a century to produce. See *Missionary Review*, Apr. 1918; Goldie: May 1927; Goldie–Scriven official correspondence with New Zealand Feb. 2, 1950.

63. This unit is based on the official records of the decade, the minutes of Synod, annual reports and statistics and the 1928 Report of the official enquirer for the Board.

CHAPTER 6. PROBLEMS OF THEORY AND PRACTICE

1. Codrington analysed the languages of Bugotu, Gao, Savo, Florida and Vaturanga, which cluster together geographically in the centre of the Group. Lexical evidence in a comparative study of seventy key words suggests a greater affinity of Vaturanga, Bugotu and Florida with far-distant Fiji than with their near neighbours Savo and Gao. This is supported also by certain grammatical features like consonantal and syllabic verbal suffixes (Codrington: 1885). I myself listed some fifty Malaita words identical with Fijian, only a few of which could have been from culture contact. In New Georgia I recognized numerous constructions and concepts as similar to those of Fiji, though different from those of nearer Solomon Islands. A spirit concept of the Shortlands (*nitu*) compares with that of the western tribes of Fiji. Some localities have customary similarities with Fiji, e.g. widow-strangling in Simbo, Bogotu and Sa'a (Moss: 1925). For Roviana *gila*, *gelia* and *gania* (know, dig and eat) the 'g' merely becomes a 'k' for Fijian (Bauan) kila, kelia and kania.
2. This was a useful concept in that it helped the westerner to see the importance of collective factors in an excessively individualistic world. It also preserved for the 'primitive', at least theoretically, the right to organize his own life as he desired. It recognized the wrongness of *imposed* culture change.
3. Myrdal: 1956, pp. 9–10.
4. Ibid., p. 9.
5. Ibid., p. 11.
6. Tippett: 1963.
7. Myrdal: 1956, p. 174.
8. By encouraging technical advice, advising on and introducing equipment, assisting in the improvement of crops, sale of produce and educating farmers. (White Paper 6.)
9. By improving yields and nutritional values, introducing new foods, and ensuring adequate all the year supplies. (White Paper 6.)
10. White Paper 5.
11. Lever's Pacific Plantations have replanted 2,000 acres but there has been very little beyond this.
12. "Government officials were only tax-collectors" was a recurring testimony from long-term resident European informants.
13. They played an improvised form of softball with a stick and ball or the hand and a lime fruit. The manner in which the fielding team formed up in a system to throw out an opponent caught between bases was a perfect example of unselfish play and automatic co-operation.
14. Correspondence exists from both field and board, and reports of addresses at conference to this effect; but frequently when the principle was stated, a rider was added to say the time was not yet.
15. The statistics are set out in Coaldrake: n.d. pp. 34, 54.
16. Goldie, an effective pioneer, was talking in 1927 of "our object is a self-directing and self-supporting church in the Solomons in the near future" (Conference Address 1927). Thirteen years later he was saying exactly the same thing (Correspondence to Gen. Sec.) but never at any time was he prepared to act on the ideal.
17. Official correspondence of the Gen. Sec. Feb. 8, 1928.
18. *Proc. 1962 Synod* p. 17.
19. Stace: 1954, p. 25.
20. Sidney J. W. Clark, who was the inspiration of much that Roland Allen wrote, retired early from business to devote his mature years to the study of missionary policies and principles. He knew many of the great mission fields of the world and specialized in the study of village communities. In North China alone he visited six hundred market towns and eleven thousand villages which they served. His work *The Indigenous Church* was based on experiences

in China, India, Burma, Malay Peninsula, Manchuria, Korea and Japan. This theoretical concept is stated on p. 17.

21. Clark's principles for planting an indigenous Church are applied when some (however few) emerge from heathenism with new life. This group is to grow like a tree (not a foreign stick). Four principles are to be kept in mind. (1) The young Church must depend on God, not on a foreign mission, (2) Christian interdependence within the fellowship must be cultivated, (3) a translation of the Word of God should be made available as soon as possible, the first converts teaching others to read, and (4) as Christian experience expands, so must Christian service; preaching and teaching must lead to action. This leads to growth. Clark differentiates between a Church *trained to be left*, when the missionary moves on, and a Church *trained to be dependent*. (Ibid., pp. 19–24.)

22. Ghana Assembly Papers: 1958, p. 182.

23. The sound of my typewriter in Fouia was an open invitation for all and sundry to bring us documents to be typed—lists of birthdays, prayers for memorizing and the biggest assignment of all, the prayer syllabus of the Mothers' Union, which links Anglican dioceses the wide world over in a wave of prayer. It covers the calendar year. Each group is remembered in prayer for five days, seventy-two units in all, each covering two to five dioceses. Each union had a link branch in another country. The Fouia branch was linked with St Mary's, Caulfield, in my home State of Victoria, Australia. The membership strength of the Mothers' Union in the Solomons is as follows:

Malaita	147
Gela	190
Ysabel	766
Guadalcanal	35

Total 1,138

24. The M.W.F. met at Rarumana every Thursday afternoon. Attendance ranged from fifteen to thirty women, and the meeting comprised a devotional and work project of some kind, usually sewing for church funds, mat-making, or the preparation of pandanus leaves for this. The gathering usually finished with outdoor games, even the older women taking part. Every second week the women met to plan a fortnight's programme. They devoted one day a week to their own M.W.F. garden—a money-making venture, which paid for the cost of sewing materials.

CHAPTER 7. PROBLEMS OF ENCOUNTER

1. *tapu* is the Polynesian form of the word which appears as 'taboo in the Oxford Dictionary. The more common Melanesian form is *tabu*, remembering that the 'b' sometimes has the value of the English 'mb'. The 't' is sometimes dropped, so that another form is *'ambu*. In the passages cited the missionary used the Polynesian form. There are many Polynesian communities in Melanesia.

2. Penny: 1888, ch. 9.

3. Codrington: 1894, ch. 5.

4. Penny: 1888, p. 185.

5. Penny seems to use the term *tindalo* either for the *shrine* or for the spirit for whom it was the vehicle. They are related, of course, for to destroy the shrine is a symbolic disposal of the *mana* of the spirit in that repository.

6. Note that they did not say the sacred things were fakes, but that they had been deprived of *mana*. This is Melanesian reporting.

7. Penny: 1888, pp. 207–08.

8. Since the completion of this manuscript a report has come to hand from the W.C.C. Consultation on Evangelism in West Africa. I note they discussed this very point, with the following result:

It is essential that baptism be seen as a manifestation of the grace of God in Jesus Christ, and as the point of departure for the new life in which the convert will step by step discover what the God who loves him asks of him. On no account may baptism be made to appear as a kind of diploma attesting that the convert knows all about God and the practice of his faith. (P. 5.)

9. E. Wilson: 1935, pp. 95–97.
10. *Not in Vain*, 1916–17.
11. District Report, 1917.
12. Metcalfe MS.
13. McGavran: 1957, pp. 13–15.
14. I found this opinion in all Christian groups, including the Roman Catholic. An R.C. leader claimed that the indifference of the whites to religion was a great hindrance to the growth of the Church. See Raucaz: 1928, p. 58.
15. Allen: 1950, p. 49.
16. This was stated to be so by Synod Resolution, 1961. but in actual practice I did find permit-holders were sometimes excluded from membership and classified as adherents. Usually such persons became nominals and ceased attending church at all.

CHAPTER 8. PROBLEMS OF INSTITUTIONS AND EDUCATION

1. *White Paper on Education*, par 15, p. 6.
2. *Proc. 1962 Synod*, pp. 14–15.
3. The attitude is a logical reaction to the dogmatism and paternalism of màny administrators, educationalists, agriculturalists, and others of scientific training, many of whom treat the indigenous adults as children. Scientific dogmatism and the capacity to transmit ideas across cultural barriers vary inversely, unless men are trained in group dynamics.
4. Coaldrake: n.d., p. 52.
5. This is not a recent problem nor peculiar to the Solomons. A missionary scholar in China once wrote:

   Few of those who get the benefit of mission education are willing to go to the Theological College. There are more attractive openings for them, especially in the city. And even those who live farther afield show signs of diminishing willingness to engage professionally in the service of the Church.

   We shall get better results when we start at the other end and give a little training to living souls, who are keen to propagate life, than a lot of those who, having perhaps no real spiritual life, feel under little compulsion to do more than the best they can for themselves with the education they receive.
6. As the Bishop put it in his charge to Synod, 1962. (Clark: 1933, p. 5.)
7. In my own missionary experience I found this essential when I was removed from village work to a central institution. I organized it in two ways (1) by offering myself for regular village preaching off the main roads but within Sunday travelling range, and (2) by arranging with my fellow missionaries for my itineration through their rural areas during the institutional term vacations. These were essential to keep myself in touch with village life and thought. They also had value in showing me how to keep my institutional courses relevant to the village needs. But the contacts had to be regular.
8. When Dr. E. W. Wallace was retiring from an important educational post on the mission field in 1930, he expressed the view, based on his long experience that

   Christian education must be an expression of the life of the Christian community, directed, supported and patronized by it, and full responsibility for the policies of Christian schools must be borne by Church. (Bull. National Christian Council, 1930.)
9. F. Williams: 1951.
10. As secretary of the Methodist Young People's Dept., Great Britain, in the 'Foreword' of Blamires: 1951, p. ix.
11. This work was translated and printed in the Babatana language. It had also been translated into Roviana, but as far as I know, not printed. The book has a tremendous appeal to Melanesians. If fits their orientation of encounter.

12. The writer knows one Melanesian area where group dynamics were applied in the following way. Two progressive groups were encouraged to stand on their own feet as independent pastorates. They paid their own ministers, handled their own finances, made their contributions to central funds, built up their own reserves and kept their buildings in order. Their initiative and independence soon became a matter for admiration. They gained prestige thereby in the eyes of other villages, who after a few years began to desire to administer their own affairs. In this way the villages in general became psychologically ready for organic development. There is a completely self-supporting and self-determining Church in almost every local unit of that Group today.

13. He claimed the method was experimental in the first place, having no biblical commission. It had become a vested right. He differentiated between institutions that were foreign and those which grew from the activity of the young Church. His objections to typical mission educational institutions may be summarized thus:

1. It takes education out of the hands of the local Church.
2. It absorbs men and means needed for evangelism.
3. It is out of proportion and not needed for Church growth.
4. It plants no indigenous Church free from foreign funds and control.
5. It presupposes that education is Christian because it is organized by a Christian Board or Society, but the teaching is mostly non-religious.
6. Even if its motive is evangelistic, it is the most expensive and least fruitful form of evangelism.
7. Leaders trained in such foreign institutions are separated from the true life of the local Church. The real leaders of the Church are not often graduates of such institutions.
8. The criterion is not the prosperity of mission school graduates, but their value to the local Church. "The results are pitifully meagre" and include "some of our bitterest opponents".

From this, the Mission Secretary concludes (and the italics are his):
Our schools are not vitally essential to the growth and development of the churches. (p. 20)
He also points out that the reasons given in justification of the policy of large foreign-supported educational institutions are four:

1. They educate national leaders.
2. They convert non-Christian students.
3. They influence the more enlightened nationals in favour of Christianity.
4. They permeate society with moral and religious ideas that prepare the way for Christianity.

In reply he says the policy has proved expensive and unfruitful. The leaders trained were more foreign than the foreign missionaries. The Church that comes from this kind of policy is foreignized and divorced from the life of the people.
It is interesting to have this view stated by one who was a mission secretary, and who saw the institutionalism of his own organization as hindering the emergence of the local Church. (Mission Secretary: 1930.)

14. A pattern known as *practising acquaintance* was given to rural folk by the missionary, a simple phonetic script to permit reading the Word, elementary first-aid to help Christians do the right thing, as a simple service growing from the Infant Church, that could grow with the Church and in time provide education and medicine that were indigenous. The missionary task was to plant an indigenous tree and nurse it through the early days, so that it could produce its own fruit. This was a reaction against the 'foreign fruit' of the institutions. (Clark: 1933, pp. 13-24.) See also Peill & Rowlands: 1930, and Rowlands: 1931, for descriptions of indigenous church-planting.

15. Citing Hamilton: 1928
. . . instead of being indigenous, it is only a foreignized Church in the midst of a hostile heathenism . . . Instead of being a native plant growing under normal conditions, the Church becomes an exotic hot-house growth, always needing shelter from cold blasts of heathen hatred.

16. McNairn: 1934.

17. Clark: 1928, 1933.
18. Allen's work is now being rediscovered and has recently been all reprinted in America. Had the Church been ready to act on his insights when they first appeared in print, the situation regarding the young Churches would have been very different today. For Clark's influence on Allen, see Allen: 1937, Dedication to Clark.
19. Blamires: 1951.
20. Citing Clark: 1933, p. 7
    If we stop in order that we may consolidate, we shall find that we are in danger of exchanging work which is *spontaneous* in its growth for that which moves only in response to *external* impulses. . . . Life does not stop to consolidate; it either grows or it dies. It is always so with *living* things. Extension *is* consolidation. When the Christian man stops to consolidate he goes backward. (Italics his).
    More recently McGavran has challenged the Methodist Gold Coast historian, Southon, who attributes slow growth in the 'second phase' of his narrative, among other things, to "the need for consolidation of the Church". McGavran admits the need for consolidation but objects to the idea "that expansion *had* to be succeeded by a period of consolidation during which expansion necessarily suffered". He goes on to add that this belief is "one of the most common and disastrous assumptions of missionary thinking" (MS. n.d. pp. 19–20). Again, under the term *gradualism* the same writer tells of a Puerto Rico minister, who satisfied himself with a good but limited intake of converts, and changed from the evangelical to the consolidating role, leaving the ever-ripening fields about him to other denominations (1959: p. 105). In a more recent symposium McGavran has made a plea for honest speaking of non-growth as non-growth (1965: pp. 238–39).
21. Mission Secretary (1930, p. 21), bemoaning the foreignized Church that resulted from foreign institutions, foreign buildings, foreign teachers, foreign funds and dependence on foreign aid, narrated an account of a conference where the reduction of mission aid was being discussed. The opposition came from the mission school graduates, one of whom said, "The Church is like a child needing the constant support and aid of an elder brother." That Church, said Mission Secretary "is more than half a century old. Those men could think of nothing but continued dependence on the foreign agency. They had been trained and supported by foreigners, and they know no alternative." He went on to suggest that the fault was not theirs but that of the Mission system.
22. White Paper 5 says the present policy will be maintained, thanks the Missions for filling "gaps which the Government medical service could not bridge for lack of funds", and for training nurses and midwives. It hopes the Churches will consult the Government before extending medical services (Par. 7). It will continue to depend on Mission hospitals for training purposes (Par. 18) in order to attain to the staff required by 1970. It depends on the Church to continue its rural work for many years (Par. 23) but wants the Church medical policies co-ordinated with those of the Government and Local Councils. Church hospitals training nurses come under the Nurses and Midwives Board. Mission hospital expansion is anticipated (Par, 43) and suggestions are made for the expansion of Church medical activity in medical education and rural services (Par. 44). The White Paper is thoroughly appreciative and recognizes that the Church pioneered the work (Par. 7) but the Government assumes the role of co-ordinator, as of course it should (Par. 50: 5) though in one sense this requires a medical missionary to serve two masters. The programme until 1970 assumes the use (among other things) of "the resources of the Churches" (Par. 67).
    White Paper No. 3 is of similar structure. It recognizes the pioneering and continuing role of the Churches while "the Government was unable to assist" (Par. 6) and still cannot play a leading role through lack of funds (Par. 15). Government depends on the Churches for training women teachers (Par. 52) but schools are subject to inspection (Par. 58) and have to meet Government requirements in management and policy (Pars. 31 and 32). Here again is the

potential two-master problem. Here too is Mission involvement for a five-year period.

23. Huddleston: 1957, p. 60.
24. Stace: 1954. See p. 7 and Par. 5 in the summary on p. 24.
25. Care must be taken to assure that conversion and civilization are not equated. A Mission exists to plant a Church and to nurse it only so much as is required to help it emerge as indigenous. It is wrong to think of health projects, industrial and other ventures as Christianity, especially when they are confined to mission stations. Jacomb (1919 p. 143) made this wrong appraisal of Melanesia:

> This raising of the standard of civilization is the test by which a tribe's conversion must be measured. . . . An honest, clean, industrious, healthy life in this world is Christianity, and leads to Heaven.

Jacomb's appraisals were formed on a basis of station observations.

At the very opposite extreme we have the following appraisal by Roland Allen (1930: pp. 185–86):

> We have done everything for them. We have taught them, baptized them, shepherded them. We have managed their funds, ordered their services, built their churches, provided their teachers. We have nursed them, fed them, doctored them. We have done everything for them except acknowledge any equality. We have done everything for them, but very little with them. We have done everything for them, except give place to them. We have treated them as 'dear children', but not as 'brethren'.

We ought to test our institutions and policies to see that their good motives do not obstruct the very end we desire—to plant an indigenous Church.

CHAPTER 9. THE TRANSMISSION AND CONTROL OF AUTHORITY AND LEADERSHIP

1. Goldie: 1908, p. 24.
2. Russell: 1950, p. 6.
3. Guppy: 1887.
4. Allen: 1950, pp. 11–12.
5. For further development of this form of authority see Hogbin: 1938, pp. 289–305. The locality here is Guadalcanal.

CHAPTER 10. THE HEAD-HUNTING AND SLAVERY COMPLEX AND SOCIO-RELIGIOUS CHANGE

1. Some slavery patterns had quite different motivation from that discussed in this chapter, as for instance the Ugi purchases of slaves from San Cristoval for purposes of adoption as a corrective to their custom of infanticide. See Guppy: 1887, p. 35, etc.
2. Ysabel learnt to hunt for heads from the experience of Roviana invasions. Gao and Bugotu extended the practice in the fifties and sixties of the last century. The Roviana people mounted tomahawk heads on long handles, using the term *kilakila*, the diffusion of which can be traced as far as Sa'a and Ulawa. Gao extended raiding to the artificial islands of Malaita by carrying off forty heads during a 'friendly' entertainment (Ivens: 1930, pp. 186–87). The Bugotu people began collecting heads for canoe houses after the Roviana pattern, but drank the blood of the victim to acquire his strength or *mana* (Bogesi: 1948, p. 224).
3. Penny: 1888, pp. 46–50. Penny climbed up into one of these houses, 150 feet above the ground, lower branches removed to 80 feet, well supplied with water, food, sandtray for fire, space of 450 square feet and accommodation for forty people. Ascent was by means of a vine ladder.
4. Guppy: 1887, p. 33.
5. Ibid., p. 16.
6. Woodford: 1890, p. 153.
7. Letter Oct. 8, 1901.

8. Knibbs: 1929, p. 38.
9. Guppy: 1887, p. 34.
10. Ibid., pp. 16, 33 etc.
11. Penny: 1888, describes one on p. 46.
12. Somerville: 1897, pp. 374–75.
13. Rooney. Letter Jul. 4, 1904.
14. Rivers: 1922, p. 109.
15. Hocart: 1931, pp. 303 ff.
16. Goldie: 1908, p. 27.
17. Both of these are also Fijian customs. For full descriptions see Knibbs: 1929, pp. 37–38 and Penny: 1888, p. 46.
18. Woodford: 1890, p. 155, for example, if a pig and a human being were being offered together they had to be of opposite sex.
19. Brown: 1910, p. 208. If a workman died during the construction of a canoe, all work stopped until a human sacrifice had been offered, and the weapon used to kill the victim was placed in the bow of the canoe (Shortlands).
20. Penny: 1888, p. 46.
21. Angas: 1865, p. 365.
22. Thurnwald: 1934.
23. Oliver: 1955, pp. 295–96.
24. Knibbs: 1929, pp. 44–45.
25. Somerville: 1897, pp. 398–99.
26. Brown: 1908, p. 517.
27. Hopkins: 1928, p. 201.
28. Rivers: 1922, ch. 8.
29. Ibid., pp. 98–102. It has also been maintained that much the same situation has arisen in Choiseul because of the loss of the feuding pattern, a similar network of relationships involving economic exchanges of shell wealth, of feasting and of facilities for the selection and development of local leadership:
    It was never simply the feasting and gift exchange as such that made big men, but rather the activities which gave rise to the exchanges. Many exchanges were terminal points in series of transactions, which often began in contractual alliances between groups united in part by their support of a big man (Scheffler: 1964b, p. 793; and 1964c, p. 400).
30. Rivers: 1922, p. 108.
31. Thurnwald: 1934, and 1936.
32. Thurnwald: 1936a, p. 14.
33. Thurnwald: 1936b, p. 349.
34. Thurnwald: 1936a, p. 12.
35. Thurnwald: 1934.
36. Thurnwald: 1936a, p. 15; 1936b, p. 354.
37. Hocart: 1925, pp. 231–253.
38. Hocart: 1931, p. 308.
39. Hocart: 1922, pp. 105–12.

CHAPTER 11. HOW VILLAGE STRUCTURE REFLECTS
CHRISTIAN PATTERNS

1. I. M. C. Tambaram: 1938, pp. 93–97.
2. See Hopkins: 1949, for the full story of Father Jack.

CHAPTER 12. EXCHANGE ECONOMY AND
CHRISTIAN INNOVATION

1. Belshaw: 1954, p. 1.
2. Ibid., p. 5.
3. Ivens: 1930, p. 55.
4. Custom money that came my way in Malaita included the following: *Abe waro*—a pair of ceremonial armbands worn above the elbows, made from tiny shell discs, threaded into a design, Cash value £4. *Roro dara*—a forehead ornament of similar skilled manufacture—£5. *Alualu*—a long necklace of

threaded porpoise teeth. Cash value £2. Smaller quantities of teeth also have fixed value. *Tavuli aia*—shell-money in fathom lengths, worth 10s. a length but usually in sets of 10 lengths at £5. Five of these required for a bride. *Kome*—a trocus shell armlet, called a custom ring, given to a girl when a man is coming with her bride-price.

5. Forde: 1948, p. 202.
6. This rise was reported both among the salt-water people and bushmen. The increase of western money was perhaps not the only reason for it. The Langalanga people had an increased production because the pacification of the island permitted wider distribution of their money in safety. But the increased price of brides led many a young man to remain unmarried. Ivens: 1930, p. 46.
7. Penny: 1888, pp. 85–88.
8. One fathom of red shell-money was valued at 50 yams or 100 coconuts. Coconuts were scarce in the artificial islands of Malaita. White shell-money was worth much less than red.
9. Other localities are Sio in the northwest, Funafou, Urassi, Sulufou, Atta, Fera Subua, Kwai, Nongasila and Uru on the east coast.
10. The shells are *kakandu* (Arca granosa) white, *romu* (Chama pacifica) red, and a species of mussel known as *kurila*, black (Woodford: 1908, p. 83).
11. Showing how the pattern differed from that of Roviana where the diving was done by slaves. This division of labour in Malaita was noted by Penny: 1888, p. 85 f.
12. Although Ivens thought the widespread travelling dated only from the days of law and order, we have this specific statement from Woodford, who knew the former times.
13. When the shell fragments were reduced to the size of 3d. bits they were *fulo-mbato* and made with a hammerhead (*fauni*) on an anvil (*fau'ui* or *fauli-ui*), then chipped into discs on a soft wood instrument (*ma'ai*) with countersunk holes, and ground flat with a stone (*fou'sava*) placed in a coconut-shell container (*teo'le'futa*) for the drilling of the central hole with a pump-drill (*futa*), tipped with flint (*landi*). The flywheel of the drill is a disc of turtle-bone (*taka*), the handle is *randi* and the spindle *futa*. The flint points are sharpened with a freshwater shell (*kee*). The bored discs are threaded on fibre (*lili*), and the rough edges of a number smoothed together on a board (*mbambaliara*) with a grooved stone (*fouliara*), sand and water. The strung discs are called *bata*—money. The various lengths and various patterns all have names. Such differentiation shows the highly developed nature of this industry. (Woodford: 1908, pp. 81–84.)
14. For a dispute on this subject, see the Deck–Hogbin controversy 1934–35.
15. The ceremonial currency of Bougainville has been described by Blackwood: 1935, pp. 446–49. Two types *beroan* and *imun* are discussed. The former is used in marriage, funerary procedure, ceremonial compensations, payment for pigs and sacred carvings, and for teaching magical formulae and processes. The latter is used in marriage transactions, funerary rites, peace offerings, in payment for bull-roarers, slitgongs, initiation paraphernalia and for removing certain taboos. In other words this custom money is used for magical and religious ceremonial and for restoring and maintaining human relationships. This is quite distinct from secular trade. The *beroan* comprises shell-discs in fathom lengths, and comes from a New Britain trade circuit reaching as far as New Ireland and Manus. The *imun* is of local, but ancient origin and consists of teeth (dog, porpoise or flying fox) set in twisted fibre. They can be bought only with pigs and are never used for personal adornment. This circuit extends to the southeast as far as Ysabel and Florida.
16. Metcalfe MS *Our Time at Teop*, p. 25.
17. Brideprice in Choiseul was in terms of *kesa*, three sets of three soapstone cylinders, supposedly not made by man but received from the gods. They were obtained from Nuatabu (Holy Island) and bought only with pigs (Metcalfe). For another account see Scheffler: 1964a.
18. Belshaw: 1950, p. 179.
19. For a further development of this matter of village absenteeism, and notes on two commissions on the subject, see Tippett: 1956. pp. 173–76. Many

N

Malaita villages have the percentage absenteeism to put them in the category which endangers their home social structure.

20. Cameron: 1923, p. 281.   20a. Miller: 1939: 82-8
21. Elkin: 1943, p. 25.
22. Stace: 1954, p. 27.
23. My last figures (1962) show only about 600 tons of copra handled by all the co-operatives in the Solomons, and these are mostly in the west and central areas—none at all in Florida and Malaita. B.S.I.P. Reports 1961–62, p. 38.
24. There is in point of fact one co-operative in the area, but its basis is fishing, not copra. This shows there is no hostility to the idea of a co-operative *per se*.
25. Six new societies were established in the eastern district where there had been none before. Five of them liquidated "through wilful mismanagement, peculation or indiscriminate credit dealing contrary to their own byelaws"; the sixth was "suspended for re-organization". B.S.I.P. Rep. 1961–62, p. 38.
26. White Paper No. 6, p. 6.
27. Belshaw: 1954, pp. 162–63.
28. B.S.I.P. Reports 1961–62, p. 38.
29. It also shows how general statistics can be misleading without their regional breakdowns. The same thing applies to church statistics in the Western Solomons just before the war when growth was all in one area.
30. It employs the system of communal levies, each baptized person contributing 2s. a year, those higher up the ecclesiastical scale being responsible for greater amounts. It also proposes the acquisition of money by the sale of copra, porpoise teeth, shell and produce, suggests the organization of village plantations and projects, claims a 2s. contribution and a 3s. thankoffering from village absentees, and suggests a thankoffering of 1s. from those recovering from sickness. It also recommends a tithe of garden produce and handwork. These suggestions are all in accord with indigenous patterns.
31. It was the rebellious Israel that vexed the Spirit of God and turned His resources against them (Isa. 63:10). The evangelists were to reject those who showed them the spirit of rejection (Matt. 10: 12–14). Paul warned the Thessalonians to "quench not the Spirit" (1 Thes. 5: 19).
32. The people of the Saposa Islands supplied fish to the Hahon folk of the northern foothills. Metcalfe at Wakekakau noted the arrival of three canoes from Kirivi "whose owners had come to barter fish for taro". He was amazed at their businesslike operations. (MS. *Our Time at Teop*, p. 30.) In the same manuscript (p. 13) Metcalfe recorded this:
    People high up on Mt. Balbi's slopes dig the clay and burn it (for the manufacture of red ochre). The Wakekakau buy it and trade it to the folk at Tearaka. These trade it to the people from Buka, who bring their clay pots for sale every year. The Buka people then trade the red ochre to the people of Nissan for pigs. The red ochre is used at their feasts and in their various forms of ritual.
    This is interesting because it shows another commodity beside pots which passes through a series of exchanges en route to distant Nissan.
33. Blackwood: 1935, pp. 439–61—a very good source for this subject. The hill people involved in this case of trade with Petats were from Gagan, Potaki and Sapani. Blackwood also has a great deal more detail of the Lontis case just outlined.
34. *The Open Door* xi, 4, pp. 10–11; xii. i, pp. 13–14.
35. Cropp: 1931a, pp. 10–11.
36. McHardy: 1935, see pp. 184, 175, 121 in particular, but also 36, 38 48, 50, 115 and 136.
37. Voyce: 1933a, pp. 10–11; 1933b, pp. 13–14.
38. Oliver: 1955, p. 295.
39. Ibid., p. 299.

CHAPTER 13. FEUD AND RECONCILIATION

1. This feud has been documented from the personal records of the eyewitnesses. I am also indebted to Rev. J. R. Metcalfe for the clarification of many factual

points and for supplying details about various episodes in the table of events (letter Nov. 1921, pp. 1–4 and interviews).

2. I use the terms *clan* and *village* in order to retain the archival quality of my sources. I am aware that anthropologically much further research is now possible, because of Scheffler's work on kin structure and social organization in Choiseul. The next step would seem to be to identify the clans and villages of the archival records with the technical terminology of the corporate groups discussed by Scheffler. I did not have his work when I was in the Solomons.

3. In some places there is evidence that this was the regular pattern. In Simbo, for instance, revenge was generally exacted by a third party 'hired' by the *bangara* of the injured group, if it was not practicable to effect a reconciliation by means of an exchange of shell valuables (Scheffler: 1962, p. 151).

4. Fox: 1924, pp. 206–07.

5. In the case of a raid when assistance was recruited this was done through a *ruata*, an economic contract involving the gift of shell valuables and a feast. This economic and social obligation had to be met upon the completion of the act of vengeance, the price having previously been set by negotiation. If the feud reached a major warfare, those whose aid had been enlisted might themselves enlist others. They themselves would have to meet the obligations of this sub-contract, which might perhaps be necessary to permit their meeting of their promise of military aid to the original organizers. The principal organizer might himself refrain from joining in the raid, so as to be sure to survive to meet his economic obligations (Scheffler: 1964b, p. 796).

6. No government official visited Lauru for long enough to make a proper survey or organize the place into administrative districts before 1941. The missionaries tried to keep law and order, though they had neither the authority nor the power to do so (Metcalfe MS. *The Three Brothers*). The Government took forty years to attempt a medical survey (Metcalfe correspondence: Mar. 1, 1941).

7. Fox: 1924. On p. 307 Fox points out some cruel things done in what are sometimes called the 'good old fighting days'.

8. It must be acknowledged, as Scheffler has pointed out (1964b, p. 799), that the role of the *go-between* was already known in Choiseul society. It was a regular social mechanism for acquiring prestige. Although the vengeance system was functionally necessary in pagan society for economic and political purposes, there was a general reluctance to engage in warfare on too wide a scale. It was costly in food requirements, in shell wealth and in human life. Therefore as the war debts and economic burden increased, so too did the social pressure on the leader to terminate the war. At such times (ibid. p. 797) peacemakers were popular.

It must be seen then that the Christian teacher assumed this known role and won prestige thereby. Christianity pressed its claims as a religion of peace and offered a Saviour who was Lord and Prince of Peace. The reader should note that this was an internal feature in Choiseul. It may have applied elsewhere, but it certainly differed from those places whose war-pattern was not internal feuding but external head-hunting.

9. Binet: 1932, pp. 4–6 (includes a translation of Tozaka's own account of the events).

10. Binet: 1925, pp. 8–10. This is a very good account with detail of the economic measuring procedure. It is interesting to compare Binet's personal experiences of nearly half a century ago with data about the *kesa* recently collected by Scheffler (1963 and 1964a).

11. Binet: 1923, pp. 12–14.

12. Binet: 1932, pp. 4–6.

13. Binet: 1925, pp. 8–10.

14. Metcalfe's private correspondence has much detail about his own efforts at persuading various parties to agree to the manumission of slaves (see especially his Nov. 1921 letter pp. 9, 10, 15 and 16). He was still pushing this programme a year later (letter Oct. 15, 1922). In the same letter Metcalfe was critical of the Government for executing a murderer after the peace had been effected, and raised the question: Is an *individual* responsible in an inter-

tribal blood-feud? A number of issues are involved here. Were there economic factors involved in the manumission of slaves which were unknown to the missionaries? In the light of Scheffler's research I think this probable. The Government action was unwise. Had the blame for this been attributed to one of the parties in the feud, war might well have commenced again. It rather suggests that the general desire for peace was genuine. Metcalfe's question is well asked. The retaliation did not require the life of the actual culprit—any kinsman would do. The guilt was the guilt of the group rather than the individual.

15. Scheffler: 1964c, pp. 401–02.

CHAPTER 14. COMPARATIVE ANALYSIS OF
NATIVISTIC MOVEMENTS

1. Belshaw: 1958, p. 492.
2. The principal informant on the Pokokoqoro Cult is Rev. J. R. Metcalfe, with whom the writer had several interviews. He also made available his private correspondence over the vital years, and a MS. on *Cargo Cults in the Solomons*.
3. Worsley: 1957, p. 182.
4. Fox: 1962, ch. 15.
5. Allen: 1950, p. 27.
6. Fox: 1958, p. 176.
7. This was a serious problem wherever there was an American army camp. I lived beside one myself at the time. I have known American soldiers to pay $10 for a fowl, and $10 for a few minutes of physical sex satisfaction. I know of a case of a woman who earned $20 a day over a period for washing clothes at a fixed price per garment however small.
8. B.S.I.P. Reports.
9. The leaders arrested in 1947 had been charged with terrorism, robbery, illegal drilling, etc. Nine were sentenced to six years and four to lesser terms. When the lookout towers and barracks were destroyed, and the Florida, Ysabel and Guadalcanal groups dropped out, the Malaita core was driven underground again.
10. B.S.I.P. Reports 1948. pp. 26 ff.; 1949–50, pp. 40 ff.
11. Worsley: 1957, p. 174. For the story of Vouza see Macquarrie: 1945. Vouza is now at the village of Roroni in Guadalcanal .He keeps the village in good order, despite the various Christian denominations in it. This is a case of village cohesion round a powerful personality. He gave me a most interesting interview.
12. Allen: 1950, p. 60.
13. Belshaw: 1958, pp. 488–89.
14. Allen: 1950, pp. 60–61.
15. Belshaw: 1958, p. 489.
16. B.S.I.P. Reports. Citing 1948,
   One of the Marching Rule's policies throughout has been to prevent workers engaging on the copra plantations, thereby gravely slowing up the work of restoring them after the damage done by neglect during the military occupation.
   Citing 1949–50 Report,
   Marching Rule, by actively preventing labourers from working in plantations had seriously hindered the economic recovery of the protectorate. . . .
   This was true, but officialdom wanted to restore 'prosperity' on the old pattern, Marching Rule wanted to right the wrongs of the old pattern.
17. The *Pacific Islands Monthly* reported this and expressed the opinion that the matter would come up again and be approved. It claimed that the population of San Cristoval had dropped from 43,000 to 4,000 in 25 years and that in some places deaths outnumbered births by seven to one. *P.I.M.* Dec. 1931.
18. *P.I.M.* July 1931, Jan. 1932, May 1932.
19. This theory was advocated by Scholefield in 1919 (*The Pacific; its Past and Future*) and is critically examined in Tippett: 1956, pp. 138–39.
20. Allen: 1950, pp. 76–77.

21. Belshaw also traced economic and political forces to pre-war times, especially to the abuses caused by 'police boys' sent out to the villages to do the work of administrators. He spoke of unrest in Gela, demands for higher wages and representation. He felt that there was hatred of the white man everywhere. This was stimulated more by the coming of the Americans, the dollar inflation, and much of their "uninformed and irresponsible critical talk". Belshaw: 1947, pp. 187, 189, 191, 192.

22. *A.B.M. Review* 1950, "Cults: Nationalism in the Pacific".

23. Allen: 1950, p. 41.

24. S.S.E.M. *Association Guide Book*, p. 1.

25. Belshaw: 1958, p. 487.

26. Correspondence from Cornwell.

27. Belshaw: 1958, p. 488.

28. Worsley: 1957, p. 120.

29. Press report in *The Age*, Jul. 23, 1965.

30. Most of the description of the Hahalis Welfare Society on these pages, except for the opening paragraph, is based on material supplied by Rev. Gordon A. R. Cornwell, who was an eye-witness. Unfortunately I was unable to visit Buka, so I am deeply indepted to him for his help. I hope that some day he will produce a full monograph on this theme, from a missionary point of view.

31. Press report in *The Age*, Jul. 23, 1965.

32. European influence through trading posts was established in Buka from 1884. Worsley: 1957, p. 114.

33. This reconstruction of Teosin's feelings is based on his own testimony to Cornwell, who had his confidence to some extent.

34. Linton: 1958, p. 473.

35. The 1913 movement was millenarian. It did not end with executions. One leader, Muling, was still involved in 1932. Pako, who prophesied a cargo ship, rejected Christianity, united Buka under its own flag. The leaders were arrested. Pako died in exile. Two years later Sanop arose and proclaimed the cargo ship again. He was imprisoned. Belief circulated that Pako was executed. His ghost appeared to Sanop, saying the time was at hand. With the arrival of the Japanese this was proclaimed again. (Worsley: 1957, pp. 114–22.)

CHAPTER 15. ETOISM: THE PROPHET AND THE SITUATION

1. My informant called it *The Mysteries of the Mind*, and said it was about West Indian Negro Holy Rollers. I doubt if he had read it but he was convinced of its influence. The book was however a post-war influence (Sargant: 1957).

2. I investigated all these factors. The mission sister was least substantiated as a cause. The mission sister was quite 'famous' and there is official correspondence about her behaviour, but not all the things said about her could be proved.

3. Eto: 1949.

4. Numerous long reports by the missionaries concerned are in the official file at Munda. I appreciate the chairman's readiness to open the file to me, but do not feel disposed to cite from it.

5. Vula and Buadromo: 1961. Report in official file at Munda.

6. Leadley: 1961.

7. Elkin: 1937, p. 541.

8. I can cite cases of S.D.As. following up this same line through the woman (normally matrilocal) living with her husband's people in a village of another denomination. From one station in particular they do not hesitate to 'fish' for the husband and the nuclear family, though it segregate them from the communal religious life altogether.

CHAPTER 16. THE GROUP EXPERIENCES OF ETOISM

1. Corte: 1958. The position taken is as follows: Jesus claims unlimited power over devils and their chief, Satan. His messianic work includes the conquest of Satan. He bequeaths the power over devils to his followers and sends out apostles to the work of conquest (p. 49). The existence of Satan and demons is

accepted, also the reality of demon-possession and the Christian involvement in overcoming it (p. 51). Satan is conceptualized personally, with a hierarchy of demons behind him. Conflict is not in the abstract, but conquest is possible through Christ (p. 58). After conversion there is still temptation (p. 64).

2. M.M. Prayer Book, pp. 17, 56, 106, 116, 127, 131. Brotherhood Book, pp. 12–13.

3. Perhaps this is the effect of the new Book of Offices that appeared in 1936, which has virtually no references to Satan and his works. One survives in the Collect for the 18th Sunday after Trinity. If the collects are used, this would be used once a year. The renouncement of the world, the flesh and the devil has been eliminated from the adult baptismal service, which now demands repentance, faith in Christ, and readiness to seek the help of the Holy Spirit.

4. Sargant: 1957.

5. Ibid., 1960 edition, p. 115.

6. His letter, Sept. 14, 1960, is in the file at Munda.

7. Sargant: 1960, pp. 67–68.

8. Ibid., p. 81.

9. Ibid., pp. 62–63.

10. Ibid., pp. 92–93.

11. Ibid., pp. 142–43, 194–95.

12. Ibid., p. 101.

13. The sermon appeared in the original Vol. III of Wesley's Sermons. It is sermon No. 33 in the current edition *Sermons on Several Occasions*, sometimes spoken of as his *Forty-four Sermons*, and recognized as Methodist standard doctrine.

14. As, for example, in his sermon on "Christian Perfection", No. 35 in the same volume, p. 474.

15. July 6, 1960, two months before Eto's letter of rejection. In the file at Munda. 8 points were made.

16. Obedience to the Church was one of the points in the chairman's pastoral letter. However, it was the point for which he cited no scriptural proof-text. The fact that the village people still saw the organization as a Mission and not a Church operated against the missionaries at this point.

17. I quote their actual words as given to me by informants: "We carried on for the Mission during the war. Now they have neglected us." This shows how very far they were from church-thinking. A wrong attitude in every way.

18. Danho: 1958, p. 41.

CHAPTER 17. THEOLOGICAL ANALYSIS OF ETOISM

1. Dracaena leaves were used in divination, rain-making, shamanistic rites, funerary rites, women's menstruation ceremonies, snake cults, war-magic, gardening and fishing magic, taboos, exorcism, acquisition of mana, protective magic, cures for certain sicknesses, for driving off evil spirits and several forms of sorcery. Many of these uses were common from Bougainville to San Cristoval.

2. Unfortunately I was unable to arrange a personal meeting with the malarial officer, but I have checked all the details I can from those who had it direct from him. I found them reliable witnesses in other things.

3. The Chairman's pastoral letter, July 6, 1960, said of the nature of prayer: We destroy its true nature when we encourage people to count up their prayers and to repeat them over and over again (Matt. 6: 7).

4. Sundkler: 1961, p. 298.

CHAPTER 18. THE PROCESS FROM ANIMIST TO CHRISTIAN FORMS

1. The importance of this process lies in whether or not it leads to theological difference between the missionaries and the emerging church. A negative attitude against the use of animistic forms in the young church may lead to a superficial acceptance of western forms and theology, driving the ghost cult

underground, only to find it later emerges in a syncretistic or neo-pagan break-away.

Various courses tried in the African situation have been listed by Pauw (1963):

1. Fellowship with mission churches but also recognizing traditional African belief and ritual. (Not scriptural.)
2. Retaining traditional forms but purging them of paganism.
3. Retaining ritual form and occasion with new Christian meaning.
4. Disregarding ancestor cult as something that must die out in time.
5. Continual encounter.

In the Solomons, the Melanesian Mission offers the best scope for the study of the third category. But this is not to say they have ignored the fifth. If encounter can be faced and won *within* culturally intelligible forms, this is all to the good. If contrary to these forms, it will be a foreign-indigenous encounter.

2. This in itself is a wonderful story. He was born a twin and custom demanded that mother and infants be buried alive. A Christian teacher, who had hidden in the bushes, dug up the bodies, but he alone was saved. An identical incident is reported from the west. Both men entered the Church.

3. As an example: A woman is killed by sorcery. The chances of proof under western law are remote, so that without a conviction all the social injuries continue to be felt and nothing is done. Supposing the offender is convicted and dealt with, the social injustices are still not righted—the husband has lost his wife and the children their mother. Even pagan law would have made some physical adjustment as compensation to them. Hogbin has developed this point.

4. *Southern Cross Log,* Feb. 1897, p. 32.
5. Hocart: 1925, pp. 234-35.
6. Confession among the South Seas Evangelicals is discussed by Hogbin at some length (1939. pp. 194, 197-98).
7. Unfortunately I did not witness this ceremony, but one of the Melanesian priests described it in detail. His account fits descriptions left by several missionary writers, for instance, Hopkins: 1927, pp. 46-47. The same pattern is widely used by other churches in New Guinea areas which are currently being won for Christ (e.g. Frerichs: 1957, pp. 144-45).
8. Lesser excommunication "excludes the sinner from participating in the public services of the Church". Restoration requires a public and open confession before the congregation.
9. These terms were laid down at the First Synod of the Diocese of Melanesia, held at Siota (Fourth Confce of Mel. Mission. 1921).
10. *Handbook of Rules, Regulations and Procedures* (1963). Discipline of a catechist is possible on the score that it renders him unsuited for his office. An individual's membership would have to be discussed at the Leaders' Meeting, or a general question of paganism could be discussed under the question on the spiritual state of the work. No minister or catechist could act without the preliminary warnings, or without the verdict of the meeting. An important person with an economic hold over his village would be difficult to discipline.

CHAPTER 20. THE BIBLE IN THE VILLAGE SITUATION

1. Wolfensberger: 1963.
2. Hogbin: 1939, pp. 184-90.
3. Corte: 1958.
4. Wesley: 1952 edition. See sermon on "Christian Perfection" pp. 457-77. This is beautifully expressed in Charles Wesley's 28-verse hymn "The Promise of Sanctification", with phrases like, "Open my faith's interior eye", and "Confound, o'erpower me with Thy grace". Thus is holiness an experience.
5. Turner's *Profile Through Preaching* has come into the writer's hands since this study was written. In an analysis of the use of Scripture in the Independent African *Church of Our Lord*, although Turner's statistical tables are differently computed from mine, *James* also heads the frequency table and

Romans, I Corinthians and *Hebrews* are all in the first ten places for all the books of the whole Bible. Again one is surprised at the comparatively low score of the *Book of Acts* (pp. 19–21). Turner attributes the popularity of James to its pithy disconnected form, aphorisms, epigrams and similes, and the practical nature of its contents. These would appeal to a proverb-loving people whose pre-Christian religion was essentially practical. This point might well apply also in the Solomons. In the case of *Hebrews*, Turner discovered that the emphasis was on the practical digressions and not the main argument. However, in the Rarumana tests the role of Christ as the superior High Priest was prominent and the typology appealed to them. The most frequent user of this book was the catechist. It may be that he was using the book for his private devotions at the time, but I would not be surprised if he found comfort in the superior sacrifice and priesthood of Christ to answer for the cultural losses by the disappearance of actual physical sacrifices. In the Anglican area this had been met by a strong emphasis on Holy Communion. I know this man felt very much the loss of his customs, and in *Hebrews* he found an answer.

In his concluding profile of *The Church of Our Lord* (pp. 78–79), Turner indicates its desire to be a biblical Church. We can say the same of the congregation at Rarumana, with this proviso—their capacity has been limited by the portions of the Bible translated. Turner also found the preference among biblical literature types was for practical teaching, religious ormoral. This is so also for Rarumana, but it differs from what I have found in other parts of Melanesia and I think it needs an explanation. I do not mean that the Fijians, for instance, are not given to proverbs and practical sayings—they certainly are—but these are not nearly as prominent as dynamic narrative and encounter. I think the concentration on the ethical and didactic in Rarumana is a second choice, in the face of mission policy and training. The people in Rarumana have lost something and their leaders know it.

6. *Kalendar and Lectionary.*

7. ibid. It also provides special collects, information regarding feasts, &c.

8. As an actual example, one young man read Acts 21 : 15–26 in English—why in English I do not know, for he obviously did not understand it. I would not have understood what he was trying to read without my own English Bible. Many words had no meaning at all, 'circumcision', 'vow' and 'saluted' were like foreign words. Many he read as other English words with quite different meaning—'certain' became 'curtain', 'purification' became 'putrifaction', 'fornication' was simply 'nation', 'carriages' became 'chariots', and the 'disciples of Caesarea' were spoken of as the 'disciples of Caesar'. There were others, but these I wrote down immediately I left the church. As an English Bible reading it was painful, as an act of worship a failure. Fortunately the young man was only assigned the opportunity once, and I trust that when next asked the priest will tell him to read in his own language. Once or twice I had the feeling that a 'capacity' to read in English was a mark of prestige. If it takes attention off the word being read and puts it on the reader, it is manifestly out of place in worship.

9. The Methodists are about to print the complete Book of Psalms in the Roviana language, a missionary having been set aside for the task.

10. Fox–Durrad Aug. 28, 1950. The reference is:
    We now put little weight on Scriptures: we have done no translating for years; the old prayer books had the epistles and gospels, the later ones have not, in many villages no portions of Scripture can be read or are read to the people.
    It is good when missionaries are aware of such shortcomings, because it is only thus that things do get done. My impression was that the Melanesian Mission had done good linguistic and translation work, in a difficult area with considerable segmentation of language regions.

11. A Methodist islander in the west was bemoaning the flooding of the area with Mormon, Jehovah's Witnesses, Osborn and Oral Roberts material (I use only the names he himself mentioned) and said, "We see these books. We see the words of the Bible, and we believe them."

CHAPTER 21. MEASURING CONGREGATIONAL PIETY BY
MEANS OF CURVES

1. This figure is as near as I could arrive at the number of persons who could actually have attended church. The population was 199, but some were away in employment or in school, and there were occasional visitors.
2. There are two possible errors, those absent due to domestic duties and any sick or aged unable to attend. The effect of these errors was not very noticeable.
3. We are confronted with a difference between the legal provision and the rural practice. No doubt the procedures laid down in *Rules, Regulations and Procedures* are followed on the station compounds, but they are certainly not universally used. Reception into membership or confirmation provides for for three steps—preparation of the candidate by the catechist, the theological scope of which is laid down in the regulations. The case is then examined by the Leaders' Meeting on a basis of moral life, financial stability, church attendance, and good name. There is no reference here to religious experience. The minister then tests the candidates' memory work and knowledge on a basis of set questions. They are tests of knowledge rather than of faith. In the reception of members service, the liturgy for which is set out, the new member makes his confession of faith and devotional promises in the form of standard liturgical responses. The service is in English and the liturgical questions are asked by the Chairman of the District. This must tend to paternalism. A Church of over sixty years' status should have the village ministers doing this. In a Church of some 20,000 odd persons, with about 8,000 on the youth-roll shortly to be received as members, and over 5,000 classed as adherents, which probably means marginals, and these distributed through some 247 village congregations, there should be some more efficient means for receiving new members or full members than by a single individual, who has a heavy administrative load in any case. There is an indigenous ministry of fifteen— small indeed for the strength of the church—but why should they not receive members in line with regular Methodist practice?
4. Praise is expressed by the word *vahesi* (*vahesia, vinahesi*). After my two weeks sample suggested this shortcoming, a careful check was kept on the use of this word in the prayers. Except in the Lord's Prayer, in which *vinahesi* is used for glory, over sixty prayers were offered before the word for praise was used spontaneously.
5. A similar check to that used for 'praise' was taken for 'confess' and 'confession' (*helahela, helahelae*). We did not record the word as used in prayer, nor do I remember it in any of the hymns.
6. Montgomery: 1896, p. 254.
7. It should be remembered that a priest was stationed at Fouia. The village may be typical of some other villages where the Anglicans had resident priests, but we cannot expect it to be typical of villages on the fringe of a pastorate, which have Holy Communion perhaps once a month or less. Such a place might produce quite a different curve.
8. Praise and adoration, confession of sin, creedal statement of belief, personal dedication and specific intercessions are all provided. In the Methodist village, prayers though much longer, are almost entirely intercession, and just as stereotyped as the formal printed prayers.

CHAPTER 22. HALF-CHRISTIAN, HALF-PAGAN VILLAGES

1. The skull was that of the grandfather's father's father.
2. This is a significant testimony, because the informant himself was converted from the priestly line.
3. When Martin Dyson arrived in Samoa in 1857, he was shocked at the number of small villages which were fractured by denominational divisions that had affiliated themselves with pre-Christian kin rivalries. He narrated a case of one kin segment leaving one denomination for a purely secular quarrel with a sociological base which had no bearing at all on religion.
   In Fiji, where Methodism is strongly entrenched, I personally have observed

that the occasional divided village, more often than not, has a sociological non-religious rivalry as its basic structure.

4. My statistics are the best I can obtain, checked where possible, but they are estimates only and from indigenous informants. The figure of 700 for Sulufou is suspect, but it could be so. The island is certainly the most over-crowded area of human habitation I have known. The list shows about 2,400 people living in these little artificial islands. I think the figures are reasonable. The Anglican priest has a criterion for estimating. He provides Holy Communion where there are sixty communicants, otherwise they have to go to near-by islands.

CHAPTER 23. URBAN AND INDUSTRIAL SITUATIONS

1. Clark: 1928, pp. 12 ff.
2. Peill: 1930.
3. Rowlands: 1930.
4. In the course of this research the writer accumulated a great deal of material on the comity agreements and denominational relationships. Owing to the length of this manuscript, this had to be eliminated. It is indeed the subject for a whole monograph.
5. Many day to day adjustments are called for, speaking of adult labour force as "the boys", of adult cooks and domestic workers as "house boys", of talking in a superior manner about "the natives" in their presence, all of which betray a paternalistic and superior attitude. One of the first impressions I had when I arrived in Honiara was that of returning in time to a day I had hoped was dead.
6. A recruiter who was operating in the Tai Lagoon while I was there was obtaining more pagan than Christian labour from that locality.
7. This presupposes that the man has a Christian experience. If not, then he should be the object of personal evangelism. The Christian group will find it hard to prosper if their accepted leaders are not Christian.
8. Clark: 1928, pp. 28 and 29.
9. The theology of this position has biblical roots. Moses' farewell blessing to to Asher was "as thy days so shall thy strength be" (Deut. 33: 25). The Christian Church has had no reason to doubt this aspect of the goodness and providence of God. Yet Christian missions are so frequently straining at raising standards for tomorrow's leadership that they fail to make use of the indigenous leadership available for today on its own levels. This is just another aspect of our paternalism.
10. The story of this interesting leader has been published (Macquarrie: 1945), although the building of this village belongs to his later years. I visited this village without warning and believe I found things as they normally are. Most of the people were out engaged on a communal project but they had left the streets well swept, and many of the domestic units were hedged with crotons and Vouza's own house had a quantity of modern equipment—sleeping nets, sewing machine, and so on. An armchair from some wartime aircraft was set up for comfort by the window. There were two church buildings and each denominational group had its residential segment. The original group was Anglican. The South Sea Evangelicals had come from Ngalibia River country in Qasibatu. The Roman Catholics comprised three families. One of my committee men drove me out to this village on my last day in Honiara, when I asked to see another village which differed from the types I had come to know.
11. Even in cases of the youths who have signed up to escape village authority or their low social status, for they would unconsciously retain their traditional solidarity with folk at home.
12. Green: 1951, p.148.
13. Hogbin: 1939, pp. 163–65.
14. Fichter: 1957.
15. I have used five categories because my data fell naturally into such a breakdown of classes. The fact that Fichter shows that 42 per cent (and 68 per cent

if the dormant class be excluded) classify as modal rather suggests a subdivision would have been possible. Working with nuclear, modal and marginal Christians, one gets a curve like my hypothetical average. This is to ignore the fact that 39 per cent have drifted away from church. They have not joined another church, and if pressed would say they were Catholics. This gives a bi-modal curve and explains why I avoid the term 'modal'.

16. Fichter: 1957, pp. 429-32.
17. Black: 1936, pp. 171-81.

CONCLUSION

1. The Christian does not escape the necessity for encounter even with considerable education and intellectual development. David Paton wrote of the situation in China:

> There are Chinese intellectuals: most of them have no theology worth speaking of, and what they have is seriously, not to say appallingly, heretical. There are orthodox Christians: they are mostly simple minded fundamentalists or educated clergy whose thought is not at bottom their own or Chinese, but remains woodenly in western categories. There is a vacuum. It has been filled mainly by dialectical materialism. If there are signs of a beginning of a theological movement, it is due principally to the realization, tragically belated, that Marxism must be encountered and mastered. (1953: p. 50.)

He thought in terms of *vacuum* and *encounter*. Time after time, in this research I have felt that the experiences of China have something to say to Melanesia.

2. Paton: 1953, p. 34.

BIBLIOGRAPHY

(This list is confined to sources consulted and references cited)

Administration: Official
  Handbook of B.S.I.P., Tulagi, 1911
  British Solomon Islands Reports, Her Majesty's Stationery Office, London, 1948, 1949–50, 1951–52, 1953–54, 1955–56, 1957–58, 1959–60, 1961–62 (Files used Western Pacific High Commission, Suva, Fiji), Apr. 1, 1903–Mar. 31, 1905
—— B.S.I.P. *White Papers* (British Solomon Islands Protectorate, Honiara), No. 3 *Educational Policy*, Aug. 1962, No. 5 *Medical & Public Health Policy*, Apr. 1964, No. 6 *Agricultural & Fisheries Policy*, Sept. 1964
Allen, C. H.
  The Marching Rule Movement in the British Solomon Islands Protectorate: An Analytical Survey. Cambridge University research scholarship in anthropology, original in Haddon Library. Microfilm used at Australian National University, Canberra, 1950
Allen, Roland
  Missionary Methods: St. Paul's or Ours? World Dominion Press, London, 1930
—— *Spontaneous Expansion of the Church*, World Dominion Press, London, 1949
—— *Sidney James Wells Clark*, World Dominion Press, London, 1937
Angas, G. F.
  Polynesia: A Popular Description . . . of the Islands of the Pacific, Society for Promoting Christian Knowledge, London, 1865
Anon.
  "A New Venture in Evangelism", *The Open Door*, vol. 32, 1953
—— "Cults: Nationalism in the Pacific", Field Survey No. 7, *A.B.M. Review*, vol. 40, 1952, pp. 101–3
—— "Levers Want Indian Labour in the Solomons", *Pacific Islands Monthly*, Dec. 1931
—— "Thirteen Points: Woes of the Solomon Islands", *Pacific Islands Monthly*, July 1931
—— *The Island Mission: Being a History of the Melanesian Mission from its Commencement.* Reprinted from *Mission Life*, William Macintosh, London), 1869
Armstrong, E. S.
  The History of the Melanesian Mission, Isbister & Co., Covent Garden, 1937
Artless, Stuart W.
  The Story of the Melanesian Mission, Melanesian Mission, London, 1937
Australian Association for the Advancement of Science
  Transactions, 1911
A.B.M. Review
  Files used at the La Trobe Library, Melbourne, No. 7, 1952

Australasian Methodist Missionary Review
Files used at Methodist Overseas Missions, Melbourne, covering the
period of Australian control of the Methodist Mission in the Solomons
1896 (July), 1898 (Dec.), 1899 (Nov.)
1901—(Apr., May, July, Aug., Sept., Oct., Dec.)
1902—(Feb., Mar., May, June, July, Aug., Sept., Oct., Nov.)
1903—(Sept., Dec.)
1904—(Mar., Apr., May, June, July, Oct., Nov.)
1905—(Feb., Apr., May, June, Aug.)
1906—(Mar., May, Oct., Nov.)
1907—(Apr., Oct., Nov.)
1908—(Feb., Mar., May, Aug., Sept.)
1909—(Feb.)
1910—(Mar., May, June, July, Aug., Oct.)
1911—(Feb., Mar., Apr., June, Aug., Oct., Dec.)
1912—(Jan., Apr., Aug., Oct., Nov.)
1913—(Aug.)
1914—(June, July)   1915—(June)
1916—(Oct.)   1917—(Jan., Mar.)
1918—(Mar., Aug., Nov., Dec.)
Barnett, Homer G.
Innovation: The Basis of Cultural Change, McGraw-Hill Book Co.,
Inc., New York, 1953
Beckett, —
Address at New South Wales Conference Foreign Mission Meeting,
Australasian Methodist Missionary Review, Apr., 1901
Belshaw, Cyril S.
"Native Politics in the Solomon Islands", *Pacific Affairs*, vol. 20. 2,
pp. 187–93, 1947
—— "Changes in Heirloom Jewellery in the Central Solomons", *Oceania*,
vol. 20. 3, Mar. 1950, pp. 169–84
—— *Changing Melanesia: Social Economics of Culture Contact*, Geoffrey
Cumberlege, O.U.P., Melbourne, 1954
—— "The Significance of Modern Cults in Melanesian Development",
Reader in Comparative Religion, Row, Peterson & Co., Evanston,
pp. 486–92, 1958, from *The Australian Outlook*)
Bensley, A. A.
"Easter and Other Occasions", *The Open Door*, vol. 12. 1, 1933
Binet, V. le C.
"Peace Celebrations at Senga", *The Open Door*, vol. 2. 2, 1923
—— "The Tale of Two Tally Sticks", *The Open Door*, vol. 4. 2, pp. 8–10,
1925
—— "The Anniversary of Peace on Choiseul", *The Open Door*, vol. 11. 2,
1932
Black, Robert H.
"Christianity as a Cross-cultural Bond in the British Solomon Islands
Protectorate as seen in the Russell Islands", *Oceania*, vol. 33. 3,
pp. 171–81, 1963
Blackwood, Beatrice
*Both Sides of Buka Passage: An Ethnographic Study of Social, Sexual
and Economic Questions in the North-western Solomon Islands*,
Clarendon Press, Oxford, 1935
Blamires, Edgar P.
Changing Strategy in Evangelism, Epworth Press, London, 1951

O

Bogesi, George
    "Santa Isabel, Solomon Islands", *Oceania*, vol. 18. 3–4, pp. 208–32, 327–57, 1948
British & Foreign Bible Society
    Na Vinatatara Vaqurana Pa Zinama Roviana, Roviana New Testament, Council of the B.F.B.S., Sydney, 1953
British Solomon Islands Society for Advancement of Science & Industry
    Transactions, vol. 2, Honiara, 1955
Brown, George
    Official Correspondence with Goldie in letter books in Methodist Overseas Missions Archives, Sydney.
—— Correspondence in *Australasian Methodist Missionary Review*
—— "Proposed New Mission", *ibid.*, Dec. 1901
—— "Mission to the Solomons", *ibid.*, July, 1901
—— "General Secretary's Report", *ibid.*, Sept., 1901
—— "The Solomon Islands", *ibid.*, Oct., 1901
—— "The New Georgia Mission", *ibid.*, Sept., Oct., Nov., 1902   ,
—— *George Brown: Pioneer, Missionary and Explorer: An Autobiography*, Hodder and Stoughton, London, 1908
—— *Melanesians and Polynesians: Their Life Histories Described and Compared*, Macmillan & Co., London, 1910
Buadromo, I See 'Vula'
Burton, John W.
    The Pacific Islands: A Missionary Survey, World Dominion Press, London, 1930
—— *The First Century of Missionary Adventure of Australian Methodism: 1855–1955*, Methodist Overseas Missions, Sydney, 1955
Calverton, V. F.
    The Making of Man: An Outline of Anthropology, The Modern Library, New York, 1931
Cameron, Charlotte
    Two Years in the Southern Seas, T. Fisher Unwin Ltd., London, 1923
Capell, A
    "The Word 'Mana': A Linguistic Study", *Oceania*, vol. 9. 1, pp. 89–96, 1938
—— "Notes on the Islands of Choiseul and New Georgia, Solomon Islands", *Oceania*, vol. 14. 1, pp. 20–29, 1943
Carter, G. G.
    Correspondence, Reports, Statements on Etoism (at Munda)
—— "The Chairman's Address to Synod", Methodist Solomon Islands District; Duplicated, 1964
Church of England
    The English Hymnal, Oxford University Press—A. R. Mowbray & Co. Ltd., London, 1962
Churchill, W.
    Beach-la-mar Vocabulary, Carnegie Institute, Washington, D.C.
Clark, Sidney J. W.
    The Indigenous Church, World Dominion Press, London, 1928
—— *The First Stage in the Christian Occupation of Rural China*, World Dominion Press, London, c. 1930
—— *Indigenous Fruits*, World Dominion Press, London, 1933
Coaldrake, F. W.
    Flood Tide in the Pacific: Church and Community Cascade into a New Age, Australian Board of Missions, Sydney, n.d. c. 1963

Codrington, R. H.
  The Melanesian Languages, Clarendon Press, Oxford, 1885
—— *The Melanesians: Studies in their Anthropology and Folk-Lore*, Clarendon Press, Oxford, 1891
—— (translat. *Story of a Melanesian Deacon: Clement Marau*, written by himself. Society for Promoting Christian Knowledge, Brighton, 1894
Collinson, Clifford W.
  Life and Laughter 'midst the Cannibals, Hurst and Blackett, London, 1927 (read, but not used as a source
Colwell, James (Ed.)
  A Century in the Pacific, Charles H. Kelly, London, 1944
Cormack, James E.
  Isles of Solomon, Review and Herald, Washington, D.C., 1944
Cornwall, G.A.R.
  Correspondence and MSS.
Corte, Nicolas
  Who is the Devil? Roman Catholic Fact and Faith Book No. 21 (translation of *Satan, l'adversaire*), Burns & Oates, London, 1958
Creighton, Louise
  G. A. Selwyn, D.D., Bishop of New Zealand and Lichfield, Society for the Propagation of the Gospel in Foreign Parts, Westminster, 1923
Cropp, A. H.
  "A Missionary on Tour: Wonderful Openings on Buka", *The Open Door*, vol. 10. 1, 1931
—— "Itinerating on Bougainville", *The Open Door*, vol. 10. 2, 1931
—— "Quaint Customs (Buka)", *The Open Door*, vol. 10. 5, 1932
Danho, Josué
  "Encounter between Christian and Non-Christian" in *The Ghana Assembly of the International Missionary Council, 28 Dec. 1957–8 Jan. 1958*, Selected papers. Edinburgh House Press for the I.M.C., London, 1958
Danks, B.
  "The Solomon Islands", *Australasian Methodist Missionary Review*, Dec. 1901
—— *Methodist Missions in the South Seas: 1821–1909*, Methodist Missionary Society of Australasia, Sydney, 1909
Deck, Norman
  Controversy with H. Ian Hogbin. Correspondence in *Oceania*, vol. 5: 2, 3, 4. Dec. 1934, Mar., June, 1935, pp. 242–45, 368–70, 488–89
Deck, Northcote
  Dr. Deck's Letter—quarterly letter published by South Seas Evangelical Mission representative in the Solomons for about twenty years from c. 1907
—— *South from Guadalcanal: The Romance of Rennell Island*, Evangelical Publishers, Toronto, 1945
Donovan, Robert J.
  P.T. 109: John F. Kennedy in World War II, McGraw-Hill Book Co., Inc., New York, 1961
Dovey, J. Whitsed
  The Cross across the Pacific, Report of the Missionary Conference at Morpeth, N.S.W. Feb. 23–28, 1948 (National Missionary Councils of Australia and New Zealand)

—— *The Gospel in the South Pacific*, World Dominion Press, London, 1950
Dunbabin, T.
  Slavers of the South Seas, Angus and Robertson, Sydney, 1935
Durrad, W. J.
  "The Depopulation of Melanesia", in *Essays on the Depopulation of Melanesia*, Ed. W. H. R. Rivers, Cambridge University Press, pp. 3–24, 1922
—— See also 'Fox'
Edge-Partington J. and T. A. Joyce
  "Note on Funerary Ornaments from Rubiana", *Man*, vol. 4, 1904, pp. 129–31
Edge-Partington, T. W.
  "Ingava, Chief of Rubiana, Solomon Islands: Died 1906", *Man*, vol. 7, 1907, pp. 22–23
Elkin, A. P.
  Review of R. C. Thurnwald's "Profane Literature of Buin, Solomon Islands", in *Oceania*, vol. 7. 2, p. 272, 1936
—— Review of R. C. Thurnwald's "The Price of the White Man's Peace", in *Oceania*, vol. 7. 2, pp. 272–73, 1936
—— "The Reaction of Primitive Races to the White Man's Culture", *The Hibbert Journal*, vol 35. 4, pp. 537–45, July, 1937
—— *Wanted—A Charter for the Native People of the Southwest Pacific*, Australian Publishing Co., Pty., Ltd., Sydney, 1943
—— "Anthropology and the peoples of the Southwest Pacific: The Past, Present and Future". *Oceania*, vol 14. 1, pp. 1–19, 1943
Erskine, John E.
  Journal of a Cruise Among the Islands of the Western Pacific, etc. John Murray, London, 1853
Eto, Silas
  "A Native Chief Takes Stock", *The Open Door*, vol. 29. 3, 1949, with editorial comment.
—— Correspondence at Methodist Mission, Munda.
Fairweather, E. R. (Ed.)
  Anglican Congress, 1963: Report of Proceedings (Anglican Congress Editorial Committee)
Fichter, Joseph H.
  "The Marginal Catholic: An Institutional Approach" in *Religion, Society and the Individual*, ed. J. Milton Yinger, The Macmillan Co., New York, 1957, pp. 423-433
Fiji Society for Science and Industry
  Transactions and Proceedings, 1947
Fison, Lorimer
  "The Murder of Bishop Patteson", *The Herald*, 1871
—— Speech delivered at St. James at a public meeting regarding the death of Bishop Patteson. Press clippings, source not specified.
    Both these items are in a Fison Press Clippings Book in the writer's possession.
Fleury, R.
  Correspondence on Etoism at Methodist Mission, Munda.
Forde, C. Daryll
  Habitat, Economy and Society: A Geographical Introduction to Ethnology Methuen & Co., London, 1948; pp. 173–219 concern the Solomon Islands

Fox, Charles E.
The Threshold of the Pacific: An Account of the Social Organization, Magic and Religion of the People of San Cristoval in the Solomon Islands, Kegan Paul, Trench, Trubner & Co. Ltd., London, 1924
―― *Fox–Durrad Papers*, Correspondence and other documents at the Turnbull Library, Wellington, New Zealand. c. 1950
―― *Lord of the Southern Isles: Being the Story of an Anglican Mission in Melanesia: 1849–1949*, A. R. Mowbray & Co. Ltd., London, 1958
―― *Kakamora*, Hodder and Stoughton, London, 1962
Frater, A. S.
"Depopulation of the New Hebrides", *Transactions and Proceedings of the Fiji Society for Science and Industry*, 1947, pp. 166–85
Frerichs, A. C.
Anutu Conquers in New Guinea, The Wartburg Press, Columbus, Ohio, 1957
Fuller, Columbus C.
"The Industrial Missions", *Australian Methodist Missionary Review*, Aug. 1908
Goldie, John F.
Correspondence from the Solomon Islands to Mission headquarters in Sydney (Methodist Overseas Missions Archives, Sydney) and Auckland (Foreign Mission Office, Auckland) and published in *Australasian Methodist Missionary Review*
―― "Report from the Solomons", in *ibid*. Mar., 1904
―― "The People of New Georgia, their Manners and Customs, and Religious Beliefs", *Proceedings of the Royal Society of Queensland*, vol. 22. 1, pp. 23–30, H. Pole & Co., Brisbane, 1908
―― "The Solomon Islands", in Colwell's *A Century in the Pacific*, Charles H. Kelly, London, pp, 559–85, 1914
―― "The Frontiers of the Kingdom" (25th Anniversary of the Mission), in *New Zealand Methodist Times*, May 7, 1927
―― "Early Days at Roviana", *The Open Door*, vol. 5. 4, 1927
―― "Roviana Circuit Report, 1937", *The Open Door*, vol. 16. 4, 1938
Green, Brian
The Practice of Evangelism, Moorhouse Lecture, Melbourne, 1951, Hodder & Stoughton, London, 1951
Grover, John C.
"A Concise History of the Search for Gold in the Solomons", *Transactions of the British Solomons Society for the Advancement of Science and Industry*, vol. 2, Honiara, 1952–54
Guppy, H. B.
The Solomon Islands and their Natives, Swan Sonnenschein Lowrey & Co., London, 1887
Hall, A. H.
"Moving Back to Kokengolo", *The Open Door*, vol. 29. 4, 1950
―― Correspondence on Etoism at Methodist Mission, Munda
Hamilton, Floyd E.
"The True Task of the Christian Church", *World Dominion*, 1928
Hayward, Victor E. W.
African Independent Church Movements, Edinburgh House Press, London, for the World Council of Churches, Commission on World Mission and Evangelism, 1963
Hocart, A. M.
"The Cult of the Dead in Eddystone of the Solomons", *Journal of*

the Royal Anthropological Institute of Great Britain and Ireland,
vol. 52, 1922, pp. 71–112, 259–305.
—— "Medicine and Witchcraft in Eddystone of the Solomons", *ibid.*
vol. 55, 1925, pp. 229–70
—— "Warfare in Eddystone of the Solomons", *ibid.* vol. 61, 1931, pp.
301–24
—— "The Mechanism of the Evil Eye", *Folklore*, vol. 49, 1938, pp. 156–57
Hogbin, H. Ian
    "Culture Change in the Solomon Islands: Report on Field Work in
    Guadalcanal and Malaita", *Oceania*, vol. 4, 1933–34, pp. 233–67
—— Controversy with N. Deck of the South Seas Evangelical Mission.
    See *Oceania*, vol. 5, Dec. 1934; Mar. 1935; June 1935
—— "Sorcery and Administration", *Oceania*, vol. 6. 1, 1935, pp. 1–32
—— "Mana", *Oceania*, vol. 6. 3, 1963
—— "The Hill People of Northeast Guadalcanal and Florida, Solomon
    Islands", *Oceania*, vol. 8. 1, 1937, pp. 62–89
—— "Social Advancement in Guadalcanal", *Oceania*, vol. 8. 3, 1938,
    pp. 289–305
—— "Social Organization in Guadalcanal", *Oceania*, vol. 8. 4, 1938,
    pp. 398–400
—— *Experiments in Civilization: The Effects of European Civilization on
    a Native Community of the Solomon Islands*, George Routledge & Sons
    Ltd., London, 1939
—— "Native Councils and Native Courts in the Solomon Islands", *Oceania*,
    vol. 14, 1944, pp. 257–83
—— *A Guadalcanal Society: The Kaoka Speakers*, Holt, Rinehart
    and Winston, New York, 1964, in the series "Case Studies in
    Anthropology"
Hopkins, A. I.
    "The Kanakas' Return", *Southern Cross Log*, Dec. 1907, pp. 97–99
—— "Depopulation of the Solomon Islands", Essay iv in W. H. R. Rivers'
    Essays on the Depopulation of Melanesia, University Press, Cambridge,
    1922
—— *In the Isles of King Solomon: Twenty-five Years Among the Primitive
    Solomon Islanders*, Seeley, Service & Co., London, 1928
—— (with Johann Flierl) "Native Life in the South West Pacific: From
    two points of view", *International Review of Missions*, vol. 17, 1928,
    pp. 538–49
—— *From Heathen Boy to Christian Priest*, Society for the Propagation of
    Christian Knowledge, London, 1949 edition
How, F. H.
    Bishop John Selwyn: A Memoir, Isbister & Co., Ltd., Covent Garden,
    1899
Huddleston, Trevor
    Naught for Your Comfort, Collins's Fontana Books, London, 1957
Im Thurn, Everard
    "Preface" in Rivers's *Essays on the Depopulation of Melanesia*,
    University Press, Cambridge, 1922
International Missionary Council
    International Review of Missions
—— *I.M.C. Research Pamphlets* (Now C.W.M.E. pamphlets)
—— *The World Mission of the Church* (Tambaram findings and recommend-
    ations—Madras Conference), 1938
—— *The Ghana Assembly of the I.M.C.*, 1957–58

Ivens, W. G.
Melanesians of the Southeast Solomon Islands, Kegan Paul, Trench, Trubner & Co. Ltd., London, 1927
—— *The Island Builders of the Pacific: How and Why the People of Mala Construct their Artificial Islands, etc.*, Seeley, Service & Co. Ltd., London, 1930
—— *A Vocabulary of the Lau Language, Big Mala, Solomon Islands.* Memoir 11, Supplements to Journal of the Polynesian Society, vols. 41–42, 1934
Jacomb, Edward
The Future of the Kanaka, P. S. King & Son, Westminster, 1919
Joyce, T. A. See 'Edge-Partington'
Knibbs, S. G. C.
The Savage Solomons as they were: A record of a head-hunting people gradually emerging from a life of savage cruelty and bloody customs, with a description of their manner and ways, etc., Seeley, Service & Co., London, 1929
Lambert, S. M.
A Doctor in Paradise, Georgian House, Melbourne, 1946
Lansley, Gerald
"Foreword" in Blamire's *Changing Strategy in Evangelism*, Epworth Press, London, 1951
Leadley, E. C.
"The Skull Houses", *The Open Door*, vol. 15. 4, 1937
—— "Higaloze", *The Open Door*, vol. 16. 1, 1937
—— *Report on the New Way of Worship* (Report on Etoism duplicated by Methodist Mission, Munda), 1961
Lessa, William A. and Evon Z. Vogt
Reader in Comparative Religion, Row, Peterson & Co., Evanston, Illinois, 1958
Linton, Ralph
"Nativistic Movements" in *Reader in Comparative Religion*, Row, Peterson & Co., Evanston, 1958, pp. 466–74 (from *American Anthropologist*)
Luxton, C. T. J.
Isles of Solomon: A Tale of Missionary Adventure, Methodist Foreign Mission Society of New Zealand, Auckland, N.Z., 1955
McGavran, Donald Anderson
The Bridges of God: A Study in the Strategy of Missions, World Dominion Press, London, 1957
—— *How Churches Grow: The New Frontiers of Mission*, World Dominion Press, London, 1959
—— *How to do a Survey in Church Growth*, Institute of Church Growth, Eugene, Oregon, 1963
—— *Church Growth and Christian Mission* Symposium edited by McGavran, Harper & Row, New York, 1965
—— *Gold Coast Methodism: Case Study in Church Growth*—Unpublished manuscript. n.d.
McHardy, Emmet
Blazing the Trail: Letters from the North Solomons, Rt. Rev. T. J. Wade, S.M., Church Hill, 1935
McNairn, A. Stuart
The Native Church—Exotic or Indigenous, World Dominion Press, London, 1934

Macquarrie, Hector
> *Vouza and the Solomon Islands,* V. Gollancz, London, 1945
Man
> vol. 4, 1904; vol. 5, 1905; vol. 8, 1908; vol. 11, 1911
Marau, Clement
> Translation of Autobiography: see R. H. Codrington
Marett, R. R.
> *The Threshold of Religion,* The Macmillan Co., New York, 1909
Melanesian Mission
> *Journal of the Mission Voyage to the Melanesian Islands of the Schooner 'Southern Cross' made in May–October, 1866,* 'Daily Southern Cross' Office, Auckland, N.Z., 1866
—— *Southern Cross Log:* English and colonial editions of this journal exist.
> 1895—May 1904, Auckland
> June 1904—April 1913, Sydney
> Since May 1913, Auckland
> *Report of the Fourth Conference of the Melanesian Mission and of the First Synod of the Missionary Diocese of Melanesia, held at Siota, Oct. 24–Nov. 8, 1921*
—— *Melanesia Today: A Study Circle Book,* Society for Promoting Christian Knowledge, London, 1927
—— *In the Solomons and Other Islands of Melanesia,* Melanesian Mission, Sydney, 1943
—— *Na Book Fooalaa: Maluta ni Fooalaa Gi Ni Lau,* Melanesian Mission Press, Taroaniara, 1962
> Prayer book, including a translation of 62 psalms and about a hundred collects. Lau Language.
—— *A Book of Common Prayer: Authorized for Use in the Churches and Chapels of the Diocese of Melanesia,* Melanesian Mission Press, Taroaniara, 1962
—— *Morning and Evening Prayers Simplified*: known locally as "The Brotherhood Book" and including 49 hymns, Melanesian Mission Press, Taroaniara, 1962
—— The *"Companions of the Brothers",* also called *"The Company of Companions"*: Rules, order of admission and offices, Melanesian Mission Press, Taroaniara, 1963
—— *Jehovah's Witnesses, or Buy a Book,* Melanesian Mission Press, Taroaniara, n.d. c. 1964
—— *Taroaniara,* Melanesian Mission Press, Taroaniara, n.d. c. 1964
—— *Proceedings of the Diocesan Synod held at St Mary's School, Maravovo, July 5th to July 15th, 1962*—together with reports and other documents presented to Synod, The Church of the Diocese of Melanesia and printed at Taroaniara, 1965
Metcalfe, John F.
> Private Documents
>> *Personal correspondence* from the Solomon Islands from 1920 to the beginning of the War (Files)
>> *Reports* and *Correspondence* after the War (Files)
>> *Biographical Notes on Solomon Island Teachers* (Files)
—— Unpublished Manuscripts
>> "The Three Brothers"
>> "Methodism in Marovo"
>> "Methodism in Guadalcanal"

"Thoughts on Etoism"
"Harry Raeno"
"Solomon Damusoe"
"The Vurulata-Senga Feud"
"The Gumi Family"
"The Two Friends"
"Timothy Loe"
"Cargo Cults in the Solomons"
"Our Time at Teop"
"History of Choiseul" (including a policy statement on industrial missions)
—— *Data of the Methodist Mission to the Solomon Islands*, a manuscript volume of regional comparative chronology, which also contains records of mission staff, workers from other Pacific Islands, Solomon Island ministers and teachers
—— The Metcalfe Collection also includes the following items not written by Metcalfe himself, but used by the writer:
  Bougainville–Buka Circuit Reports & Statistics 1931–33
  Leadley Report on the New Way of Worship Feb. 2, 1961 (Etoism)
  "Extracts from Report of Commission of Enquiry into Policies & Activities of Missions in the District of Kieta, by Judge Phillips of Rabaul, Apr. 22, 1929"
Methodist Church
  (a) Documents produced by the controlling body in Australia
    General Conference Minutes, 1888, 1901
    "Annual Meeting Report", *Australasian Methodist Missionary Review*, Mar. 1902
    "Abstract of Report", *ibid.*, Feb. 1904
    "Report of the Board of Management", Sydney, 1907
    "Report for 1918" (Sydney), "Report to Board", 1916
    "Correspondence of the Missionaries released to *Sydney Morning Herald*", 1912 (S.M.H., Oct. 1, 1912)
  (b) Documents produced by the controlling body in New Zealand
    New Zealand Methodist Conference Minutes, 1921
    Annual Reports published 1922, 1923, 1924, 1925, 1928, 1929, 1930, 1931, 1932, 1933, 1934, 1935, 1936, 1937, 1938, 1939, 1940, 1941
    Reports of the Foreign Mission Board, 1928, 1929
  (c) Documents produced by the controlling body in the Solomon Islands, first known as the Mission, now as Solomon Islands District
    The Methodist Messenger, duplicated magazine of the Methodist Church in the Western Solomons, issued from 1959 to 1964, now replaced by *Onward*, with a Solomon Islands news sheet
    Handbook of Rules, Regulations & Procedures (duplicated at Munda) 1963
    "Development towards a Melanesian Conference from 1946", an unsigned report which appears to have been written about 1960
    "The Chairman's Address to Synod" (duplicated at Munda) 1964
    Files at the Head Station, Munda, New Georgia:
    "District History" (2 files)
    "Historical Articles & Notes on Personalities"

Methodist Church (*continued*)
    "Reports & Minutes of Synod 1928–44"
    "Reports & Minutes of United Methodist Synod of Melanesia"
    Roviana and District Reports, 1917
    File marked "Pentecostalism" (Etoism)
    Vernacular Publications (Roviana Language)
        Na Buka Kinera Lotu te Jisu Karisito pa Zinama Roviana,
        Epworth Printing & Publishing Co., Sydney, 1912
        Na Kinera Lotu te Jisu Karisito tadi na Ekelesia Metodisi,
        Epworth Printing & Publishing Co., Sydney, 1918 and 1924
        editions
        *Kaiqa Pule Kinera Lotu te Jisu Karisito tadi na Ekelesia
        Metodisi*, Spectator Publishing Co., Melbourne, 1920
        Sa Buka Kera Metodisi, Government Printing Office, Honiara,
        1963
    (d) *Official Correspondence* from the District
        In the Methodist Mission Archives, Sydney
        In the Methodist Mission Archives, Fiji
        In the Methodist Mission Office, Auckland
        In the Western Pacific High Commission Archives, Suva, Fiji
Miller, F. S.
    The Gospel in Korea, Fleming H. Revell, New York, 1939
Mission Secretary, A
    Education and the Missionary Task, World Dominion Press, London,
    1930
Mitchell, Doris M.
    Challenge in Melanesia, Australian Board of Missions, Sydney, 1958
Montgomery, H. H.
    *The Light of Melanesia: A Record of Thirtyfive Years' Mission Work
    in the South Seas*, Society for Promoting Christian Knowledge,
    London, 1896
Moss, Rosalind
    The Life After Death in Oceania and the Malay Archipelago, Humphrey
    Milford, O.U.P., Oxford, 1925
Myrdal, Gunnar
    An International Economy: Problems and Prospects, Harper &
    Brothers, New York, 1956
Mytinger, C.
    Head-hunting in the Solomon Islands Around the Coral Sea, Macmillan
    & Co., London, 1943
Newbolt, M. R. (Ed.)
    John Steward's Memories, Phillipson & Golder Ltd., Chester, 1939
Nicholson, R. C.
    Correspondence in *Australasian Methodist Missionary Review*
    —— *The Son of a Savage: The Story of Daniel Bula*, The Epworth Press,
    London, 1924
Oceania
    *A Journal Devoted to the Study of the Native Peoples of Australia,
    New Guinea and the Islands of the Pacific Ocean*, Australian National
    Research Council, Sydney, 4, 1933–34; 5, 1934–35; 6, 1935–36;
    8, 1937–38; 9, 1938–39; 14, 1943–44; 18, 1947–48; 20, 1949–50;
    21, 1950–51; 33, 1962–63
Oliver, Douglas L.
    A Solomon Islands Society: The Siuai of Bougainville, Harvard
    University Press, Cambridge, 1955

The Open Door
  Quarterly journal of the New Zealand Methodist Missionary Society.
  Complete file at Foreign Mission Office, Auckland. Sept. 1923;
  Dec. 1925; Mar. 1927; Dec. 1930; Mar., June, Sept. 1931; June,
  Sept. 1932; Mar., June 1933; June 1934; Mar. 1935; Mar., June 1937;
  Mar. 1938; Dec. 1941; Mar. 1952; Mar. 1953; Sept. 1954
Orchard, R. K. (Ed.)
  *The Ghana Assembly of the International Missionary Council: 28 Dec.
  1957 to 8 Jan. 1958* (Select papers with an essay on the role of the
  I.M.C.), Edinburgh House Press, London, 1958
Pacific Affairs
  Journal. Files used at La Trobe Library, Melbourne, 9, 1936; 20, 1947
Pacific Islands Monthly
  Files used at La Trobe Library, Melbourne
  Controversy on Mission Trading—correspondence published Dec.
  1931; Jan. 1932; Apr. 1932; May 1932; Aug. 1932
  "Levers Want Indian Labour for the Solomons", Dec. 1931
  "Thirteen Points: Woes of the Solomon Islands", July 1931
Page, Jessie
  Bishop Patteson, the Martyr of Melanesia, S. W. Partridge & Co. Ltd.,
  Old Bailey, London, n.d.
Parrinder, Geoffrey
  Witchcraft, Penguin Books Ltd., London, 1958
Paton, David M.
  Christian Missions and the Judgement of God, Student Christian
  Movement Press, London, 1953
Paton, Frank H. L.
  *Patteson of Melanesia: A Brief Life of John Coleridge Patteson,
  Missionary Bishop*, Society for Promoting Christian Knowledge,
  London, n.d.
Pauw, B. A.
  "African Christians and their Ancestors" in V. E. W. Hayward's
  African Independent Church Movements, Edinburgh House Press,
  London, pp. 33–46, 1963
Peill, S. E. and W. F. Rowlands
  Church Planting, World Dominion Press, London, n.d., but probably
  1930. Contains "Conditions of the Birth of a Living Church" (Peill)
  and "Church Planting in Siaochang, North China" (Rowlands)
Penny, Alfred
  Ten Years in Melanesia, Wells Gardner, Darton & Co., London,
  1888
Piolet, J. B. (Ed.)
  La France au dehors: les missions Catholiques françaises au XIX siècle,
  vol. 4, *Oceania*, A. Colin, Paris, 1902
Polynesian Society
  Journal of the Polynesian Society, vols. 41–42, 1934; 57, 1948
Raucas, L. M.
  In the Savage South Solomons: The Story of a Mission (Translation
  from the French), M. H. Gill & Son Ltd., Dublin, 1928
Rishworth, E. M.
  "Mrs. J. F. Goldie—An Appreciation", *The Open Door*, vol. 28,
  Mar. 1949
Rivers, W. H. R.
  The History of Melanesian Society, 2 vols., The University Press,

Cambridge, 1914
—— (Ed.) *Essays on the Depopulation of Melanesia*, The University Press, Cambridge, 1922
—— "The Psychological Factor", Essay VIII in *ibid.*, 1922
—— *Social Organization*, Kegan Paul, Trench, Trubner & Co., London, 1924

Robson, R. W.
Pacific Islands Year Book, 8th ed., Pacific Publications Pty. Ltd., Sydney, 1959

Roman Catholic Vicariate of the South Solomons
Official Statistics, 1964

Rooney, S. R.
Correspondence in *Australasian Methodist Missionary Review*
—— "Notes on Some Customs & Beliefs of the Natives of Choiseul Island", Australian Association for the Advancement of Science, *Transactions & Proceedings*, vol. 13, Sydney, 1911

Rowlands, W. F.
Indigenous Ideals in Practice: Evangelistic Policy and Work in the Siaochang Field in North China, World Dominion Press, London, 1931
—— See also Peill & Rowlands: *Church Planting*

Royal Anthropological Institute of Great Britain & Ireland
Journals, vols. 26, 1897; 52, 1923; 55, 1926; 61, 1932; 65, 1936; 67, 1938; 70, 1941

Russell, T.
"The Culture of Marovo, British Solomon Islands", *Journal of the Polynesian Society*, vol. 57, 1948, pp. 306–29
—— "The Fataleka of Malaita", *Oceania*, vol. 21, Sept. 1950

Rycroft, Harold R.
From Savagery to Christ: The Story of David Vule, The Epworth Press, London, 1926

Sargant, William
Battle for the Mind: A Physiology of Conversion and Brain-washing, Wm. Heinemann Ltd., London, 1957 (1960 revision by Pan Books Ltd., London, used for citing)

Scheffler, Harold W.
"Kindred and Kin Groups in Simbo Island Social Structure", *Ethnology*, vol. 1, No. 2, April 1962, pp. 135–57
—— "Choiseul Island Descent Groups", *Journal of the Polynesian Society*, vol. 72, No. 3, Sept. 1963, pp. 177–87
—— "Political Finance in Melanesia: Big Men and Discs of Shell", *Natural History Magazine*, 1964 (a), pp. 20–25
—— "The Genesis and Repression of Conflict: Choiseul Island", *American Anthropologist*, vol. 66, No. 4, Aug. 1964 (b), pp. 789–804
—— "The Social Consequences of Peace on Choiseul Island", *Ethnology*, vol. 3, No. 4, Oct. 1964 (c) pp. 398–403

Scholefield, Guy H.
The Pacific: Its Past and Future, and the Policy of the Great Powers from the 18th Century, J. Murray, London, 1919

Selwyn, J. R.
Pastoral Work in the Colonies and the Mission Field, Society for Promoting Christian Knowledge, Brighton, 1897

Sinker, William
By Reef and Shoal: Being an Account of a Voyage amongst the islands

of the Southwest Pacific, Society for Promoting Christian Knowledge, Brighton, 1913
Somerville, H. Boyle T.
"Ethnological Notes on New Georgia", *Journal of the Royal Anthropological Institute of Great Britain and Ireland*, vol. 26, 1897, pp. 357–412
South Seas Evangelical Mission
Dr. Deck's Letter
Journal—*Not in Vain*
Fellowship of South Sea Evangelical Churches, also known as "The Association Guide Book", South Seas Evangelical Mission, Sydney, n.d.
Southern Cross Log
Journal of the Melanesian Mission
1896, 1897, 1900, 1902, 1906, 1907, 1908
Stace, V. D.
The Pacific Islander and Modern Commerce, S.P.C. Technical Paper No. 54, South Pacific Commission, Noumea, 1954
Steward, John
"The Brothers" in Newbolt's *John Steward's Memories*, Phillipson & Golder Ltd., Chester, 1939, pp. 111–22
——— "The Melanesian People" in *ibid.*, pp. 123–235
Stubbs, D. C.
"Anthropology and Missions, with Special Reference to Malaita", Typescript at Methodist Mission, Munda
Sullivan, Violet M.
The Chief Surrenders: A Solomon Islands Story, S. John Bacon, Melbourne, for the S.S.E.M., n.d.
Sundkler, Bengt G. M.
Bantu Prophets in South Africa, Oxford University Press, for the International African Institute, London, 1961
Taylor, John V.
The Growth of the Church in Buganda: An Attempt at Understanding, Student Christian Movement Press, London, 1958
——— and Dorothea Lehmann
Christians of the Copperbelt, Student Christian Movement Press, London, 1961
Third Division Histories Commission
Stepping Stones to the Solomons (unofficial history of 29th Batn., 2nd N.Z. Exped. Force in the Pacific), A. H. & A. W. Reed, Wellington, for the Histories Commission, 1947
Thurnwald, R. C.
"Pigs and Currency in Buin", *Oceania*, vol. 5. 2, 1934, pp. 119–41
——— *Profane Literature of Buin, Solomon Islands* (Yale University Publication in Anthropology, No. 8, 1936), Yale University Press, New Haven, 1936
——— "The Price of the White Man's Peace", *Pacific Affairs*, vol. 9. 3, 1936, pp. 347–57. (See 'Elkin' for reviews)
Tippett, A. R.
The Nineteenth-century Labour Trade in the Southwest Pacific: A Study of Slavery and Indenture as the Origin of Present-day Racial Problems, M.A. Thesis in History at American University, Washington D.C., 1956
——— "Probing Missionary Inadequacies at the Popular Level", *Inter-*

national Review of Missions, vol. 49, 1960, pp. 411–19

—— "Initiation Rites and Functional Substitutes", *Practical Anthropology*, Mar. 1963, pp. 66–70

—— "Church Growth or Else!" *World Vision Magazine*, Feb. 1966, pp. 12–13, 28

Tucker, H. W.
   Life and Episcopacy of George Augustus Selwyn, Bishop of New Zealand, etc., 2 vols., William Wells Gardner, London, 1879 (with the text of many Selwyn letters)

Turner, Harold W.
   Profile Through Preaching: A Study of Sermon Texts used in a West African Independent Church, Edinburgh House Press for C.W.M.E. of the W.C.C., 1965

U.S. Consular Despatch
   From T. Canasius to Department of State, Apr. 17, 1884, in National Archives, Record Group 84, Washington, D.C.

Vance, Robert C.
   The Hunter Hunted, South Seas Evangelical Mission, Sydney, n.d.

Voyce, A. H.
   "Our Responsibilities in Bougainville", *The Open Door*, vol. 11. 4, 1933

—— "Retrospect and Prospect", *The Open Door*, vol. 12, 1933

—— "A Field White Unto Harvest in Northern Bougainville", *The Open Door*, vol. 13. 4, 1935

—— "The Semi-Jubilee of Methodism on Bougainville", *The Open Door*, vol. 20. 3, 1941

—— "To Him be the Glory!", *The Open Door*, vol. 30. 4, 1952

Vula, Aisake and I. Buadromo
   Visitation of Roviana Lagoon and Rendova Island, Report on Etoism at Methodist Mission, Munda

Ward, John M.
   British Policy in the South Pacific (1786–1893), Australasian Publishing Co., Pty., Ltd., Sydney, 1948

Waterhouse, J. H. L.
   A Roviana and English Dictionary with an English-Roviana Index, List of Natural History Objects and Appendix of Old Customs, 1928 (Revised by L. M. Jones, 1949), Epworth Printing and Publishing House, Sydney

Waterson, Clara
   With God in the Solomons, South Seas Evangelical Mission, Sydney, n.d.

Welbourn, F. B.
   "The Importance of Ghosts" in V. E. W. Hayward's *African Independent Church Movements*, Edinburgh House Press, London, 1963, pp. 15–26

Wench, Ida
   Mission to Melanesia, Elek Books, London, 1961

Wesley, John
   Sermons on Several Occasions: First Series, also known as Forty-four Sermons, Epworth Press, London, 1952 edition used

White Papers
   B.S.I.P. White Papers are listed under 'Administration'

Williams, F. E.
   The Blending of Cultures: An Essay on the Aims of Native Education,

Papua and New Guinea Official Research Publication, W. A. Bock, Government Printer, Port Moresby, 1951

Williams, W.
Letter from the President General to the Methodist People, Pamphlet, Epworth Press, Sydney, 1907

Williamson, Robt.
"Solomon Island Notes" (Taboos, etc.) *Man*, vol. 11, 1911, pp. 65–68
—— *The Ways of the South Seas Savage: A record of travel and observation among the savages of the Solomon Islands, etc.*, Seeley, Service & Co., London, 1914

Wilson, Cecil
General Reports in *Southern Cross Log*, 1906, 1907, 1908

Wilson, Ellen
Dr. Welchman of Bugotu, Society for Promoting Christian Knowledge, London, 1935

Wolfensberger, G. H.
The Bible in the Missionary Situation, article duplicated by Study Secretariat of the United Bible Societies, Geneva, 1963

Woodford, Charles M.
A Naturalist Among the Head-Hunters: being an account of three visits to the Solomon Islands: 1886, 1887, 1888, George Philip & Son, London, 1890
—— "Note on Funerary Ornaments from the Solomon Islands", *Man*, vol. 5, 1905, pp. 38–39
—— "Notes on the Manufacture of the Malaita Shell Bead Money of the Solomon Group", *Man*, vol. 8, 1908, pp. 81–84
—— "The Solomon Islands", Essay VI in Rivers: *Essays on the Depopulation of Melanesia*, University Press, Cambridge, 1922

World Council of Churches
D.W.M.E. Consultation Statements
On Church Growth, Iberville, Canada, 1963
On the Evangelization of West Africa Today, Yaounde, Cameroun, 1965

Worrall, H.
Correspondence *re* Solomon Islanders in Fiji in Methodist Mission Archives, Sydney. Worrall's note-book is also there

Worsley, Peter
The Trumpet Shall Sound: A Study of Cargo Cults in Melanesia, MacGibbon & Kee, London, 1957. Chapter 6 deals with Buka cults, and chapter 11 with Marching Rule

Wright, L. W. S.
"Notes on the Hill People of Northeastern Guadalcanal", *Oceania*, vol. 9. 1, 1938, pp. 97–100

Yinger, J. Milton
Religion, Society and the Individual. An Introduction to the Sociology of Religion, The Macmillan Co., New York, 1957

Yonge, C. M.
Life of John Coleridge Patteson: Bishop of the Melanesian Islands, Macmillan & Co., London, 1874 (2 vols.)

Young, Florence S. H.
Pearls from the Pacific, Marshall Brothers Ltd., London, n.d.

INDEX OF PERSONS

ABRAHAM, C. J. 356
Allen, C. H. 144, 204, 208, 362, 365, 370, 371, 378
Allen, Roland 131, 360, 364, 365, 378
Angarau, Samuela 358
Angas, G. F. 366, 378
Aranai 191, 193, 194
Armstrong, E. S. 346, 354, 355, 356, 357, 378
Artless, S. W. 355, 378
Ayres, B. vii

BARNETT, H. G. 379
Baulee 108
Beauclerc, G. A. F. W. 54, 358
Beckett, – 358, 379
Belangana 358
Belshaw, Cyril S. 34, 171, 172, 177, 182, 201, 355, 366, 367, 368, 370, 371, 379
Benskin, J. 358
Bensley, A. A. 359, 379
Bera 55
Biliki 192, 193
Binet, V. le C. 198, 379
Black, R. H. 341, 342, 343, 377, 379
Blackwood, B. 187, 367, 368, 379
Blamires, P. 132, 362, 364, 379, 385
Bogesi, George 354, 365, 380
Brown, G. 54, 55, 354, 358, 366, 380
Brunner, Emil 110
Buadromo, Iliesa 371, 380, 392
Buki 192, 193, 194

Bula, D. 59, 60, 61, 62, 388
Burton, John W. 380

CAMERON, C. 368, 380
Canasius, T. 354
Capell, A. 353, 380
Carter, G. vii, 380
Cheyne, G. 147
Clark, Sidney, J. W. 92, 93, 125, 131, 132, 134, 331, 360, 361, 362, 363, 364, 376, 380
Coaldrake, F. 357, 360, 362, 380
Codrington, R. H. 50, 346, 353, 360, 361, 381
Cornwell, G. A. R. vii, 371, 381
Corte, N. 371, 373, 381
Cropp, A. H. 187, 368, 381

DALEALE 191, 193
Damusoe, Solomon 110
Danho, Josue 247, 372, 381
Danks, B. 355, 358, 359, 381
Davis, – 152
Deck, Norman 367, 381
Deck, Northcote 110, 272, 381, 391
Didimari 192, 193
Donovan, R. J. 381
Dorovoqa 191, 194
Dovey, J. W. 381
Dunbabbin, T. 354, 382
Durrad, W. J. 355, 374, 382

EDGE-PARTINGTON, T. W. 382
Elkin, A. P. 179–80, 229, 368, 382

Erovo 158
Eto, Silas 90, 143, 144, 201, 214, 219–66, 284, 349, 371, 372, 382

FAIDANGI, ABRAHAM 109
Fichter, J. 339, 340, 377, 382
Firth, Raymond 175
Fison, Lorimer 21, 382
Floyd, William 357
Forde, C. D. 353, 367, 382
Fox, C. E. vii, 50, 193, 204, 252, 346, 354, 355, 356, 357, 369, 370, 374, 383
Frater, A. S. 354, 383
Frerichs, A. C. 373, 383
Frum, John 90, 229
Fuller, C. C. 383

GATTY, HAROLD vii
Gandapeta, Stephen 59
Gemu 140, 142, 143, 247
Gemu, Joni 140, 142
George, Timothy 201
Gina 61, 354
Gnu 191
Goldie, Mrs John F. (Helena) 287, 288, 359
Goldie, John F. 3, 10, 23, 24, 25, 54, 55, 59, 60, 61, 110, 142, 221, 223, 226, 229, 237, 238, 244, 353, 355, 358, 359, 360, 365, 366, 383
Gorai 144
Gove 139, 140
Green, Brian 336, 376, 383
Grover, J. C. 383
Gumi 141, 247
Guppy, H. B. 20, 21, 148, 354, 355, 365, 366, 383

HALL, A. H. 383
Hamilton, – 363, 383
Hayward, V. E. W. 383

Hill, A. T. vii, xvii, 48
Hilliard, David vii, 355
Hocart, A. M. 15, 16, 158, 366, 373, 383, 384
Hogbin, H. I. 16, 297, 353, 354, 365, 367, 373, 376, 384
Hopi, Joni 198
Hopkins, A. I. 9, 39, 346, 354, 366, 373, 384
Huddleston, T. 134, 365, 384

IM THURN, E. 384
Iqava (Ingava, Hiqava) 56, 58, 139, 140, 142, 144, 152, 382
Ivens, W. G. 18, 172, 354, 365, 366, 367, 385

JACOMB, EDWARD 365, 385
Jipe 192, 194
Jones, – 357
Jones, L. M. 392
Julamana, Brown 206

KALEKONA 103, 107
Kasa 141
Kiau, Chilion 24
Kiriau, George vii
Kisini, Isaac 61
Knibbs, S. G. C. 148, 366, 385
Kodosiko 191
Kopuria, Ini 50, 51, 357
Koroso 192, 193, 194

LAKEMPA, MOSES 61
Lalaku 192, 194
Lambert, S. M. 21, 354, 385
Lansley, Gerald 129, 385
Lawry, W. 34
Leadley, E. C. 354, 371, 385, 387
Leembruggen, W. 63
Lehmann, D. 391

Lekezoto 192
Lembu 61
Lepo 158
Liliboa 192, 194, 197, 198
Linton, Ralph 215, 371, 385
Lipa 192
Luxton, C. T. J.   346, 355, 358, 359, 385

MCGAVRAN, D. A.   III, 132, 362, 364, 385
McHardy, Emmet   64, 65, 188, 368, 385
McNairn, A. Stuart   363, 385
Macquarrie, H.   376, 386
Mali, Ani   139, 140, 142
Mapuro   248, 250
Marita   105, 107
Mahaffy, –   358
Marsden, S.   40
Marau, Clement   44, 104, 105, 106, 107, 381, 386
Marett, R. R.   6, 353, 386
Maro   158
Matemata   158
Mere   139, 142
Mendaña   10
Metcalfe, J. R.   vii, 358, 359, 362, 367, 368, 369, 370, 386, 387
Mitchell, D. M.   388
Montgomery, H. H.   357, 388
Morgan, G.   vii
Moss, R.   354, 360, 388
Mulakana   110
Muling   371
Myrdal, Gunnar   83, 84, 85, 86, 360, 388
Mytinger, C.   388

NEQOBANGARA   191
Newbolt, M. R.   357, 388, 391
Newman, –   106
Nina   158
Ngalarusa   192

Ngalatoto   192
Ngavala   191, 193
Nicholson, R. C.   3, 56, 346, 355, 359, 388
Njukili   158
Nodoro   191, 193
Nubui   158

OLIVER, DOUGLAS L.   4, 353, 366, 368, 388
Orchard, R. K.   389

PABULU   192, 193, 194
Paddon, –   355
Page, J.   356, 389
Pakavai   191, 193
Pako   371
Panda   158
Papaqui   192
Parasusu   191
Parrinder, Geoffrey   354, 389
Paruku   192, 194
Paton, D. M.   349, 377, 389
Paton, F. L.   389
Patteson, J. C.   21, 34, 35, 36, 39, 40, 42, 43, 90, 102, 234, 269, 389, 393
Paukubatu   201, 203
Pausu, David   61
Pauw, B. A.   373, 389
Peill, S. E.   331, 363, 376, 389, 390
Penjaeqole   191
Penny, A.   42, 102, 103, 108, 147, 151, 175, 356, 361, 365, 366, 367, 389
Pepele   158
Pero   158
Peter, Simon   110
Pio, Riti   140, 142
Piolet, J. B.   354, 389
Pivo, Mark   61
Pokokoqoro   73, 201, 202, 203
Pondekana   191, 193, 194
Pritt, L.   36

QALABOE 191, 193
Qalonioro 191
Que 140, 142

RAUCAS, L. N. 354, 362, 389
Reynolds, – vii
Rishworth, E. M. 389
Rivers, W. H. R. 26, 152, 153, 355, 357, 366, 389
Roberts, Oral 223, 374
Robson, R. W. 390
Rogani 103
Roke 191, 194
Rona 158
Rooney, S. R. 55, 56, 358, 359, 366, 390
Rowlands, W. E. 331, 363, 376, 389, 390
Russell, T. 365, 390
Rycroft, H. R. 346, 390

SANOP 371
Sapibuana, Charles 43, 102, 103
Sargant, W. 223, 235, 236, 237, 238, 239, 240, 372, 390
Sasa, Pio 140, 142
Scheffler, Harold W. 366, 367, 369, 370, 390
Scholefield, G. H. 370, 390
Scriven, – 359
Selwyn, G. A. 33, 36, 38, 40, 43, 90, 269, 355, 356, 392
Selwyn, J. R. 356, 384, 390
Semote 191
Shakespeare
  Julius Caesar 359
  Tales From Shakespeare 359
Siama 14, 109
Sinker, W. 390
Sito 23
Soga 43, 44
Soge 158
Somerville, H. B. T. 366, 391
Stace, V. D. 360, 365, 368, 391

Steward, John, 46, 50, 51, 357, 388, 391
Suna 158
Sundkler, B. 236, 264, 372, 391

TABIPUDA 192, 193
Takokolo 191, 192, 193
Taloifuila, Jack 48, 169, 170, 366
Tambukoru 104
Taravai 158
Taveqa 192, 193
Taylor, J. V. 391
Teosin 201, 211, 212, 371
Thurnwald, R. C. 155, 156, 366, 391
Tippett, A. R. 353, 360, 370, 391, 392
Tozaka, Amos 194, 197–8, 369
Tucker, H. W. 392
Turner, H. W. 373, 392

ULU 358

VAIKUMU 191, 193, 194
Vaiva 191
Van Gennep, Arnold 13
Vance, R. C. 392
Verguet, – 354
Vouza, J. C. 206, 370, 376, 386
Vovoso, Pcqu 139, 140, 142
Voyce, Mrs. A. H. 359
Voyce, A. H. vii, 188, 368, 392
Vula, A. 371, 380, 392
Vule, David 359, 390
Vuvulenga 192, 194

WALLACE, E. W. 362
Ward, J. M. 392
Wate, Joseph 48
Waterhouse, J. H. L. 238, 392
Waterson, C. 392
Watson, A. C. vii
Welbourn, F. B. 353, 392

Welchman, H. 43, 44, 108, 109, 393
Wench, Ida 393
Wesley, Charles 373
Wesley, John 214, 221, 226, 233, 236, 237, 238, 239, 240, 249, 273, 280, 287, 392
Bicentenary 72, 239, 287
Wheatley, Norman 56, 358
Wickham, Frank 358
Williams, F. E. 128, 362, 392
Williams, H. 40, 43
Williams, John 34
Williams, W. 393
Williamson, Robert 5, 353, 393
Wilson, Cecil 38, 39, 45, 46, 55, 90, 357, 358, 393

Wilson, E. 354, 357, 362, 393
Wolfensberger, G. H. 297, 373, 393
Woodford, Charles M. 147, 354, 358, 365, 366, 393
Worrall, H. 54, 393
Worsley, Peter 204, 210, 370, 371, 393
Wright, L. W. S. 393

YINGER, J. M. 382, 393
Yonge, C. M. 393
Young, F. S. H. 393

ZIO, JOELI vii, 253
Zuvulu 61

GENERAL INDEX

ABSENTEEISM 52, 177–80, 189, 368

Acculturation 20–26, 34–35, 154–55, 156–59, 171–89, 330–45, 348–49, 351–52

Achievements, mission 346–7

Administration

Documents 378

Policy xv/xvi, 25–26, 86–88, 98–99, 111–12, 115–18, 119–20, 123, 133–34, 152–53, 155, 204–09, 347, 369

Afterlife, belief in 7, 9–10

Agents (of the Mission)

Fijians 55, 56, 61–63, 70, 80, 120, 224–25, 380, 392

Samoans 56, 61

Tongans 61, 70

Agriculture 66–69, 86–88, 182, 360

Anti-authoritarianism 340

Arms trade 42, 151–52, 171

Art, indigenous 168

Artificial Islands 166–70, 172, 175–76, 323 ff., 367, 385

Authority 94, 139, 157, 348, 365

Transmission of 139–46

BABY GARDEN 202, 209–12, 216

Baha'i 50, 98, 184

Baptism 38, 42–43, 57 ff., 64–65

Forms of 275, 279

Battle for the Mind 219, 223, 235–39, 242–44, 252, 390

Bell murder case 208

Bible 129, 287, 288, 297–307, 373–74

Bible Reading Association 304

B.F.B.S. 380

Eto's interpretation of 299

Reading 280–81

Selection sampling 299–303, 349

Bishops, Melanesian Assistant, 30–31

Bush people 163, 175, 185, 206, 320, 367

Boys' Brigade 31, 181, 182–83

Bride-price 98, 174, 176, 367

Brotherhood, Melanesian 31, 38, 45, 50–53, 120, 319, 350, 357, 386, 391

CANEFIELDS 20, 46

Cannibalism 9, 10, 147 ff.

Canoe rites 12, 13

Catechism 36, 64, 275, 287

Ceremonial inhumanity 8–10, 147–59, 346

Change, culture (see Acculturation)

Change, semantic 275–76

Chaplaincy 332

Christians

Nominal 85, 126, 282, 308, 309, 311, 315, 316, 329, 338–41, 350, 351, 352

Nuclear 311, 315, 316, 338–41, 352

Marginal 85, 283, 309, 313–16, 329, 338–41, 350–52

Second generation 308 ff.

Christopaganism (see also Syncretism) xiii, 250, 282, 343–45, 350–51, 352
Church, Congregational 96
Church, indigenous xiii, 63, 72, 83, 84, 85, 88–93, 124–28, 182–85, 283–85, 332–33, 360–61, 362, 363, 372
Church as peacemaker 62, 196–200
Church association 124, 165, 181, 183–84
Church growth xv–xvi, 29–32, 81, 125–28, 132–33, 195, 196, 241, 243, 309, 331, 359
  Conversion (quantitative) 29, 30–31, 61, 62, 63, 64–65, 184, 185–89, 199–200, 346, 347
  Migration (transfer) 32, 330, 331–34
  Organic xvi, 31, 62, 63, 124, 133, 134, 181, 182, 184, 330, 346, 347, 352
  Quality 29, 31, 124, 130–31, 179, 184, 199–200, 241, 245–46, 273, 282–85, 346, 347, 352
Church Missionary Society 43
Church of our Lord 373–74
Church records 64
Civilizing, policy of 40–41
Clergy, indigenous (see also Ministry) 31, 38–39, 45, 90, 319, 347, 376
Cohesion (social) 11, 199–200, 273, 274, 348
Collective man 336, 337, 351
Colonialism 24, 25, 67, 332, 348, 376
Colony, Roviana 154–56
Comity xv, 34, 37, 55, 332
Confession 65, 276–77, 279, 375

Confession, General 274, 277, 280
Communal weekday piety 314, 316, 317
Companions, Company of 51, 318, 319, 350, 386
Consolidation, fallacy of 132, 364
Contact, lines of 59–60
Contrasting assumptions 340
Construction and reconstruction 92–93
Conversion xvi–xvii, 18, 43, 44, 49, 57–62, 102–11, 320–22, 336–37
Co-existence (Christian-pagan villages) xvi, 80, 122, 270, 272, 319–29, 334, 349–50
Co-operative societies 180–82, 183, 367, 368
Criteria for Mission Institutions 125–28, 347–48
Curers, Christopagan 343–45, 350–57
Custom, economic dimensions of 173–77
Custom marriage 342–43
Custom money 8, 155, 173–77, 198, 366, 367, 368, 369
Custom sickness 343–44

DEAD, cult of the 158
Death 6
Decision 96
Denominationalism 338, 341, 342, 343, 351–52
Depopulation 21, 41–42, 152 ff., 370, 382, 390, 393
District Council 124
Discipline, Church 283–85, 373
District representatives 113
Divination 12–13, 14–15, 18, 115, 280–81, 372
Dracaena 11–12, 15, 250, 372

Drift, marginal-nominal 310 ff., 350
Dunning 103
Dysfunctional parish 340
EDUCATION xvi, 87, 119–35, 348, 362–65
In the Church 128–31
Institutions 122, 125–28, 132–33, 363
Theological 125
Elders, tribal 57, 58, 157, 158
élite xvi, 341–42, 343
Enclosure, congregational xvi–xvii, 30, 49
Enthusiasm 214, 223, 227–29, 233, 239–41, 294
Early stick tapping 221
The Round 225, 232, 250
Effect of the Book 235–39
Wesley and enthusiasm 239–41
Ethnic awareness 65
Etoism (C.F.C. Christian Fellowship Church, Western Solomons Schism) 73, 75, 85, 86, 90, 92, 142, 143, 154, 201, 202, 203, 212–16, 219–66, 277, 280, 284, 286, 287, 288, 349
Conclusions 265, 266
Diffusion of 229–31
Fijians' Report 224–25, 371, 392
Fraternal investigator's report 227–29, 233
Group experiences 232, 47
Historical sequence 220–26
Hymns 253–64
Pagan elements 248–52
Problems 212–16, 219–20
Prophet (see S. Eto) 226, 227
Theological analysis 248, 264

Evangelism 50–53
Exchange economy 171–89, 348–9
Latent factors 176, 184
Exorcism 14, 19, 123, 173
Expurgation 128–29

FEAR 7, 248
Felling the Suqu 198, 199
Festivals, Christian 67, 75
Feuding 22–24, 62, 150, 190–200, 346, 349, 366
Fijians 55, 56, 61–63, 70, 80, 121, 224–25, 248, 371, 380, 392
First fruit 168
Foreign concepts 69
Formalism 277 ff.
Functional substitutes 12, 25, 26, 101, 153, 154, 173, 174, 176, 200, 269–72, 286, 298
Free speech 117–18, 348

GHOSTS 4–8, 15, 17, 18, 19, 153, 155, 173, 230, 250, 270, 280, 271
Girls' Life Brigade 183
Goblins (imps) 6, 354
Gods and spirits
Bangara 3, 353
Bangara La'ata 3
Crator 3
Hongging 4
Koevasi 3
Outsider, The Great 3, 7
Panannga 4
Sivatohu 3
Spirit, The Great 3
Supreme Being 4
Tantanu 4
Tantanu Mekusim 4
Goldie College 224, 231
Gradualism 364
Group dynamics 93, 131, 363
Groups, pressure 111–17, 351

HAHALIS WELFARE SOCIETY 74,
  82, 83, 201, 202, 209–12,
  216
Headhunting 7, 12, 26, 147–
  59, 346, 348
History
  Anglican 33–53
  Methodist 54–76
Holy Communion 69, 70, 75,
  91, 163–65, 247, 274, 277,
  278, 280, 281, 298, 303, 305,
  306, 375
Holy Island 367
Holy water 252, 278
Hymns 158, 286–96
  Etoist 233, 253–64
  Indigenous 288
  Selection sampling 289–96,
  349
  Theological significance of
  286–88

ICONOCLASM 105–11
Incantations (charms) 11, 12,
  269
Individualism and co-operation
  179
Industrial missions 45–46, 56–
  57, 66–69, 383
Infanticide 61, 270
Inflorescence 175
Incorporation (expansion) 128
Incorporation (see Rites)
Innovation (advocating and
  accepting) 86–88, 171–89,
  193, 220, 241, 333, 335
  Modification 87
  Rejection 173, 184–85
Institutionalism 131–35, 348,
  362–65
Integration 83
International Missionary Coun-
  cil (I.M.C.) 384, 389
  Ghana statement 95, 361,
  384, 389

Tambaram 366, 384
Island of Skulls 7–8
Itineration 64–65, 71, 121, 127

JEHOVAH'S WITNESSES 50, 184,
  223, 307, 323, 374, 386
Justice, Social 23–24, 113–15,
  207–09, 273–74, 348

KESA 3, 367, 369
Knowledge, specialist 172–73
Kwato 96

LABOUR 172, 207
  Diffusion of magic by 339
  Groups 334
  Indentured 48, 54, 113, 171,
  177–80, 207, 376
  Trade 20–21, 42, 151, 171
Language problem 36, 64
Leadership xvi–xvii, 62–63,
  73, 120, 121, 125, 127, 129,
  139–46, 334–36, 350, 366,
  376
Lectionary 303, 304, 318, 374
Literature, preparation of 36,
  45, 64, 130
Liturgy 36, 65, 97, 234, 269–
  70, 275, 280, 304–05, 372,
  375
  Benediction 296
  Chants 296
  Commandments 280
  Creed 275, 280, 296
  Gloria 280, 296
  Jubilate 280, 296
  Litany 65, 274
  Lord's Prayer 275, 280, 296
  Magnificat 280, 296, 305
  Nunc Dimitis 280, 296, 305
  Psalms 304–05
  Venite 280, 296
Liquor 25, 111, 115–17
Liquor Bill 84

Local Church xvi, 347–48, 349–50, 352
London Missionary Society 34, 96
(Congregationals), 331

MAGIC 9–16
Counter 6, 10, 11, 15, 16, 114, 115, 250, 350
Curative 158–59, 350–51, 366
Imitative 155, 156
Shamanism 14, 109
"Strength of Ten" 203
War 5, 9
(see also Rites)
Magical practitioners 10, 100, 101, 109
Maintenance 128
Mana 4–16, 19, 22, 58, 79, 100–18, 101, 102, 103, 104–06, 110, 151–52, 153, 158–59, 197, 252, 269, 270, 278, 286, 353, 354, 361, 365
Maoris 43
Marching Rule 82, 90, 98, 114, 165, 181, 184, 201, 202, 204–09, 214, 222, 338, 370, 378
Causes 208
Goals 206
Tax 208
Marginality 85, 283, 329, 338, 339–41, 350, 352, 375
Markets 185–89, 331
Master tribes 148
Materialism (secularism) xvi, 80, 95, 112–13, 332, 351
Mau Mau 237
Mediator (Go-between) 197–98, 369
Medicinal plants 11–12, 15
Medical work xvi, 64, 70, 86, 121, 348, 363, 364, 365
Melanesian Mission 33–53, 357, 386

Brotherhood 31, 38, 45, 50–53, 120, 319, 350, 357
Clergy, Indigenous 31, 38, 39, 45, 90, 319, 347, 375
Companions 51, 318, 319, 350
Ethos 35–36, 355
History 33–53, 378, 386
Method 34, 35
Mothers' Union 97, 318, 361
Reasons for slow growth 39–42
Sources 386
Staffing problems 46
Merit 7
Messianism 212, 259–60
Methodist Church
Australian 54, 61, 62, 357–60, 379, 380
Ministry, indigenous 72, 73, 91, 92, 97
Mission 45, 54–63, 66, 67, 127–28, 379, 380, 383, 386–88
New Zealand 61–76, 359
N.Z. Board Report 1928 69–76, 131–35
Wesleyan Church 358
Wesleyan Missionary Society 34
Women's Fellowship 97
Methodist Union 358
Methodology xiii–xv
Migration 330–31, 332–33
Millenarianism 203–04, 225, 371
Minister—adherent ratio 91
Mission administration 127–28, 132–33
Mission or Church xv–xvi, 124–25, 127–28, 131–35
Mission ships 127
Mission stations vii, 47
Model villages and plantations 70

Mormonism 223, 374
Murderers, professional 191,
     192, 193, 194
Myths 3–4

NATIONALISM 208–09, 262, 349
Nativistic movements 73, 201–
     16, 219–66, 282, 370–71,
     338, 349
Anti-white 207–08, 209–11
Buka cults 371
Chair and Rule Movement
     206, 208
Continuity of 216, 371
Freedom Movement 205–06
Lontis Cult 209
Needs 6
Neo-Paganism (resurgence of
     practices) xiii, 281–85,
     373
Nominality 85, 126, 282, 283,
     308, 309, 329, 339–41, 350,
     352, 375

OBSTRUCTORS 133
Oceania 388
"Opening a village" 52
Opportunity (for evangelism)
     65, 68–69, 71, 187, 309,
     327, 330–31, 351
Opinion
     Groups 111–18
     Indigenous 113–15
     Public xvi
Organization 36–37, 50–51,
     172, 180–85
     Marching Rule 204–05
     Religio - economic 182–85,
          189
     Socio-economic 180–82, 189
Orphans 57
Outreach 132, 332
Ownership, private 25

PAGANISM, MODIFIED 320

Participation 286, 352
Paternalism 63, 88–90, 91–92,
     134, 227, 228, 332, 347–48,
     350, 362, 365, 376
Peace-making 194–96
     Ceremony of 197–99
     Netogiation 197
     Symbolism of 197–200
People movements 42, 43, 60
Perfectionism 91
Piety curves 308–18, 349, 350
Pilgrim's Progress 130, 359
Pilot projects 131, 134
Plantation communities 341–
     45, 351
Polynesian society 389
Practising acquaintance (pol-
     icy) 363
Prayers 3, 6, 11, 15, 105,
     269–72, 272–75, 276–76,
     278
Prestige 173, 174, 177, 187
Priest (pagan) 105, 106, 108,
     158, 173, 321, 324–29
     "buying back" 324–29
Priorities 49, 66–67, 71, 128
Programs, co-operative 166–
     70
Psychological factor 25–26
Pokokoqoro cult 201–04, 210,
     214, 338, 370
Power encounter 5–6, 8, 43–
     44, 60–61, 79, 100–11, 233–
     35, 251–52, 278–79, 297–98,
     312, 372
Punitive expeditions 21–24,
     62, 171, 191, 193fi

QUAKERS 238

RECONCILIATION 17, 18, 19, 62,
     190, 194–99, 228–29, 277,
     322, 325, 326, 368–70
Reconstruction 92–93, 134

Redemption 17, 18
Relative morality 340
Religion and Morals, diffusion of 338–39
Remote control (policy) 37, 39–42, 45
Residential segment (Vasina) 160–63
Responsibility, communal 177–80, 350
Revitalization (renewal) 215, 348, 350, 352
Rites, indigenous
  Fishing 4, 11–13
  Funerary 150, 153
  Harvesting 13, 19
  Housebuilding 12–13
  Planting 4, 11–12, 19
  Purifications 19
  Rain-making 342, 343
Rites of incorporation 13
Rites of re-incorporation (Christian) 342
Roman Catholics 7, 9, 33, 34, 37, 49, 50, 64–65, 68, 94, 184, 187, 188, 211, 212, 222, 275, 278, 298, 323, 331, 339–40, 341–42, 358, 362, 376
  Growth in Malaita 47, 49
  Roviana, colonization 154–56
  Language 144
  Reasons for choice 55, 156
Royal Anthropological Institute 390

SACRED THINGS
  Creatures 6, 8
  Objects 3, 4, 5, 7, 8, 14, 15, 103, 104, 105, 108, 110, 248, 284, 285, 320
  Destruction of 60, 61, 100–11
  Occasions 7

Places 4, 5, 6, 7, 13, 19, 103, 104–05, 109, 150, 249–50, 320
Tree 4, 8, 13, 100–02
Words 232
Sacrifice 4–6, 9, 11, 13, 15, 18, 61, 101, 102, 107, 150, 151, 155, 298
Human 13
Salt - water People 163–70, 206, 320, 323, 367
Salvation 16–19, 298
Samoans 56, 61
Seventh Day Adventists 49, 68, 94, 184, 211, 212, 222, 229, 251, 323, 331, 341, 342, 358, 371
Shamanism 14, 109
Shrine (vehicle) 6, 19, 361
Shrinkage (membership) 179, 340
Sin 16–19
Skull cult 4–5, 7–10, 101, 108, 148, 149, 150, 152, 250
Slavery 9, 11–12, 20–21, 57, 61, 147–59, 346, 365–366, 367
  Bondsmen 155
  Female 150
  Manumission 199, 369–70
  Religious role 157–59
Small groups, rights of 98–99
Social balance xvi
Social structure 154, 351
  Cleavage in 321, 375–76
  Family pattern 139–46, 229, 231
  Feuding pattern 190–200
  Headhunting and slaving pattern 147–59
  Industrial collective man 335–37
  Kin substructure 322–29
  Marriage pattern 176
  Power encounter in 106–07
  Trade patterns 185–89, 348–49, 366–68

Village structure 160–70, 366
Plantation 341–45
Sodalites 57–62, 148
Sondo (Abode of Dead)   10
Sorcerer 100–01, 191
Sorceresses 11, 14, 58
Sorcery 10–16, 114–15, 190, 191, 193, 224, 249, 273, 278, 284, 343–44, 350–51, 354
Eto accused of 249
Evil eye 16, 249
Forms of 15
Soul-stuff (soul value) 7–8
Southern Cross 50, 355, 356, 386, 391
South Seas Evangelical Mission 49, 97, 98, 184, 208, 209, 272, 276–77, 280, 297, 298, 299, 306, 323, 331, 341, 342, 376, 381, 392
Spirits 4–7, 9, 104–05, 106–11, 272, 320, 354
Little 7
Spirits, possession 14, 79, 250–51
Standards xvii
Static and dynamic thinking 83–86, 347
Statistics, Church 33, 42–43, 48–49, 51–52, 59–60, 61, 63, 65, 71–72, 73–76, 75–76, 182, 183–84, 219, 355–57
Need for accuracy in 31, 32, 355
Stewardship 215, 347
Sunday Schools 75, 89
Surville Expedition (1769) 147
Symbolism (Symbolic Acts) 11, 18–19, 108, 197–200, 269, 277–81
Syncretism 134, 155, 209–11, 215–16, 249–50, 343–45, 350–51
Reasons for 282–85

TABOO 25, 60, 62, 79, 100–02, 103, 110, 148, 181, 216, 248, 249, 361
Technical projects 66–71
Tension (communal/family) 317
Theology, Christian xiv, 12, 13, 286–96, 349
Pagan 16–19
Tongans 61, 70
Trade exchange 26, 148ff., 155, 171–89, 366–68
Trade partners 188
Traders 21–22, 42, 151, 152, 207
Training courses 64–65
Translation 130, 280
Twelve Rules of a Helper 221

UNITY 81, 93–99, 278–81, 351–52
Urbanization 80, 94, 95, 99, 330–41

VALUES, CULTURAL 145
Village union 124, 165, 181, 183
Villages studied in depth
Fouia 48, 163–66, 178, 179, 180–81, 292–95, 303–07, 315–18, 361
Honiara vii, 80, 98, 111–13, 127, 169, 177–78, 179–80, 330–41, 351, 376, 377
Rarumana 89, 98–99, 154, 160–63, 172, 178, 179, 288, 292, 295, 296, 299–303, 310–14, 361
Sulufou 166–70, 172
Voids, cultural (vacuums) 85, 152–54, 200, 212, 214, 246,

247, 269, 272, 348, 377
Spiritual   277
Volunteer Labour Corps   204
Voodooism   236

WAR   147ff., 190–96
War Demon   155
Wealth, concepts of   172–73
Women's Work   97
    Anglican "Mothers' Union"
    97, 361

Methodist "Women's Fellow-
    ship"   97, 361
World Council of Churches   ix,
    xiii, xv, 29, 93, 97, 297,
    353, 383, 392, 393
    Consultations   361
    Iberville   29
    Samoa   96
    West Africa   361
    Division World Mission and
    Evangelism   xiii

Alan R. Tippett is currently professor of Anthropology and Oceanic Studies at the School of World Mission and Institute of Church Growth at Fuller Theological Seminary. Dr. Tippett held pastorates in Victoria, Australia, 1935-1940, and served as a missionary of the Australian Methodist Church to the Fiji Islands, 1941-1961. His missionary experience includes the superintendency of a theological seminary. Besides numerous missiological and anthropological articles, Dr. Tippett authored *The Christian: Fiji 1835-67* (1954), *Fijian Material Culture–Culture Context, Function and Change* (1968), *Verdict Theology in Missionary Theory* (1969), *Church Growth and the Word of God* (1970), *Peoples of Southwest Ethiopia* (1970), *People Movements in Southern Polynesia* (1971), *God, Man and Church Growth* (1973), and eight books in the Fijian language. He is editor of *Missiology,* a periodical by the American Society of Missiology.

Other Books by the William Carey Library

General

Church Growth and Group Conversion by Donald A. McGavran $2.45p
The Evangelical Response to Bangkok edited by Ralph D. Winter
$1.95p
Growth and Life in the Local Church by H. Boone Porter $2.95p
Message and Mission: the Communication of the Christian Faith by
Eugene Nida $3.95p
Reaching the Unreached: A Preliminary Strategy for World
Evangelization by Edward Pentecost $5.95p
Verdict Theology in Mission Theory by Alan Tippett $4.95p

Area and Case Studies

Aspects of Pacific Ethnohistory by Alan R. Tippett $3.95p
The Baha'i Faith: Its History and Teachings by William Miller $8.95p
A Century of Growth: the Kachin Baptist Church of Burma by Herman
Tegenfeldt $9.95c
Church Growth in Japan by Tetsunao Yamamori $4.95p
A New Day in Madras by Amirtharaj Nelson $7.95p
People Movements in the Punjab by Margaret and Frederick Stock
$8.95p
The Protestant Movement in Italy by Roger Hedlund $3.95p
Protestants in Modern Spain: the Struggle for Religious Pluralism by
Dale G. Vought $3.45p
The Religious Dimension in Hispanic Los Angeles: A Protestant Case
Study by Clifton Holland $9.95p
Taiwan: Mainline Versus Independent Church Growth by Allen J.
Swanson $3.95p
Understanding Latin Americans by Eugene Nida $3.95p

Theological Education by Extension

Designing a Theological Education by Extension Program by Leslie D.
Hill $2.95p
An Extension Seminary Primer by Ralph Covell and Peter Wagner
$2.45p
The World Directory of Theological Education by Extension by Wayne
Weld $5.95p

Textbooks and Practical Helps

Becoming Bilingual: A Guide to Language Learning by Donald Larson
and William A. Smalley $5.95xp
God's Word in Man's Language by Eugene Nida $2.95p
An Inductive Study to the Book of Jeremiah by F.R. Kinsler $4.95p
Bibliography for Cross-Cultural Workers by Tippett $3.95p $5.95c
Principles of Church Growth by Weld and McGavran $4.95xp
Manual of Articulatory Phonetics by William A. Smalley $4.95xp
The Means of World Evangelization: Missiological Education at the
Fuller School of World Mission edited by Alvin Martin $9.95p
Readings in Missionary Anthropology edited by William Smalley
$4.95xp